Historical
Viewpoints

Historical Viewpoints

SECOND EDITION

Volume One to 1877
Notable Articles from American Heritage

Editor
John A. Garraty

Columbia University

Harper & Row, Publishers
New York, Evanston, San Francisco, London

Sponsoring Editor: John G. Ryden
Special Projects Editor: Mary Lou Mosher
Project Editor: Robert Ginsberg
Designer: Rita Naughton
Production Supervisor: Will C. Jomarrón

Cover: Detail from "Rustic Dance After a Sleigh Ride" by William Sidney Mount, courtesy of The Museum of Fine Arts, Boston.

All articles have appeared in *American Heritage, The Magazine of History,* some under different titles.

Historical Viewpoints, Second Edition. Volume One to 1877.

Copyright © 1970, 1975 by Harper & Row, Publishers, Inc.

All rights reserved. Printed in the United States of America. No part of this book may be used or reproduced in any manner whatsoever without written permission except in the case of brief quotations embodied in critical articles and reviews. For information address Harper & Row, Publishers, Inc., 10 East 53rd Street, New York, N.Y. 10022.

Library of Congress Cataloging in Publication Data

Garraty, John Arthur, 1920–   comp.
   Historical viewpoints.

   1.   United States—History—Addresses, essays, lectures.   I.   American heritage.   II.   Title.
EI78.6.G26   1975   973'.08   74-20645
ISBN 0-06-042258-0 (v. 1)

Acknowledgments

"Myths That Hide the American Indian," © 1956 by Oliver La Farge. Reprinted by permission of J. Pendaries La Farge.

"The Great Debate over Indian Policy," © 1963 by Lewis Hanke. Reprinted by permission.

"America and the Elizabethan Imagination," © 1959 by A. L. Rowse. Reprinted by permission.

"William Byrd II of Virginia," © 1959 by Marshall Fishwick. Reprinted by permission.

"The Frontier and the American Character," by Ray Allen Billington, © 1958 by American Heritage Publishing Co., Inc.

"The Middle Passage" from *Black Cargoes* by Daniel P. Mannix and Malcolm Cowley. Copyright © 1962 by Daniel P. Mannix. Reprinted by permission of The Viking Press, Inc.

"The Scotch-Irish in America," by James G. Leyburn, © 1970 by American Heritage Publishing Co., Inc.

"George III, Our Last King," by J. H. Plumb, © 1960 by American Heritage Publishing Co., Inc.

"James Otis and the Writs of Assistance," by Richard B. Morris, © 1962 by American Heritage Publishing Co., Inc.

"The Anatomy of *Common Sense*," © 1973 by Bernard Bailyn. Reprinted by permission. The article first appeared in the Library of Congress's *Fundamental Testaments of the American Revolution* (Washington, 1973).

"England's Vietnam: The American Revolution," by Richard M. Ketchum, © 1971 by American Heritage Publishing Co., Inc.

"Shays' Rebellion," by Alden T. Vaughan, © 1966 by American Heritage Publishing Co., Inc.

"The Constitution: Was It an Economic Document?" © 1958 by Henry Steele Commager. Reprinted by permission.

"The Search for a Usable Past," © 1965 by Henry Steele Commager. Reprinted by permission.

"The Case of the Missing Commissions" by John A. Garraty (reprinted under the title "Marbury v. Madison") from *Quarrels That Have Shaped the Constitution,* edited by John A. Garraty. Copyright © 1963 by Harper & Row, Publishers, Inc. By permission of the publishers.

"Madison and the War of 1812," by Irving Brant, © 1959 by American Heritage Publishing Co., Inc.

"Was Jackson Wise to Dismantle the Bank?" by Bray Hammond, © 1956 by American Heritage Publishing Co., Inc.

"Religion on the Frontier," © 1958 by Bernard A. Weisberger. Reprinted by permission.

"The Education of Women," by Elaine Kendall, © 1973 by American Heritage Publishing Co., Inc.

"Ralph Waldo Emerson" (original title "Have Courage!"), copyright © 1968 by Nelson Doubleday, Inc. from the book *Ralph Waldo Emerson: Essays & Journals,* edited by Lewis Mumford. Reprinted by permission of Doubleday & Company, Inc.

"Poverty in America," by David J. Rothman, © 1972 by American Heritage Publishing Co., Inc.

"Samuel Slater Imports a Revolution," by Arnold Welles, © 1958 by American Heritage Publishing Co., Inc.

"There Was Another South," by Carl N. Degler, © 1960 by American Heritage Publishing Co., Inc.

"The Needless Conflict," by Allan Nevins, © 1956 by American Heritage Publishing Co., Inc.

"Soldiering in the Civil War," by Bruce Catton, © 1957 by American Heritage Publishing Co., Inc.

"How Lincoln Would Have Rebuilt the Union," by James G. Randall and R. N. Current, © 1955 by Dodd, Mead & Company, Inc. Reprinted by permission of Dodd, Mead & Company, Inc. from *The Last Full Measure* by James G. Randall and R. N. Current.

"Why They Impeached Andrew Johnson," by David Herbert Donald, © 1956 by American Heritage Publishing Co., Inc.

Picture Credits

1, Collection of Warren Clifton Shearman. 4 (left) Culver Pictures, Inc. 4 (right) California Historical Society, San Francisco. 14, Gilcrease Institute of American History & Art. 21, New York Public Library. 28, John Carter Brown Library, Providence. 36, New York Public Library. 39, Culver Pictures, Inc. 43, New York Public Library. 47, Collection of Mr. and Mrs. Samuel Schwartz. 53, By permission of the owners, Mr. and Mrs. William Byrd. 57, Library of Congress. 60, Culver Pictures, Inc. 65, New York Public Library, Picture Collection. 73, *Abstract of Evidence on . . . Slave Trade, 1792.* 76, New Haven Colony Historical Society. 82, *Harper's Weekly,* June 2, 1860. 85, American Antiquarian Society. 90, Manchester Historic Association. 93, New York Public Library. 99, Library of Congress. 102, Colonial Williamsburg Collection. 103, By Permission of the Trustees of the British Museum. 107, National Maritime Museum. 114, Collection of Mrs. Carlos A. Hepp. 115, Massachusetts Historical Society. 124, Historical Society of Pennsylvania. 137, British Museum. 142, Metropolitan Museum of Art. 149, British Museum. 158, Culver Pictures, Inc. 162, Culver Pictures, Inc. 168, Free Library of Philadelphia (Picture Collection). 169, Independence National Historical Park Collection, Philadelphia. 173, National Archives. 181, Collection of Davenport West, Jr. 190, Courtesy, Henry Francis du Pont Winterthur Museum. 202, Colonial Williamsburg Photo. 206, Washington and Lee University Collection. 213, Colonial Williamsburg Photo. 220, Courtesy of The New-York Historical Society. 224, Courtesy of The New-York Historical Society. 233, Courtesy of the Museum of Fine Arts, Boston: M. & M. Karolik Collection. 237, Courtesy of The New-York Historical Society. 241, Courtesy of The New-York Historical Society. 250, Emma Willard School, Troy, New York. 258, Shelburne Museum, Shelburne, Vermont. 265, Culver Pictures, Inc. 279, Culver Pictures, Inc. 283, National Cyclopedia of American Biography (James T. White Co.). 287, Rhode Island Historical Society. 293, Gibbes Art Gallery, Charleston. 294, Chicago Historical Society. 295, Library of Congress. 298, National Archives. 303, Cook Collection, Valentine Museum. 308, National Archives. 309, Collection of Frederick H. Meserve. 314, John N. Holloway, *History of Kansas,* 1868. 319, Library of Congress. 323, Courtesy of the Museum of Fine Arts, Boston: M. & M. Karolik Collection. 324, Library of Congress. 326, Cooper-Hewitt Museum of Design, Smithsonian Institution. 351, Library of Congress. 356, Free Library of Philadelphia.

Contents

John A. Garraty Introduction   viii

Part One A NEW WORLD

Oliver La Farge Myths That Hide the American Indian   2
Lewis Hanke The Great Debate over Indian Policy   16
A. L. Rowse America and the Elizabethan Imagination   34

Part Two COLONIAL LIFE

Marshall Fishwick William Byrd II of Virginia   48
Ray Allen Billington The Frontier and the American Character   58
Daniel P. Mannix and Malcolm Cowley The Middle Passage   70
James G. Leyburn The Scotch-Irish in America   86

Part Three THE BIRTH OF A NATION

J. H. Plumb George III, Our Last King   100
Richard B. Morris James Otis and the Writs of Assistance   110
Bernard Bailyn The Anatomy of *Common Sense*   122
Richard M. Ketchum England's Vietnam: The American Revolution   140
Alden T. Vaughan Shays' Rebellion   152
Henry Steele Commager The Constitution: Was It an Economic Document?   166

Part Four NATIONAL GROWING PAINS

Henry Steele Commager The Search for a Usable Past   182
John A. Garraty Marbury v. Madison   198
Irving Brant Madison and the War of 1812   210
Bray Hammond Was Jackson Wise to Dismantle the Bank?   222

Part Five ANTEBELLUM SOCIETY

Bernard A. Weisberger Religion on the Frontier   234
Elaine Kendall The Education of Women   248
Lewis Mumford Ralph Waldo Emerson   262
David J. Rothman Poverty in America   274
Arnold Welles Samuel Slater Imports a Revolution   280
Carl N. Degler There Was Another South   290

Part Six CIVIL WAR AND RECONSTRUCTION

Allan Nevins The Needless Conflict   304
Bruce Catton Soldiering in the Civil War   316
James G. Randall and R. N. Current How Lincoln Would Have Rebuilt the
   Union   328
David Herbert Donald Why They Impeached Andrew Johnson   348

Introduction

There are almost as many kinds of history as there are historians. In addition
to the differences between political history and the social, economic, and
cultural varieties, the discipline lends itself to such classifications as analytical,
narrative, statistical, impressionistic, local, comparative, philosophical, synthetic,
and many others. Often the distinctions between one and another kind of history
are overemphasized. No one can write good political history without some
consideration of social, economic, and cultural questions; narrative history
requires analysis to be meaningful; impressionistic treatments of past events
are, in a way, statistical histories based on very tiny samples. Nevertheless, the
types exist and serve different purposes. Each focuses on part of the total
human experience and sees it from a particular perspective; each, when well
done, adds its own contribution to the total record. It is therefore foolish to
argue that any kind of historical approach is inherently better than all the others.
Some are perhaps more generally useful (that is, more interesting to a wider
segment of the population) or more suggestive at a particular time and place
than others, but the distinctions are like those between a miniature and a mural,
a sonnet and an epic poem. No one would suggest that "The Moonlight
Sonata" was a waste of Beethoven's time because he was capable of producing
the *Choral* symphony, or that Mozart should not have written "Eine Kleine
Nachtmusik" because he had within him *Don Giovanni,* and in the same way a
monograph or an article of twenty pages can be as well worth doing and as
satisfying to read as Edward Gibbon's *Decline and Fall of the Roman Empire*.

The most useless and confusing distinction commonly drawn between
varieties of history is that separating "scholarly" from "popular" history. These
terms came into existence during the latter half of the nineteenth century.
Before that time, all history was popular in the sense that those who wrote it,
viewing themselves as possessors of special information acquired through
scholarship or through having observed firsthand the events they described,
aimed to transmit that knowledge to anyone interested in the subject. But when
history became "scientific" and professionalized, historians began to write
primarily for other historians. They assumed that nonspecialists had no interest
in their work or were incapable of understanding it, and even argued that to

write history for the general reader was to prostitute one's talents. Therefore, although with many notable exceptions, the best-trained and most knowledgeable and intelligent historians tended to forswear the task of transmitting their scholarly findings to ordinary readers.

Of course popular history continued to be written and read, but most of it was produced by amateurs, and thus its quality varied greatly. The scholarly prejudice against "popularizers" had a solid basis in fact. Too often popular history was—and still is—shallow, error-ridden, out-of-date before publication, a mere rehash of already written books, an exasperating mixture, as one critic has said, of "something we all knew before" and "something which is not so." Much of it was written by journalists and novelists who often lacked the patience, the professional skills, and the knowledge of sources that are as necessary for the writing of good history as narrative power, imagination and lucidity of style.

It was chiefly with the hope of encouraging professional historians to broaden their perspectives that, beginning in the 1930's, a group of historians led by Professor Allan Nevins of Columbia University began to think of founding a general circulation magazine of American history. Their aim was a magazine in which solidly researched and significant articles would be presented in a way that would interest and educate readers who were not professional students of the past. Nevins himself, one of the great historians of the twentieth century, epitomized the combination these men sought to produce. He was a prodigious scholar, author of dozens of learned volumes, and trainer of literally hundreds of graduate students, but he was also a fluent and graceful writer whose work was widely read and appreciated. Nevins' books won Pulitzer Prizes as well as academic renown.

The example provided by Nevins and a few other outstanding historians of his generation, such as Samuel Eliot Morison, undoubtedly influenced the gradual revival of concern for popular history that has occurred in recent times on the part of professional academic scholars. So did the increasing sophistication of the general reading public, which made it less difficult for these experts to write this type of history without sacrificing their intellectual standards. In any case, in 1954 the Nevins group—the Society of American Historians—joined the American Association for State and Local History in sponsoring the hard-cover magazine they had envisioned: *American Heritage.*

The success of *American Heritage* was rapid and substantial. It achieved a wide circulation, and a galaxy of the best professional historians began to publish in its pages. Its articles, at their best, have been authoritative, interesting, significant, and a pleasure to read. They have ranged over the whole course of American history from the pre-colonial era to the present, and have dealt with every aspect of American development from politics to painting and from economics to architecture.

The present selection from among the hundreds of essays and book excerpts that have appeared in *American Heritage* since 1954 does not pretend to offer "the best" of these articles, although any such collection would undoubtedly include many of those I have chosen. It seeks rather to provide a balanced assortment of articles to supplement and enrich general college courses in American history. Keeping in mind the structure of these courses and the topics they tend to emphasize, I have reprinted here articles which, in my opinion, will add depth and breadth to the student's understanding.

This is—by definition—popular history, but it is also history written by experts. The articles differ in purpose and approach. Some present new findings, some re-examine old questions from a fresh point of view, others magisterially distill and synthesize masses of facts and ideas. From the total the reader may extract, along with the specifics of the individual essays, a sense of the variety and richness of historical literature. He will observe how forty-odd historians (and not all of them academic scholars) have faced the task of presenting knowledge not to other historians alone but to an audience of intelligent and interested general readers. Since most of the students enrolled in college history courses are not specialists—even those who intend to become professional historians stand at the very beginning of their training— this approach seems to me ideally adapted to their needs. Many, though by no means all, of the subjects treated in these essays have also been covered in articles in professional historical periodicals, often written by the same historians. But as here presented, without sacrifice of intellectual standards, the material is not so much easier to grasp as it is more meaningful. Details are clearly related to larger issues; historical characters are delineated in the round, not presented as stick figures or automatons; too much previous knowledge is not assumed. I once read the draft of an essay on the history of the Arabs which contained the sentence, "The life and philosophy of Mohammed are well-known," and which then went on to other less universally understood topics. Such essays no doubt have their place, but that place is not in collections designed for beginners, whatever the subject.

Finally, I believe that at least some of the essays I have included here illustrate the truth that history is, at its best, an art as well as a science. After all, the ancients gave history its own Muse, Clio. From reading the following pages, I hope and expect that students will come to realize that history is a form of literature, that it can be *enjoyed,* not merely assimilated. Even those who see college history courses exclusively as training grounds for future professionals surely will not object if their students enjoy these readings while they learn.

This second edition has been inspired by the encouraging reception afforded *Historical Viewpoints* and by the fact that so many interesting new articles have been published in *American Heritage* since the book came out in 1970. This edition contains twelve new essays. Some replace articles in the first edition; I have included these new selections because they seemed better suited to current historical interests. Others represent additional material offered to provide more depth and variety to the volume. In particular, I have added essays that deal with social history, women, blacks, and of course ones that deal with the most recent past. Thus I hope that the book will serve even better than its predecessor the needs and interests of contemporary students of American history.

JOHN A. GARRATY
August 1974

Part One

A New World

Perils of the Sea of Darkness,
*by sixteenth-century Flemish
engraver Theodore de Bry,
combines truth and fantasy
to symbolize the Old World's
fascination with the new.*

Oliver La Farge
Myths That Hide the American Indian

As Oliver La Farge explains in this essay, the true character of the civilization of the American Indian has, from the time of Columbus, been shrouded in myth. White men have seen the Indians as they wished to see them, not as they were. Naturally, there are good reasons for this as well as bad: the tribes left no written records; they were scattered and isolated over a vast continent; and they differed one from another greatly in culture and social structure.

Years of patient research by archaeologists, anthropologists, and other students have gone into the work of reconstructing their way of life. As La Farge's essay shows, that task, if not completed, has been substantially advanced. Its importance, of course, is enormous, and not merely because of our interest in the first settlers of America. Only by understanding the Indians can the early history of the European in the New World be fully grasped.

An anthropologist by training, La Farge was an admirable exemplar of the role of the specialist in writing history for the general public. Besides his many scientific works, and a Pulitzer Prize winning novel, *Laughing Boy,* in articles like this one he brought to thousands of readers objective and yet moving portraits of Indian life.

*E*ver since the white men first fell upon them the Indians of what is now the United States have been hidden from white men's view by a number of conflicting myths. The oldest of these is the myth of the Noble Red Man or the Child of Nature, who is credited either with a habit of flowery oratory of implacable dullness or else with an imbecilic inability to converse in anything more than grunts and monosyllables.

That first myth was inconvenient. White men soon found their purposes better served by the myth of ruthless, faithless savages, and later, when the "savages" had been broken, of drunken, lazy good-for-nothings. All three myths coexist today, sometimes curiously blended in a schizophrenic confusion such as one often sees in the moving pictures. Through the centuries the mythical figure has been variously equipped; today he wears a feather headdress, is clothed in beaded buckskin, dwells in a tepee, and all but lives on horseback.

It was in the earliest period of the Noble Red Man concept that the Indians probably exerted their most important influence upon Western civilization. The theory has been best formulated by the late Felix S. Cohen, who, as a profound student of law concerning Indians, delved into early white-Indian relations, Indian political economy, and the white men's view of it. According to this theory, with which the present writer agrees, the French and English of the early seventeenth century encountered, along the East Coast of North America from Virginia southward, fairly advanced tribes whose semi-hereditary rulers depended upon the acquiescence of their people for the continuance of their rule. The explorers and first settlers interpreted these rulers as kings, their people as subjects. They found that even the commonest subjects were endowed with many rights and freedoms, that the nobility was fluid, and that commoners existed in a state of remarkable equality.

Constitutional monarchy was coming into being in England, but the divine right of kings remained firm doctrine. All European society was stratified in many classes. A somewhat romanticized observation of Indian society and government, coupled with the idea of the Child of Nature, led to the formulation, especially by French philosophers, of the theories of inherent rights in all men, and of the people as the source of the sovereign's authority. The latter was stated in the phrase, "consent of the governed." Both were carried over by Jefferson into our Declaration of Independence in the statement that "all men are created equal, that they are endowed by their Creator with certain unalienable Rights" and that governments derive "their just powers from the consent of the governed. . . ."

Thus, early observations of the rather simple, democratic organization of the more advanced coastal tribes, filtered through and enlarged by the minds of European philosophers whose thinking was ripe for just such material, at least influenced the formulation of a doctrine, or pair of doctrines, that furnished the intellectual base for two great revolutions and profoundly affected the history of mankind.

In the last paragraph I speak of "the more advanced" tribes.

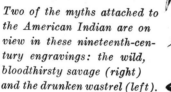
Two of the myths attached to the American Indian are on view in these nineteenth-century engravings: the wild, bloodthirsty savage (right) and the drunken wastrel (left).

Part of the myth about the first Americans is that all of them, or most of them, had one culture and were at the same stage of advancement. The tribes and nations that occupied North America varied enormously, and their condition was anything but static. The advent of the white men put a sudden end to a phase of increasingly rapid cultural evolution, much as if a race of people, vastly superior in numbers, in civilization, and above all in weapons, had overrun and conquered all of Europe in Minoan times. Had that happened, also, the conquerors would undoubtedly have concluded, as so many white men like to conclude about Indians, that that peculiar race of light-skinned people was obviously inferior to their own.

Human beings had been in the New World for at least 15,000 years. During much of that time, as was the case in the beginning everywhere, they advanced but little from a Palaeolithic hunting culture. Somewhere around 2,500 B.C. farming began with the domestication of corn either in Peru or in Meso-America* in the vicinity of western Guatemala. Farming brought about the sedentary life and the increased food supply necessary for cultural progress. By the time of the birth of Christ, the influence of the high cultures, soon to become true civilizations, in Meso-America was beginning to reach into the present United States. Within the next 1,500 years the Indians of parts of North America progressed dramatically. When the white men first landed, there were three major centers of high culture: the Southeast-Mississippi Valley, the Southwest, and the Northwest Coast. None of the peoples of these regions, incidentally, knew about war bonnets or lived in tepees.

The Southeast-Mississippi Valley peoples (for brevity, I shall refer to the area hereafter simply as "Southeast") seem to have had the

* Meso-America denotes the area in which the highest civilizations north of Peru developed, extending from a little north of Mexico City into Honduras.

strongest influences from Meso-America, probably in part by land along the coast of Texas, in part by sea across the Gulf of Mexico, whether direct from Mexico or secondhand through the peoples of the West Indies. There is a striking resemblance between some of their great earthen mounds, shaped like flat-topped pyramids, with their wood-and-thatch temples on top, and the stone-and-mortar, temple-topped pyramids of Meso-America. Some of their carvings and engravings strongly suggest that the artists had actually seen Meso-American sculptures. The list of similarities is convincingly long.

There grew up along the Mississippi Valley, reaching far to the north, and reaching also eastwards in the far south, the high culture generally called "Mound Builder." It produced a really impressive art, especially in carving and modeling, by far the finest that ever existed in North America. The history of advancing civilization in the New World is like that of the Old—a people develops a high culture, then barbarians come smashing in, set the clock part way back, absorb much of the older culture, and carry it on to new heights. A series of invasions of this sort seems to have struck the Mound Builders in late prehistoric times, when they were overrun by tribes mainly of Muskhogean and Iroquoian linguistic stock. Chief among these were the ancestors of the well-known Five Civilized Tribes—the Seminoles, Creeks, Choctaws, Chickasaws, and Cherokees. When white men first met them, their culture was somewhat lower than that of the earlier period in the land they occupied. Nonetheless, they maintained, in Florida, Alabama, Mississippi, Louisiana, and Georgia, the highest level east of the Rockies. A late movement of Iroquoian tribes, close relatives of the Cherokees, among them the Iroquois themselves, carried a simpler form of the same culture into Pennsylvania, New York, Ohio, and into the edge of Canada.

All of these people farmed heavily, their fields stretching for miles. They were few in a vast land—the whole population of the present United States was probably not over a million. Hunting and fishing, therefore, were excellent, and no reasonable people would drop an easy source of abundant meat. The development of their farming was held in check quantitatively by the supply of fish and game. They farmed the choice land, and if the fields began to be exhausted, they could move. They moved their habitations somewhat more freely than do we, but they were anything but nomadic. The southern tribesmen lived neither in wigwams nor tepees, but in houses with thatched roofs, which in the extreme south often had no walls. They had an elaborate social structure with class distinctions. Because of their size, the white men called their settlements "towns." The state of their high chiefs was kingly. They were a people well on the road toward civilization.

The Natchez of Mississippi had a true king, and a curious, elaborate social system. The king had absolute power and was known as the Sun. No ordinary man could speak to him except from a distance, shouting and making obeisances. When he went out, he was carried on a litter, as the royal and sacred foot could not be allowed to touch the ground. The Natchez nation was divided into two groups, or moieties: the aristocracy and the common people. The higher group was subdivided into Suns (the royal family), Nobles, and Honored Ones. The common people were known simply as Stinkers. A Stinker could marry anyone he pleased, but all the aristocrats had to marry out of their moiety, that is, marry Stinkers. When a female aristocrat married a Stinker man, her children belonged to her class; thus, when a Sun woman married a Stinker, her children were Suns. The children of the men, however, were lowered one class, so that the children of a Sun man, even of the Sun himself, became Nobles, while the children of an Honored One became lowly Stinkers.

This system in time, if nothing intervened, would lead to an overwhelming preponderance of aristocrats. The Natchez, however, for all their near-civilization, their temples, their fine crafts and arts, were chronically warlike. Those captives they did not torture to death they adopted, thus constantly replenishing the supply of Stinkers (a foreigner could become nothing else, but his grandchildren, if his son struck a royal fancy, might be Suns).

The Indians of the Southeast knew the Mexican-West Indian art of feather weaving, by means of which they made brilliant, soft cloaks. The Sun also wore a crown of an elaborate arrangement of feathers, quite unlike a war bonnet. In cloak and crown, carried shoulder-high on a litter, surrounded by his retainers, his majesty looked far more like something out of the Orient than anything we think of ordinarily when we hear the word "Indian."

The Natchez were warlike. All of the southeasterners were warlike. War was a man's proper occupation. Their fighting was deadly, ferocious, stealthy if possible, for the purpose of killing—men, women, or children, so long as one killed—and taking captives, especially strong males whom one could enjoy torturing to death. It is among these tribes and their simpler relatives, the Iroquois, that we find the bloodthirsty savage of fiction, but the trouble is that he is not a savage. He is a man well on the road toward civilization.

With the Iroquois, they shared a curious pattern of cruelty. A warrior expected to be tortured if captured, although he could, instead, be adopted, before torture or at any time before he had been crippled. He entered into it as if it were a contest, which he would win if his captors failed to wring a sign of pain from him and if he kept taunting them so long as he was conscious. Some of the accounts of such torture among the Iroquois, when the victim was a member of a tribe speaking the same language and holding to the same customs, are filled with a quality of mutual affection. In at least one case, when a noted enemy proved to have been too badly wounded before his capture to be eligible for adoption, the chief, who had hoped that the man would replace his own son, killed in battle, wept as he assigned him to his fate. At intervals between torments so sickening that one can hardly make one's self read through the tale of them, prisoner and captors exchanged news of friends and expressions of mutual esteem. Naturally, when tribes who did not hold to these customs, including white men, were subjected to this treatment it was not well received.

This pattern may have come into North America from a yet more advanced, truly civilized source. The Mexicans—the Aztecs and their neighbors—expected to be sacrificed if they were captured, and on occasion might insist upon it if their captors were inclined to spare them. They were not tortured, properly speaking, as a general rule, but some of the methods of putting them to death were not quick. What we find in North America may have been a debasement of the Mexican practices developed into an almost psychopathic pleasure among people otherwise just as capable of love, of kindness, of nobility, and of lofty thought as any anywhere—or what the conquistadores found in Mexico may have been a civilized softening of earlier, yet more fearful ways. The Aztecs tore fantastic numbers of hearts from living victims, and like the people of the Southeast, when not at war said "We are idle." They were artists, singers, dancers, poets, and great lovers of flowers and birds.

The Iroquois and Muskhogeans had a real mental sophistication. We observe it chiefly in their social order and what we know of their religions. The Iroquois did not have the royalty and marked divisions of classes that we find farther south, but their well-organized, firmly knit tribes were what enabled them, although few in numbers, to dominate the Algonkians who surrounded them. The Iroquois came nearer to having the matriarchy that popular fable looks for among primitive people than any other American tribe. Actual office was held by the men, but the women's power was great, and strongly influenced the selection of the officers.

Five of the Iroquois tribes achieved something unique in North America, rare anywhere, when in the sixteenth century they formed the League of the Five Nations—Senecas, Onondagas, Mohawks, Cayugas, and Oneidas—to which, later, the Tuscaroras were added. The league remained united and powerful until after the American Revolution, and exists in shadowy form to this day. It struck a neat balance between sovereignty retained by each tribe and sovereignty sacrificed to the league, and as so durable and effective a union was studied by the authors of our Constitution.

The league was founded by the great leader Hiawatha. Any resemblance between the fictional hero of Longfellow's poem and this real, dead person is purely coincidental. Longfellow got hold of the name and applied it to some Chippewa legends, which he rewrote thoroughly to produce some of the purest rot and the most heavy-footed verse ever to be inflicted upon a school child.

The Iroquois lived in "long houses," which looked like extended Quonset huts sheathed in bark. Smaller versions of these, and similarly covered, domed or conical structures, are "wigwams," the typical housing of the Northeast. Many people use the word "wigwam" as synonymous with "tepee," which is incorrect. A tepee, the typical dwelling of the Plains Indians of a later period, is a functional tent, usually covered with hides or, in recent years, canvas, and one of its essential features is that it is the shelter of constantly mobile people.

A tepee, incidentally, is about the most comfortable tent ever invented, winter or summer—provided you have two or three strong, competent women to attend to setting it up and striking it.

The great tribes we have been discussing showed their sophistication in a new way in their response to contact with Europeans. Their tribal organizations became tighter and firmer. From south to north they held the balance of power. The British success in establishing good relations with many of them was the key to driving the French out of the Mississippi area; to win the Revolution, the Americans had to defeat the Iroquois, whose favor up to then had determined who should dominate the Northeast. The southern tribes radically changed their costume, and quickly took over cattle, slaves, and many arts. By the time Andrew Jackson was ready to force their removal, the Cherokees had a stable government under a written constitution, with a bicameral parliament, an alphabet for writing their language, printing presses, a newspaper, schools, and churches.

Had it not been for the white men's insatiable greed and utter lawlessness, this remarkable nation would have ended with a unique demonstration of how, without being conquered, a "primitive" people could adapt itself to a new civilization on its own initiative. They would have become a very rare example of how aborigines could receive solid profit from the coming of the white men.

After the five Civilized Tribes were driven to Oklahoma, they formed a union and once again set up their governments and their public schools. Of course we could not let them have what we had promised them; it turned out that we ourselves wanted that part of Oklahoma after all, so once again we tore up the treaties and destroyed their system. Nonetheless, to this day they are a political power in the state, and when one of their principal chiefs speaks up, the congressmen do well to listen.

The tribes discussed until now and their predecessors in the same general area formed a means of transmission of higher culture to others, east and west. Their influence reached hardly at all to the northwards, as north of the Iroquois farming with native plants was difficult or impossible. On the Atlantic Coast of the United States the tribes were all more or less affected. Farming was of great importance. Even in New England, the status of chiefs was definite and fairly high. Confederacies and hegemonies, such as that of the Narragansetts over many of the Massachusetts tribes, occurred, of which more primitive people are incapable. Farther south, the state of such a chief as Powhatan was royal enough for Europeans to regard him as a king and his daughter as a true princess.

To the westward, the pattern of farming and sedentary villages extended roughly to the line that runs irregularly through Nebraska and Kansas, west of which the mean annual rainfall is below twenty inches. In wet cycles, there were prehistoric attempts to farm farther west, and in historic times the Apaches raised fair crops in the eastern foothills of the southern tip of the Rockies, but only the white men combined the mechanical equipment and the stupidity to break the turf and exhaust the soil of the dry, high plains.

An essay as short as this on so large a subject is inevitably filled with almost indefensible generalizations. I am stressing similarities, as in the case of the Iroquois-Southeast tribes, ignoring great unlikenesses. Generalizing again, we may say that the western farmers, whose cultures in fact differed enormously, also lived in fairly fixed villages. In the southern part, they built large houses covered with grass thatch. At the northwestern tip of the farming zone we find the Mandans, Hidatsa, and Crows, who lived in semi-subterranean lodges of heavy poles covered with earth, so big that later, when horses came to them, they kept their choice mounts inside. These three related, Siouan-speaking tribes living on the edge of the Plains are the first we have come to whose native costume, when white men first observed them, included the war bonnet. That was in the early nineteenth century; what they wore in 1600, no one knows.

The western farmers had their permanent lodges; they also had tepees. Immediately at hand was the country of the bison, awkward game for men on foot to hunt with lance and bow, but too fine a source of meat to ignore. On their hunting expeditions they took the conical tents. The size of the tepees was limited, for the heavy covers and the long poles had to be dragged either by the women or by dogs. Tepee life at that time was desirable only for a short time, when one roughed it.

The second area of Meso-American influence was the Southwest, as anthropologists define it—the present states of New Mexico and Arizona, a little of the adjacent part of Mexico, and various extensions at different times to the north, west, and east. We do not find here the striking resemblances to Meso-America in numbers of culture traits we find in the Southeast; the influence must have been much more indirect, ideas and objects passing in the course of trade from tribe to tribe over the thousand miles or so of desert northern Mexico.

In the last few thousand years the Southwest has been pretty dry, although not as dry as it is today. A dry climate and a sandy soil make an archaeologist's paradise. We can trace to some extent the actual transition from hunting and gathering to hunting plus farming, the appearance of the first permanent dwellings, the beginning of pottery-making, at least the latter part of the transition from twining and basketry to true weaving. Anthropologists argue over the very use of the term "Southwest" to denote a single area, because of the enormous variety of the cultures found within it. There is a certain unity, nonetheless, centering around beans, corn, squashes, tobacco, cotton, democracy, and a preference for peace. Admitting the diversity, the vast differences between, say, the Hopi and Pima farmers, we can still think of it as a single area, and for purposes of this essay concentrate on the best-studied of its cultures, the Pueblos.

The name "Pueblo" is the Spanish for "village," and was given to that people because they lived—and live—in compact, defensible settlements of houses with walls of stone laid up with adobe mortar or entirely of adobe. Since the Spanish taught them how to make rectangular bricks, pure adobe construction has become the commoner type. They already had worked out the same roofing as was usual in Asia Minor and around the Mediterranean in ancient times. A modern Pueblo house corresponds almost exactly to the construction of buildings dating back at least as far as 600 B.C. in Asia Minor.

The Pueblos, and their neighbors, the Navahos, have become well enough known in recent years to create some exception to the popular stereotype of Indians. It is generally recognized that they do not wear feathers and that they possess many arts, and that the Pueblos are sedentary farmers.

Farming has long been large in their pattern of living, and hunting perhaps less important than with any people outside the Southwest. Their society is genuinely classless, in contrast to that of the Southeast. Before the Spanish conquest, they were governed by a theocracy. Each tribe was tightly organized, every individual placed in his niche. The power of the theocracy was, and in some Pueblos still is, tyrannical in appearance. Physical punishment was used to suppress the rebellious; now more often a dissident member is subjected to a form of being sent to Coventry. If he be a member of the tribal council, anything he says at meetings is pointedly ignored. If he has some ceremonial function, he performs it, but otherwise he is left in isolation. I have seen a once self-assertive man, who for a time had been a strong leader in his tribe, subjected to this treatment for several years. By my estimation, he lost some thirty pounds, and he became a quiet conformist.

The power of the theocracy was great, but it rested on the consent of the governed. No man could overstep his authority, no one man had final authority. It went hard with the individual dissident, but the will of the people controlled all.

The Pueblos had many arts, most of which still continue. They wove cotton, made handsome pottery, did fine work in shell. Their ceremonies were spectacular and beautiful. They had no system of torture and no cult of warfare. A good warrior was respected, but what they wanted was peace.

The tight organization of the Pueblo tribes and the absolute authority over individuals continues now among only a few of them. The loosening is in part the result of contact with whites, in part for the reason that more and more they are building their houses outside of the old, solid blocks of the villages, simply because they are no longer under constant, urgent need for defense.

It is irony that the peace-loving southwestern farmers were surrounded by the worst raiders of all the wild tribes of North America. Around A.D. 1100 or 1200 there began filtering in among them bands of primitives, possessors of a very simple culture, who spoke languages of the Athabascan stock. These people had drifted down from western Canada. In the course of time they became the Navahos and the Apaches. For all their poverty, they possessed a sinew-backed bow of Asiatic type that was superior to any missile weapon known to the Southwest. They traded with the Pueblos, learned from them, stole from them, raided them. As they grew stronger, they became pests. The Navahos and the northeastern branch of the Apaches, called Jicarilla Apaches, learned farming. The Navahos in time became artists, above all the finest of weavers, but they did not give up their raiding habits.

These Athabascans did not glorify war. They made a business of it. Killing enemies was incidental; in fact, a man who killed an enemy had to be purified afterwards. They fought for profit, and they were about the only North Americans whose attitude toward war resembled professional soldiers'. This did not make them any less troublesome.

The last high culture area occupied a narrow strip along the Pacific Coast, from northern California across British Columbia to southern Alaska, the Northwest Coast culture. There was no Meso-American influence here, nor was there any farming. The hunting and fishing were so rich, the supply of edible wild plants so adequate, that there was no need for farming—for which in any case the climate was unfavorable. The prerequisite for cultural progress is a food supply so lavish that either all men have spare time, or some men can specialize in non-food-producing activities while others feed them. This condition obtained on the Northwest Coast, where men caught the water creatures from whales to salmon, and hunted deer, mountain sheep, and other game animals.

The area was heavily forested with the most desirable kinds of lumber. Hence wood and bark entered largely into the culture. Bark was shredded and woven into clothing, twined into nets, used for padding. Houses, chests, dishes, spoons, canoes, and boats were made of wood. The people became carvers and woodworkers, then carried their carving over onto bone and horn. They painted their houses, boats, chests, and their elaborate wooden masks. They made wooden armor, including visored helmets, and deadly wooden clubs. In a wet climate, they made raincloaks of bark and wore basketry hats, on the top of which could be placed one or more cylinders, according to the wearer's rank. The chiefs placed carvings in front of their houses that related their lineage, tracing back ultimately to some sacred being such as Raven or Bear—the famous, so-called totem poles.

I have said that the finest prehistoric art of North America was that of the Mound Builders; in fact, no Indian work since has quite equaled it—but that is, of course, a matter of taste. The greatest historic Indian art was that of the Northwest Coast. Their carvings, like the Mound Builder sculptures, demand comparison with our own work. Their art was highly stylized, but vigorous and fresh. As for all Indians, the coming of the white men meant ruin in the end, but at first it meant metal tools, the possession of which resulted in a great artistic outburst.

Socially they were divided into chiefs, commoners, and slaves. Slaves were obtained by capture, and slave-raiding was one of the principal causes of war. Generosity was the pattern with most Indians, although in the dry Southwest we find some who made a virtue of thrift. In the main, a man was respected because he gave, not because he possessed. The Northwest Coast chiefs patterned generosity into an ugliness. A chief would invite a rival to a great feast, the famous potlatch. At the feast he would shower his rival and other guests with gifts, especially copper disks and blankets woven of mountain sheep wool, which were the highest units of value. He might further show his lavishness by burning some possessions, even partially destroy a copper disk, and, as like as not, kill a few slaves.

If within a reasonable time the other chief did not reply with an even larger feast, at which he gave away or destroyed double what his rival had got rid of, he was finished as a chief—but if he did respond in proper form, he might be beggared, and also finished. That was the purpose of the show. Potlatches were given for other purposes, such as to authenticate the accession of the heir to a former chief, or to buy a higher status, but ruinous rivalry was constant. They seem to have been a rather disagreeable, invidious, touchy people. The cruelty of the southeasterners is revolting, but there is something especially unpleasant about proving one's generosity and carelessness of possessions by killing a slave—with a club made for that special purpose and known as a "slave-killer."

The Meso-American culture could spread, changing beyond recognition as it did so, because it carried its food supply with it. The Northwest Coast culture could not, because its food supply was restricted to its place of origin.

North and east of the Northwest Coast area stretched the sub-Arctic and the plains of Canada, areas incapable of primitive farming. To the south and east were mountains and the region between the Rockies and the Coastal ranges called the Great Basin. Within it are large stretches of true desert; most of it is arid. Early on, Pueblo influences reached into the southern part, in Utah and Nevada, but as the climate grew drier, they died away. It was a land to be occupied by little bands of simple hunters and gatherers of seeds and roots, not strong enough to force their way into anywhere richer.

In only one other area was there a natural food supply to compare with the Northwest Coast's, and that was in the bison range of the Great Plains. But, as already noted, for men without horses or rifles, hunting bison was a tricky and hazardous business. Take the year 1600, when the Spanish were already established in New Mexico and the English and French almost ready to make settlements on the East Coast, and look for the famous Plains tribes. They are not there. Some are in the mountains, some in the woodlands to the northeast, some farming to the eastward, within the zone of ample rainfall. Instead we find scattered bands of Athabascans occupying an area no one else wanted.

Then the white men turned everything upside down. Three elements were most important in the early influence: the dislodgment of eastern tribes, the introduction of the horse, and metal tools and firearms. Let us look first at the impact on the centers of high culture.

White men came late to the Northwest Coast, and at first only as traders. As already noted, early contact with them enriched the life of the Indians and brought about a cultural spurt. Then came settlers. The most advanced, best organized tribes stood up fairly well against them for a time, and they are by no means extinct, but of their old culture there are now only remnants, with the strongest survivals being in the arts. Today, those Indians who are in the "Indian business," making money from tourists, dress in fringed buckskin and war bonnets, because otherwise the tourists will not accept them as genuine.

The tribes of the Atlantic Coast were quickly dislodged or wiped out. The more advanced groups farther inland held out all through colonial times and on into the 1830's, making fairly successful adjustments to the changed situation, retaining their sovereignty, and enriching their culture with wholesale taking over of European elements, including, in the South, the ownership of Negro slaves. Finally, as already noted, they were forcibly removed to Oklahoma, and in the end their sovereignty was destroyed. They remain numerous, and although some are extremely poor and backward, others, still holding to their tribal affiliations, have merged successfully into the general life of the state, holding positions as high as chief justice of the state supreme court. The Iroquois still hold out in New York and in Canada on remnants of their original reservations. Many of them have had remarkable success in adapting themselves to white American life while retaining considerable elements of their old culture. Adherents to the old religion are many, and the rituals continue vigorously.

The British invaders of the New World, and to a lesser degree the French, came to colonize. They came in thousands, to occupy the land. They were, therefore, in direct competition with the Indians and acted accordingly, despite their verbal adherence to fine principles of justice and fair dealing. The Spanish came quite frankly to conquer, to Christianize, and to exploit, all by force of arms. They did not shilly-shally about Indian title to the land or Indian sovereignty, they simply took over, then granted the Indians titles deriving from the Spanish crown. They came in small numbers—only around 3,000 settled in the Southwest—and the Indian labor force was essential to their aims. Therefore they did not dislodge or exterminate the Indians, and they had notable success in modifying Indian culture for survival within their regime and contribution to it.

In the Southwest the few Spaniards, cut off from the main body in Mexico by many miles of difficult, wild country, could not have survived alone against the wild tribes that shortly began to harry them. They needed the Pueblo Indians and the Pueblos needed them. The Christian Pueblos were made secure in their lands and in their local self-government. They approached social and political equality. During the period when New Mexico was under the Mexican Republic, for two years a Taos Indian, braids, blanket, and all, was governor of the territory. Eighteen pueblos survive to this day, with a population now approaching 19,000, in addition to nearly 4,000 Hopis, whose culture is Pueblo, in Arizona. They are conservative progressives, prosperous on the whole, with an excellent chance of

Alfred Jacob Miller's painting of a
Plains warrior—the myth still endures.

surviving as a distinctive group for many generations to come. It was in the house of a Pueblo priest, a man deeply versed in the old religion as well as a devout Catholic, that I first saw color television.

The Spanish, then, did not set populations in motion. That was done chiefly from the east. The great Spanish contribution was loosing the horses. They did not intend to; in fact, they made every possible effort to prevent Indians from acquiring horses or learning to ride. But the animals multiplied and ran wild; they spread north from California into Oregon; they spread into the wonderful grazing land of the high Plains, a country beautifully suited to horses.

From the east, the tribes were pressing against the tribes farther west. Everything was in unhappy motion, and the tribes nearest to the white men had firearms. So the Chippewas, carrying muskets, pushed westward into Minnesota, driving the reluctant Dakotas, the Sioux tribes, out of the wooded country into the Plains as the horses spread north. At first the Dakotas hunted and ate the strange animals, then they learned to ride them, and they were off.

The Sioux were mounted. So were the Blackfeet. The semi-civilized Cheyennes swung into the saddle and moved out of the farming country onto the bison range. The Kiowas moved from near the Yellowstone to the Panhandle; the Comanches came down out of the Rocky Mountains; the Arapahos, the Crows, abandoning their cornfields, and the Piegans, the great fighting names, all followed the bison. They built their life around the great animals. They ate meat lavishly all year round; their tepees, carried or dragged now by horses, became commodious. A new culture, a horse-and-bison culture, sprang up overnight. The participants in it had a wonderful time. They feasted, they roved, they hunted, they played. Over a serious issue, such as the invasion of one tribe's territory by another, they could fight deadly battles, but otherwise even war was a game in which shooting an enemy was an act earning but little esteem, but touching one with one's bare hand or with a stick was the height of military achievement.

This influx of powerful tribes drove the last of the Athabascans into the Southwest. There the Apaches and the Navahos were also mounted and on the go, developing their special, deadly pattern of war as a business. In the Panhandle country, the Kiowas and Comanches looked westward to the Spanish and Pueblo settlements, where totally alien peoples offered rich plunder. The Pueblos, as we have seen, desired to live at peace. The original Spanish came to conquer; their descendants, becoming Spanish-Americans, were content to hold what they had, farm their fields, and graze their flocks. To the north of the two groups were Apaches and Utes; to the east, Kiowas and Comanches; to the south, what seemed like unlimited Apaches; and to the west the Navahos, of whom there were several thousands by the middle of the seventeenth century.

The tribes named above, other than the Kiowas and Comanches, did not share in the Plains efflorescence. The Navahos staged a different cultural spurt of their own, combining extensive farming with constant horseback plundering, which in turn enabled them to become herdsmen, and from the captured wool develop their remarkable weaving industry. The sheep, of course, which became important in their economy, also derived from the white men. Their prosperity and their arts were superimposed on a simple camp life. With this prosperity, they also developed elaborate rituals and an astoundingly rich, poetic mythology.

The Dakotas first saw horses in 1722, which makes a convenient peg date for the beginning of the great Plains culture. A little over a hundred years later, when Catlin visited the Mandans, it was going full blast. The memory of a time before horses had grown dim. By 1860 the Plains tribes were hard-pressed to stand the white men off; by 1880 the whole pattern was broken and the bison were gone. At its height, Plains Indian culture was brittle. Materially, it depended absolutely on a single source of food and skins; in other aspects, it required the absolute independence of the various tribes. When these two factors were eliminated, the content was destroyed. Some Indians may still live in tepees, wear at times their traditional clothing, maintain here and there their arts and some of their rituals, but these are little more than fringe survivals.

While the Plains culture died, the myth of it spread and grew to become embedded in our folklore. Not only the Northwest Coast Indians but many others as unlikely wear imitations of Plains Indian costume and put on "war dances," to satisfy the believers in the myth. As it exists today in the public mind, it still contains the mutually incongruous elements of the Noble Red Man and the Bloodthirsty Savage that first came into being three centuries and a half ago, before any white man had ever seen a war bonnet or a tepee, or any Indian had ridden a horse.

Lewis Hanke
The Great Debate over Indian Policy

One of the most difficult problems that historians face, especially when dealing with distant events and cultures foreign to their own, is assimilating the point of view of the actors whose behavior they seek to describe and explain. Those who write about the European settlement of the New World confront this problem in one of its most knotty aspects, because from the perspective of our own times the actions of the Europeans appear so inhumane as to defy explanation, let alone justification. How can their "settlement" of the Americas be described as anything but naked, unprovoked aggression, their treatment of the native inhabitants in less blunt terms than cruel and callously overbearing? Yet we know that these Europeans were human beings, most of them—we may safely assume—no better or worse than ourselves. The historian's task is to show why they behaved as they did, and this involves understanding their values and assumptions as well as their motives. The good historian does not suspend judgment but attempts to judge the subjects under investigation only after internalizing as much as possible of the mental and emotional baggage that they carried through life.

The following essay by Lewis Hanke of the University of Massachusetts, an expert on the history of Spanish colonization and recently President of the American Historical Association, goes far toward making the behavior of the Europeans in America less incredible in modern eyes. His hero, Bartolomé de Las Casas, about whom he has written extensively, was throughout most of his long life a defender of the rights of the Indians and an admirer of their culture and their artistic achievements. But many of Las Casas' ideas and assumptions seem as narrow-minded as those of his contemporaries who considered the Indians subhuman, fit only for slavery or extinction. The essay deals on one level with the struggle waged among the Spaniards over Indian policy, but at a deeper and more important level it throws light on the whole history of the New World and on human nature itself.

When Hernando Cortés and his little band of Spaniards fought their way in 1519 from the tropical shores of Mexico up to the high plateau and first saw stretched below them the Aztec capital Tenochtitlán, gleaming on its lake under the morning sun, they experienced one of the truly dramatic moments in the history of America. Fortunately we have the words of a reporter worthy of the scene, the foot soldier Bernal Díaz del Castillo, whose *True History of the Conquest of New Spain* is one of the classics of the Western world. He wrote:

"Gazing on such wonderful sights we did not know what to say or whether what appeared before us was real; for on the one hand there were great cities and in the lake ever so many more, and the lake itself was crowded with canoes, and in the causeway were many bridges at intervals, and in front of us stood the great City of Mexico, and we—we did not number even four hundred soldiers!"

That was a soldier's memory, and even today the Spanish conquest of the New World is widely believed, especially by English-speaking peoples, to have been a purely military exploit of a peculiarly ruthless nature. That the period of discovery and conquest was full of violence is certain.

But what deserves more notice is quite another aspect of this turbulent period: the great struggle among the Spaniards themselves to determine how to apply Christian precepts to relations with the natives they encountered as they crossed the rivers, plains, swamps, and mountains of the New World. The going forth together of the Spanish standard and the Roman Catholic cross is well known. But too often the cross is dismissed as merely a symbol of a national church as much bent on "conquest" as the standard-bearers. The real effort to convert the natives, which moved many Spaniards and greatly concerned the Crown of Spain, and the powerful role religious conscience played throughout the conquest have been largely overlooked. Other nations sent out bold explorers and established empires. But no other European nation plunged into the struggle for Christian justice, as she understood it, that Spain engaged in shortly after Christopher Columbus first reached the New World.

So the story deserves to be told of Bartolomé de Las Casas, perhaps the most loved and hated and certainly the most influential of many Spaniards who believed the Spanish mandate in America to be primarily an obligation to convert the Indians peacefully to the Christian faith. He gave fifty strenuous years of his life to protect the natives from the treatment his fellow countrymen accorded them.

But, to be understood, he must be seen against the background of the Spanish colonial effort as a whole. Like many others who opposed a purely military conquest, Las Casas represented the church that the Spanish Crown sent to the New World in double harness with the conquistadors. For this conquest was unique. The Spaniards, with the approval of the Pope and carrying out the commands of their King, were to claim the new lands and the tribute of their inhabitants for the Spanish Crown (a worldly purpose) and bring these inhabitants into the knowledge of Christ (a spiritual purpose). The dual motivation behind the enterprise made conflict inevitable—conflict not only between the Spanish and the natives they were dealing with, but also among the Spaniards themselves, for although practically all Spaniards accepted both purposes as good, they could never agree for long on how best to achieve them.

From our vantage point, four hundred years later, we can see the tragedy of the Spanish conquest: the Crown and the nation were attempting the impossible. On the one hand, they sought imperial dominion, prestige, and revenue; on the other, the voluntary commitment of many peoples culturally different from themselves to the new religion they offered or imposed. The tragedy of the Indians was that in order to accomplish either objective the Spaniards were bound to overthrow established Indian values and to disrupt or destroy Indian cultures and civilizations, as they did in spectacular fashion in Mexico and Peru.

But from Spanish documents alone—the voices of the conquered can be heard only through Spanish materials—we may reconstruct the extraordinary story of how Christian conscience worked as a leaven during the onrushing conquest, insisting on judging men's deeds and the nation's policies. The struggle centered upon the aborigines. Influenced by the wealth of medieval legends that for centuries had circulated in Europe, the Spaniards expected to meet in America giants, pygmies, griffins, wild men, human beings adorned with tails, and other fabulous folk. When Cortés embarked from Cuba upon the conquest of Mexico, Governor Diego Velázquez instructed him to look in Aztec lands for strange beings with great flat ears and doglike faces. Francisco de Orellana was so sure that he had met warrior women on his famous voyage of 1540–41 that the mightiest river in South America was named the Amazon.

The plumed and painted peoples actually encountered soon perplexed the Spanish nation, from King to common citizen. Who were they and where did they come from? What was their nature, especially their capacity for European civilization and Christianity, and how should they be dealt with? Few significant figures of the conquest failed to deliver opinions, and the Council of the Indies held long formal inquiries on the subject. The voices of dogmatic and troubled individuals—ecclesiastics, soldiers, colonists, and royal officials in America as well as men of action and thought in Spain—rose continually in a dissident chorus of advice to Crown and Council.

Against this background of national excitement Bartolomé de Las Casas arose to devote his life to the Indians. His contemporaries saw him variously as a saintly leader, a dangerous fanatic, or a sincere fool; and, because his reputation is bound up with judgments on the conquest as a whole, his memory is kept green even today by support and attack. Of Las Casas the man, despite his powerful role, we know little. Neither friend nor enemy described his appearance, and no painter recorded it during his life. He wrote no autobiography; we must depend largely upon his historical and polemical writings for knowledge of his life and ideas.

We do know that he was born in Seville in 1474 and was there when Columbus, returning from his first voyage in 1493, triumphantly exhibited through the streets natives and parrots from the New World. His father accompanied Columbus on the second voyage and is supposed to have given the boy an Indian slave to serve as a page during his student days. Bartolomé went to America, probably with Nicolás de Ovando in 1502, and, even though he had already received minor orders, he was little better than the rest of the gentlemen-adventurers who rushed to the New World, bent on speedily acquiring fortunes. He obtained Indian slaves, worked them in mines, and attended to the cultivation of his estates. While he did not mistreat his Indians, their lowly lot seems not to have disturbed him. In 1512 he participated in the conquest of Cuba and was rewarded with both land and the service of some Indians.

It was against such men as Las Casas that a young Dominican friar named Antonio de Montesinos delivered two indignant sermons in Hispaniola in 1511. This first public cry on behalf of human liberty in the New World, whose texts were ''I am a voice crying in the wilderness'' and ''Suffer me a little and I will show thee that I have yet to speak on God's behalf,'' stunned and then enraged the colonists, for Montesinos declared they were in mortal sin by reason of their cruelty to the Indians. Of Montesinos, whom the King shortly commanded to be silent, we know little except this brave moment of protest, which has been called one of the great events in the spiritual history of mankind. Las Casas shared the resistance of the other colonists to the cry. Like them, he took no steps to change his way of life, and for more than two years after the sermons he continued as a gentleman-ecclesiastic, although on one occasion a priest refused him the sacraments because he held slaves. The ensuing dispute disturbed without convincing him.

But the seed of a great decision was growing within this obstinate man, as yet unaware that he was destined to become the greatest Indian champion of them all. One day in the spring of 1514, while he was preparing a sermon for Whitsunday at the newly established Cuban settlement of Sancti Espiritus, his eye fell upon this verse in Ecclesiasticus: ''He that sacrificeth of a thing wrongfully gotten, his offering is ridiculous, and the gifts of unjust men are not accepted.''

Pondering on this text and on the doctrines preached by the Dominicans, he became increasingly convinced ''that everything done to the Indians thus far was unjust and tyrannical.'' The scales fell from his eyes. He saw at last what was to be forever after the truth for him, and experienced as complete a change of life as did Saul of Tarsus on the road to Damascus.

Characteristically, he entered upon the new life immediately. He freed his Indians and preached a sermon at Sancti Espiritus against his fellow Spaniards. It shocked them as much as Montesinos had shocked his congregation. The path thus chosen in his fortieth year Las Casas was to follow for the more than fifty years that remained to him; the energy and skill hitherto employed for his own comfort and enrichment led him to far places, and many times across the Ocean Sea, to attack and astonish generations of his countrymen.

As one of the dominating personalities of Spain's most glorious age, he wrote more copiously, spoke more vigorously, and lived longer than any other prominent figure of the conquest. He was no ivory-tower scholar but a tenacious fighter always eager to put into practice the doctrines he preached. And, though he insisted that all dealing with Indians should be peaceful, those of his fellow Spaniards who opposed his views found him an aggressive and unrelenting opponent.

One of his first projects, undertaken in 1521, was an attempt to colonize the northern coast of Venezuela with Spanish farmers who were to till the soil, treat the Indians kindly, and thus lay the basis for an ideal Christian community. The colony was a complete failure, largely because the Spaniards involved sought to enrich themselves rather than to put into effect the aspirations of Las Casas. Deeply discouraged, he entered the Dominican Order and for ten years, meditating and studying, remained apart from the affairs of the world. Then he took up the battle again. Until his death in 1566 at the age of ninety-two, he fought the good fight in divers ways and places; in Nicaragua he sought to block wars he considered unjust; in Mexico he engaged in bitter debates with other ecclesiastics over justice for the Indians; in Guatemala he promoted a plan for the peaceful conquest and Christianization of the Indians; before the royal court in Spain he agitated successfully on behalf of many laws to protect the American natives. He even served as bishop for awhile, at Chiapa in southern Mexico. During his last two decades, after his final return to Spain in 1547 at the age of seventy-three, he became a sort of attorney-at-large for the Indians.

It was during this last period also that he produced and published some of his most important works. Of those writings published in his own lifetime, the tract that most immediately inflamed Spaniards was the *Very Brief Account of the Destruction of the Indies*. This thundering denunciation of Spanish cruelty and oppression, full of harsh accusations and horrifying statistics on the number of Indians killed, was printed in 1552 in Seville. Even though Las Casas believed treatment of the Indians was "less bad" in Mexico, the work is a thoroughgoing indictment of Spanish action in all parts of the "Indies."

Translations of the *Very Brief Account* brought out in English, Dutch, French, German, Italian, and Latin powerfully influenced the world to believe that Spaniards were inherently cruel. The De Bry drawings that illustrated many of the texts, depicting Spaniards hunting Indians with mastiffs and butchering even women and children, graphically underlined the charges. Thus the political use

The Spanish inscription under this late eighteenth-century
portrait of Bartolomé de Las Casas reads: "Order of
Preachers, Bishop of Chiapas. Most zealous apostle and defender of the welfare of the Indians."

the enemies of Spain made of the writings of Las Casas helped usher in the modern age of propaganda For, ironically enough, his zeal to touch the consciences of his own king and countrymen by stressing the cruelties of the conquistadors was largely responsible for that dark picture of Spain's work in America which has for hundreds of years borne the name, "The Black Legend"—*La leyenda negra*— which is still widely believed, at least in English-speaking lands.

Although Las Casas' principal aim was to shame the Spanish conscience, he was also a historian, and his *Historia de las Indias* remains one of the basic documents of the discovery and early conquest of America. He has also been recognized as an important political theorist, and as one of the first anthropologists of America. Although sixteenth-century Spain was a land of eminent scholars and bold thinkers, few of his contemporaries matched the wide range of Las Casas' learning or the independence of his judgments.

Two of his major convictions show how he challenged the Christian conscience of his time to confront the great issues presented by the Spanish conquest. The first was that Christianity must be preached to the Indians by peaceful means alone. The second was that the Indians were human beings to be educated and Christianized, not half-men to be enslaved and kept down in what one sixteenth-century Englishman described as "ethnique darkness."

To prove his first point Las Casas wrote an enormous treatise, *The Only Method of Attracting All People to the True Religion*; though only a portion has been preserved, that remnant is a large volume. The doctrine he enunciated in this first of his many polemical writings was simple enough. He quoted, as did Pope Paul III in the bull "Sublimis Deus," the words of Christ, "Go ye and teach all nations," and agreed that "nations" included the American Indians. As the Pope declared in Rome in that momentous pronouncement on June 9, 1537, at about the time that Las Casas was preaching the same doctrine in Guatemala:

> The sublime God so loved the human race that he not only created man in such wise that he might participate in the good that other creatures enjoy, but also endowed him with capacity to attain to the inaccessible and invisible Supreme Good and behold it face to face . . . all are capable of receiving the doctrines of the faith . . . We . . . consider that the Indians are truly men and that they are not only capable of undertaking the Catholic faith, but according to our information, they desire exceedingly to receive it . . . The said Indians and all other people who may later be discovered by Christians are by no means to be deprived of their liberty or the possession of their property, even though they be outside the faith of Jesus Christ; and they may and should, freely and legitimately, enjoy their liberty and the possession of their property; nor should they be in any way enslaved; should the contrary happen it shall be null and of no effect. . . . By virtue of our

apostolic authority, we declare . . . that the said Indians and other peoples should be converted to the faith of Jesus Christ by preaching the word of God and by the example of good and holy living.

Las Casas applied this doctrine even more specifically than the Pope. He declared that wars against the Indians were unjust and tyrannical; hence the gold, silver, pearls, jewels, and lands wrested from them were wrongfully gotten and must be restored. To subdue and convert the natives by force was not only unlawful, it was also unnecessary. For once the Indians accepted Christianity, their next and inevitable step would be to acknowledge the King of Spain as their sovereign.

Again and again Las Casas returned to his central theme. The proper method for conversion was "bland, suave, sweet, pleasing, tranquil, modest, patiently slow, and above all peaceful and reasonable." Moreover, following Saint Augustine, he insisted that faith depended upon belief, which presupposed understanding. This brought him into conflict with those who favored wholesale baptism of Indians without too many questions asked or catechisms learned. The friars who bore the brunt of the frontier missionary campaigns went about their work with uplifted hearts and a firm conviction that the souls of the Indians constituted the true silver to be mined in America. Indeed, the conquest presented them with a wonderful opportunity, for, though Luther was challenging the Church in Europe, they were determined to build it anew and make it unassailable in the New World. They recorded impressive baptismal statistics. The Franciscans, who believed in mass baptism and sprinkled holy water over Indian heads until their hands could no longer hold the hyssop, calculated that in Mexico alone, between 1524 and 1536, they had saved four million souls. Urged on by flaming zeal, they were exasperated by Las Casas, who wanted each Indian properly instructed in the faith before baptism.

Influenced by Las Casas' doctrine of peaceful persuasion, his Dominican brothers actually tried to put it into effect beginning in 1537, in the spirit of one of Las Casas' favorite authorities, St. John Chrysostom, who had declared: "Men do not consider what we say but what we do—we may philosophize interminably, but if when the occasion arises we do not demonstrate with our actions the truth of what we have been saying, our words will have done more harm than good." For this demonstration of Las Casas' ideas they chose the only land left unconquered in that region, the province of Tuzutlán in present-day Guatemala. It was a mountainous, rainy tropical country filled with fierce beasts, snakes, and large monkeys. Worst of all, it lacked salt. The ferocious natives there were impossible to subjugate, or so believed the conquistadors, who had invaded the region three times and had as often returned "holding their heads." *Tierra de guerra*, they named it—"Land of War."

To this province and people Las Casas offered to go, to induce them voluntarily to become vassals of the King of Spain and pay him tribute according to their ability, to teach them and to preach the Christian faith. All this he proposed to do without arms or soldiers, his only weapon being the word of God and the "reasons of the Holy Gospel." Governor Alonso Maldonado speedily granted his two modest requests: that Indians won over by peaceful methods should not be parceled out to serve Spaniards but should be declared direct dependents of the King, with only moderate tribute to pay; and that for five years no Spaniards except Las Casas and his brother Dominicans should enter the province, so that secular Spaniards might not disturb the Indians or "provoke scandal."

It would be gratifying to report that the experiment in Guatemala went smoothly, but the facts are otherwise. For ten years the colonists in the nearby capital and the ecclesiastics fought stubbornly over the peaceful preaching of the faith. During this time the municipal council of Santiago informed the King that Las Casas was an unlettered friar, an envious, turbulent, most unsaintly fellow, who kept the land in an uproar and would, unless checked, destroy Spanish rule in the New World; furthermore, that the so-called "peaceful" Indians revolted every day and killed many Spaniards. But royal orders continued to flow from Spain supporting the Dominicans and—amid the sardonic laughter of the colonists—the Land of War was officially christened "the Land of True Peace."

In 1544 Las Casas was appointed Bishop of Chiapa, a region which included Tuzutlán. His battle with the colonists grew so hot that a royal investigator was sent to that area in 1547 to look into alleged mistreatment of the Dominicans by the Spanish colonists and reported that much supporting evidence could be found. For a time the Bishop himself fled to Nicaragua to escape his irate flock, many of whom, including the judges of the royal *audiencia*, he had excommunicated.

The end of the experiment is chronicled in a sad letter the friars sent to the Council of the Indies in May, 1556. Writing so that the King might clearly understand what had happened, they described the strenuous work they had done for years, despite the great heat and difficulty of the land. But always "the devil was vigilant" and finally he had stirred up the pagan priests, who called in some neighboring infidel Indians to help provoke a revolt in which the friars and their followers were burned out of their homes and some thirty were killed by arrows, one being sacrificed before a pagan idol. Among those who died was a zealous missionary able to preach in seven Indian languages. The Spaniards in Santiago, citing the royal order forbidding them to enter the territory, had unctuously declined the friars' request for help. The story ended when the King ordered the punishment of the rebellious Indians; the Land of True Peace became even poorer, and the peaceful conversion of Indians there ceased.

Despite this failure, Las Casas, remaining true to his idea, returned to Spain in 1547 to urge his point of view before King and Council. Now seventy-three, after nearly half a century of experience in Indian affairs, he arrived just in time to direct the campaign for his second great conviction: that the aborigines were human beings with the same essential rights as Spaniards. It was a dangerous moment for the Indians, for the ancient theory of Aristotle—that some men are by nature slaves—had been invoked, had been gratefully received by colonists and officials, and had been found conveniently applicable to Indians from the coasts of Florida to the mountains of far-distant Chile. The proposal that someone else should do the physical work of the world appealed strongly to sixteenth-century Spaniards, whose taste for martial glory and religious conquest and distaste for labor came from their forefathers, who had struggled for centuries to eject the Moslems from Spain. And when to this doctrine was linked the concept that the inferior beings were actually benefited by the labor they performed, the proposition became invincibly attractive.

The Aristotelian doctrine had first been applied to the American Indians in 1519, when Las Casas at the age of forty-five clashed with Juan Quevedo, Bishop of Darién, at Barcelona before the young Emperor Charles V. Las Casas had denounced the bishop for invoking such a non-Christian idea and had dismissed Aristotle as a "gentile burning in Hell, whose doctrine we need not follow except in so far as it conforms to Christian truth." At the same time Las Casas enunciated the basic concept which would guide his action on behalf of the Indians all the rest of his agitated life: "Our Christian religion is suitable for and may be adapted to all the nations of the world, and all alike may receive it; and no one may be deprived of his liberty, nor may he be enslaved on the excuse that he is a natural slave, as it would appear that the reverend bishop of Darién advocates." But no decision had emerged from the debate; the episode was merely a prelude to the important drama that unfolded thirty years later when Las Casas confronted the scholar Juan Ginés de Sepúlveda in Valladolid, the somber Spanish capital on the desolate plain of Castile.

This great dispute originated when the Council of the Indies declared to the King on July 3, 1549, that the dangers both to the Indians and to the King's conscience which the conquests incurred were so great that no future military expedition should be licensed without his express permission and that of the Council. The Council declared:

> The greed of those who undertake conquests and the timidity and humility of the Indians is such that we are not certain whether any instruction will be obeyed. It would be fitting for Your Majesty to order a meeting of learned men, theologians, and jurists . . . to . . . consider the manner in which these conquests should be carried on . . . justly and with security of conscience.

Accordingly, in April of 1550 the King, Charles I of Spain and Charles V of the Holy Roman Empire, ordered that all New World conquests be suspended until a special group of theologians and counselors—to be convened that very year—should decide upon a just method of conducting them.

In 1550 Charles' influence was felt in every country of Europe. His possessions stretched to the Netherlands in the north and Milan in the south; in the New World his bold captains had raced over a vast territory from northern Mexico some seven thousand miles south to Buenos Aires, and his ships had even reached Manila far across the Pacific. In the fifty-eight years since Columbus' landfall Spaniards had discovered one thousand times more new land than had been explored in the previous one thousand years of medieval Europe. In the New World great Indian empires—the Inca and the Aztec being the most notable—had toppled before Spanish soldiers, while in the Old, Charles sturdily fought back both Protestants and Turks. Probably never before had such a mighty sovereign ordered his conquests to cease until it should be decided if they were just.

We do not know where in Valladolid the sessions of the "Council of Fourteen"—which began in mid-August—were held. Perhaps the Council sat in the halls of the ancient university or in the Dominican monastery of San Gregorio, whose imposing buildings still stand. Among the judges were outstanding theologians and veteran members of the councils of Castile and of the Indies; this was the last significant dispute on the nature of the Indians and the justice of Spain's dominion over America.

Las Casas was bold indeed to engage Sepúlveda in learned combat, for this humanist scholar, who had given comfort to Spanish officials and conquistadors by composing a treatise defending the Spanish conquest, had one of the best trained minds of his time. During years of study in Italy he had become one of the principal scholars in the recovery of the "true" Aristotle, and he enjoyed great prestige at court. In 1548, not long before joining battle with Las Casas, he had published in Paris his Latin translation of Aristole's *Politics*, which he considered his principal contribution to knowledge.

The disputants had been summoned to Valladolid to answer the question, Is it lawful for the King of Spain to wage war on the Indians before preaching the faith to them in order to subject them to his rule, so that afterward they may be more easily instructed in the faith? Sepúlveda had come to prove that this was "both lawful and expedient." Las Casas was there to declare it "inquitous, and contrary to our Christian religion."

On the first day of the dispute Sepúlveda spoke for three hours, giving a résumé of his work "Demócrates." On the second day Las Casas appeared, armed with a monumental treatise, still unpublished, which he proceeded to read word for word. This scholastic onslaught continued for five days, until the reading was completed or—as

Sepúlveda suggested—until the members of the Council could bear no more. The two principals did not appear together, but the judges discussed the issues with them separately and also carried on discussions among themselves.

Sepúlveda's fundamental idea was simple. It was lawful and necessary to wage war against the natives for four reasons: (1) For the gravity of the sins which the Indians had committed, especially their idolatries and their "sins against nature"—cruelty to their fellows, cannibalism, and use of human sacrifice in religious ceremonies; (2) On account of the rudeness of their natures, which obliged them to serve persons, like the Spaniards, having a more refined nature; (3) In order to spread the faith, which would be more easily accomplished by the prior subjugation of the natives; (4) To protect the weak among the natives themselves.

The arguments of Las Casas require little detailed analysis: he simply called for justice for the Indians. But the judges at Valladolid, like the later Scottish philosopher who declared, "Blessed are they that hunger and thirst after justice, but it is easier to hunger and thirst after it than to define it," inquired of Las Casas exactly how the conquest ought to proceed. He replied that, when no danger threatened, preachers alone should be sent. In particularly dangerous parts of the Indies, fortresses should be built on the borders, and little by little the people would be won over to Christianity by peace, love, and good example. It is clear that Las Casas, despite the failure at Tuzutlán, never abandoned his hopes for peaceful colonization and persuasion.

The focal point of the argument was Sepúlveda's second justification for the Spaniards' rule: the "natural rudeness and inferiority" of the Indians, which, he declared, accorded with the doctrine of philosophers that some men are born to be natural slaves. Indians in America were without exception rude persons born with a limited understanding, he claimed, and therefore they were to be classed as *servi a natura*, bound to serve their superiors and natural lords, the Spaniards. These inferior people "require, by their own nature and in their own interests, to be placed under the authority of civilized and virtuous princes or nations, so that they may learn, from the might, wisdom, and law of their conquerors, to practice better morals, worthier customs and a more civilized way of life." The Indians are as inferior "as children are to adults, as women are to men, as different from Spaniards as cruel people are from mild people."

Compare then those blessings enjoyed by Spaniards of prudence, genius, magnanimity, temperance, humanity, and religion with those of the *homunculi* [little men] in whom you will scarcely find even vestiges of humanity, who not only possess no science but who also lack letters and preserve no monument of their history except certain vague and obscure reminiscences of some things in certain paintings. Neither do they have written laws, but barbaric institutions and customs. They do not even have private property.

The fatuity of Sepúlveda's utterances is the more striking when one considers how much information on Indian culture and intellectual capacity was then available. It had been thirty years since the German artist Albrecht Dürer had seen the artistic booty that Cortés had dispatched from Montezuma's Mexico to Charles V and had

The title page of the earliest printed Spanish–Mexican Indian dictionary, published in 1555 by the scholar–friar Alonso de Molina.

written in his diary: ". . . I saw among them amazing artistic objects, and I marvelled over the subtle ingenuity of the men in these distant lands, indeed I cannot say enough about the things that were brought before me." Few were equipped to judge as expertly as Dürer the artistic accomplishments of the New World, but by 1550 much of the Aztec, Maya, and Inca culture had come to the notice of Spaniards, and a mass of material rested in the archives of the Council of the Indies. The mathematical achievements of the Mayas and the art and engineering feats of the Incas were not fully appreciated then, but much information was available. Even Cortés, whom Sepúlveda so admired, had been much impressed by some of the Indian laws and achievements, which surprised him since he considered them "barbarians lacking in reason, and in knowledge of God, and in communication with other nations."

But Spaniards who had not been to America had no basis for understanding Indians or assessing their cultural power and potentiality, and many were ready to agree with Sepúlveda when he asked: "How can we doubt that these people, so uncivilized, so barbaric, so contaminated with many sins and obscenities . . . have been justly conquered by such an excellent, pious, and most just king as was Ferdinand the Catholic and as is now Emperor Charles, and by such a humane nation which is excellent in every kind of virtue?"

In reply to Sepúlveda's wholesale denigration of the Indians, Las Casas presented to the judges his 550-page Latin manuscript "Apologia," sixty-three chapters of close reasoning and copious citations dedicated to demolishing the arguments of his opponent. He also seems to have presented a summary, perhaps for those judges who might falter in plowing through his detailed treatise.

Bringing into court his long experience in the Indies, he stressed heavily that "God had deprived Sepúlveda of any personal knowledge of the New World." Painting a glowing picture of Indian ability and achievement, he drew heavily upon his earlier *Apologetic History*, a tremendous accumulation of 870 folio pages on Indian culture that he had begun in 1527 and completed some twenty years later, to refute the charge that the Indians were semi-animals whose property and services could be commandeered by Spaniards and against whom war could justly be waged. Here he advanced the astonishing idea that the American Indians compared favorably with the Egyptians, Greeks, and Romans—were indeed superior to them in some ways—and in fact fulfilled every one of Aristotle's requirements for the good life. In several aspects, he insisted, they even surpassed the Spaniards themselves! His closing argument pulled no punches:

> Doctor Sepúlveda founds these rights upon our superiority . . . and upon our having more bodily strength than the Indians . . . This is simply to place our kings in the position of tyrants. The right of those kings rests upon their extension of the gospel in the New World, and their good government of the Indian nations. These duties they would be bound to fulfill

even at their own expense; much more so considering the treasures they have received from the Indies. To deny this doctrine is to flatter and deceive our monarchs, and to put their salvation in peril. The doctor perverts the natural order of things, making the means the end, and what is accessory, the principal. . . . He who is ignorant of this, small is his knowledge, and he who denies it is no more of a Christian than Mahomet was.

The judges at Valladolid, probably exhausted and confused by this mighty conflict, fell into argument with one another and reached no collective decision. Both disputants claimed victory, but the facts now available do not conclusively support either one. The judges went home after the final meeting, and for years afterward the Council of the Indies struggled to get them to write out their opinions. In vain. We can sympathize with the judges, for they had been besieged by two formidable men committed to two conflicting visions of Indian reality, and each had insisted that the whole structure of Spain's action in America must conform to his single vision.

After the last meeting, Las Casas and his companion, Rodrigo de Andrada, made final arrangements with the San Gregorio monastery in Valladolid to spend the rest of their lives there. According to the contract drawn up on July 21, 1551, they were to be accorded three new cells—one of them presumably for the large collection of books and manuscripts Las Casas had amassed—a servant, first place in the choir, freedom to come and go as they pleased, and burial in the San Gregorio sacristy.

Las Casas did not, however, settle down to a life of quiet contemplation. The failure of the Valladolid disputation to produce a resounding public triumph for his ideas may have convinced him that his efforts on behalf of the Indians needed a more permanent record. He was now seventy-eight years old, weary from half a century of involvement in Indian affairs, and he probably hoped to use the printing press to place his propositions and projects before Spaniards whom he could not otherwise reach. At any rate, he left San Gregorio and sallied forth the next year, 1552, to Seville, where he spent many months recruiting friars for America and preparing a series of nine remarkable treatises, printed there in 1552 and early 1553, which served · as textbooks and guides to friars scattered over the vast stretches of America.

But his opponents made use of them too. His summaries of the debates with Sepúlveda—printed in Seville and later translated in England—of course included Sepúlveda's arguments. These, ironically, so impressed the town council of Mexico, the richest and most important city in all the Indies, that it voted in February of 1554 to buy Sepúlveda "jewels and clothing from this land to the value of two hundred pesos" in recognition of his soundness and "to encourage him in the future." Sepúlveda himself fired a new salvo by issuing a reply to Las Casas under the somewhat pejorative title, "Rash, Scandalous and Heretical Propositions which Dr. Sepúlveda Noted in the Book on the Conquest of the Indies which Friar Bartolomé de Las Casas Printed Without a License."

Las Casas never wavered in his convictions, and in his will, dated March 17, 1564, prophesied darkly: "Surely God will wreak his fury and anger against Spain some day for the unjust wars waged against the Indians." In the last few months of his life he made a final appeal to Rome for support, but his long and passionate crusade ended when death overtook him in July, 1566.

The struggle itself did not end. In fact, the Crown pursued a steady course during the years after Valladolid in the direction of the doctrine set forth by Las Casas: friendly persuasion and not general warfare to attract the Indians to the faith. And though Sepúlveda's views had been widely circulated in manuscript form and presented in detail at the Valladolid meeting, his treatise "Demócrates," which had set off the controversy, was never approved for publication. The generous terms of the standard law on new discoveries—promulgated in July of 1573 by Charles' successor, Philip II, and designed to regulate all future discoveries and conquests—were probably attributable to the battle Las Casas fought at Valladolid.

The law decreed particularly that, instead of "conquest" the term "pacification" should henceforth be used. The vices of the Indians were to be dealt with very gently at first "so as not to scandalize them or prejudice them against Christianity." If, after all the explanations, natives still opposed a Spanish settlement and the preaching of Christianity, the Spaniards might use force but were to do "as little harm as possible," a measure that Las Casas would never have approved. No license was given to enslave the captives. In theory this general order governed conquests as long as Spain ruled her American colonies, although some Spaniards could always be found who thought that the Indians should be subjugated by arms because they were not Christians.

What if Spain had followed the precepts of Las Casas to the letter? Would every friar eventually have been enslaved or killed, and Spanish America overrun by other, less squeamish Europeans? We shall never know, for the history of the expansion of Europe includes no examples of the wholly peaceful penetration of new lands. We do know, however, that for generations the Dominican attempt to preach the faith peacefully in Guatemala influenced Spaniards throughout Spain's vast American empire to use persuasion rather than a "fire and sword" policy in bringing Catholicism to the Indians.

In the end, no simplification of the Valladolid controversy is satisfactory. For in this struggle between learned, bitterly divided men of the same nation, other considerations besides theories on the nature of the Indians—economic striving, personality clashes, and the Crown's interest—all played a part. But it was significant that the Crown permitted fundamental disputes in those tumultuous years in which its policies were evolving. To Spain's everlasting credit she allowed men to insist that all her actions in America be just, and at times she listened to those voices.

The attempt in 1573 to regulate all future conquests and the many other laws on behalf of the Indians would never have been promulgated if Sepúlveda's ideas on just war against the Indians had triumphed. Nor would this passage have appeared in the fundamental code, the Laws of the Indies, printed in 1681: "War cannot and shall not be made on the Indians of any province to the end that they may receive the Holy Catholic Faith or yield obedience to us, or for any other reason."

But the Valladolid dispute lives on principally because of the ideas on the nature of man which Las Casas enunciated there. One fine passage shows the great eloquence of which he was sometimes capable:

> Thus mankind is one, and all men are alike in that which concerns their creation and all natural things, and no one is born enlightened. . . . All of us must be guided and aided at first by those who were born before us. And the savage peoples of the earth may be compared to uncultivated soil that readily brings forth weeds and useless thorns, but has within itself such natural virtue that by labor and cultivation it may be made to yield sound and beneficial fruits.

No single individual completely typifies the nation which established Spanish power in the New World. Rather, the sixteenth-century Spanish character may be likened to a medal stamped on each of its sides with a resolute face. One is that of an imperialistic conquistador; the other, that of a friar devoted to God. Both were imprisoned within the thinking of their own kind and their own time. Neither, when he was most himself, could wholly understand or forgive the other. Yet they were sent yoked together into a new world and together were responsible for the action and the achievement of Spain in America. Even to begin to understand the extremely complex movement of men and ideas which is called the Spanish conquest, we must see that both these bold faces were truly Spanish.

The struggle which Montesinos started in Cuba and Las Casas and many others carried forward throughout the Spanish empire in America is not yet over. The dust on centuries-old manuscripts that recount the Spanish struggle for Christian justice cannot obscure the vitality of the issues, which still disturb the world today. The cry of Montesinos denouncing the enslavement of Indians and the loud voice of Las Casas proclaiming that all the peoples of the world are men are valid today and will still be valid tomorrow, for they are timeless.

And in the perspective of centuries the decision of the Spaniards not to stigmatize the Indians as natural slaves may be seen as a milestone on the long road, still under construction, which winds slowly toward civilizations based on the dignity of all men.

A.L. Rowse

America and the Elizabethan Imagination

The history of America has often been explained in terms of the impact of a virgin continent upon European, African, and other immigrants, an impact at once physical and psychological. Less frequently stressed, but equally significant, was the impact of that continent, with all its wonders, on those peoples, especially the western Europeans, who did not migrate to the New World. The effects of America on Europe were staggering, and not confined to the obvious political, economic, and social aspects of life. True enough, the wealth of the New World provided a tremendous stimulus to Europe. But in some ways America's most profound effects were upon the imaginations of creative men and women.

The British historian, A. L. Rowse of Oxford University, treats this subject in the following essay, part of his general study of *The Elizabethans and America*. He mentions the impact of the humble potato on England and Ireland, but his main concern is with the reactions of poets, philosophers, political thinkers, scientists, and other intellectuals. The stimulation that America provided undoubtedly helped produce the great flowering of Elizabethan culture that we associate with the age of Shakespeare; Professor Rowse, for example, shows how extensively contemporary information about the New World influenced *The Tempest*. Moreover, he makes clear, the effects were pervasive. America kindled the imagination of the Elizabethans and in countless ways contributed to one of the greatest outpourings of creative activity in all history.

During the reign of Elizabeth I, as the interest in and knowledge of America gathered momentum, so their reverberation in literature and the arts became louder, more frequent, and more varied. On the one hand, there were the writings and reports of those who had been there, as collected by Hakluyt and Purchas; the books written by people like Captain Smith and Morton and Strachey; the histories and journals of Bradford and Winthrop; the numerous tracts and sermons devoted to the subject. On the other, there is the reflection of America in the mirror of the imagination, in the poetry and prose of Spenser and Sidney, Raleigh and Chapman, Shakespeare and Drayton, Bacon and Donne. Sometimes these things run into one another: in the case of Raleigh, for example, who always straddles all fences. But it is fascinating to observe how not only the content of the voyagers' accounts but their very phrases will appear in the lines of the poets; how the words of Raleigh's sea captain, Barlow, take wing in the verse of his master or reappear in Drayton's ode "To the Virginian Voyage," or how Strachey's account of the hurricane off Bermuda is echoed in *The Tempest*.

The transition from the factual world of translations and reports to the realm of the imagination may be seen first in the circle of Philip Sidney, to whom Hakluyt dedicated his *Divers Voyages*. When we read Sidney's *Arcadia*, whose author was so much interested in America and several times thought of coming here, we recognize the atmosphere of the voyages. It begins with a shipwreck, with the wrack floating in a sea of very rich things and "many chests which might promise no less." The capture of prizes dominates the first chapters, with the arrival of Musidorus in a strange country, having lost his friend Pyrocles, who subsequently turns up. It is like the beginning of *The Tempest*, or episodes of *A Winter's Tale* and *Pericles*. The influence of the voyages speaks in them all, inciting the imagination to strange scenes and countries across the seas.

The atmosphere of *Arcadia* is quite like that of *The Faërie Queene* —the dreamlike timelessness of a fairy world of romance. Spenser was a friend of both Sidney and Raleigh, and the introductory stanzas to Book II acknowledge the impulse of the expansion:

But let that man with better sense advise
That of the world least part to us is red;
And daily how through hardy enterprise
Many great regions are discovered,
Which to late age were never mentioned.
Who ever heard of th' Indian Peru?
Or who in venturous vessel measured
The Amazon huge river now found true?
Or fruitfullest Virginia who did ever view?

Yet all these were men no man did them know,
Yet have from wisest ages hidden been;
And later times things more unknown shall show.

DIVERS

voyages touching the diſcouerie of
America, *and the Ilands adiacent*
vnto the ſame, made firſt of all by our
*Engliſhmen, and afterward by the French-
men and Britons:*

And certaine notes of aduertiſements for obſerua-
tions, neceſſarie for ſuch as ſhall heereafter
make the like attempt,

With two mappes annexed heereunto for the
plainer vnderſtanding of the whole
matter.

Imprinted at Lon-
don for Thomas VVoodcocke,
dwelling in paules Church-yard,
at the ſigne of the blacke beare.

1582.

*The title page from Hakluyt's
1582 edition of* Divers Voyages.

In the Old World, America was regarded as overflowing with gold as some still believe it to be. Marlowe has several references to this in *Tamburlaine:*

> *Desire of gold, great sir?*
> *That's to be gotten in the Western Ind:*

The thought is expressed by Greene, Peele, Lyly, Massinger, Chapman. It appears in Shakespeare, where sooner or later everything gets expression. We must remember that America, in this connotation, often appears as India, with or without the adjective "Western." This is made sufficiently clear by the dominant association with "mines." "As bountiful as mines of India," he writes. Henry VIII's meeting with Francis I at the Field of the Cloth of Gold

> *Made Britain India; every man that stood*
> *Showed like a mine.*

In *Twelfth Night*, when Maria appears to lay down the letter that entraps Malvolio, Sir Toby belches, "How now, my metal of India," *i.e.,* piece of gold. When Malvolio falls into the trap and is utterly bemused, Maria reports, "He does smile his face into more lines than is in the new map with the augmentation of the Indies." That was the map that went with the first volume of the enlarged edition of Hakluyt published in 1598. Shakespeare derived inspiration and profit from reading Hakluyt. The theme of digging for gold is an important element in *Timon*—at a time, too, when the Jamestown colony was temporarily given over to a frantic search for it. One writer declared in 1608 that there was then "no talk, no hope, no work but to dig gold, wash gold, refine gold, load gold." And this was about the date when *Timon* was written. The combination of the gold theme with digging for roots for subsistence comes straight from the voyages.

The theme is extended in the scenes that Chapman, Raleigh's poet, contributed to Ben Jonson and John Marston's *Eastward Ho!* The absurd Sir Petronel Flash's money is bestowed on a ship bound for Virginia. Security comments: "We have too few such knight adventurers: who would not sell away competent certainties to purchase, with any danger, excellent uncertainties?" This was precisely what many did for Virginia, and New England too. Seagull helps with a lot of mariners' tales about Virginia to gull the public. "Come, boys," he says, "Virginia longs till we share the rest of her maidenhead." That was a regular phrase with the voyagers—Raleigh's phrase for Guiana.

On this Spendall asks: "Why, is she inhabited already with any English?" Seagull: "A whole country of English is there, man, bred of those that were left there in '79." (Actually the date was '87; but we do not go to dramatists for dates any more than to historians for dramatics.) "They have married with the Indians and make 'em bring forth as beautiful faces as any we have in England, and therefore the Indians are so in love with 'em that all the treasure they have they lay at their feet." Scapethrift: "But is there such treasure there, captain, as I have heard?" Seagull: "I tell thee, gold is more plentiful there than copper is with us; and for as much red copper as I can bring, I'll have thrice the weight in gold. Why, man, all their dripping pans and their chamber pots are pure gold; and all the chains with which they chain up their streets are massy gold; all the prisoners they take are fettered in gold; and for rubies and diamonds they go forth on holidays and gather 'em by the seashore . . ." Scapethrift asks, "And is it a pleasant country withal?" Captain Seagull replies: "As ever the sun shined on: temperate and full of all sorts of excellent viands."

These leads—Spenser, Marlowe, Chapman—all point to Raleigh, as they were all his friends; he stands at the crossroads in literature, as he did in these actions. The captains he sent to reconnoiter Virginia in 1584 reported as follows:

The second of July we found shoal water, where we smelt so sweet and so strong a smell as if we had been in the midst of some delicate garden abounding with all kind of odoriferous flowers, by which we were assured that the land could not be far distant . . . We viewed the land about us, being, whereas we first landed, very sandy and low towards the water's side, but so full of grapes as the very beating and surge of the sea overflowed them; of which we found such plenty, as well on every little shrub as also climbing towards the tops of high cedars that I think in all the world the like abundance is not to be found. Under the bank or hill whereon we stood, we beheld the valleys replenished with goodly cedar trees.

In the poem Raleigh was writing some years later to recover the Queen's favor (but never finished), *Cynthia, the Lady of the Sea,* we read:

On highest mountains where those cedars grow
Against whose banks the troubled ocean bet
And were the marks to find thy hoped port
Into a soil far off themselves remove.

And when we come to Drayton's ode, "To the Virginian Voyage," we find:

When as the luscious smell
Of that delicious land
Above the sea that flows
The clear wind throws,
Your hearts to swell
Approaching the dear strand.
And the ambitious vine
Crowns with his purple mass
The cedar reaching high
To kiss the sky,
The cypress, pine,
And useful sassafras.

Of the motives that could lead men to leave home Raleigh speaks, in his own case:

My hopes clean out of sight with forced wind
To kingdoms strange, to lands far off addressed . . .

And he sums them all up in one famous line:

To seek new worlds for gold, for praise, for glory.

There was a whole succession of literary men who went as officials to Virginia: William Strachey, John Pory, Christopher Davison, George Sandys. Donne, who was hard up before he condescended to enter the Church, sought to be made secretary. Strachey, a Cambridge man, moved in a literary and dramatic circle in London. He was a shareholder in the Children of the Queen's Revels and so came to Blackfriars two or three times a week, where he would meet Shake-

In 1609 Sea Venture *was wrecked in a hurricane off Bermuda. On board was William Strachey, whose recounting of the adventure provided
Shakespeare with the plot for* The Tempest.

speare. In 1609 he went out with Gates and Somers in the *Sea Venture*, which was famously wrecked on Bermuda, though all were
saved and spent an agreeable winter there. The extraordinary happening made a strong impression on people's minds at home, and
several accounts of it appeared, the most detailed being Strachey's
letter to a noble lady, which circulated in manuscript. It is not surprising that the most impressionable mind in that circle was struck
by it, for this was the germ of *The Tempest*.

It is somehow right that, just as More's *Utopia* provides the first
expression of genius of the New World in our period, so *The Tempest*
provides the last; that these two transcendent minds should have
risen to the full height of the theme. For there is far more of the
New World in Shakespeare's play than the original suggestion from
Strachey's letter: the storm with its veracious details, St. Elmo's
fire flaming amazement along the mainmast: the wreck and not a
hair of the people hurt; the enchanted island full of noises, for
Bermuda was believed to be haunted by evil spirits. The whole play
sings of the sea; the loveliest songs are of the sea:

> *Full fathom five thy father lies,*
> *Of his bones are coral made;*
> *Those are pearls that were his eyes:*
> *Nothing of him that doth fade*
> *But doth suffer a sea-change*
> *Into something rich and strange.*

Not only that, but with the creation of Caliban, the primitive savage, possessor of the island, and his relation to Prospero, the very civilized and lordly person who dispossesses him, the whole question of what happens when civilization makes its impact upon primitive society is placed before us in a way we can never forget. Our sympathies are not with Prospero—and perhaps in the subconscious corridors of the mind we think of what happened to the redskins. There is something deeply affecting about Caliban:

> *. . . When thou camest first,*
> *Thou strok'dst me and mad'st much of me: would'st give me*
> *Water with berries in't and teach me how*
> *To name the bigger light, and how the less.*
> *That burn by day and night . . .*

This is what had happened time and again, generation after generation, with tribe after tribe, all along the coasts of America when the Indians came in contact with the white men and their superior knowledge. We read in Hakluyt and Captain Smith with what avidity they learned about the stars and the firmament, watched the white men's instruments, were impressed by lodestone and magnet, optic glass and clock.

> *. . . and then I lov'd thee*
> *And show'd thee all the qualities o' the isle,*
> *The fresh springs, brine-pits, barren place, and fertile.*

That, too, had often happened—we remember how Squanto showed the Pilgrims where best to take their fish and how to set Indian corn, and enabled them to subsist through the hard first years. In one sense the Indians were quick to learn; in another, they never learned— the gulf between their primitive cast of mind and that of the white man was too deep to bridge. And so the red man lost in the struggle for existence. Nor did he profit from his knowledge, in spite of his experiences at the hand of the white man. After Prospero comes the drunken Stephano:

> CALIBAN: *I prithee, let me bring thee where crabs grow;*
> *And I with my long nails will dig thee pig-nuts;*
> *Show thee a jay's nest and instruct thee how*
> *To snare the nimble marmozet; I'll bring thee*
> *To clust'ring filberts and sometimes I'll get thee*
> *Young scamels from the rocks . . .*

In spite of what he has suffered at the hand of Prospero, Caliban now wants Stephano to be his god:

> *I'll show thee every fertile inch o' the island;*
> *And I will kiss thy foot: I prithee, be my god.*

We are reminded of the native Californians who embarrassed Drake and his men by taking them for gods.

The idea of an original state of nature was to have an important development in political speculation and theorizing about society, and it was given immense impetus by what men discovered in the New World. It was brought home vividly to me years ago when I saw John Locke's library as it had come down in the possession of his representatives: we take it for granted that he was a generalizing and abstract thinker, as he was, but his library was full of the American voyages. There, made visible, was an example of the way early anthropology went into political theory.

Tudor folk were fascinated by the trappings of Indian life and the spectacle of Indians, from the time Cabot brought some back to the streets of Westminster, and a Brazilian chief was presented at the court of Henry VIII. In 1614—when the great Virginian venture was much in mind—two masques were given by the Inns of Court. Bacon's *Masque of Flowers* argued the merits and demerits of Virginia's chief product, tobacco, before the antitobacconist James I. Chapman's masque, a much grander affair dressed by Inigo Jones, had the masquers attired in Indian costume, "with high sprigged feathers on their heads, hair black and large waving down to their shoulders." The musicians were attired like Virginian "priests"—no doubt from John White's drawing. But the serious-minded Chapman addressed himself to a searching theme, the problem posed by the diversity of religion revealed by a new world, of which Holy Scripture, which held the key to all human history, had no knowledge. The orthodox poet spoke through Eunomia, representing civilized order:

Virginian princes, you must now renounce
Your superstitious worship of these Suns,
Subject to cloudy darkenings and descents,
And of your fit devotions turn the event
To this our British Phoebus, whose bright sky
(Enlightened with a Christian piety)
Is never subject to black error's night,
And hath already offered heaven's true light
To your dark region.

There were people, even then, who speculated sensibly whether the American Indians had not come across the narrow divide of the Bering Strait from Asia. Some reflection of these speculations may be seen in Bacon's *jeu d'esprit*, *The New Atlantis*. Naturally the influence of the voyages and of reading Hakluyt is apparent, and Bacon had a direct interest in colonization by this time: he was one of the Council for Newfoundland. Bacon's utopian island was in the Pacific, which might still have islands and continents not yet come to light—Australia was yet to come out of it. But he refers to the inundation of an Atlantic continent, and the shrinking Atlantic shelf of America. Hence the American Indians were but remnants of a people: "Marvel you not at the thin population of America, nor at the rudeness and ignorance of the people; for you must accept your inhabitants of America as a young people: younger a thousand years, at the least, than the rest of the world."

The mind of the poet Donne was markedly stimulated by the geographical curiosity of the time. This is reflected in the unexpected images he reaches out for on the subject of love:

Let sea-discoverers to new worlds have gone,
Let maps to others worlds on worlds have shown,
Let us possess one world, each hath one and is one.

Where we can find two better hemispheres
Without sharp North, without declining West?

Or in addressing his mistress, going to bed, in somewhat unusual terms:

O my America! my new-found-land,
My kingdom, safeliest when with one man manned!

Many were the sermons that were preached to speed the Virginia enterprise; but Donne's sermon is the finest specimen of the class, in which it is elevated to literature. As we should expect, he raised the issues presented by colonization to a higher plane. He warned those going against seeking independence or exemption from the laws of England. "If those that govern there would establish such a government as should not depend upon this, or if those that go thither propose to themselves an exemption from laws to live at their liberty, this is to . . . divest allegiance and be under no man." And Donne had something to say which is very much to the point in the modern discussion about colonialism. The law of nations ordains "that every man improve that which he hath . . . the whole world, all mankind must take care that all places be improved as far as may be to the best advantage of mankind in general."

With a New World being discovered, there was not only an immense extension of geographical knowledge, but a comparable impetus to improve its quality and techniques. England was backward in this art, as in so much else; but now her geographers profited from their contacts with these leaders of thought, while they made use of the information gathered by the English voyagers in constructing their maps—Ortelius, of Anthony Jenkinson, for Russia and Persia; Mercator, of Drake, for America and the Pacific. Though English map makers in this field were not yet comparable, they were beginning. Frobisher's and Gilbert's voyages to North America led to a considerable increase of information about the northern areas, reflected in the maps of Michael Lok and Thomas Best. A number of John Dee's maps of these regions remain, and illustrate, as everything about him does, his curious mixture of shrewd criticism and crazy credulity. His map of North America based on Gilbert's explorations, for example, has a proper realization of the width of the continent across Canada; but theorist that he was, he had no compunction in tracing a waterway right across, to debouch with the Colorado into Southern California. By the end of the century, much more exact and useful contributions were being made to navigation

John Smith's Generall Historie
*(1624), the title page of which
is reproduced here, attracted
wide interest in England. The
portraits are those of Elizabeth, James I, and Charles I.*

and cosmography by such men as John Davis and Edward Wright.

Hariot appears as the most complete, all-round scientist of that time, with his interest alike in mathematics and astronomy, anthropology and navigation. He set forth a model of first-class scientific method with his *Brief and True Report of the new found land of Virginia*. It is the work of a superior mind; no Elizabethan quaintness in this; no fancy, let alone fantasy; all is in due order based on close observation, accurately brought into correlation with existing categories. It gives an account of the flora and fauna: the commodities of the country with their qualities and uses; methods of agriculture and properties of the soil, plants and fruits and roots; the beasts, fowl, and fish; ending with the nature and manners of the people, for Hariot had learned enough of their language to communicate with them about their notions and beliefs.

This concise little work, important as it is, is only a fragment of the materials collected by Hariot and John White at Roanoke. White was similarly engaged in mapping the coasts and sounds and rendering the life of the place in his water colors of the plants and fishes, the characters and ways of the natives. But after the hurricane that decided the colony to leave, many of their maps and papers were lost in the sea in the hurried transfer of their goods to Drake's ships. Others of White's papers left on Roanoke were spoiled by the Indians. But what remains is considerable.

The impact of America upon natural history in general, and botany in particular, was no less exciting. A wide range of new plants and animals provided continuing stimulus to the scientific curiosity, as well as the fancy, of naturalists in England as elsewhere. And this is reflected in their books. From the New World came the giant sunflower, nasturtium, Michaelmas daisy, lobelia, evening primrose, and so on. But by far the most important introductions were tobacco and the potato: these affected history.

The medicinal properties of tobacco were considered valuable. Hariot reported that it "purgeth superfluous phlegm and other gross humours, and openeth all the pores and passages of the body: by which means the use thereof not only preserveth the body from obstructions, but also (if any be, so that they have not been of too long continuance) breaketh them."

The habit of smoking spread rapidly among the courtiers and the upper class, popularized by Raleigh and those in touch with the colonies. It was noted as a piece of arrogance on Raleigh's part that "he took a pipe of tobacco before he went to the scaffold"; it is more likely to have been to steady his nerves, or as a last pleasure on earth. Even before the end of the Queen's reign, the habit was spreading to the lower orders. All this was good for Virginia: it put the colony on its feet and enabled it to survive.

The potato has had even more effect in history. In *The History and Social Influence of the Potato*, Redcliffe N. Salaman writes: "The introduction of the potato has proved to be one of the major events in man's recent history, but, at the time, it was a matter of relatively little moment and called forth no immediate public comment." To the Elizabethans the innocuous potato was not only sustaining, but stimulating to lust. We remember that when Falstaff, with the worst intentions, gets Mistress Ford and Mistress Page to come in to him, he calls on the sky to rain potatoes. Amid so much that is earthy, not to say murky, about this root, Dr. Salaman thinks it quite probable that Raleigh did introduce the growing of potatoes into Ireland—one more of the many things he has to answer for. This certainly had remote and far-reaching consequences, setting in motion the cycle that ultimately led to the mass migration of the Irish, during and after the Famine, to America.

It was from Ireland, too, that John White's drawings of American life turned up, having long ago disappeared from view. In the end, it is through such things as these—Powhatan's mantle, a wampum girdle or a shell necklace, the things the Elizabethans held in their hands and brought home, the flotsam and jetsam of time—that we are most directly in touch with that early American life, as well as through those fragments of memory that have entered into folklore, the unforgotten impression that Pocahontas made on the English people in her day—still alive in the famous inn sign, "La Belle Sauvage." I write these words not far from a village in Cornwall still called after her, Indian Queen's. For what enters into the unconscious life of the mind and is carried on in folklore is the best evidence of the strength of common memories, common affections, and common ancestry.

Fox hunting was a passion which colonial gentry gladly indulged. This rendering of a hunting party is a detail from an overmantel painting of the late seventeenth century.

Part Two
Colonial Life

Marshall Fishwick

William Byrd II
of Virginia

Whether William Byrd II was actually as unique a person as he seems can never be known, for it is only because of his marvelously candid diary that we know him as well as we do. Perhaps if others among the privileged but hard-working tobacco planters of eighteenth-century Virginia had left similar records we would have had to conclude that Byrd was merely typical. In any case, Byrd the historical figure is important not because of his personal qualities, fascinating as these were, but because of what the story of his life tells us about the society of colonial Virginia.

If Byrd was, as Professor Marshall Fishwick, director of the American Studies Institute, Lincoln University, notes in the following essay, a "Renaissance man," he was one no doubt in part because the world he inhabited demanded versatility and rewarded achievement. His career helps explain the extraordinary self-confidence, imagination, and energy of several generations of Americans, not only his own but even more those which immediately followed, and which, in the single case of his native Virginia, produced Washington, Jefferson, Madison, Patrick Henry, and a host of others—the great Virginia leaders of the American Revolution.

*H*e could never resist an old book, a young girl, or a fresh idea. He lived splendidly, planned extensively, and was perpetually in debt. Believing perhaps, like Leonardo, that future generations would be more willing to know him than was his own, he wrote his delicious, detailed diaries in code. Only now that they have been translated, and time has put his era in perspective, do we see what William Byrd of Westover was: one of the half-dozen leading wits and stylists of colonial America.

In the popular imagination, to be an American hero means to rise from rags to riches. William Byrd reversed the pattern, as he did so many other things: born to wealth, he never seemed able to hold on to it. His father, William Byrd I (1653–1704), was one of the most powerful and venerated men of his generation. Not only had he inherited valuable land on both sides of the James River, he had also won the hand of Mary Horsmanden, and a very dainty and wealthy hand it was, too. Some of the bold and red knight-errant blood of the Elizabethans flowed through the veins of William Byrd I. He had the same knack as did Captain John Smith (in whom that blood fairly bubbled) for getting in and out of scrapes. For example, William Byrd I joined Nathaniel Bacon in subduing the Indians, but stopped short of joining the rebellion against Governor William Berkeley, withdrawing in time to save his reputation and his neck. Later on he became receiver-general and auditor of Virginia, a member of the Council of State, and the colony's leading authority on Indians. The important 1685 treaty with the Iroquois bore his signature. Death cut short his brilliant career soon after his fiftieth birthday, and suddenly thrust his son and namesake into the center of the colonial stage. The boy, who had spent much of his time in England getting an education and, later, as an agent for Virginia, must now return to America and assume the duties of a man.

No one can read the story of young Will Byrd's early years, and his transformation, without thinking of Will Shakespeare's Prince Hal. If ever a young Virginian behaved scandalously in London, it was Will Byrd. "Never did the sun shine upon a Swain who had more combustible matter in his constitution," Byrd wrote of himself. Love broke out upon him "before my beard." Louis Wright, to whose editing of Byrd's diaries we are indebted for much of our knowledge of the man, says that he was notoriously promiscuous, frequenting the boudoirs of highborn and lowborn alike. Indeed, as his diary shows, he was not above taking to the grass with a *fille de joie* whom he might encounter on a London street.

Once, when he arrived for a rendezvous with a certain Mrs. A-l-n, the lady wasn't home, so he seduced the chambermaid. Just as he was coming down the steps Mrs. A-l-n came in the front door. Then Will Byrd and Mrs. A-l-n went back up the stairs together. Several hours later, he went home and ate a plum cake.

On his favorites he lavished neoclassic pseudonyms and some of the era's most sparkling prose. One such lady (called "Facetia" and believed to have been Lady Elizabeth Cromwell) was his preoccupation during 1703. When she left him to visit friends in Ireland, Will Byrd let her know she would be missed:

> The instant your coach drove away, madam, my heart felt as if it had been torn up by the very roots, and the rest of my body as if severed limb from limb. . . . Could I at that time have considered that the only pleasure I had in the world was leaving me, I had hung upon your coach and had been torn in pieces sooner than have suffered myself to be taken from you.

Having said all the proper things, he moved on to relate, in a later letter, some of the juicier bits of London gossip. Mrs. Brownlow had finally agreed to marry Lord Guilford—"and the gods alone can tell what will be produced by the conjunction of such fat and good humour!" The image is Falstaffian, as were many of Byrd's friends. But with news of his father's death he must, like Prince Hal, scorn his dissolute friends and assume new duties. With both Hal and Will the metamorphosis was difficult and partial, but nonetheless memorable.

The Virginia to which in 1705 William Byrd II returned—the oldest permanent English settlement in the New World and the first link in the chain that would one day be known as the British Empire—was a combination of elegance and crudity, enlightenment and superstition. While some of his Virginia neighbors discussed the most advanced political theories of Europe, others argued about how to dispose of a witch who was said to have crossed over to Currituck Sound in an eggshell. In 1706, the same year that Byrd was settling down in Virginia after his long stay in England, a Virginia court was instructing "as many Ansient and Knowing women as possible . . . to search her Carefully For teats spotts and marks about her body." When certain mysterious marks were indeed found, the obvious conclusion was drawn, and the poor woman languished in ye common gaol. Finally released, she lived to be eighty and died a natural death.

Other Virginia ladies faced problems (including, on occasions, Will Byrd) that were far older than the colony or the witch scare. A good example was Martha Burwell, a Williamsburg belle, who rejected the suit of Sir Francis Nicholson, the governor, so she might marry a man more to her liking. If she did so, swore the enraged Nicholson, he would cut the throat of the bridegroom, the clergyman, and the issuing justice. Unaware that females are members of the weaker sex, Martha refused to give in—even when Nicholson threw in half a dozen more throats, including those of her father and brothers. She married her true love. No throats were cut—but visitors to the Governor's palace in Williamsburg observed that His Excellency made "a Roaring Noise."

In those days Tidewater Virginia was governed by benevolent paternalists. The aristocrats intermarried, and the essential jobs—sheriff, vestryman, justice of the peace, colonel of militia—stayed in the family. The support of the gentry was the prerequisite to social and political advancement. Wealth, status, and privilege were the Tidewater trinity, and it was a case of three in one: wealth guaranteed status; status conveyed privilege; and privilege insured wealth.

Will Byrd both understood and mastered the world to which he had returned. He retained the seat in the House of Burgesses which he had won before going to England, and turned his attention to finding a suitable wife. Like many of his contemporaries, he confined "romantic love" to extracurricular affairs, and called on common sense to help him in matrimony. Both Washington and Jefferson married rich widows. Ambitious young men found they could love a rich girl more than a poor one, and the colonial newspapers reported their marriages with an honesty that bordered on impropriety. One reads, for example, that twenty-three-year-old William Carter married Madam Sarah Ellson, widow of eighty-five, "a sprightly old Tit, with three thousand pounds fortune."

Will Byrd's choice was the eligible but fiery Lucy Parke, daughter of the gallant rake Daniel Parke, who had fought with Marlborough on the Continent and brought the news of Blenheim to Queen Anne. Many a subsequent battle was fought between Lucy Parke and William Byrd after their marriage in 1706, though neither side was entirely vanquished. Byrd was quick to record his victories, such as the one noted in his diary for February 5, 1711: "My wife and I quarrelled about her pulling her brows. She threatened she would not go to Williamsburg if she might not pull them; I refused, however, and got the better of her and maintained my authority."

That Mrs. Byrd had as many good excuses for her fits of temper and violence as any other lady in Virginia seems plain—not only from her accusations, but from her husband's admissions. From his diary entry of November 2, 1709, for example, we get this graphic picture of life among the planters:

In the evening I went to Dr. [Barrett's], where my wife came this afternoon. Here I found Mrs. Chiswell, my sister Custis, and other ladies. We sat and talked till about 11 o'clock and then retired to our chambers. I played at [r-m] with Mrs. Chiswell and kissed her on the bed till she was angry and my wife also was uneasy about it, and cried as soon as the company was gone. I neglected to say my prayers which I should not have done, because I ought to beg pardon for the lust I had for another man's wife. However I had good health, good thoughts, and good humor, thanks be to God Almighty.

As we read on, we begin to realize that we are confronting a Renaissance man in colonial America—a writer with the frankness of Montaigne and the zest of Rabelais. Philosopher, linguist, doctor, scientist, stylist, planter, churchman, William Byrd II saw and reported as much as any American who died before our Revolution.

Here was a man who, burdened for most of his life with the responsibility of thousands of acres and hundreds of slaves, never became narrow or provincial. Neither his mind, nor his tongue, nor his pen—the last possibly because he wrote the diaries in code—was restrained by his circumstances, and no one at home or abroad was immune from the barbs of his wit. When we read Byrd, we know just what Dean Swift meant when he said: "We call a spade a spade."

One of Byrd's most remarkable achievements, and one not nearly well enough known and appreciated, is his sketch of himself, attached to a letter dated February 21, 1722. For honesty and perception, and for the balance that the eighteenth century enthroned, it has few American counterparts.

Poor Inamorato [as Byrd calls himself] had too much mercury to fix to one thing. His Brain was too hot to jogg on eternally in the same dull road. He liv'd more by the lively moment of his Passions, than by the cold and unromantick dictates of Reason . . . He pay'd his Court more to obscure merit, than to corrupt Greatness. He never cou'd flatter any body, no not himself, which were two invincible bars to all preferment. . . . His religion is more in substance than in form, and he is more forward to practice vertue than profess it . . . He knows the World perfectly well, and thinks himself a citizen of it without the . . . distinctions of kindred sect or Country.

He goes on to explain why, for most of his life, he began his day by reading ancient classics, and frowned upon morning interruptions:

A constant hurry of visits & conversations gives a man a habit of inadvertency, which betrays him into faults without measure & without end. For this reason, he commonly reserv'd the morning to himself, and bestow'd the rest upon his business and his friends.

The reason for his own candor is clearly stated:

He Lov'd to undress wickedness of all its paint, and disguise, that he might loath its deformity.

The extent of his philosophizing and his admitted heresy is made clear by this remarkable passage:

He wishes every body so perfect, that he overlooks the impossibility of reaching it in this World. He wou'd have men Angells before their time, and wou'd bring down that perfection upon Earth which is the peculiar priviledge of Heaven.

Byrd left us a scattered and largely unavailable body of literature —vers de société, historical essays, character sketches, epitaphs, letters, poems, translations, and humorous satires. Of this work Maude Woodfin, one of the few scholars to delve adequately into Byrd's work, wrote:

"There is a distinctly American quality in these writings of the latter half of Byrd's life, in direct contrast to the exclusively English quality in the writings of his earlier years. Further study and time will doubtless argue that his literary work in the Virginia period from 1726 on, with its colonial scene and theme, has greater literary merit than his work in the London period."

Byrd has a place in our architectural history as well. His manor

This portrait of William Byrd was painted in London by Sir Godfrey Kneller between 1715 and 1720 when the aristocratic Virginian was in his prime.

house, Westover, is in many ways the finest Georgian mansion in the nation. Triumphant architectural solutions never came quickly or easily: only first-rate minds can conjure up first-rate houses. In the spring of 1709, we know from Byrd's diary, he had workmen constructing brick. Five years later, stonecutters from Williamsburg were erecting the library chimney. There were interruptions, delays, faulty shipments, workmen to be trained. But gradually a masterpiece—noble in symmetry, proportion, and balance—emerged.

Built on a little rise a hundred yards from the James River, Westover has not changed much over the generations. The north and south façades are as solid and rhythmical as a well-wrought fugue, and the beautiful doorways would have pleased Palladio himself. Although the manor is derived from English standards (especially William Salmon's *Palladio Londinensis*), Westover makes such superb use of the local materials and landscape that some European critics have adjudged it esthetically more satisfying than most of the contemporary homes in England.

Like other buildings of the period, Westover was planned from the outside in. The main hallway, eighteen feet wide and off center, goes the full length of the house. The stairway has three runs and a balustrade of richly turned mahogany. The handsomely paneled walls of the downstairs rooms support gilded ceilings. Underneath the house is a complete series of rooms, converging at the subterranean passage leading to the river. Two underground chambers, which could be used as hiding places, are reached through a dry well. Since he liked nothing less than the idea of being dry, William Byrd kept both chambers stocked with claret and Madeira.

Westover takes its place in the succession of remarkable Virginia manors that remain one of the glories of the American past. It was completed probably by 1736, after Stratford Hall, with its masculine vigor, and Rosewell, with its mahogany balustrade from San Domingo. Westover would be followed by Brandon, with chaste cornices and fine simplicity; Gunston Hall, with cut-stone quoins and coziness; Sabine Hall, so reminiscent of Horace's villa at Tivoli; and Pacatone, with its wonderful entrance and its legendary ghosts.

These places were more than houses. They were little worlds in themselves, part of a universe that existed within the boundaries of Virginia. The planters lavished their energy and their lives on such worlds. They were proud of their crops, their horses, their libraries, their gardens. Byrd, for example, tells us about the iris, crocus, thyme, marjoram, phlox, larkspur, and jasmine in his formal two-acre garden.

At Westover one might find the Carters from Shirley, the Lees from Stratford, the Harrisons from Randolph, or the Spotswoods from Germanna. So might one encounter Byrd's brother-in-law, that ardent woman-hater, John Custis, from Arlington. Surely the ghost of William Byrd would not want any tale of Westover to omit a short tribute to Custis' irascible memory.

While other founding fathers left immortal lines about life and liberty to stir our blood, Custis left words to warm henpecked hearts. With his highhanded lady he got on monstrous poor.

After one argument Custis turned and drove his carriage into the Chesapeake Bay. When his wife asked where he was going, he shouted, "To Hell, Madam." "Drive on," she said imperiously. "Any place is better than Arlington!" So that he might have the last word, Custis composed his own epitaph, and made his son execute it on pain of being disinherited:

UNDER THIS MARBLE TOMB LIES THE BODY
OF THE HON. JOHN CUSTIS, ESQ.,

* * * *

AGE 71 YEARS, AND YET LIVED BUT SEVEN YEARS,
WHICH WAS THE SPACE OF TIME HE KEPT
A BACHELOR'S HOME AT ARLINGTON
ON THE EASTERN SHORE OF VIRGINIA.

Still Custis came to Westover, like all others who could, to enjoy the fairs, balls, parlor games, barbecues—but above all, the conversation.

One should not conclude that entertaining friends was the main occupation of William Byrd. As soon as he awoke he read Latin, Greek, or Hebrew before breakfast. His favorite room was not the parlor but the library, in which were collected over 3,600 volumes dealing with philosophy, theology, drama, history, law, and science. Byrd's own writings prove his intimate knowledge of the great thinkers and writers of the past.

Of those works, none except his diary is as interesting as his *History of the Dividing Line*. On his fifty-third birthday, in 1727, Byrd was appointed one of the Virginia commissioners to survey the disputed Virginia–North Carolina boundary; the next spring saw the group ready to embark on their task. Byrd's *History*, which proves he was one of the day's ablest masters of English prose, is a thing of delight. For days comedy and tragedy alternated for supremacy. Indians stole their food. Bad weather and poor luck caused Byrd to swear like a trooper in His Majesty's Guards. To mend matters, Byrd's companions arranged a party around a cheerful bowl, and invited a country bumpkin to attend. She must have remembered the party for a long time: ". . . they examined all her hidden Charms and play'd a great many gay Pranks," noted Byrd, who seems to have disapproved of the whole affair. "The poor Damsel was disabled from making any resistance by the Lameness of her Hand."

Whenever matters got too bad, the party's chaplain "rubbed up" his aristocratic swamp-evaders with a seasonable sermon; and we must adjudge all the hardships a small price to pay for the *History*. This was followed by *A Journey to Eden*, which tells of Byrd's trip to survey twenty thousand acres of bottom land. On September 19, 1733, Byrd decided to stake out two large cities: "one at Shacco's, to be called Richmond, and the other at the point of the Appomattuck River, to be called Petersburg."

It is a generally accepted belief that only in politics did eighteenth-century America reach real distinction. But as we look more closely at our colonial literature and architecture, and apply our own criteria rather than those imposed upon us by the English, we find that this may not be so. How, for example, could we have underestimated William Byrd's importance all these years? There are several answers. He never pretended to be a serious writer (no gentleman of his time and place would), any more than Jefferson would have set himself up as a professional architect. But at least we have Jefferson's magnificent buildings to refute the notion that he was a mere dabbler, and for years we had little of Byrd's prose. Because he did ''call a spade a spade,'' many of his contemporaries, and even more of their descendants, have not wanted his work and allusions made public. Byrd had been dead almost a century when Edmund Ruffin published fragments of his writings in the *Virginia Farmers' Register*. Only in our own generation have the diaries been deciphered: not until 1941 did a major publisher undertake to see part of them into print; not until 1958 did we have *The London Diary* (1717–21); not even now can we read all that Byrd left for us.

No amount of reappraisal can turn Byrd into a figure of the highest magnitude. What it might do is to reveal a man who for candor, self-analysis, and wit is unsurpassed—this in an age that produced Washington, Adams, Franklin, Henry, and Jefferson. Could any other colonial American, for example, have written such a delightful and ribald satire on women as ''The Female Creed,'' which has an eighteenth-century lady profess: ''I believe in astrologers, coffee-casters, and Fortune-tellers of every denomination, whether they profess to read the Ladys destiny in their faces, in their palms or like those of China in their fair posteriors.''

Nor will one often encounter in a colonial writer the desire to exhume his father's corpse, and then to report: ''He was so wasted there was not one thing to be distinguished. I ate fish for dinner.''

When William Byrd II died in the summer of 1744, the pre-Revolutionary ethos and attitudes were dying too. They have not attracted historians and novelists as have the earlier adventurous days of settlement or the later days that tried men's souls. The period from 1700 to 1750 remains the forgotten one in American history and literature, despite much excellent but rather specialized work in it since 1930.

When we know more of that important and colorful half century, William Byrd's reputation will rise. In him we shall find the most complete expression of a man who lived with us but belongs to the world. In his work we shall see, more clearly than in that of his contemporaries, the emerging differences between England and the American colonies destined to grow into their own nationhood. Beside him, the so-called Connecticut Wits of the late eighteenth century seem to be lacking half their title. Compared to his prose, the tedious sermonizing of the Puritan and Anglican ministers seems like copybook work in an understaffed grammar school. Not that William Byrd was a saint, or a model husband—as he would have been the first to point out. But as with the saints, we admire him all the more because he tells us about his faults and lets us tabulate the virtues for ourselves. All told, we can say of him what Abraham Lincoln supposedly said when he saw Walt Whitman far down the corridors of a building: "There goes a man." William Byrd of Westover would have settled for this.

The Latin motto of William Byrd's coat of arms reads, appropriately enough, "No guilt to make one pale."

Ray Allen Billington
The Frontier and the American Character

New ways of looking at the past, called "interpretations," are a constant source of stimulation and controversy among historians. Most interpretations are produced not so much by the discovery of new facts as by present-mindedness; current events cause us to see the past in a new light, or, to put it differently, our search for the causes of contemporary events often leads us to change our understanding of the effects of past events.

Of all interpretations of American history, none has been more provocative of research and controversy than Frederick Jackson Turner's "frontier thesis." In a paper published in 1893, Turner argued that the whole character of American civilization had been shaped from earliest colonial times by the existence of undeveloped land and resources, and by their exploitation by pioneers. At a time when Americans were becoming aware that the western frontier was disappearing, this idea proved enormously persuasive; for years the Turner thesis dominated the writing of American history. Eventually, however, a new generation of scholars began to uncover its weaknesses and contradictions, and today the interpretation seems only one among many. The role of the frontier is generally accepted as having been important, but it is not seen as "explaining" American development, as Turner suggested.

The leading modern expert on the history of the frontier is Ray Allen Billington, Senior Research Fellow at the Huntington Library. Billington has written the definitive biography of Turner and is master of the complex and voluminous literature on the Turner thesis that has been published in this century. In this essay he sums up and balances this continuing discussion of Turner's ideas. If this is not the last word that will be written about the effects of the frontier on America, it is the best and fairest general judgment of the subject that we have.

Since the dawn days of historical writing in the United States, historians have labored mightily, and usually in vain, to answer the famous question posed by Hector St. John de Crèvecœur in the eighteenth century: "What then is the American, this new man?" Was that composite figure actually a "new man" with unique traits that distinguished him from his Old World ancestors? Or was he merely a transplanted European? The most widely accepted—and bitterly disputed—answer was advanced by a young Wisconsin historian named Frederick Jackson Turner in 1893. The American was a new man, he held, who owed his distinctive characteristics and institutions to the unusual New World environment—characterized by the availability of free land and an ever-receding frontier—in which his civilization had grown to maturity. This environmental theory, accepted for a generation after its enunciation, has been vigorously attacked and vehemently defended during the past two decades. How has it fared in this battle of words? Is it still a valid key to the meaning of American history?

Turner's own background provides a clue to the answer. Born in Portage, Wisconsin, in 1861 of pioneer parents from upper New York state, he was reared in a land fringed by the interminable forest and still stamped with the mark of youth. There he mingled with pioneers who had trapped beaver or hunted Indians or cleared the virgin wilderness; from them he learned something of the free and easy democratic values prevailing among those who judged men by their own accomplishments rather than those of their ancestors. At the University of Wisconsin Turner's faith in cultural democracy was deepened, while his intellectual vistas were widened through contact with teachers who led him into that wonderland of adventure where scientific techniques were being applied to social problems, where Darwin's evolutionary hypothesis was awakening scholars to the continuity of progress, and where searchers after truth were beginning to realize the multiplicity of forces responsible for human behavior. The young student showed how well he had learned these lessons in his master's essay on "The Character and Influence of the Fur Trade in Wisconsin"; he emphasized the evolution of institutions from simple to complex forms.

From Wisconsin Turner journeyed to Johns Hopkins University, as did many eager young scholars of that day, only to meet stubborn opposition for the historical theories already taking shape in his mind. His principal professor, Herbert Baxter Adams, viewed mankind's development in evolutionary terms, but held that environment had no place in the equation; American institutions could be understood only as outgrowths of European "germs" that had originated among Teutonic tribes in the forests of medieval Germany. To Turner this explanation was unsatisfactory. The "germ theory" explained the similarities between Europe and America, but what of the many differences? This problem was still much in his mind when he returned to the University of Wisconsin as an instructor in 1889. In two remarkable papers prepared during the next few years he set forth his answer.

Frederick Jackson Turner, photographed about 1890.

The first, "The Significance of History," reiterated his belief in what historians call "multiple causation"; to understand man's complex nature, he insisted, one needed not only a knowledge of past politics, but a familiarity with social, economic, and cultural forces as well. The second, "Problems in American History," attempted to isolate those forces most influential in explaining the unique features of American development. Among these Turner believed that the most important was the need for institutions to "adapt themselves to the changes of a remarkably developing, expanding people."

This was the theory that was expanded into a full-blown historical hypothesis in the famous essay on "The Significance of the Frontier in American History," read at a conference of historians held in connection with the World Fair in Chicago in 1893. The differences between European and American civilization, Turner stated in that monumental work, were in part the product of the distinctive environment of the New World. The most unusual features of that environment were "the existence of an area of free land, its continuous recession, and the advance of American settlement westward." This free land served as a magnet to draw men westward, attracted by the hope of economic gain or adventure. They came as Europeans or easterners, but they soon realized that the wilderness environment was ill-adapted to the habits, institutions, and cultural baggage of the stratified societies they had left behind. Complex political institutions were unnecessary in a tiny frontier outpost; traditional economic practices were useless in an isolated community geared to an economy of self-sufficiency; rigid social customs were outmoded in a land where prestige depended on skill with the axe or rifle rather than on hereditary glories; cultural pursuits were unessential in a land where so many material tasks awaited doing. Hence in each pioneer settlement there occurred a rapid reversion to the primitive. What little government was necessary was provided by simple associations of settlers; each man looked after his family without reliance on his fellows; social hierarchies disintegrated, and cultural progress came to a halt. As the newcomers moved backward along the scale of civilization, the habits and customs of their traditional cultures were forgotten.

Gradually, however, newcomers drifted in, and as the man-land ratio increased, the community began a slow climb back toward civilization. Governmental controls were tightened and extended, economic specialization began, social stratification set in, and cultural activities quickened. But the new society that eventually emerged differed from the old from which it had sprung. The abandonment of cultural baggage during the migrations, the borrowings from the many cultures represented in each pioneer settlement, the deviations natural in separate evolutions, and the impact of the environment all played their parts in creating a unique social organism similar to but differing from those in the East. An "Americanization" of men and their institutions had taken place.

Turner believed that many of the characteristics associated with the American people were traceable to their experience, during the three centuries required to settle the continent, of constantly "beginning over again." Their mobility, their optimism, their inventiveness and willingness to accept innovation, their materialism, their exploitive wastefulness—these were frontier traits; for the pioneer, accustomed to repeated moves as he drifted westward, viewed the world through rose-colored glasses as he dreamed of a better future, experimented constantly as he adapted artifacts and customs to his peculiar environment, scorned culture as a deterrent to the practical tasks that bulked so large in his life, and squandered seemingly inexhaustible natural resources with abandon. Turner also ascribed America's distinctive brand of individualism, with its dislike of governmental interference in economic functions, to the experience of pioneers who wanted no hindrance from society as they exploited nature's riches. Similarly, he traced the exaggerated nationalism of the United States to its roots among frontiersmen who looked to the national government for land, transportation outlets, and protection against the Indians. And he believed that America's faith in democracy had stemmed from a pioneering experience in which the leveling influence of poverty and the uniqueness of local problems encouraged majority self-rule. He pointed out that these characteristics, prominent among frontiersmen, had persisted long after the frontier itself was no more.

This was Turner's famous "frontier hypothesis." For a generation after its enunciation its persuasive logic won uncritical acceptance among historians, but beginning in the late 1920's, and increasingly after Turner's death in 1932, an avalanche of criticism steadily mounted. His theories, critics said, were contradictory, his generalizations unsupported, his assumptions inadequately based; what empirical proof could he advance, they asked, to prove that the frontier experience was responsible for American individualism, mobility, or wastefulness? He was damned as a romanticist for his claim that democracy sprang from the forest environment of the United States and as an isolationist for failing to recognize the continuing impact of Europe on America. As the "bait-Turner" vogue gained popularity among younger scholars of the 1930's with their international, semi-

Marxian views of history, the criticisms of the frontier theory became as irrational as the earlier support given by overenthusiastic advocates.

During the past decade, however, a healthy reaction has slowly and unspectacularly gained momentum. Today's scholars, gradually realizing that Turner was advancing a hypothesis rather than proving a theory, have shown a healthy tendency to abandon fruitless haggling over the meaning of his phrases and to concentrate instead on testing his assumptions. They have directed their efforts primarily toward re-examining his hypothesis in the light of criticisms directed against it and applying it to frontier areas beyond the borders of the United States. Their findings have modified many of the views expressed by Turner but have gone far toward proving that the frontier hypothesis remains one essential tool—albeit not the only one—for interpreting American history.

That Turner was guilty of oversimplifying both the nature and the causes of the migration process was certainly true. He pictured settlers as moving westward in an orderly procession—fur trappers, cattlemen, miners, pioneer farmers, and equipped farmers—with each group playing its part in the transmutation of a wilderness into a civilization. Free land was the magnet that lured them onward, he believed, and this operated most effectively in periods of depression, when the displaced workers of the East sought a refuge from economic storms amidst nature's abundance in the West. "The wilderness ever opened the gate of escape to the poor, the discontented and oppressed," Turner wrote at one time. "If social conditions tended to crystallize in the east, beyond the Alleghenies there was freedom."

No one of these assumptions can be substantiated in the simplified form in which Turner stated it. His vision of an "orderly procession of civilization, marching single file westward" failed to account for deviations that were almost as important as the norm; as essential to the conquest of the forest as trappers or farmers were soldiers, mill-operators, distillers, artisans, storekeepers, merchants, lawyers, editors, speculators, and town dwellers. All played their role, and all contributed to a complex frontier social order that bore little resemblance to the primitive societies Turner pictured. This was especially the case with the early town builders. The hamlets that sprang up adjacent to each pioneer settlement were products of the environment as truly as were the cattlemen or Indian fighters; each evolved economic functions geared to the needs of the primitive area surrounding it, and, in the tight public controls maintained over such essential functions as grist-milling or retail selling, each mirrored the frontiersmen's community-oriented views. In these villages, too, the equalitarian influence of the West was reflected in thoroughly democratic governments, with popularly elected councils supreme and the mayor reduced to a mere figurehead.

The pioneers who marched westward in this disorganized procession were not attracted by the magnet of "free land," for Turner's assumption that before 1862 the public domain was open to all who could pay $1.25 an acre, or that acreage was free after the Homestead Act was passed in that year, has been completely disproved. Turner failed to recognize the presence in the procession to the frontier of that omnipresent profit-seeker, the speculator. Jobbers were always ahead of farmers in the advance westward, buying up likely town sites or appropriating the best farm lands, where the soil was good and transportation outlets available. When the settler arrived his choice was between paying the speculator's price or accepting an inferior site. Even the Homestead Act failed to lessen speculative activity. Capitalizing on generous government grants to railroads and state educational institutions (which did not want to be bothered with sales to individuals), or buying bonus script from soldiers, or securing Indian lands as the reservations were contracted, or seizing on faulty features of congressional acts for the disposal of swampland and timberland, jobbers managed to engross most of the Far West's arable acreage: for every newcomer who obtained a homestead from the government, six or seven purchased farms from speculators.

Those who made these purchases were not, as Turner believed, displaced eastern workers fleeing periodic industrial depressions. Few city-dwelling artisans had the skills or inclination, and almost none the capital, to escape to the frontier. Land prices of $1.25 an acre may seem low today, but they were prohibitive for laborers earning only a dollar a day. Moreover, needed farm machinery, animals, and housing added about $1,000 to the cost of starting a farm in the 1850's, while the cheapest travel rate from New York to St. Louis was about $13 a person. Because these sums were always beyond the reach of factory workers (in bad times they deterred migration even from the rural East), the frontier never served as a "safety valve" for laborers in the sense that Turner employed the term. Instead, the American frontiers were pushed westward largely by younger sons from adjacent farm areas who migrated in periods of prosperity. While these generalizations apply to the pre-Civil War era that was Turner's principal interest, they are even more applicable to the late nineteenth century. During that period the major population shifts were from country to city rather than vice versa; for every worker who left the factory to move to the farm, twenty persons moved from farm to factory. If a safety valve did exist at that time, it was a rural safety valve, drawing off surplus farm labor and thus lessening agrarian discontent during the Granger and Populist eras.

Admitting that the procession to the frontier was more complex than Turner realized, that good lands were seldom free, and that a safety valve never operated to drain the dispossessed and the malcontented from industrial centers, does this mean that his conclusions concerning the migration process have been completely discredited? The opposite is emphatically true. A more divergent group than Turner realized felt the frontier's impact, but that does not minimize the extent of the impact. Too, while lands in the West were almost never free, they were relatively cheaper than those in Europe or the East, and this differential did serve as an attracting force. Nor can pages of statistics disprove the fact that, at least until the Civil War, the frontier served as an indirect safety valve by attracting displaced eastern farmers who would otherwise have moved into industrial cities; thousands who left New England or New York for the Old Northwest in the 1830's and 1840's, when the "rural decay" of the Northeast was beginning, would have sought factory jobs had no western outlet existed.

The effect of their exodus is made clear by comparing the political philosophies of the United States with those of another frontier country, Australia. There, lands lying beyond the coastal mountains were closed to pioneers by the aridity of the soil and by great sheep ranchers who were first on the scene. Australia, as a result, developed an urban civilization and an industrialized population relatively sooner than did the United States; and it had labor unions, labor-dominated governments, and political philosophies that would be viewed as radical in America. Without the safety valve of its own West, feeble though it may have been, such a course might have been followed in the United States.

Frederick Jackson Turner's conclusions concerning the influence of the frontier on Americans have also been questioned, debated, and modified since he advanced his hypothesis, but they have not been seriously altered. This is true even of one of his statements that has been more vigorously disputed than any other: "American democracy was born of no theorist's dream; it was not carried in the *Susan Constant* to Virginia, nor in the *Mayflower* to Plymouth. It came out of the American forest, and it gained a new strength each time it touched a new frontier." When he penned those oft-quoted words, Turner wrote as a propagandist against the "germ theory" school of history; in a less emotional and more thoughtful moment, he ascribed America's democratic institutions not to "imitation, or simple borrowing," but to "the evolution and adaptation of organs in response to changed environment." Even this moderate theory has aroused critical venom. Democracy, according to anti-Turnerians, was well advanced in Europe and *was* transported to America on the *Susan Constant* and the *Mayflower*; within this country democratic practices have multiplied most rapidly as a result of eastern lower-class pressures and have only been imitated in the West. If, critics ask, some mystical forest influence was responsible for such practices as manhood suffrage, increased authority for legislatures at the expense of executives, equitable legislative representation, and women's political rights, why did they not evolve in frontier areas outside the United States—in Russia, Latin America, and Canada, for example—exactly as they did here?

The answer, of course, is that democratic theory and institutions were imported from England, but that the frontier environment tended to make them, in practice, even more democratic. Two conditions common in pioneer communities made this inevitable. One was the wide diffusion of land ownership; this created an independent outlook and led to a demand for political participation on the part of those who had a stake in society. The other was the common

*A contemporary etching of a wagon train
encampment along the Laramie River.*

social and economic level and the absence, characteristic of all primitive communities, of any prior leadership structure. The lack of any national or external controls made self-rule a hard necessity, and the frontiersmen, with their experience in community co-operation at cabin-raisings, logrollings, corn-huskings, and road or school building, accepted simple democratic practices as natural and inevitable. These practices, originating on the grass roots level, were expanded and extended in the recurring process of government-building that marked the westward movement of civilization. Each new territory that was organized—there were 31 in all—required a frame of government; this was drafted by relatively poor recent arrivals or by a minority of upper-class leaders, all of whom were committed to democratic ideals through their frontier community experiences. The result was a constant democratization of institutions and practices as constitution-makers adopted the most liberal features of older frames of government with which they were familiar.

This was true even in frontier lands outside the United States, for wherever there were frontiers, existing practices were modified in the direction of greater equality and a wider popular participation in governmental affairs. The results were never identical, of course, for both the environment and the nature of the imported institutions varied too greatly from country to country. In Russia, for instance, even though it promised no democracy comparable to that of the United States, the eastward-moving Siberian frontier, the haven of some seven million peasants during the nineteenth and early twentieth centuries, was notable for its lack of guilds, authoritarian churches, and all-powerful nobility. An official visiting there in 1910 was alarmed by the "enormous, rudely democratic country" evolving under the influence of the small homesteads that were the normal living units; he feared that czarism and European Russia would soon be "throttled" by the egalitarian currents developing on the frontier.

That the frontier accentuated the spirit of nationalism and individualism in the United States, as Turner maintained, was also true. Every page of the country's history, from the War of 1812 through the era of Manifest Destiny to today's bitter conflicts with Russia, demonstrates that the American attitude toward the world has been far more nationalistic than that of non-frontier countries and that this attitude has been strongest in the newest regions. Similarly, the pioneering experience converted settlers into individualists, although through a somewhat different process than Turner envisaged. His emphasis on a desire for freedom as a primary force luring men westward and his belief that pioneers developed an attitude of self-sufficiency in their lone battle against nature have been questioned, and with justice. Hoped-for gain was the magnet that attracted most migrants to the cheaper lands of the West, while once there they lived in units where co-operative enterprise—for protection against the Indians, for cabin-raising, law enforcement, and the like—was more essential than in the better established towns of the East. Yet the fact remains that the abundant resources and the greater social mobility of frontier areas did instill into frontiersmen a uniquely American form of individualism. Even though they may be sheeplike in following the decrees of social arbiters or fashion dictators, Americans today, like their pioneer ancestors, dislike governmental interference in their affairs. "Rugged individualism" did not originate on the frontier any more than democracy or nationalism did, but each concept was deepened and sharpened by frontier conditions.

His opponents have also cast doubt on Turner's assertion that American inventiveness and willingness to adopt innovations are traits inherited from pioneer ancestors who constantly devised new techniques and artifacts to cope with an unfamiliar environment. The critics insist that each mechanical improvement needed for the conquest of the frontier, from plows to barbed-wire fencing, originated in the East; when frontiersmen faced such an incomprehensible task as conquering the Great Plains they proved so tradition-bound that their advance halted until eastern inventors provided them with the tools needed to subdue grasslands. Unassailable as this argument may be, it ignores the fact that the recurring demand for implements and methods needed in the frontier advance did put a premium on inventiveness by Americans, whether they lived in the East or West. That even today they are less bound by tradition than other peoples is due in part to their pioneer heritage.

The anti-intellectualism and materialism which are national traits can also be traced to the frontier experience. There was little in pioneer life to attract the timid, the cultivated, or the aesthetically sensitive. In the boisterous western borderlands, book learning and intellectual speculation were suspect among those dedicated to the material tasks necessary to subdue a continent. Americans today reflect their background in placing the "intellectual" well below the "practical businessman" in their scale of heroes. Yet the frontiersman, as Turner recognized, was an idealist as well as a materialist. He admired material objects not only as symbols of advancing civilization but as the substance of his hopes for a better future. Given economic success he would be able to afford the aesthetic and intellectual pursuits that he felt were his due, even though he was not quite able to appreciate them. This spirit inspired the cultural activities—literary societies, debating clubs, "thespian groups," libraries, schools, camp meetings—that thrived in the most primitive western communities. It also helped nurture in the pioneers an infinite faith in the future. The belief in progress, both material and intellectual, that is part of modern America's creed was strengthened by the frontier experience.

Frederick Jackson Turner, then, was not far wrong when he maintained that frontiersmen did develop unique traits and that these, perpetuated, form the principal distinguishing characteristics of the American people today. To a degree unknown among Europeans, Americans do display a restless energy, a versatility, a practical ingenuity, an earthy practicality. They do squander their natural resources with an abandon unknown elsewhere; they have developed a mobility both social and physical that marks them as a people apart. In few other lands is the democratic ideal worshiped so intensely, or nationalism carried to such extremes of isolationism or international arrogance. Rarely do other peoples display such indifference toward intellectualism or aesthetic values; seldom in comparable cultural areas do they cling so tenaciously to the shibboleth of rugged individualism. Nor do residents of non-frontier lands experience to the same degree the heady optimism, the rosy faith in the future, the belief in the inevitability of progress that form part of the American creed. These are pioneer traits, and they have become a part of the national heritage.

Yet if the frontier wrought such a transformation within the United States, why did it not have a similar effect on other countries with frontiers? If the pioneering experience was responsible for our democracy and nationalism and individualism, why have the peoples of Africa, Latin America, Canada, and Russia failed to develop identical characteristics? The answer is obvious: in few nations of the world has the sort of frontier that Turner described existed. For he saw the frontier not as a borderland between unsettled and settled lands, but as an accessible area in which a low man-land ratio and abundant natural resources provided an unusual opportunity for the individual to better himself. Where autocratic governments controlled population movements, where resources were lacking, or where conditions prohibited ordinary individuals from exploiting nature's virgin riches, a frontier in the Turnerian sense could not be said to exist.

The areas of the world that have been occupied since the beginning of the age of discovery contain remarkably few frontiers of the American kind. In Africa the few Europeans were so outnumbered by relatively uncivilized native inhabitants that the need for protection transcended any impulses toward democracy or individualism. In Latin America the rugged terrain and steaming jungles restricted areas exploitable by individuals to the Brazilian plains and the Argentine pampas; these did attract frontiersmen, although in Argentina the prior occupation of most good lands by government-favored cattle growers kept small farmers out until railroads penetrated the region. In Canada the path westward was blocked by the Laurentian Shield, a tangled mass of hills and sterile, brush-choked soil covering the country north and west of the St. Lawrence Valley. When railroads finally penetrated this barrier in the late nineteenth century, they carried pioneers directly from the East to the prairie provinces of the West; the newcomers, with no prior pioneering experience, simply adapted to their new situation the eastern institutions with which they were familiar. Among the world's frontier nations only Russia provided a physical environment comparable to that of the United States, and there the pioneers were too accustomed to rigid feudal and monarchic controls to respond as Americans did.

Further proof that the westward expansion of the United States has been a powerful formative force has been provided by the problems facing the nation in the present century. During the past fifty years the American people have been adjusting their lives and institutions to existence in a frontierless land, for while the superintendent of the census was decidedly premature when he announced in 1890 that the country's "unsettled area has been so broken into by isolated bodies of settlement that there can hardly be said to be a frontier line" remaining, the era of cheap land was rapidly drawing to a close. In attempting to adjust the country to its new, expansionless future, statesmen have frequently called upon the frontier hypothesis to justify everything from rugged individualism to the welfare state, and from isolationism to world domination.

Political opinion has divided sharply on the necessity of altering the nation's governmental philosophy and techniques in response to the changed environment. Some statesmen and scholars have rebelled against what they call Turner's "Space Concept of History," with all that it implies concerning the lack of opportunity for the individual in an expansionless land. They insist that modern technology has created a whole host of new "frontiers"—of intensive farming, electronics, mechanics, manufacturing, nuclear fission, and the like—which offer such diverse outlets to individual talents that governmental interference in the nation's economic activities is unjustified. On the other hand, equally competent spokesmen argue that these newer "frontiers" offer little opportunity to the individual—as distinguished from the corporation or the capitalist—and hence cannot duplicate the function of the frontier of free land. The government, they insist, must provide the people with the security and opportunity that vanished when escape to the West became impossible. This school's most eloquent spokesman, Franklin D. Roosevelt, declared: "Our last frontier has long since been reached. . . . Equality of opportunity as we have known it no longer exists. . . . Our task now is not the discovery or exploitation of natural resources or necessarily producing more goods. It is the sober, less dramatic business of administering resources and plants already in hand, of seeking to re-establish foreign markets for our surplus production, of meeting the problem of under-consumption, of adjusting production to consumption, of distributing wealth and products more equitably, of adapting existing economic organizations to the service of the people. The day of enlightened administration has come." To Roosevelt, and to thousands like him, the passing of the frontier created a new era in history which demanded a new philosophy of government.

Diplomats have also found in the frontier hypothesis justification for many of their moves, from imperialist expansion to the restriction of immigration. Harking back to Turner's statement that the perennial rebirth of society was necessary to keep alive the democratic spirit, expansionists have argued through the twentieth century for an extension of American power and territories. During the Spanish-American War imperialists preached such a doctrine, adding the argument that Spain's lands were needed to provide a population outlet for a people who could no longer escape to their own frontier. Idealists such as Woodrow Wilson could agree with materialists like J. P. Morgan that the extension of American authority abroad, either through territorial acquisitions or economic penetration, would be good for both business and democracy. Later, Franklin D. Roosevelt favored a similar expansion of the American democratic ideal as a necessary prelude to the better world that he hoped would emerge from World War II. His successor, Harry Truman, envisaged his "Truman Doctrine" as a device to extend and defend the frontiers of democracy throughout the globe. While popular belief in the superiority of America's political institutions was far older than Turner, that belief rested partly on the frontier experience of the United States.

These practical applications of the frontier hypothesis, as well as its demonstrated influence on the nation's development, suggest that its critics have been unable to destroy the theory's effectiveness as a key to understanding American history. The recurring rebirth of society in the United States over a period of three hundred years did endow the people with characteristics and institutions that distinguish them from the inhabitants of other nations. It is obviously untrue that the frontier experience alone accounts for the unique features of American civilization; that civilization can be understood only as the product of the interplay of the Old World heritage and New World conditions. But among those conditions none has bulked larger than the operation of the frontier process.

Daniel P. Mannix
and Malcolm Cowley
The Middle Passage

To Europeans like William Byrd, America offered an environment of unparalleled freedom and stimulation; for those of lesser fortune, as the historical record shows, it supplied only somewhat less opportunity for self-expression and improvement. But for Africans—roughly ten per cent of all the colonists by the middle of the eighteenth century—America meant the crushing degradation of slavery. Until recently, without excusing or justifying slavery, most historians have tended not so much to ignore as to compartmentalize (one is almost tempted to say "segregate") the history of the Negro from the general stream of American development. When generalizing about American "free institutions," "opportunity," and "equality," the phrase "except for blacks" needs always to be added if the truth is to be told.

Historical arguments have developed about the condition of slaves in America, about the differences between the British-American and Latin American slave systems, and about other aspects of the history of the Negro in the New World. But there has been only unanimity among historians about the horrors associated with the capture of blacks in Africa and with the dread "middle passage" over which the bondsmen were shipped to the Americas. In this essay the literary critic Malcolm Cowley and the historian Daniel P. Mannix combine their talents to describe what it meant to be wrenched from one's home and native soil, herded in chains into the foul hold of a slave ship, and dispatched across the torrid mid-Atlantic into the hell of slavery.

*L*ong before Europeans appeared on the African coast, the merchants of Timbuktu were exporting slaves to the Moorish kingdoms north of the Sahara. Even the transatlantic slave trade had a long history. There were Negroes in Santo Domingo as early as 1503, and the first twenty slaves were sold in Jamestown, Virginia, about the last week of August, 1619, only twelve years after the colony was founded. But the flush days of the trade were in the eighteenth century, when vast supplies of labor were needed for the sugar plantations in the West Indies and the tobacco and rice plantations on the mainland. From 1700 to 1807, when the trade was legally abolished by Great Britain and the United States, more than seventy thousand Negroes were carried across the Atlantic in any normal year. The trade was interrupted by wars, notably by the American Revolution, but the total New World importation for the century may have amounted to five million enslaved persons.

Most of the slaves were carried on shipboard at some point along the four thousand miles of West African coastline that extend in a dog's leg from the Sahara on the north to the southern desert. Known as the Guinea Coast, it was feared by eighteenth-century mariners, who died there by hundreds and thousands every year.

Contrary to popular opinion, very few of the slaves—possibly one or two out of a hundred—were free Africans kidnapped by Europeans. The slaving captains had, as a rule, no moral prejudice against man-stealing, but they usually refrained from it on the ground of its being a dangerous business practice. A vessel suspected of man-stealing might be "cut off" by the natives, its crew killed, and its cargo of slaves offered for sale to other vessels.

The vast majority of the Negroes brought to America had been enslaved and sold to the whites by other Africans. There were coastal tribes and states, like the Efik kingdom of Calabar, that based their whole economy on the slave trade. The slaves might be prisoners of war, they might have been kidnapped by gangs of black marauders, or they might have been sold with their whole families for such high crimes as adultery, impiety, or, as in one instance, stealing a tobacco pipe. Intertribal wars, the principal source of slaves, were in many cases no more than large-scale kidnapping expeditions. Often they were fomented by Europeans, who supplied both sides with muskets and gunpowder—so many muskets or so much powder for each slave that they promised to deliver on shipboard.

The ships were English, French, Dutch, Danish, Portuguese, or American. London, Bristol, and finally Liverpool were the great English slaving ports. By 1790 Liverpool had engrossed five eighths of the English trade and three sevenths of the slave trade of all Europe. Its French rival, Nantes, would soon be ruined by the Napoleonic wars. During the last years of legal slaving, Liverpool's only serious competitors were the Yankee captains of Newport and Bristol, Rhode Island.

Profits from a slaving voyage, which averaged nine or ten months, were reckoned at thirty per cent, after deducting sales commissions, insurance premiums, and all other expenses. The Liverpool merchants became so rich from the slave trade that they invested heavily in mills, factories, mines, canals, and railways. That process was repeated in New England, and the slave trade provided much of the capital that was needed for the industrial revolution.

A slaving voyage was triangular. English textiles, notions, cutlery, and firearms were carried to the Guinea Coast, where they were exchanged for slaves. These were sold in America or the West Indies, and part of the proceeds was invested in colonial products, notably sugar and rice, which were carried back to England on the third leg of the voyage. If the vessel sailed from a New England port, its usual cargo was casks of rum from a Massachusetts distillery. The rum was exchanged in Africa for slaves—often at the rate of two hundred gallons per man—and the slaves were exchanged in the West Indies for molasses, which was carried back to New England to be distilled into rum. A slave ship or Guineaman was expected to show a profit for each leg of its triangular course. But the base of the triangle, the so-called Middle Passage from Africa to the New World with a black cargo, was the most profitable part of the voyage, at the highest cost in human suffering. Let us see what happened in the passage during the flush days of the slave trade.

As soon as an assortment of naked slaves was carried aboard a Guineaman, the men were shackled two by two, the right wrist and ankle of one to the left wrist and ankle of another; then they were sent below. The women—usually regarded as fair prey for the sailors —were allowed to wander by day almost anywhere on the vessel, though they spent the night between decks, in a space partitioned off from that of the men. All the slaves were forced to sleep without covering on bare wooden floors, which were often constructed of unplaned boards. In a stormy passage the skin over their elbows might be worn away to the bare bones.

William Bosman says, writing in 1701, "You would really wonder to see how these slaves live on board; for though their number sometimes amounts to six or seven hundred, yet by the careful management of our masters of ships"—the Dutch masters, in this case—"they are so regulated that it seems incredible: And in this particular our nation exceeds all other Europeans; for as the French, Portuguese and English slave-ships, are always foul and stinking; on the contrary ours are for the most part clean and neat."

Slavers of every nation insisted that their own vessels were the best in the trade. Thus, James Barbot, Jr., who sailed on an English ship to the Congo in 1700, was highly critical of the Portuguese. He admits that they made a great point of baptizing the slaves before taking them on board, but then, "It is pitiful," he says, "to see how they crowd those poor wretches, six hundred and fifty or seven hundred in a ship, the men standing in the hold ty'd to stakes, the women between decks and those that are with child in the great cabin and the children in the steeridge which in that hot climate occasions an intolerable stench." Barbot adds, however, that the Portuguese provided the slaves with coarse thick mats, which were "softer for the poor wretches to lie upon than the bare decks . . . and it would be prudent to imitate the Portuguese in this point." The English, however, did not display that sort of prudence.

There were two schools of thought among the English slaving captains, the "loose-packers" and the "tight-packers." The former argued that by giving the slaves a little more room, better food, and a certain amount of liberty, they reduced the death rate and received a better price for each slave in the West Indies. The tight-packers answered that although the loss of life might be greater on each of their voyages, so too were the net receipts from a larger cargo. If many of the survivors were weak and emaciated, as was often the case, they could be fattened up in a West Indian slave yard before being offered for sale.

The argument between the two schools continued as long as the trade itself, but for many years after 1750 the tight-packers were in the ascendant. So great was the profit on each slave landed alive that hardly a captain refrained from loading his vessel to its utmost capacity. Says the Reverend John Newton, who was a slaving captain before he became a clergyman:

> The cargo of a vessel of a hundred tons or a little more is calculated to purchase from 220 to 250 slaves. Their lodging rooms below the deck which are three (for the men, the boys, and the women) besides a place for the sick, are sometimes more than five feet high and sometimes less; and this height is divided toward the middle for the slaves to lie in two rows, one above the other, on each side of the ship, close to each other like books upon a shelf. I have known them so close that the shelf would not easily contain one more.
>
> The poor creatures, thus cramped, are likewise in irons for the most part which makes it difficult for them to turn or move or attempt to rise or to lie down without hurting themselves or each other. Every morning, perhaps, more instances than one are found of the living and the dead fastened together.

This diagram is a typical example of the "tight packing" techniques of many slavers.

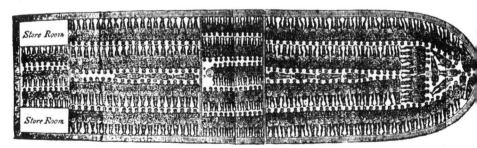

Newton was writing in 1788, shortly before a famous parliamentary investigation of the slave trade that lasted four years. One among hundreds of witnesses was Dr. Alexander Falconbridge, who had made four slaving voyages as a surgeon. Falconbridge testified that "he made the most of the room," in stowing the slaves, "and wedged them in. They had not so much room as a man in his coffin either in length or breadth. When he had to enter the slave deck, he took off his shoes to avoid crushing the slaves as he was forced to crawl over them." Falconbridge "had the marks on his feet where the slaves bit and pinched him."

Captain Parrey of the Royal Navy was sent to measure the slave ships at Liverpool and make a report to the House of Commons. That was also in 1788. Parrey discovered that the captains of many slavers possessed a chart showing the dimensions of the half deck, lower deck, hold, platforms, gunroom, orlop, and great cabin, in fact of every crevice into which slaves might be wedged. Miniature black figures were drawn on some of the charts to illustrate the most effective method of packing in the cargo.

On the *Brookes*, which Parrey considered to be typical, every man was allowed a space six feet long by sixteen inches wide (and usually about two feet seven inches high); every woman, a space five feet ten inches long by sixteen inches wide; every boy, five feet by fourteen inches; every girl, four feet six inches by twelve inches. The *Brookes* was a vessel of 320 tons. By a new law passed in 1788 it was permitted to carry 454 slaves, and the chart, which later became famous, showed where 451 of them could be stowed away. Parrey failed to see how the captain could find room for three more. Nevertheless, Parliament was told by reliable witnesses, including Dr. Thomas Trotter, formerly surgeon of the *Brookes*, that before the new law she had carried 600 slaves on one voyage and 609 on another.

Taking on slaves was a process that might be completed in a month or two by vessels trading in Lower Guinea, east and south of the Niger delta. In Upper Guinea, west and north of the delta, the process was longer. It might last from six months to a year or more on the Gold Coast, which supplied the slaves most in demand by the English colonies. Meanwhile the captain was buying Negroes, sometimes one or two a day, sometimes a hundred or more in a single lot, while haggling over each purchase.

Those months when a slaver lay at anchor off the malarial coastline were the most dangerous part of her voyage. Not only was her crew exposed to African fevers and the revenge of angry natives; not only was there the chance of her being taken by pirates or by a hostile man-of-war; but there was also the constant threat of a slave mutiny. Captain Thomas Phillips says, in his account of a voyage made in 1693–94:

> When our slaves are aboard we shackle the men two and two, while we lie in port, and in sight of their own country, for 'tis then they attempt to make their escape, and mutiny; to prevent

which we always keep centinels upon the hatchways, and have a chest full of small arms, ready loaden and prim'd, constantly lying at hand upon the quarter-deck, together with some granada shells; and two of our quarter-deck guns, pointing on the deck thence, and two more out of the steerage, the door of which is always kept shut, and well barr'd; they are fed twice a day, at 10 in the morning, and 4 in the evening, which is the time they are aptest to mutiny, being all upon the deck; therefore all that time, what of our men are not employ'd in distributing their victuals to them, and settling them, stand to their arms; and some with lighted matches at the great guns that yaun upon them, loaden with partridge, till they have done and gone down to their kennels between decks.

In spite of such precautions, mutinies were frequent on the Coast, and some of them were successful. Even a mutiny that failed might lead to heavy losses among the slaves and the sailors. Thus, we read in the Newport, Rhode Island, *Mercury* of November 18, 1765:

By letters from Capt. Hopkins in a Brig belonging to Providence arrived here from Antigua from the Coast of Africa we learn That soon after he left the Coast, the number of his Men being reduced by Sickness, he was obliged to permit some of the Slaves to come upon Deck to assist the People: These Slaves contrived to release the others, and the whole rose upon the People, and endeavoured to get Possession of the Vessel; but was happily prevented by the Captain and his Men, who killed, wounded and forced overboard, Eighty of them, which obliged the rest to submit.

There are scores of similar items in the colonial newspapers.

William Richardson, a young sailor who shipped on an English Guineaman in 1790, tells of going to the help of a French vessel on which the slaves had risen while it was at anchor. The English seamen jumped into the boats and pulled hard for the Frenchman, but by the time they reached it there were "a hundred slaves in possession of the deck and others tumbling up from below." The slaves put up a desperate resistance. "I could not but admire," Richardson says, "the courage of a fine young black who, though his partner in irons lay dead at his feet, would not surrender but fought with his billet of wood until a ball finished his existence. The others fought as well as they could but what could they do against fire-arms?"

There are fairly detailed accounts of fifty-five mutinies on slavers from 1699 to 1845, not to mention passing references to more than a hundred others. The list of ships "cut off" by the natives—often in revenge for the kidnapping of free Africans—is almost as long. On the record it does not seem that Africans submitted tamely to being carried across the Atlantic like chained beasts. Edward Long, the Jamaica planter and historian, justified the cruel punishments inflicted on slaves by saying, "The many acts of violence they

*In 1839 some 53 captives revolted aboard the
slaver* Amistad. *They were recaptured but later
freed in a case that reached the Supreme Court.*

have committed by murdering whole crews and destroying ships when
they had it in their power to do so have made these rigors wholly
chargeable on their own bloody and malicious disposition which calls
for the same confinement as if they were wolves or wild boars.'' For
''wolves or wild boars'' a modern reader might substitute ''men who
would rather die than be enslaved.''

With the loading of the slaves, the captain, for his part, had finished what he regarded as the most difficult part of his voyage. Now
he had to face only the ordinary perils of the sea, most of which were
covered by his owners' insurance against fire, shipwreck, pirates and
rovers, letters of mart and counter-mart, barratry, jettison, and
foreign men-of-war. Among the risks not covered by insurance, the
greatest was that of the cargo's being swept away by disease. The un-
derwriters refused to issue such policies, arguing that they would
expose the captain to an unholy temptation. If insured against disease
among his slaves, he might take no precautions against it and might
try to make his profit out of the insurance.

The more days at sea, the more deaths among his cargo, and so the
captain tried to cut short the next leg of his voyage. If he had shipped
his slaves at Bonny, Old Calabar, or any port to the southward, he
might call at one of the Portuguese islands in the Gulf of Guinea for
an additional supply of food and fresh water, usually enough, with
what he had already, to last for three months. If he had traded to the
northward, he made straight for the West Indies. Usually he had from
four to five thousand nautical miles to sail—or even more, if the passage was from Angola to Virginia. The shortest passage—that from the
Gambia River to Barbados—might be made in as little as three weeks,
with favoring winds. If the course was much longer, and if the ship was
becalmed in the doldrums or driven back by storms, the voyage might
take more than three months, and slaves and sailors would be put on
short rations long before the end of the Middle Passage.

On a canvas of heroic size, Thomas Stothard, Esquire, of the Royal Academy, depicted *The Voyage of the Sable Venus from Angola to the West Indies*. His painting is handsomely reproduced in the second volume of Bryan Edwards' *History of the British Colonies in the West Indies* (1793), where it appears beside a poem on the same allegorical subject by an unnamed Jamaican author, perhaps Edwards himself.

The joint message of the poem and the painting is simple to the point of coarseness: that slave women are preferable to English girls at night, being passionate and accessible; but the message is embellished with classical details, to show the painter's learning.

Meanwhile the Sable Venus, if she was a living woman carried from Angola to the West Indies, was roaming the deck of a ship that stank of excrement; as was said of any slaver, "You could smell it five miles down wind." She had been torn from her husband and her children, she had been branded on the left buttock, and she had been carried to the ship bound hand and foot, lying in the bilge at the bottom of a dug-out canoe. Now she was the prey of the ship's officers.

Here is how she and her shipmates spent the day.

If the weather was clear, they were brought on deck at eight o'clock in the morning. The men were attached by their leg irons to the great chain that ran along the bulwarks on both sides of the ship; the women and half-grown boys were allowed to wander at will. About nine o'clock the slaves were served their first meal of the day. If they were from the Windward Coast—roughly, the shoreline of present-day Liberia and Sierra Leone—the fare was boiled rice, millet, or corn meal, sometimes cooked with a few lumps of salt beef abstracted from the sailors' rations. If they were from the Bight of Biafra, at the east end of the Gulf of Guinea, they were fed stewed yams, but the Congos and the Angolas preferred manioc or plantains. With the food they were all given half a pint of water, served out in a pannikin.

After the morning meal came a joyless ceremony called "dancing the slaves." "Those who were in irons," says Dr. Thomas Trotter, surgeon of the *Brookes* in 1783, "were ordered to stand up and make what motions they could, leaving a passage for such as were out of irons to dance around the deck." Dancing was prescribed as a therapeutic measure, a specific against suicidal melancholy, and also against scurvy—although in the latter case is was a useless torture for men with swollen limbs. While sailors paraded the deck, each with a cat-o'-nine-tails in his right hand, the men slaves "jumped in their irons" until their ankles were bleeding flesh. Music was provided by a slave thumping on a broken drum or an upturned kettle, or by an African banjo, if there was one aboard, or perhaps by a sailor with a bagpipe or a fiddle. Slaving captains sometimes advertised for "A person that can play on the Bagpipes, for a Guinea ship." The slaves were also told to sing. Said Dr. Claxton after his voyage in the *Young Hero*, "They sing, but not for their amusement. The captain ordered them to sing, and they sang songs of sorrow. Their sickness, fear of being beaten, their hunger, and the memory of their country, etc., are the usual subjects."

While some of the sailors were dancing the slaves, others were sent below to scrape and swab out the sleeping rooms. It was a sickening task, and it was not well performed unless the captain imposed an iron discipline. James Barbot, Sr., was proud of the discipline maintained on the *Albion-Frigate*. "We were very nice," he says, "in keeping the places where the slaves lay clean and neat, appointing some of the ship's crew to do that office constantly and thrice a week we perfumed betwixt decks with a quantity of good vinegar in pails, and red-hot iron bullets in them, to expel the bad air, after the place had been well washed and scrubbed with brooms." Captain Hugh Crow, the last legal English slaver, was famous for his housekeeping. "I always took great pains," he says, "to promote the health and comfort of all on board, by proper diet, regularity, exercise, and cleanliness, for I considered that on keeping the ship clean and orderly, which was always my hobby, the success of our voyage mainly depended." Certainly he lost fewer slaves in the Middle Passage than the other captains, some of whom had the filth in the hold cleaned out only once a week.

At three or four in the afternoon the slaves were fed their second meal, often a repetition of the first. Sometimes, instead of African food, they were given horse beans, the cheapest provender from Europe. The beans were boiled to a pulp, then covered with a mixture of palm oil, flour, water, and red pepper, which the sailors called "slabber sauce." Most of the slaves detested horse beans, especially if they were used to eating yams or manioc. Instead of eating the pulp, they would, unless carefully watched, pick it up by handfuls and throw it in each other's faces.

That second meal was the end of their day. As soon as it was finished they were sent below, under the guard of sailors charged with stowing them away on their bare floors and platforms. The tallest men were placed amidships, where the vessel was widest; the shorter ones were tumbled into the stern. Usually there was only room for them to sleep on their sides, "spoon fashion." Captain William Littleton told Parliament that slaves in the ships on which he sailed might lie on their backs if they wished—"though perhaps," he conceded, "it might be difficult all at the same time."

After stowing their cargo, the sailors climbed out of the hatchway, each clutching his cat-o'-nine-tails; then the hatchway gratings were closed and barred. Sometimes in the night, as the sailors lay on deck and tried to sleep, they heard from below "an howling melancholy noise, expressive of extreme anguish." When Dr. Trotter told his interpreter, a slave woman, to inquire about the cause of the noise, "she discovered it to be owing to their having dreamt they were in their own country, and finding themselves when awake, in the hold of a slave ship."

More often the noise heard by the sailors was that of quarreling among the slaves. The usual occasion for quarrels was their problem of reaching the latrines. These were inadequate in size and number, and hard to find in the darkness of the crowded hold, especially by men who were ironed together in pairs.

In squalls or rainy weather, the slaves were never brought on deck. They were served their two meals in the hold, where the air became too thick and poisonous to breathe. Dr. Falconbridge writes:

For the purpose of admitting fresh air, most of the ships in the slave-trade are provided, between the decks, with five or six air-ports on each side of the ship, of about six inches in length and four in breadth; in addition to which, some few ships, but not one in twenty, have what they denominate wind-sails [funnels made of canvas and so placed as to direct a current of air into the hold]. But whenever the sea is rough and the rain heavy, it becomes necessary to shut these and every other conveyance by which the air is admitted. . . . The negroes' rooms very soon become intolerably hot. The confined air, rendered noxious by the effluvia exhaled from their bodies and by being repeatedly breathed, soon produces fevers and fluxes which generally carry off great numbers of them.

Dr. Trotter says that when tarpaulins were thrown over the gratings, the slaves would cry, "Kickeraboo, kickeraboo, we are dying, we are dying." Falconbridge gives one instance of their sufferings:

Some wet and blowing weather having occasioned the portholes to be shut and the grating to be covered, fluxes and fevers among the negroes ensued. While they were in this situation, I frequently went down among them till at length their rooms became so extremely hot as to be only bearable for a very short time. But the excessive heat was not the only thing that rendered their situation intolerable. The deck, that is, the floor of their rooms, was so covered with the blood and mucus which had proceeded from them in consequence of the flux, that it resembled a slaughter-house.

While the slaves were on deck they had to be watched at all times to keep them from committing suicide. Says Captain Phillips of the *Hannibal*, "We had about 12 negroes did wilfully drown themselves, and others starv'd themselves to death; for," he explained, " 'tis their belief that when they die they return home to their own country and friends again."

This belief was reported from various regions, at various periods of the trade, but it seems to have been especially strong among the Ibos of eastern Nigeria. In 1788, nearly a hundred years after the *Hannibal's* voyage, Dr. Ecroide Claxton was the surgeon who attended a shipload of Ibos. Some, he testified,

wished to die on an idea that they should then get back to their own country. The captain in order to obviate this idea, thought of an expedient viz. to cut off the heads of those who died intimating to them that if determined to go, they must return without heads. The slaves were accordingly brought up to witness the operation. One of them by a violent exertion got loose and flying to the place where the nettings had been unloosed in order to empty the tubs, he darted overboard. The ship brought to, a man was placed in the main chains to catch him which he perceiving, made signs which words cannot express expressive of his happiness in escaping. He then went down and was seen no more.

Dr. Isaac Wilson, a surgeon in the Royal Navy, made a Guinea voyage on the *Elizabeth*, captain John Smith, who was said to be very humane. Nevertheless, Wilson was assigned the duty of flogging the slaves. "Even in the act of chastisement," Wilson says, "I have seen them look up at me with a smile, and, in their own language, say 'presently we shall be no more.'" One woman on the *Elizabeth* found some rope yarn, which she tied to the armorer's vise; she fastened the other end round her neck and was found dead in the morning.

On the *Brookes* when Thomas Trotter was her surgeon, there was a man who, after being accused of witchcraft, had been sold into slavery with all his family. During the first night on shipboard he tried to cut his throat. Dr. Trotter sewed up the wound, but on the following night the man not only tore out the stitches but tried to cut his throat on the other side. From the ragged edges of the wound and the blood on his fingers, he seemed to have used his nails as the only available instrument. His hands were then tied together, but he refused all food, and he died of hunger in eight or ten days.

Besides the propensity for suicide, another deadly scourge of the Guinea cargoes was a phenomenon called "fixed melancholy." Even slaves who were well fed, treated with kindness, and kept under relatively sanitary conditions would often die, one after another, for no apparent reason; they had simply lost the will to live. Dr. Wilson believed that fixed melancholy was responsible for the loss of two thirds of the slaves who died on the *Elizabeth*. "No one who had it was ever cured," he says, "whereas those who had it not and yet were ill, recovered. The symptoms are a lowness of spirits and despondency. Hence they refuse food. This only increases the symptoms. The stomach afterwards got weak. Hence the belly ached, fluxes ensued, and they were carried off." But in spite of the real losses from despair, the high death rate on Guineamen was due to somatic more than to psychic afflictions.

Along with their human cargoes, crowded, filthy, undernourished, and terrified out of the wish to live, the ships also carried an invisible cargo of microbes, bacilli, spirochetes, viruses, and intestinal worms from one continent to another; the Middle Passage was a crossroad and market place of diseases. From Europe came smallpox, measles (somewhat less deadly to Africans than to American Indians), gonorrhea, and syphilis (which last Columbus' sailors had carried from America to Europe). The African diseases were yellow fever (to which the natives were resistant), dengue, blackwater fever, and malaria (which was not specifically African, but which most of the slaves carried in their blood streams). If anopheles mosquitoes were present, malaria spread from the slaves through any new territories to which they were carried. Other African diseases were amoebic and bacillary dysentery (known as "the bloody flux"), Guinea worms, hookworm (possibly African in origin, but soon endemic in the warmer parts of the New World), yaws, elephantiasis, and leprosy.

The particular affliction of the white sailors after escaping from the fevers of the Guinea Coast was scurvy, a deficiency disease to which they were exposed by their monotonous rations of salt beef and sea biscuits. The daily tot of lime juice (originally lemon juice) that prevented scurvy was almost never served on merchantmen during the days of the legal slave trade, and in fact was not prescribed in the Royal Navy until 1795. Although the slaves were also subject to scurvy, they fared better in this respect than the sailors, partly because they made only one leg of the triangular voyage and partly because their rough diet was sometimes richer in vitamins. But sailors and slaves alike were swept away by smallpox and "the bloody flux," and sometimes whole shiploads went blind from what seems to have been trachoma.

Smallpox was feared more than other diseases, since the surgeons had no way of curing it. One man with smallpox infected a whole vessel, unless—as sometimes happened—he was tossed overboard when the first scabs appeared. Captain Wilson of the *Briton* lost more than half his cargo of 375 slaves by not listening to his surgeon. It was the last slave on board who had the disease, says Henry Ellison, who made the voyage. "The doctor told Mr. Wilson it was the small-pox," Ellison continues. "He would not believe it, but said he would keep him, as he was a fine man. It soon broke out amongst the slaves. I have seen the platform one continued scab. We hauled up eight or ten slaves dead of a morning. The flesh and skin peeled off their wrists when taken hold of, being entirely mortified."

But dysentery, though not so much feared, probably caused more deaths in the aggregate. Ellison testified that he made two voyages on the *Nightingale*. On the first voyage the slaves were so crowded that thirty boys "messed and slept in the long boat all through the Middle Passage, there being no room below"; and still the vessel lost only five or six slaves in all, out of a cargo of 270. On the second voyage, however, the *Nightingale* buried "about 150, chiefly of fevers and flux. We had 250 when we left the coast."

The average mortality in the Middle Passage is impossible to state accurately from the surviving records. Some famous voyages were made without the loss of a single slave. On one group of nine voyages between 1766 and 1780, selected at random, the vessels carried 2,362 slaves and there were no epidemics of disease. The total loss of slaves was 154, or about six and one-half per cent. That figure is to be compared with the losses on a list of twenty voyages compiled by Thomas Clarkson, the abolitionist, in which the vessels carried 7,904 slaves with a mortality of 2,053, or twenty-six per cent. Balancing high and low figures together, the English Privy Council in 1789 arrived at an estimate of twelve and one-half per cent for the average mortality among slaves in the Middle Passage. To this figure it added four and one-half per cent for the deaths of slaves in harbors before they were sold, and thirty-three per cent for deaths in the so-called ''seasoning'' or acclimatizing process, making a total of fifty per cent. If these figures are correct, only one slave was added to the New World labor

In April of 1860 these despondent and emaciated
slaves reached Key West in the bark Wildfire.
From an etching published in Harper's Weekly.

force for every two purchased on the Guinea Coast.

To keep the figures in perspective, it might be said that the mortality among slaves in the Middle Passage was possibly no greater than that of white indentured servants or even of free Irish, Scottish, and German immigrants in the North Atlantic crossing. On the better-commanded Guineamen it was probably less, and for a simple economic reason. There was no profit on a slaving voyage until the Negroes were landed alive and sold; therefore the better captains took care of their cargoes. It was different on the North Atlantic crossing, where even the hold and steerage passengers paid their fares before coming aboard, and where the captain cared little whether they lived or died.

After leaving the Portuguese island of São Tomé—if he had watered there—a slaving captain bore westward along the equator for a thousand miles, and then northwestward toward the Cape Verde Islands. This was the tedious part of the Middle Passage. "On leaving the Gulf of Guinea," says the author of a *Universal Geography* published in the early nineteenth century, ". . . that part of the ocean must be traversed, so fatal to navigators, where long calms detain the ships under a sky charged with electric clouds, pouring down by torrents of rain and of fire. This *sea of thunder*, being a focus of mortal diseases, is avoided as much as possible, both in approaching the coasts of Africa and those of America." It was not until reaching the latitude of the Cape Verde Islands that the vessel fell in with the northeast trades and was able to make a swift passage to the West Indies.

Dr. Claxton's ship, the *Young Hero*, was one of those delayed for weeks before reaching the trade winds. "We were so streightened for provisions," he testified, "that if we had been ten more days at sea, we must either have eaten the slaves that died, or have made the living slaves *walk the plank*," a term, he explained, that was widely used by Guinea captains. There are no authenticated records of cannibalism in the Middle Passage, but there are many accounts of slaves killed for various reasons. English captains believed that French vessels carried poison in their medicine chests, "with which they can destroy their negroes in a calm, contagious sickness, or short provisions." They told the story of a Frenchman from Brest who had a long passage and had to poison his slaves; only twenty of them reached Haiti out of five hundred. Even the cruelest English captains regarded this practice as Latin, depraved, and uncovered by their insurance policies. In an emergency they simply jettisoned part of their cargo.

Often a slave ship came to grief in the last few days of the Middle Passage. It might be taken by a French privateer out of Martinique, or it might disappear in a tropical hurricane, or it might be wrecked on a shoal almost in sight of its harbor. On a few ships there was an epidemic of suicide at the last moment.

These, however, were exceptional disasters, recounted as horror stories in the newspapers of the time. Usually the last two or three days of the passage were a comparatively happy period. All the slaves, or all but a few, might be released from their irons. When there was a remaining stock of provisions, the slaves were given bigger meals—to fatten them for market—and as much water as they could drink. Sometimes on the last day—if the ship was commanded by an easygoing captain—there was a sort of costume party on deck, with the women slaves dancing in the sailors' castoff clothing. Then the captain was rowed ashore, to arrange for the disposition of his cargo.

This was a problem solved in various fashions. In Virginia, if the vessel was small, it might sail up and down the tidal rivers, bartering slaves for tobacco at private wharves. There were also public auctions of newly imported slaves, usually at Hampton, Yorktown, or Bermuda Hundred. In South Carolina, which was the great mainland slave market, the cargo was usually consigned to a commission merchant, who disposed of the slaves at auction, then had the vessel loaded with rice or indigo for its voyage back to England.

In the smaller West Indian islands, the captain sometimes took charge of selling his own slaves. In this case he ferried them ashore, had them drawn up in a ragged line of march, and paraded them through town with bagpipes playing, before exposing them to buyers in the public square. In the larger islands, commission merchants took charge of the cargo, and the usual method of selling the slaves at retail was a combination of the "scramble"—to be described in a moment—with the vendue or public auction "by inch of candle."

First the captain, with the commission merchant at his side, went over the cargo and picked out the slaves who were maimed or diseased. These were carried to a tavern and auctioned off, with a lighted candle before the auctioneer; bids were received until an inch of candle had burned. The price of so-called "refuse" slaves sold at auction was usually less than half of that paid for a healthy Negro. "I was informed by a mulatto woman," Dr. Falconbridge says, "that she purchased a sick slave at Grenada, upon speculation, for the small sum of one dollar, as the poor wretch was apparently dying of the flux." There were some slaves so diseased and emaciated that they could not be sold for even a dollar, and these might be left to die on the wharves.

The healthy slaves remaining after the auction were sold by "scramble," that is, at standard prices for each man, each woman, each boy, and each girl in the cargo. The prices were agreed upon with the purchasers, who then scrambled for their pick of the slaves. During his four voyages Falconbridge was present at a number of scrambles. "In the *Emilia*," he says,

> at Jamaica, the ship was darkened with sails, and covered round. The men slaves were placed on the main deck, and the women on the quarter deck. The purchasers on shore were informed a gun would be fired when they were ready to open the sale. A great number of people came on board with tallies or cards in their hands, with their own names upon them, and rushed through the barricado door with the ferocity of brutes. Some had three or four handkerchiefs tied together, to encircle as many as they thought fit for their purposes.

For the slaves, many of whom believed that they were about to be eaten, it was the terrifying climax of a terrifying voyage.

The parliamentary investigations of 1788–1791 presented a complete picture of the Middle Passage, with testimony from everyone concerned except the slaves, and it horrified the English public. Powerful interests in Parliament, especially those representing the Liverpool merchants and the West Indian planters, prevented the passage of restrictive legislation at that time. But the Middle Passage was not forgotten, and in 1807 Parliament passed a law forbidding any slaver to sail from a British port after May 1 of that year. At about the same time, Congress prohibited the importation of slaves into American territory from and after January 1, 1808. All the countries of Europe followed the British and American example, if with some delay. During the next half century, however, reformers would learn that the trade was difficult to abolish in fact as well as in law, and that illegal slaving would continue as long as slavery itself was allowed to flourish.

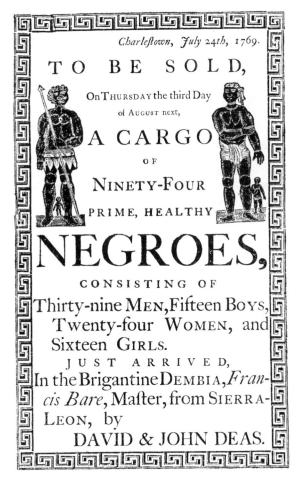

Charlestown, July 24th, 1769.

TO BE SOLD,

On THURSDAY the third Day
of AUGUST next,

A CARGO

OF

NINETY-FOUR

PRIME, HEALTHY

NEGROES,

CONSISTING OF

Thirty-nine MEN, Fifteen BOYS, Twenty-four WOMEN, and Sixteen GIRLS.

JUST ARRIVED,

In the Brigantine DEMBIA, *Francis Bare*, Master, from SIERRA-LEON, by

DAVID & JOHN DEAS.

This 1769 broadside is typical of those posted in southern ports to advertise the arrival of slave ships from Africa's west coast.

James G. Leyburn
The Scotch-Irish
in America

That we are a nation of immigrants and that each national and ethnic strain in our society has "contributed" to the shaping of American civilization are commonplace observances. We tend, however, to assume that before the arrival of the great waves of Irish and German immigrants in the 1840's the country was populated almost entirely by people of English descent. This was far from the case. There were, aside from small groups of Dutch, Portuguese, Swedish, and French settlers, the "Pennsylvania Dutch" (actually Germans) who flocked into Pennsylvania in the late seventeenth century, and far more important— because the Pennsylvania Dutch formed a relatively isolated enclave—the thousands of Scotch-Irish settlers, whose origins and influence are discussed in this essay by James G. Leyburn.

The Scotch-Irish were English in the political sense, but as Leyburn shows, they possessed a distinct culture and had a distinctive and long-lasting impact on American civilization. Leyburn, emeritus professor of sociology at Washington and Lee University, is the author of, among other books, *The Scotch-Irish: A Social History.*

Millions of Americans have Scotch-Irish ancestors, for when this country gained its independence perhaps one out of every ten persons was Scotch-Irish. Few descendants among these millions, however, know much about their ancestors—about what the hyphenated name implies, where the original Scotch-Irishmen came from and why, or what part this vigorous folk played in early American history.

Because the thirteen original American colonies were English, with government in English hands and the population predominantly from England, the tendency of our history books has been to make us see colonial history as the product of transplanted Englishmen. Every American child learns about Jamestown, Pilgrims and Puritans, Tidewater planters, landed proprietors and gentry—all English; but few schoolbooks make a child aware of the non-English "first Americans." In quite recent years our attention has been insistently called to the blacks who made up one sixth of our first census in 1790; and the very names of German, Dutch, Portuguese, Jewish, and French Huguenot elements tell us who these early Americans were. But who were the Scotch-Irish?

Next to the English they were the most numerous of all colonists, with settlements from Maine to Georgia. Some historians suggest that they were "archetypal" Americans, in the sense that their ideals and attitudes, limitations and prepossesions, virtues and vices, proved to be common national characteristics of nineteenth-century Americans. If such a claim has any validity, the people themselves deserve to be more than a vague name.

To English colonists who were their neighbors from 1717 to 1775 any idea that immigrants from northern Ireland might presage future American character would have been startling if not dismaying. Few of the settled colonists had kind words for the newcomers in those days. Pennsylvania received the largest numbers of them, and James Logan, secretary to the Penn family and an Irishman himself, lamented that "the settlement of five families of [Scotch-Irishmen] gives me more trouble than fifty of any other people." When they continued to pour into the colony, Logan, fearing that the recent Quaker element might be submerged, fumed: "It is strange that they thus crowd where they are not wanted." Cotton Mather in Massachusetts was more forthright; he fulminated against their presence as one of "the formidable attempts of Satan and his Sons to Unsettle us." On the eve of the Revolution a loyal English colonist declared the Scotch-Irish to be, with few exceptions, "the most God-provoking democrats on this side of Hell."

Such initial hostility toward a wave of foreigners was to become commonplace during the next century, when America received some thirty million immigrants from Europe. By comparison with these late-comers, however, the Scotch-Irish were fortunate, since they experienced active hostility for only a brief time. Practically all of them pushed as quickly as possible to the cheap lands of the back country, where, out of sight, they no longer offended the sensibilities of English colonists by their "oddities."

In many ways the Scotch-Irish pioneers were indeed an augury of Americans-to-be. They were probably the first settlers to identify themselves as Americans—not as Pennsylvanians or Virginians or citizens of some other colony, nor as Englishmen or Germans or any European nationality. Their daily experience of living on the outer fringe of settlement, of making small farms in the forests, of facing the danger of Indian attack and fighting back, called for qualities of self-reliance, ingenuity, and improvisation that Americans have ranked high as virtues. They were inaugurators of the heroic myth of the winning of the West that was to dominate our nineteenth-century history. Their Presbyterian Church, with its tradition of formality in worship and its insistence upon an educated ministry, was the first denomination to make tentative, if reluctant, adjustments to the realities of frontier life. Social mixing and intermarriage with their neighbors, irrespective of national background, made any such qualifier as Scotch-Irish (or northern Irish or Ulsterman) disappear within a generation.

When the Revolutionary War came, Scotch-Irishmen were the most wholehearted supporters of the American cause in each of the thirteen colonies. If before 1775 they were still regarded as aliens and immigrants, their zeal as patriots and soldiers changed all that. At home and abroad they were credited with playing a vital part in the struggle for independence. A Hessian captain wrote in 1778, "Call this war by whatever name you may, only call it not an American rebellion; it is nothing more or less than a Scotch Irish Presbyterian rebellion." King George was reported to have characterized the Revolution as "a Presbyterian war," and Horace Walpole told Parliament that "there is no use crying about it. Cousin America has run off with a Presbyterian parson, and that it is the end of it." A representative of Lord Dartmouth wrote from New York in 1776 that "Presbyterianism is really at the Bottom of this whole Conspiracy, has supplied it with Vigour, and will never rest, till something is decided upon it." Such testimony to enthusiasm for the American cause was not given to any other group of immigrants.

Upon the conclusion of the war, when the great Ohio and Mississippi valleys were opened up and the rush westward began, sons and daughters of the original Scotch-Irishmen led the way across the mountains to the new frontiers. Theodore Roosevelt is not the only historian who suggests that the institutions, attitudes, and characteristics of these trans-Allegheny pioneers constituted the practical middle ground into which the diversities of easterners and southerners might merge into something new—American culture.

The hyphenated term "Scotch-Irish" is an Americanism, generally unknown in Scotland and Ireland and rarely used by British historians. In American usage it refers to people of Scottish descent who, having lived for a time in the north of Ireland, migrated in considerable numbers to the American colonies during the half century before the Revolutionary War. Perhaps 250,000 of them actually crossed the sea to America, and they bred rapidly; their sons, like later arrivals from Ulster, constantly extended settlements westward to the Appalachians. The mountains then sent the flow of newcomers north and especially south from Pennsylvania until they constituted a dominant element in many colonies.

Only occasionally were these people then called Scotch-Irish; the usual designation was simply "Irish." "Scotch-Irish" is accurate, yet many Irish-American critics assert that it is an appellation born of snobbish pride and prejudice. . . .

Yet for all the implicit snobbishness in the double name, it directs attention to geographical, historical, and cultural facts in the background of the Scotch-Irish people. The persistence of ancestral traits of character can be exaggerated and even given a mystical quality; but there is no doubt that tradition, ancient "sets" of mind, religious convictions, limitations of outlook, and abiding prejudices gave the Scotch-Irish qualities of personality and character that affected their life in America.

The people who began to come to America in 1717 were not Scots, and certainly they were not Irish: already they were Scotch-Irish, even though this name was rarely given them. The hyphen bespeaks two centuries of historical events, many of them tragic ("dark and drublie" was the Scottish phrase), some of them heroic. The ancestors of these people had come, in the century after 1610, from the Lowlands of Scotland across the twenty-mile channel to the northern province of Ireland (Ulster) as a result of a political experiment undertaken by England. It was called the Plantation of Ulster, and it was simply one of England's many attempts to solve "the Irish problem."

For five centuries, ever since the time of Henry II (1133–89), England had tried to rule Ireland, but the Irish refused to become docile subjects. Their resistance was intensified into bitterness when England became Protestant and tried to extirpate the Roman Catholic religion in Ireland. Finally, in Queen Elizabeth's closing years, Irish earls in the north, after a desperate struggle, were defeated and exiled, and the Crown confiscated all their lands. James I, who followed Elizabeth in 1603, proposed (at the suggestion of Edmund Spenser and others of his counsellors) to settle this region with loyal English and Scottish Protestants who, in return for cheap land, would keep the Irish under control. Since the king had been James VI of Scotland before succeeding to the English crown, he was successful in persuading thousands of his Scottish subjects to cross to Ulster and start a new life there under advantageous economic circumstances.

Only a vivid modern imagination can conceive the squalor, indeed the near savagery, of the northern Irish counties around 1600. Queen

This pioneer settlement in colonial New Hampshire is reasonably typical of the rough and primitive cabins and stockades built by the earliest Scotch–Irish in America.

Elizabeth called the inhabitants "the wild Irish." She and her advisors looked upon them as Victorians did African natives and other "lesser breeds without the law." These Irishmen had no cities, no education, no refinements; they lived from hand to mouth at a primitive level (maintained, of course, by centuries of guerrilla fighting against the English). Their Catholic religion, a patriotic rallying point and a blessed solace, had acquired many elements of magic and superstition. Almost utter demoralization had ensued upon the defeat and exile of their leaders in the 1590's.

The Scots who were invited (along with English Protestants) by King James to settle Ulster and subdue its natives were thus the first Scotch-Irishmen. They came from the Lowlands, that region nearest the English border and longest in contact with English ways, language, and ideas. They were not the romantic Highland figures of Scott's novels. They were not clansmen who wore kilts and who marched, complete with dirk, sporran, brooch, and bonnet, to the skirling of bagpipes in the glens. On the contrary, they were farmers who eked out a bare living on thin soil as tenants of a laird. Three words best characterize them: they were poor, Presbyterian, and pertinacious.

Their farming methods were primitive. Crops were not rotated, and the yield was meager; starvation was always imminent in the long winters, for both man and beast. King James's offer of a new start in Ireland on larger farms whose land had lain fallow was, therefore, very appealing, all the more because lairds in the Lowlands had recently demanded higher rents and contracts that made farmers feel a loss of traditional rights and dignity.

The first Scotsmen to pioneer in Ulster succeeded well enough to allure other thousands of Lowlanders, and when, in mid-century, troubles arose with the English king and his church, the exodus increased. The new Ulstermen ran the gamut of character, as pioneers do. Their motives for migration—desire for a better living, escape from problems and debts—indicate ambition and initiative. Some of the adventurers proved to be shiftless; others had qualities needing only opportunity to bring them to full flower. Most of the "planters" took their families with them, thus proclaiming their intention to stay and establish themselves. Socially, they were generally humble folk (aristocrats rarely migrate), but with tenacious qualities indispensable for pioneers.

They were Presbyterians to a man, and Scottish Presbyterianism was unique in its intensity, even in those religious days. The Reformation in Scotland, led by John Knox, had achieved immediate and almost universal success among Lowlanders. Their Calvinist "kirk" became the Church of Scotland, a nationalist symbol for the people, who supported it all the more loyally because of the initial struggle against "popery" and the subsequent resistance against royal efforts to make it Anglican. A notable aspect of the Reformation in Scotland was the enthusiastic commitment of the people to education, not only for ministers but also for laymen. It was as if a dormant ideal had suddenly and permanently come to flower. The highest aspiration of a Lowland family was that a son might attend a university and become a minister or dominie. The passion for education carried over to northern Ireland and to America, with far-reaching results in the colonies.

It is likely that the quality of the Lowlanders that made the king most hopeful of their success in the Ulster Plantation was their well-known stubbornness and dourness ("dour" and "durable" are linguistically related). He counted on these traits to hold them in Ulster even when things went badly, and to make them keep the "wild Irish" in tow, and his confidence proved justified. Had not an elder of the kirk besought the Lord that he might always be right, "for Thou knowest, Lord, that I am unco' hard to turn"?

In the century between 1610 and 1717 perhaps as many as one hundred thousand Lowlanders came across from Scotland, and by the latter date there were some five Scots to every three Irishmen and one Englishman in Ulster. The English planters represented the Establishment: high civil officials, Anglican churchmen, businessmen, and the Army; but the preponderant Scots set the tone of the new culture of northern Ireland. It is a culture that, as the recent troubles there have painfully shown, is still self-consciously different from that of the rest of the island.

The Ulster experience was a fitting preparation for pioneering in America. The farmers had constantly to be on guard against native

Irish uprisings. Agricultural methods decidedly improved under English example. Feudalism, which still existed in Scotland, simply disappeared in Ulster, for farmers were no longer subject to an overlord or attached to one locality. The Presbyterian Church, with its members "straitly" watched over and disciplined by the session of each parish kirk, stiffened the moral fiber of the people, and with its own presbyteries, not subject to the Scottish Kirk, gave the members experience in self-government.

In one respect, however, the Scotch-Irish seemed to be deficient. The Renaissance did not reach Scotland until the eighteenth century, many years after the Lowlanders had left. From the moment of their arrival in northern Ireland comment was made by Englishmen on the apparently complete lack of aesthetic sensibility on the part of these Scots. As one observer remarked, if a Scotsman in Ulster "builds a cottage, it is a prison in miniature; if he has a lawn, it is only grass; the fence of his grounds is a stone wall, seldom a hedge. He has a sluggish imagination: it may be awakened by the gloomy or terrific, but seldom revels in the beautiful." The same limitations apparently characterized the Scotch-Irish in America.

In the very decades when at last the Ulster Plantation seemed to be achieving its purpose, with the Irish subdued, Protestantism dominant, English rule secured, and prosperity imminent, the great migration to America got under way. As usually happens when thousands of people undertake so hazardous an enterprise as crossing an ocean to find a new home, there was both a push from the old country and a pull from the new.

Paradoxically, Ulster's growing prosperity was one cause of the first wave of migration. A lucrative woolen and linen industry, developing since the 1690's, alarmed the English Parliament and led to the passage of a series of crippling protective acts whose results were resentment on the part of Ulstermen, economic depression, and recurrent unemployment. A second cause touched men personally and turned many thoughts to migration: this was the hated practice of rack-renting. The term referred to a landlord's raising rent when a long lease on his land expired—and in the decade after 1710 hundreds of leases came up for renewal. To us, such a practice seems normal; but Ulster farmers felt it to be a violation of tradition, a moral injury, because a tenant was treated impersonally. If the farmer could not or would not pay the higher rent, he had only two practical alternatives: a return to the poverty of Scotland, or migration to the New World.

Still other causes stimulated emigration. Six years in succession after 1714 brought dire drought, with depression in the flax industry and soaring costs of food. In 1716 sheep were afflicted with a destructive disease; severe frosts throughout the decade discouraged farmers; a smallpox epidemic scourged Ulster. In addition there was a goad from the Anglican religious establishment. Deserting the tolerant policy of William III, the High-Church party, ascendant during the reign of Queen Anne (1702–14), secured the passage of a Test Act, requiring all officeholders in Ireland to take the sacrament according to prescriptions of the Church of England. Although aimed at Irish Catholics, the weight of this requirement fell heavily upon substantial Presbyterians who held magistracies and other civil posts. By extension, Presbyterian ministers could no longer perform legal marriages or even bury the dead, nor could "dissenters" teach school. This unwise law, though not everywhere rigidly enforced, caused resentment among the stubborn Scots, intensified by the fact that they had been loyal to the Crown and had proved a bulwark of defense against the rampageous Irish.

For all these reasons some five thousand Ulster Scots went to America in 1717 and 1718. After that initial migration, the pull of America began to exert more effect than the push from northern Ireland. Reports coming from the colonies were highly favorable, especially from Pennsylvania. Land was cheap and plentiful, authorities were well disposed, the soil was fertile beyond all imagination, and opportunities were boundless. Only two drawbacks loomed: the perils of an ocean crossing, and the expense of the passage. The former was very real in those days; but optimism persuaded young people that the nightmare of several weeks on a tiny, overcrowded ship, with much illness, was rarely fatal and that grim memories would soon fade. As for passage money, the practice of indenture had long been

The port of Londonderry in northern Ireland in the 1700's was one of the major embarkation points for the Scotch–Irish emigrating to the New World.

a familiar device. Few who had made up their minds to go would be deterred by having to work for a master in America for a period of years to pay off their passage fee, for then came freedom and a new life in a country which, according to some, resembled paradise.

Five great waves brought a quarter million Ulster Scots to America, turned them into Scotch-Irish Americans, depressed the economy of Ulster, and depopulated parts of that province. The tides ebbed and flowed partly with conditions in Ulster, partly with upsurges of what was called migration fever. The chief waves were those of 1717–18, 1725–29, 1740–41, 1754–55, and 1771–75; and each benefited particular colonies. The first two helped fill up the back country of Pennsylvania and soon began spilling over into the Shenandoah Valley of Virginia. The third further peopled the Shenandoah Valley and spread into the piedmont and upcountry of North Carolina. That colony and South Carolina drew most of the people in the fourth wave, while the final group, coming just before the Revolutionary War, spread out widely from New York to Georgia.

In each wave, other colonies drew settlers. Because the Delaware River early proved the favorite entryway, the colonies of New Jersey, Delaware, and Maryland soon had many Ulstermen. Massachusetts reluctantly admitted a few but so disliked their uncongenial ways that later arrivals in Boston went on to New Hampshire or Maine.

Two facts about the migration are significant for American history. First, there was almost no further influx from northern Ireland after the Revolutionary War; thus, there was no addition to the Scotch-Irish element from abroad nor any inducement to maintain sentimental ties or a "national" identity with a country ruled by England. Second, the concentration of Scotch-Irishmen in the geographically central colonies of Pennsylvania and Virginia made a kind of reservoir from which the people spread north and south through all other colonies; moreover, their farms just east of the Alleghenies were nearest the Great West when that vast territory opened up after 1783. Scotch-Irishmen were thus the vanguard of the trans-Allegheny pioneers. . . .

Scotch-Irishmen struck a real blow for religious liberty in this country. In 1738 the royal governor of Virginia and the Tidewater planters actively sought to persuade newcomers to the Pennsylvania frontier to leave that crowded region and settle in the Shenandoah Valley. An ancestor of John C. Calhoun presented to Governor William Gooch a memorial drawn up by the Presbyterian Synod of Philadelphia requiring religious toleration as a prerequisite for settlement. Gooch acceded to the demand, to the benefit of Virginia and of later American freedom. . . .

In education and religion it may be asserted that many American ideals and standards derive from the happy agreement of two self-assured colonial groups, the Scotch-Irish and the New England Yankees. Alone, neither people might have been weighty enough or (in the case of the Yankees) unprovincial enough to have prevailed; but their common Calvinism and earnestness gave America its first commitment to general education as well as its tendency to identify religion with upright moral character.

For both people, schools followed churches as the first institutions to be formed. The word of God must be expounded by educated ministers, and colonists could not send their sons abroad for training. The connection between church and school, going back to the Reformation, was to remain close for descendants of both Presbyterians and Puritans until the present century. Ministers were schoolmasters as well as preachers. Curricula in Scotch-Irish log schools on the frontier resembled those of the town schools in earlier New England, with training in the three R's, the Bible, and the catechisms, while higher education was directed toward training for the ministry. The Puritans founded Harvard and Yale well before the Presbyterians established Princeton and Hampden-Sydney and Dickinson; but from these first colleges came a host of others, whose students were not wholly ministerial. Until the Civil War the great majority of colleges in the country were founded by religious denominations and still remained under their control. (The state's responsibility for higher education had not yet been widely claimed.) Of the 207 permanent colleges founded before 1861, well over half were established by Presbyterians and New Englanders; and many of them were notable as "mothers" of still other colleges.

The distinctive religious influence of the Scotch-Irish and New Englanders was not in their common Calvinism, though certainly Calvinist theology has had its effect upon America: it was rather in persuading millions of Americans that religion and character are synonyms. In most other parts of the world religion is likely to mean ritual observance, adherence to a creed, customary pious acts, or some combination of these; but when an American says that a person is deeply religious he is likely to mean first of all that he is upright and highly moral. Both Puritans and Scotch-Irish insisted upon rectitude of life and behavior, stubborn adherence to principle, scorn of compromise, and a stern severity that could be as hard upon others as upon self. Neither people could accept the idea that a man's religious duty consisted only of acts performed on Sunday or of doctrinal orthodoxy. Since America quickly became pluralistic in religion, there could never have been agreement upon ritual, creed, or observances to unify us religiously; but all Americans could agree on admirable character and high moral rectitude. What the Puritans and Scotch-Irish made of religion was immensely reinforced when the Baptist and Methodist movements, rising to ascendancy in the nineteenth century, taught the same ideas.

In certain ways the Presbyterian Church of the Scotch-Irish was the first important denomination to become "Americanized" and broadly "American." In log churches on a frontier, with a congregation of pioneer farmers, many formal traditions of the dignified Presbyterian Church quietly vanished—the Geneva gown and stock, the separate pulpit, the attendance of the minister by a beadle, the set prayers. Many of the colonial Presbyterian ministers experimented with unconventional, direct methods of evangelism, in order to speak clearly to a people losing interest in dignity for the sake of tradition. (The approval of the presbyteries for this informality was not won, however; and because the dynamic Methodists and Baptists felt free to adopt resourceful methods of evangelism, they drew thousands of adherents among descendants of the Scotch-Irish.)

The Church of England was the established religion in six colonies and the Congregational faith in three others; both, then, were identified with the upper-class English Establishment; but the Presbyterian Church was nowhere official, elite, or English. Moreover, these other two dominant churches were regional, strong only in the Tidewater and in New England; but the Presbyterian Church, like the Scotch-Irish people, was present in every colony. Its ministers were supported not by legally exacted tithes but by free contributions of members; these ministers in their work moved freely from one region to another. The organization of the church was controlled by presbyteries that ranged from New York to the South. The "federal" structure of the church of the Scotch-Irish seemed congenial to American conditions and exerted a unifying influence in our early history.

If we of the twentieth century wish to admire the Scotch-Irish as representative prototypes of later Americans, we must ruefully note that their Ulster forefathers' neglect of things aesthetic was carried over to the new country. European visitors and critics in the nineteenth century, indeed, considered all Americans deficient in such matters; but we now know how wrong they were, for our museums are full of beautiful early American art and artifacts from New England, from the Tidewater, from German farmlands, and from many other regions and districts—but not from Scotch-Irish settlements. Nothing in the background of these people in either Scotland or northern Ireland had attracted them to painting, sculpture, architecture, music, and literature, and nothing in their way of life in the colonies apparently changed their attitude. They liked what was practical and seemed indifferent to whether it was beautiful. The lists of distinguished scions of the Scotch-Irish in nineteenth-century America include no names of artists and poets.

By 1800 the young United States was growing strong and self-confident, with a continent to win. Already the authority of the thirteen original states was losing its hold over the rising generation. If a farsighted historian of the time had been inclined to identify representative types of inhabitants who would probably become the most characteristic Americans of the new century, he might well have named the restless frontiersman and the rising middle-class townsman. The former was rapidly winning the West, clearing the wilderness, exploiting America's fabulous wealth, adding romance to the American myth; the latter was establishing law and order, building industry, adding comfort to utility, and treasuring respectability and responsibility. If the same historian had sought to find the embodiment of each of his representative types, he could have pointed immediately to the descendants of the vigorous Scotch-Irish, now thoroughly American, with no further accretions from abroad. Most of them had even forgotten the adjective formerly applied to them. The daily life of being an American was too absorbing to permit adulation of one's ancestors, even though these had been the admirable Scotch-Irish.

In Daniel Berger's 1784 engraving, defiant Bostonians burn newspapers and documents carrying the stamp demanded by the act of 1765.

Part Three

The Birth of a Nation

J.H. Plumb
George III, Our Last King

One of the most difficult tasks of the historian is to deal fairly with failure, with incompetence—even with evil. He must try to honor Othello's plea and speak of men (and institutions) as they actually were—"nothing extenuate, nor set down aught in malice." In this essay one of England's premier historians, Professor J. H. Plumb of Cambridge University, succeeds brilliantly in achieving this objective.

Professor Plumb's analysis of America's last king, the unfortunate and much-maligned George III, lays bare the monarch's inadequacies but describes him with sympathy and understanding. As a result, we learn a great deal not only about George III but also about eighteenth-century British politics, and thus about the causes of the American Revolution. George III is easy to caricature or to portray as the Devil incarnate, and as Plumb points out, historians have done both these things repeatedly. Their accounts have often been entertaining, but they have explained very little about the man and his times. By treating him as he has, however, Plumb makes George III and the tragic events of the early years of his long reign plausible, and thus meaningful.

Professor Plumb has written, among many books, *The First Four Georges, England in the Eighteenth Century: 1714–1815,* and two volumes of a definitive biography of Sir Robert Walpole.

*P*oor George III still gets a bad press. In a famous television talk in London, the Prime Minister of Great Britain suggested to the President of the United States that the kind of colonial policy associated with the name of George III still distorted the American view of the nature and function of the British Empire, and Mr. Eisenhower smilingly agreed. It is not surprising. Since Jefferson's great philippic in the Declaration of Independence, few historians, English or American, have had many good words to say for him. True, he has been excused direct responsibility for many items of the catalogue of enormities that Jefferson went on to lay at his door, but to the ordinary man he remains one of England's disastrous kings, like John or the two Jameses.

Actually, . . . toward the end of his life and immediately after it his reputation improved, and even the writers of American school textbooks did not at first hold him personally responsible for the disasters that led to independence. They held his ministers responsible. It was after the publication of Horace Walpole's *Memoirs* in 1845 that George III began to be blamed. Walpole's gossip appeared to give substance to Burke's allegations that the King deliberately attempted to subvert the British constitution by packing ministries and Parliament with his personal party—the King's friends—a collection of corrupt politicians bought with place and with pension.

Later historians held that these Tory incompetents, bent on personal government for their master, pursued a ruinous policy that ended only with the breakup of the first British Empire and a return of the Whigs to power. Historians reminded themselves not only of the disasters in America, but the failure of parliamentary reform in England, of the oppressions of the Irish, the Catholics, the Dissenters; they remembered the treatment of radicals at the time of the French Revolution; they recalled the merciless suppression of trade unions; the violent opposition to the abolition of slavery. It all added up to a huge indictment of George III and a magnificent justification for Whig doctrine. Here and there a scholar urged caution, but was little heeded. What the great historians formulated, the textbook writers cribbed. When English historians found so much to condemn, why should Americans lag behind? In 1954, two American historians—Leon Canfield and Howard Wilder—could write:

In 1760, George III mounted the throne. A young man of twenty-two, he was unwilling to accept the idea that the King's power should be limited. His mother had always said to him: "George, be King!" When he became ruler this obstinate young man put his mother's advice into swift action. He set out to get his way not by ignoring Parliament but by building up a personal following. He made free use of bribes and appointments, and presently the King's friends were strong in Parliament.

The increase in royal power drove the wedge of misunderstanding deeper between England and the colonies.

The young George III was portrayed in his coronation robes by court painter Allan Ramsay.

In 1959, an English historian, Jack Lindsay, was still writing in much the same vein. These views, however, are no longer fashionable. The greatest living English historian of the eighteenth century, Sir Lewis Namier, has hammered at them for thirty years. His friend, Romney Sedgwick, with a more caustic pen and no less scholarship, has subjected them to ridicule in review after review, sinking his verbal darts into reputations as skillfully as a savage at his blowpipe. Professor Herbert Butterfield has not only traced the origins of the myths of George III's tyranny but has also shown how the now-fashionable view of George III was held by historians and textbook writers long, long ago in the early nineteenth century. So the wheel has come full circle. Will it turn again? Or will blame and justification give way simply to understanding? Shall we at last have a balanced portrait of America's last king?

On one thing historians are agreed. To understand the part played by George III in the great tragedy of his reign, one must begin with the King's own personality and with the environment in which he was reared. David and Absalom provided the pattern of family relationship of European monarchs and their sons and heirs in the eighteenth century, except that most of the monarchs were less controlled than David. Peter the Great of Russia had his son Alexis executed—slowly and painfully. The Elector of Prussia, Frederick William, insisted that his son, whom he had kept in close confinement, watch the death of his dearest friend for what only a madman could call treason. So it is not surprising to learn that George III's grandmother wished that her son, Frederick, father of George III, were in the bottommost pit of hell or that she became almost hysterical on her deathbed when she thought he might inherit some of her personal possessions. The

James Gillray did this caricature of the penny-wise and pound-foolish monarch in 1791.

Lord Chancellor had to be sent for to lull her fears.

George II's opinion of his own lackluster son matched his wife's. He quite simply hated him as he had hated his own father, who, at one time, had put him under house arrest and removed his children. (It had required all the persuasive powers of the Cabinet to get him released.) This fantastic antagonism between father and son that went on from generation to generation found a situation in English politics that fitted it like a glove. The House of Commons always harbored a number of disappointed politicians who were so hated by the ministers in power that they had few prospects of immediate advancement. But as Sir Robert Walpole bluntly phrased it: "Everybody who could get no ready money had rather have a bad promissory note than nothing." So they made their court to the heir, who found them jobs in his household, and plotted the political changes that they would make when Father died. So throughout the century a Prince of Wales as soon as he was grown up became the leader of the Opposition. At times the Opposition made such a nuisance of itself that the monarch and his ministry decided to buy it off by giving jobs to the leaders, and the astonished heir apparent found his friends deserting him with alacrity. This happened both to George III and to his father. The politics of hatred and the politics of betrayal, therefore, became a part of the environment of the adolescence and early manhood of the Hanoverian kings.

It was in an atmosphere of faction that George III was born; an environment that might have taxed the most gifted of men. Unfortunately George III was as unlucky in his heredity as in his environment. Neither George II nor his Queen, Caroline, was devoid of character or without some gifts above the commonplace. Her intelligence and his memory were unusual in monarchs, and their hatred of their son was tinged with genuine disappointment. Frederick, George III's father, was known to posterity as "Poor Fred," and the epithet was not unjust. He possessed a small talent for music, a mild interest in games, particularly cricket, and little else. The unsympathetic Lord Shelburne described his life as a "tissue of childishness and falsehood"; and his friends as well as his enemies despised him. George II married his son to Princess Augusta of Saxe-Gotha simply because there was no one else. The other Protestant princesses of sufficiently high birth had madness in their families, and George II rejected them, for as he said, "I did not think ingrafting my half-witted coxcomb upon a madwoman would mend the breed." As it turned out, it could not have made matters much worse, for an astonishing number of Princess Augusta's children and grandchildren turned out to be congenital idiots, or subject to fits of insanity, or mentally unbalanced, or blind; the rest were odd or wicked or both.

In some ways George III can be described as the best of the bunch. He was very stupid, really stupid. Had he been born in different circumstances it is unlikely that he could have earned a living except as an unskilled manual laborer. He was eleven before he could read, and he never mastered grammar or spelling or punctuation. He was lethargic, apathetic, childish, a clod of a boy whom no one could teach. His major response to life was a doting love for his brother, Edward. In late adolescence he began to wake up, largely because of a passionately romantic attachment to Lord Bute, the close friend and confidant of his mother.* Somehow Bute made the young prince conscious not only of his destiny but also of his shortcomings. The Prince promised time and time again to throw off his lethargy so that he could accomplish great things for Bute's sake. Naturally the greatest of things was to get rid of his grandfather's evil ministers and to install Bute in a position of power. The ill-spelt, ungrammatical, childish, heartfelt notes that he sent to Bute make pathetic reading. They are charged with a sense of inadequacy, a feeling of hopelessness before the immensity of the burden which destiny had laid on his shoulders, and with an anxious need for help that is almost neurotic in its intensity.

Every year his reverence for the concept of kingship grew stronger; nothing illustrates his regard more than his behavior over Lady Sarah Lennox. This charming girl of fifteen swept him off his feet just before he succeeded to the throne. He longed to marry her. Bute said no, and George III wrote that "he [i.e., Bute] has thoroughly convinced me of the impropriety of marrying a country woman; the interest of my country ever shall be my first care, my own inclinations shall ever submit to it." And submit he did and married a dull, plain, German Protestant princess who bore him the huge family that was to plague his days.

---

* The public thought she was his mistress. Almost certainly she was not. The slander deeply distressed George III and made his attachment to Bute firmer.

A sexually timid, if nonetheless passionate man, George may have found it easier to take Bute's advice than many have thought. Lady Sarah attracted lovers as a candle moths, and George, conscious of his faults and of his inadequacies, must have realized that he cut a poor figure amidst *her* brilliant courtiers. His Queen, Charlotte, attracted no one. And yet sacrifice there was, and George paid for it. Shortly after his marriage he experienced his first bout of insanity. Later in life these periods of madness grew longer. It was only during these attacks that his thoughts escaped from his strict concept of marriage, and rioted in adultery. Then, and then only, was it unsafe for a lady of his court to be alone with him.

During these years of delayed adolescence George III learned, too, that kings had to make other sacrifices. Men powerfully backed in the Lords and Commons, and with an experience of a lifetime's politics behind them, could not easily be dismissed. The great Whig families had ruled since the Hanoverian accession in 1714. They had filled the court of the Georges, monopolized the great offices of state, controlled the Cabinet, dominated the House of Lords, managed the Commons, and run the war with France which had lasted more or less for twenty years. The Duke of Newcastle, George II's Secretary of State, had held an important position in government since he had reached his majority. The Dukes of Devonshire took their high offices as if they belonged to them by hereditary right. Even the Whig career politicians, such as the Lord Chancellor Hardwicke, had been in power for so long that they had come to regard themselves as practically irreplaceable.

These men were not to be easily swept away and replaced by Bute; they possessed too much cunning, too much political experience, too many followers whom they had gratified with places. They doubted Bute's capacity to survive. And still time was on George III's side. The great Whig leaders were old men; indeed their party was known as the Old Corps. And in their long lives they had made plenty of enemies. They had disappointed some members of Parliament, made others impatient, and many disapproved of their policy. Chatham, that hawk-eyed man of destiny who had been responsible more than any other man for the sweeping English victories in the Seven Years' War, deplored their caution, ignored their advice, and treated them, as one of his colleagues grumbled, "as inferior animals." And behind Chatham was the restless brood of Grenvilles, his relations by marriage—difficult, disloyal, able and ambitious men. There was yet another powerful group, led by the immensely rich Duke of Bedford, who thought it high time for the old Whigs to retire, and let them enjoy the rich pastures of court patronage.

The King's intentions, of course, were known to all these groups in 1760. His aversion to Newcastle and to Chatham, whom he labeled "the blackest of hearts," was common court gossip. And after all, he was a young king with old ministers; many time-serving politicians thought that it might be wise to trim their sails and wait for the new breeze, from whatever quarter it might blow. Of course the old

Whigs, and even Chatham, realized they had to accept Bute and somehow or other please the King, if they were to survive. They soon had the measure of Bute. He lacked a personal following, felt unequal to the supreme task of ruling the country and running the war. His dependable allies in the House of Commons were few. He faltered; he hesitated; he failed to force a showdown and kick out the old Whigs. True, Chatham resigned in a huff because, knowing the King's pacific sentiments, the Cabinet refused to go along with him and declare war on Spain and seize her trade. Instead, as Chatham forecast, Spain declared war on England.

But Chatham gone did little to strengthen Bute. By the end of January, 1763, the consummate skill of those hoary old politicians Newcastle and Hardwicke had so undermined Bute's confidence that he was little better than a nervous wreck. He told George III that even the Angel Gabriel would find it difficult to govern England; that his own life was rendered intolerable by infamous scenes and blackened by ingratitude and that he felt himself on the brink of a precipice. George III was too young, too inept, too unpracticed in the arts of politics to help Bute, and so Bute resigned. George III tried to keep him as a private and secret adviser; the politicians would not let him. They grumbled, they nagged, they bullied. The King had to face his future on his own.

He was most reluctant to do so. Although peace had been achieved in 1763—he had ardently desired this—he soon found himself in the thick of problems which he felt too vast for his poor comprehension. Yet he knew that the fate of his people and his Empire was *his* responsibility to God. He felt so young, so hopeless, so desperately in need of help for someone who thought as he did on men and affairs yet was strong enough to force his will on the warring political factions. Although the old Whig empire had broken up under the strain of Chatham's resignation and the Treaty of Paris, yet the King found no stability. The King's necessity drove him back to Chatham. Chatham prided himself on being above party. The King's need, the nation's need, required men of ability, not politicians; sentiments that thrilled George III. But unfortunately Chatham's mental health was far from good, and no sooner had he become Prime Minister than the strain of office sent him off his head. He shut himself up, would speak to no one, and had his meals served through a trap door. The King waited and waited for him to recover for two long years, during which a leaderless ministry drove his country nearer to ruin. Chatham recovered only to resign and became a passionate supporter of the American cause and so, once more, the object of George III's hate. The ministries that followed earned neither the country's confidence nor the King's.

Thus the first ten years of George III's reign passed in political chaos; slowly, however, he learned the devious ways of politics, the price of men, and above all the necessity for a man who could manage the Commons in *his* interest. In 1770 he discovered Lord North, the eldest son of the Earl of Guilford; North, whose association with the

King was to prove so disastrous for England and so fortunate for America, was an odd character. An excellent administrator, a witty and practiced debater, full of good humor and charm, he always pleased and soothed the members of the Commons; nevertheless his soft, fat, rounded body and full, piglike face bespoke an indolence that bordered on disease, a physical incapacity that made his laborious days an intolerable burden on his spirit. Time and time again he begged the King to release him from office. The King would not, for North reverenced as he did the mystical power of monarchy and thought as he did on the two grave political problems which vexed his country—Wilkes and America.

Without North, he could see only ruin for himself and his people. The constantly changing ministries and the bitter factional strife of George III's first ten years had bedeviled both problems. John Wilkes, wit, libertine, master tactician, raised fundamental issues concerning the liberty of the British subject. None of the cases in which he was involved was clear-cut; in each the ministerial cause was handled with massive ineptitude. Wilkes divided the Whig groups in Parliament as effectively as he united the discontented in London. George hated "that devil Wilkes," and let this hatred be known to all and sundry. Thus Wilkes's supporters could talk of royal despotism and get others to believe them. In America Wilkes's name became a byword for liberty and for resistance to royal tyranny from Boston down the seaboard to Charleston.

America proved a graver problem than Wilkes; and the effect of ministerial changes far worse. After the great war with France which, through the Treaty of Paris, deprived her of Canada, the majority of Englishmen, and, indeed, many colonists, felt that some of the expenses of the conflict should be borne by the Americans. Each ministry from 1760–70 differed in its views as to how this should be done, and each had a separate solution for assuaging the bitterness aroused in the Americans by the inept attempts to get revenue. Acts passed by

George III's closest adviser, Frederick Lord North, from a mezzotint published in 1775.

one ministry were repealed by its successor, and party maneuver became more important than the fate of America. Nor was it the question of revenue alone that infuriated the colonists—the British constantly betrayed their ignorance of American needs and American aspirations. They tried to restrict settlement beyond the Allegheny Mountains, took Indian affairs into their own hands, attempted to suppress paper currency, renovated oppressive customs laws, and restricted trade with the West Indies. No Englishman realized that the American colonies were moving toward a rapid expansion in trade, wealth, and power, just as no American could conceive of the huge expense of war that arose from Britain's vast imperial connections.

By the late 1760's, hope for compromise was probably a delusive dream of men of good will such as Chatham and Franklin. But whether it had a chance or not, there can be no doubt that the known attitude of the King made matters worse. George III revered, naturally enough, the concept of kingship. Kings were God's immediate servants. Their duties were clear—to pass on all the rights, obligations, powers, territories, undiminished, to their heirs. The constitution was sacrosanct and unchangeable. And so absolutely did George III identify himself with the English Crown that any criticism of monarchical powers, any suggestion of reform or change, he regarded as a personal affront.

The King was so stupid that he could not distinguish between himself as a person and his constitutional position as ruler. Although he accepted the American policies—either of compromise or coercion—with which his ministers presented him, placing his signature first on the Stamp Act and then on its repeal, his heart was always with the physical-force party, and he moved with uttermost reluctance to the idea of compromise, which, he thought, would infuriate as well as ruin Britain.* Those politicians, therefore, who were prepared to bring the "American rebels," as the King called them, to their senses were the recipients of his warmhearted loyalty and devotion. In the small world of English political society, the King's views did not go for nothing. He was the fountain of patronage, the ultimate executive authority, the man who could make and break ministers and ministries. In consequence, the King's attitude began to polarize new attitudes in politics. He became the symbol of conservatism and reaction; his opponents, the men who thought that the liberties for which Wilkes and the Americans fought were essential, too, for all Englishmen, began to take a more radical attitude not only to the

---

* As may be seen from his letter to North of January 31, 1776: "You will remember that before the recess, I strongly advised you not to bind yourself to bring forward a proposition for restoring tranquillity to North America, not from any absurd ideas of unconditional submission my mind never harboured; but from foreseeing that whatever can be proposed, will be liable, not to bring America back to a sense of attachment to the Mother Country, yet to dissatisfy this Country, which has in the most handsome manner cheerfully carried on the contest, and therefore has a right to have the struggle continued, until convinced that it is in vain."

Crown but also to the very structure of English society. Naturally, the first effect of this was to disrupt the old political alignments; Whiggery began to break up into two groups, a right and a left wing; the Tories, who had been in opposition since 1714, now felt that they could support George III body and soul. It took many years for these new forces to push their way through into public consciousness, redefined, but George III's own personality—his meddling interference and his blind, obstinate conservatism—sharpened many men's intention to reduce the powers of the Crown even further.

The first twenty years of George III's reign were a public and a personal failure. He had done his duty conscientiously. He had tried, according to his lights, to put the government in the hands of tried and able men. The ills which assailed his country, he sincerely believed, were not of his making. Scarcely a man pitied him; the majority thought he had only himself to blame when disaster came. Yorktown ended his hopes that the tide might turn, and finished North.

During the long years of British defeat, the Old Corps of Whigs, now led by the Marquis of Rockingham, had developed a new view of the role of kingship; and their great publicist and philosopher, Edmund Burke, had persuasively pleaded for a new attitude to party and to politics. When, at last, the failures in America led the independent members of the Commons to desert North, and thereby compelled the King to send for Rockingham to take over the reins of government, George found Rockingham's terms hard to accept: freedom for America, peace with France, and hardest of all, no say in the appointment of his ministers, which he regarded as the darling prerogative of the Crown.

The King, despite himself, now had to accept what the Whigs offered him—a revolutionary action that cut at the root of royal power. He had been broken by forces that his poor brain could not understand. And, perhaps not without justice, he was held to blame for England's defeat in America by contemporaries in both countries, and by generations of historians, though justice would also demand that the shortsighted, quarrelsome, ignorant, power-seeking politicians who had made policy toward America as changeable as the British climate should be held equally responsible. We, at least, can feel pity for him —ignorant, stupid, conscientious, prejudiced, a victim of his own inadequate temperament. . . .

His motives were honorable; he gave all of his pitifully small abilities to the defense of what he thought to be the vital interests and essential rights of the British nation. Had he been as wise as Solomon, Britain and America would have gone their separate ways. The forces that crushed him would have crushed greater men. As it is, he remained a pathetic figure of tragicomedy; and, as the years passed, he acquired even a certain grandeur. There had been many worse kings to exercise rule over America and Britain. If he is to be blamed, it must be not for what he did but for what he was—an unbalanced man of low intelligence. And if he is to be praised, it is because he attempted to discharge honorably tasks that were beyond his powers.

Richard B. Morris

James Otis and the Writs of Assistance

Professor Richard B. Morris of Columbia University, author of this essay on the paradoxical figure James Otis and his fight against the British policy of issuing general search warrants in the years before the Revolution, is particularly well qualified to deal with this difficult and technical subject. He has devoted his scholarly life to the era of the Revolution and to American legal history. His many works include *The Peacemakers,* a dramatic account of the negotiations that produced the Treaty of Paris ending the Revolution, and *Government and Labor in Early America,* a study of the laws regulating labor and working conditions during the colonial era.

Besides describing a difficult subject and a complex man clearly, Morris' essay also demonstrates how effective history can be in throwing light on later events and current problems. He shows—always keeping the nuances of the question in mind—how the conflict between the rights of the individual and the rights of government (which represents the collective rights of all citizens) always exists in a state of dynamic tension. With fine balance he explains not only why Americans objected to the writs of assistance but also why, from the British viewpoint, such writs seemed perfectly reasonable. In addition, he delineates the relationship between this controversy and present-day arguments over the legitimacy of wire tapping and other "bugging" devices.

Few freedoms are more fundamental to our way of life—and few so clearly differentiate our democracy from the rival system which seeks to bury it—than the freedom from the midnight knock on the door, from the arbitrary invasion of a man's home by soldiery or police. Enshrined in the Fourth Amendment to the Constitution, the right is nevertheless still a matter of contention: almost every year that passes sees cases based upon it coming before the United States Supreme Court. Given the almost inevitable conflict between the legitimate demands of civil authority and the equally legitimate demands of individual freedom, it is likely that the controversy will be always with us.

What one famous Supreme Court justice called "the right most valued by civilized man," the right to be let alone, is a venerable one in America: long before the Revolution, violation of it by representatives of the king rankled deeply in the hearts of his American subjects; it was, indeed, one of the major reasons they eventually decided they could no longer serve him.

The issue was first expounded in the course of an extraordinary forensic argument made in the year 1761 before five scarlet-robed judges in the council chamber of the Town-house in Boston. The speaker was James Otis, Jr., then thirty-six years old, born in nearby West Barnstable and considered the ablest young lawyer at the Boston bar.

His plea for the right of privacy was at once significant and poignant. It was significant because without the burning moral issue thus precipitated, it might have been possible for the cynical to dismiss the forthcoming Revolution as a mere squabble between colonies and mother country over taxation. The poignancy of Otis' plea derives from the brilliant young lawyer's subsequent curious conduct: while many of his friends became leaders in the fight for independence, he followed a mysterious zigzag course that unfortunately, in the eyes of some of his contemporaries, cast doubt upon his loyalty to the cause of freedom.

The specific occasion of Otis' appearance was an application to the Superior Court of Massachusetts Bay by Charles Paxton, Surveyor of Customs for the Port of Boston, for writs of assistance. These were general warrants which, as they were commonly interpreted, empowered customs officers under police protection arbitrarily to enter—if necessary, to break into—warehouses, stores, or homes to search for smuggled goods. The intruders were not even required to present any grounds for suspecting the presence of the illicit items. Such writs had been authorized in England—where they were issued by the Court of Exchequer—since the time of Charles II, but nothing like them had been used in the colonies prior to the French and Indian War. The only writs theretofore procurable had been specific search warrants issued by the regular common-law courts; but these had authorized search only in places specified in the warrants and only upon specific information, supported by oath, that smuggled goods were hidden there. True, an act of King William III regulating colonial trade had given the customs officers in America the same rights of search as their opposite numbers in England enjoyed. But it was a new question whether the royal order extended to colonial courts the same authority to issue the writs that the Court of Exchequer exercised in the mother country.

During the final phase of the Second Hundred Years' War between Britain and France, however, writs of assistance had been issued in Massachusetts to facilitate the feverish if futile efforts of customs officers to stamp out illegal trade between the colonists and the enemy—in Canada and the French West Indies. These writs had been issued in the name of King George II, but that monarch died in October, 1760, and his grandson succeeded to the throne as George III. According to law, the old writs expired six months after the death of a sovereign, and new ones had to be issued in the name of his successor. Now, in February of 1761, while the issue hung in the balance—George III would not be crowned until September—Surveyor Paxton's case came to trial.

Sixty-three prominent Boston merchants joined to oppose him, retaining the brilliant, impassioned, unstable Otis—and his amiable and temperate associate, Oxenbridge Thacher—to represent them. In order to take their case, Otis resigned his office as Advocate General of the Vice-Admiralty Court, in which capacity he would have been expected to represent the Crown and present the other side of the argument. That task was now assigned to Jeremiah Gridley, a leader of the Boston bar, who appeared as counsel for the customs officers.

Behind Otis' resignation lay deep personal animosities that added drama to the legal battle. Not long before, the chief justiceship of the Superior Court—which would hear the arguments on the writs of assistance and render a decision—had fallen vacant. William Shirley, then governor of the colony, had promised the post to Otis' father, but Shirley's successor, Francis Bernard, had ignored the commitment and instead named his lieutenant governor, Thomas Hutchinson. Already the target of colonists who resented his nepotistic use of the lieutenant governorship, Hutchinson now earned additional criticism for holding two offices at the same time. And his appointment of course precipitated a feud with the influential Otises; young James, according to rumor, declared "he would set the province in flames, if he perished by the fire."

Nevertheless Hutchinson, attired in his new judicial robes, took his seat in the great Town-house council chamber as the trial opened on February 24. With him on the bench were Justices Lynde, Cushing, Oliver, and Russell. Gridley opened for the Crown. He argued that such general writs were being issued in England by the Court of Exchequer, which had the statutory authority to issue them; the province law of 1699, he continued, had granted the Superior Court jurisdiction in Massachusetts "generally" over matters which the courts of King's Bench, Common Pleas, and Exchequer "have or ought to have."

Thacher replied first. Addressing himself largely to technical issues, he denied that the Superior Court could exercise the right of the Court of Exchequer in England to issue such writs. Then Otis arose to speak. One contemporary critic described him as "a plump, round-faced, smooth skinned, short-necked, eagle-eyed politician," but to John Adams—who attended the trial, reported it in his diary, and was to write an account of it more than fifty years later—"Otis was a flame of fire."

He had prepared his argument with care. Although his oration covered some four or five hours and was not taken down stenographically, it left on Adams an indelible impression. With a "profusion of legal authorities," Adams tells us, "a prophetic glance of his eye into futurity, and a torrent of impetuous eloquence, he hurried away everything before him." Adams continued: "Every man of a crowded audience appeared to me to go away, as I did, ready to take arms against writs of assistance." And he concluded: "Then and there the child Independence was born."

More important than the electrifying effect of Otis' argument upon his auditors was its revolutionary tenor. Anticipating ideas that would be set forth in the Declaration of Independence fifteen years later, Otis argued that the rights to life, liberty, and property were derived from nature and implied the guarantee of privacy, without which individual liberty could not survive. (Venturing beyond the immediate issue, Otis declared that liberty should be granted to all men regardless of color—an abolitionist note that startled even the sympathetic Adams.)

Relying on English lawbooks to prove that only special warrants were legal, Otis attacked the writs as "instruments of slavery," which he swore to oppose to his dying day with all the powers and faculties God had given him. Defending the right of privacy, he pointed out that the power to issue general search warrants placed "the. liberty of every man in the hands of every petty officer." The freedom of one's house, he contended, was "one of the most essential branches of English liberty." In perhaps his most moving passage he was reported to have declared:

A man's house is his castle, and whilst he is quiet he is as well guarded as a prince in his castle. This writ, if it should be declared legal, would totally annihilate this privilege. Customhouse officers may enter our houses when they please; we are commanded to permit their entry. Their menial servants may enter, may break locks, bars, and everything in their way; and whether they break through malice or revenge, no man, no court, can inquire. Bare suspicion without oath is sufficient. This wanton exercise of this power is not a chimerical suggestion of a heated brain. . . . What a scene does this open! Every man, prompted by revenge, ill humor, or wantonness to inspect the inside of his neighbor's house, may get a writ of assistance. Others will ask it from self-defense; one arbitrary exertion will provoke another, until society be involved in tumult and blood.

With remarkable prescience Otis' words captured the mood of the midnight visitation by totalitarian police which would terrify a later era less sensitive to individual freedom.

At right is Joseph Blackburn's portrait of the brilliant but unstable attorney James Otis.

Otis then proceeded to denounce the Navigation Acts, which had regulated the trade of the empire since the time of Cromwell, exposing their nuisance aspects with great wit. By implication he acknowledged the widespread existence of smuggling, and went so far as to contend that "if the King of Great Britain in person were encamped on Boston Common, at the head of twenty thousand men, with all his navy on our coast, he would not be able to execute these laws. They would be resisted or eluded." Turning to the similarly unenforceable Molasses Act, passed by Parliament in 1733 to protect the British West Indies planters from the competition of the foreign West Indies, he charged that the law was enacted "by a foreign legislature, without our consent, and by a legislature who had no feeling for us, and whose interest prompted them to tax us to the quick."

The nub of Otis' argument was that, even if the writs of assistance had been authorized by an Act of Parliament, "an act against the Constitution is void. An act against natural equity is void; and if an act of Parliament should be made, in the very words of this petition, it would be void. The executive courts* must pass such acts into disuse." This contention—that Parliament was not omnipotent and could be restrained by the unwritten Constitution and a higher law—was a notion soon to be pushed further by John Adams and other members of the Massachusetts bar: the argument became familiar in the colonies well before the Declaration of Independence was adopted.

Measured by its effect on its auditors and its immediate impact on the majority of the court, Otis' speech ranks among the most memorable in American history, alongside Patrick Henry's fiery oration protest-

---

* By "executive courts" he meant the regular courts of law as distinguished from the Massachusetts legislature, known as the General Court. Otis' argument presaged a special and unique role for the United States Supreme Court, the exercise of the power to declare laws unconstitutional.

This portrait of Chief Justice Thomas Hutchinson is attributed to John Singleton Copley.

ing the Stamp Act, Fisher Ames' memorable defense of Jay's Treaty in the House of Representatives, and Daniel Webster's classic reply to Hayne. Had a decision been rendered on the spot, Otis and Thacher would have won, for all the judges save Thomas Hutchinson were against the writs; even from *his* opinion, carefully worded, opponents of the writs could take comfort: "The Court has considered the subject of writs of assistance," the chief justice announced, "and can see no foundation for such a writ: but as the practice in England is not known [owing to the interregnum], it has been thought best to continue the question to the next term, and that in the meantime opportunity may be given to know the result." But the crafty chief justice, aware that he stood alone among his colleagues, was merely buying precious time.

Another hearing was held in November, 1761. This time Robert Auchmuty joined Gridley in defense of the writs. The arguments lasted "the whole day and evening," covering much the same ground as the previous hearing. But the court had now before it information that under the new monarch, George III, writs of assistance were being issued in the mother country by the Court of Exchequer; the Massachusetts judges accordingly felt that they could no longer refuse to issue them too. Writing years later, John Adams recounted that "the Court clandestinely granted them."

Thomas Hutchinson had won a pyrrhic victory. It was he who had talked the rest of the court into agreeing to a delay to learn what the English practice was and he who was chiefly responsible for granting the writs. He was to pay dearly in personal popularity. Moreover, at the younger Otis' prompting, the legislature manifested its displeasure with the decision not only by reducing the salary of the judges of the Superior Court, but by cutting out entirely Hutchinson's allowance as chief justice. And that was only the beginning. During the riots in Boston in 1765 over the passage of the Stamp Act, Hutchinson's mansion was sacked and his library and papers scattered—out of revenge, Governor Bernard claimed, for his connection with the writs. Henceforward, Hutchinson was to be the leader of the Court party and a frank advocate of coercion to secure colonial obedience to Parliament.

As for James Otis, his initial attack upon the writs had made him the darling of the populace of Boston and the leader of the radical party. Taking the issue to the people at once—in May of 1761—he won election to the Massachusetts General Court. When the news of it reached Worcester, Brigadier Timothy Ruggles, then chief justice of the common pleas court and later a Tory exile, declared at a dinner party in John Adams' presence, "Out of this election will arise a damned faction, which will shake this province to its foundation."

Ruggles' gloomy forebodings proved even more accurate than he could have expected, for the year 1761 triggered the Revolutionary movement, and the Otises, father and son, set off the chain reaction. That same year the father was re-elected Speaker of the House. Together they succeeded in pushing through an act forbidding the courts to issue any writ that did not specify under oath the person and place to be searched. On the advice of the justices of the Superior Court, Governor Bernard refused to approve the legislation; overoptimistically he stigmatized it as a "last effort of the confederacy against the customhouse and laws of trade."

The constitutional views which Otis first expounded in the writs of assistance case were given more elaborate formulation in a forceful political tract, "A Vindication of the Conduct of the House of Representatives," which he published in 1762. Therein he enunciated the Whig view that all men are naturally equal, and that kings are made to serve the people, not people the ends of kings.

It would be gratifying to report that the man who had made a political career out of his opposition to the writs was in the forefront of the Revolution when the fighting actually got under way. Regrettably, he was not. Quick-tempered and tense, increasingly eccentric and even abusive, Otis simply was not cast in the heroic mold. Whether from self-interest, fear, expediency, irresponsibility, or family friction (his wife was a high Tory and a shrew), or from a combination of all five, Otis now followed a vacillating course that branded him a recreant to his own principles, loathed by his foes, deserted by his followers.

It all started with what looked suspiciously like a deal. In 1764 Governor Bernard appointed Otis Senior chief justice of the Court of Common Pleas and judge of probate in Barnstable County. In that same year the son issued his "Rights of the British Colonies Asserted and Proved," the most influential American pamphlet published prior to John Dickinson's "Letters from a Farmer in Pennsylvania." Written in opposition to the Sugar Act, Otis' tract took the position that Parliament had no right to tax the colonies and that taxation was "absolutely irreconcilable" with the rights of the colonists as British subjects—indeed, as human beings. Nevertheless, it gave comfort to the Court party by affirming the subordination of the colonies to Great Britain and the right of Parliament to legislate for them in matters other than taxation. Hailed by the Whigs in England, the pamphlet elicited a grudging compliment from Lord Mansfield, who quickly pounced on Otis' concession of the supremacy of the Crown. When someone said that Otis was mad, Mansfield rejoiced that in all popular assemblies "madness is catching." The evidence that the younger Otis' more conciliatory tone was the *quid pro quo* for his father's appointment is at best circumstantial, but informed people felt that the connection was obvious.

Otis pursued his irresolute, even self-contradictory course during the Stamp Act controversy. In his "Vindication of the British Colonies" he reversed his earlier position: Parliament *did* have the authority to impose taxes, he said, though he questioned whether the taxes imposed were fair. In two subsequent tracts he again shifted his ground. Arguing against the writs of assistance, he had decried laws enacted "by a foreign legislature, without our consent." Now he even accepted the theory of "virtual representation"—the fiction that the colonies were virtually represented in Parliament, in the sense that the interests of all Englishmen were theoretically represented by the whole body of Parliament—though propertyless subjects could not vote, though many Members represented "rotten boroughs," and though many English cities had no Member at all. "Representation," Otis conceded, "is now no longer a matter of right but of indulgence only." But in the second tract he swung completely around again, denied the right of taxation without representation, and demanded actual representation in Parliament.

Considering his erratic and equivocal wanderings, it is little wonder that when Otis ran again for the House he was attacked in a bit of doggerel appearing in the Boston *Evening Post* and attributed to a customs official not noted for his sobriety:

> *So Jemmy rail'd at* upper folks *while Jemmy's Dad was out,*
> *But Jemmy's Dad has now* a place, *so Jemmy's turn'd about. . . .*
> *And Jemmy is a silly dog, and Jemmy is a tool,*
> *And Jemmy is a stupid cur, and Jemmy is a fool. . . .*

The attack outraged the voters' sense of decency and "Jemmy" was elected to the House by a small majority. When he had thought himself ruined, Otis ruefully admitted, "the song of a drunkard saved me."

Sent as a Massachusetts delegate to the Stamp Act Congress in New York in 1765, Otis had the satisfaction of seeing his constitutional doctrine of no taxation without representation embodied in the Resolves adopted by that body. But the radical leaders refused to incorporate his demand for actual representation of the colonies in the House of Commons. Most of them were wary of a trap, for a grant of token representation to the colonies could not have checked the anticolonial course of the majority in Parliament.

Although far more moderate on the Stamp Act issue than either Patrick Henry or Daniel Dulany, Otis plucked up his courage and under the pseudonym "John Hampden" published in the Boston press a sweeping denial of Parliament's right to tax the colonies. But by now his waverings had placed him under suspicion. Forced to defend himself at a Boston town meeting held in the spring of 1766, and to deny charges that his behavior was the result of "weak nerves" or "cowardice," he offered to meet George Grenville in single combat on the floor of Faneuil Hall to settle the whole issue. Again returned to the House with his popularity temporarily restored, Jemmy was humiliated when Governor Bernard vetoed his selection by his colleagues as Speaker as simply "impossible." Thenceforward for several years he collaborated with Sam Adams in directing the radical party in the House.

In February, 1768, Sam Adams drew up a circular letter denouncing Lord Townshend's external tax measures—import duties on such items as glass, lead, paper, and tea—enacted by Parliament. Lord Hillsborough, Secretary of State for the colonies, promptly denounced Adams' letter, ordered the Massachusetts legislature to rescind it, and instructed the colonial governors that the assemblies of other colonies be prevented, by dissolution if necessary, from endorsing it. Otis launched into an abusive two-hour tirade against Hillsborough, ridiculing king's ministers who, like Hillsborough, had been educated by travel on the European continent as "the very frippery and foppery of France, the mere outside of monkeys." Although he withheld criticism of George III, he delivered an encomium on Oliver Cromwell and defended the execution of Charles I. That same year, following the arrival in Boston of two regiments of redcoats, Otis wrote to an English correspondent:

> You may ruin yourselves, but you cannot in the end ruin the colonies. Our fathers were a good people. We have been a free people, and if you will not let us remain so any longer, we shall be a great people, and the present measures can have no tendency but to hasten [with] great rapidity, events which every good and honest man would wish delayed for ages, if possible, prevented forever.

Unfortunately for his continued effectiveness as a political leader, no checkrein could be placed on Otis' abusive conduct toward others. "If Bedlamism is a talent, he has it in perfection," commented Tory Judge Peter Oliver, and even friendly critics agreed that Otis was unbalanced. The dispatch of troops to Boston heightened tempers. In 1769 Otis got into a coffeehouse brawl with John Robinson, a customs official. It is charitable to conclude that the caning he received accelerated his mental disintegration. In any event, two years later his family and friends requested he be examined by a sanity commission; as judge of probate, his old foe, Hutchinson, had the satisfaction of appointing its members, who found Otis to be a lunatic. Although he had intermittent lucid spells thereafter, he played no role at all during the Revolution. Instead, it was his brother Joseph who fought at Bunker Hill. James' death was appropriately dramatic. On May 23, 1783, he was standing in the doorway of a farmhouse in Andover when he was struck down by lightning. "He has been good as his word," commented Hutchinson. "Set the province in a flame and perished in the attempt."

A whole generation passed before John Adams, in a series of letters to the newspapers in 1818, established the legend of James Otis' heroic role. Even Virginians came to speak reverently of the "god-like Otis," and perhaps it is only fitting that he should be judged by his most brilliant and seminal achievement rather than by the sadder years when darkness fell upon him. It is only proper, too, that we recognize the writs of assistance case for what it was in fact—first of a series of crises which culminated at Lexington and Concord.

The attack against the writs, initiated by Otis, developed into a notable series of legal battles, fought not only in Massachusetts but throughout the colonies. Local justices of the peace in the Bay Colony refused in 1765 to grant them on the ground that they were repugnant to the common law. They continued to be issued by that province's Superior Court, but individuals sometimes managed to defy them: in 1766 a merchant named Daniel Malcolm, presumably on the advice if not the instigation of Otis, refused to admit the customs officials into part of his cellar, even though they were armed with writs of assistance, and warned them that he would take legal action against them if they entered. The customs men backed down.

Meantime opposition to the writs was spreading to other colonies. In 1766 the customs collector of New London, Connecticut, sought legal advice as to his power of search and seizure, but the judges at New Haven felt that in the absence of a colonial statute they could make no determination. The collector referred the matter to the Commissioner of Customs in England, who in turn asked the advice of Attorney General William de Grey. His opinion came as a shock to the customs officials, for he found that the Courts of Exchequer in England "do not send their Processes into the Plantations, nor is there any Process in the plantations that corresponds with the description in the act of K[ing] W[illiam]."

Aware that the ground was now cut from under them, the Lords of Treasury saw to it that the Townshend Acts passed in 1767 contained a clause specifically authorizing superior or supreme courts in the colonies to grant writs of assistance. Significantly, the American Board of Commissioners of Customs set up under the act sought between 1767 and 1773 to obtain writs in each of the thirteen colonies, but succeeded fully only in Massachusetts and New Hampshire. But as late as 1772 charges were made in Boston that "our houses and even our bed chambers are exposed to be ransacked, our boxes, chests, and trunks broke open, ravaged and plundered by wretches, whom no prudent man would venture to employ even as menial servants."

In other colonies the issue was stubbornly fought out in the courts. New York's Supreme Court granted the writs when the customs officers first applied for them in 1768, though not in the form the applications demanded; finally, the court flatly refused to issue the writs at all. In Pennsylvania the Tory Chief Justice, William Allen, refused also on the ground that it would be "of dangerous consequence and was not warranted by law." The writs were denied, too, in every southern colony save South Carolina, which finally capitulated and issued them in 1773. Significantly, the courts, though often manned by royal appointees, based their denials on the grounds advanced by Otis in the original Paxton case, going so far as to stigmatize the writs as unconstitutional.

What is important to remember throughout the controversy in which Otis played so large a part is that the colonists were seeking to define personal liberties—freedom of speech, the press, and religion—which even in England, right up to the eve of the American Revolution, were not firmly enshrined in law. Indeed, the issues of whether a person could be arrested under a general warrant or committed to prison on any charge by a privy councillor were not settled until the 1760's. Then Lord Camden took a strong stand for freedom from police intrusion. Less dramatically perhaps than in the colonies, similar issues of civil liberties were being thrashed out in the mother country, but in the colonies this struggle laid the groundwork upon which the new Revolutionary states, and later the federal government, built their safeguards for civil liberties.

In Virginia, where the issue was contested most bitterly, writs of assistance were condemned in the Bill of Rights of June 12, 1776, as "grievous and oppressive." Condemnation was also reflected in the clauses in the Declaration of Independence denouncing the King because he had made judges dependent for their tenure and their salaries upon his will alone. Five other states soon followed Virginia in outlawing the writs. Of these, Massachusetts in her constitution of 1780 provided the most explicit safeguards. The relevant section of the state constitution, notable because it served as the basis for Madison's later incorporation of such a guarantee in the federal Bill of Rights, reads as follows:

XIV. Every subject has a right to be secure from all unreasonable searches and seizures of his person, his houses, his papers and all his possessions. All warrants, therefore, are contrary to this right, if the cause or foundation of them be not previously supported by oath or affirmation; and if the order in the warrant to a civil officer, to make search in suspected places, or to arrest one or more suspected persons, or to seize their property, be not accompanied with a special designation of the persons or objects of search, arrest, or seizure; and no warrant ought to be issued but in cases, and with the formalities prescribed by the laws.

John Adams, who wrote that constitution, had remembered his lessons very well indeed.

More succinctly than the guarantee in the Massachusetts constitution, the Fourth Amendment to the federal Constitution affirmed "the right of the people to be secure in their persons, houses, papers, and effects, against unreasonable searches and seizures," and declared that "no warrants shall issue, but upon probable cause, supported by oath or affirmation, and particularly describing the place to be searched, and the persons or things to be seized."

In our own day, several members of a Supreme Court heavily preoccupied with safeguarding personal liberty have conspicuously defended the guarantees in the Fourth Amendment. It was the late Justice Louis Brandeis who, in his dissenting opinion in a wire-tapping decision of 1928 (*Olmstead v. U.S.*) opposing police intrusion without a search warrant, championed "the right to be let alone—the most comprehensive of rights and the right most valued by civilized man. . . . To protect that right," he asserted, "every unjustifiable intrusion by the Government upon the privacy of the individual, whatever the means employed, must be deemed a violation of the Fourth Amendment."

More recently Justice Felix Frankfurter has opposed searches conducted as an incident to a warrant of arrest. In a notable dissent (*Harris v. U.S.*, 1946) he pointed out that the decision turned "on whether one gives the [Fourth] Amendment a place second to none in the Bill of Rights, or considers it on the whole a kind of nuisance, a serious impediment in the war against crime. . . . How can there be freedom of thought or freedom of speech or freedom of religion," he asked, "if the police can, without warrant, search your house and mine from garret to cellar merely because they are executing a warrant of arrest?" He went on to warn: "Yesterday the justifying document was an illicit ration book, tomorrow it may be some suspect piece of literature." Again, in a more recent case (*United States v. Rabinowitz*, 1950), Justice Frankfurter dissented from a decision authorizing federal officers to seize forged postage stamps without search warrant but as an incident to arrest. He said pointedly:

> It makes all the difference in the world whether one recognizes the central fact about the Fourth Amendment, namely, that it was a safeguard against recurrence of abuses so deeply felt by the Colonies as to be one of the potent causes of the Revolution, or whether one thinks of it as merely a requirement for a piece of paper.*

Once it was a powerful monarch concerned about securing every shilling of customs revenue. Today it is a great republic legitimately concerned about the nation's security. Once it was the knock on the door. Today it is wire tapping or other electronic devices. The circumstances and techniques may differ; the issue remains the same.

* In 1957 Mrs. Dollree Mapp of Cleveland, Ohio, was arrested for possessing obscene literature seized in her home by police, apparently without a warrant. Her subsequent conviction was upheld by two state appeal courts, but on June 19, 1961, the Supreme Court reversed the conviction, declaring that evidence obtained by search and seizure in violation of the Fourth Amendment is inadmissible in a state court, as it is in a Federal court. But, in the case of Burton N. Pugach of New York City, accused of conspiring to maim the girl who had rejected him, the Supreme Court on February 27, 1961, had upheld the right of state officials and state courts to use evidence obtained by wire tapping, which many feel also violates a citizen's privacy. So the historic conflict between private right and the public good goes on.

Bernard Bailyn
The Anatomy
of Common Sense

Evidence of the truth of the old adage that the pen is sometimes mightier than the sword has never had a better witness than Tom Paine's remarkable pamphlet *Common Sense*. The impact of Paine's stirring call for a total break with Great Britain upon the Americans of 1776 has long been recognized. Historians have explained its influence variously: some stress the power of Paine's language, some the boldness of his argument, and some contend that it merely provided the spark that in the highly charged atmosphere of the times ignited the explosion. In this essay Bernard Bailyn goes beyond the issue of whether or not *Common Sense* "caused" the American people to decide for independence, which, he says, is not at this distance a very "useful" question. Instead he seeks to explain the qualities that make the pamphlet so unusual.

Bailyn, Winthrop Professor of History at Harvard University, is one of our leading authorities on the Revolutionary era. His work has recently centered on the large and interesting political literature produced by Americans in the late eighteenth century as a result of the controversies that developed between Britain and the colonies. He sees the analysis of the ideological conflicts of the day as providing the best means for understanding the psychology of the colonists and thus their motives and expectations. One volume of his massive edition of the *Pamphlets of the American Revolution* has already appeared. His *Origins of American Politics* is based mainly upon his wide reading in these materials.

*C*ommon Sense is the most brilliant pamphlet written during the American Revolution, and one of the most brilliant pamphlets ever written in the English language. How it could have been produced by the bankrupt Quaker corsetmaker, the sometime teacher, preacher, and grocer, and twice-dismissed excise officer who happened to catch Benjamin Franklin's attention in England and who arrived in America only 14 months before *Common Sense* was published is nothing one can explain without explaining genius itself. For it is a work of genius—slap-dash as it is, rambling as it is, crude as it is. It "burst from the press," Benjamin Rush wrote, "with an effect which has rarely been produced by types and papers in any age or "country." Its effect, Franklin said, was "prodigious." It touched some extraordinarily sensitive nerve in American political awareness in the confusing period in which it appeared.

It was written by an Englishman, not an American. Paine had only the barest acquaintance with American affairs when, with Rush's encouragement, he turned an invitation by Franklin to write a history of the Anglo-American controversy into the occasion for composing a passionate tract for American independence. Yet not only does *Common Sense* voice some of the deepest aspirations of the American people on the eve of the Revolution but it also evokes, with superb vigor and with perfect intonation, longings and aspirations that have remained part of American culture to this day.

What is one to make of this extraordinary document after 200 years? What questions, in the context of the current understanding of the causes and meaning of the Revolution, should one ask of it?

Not, I think, the traditional one of whether *Common Sense* precipitated the movement for independence. To accomplish that was of course its ostensible purpose, and so powerful a blast, so piercing a cry so widely heard throughout the colonies—everyone who could read must have seen it in one form or another—could scarcely have failed to move some people some of the way. It undoubtedly caused some of the hesitant and vaguely conservative who had reached no decision to think once more about the future that might be opening up in America.

For it appeared at what was perhaps the perfect moment to have a maximum effect. It was published on January 10, 1776. Nine months before, the first skirmishes of the Revolutionary War had been fought, and seven months before, a bloody battle had taken place on Breed's Hill, across the bay from Boston, which was the headquarters of the British army in America, long since surrounded by provincial troops. Three months after that, in September 1775, a makeshift American army had invaded Canada and taken Montreal. In December its two divisions had joined to attack Quebec, and though that attack, on December 30–31, had failed miserably, the remnants of the American armies still surrounded the city when Paine wrote *Common Sense,* and Montreal was still in American hands.

That a war of some sort was in progress was obvious, but it was

This engraving of Tom Paine was copied from a portrait by John Wesley Jarvis. It is said to be the only portrait drawn from life.

not obvious what the objective of the fighting was. There was disagreement in the Continental Congress as to what a military victory, if it came, should be used to achieve. A group of influential and articulate leaders, especially those from Massachusetts, were convinced that only independence from England could properly serve American needs, and Benjamin Franklin, recently returned from London, had reached the same conclusion and had found like-minded people in Philadelphia. But that was *not* the common opinion of the Congress, and it certainly was not the general view of the population at large. Not a single colony had instructed its delegates to work for independence, and not a single step had been taken by the Congress that was incompatible with the idea—which was still the prevailing view —that America's purpose was to force Parliament to acknowledge the liberties it claimed and to redress the grievances that had for so long and in so many different ways been explained to the world. All the most powerful unspoken assumptions of the time—indeed, common sense—ran counter to the notion of independence.

If it is an exaggeration, it is not much of an exaggeration to say that one had to be a fool or a fanatic in early January 1776 to advocate American independence. Militia troops may have been able to defend themselves at certain points and had achieved some limited goals, but the first extended military campaign was ending in a squalid defeat below the walls of Quebec. There was no evidence of an area of agreement among the 13 separate governments and among the hundreds of conflicting American interests that was broad enough and firm enough to support an effective common government. Everyone knew that England was the most powerful nation on earth, and if its navy had fallen into disrepair, it could be swiftly rebuilt. Anyone whose common sense outweighed his enthusiasm and imagination knew that a string of prosperous but weak communities along the Atlantic coast left uncontrolled and unprotected by England would quickly be pounced on by rival European powers whose ruling political notions and whose institutions of government were the opposite of what Americans had been struggling to preserve. The most obvious presumption of all was that the liberties Americans sought were British in nature: they had been achieved by Britain over the centuries and had been embedded in a constitution whose wonderfully contrived balance between the needs of the state and the rights of the individual was thought throughout the western world to be one of the finest human achievements. It was obvious too, of course, that something had gone wrong recently. It was generally agreed in the colonies that the famous balance of the constitution, in Britain and America, had been thrown off by a vicious gang of ministers greedy for power, and that their attention had been drawn to the colonies by the misrepresentations of certain colonial officeholders who hoped to find an open route to influence and fortune in the enlargement of Crown power in the colonies. But the British constitution had been under attack before, and although at certain junctures in the past drastic action had been necessary to reestablish the balance, no one of any importance had ever concluded that the constitution itself was at fault; no one had ever cast doubt on the principle that liberty, as the colonists knew it, rested on—had in fact been created by—the stable balancing of the three essential socio-constitutional orders, the monarchy, the nobility, and the people at large, each with its appropriate organ of government: the Crown, the House of Lords, and the House of Commons. If the balance had momentarily been thrown off, let Americans, like Britishers in former ages, fight to restore it: force the evildoers out, and recover the protection of the only system ever known to guarantee both liberty and order. America had flourished under that benign system, and it was simply common sense to try to restore its balance. Why should one want to destroy the most successful political structure in the world, which had been constructed by generations of constitutional architects, each building on and refining the wisdom of his predecessors, simply because its present managers were vicious or criminal? And was it reasonable to think that these ill-coordinated, weak communities along the Atlantic coast could defeat England in war and then construct a system of government free of the defects that had been revealed in the almost-perfect English system?

Since we know how it came out, these seem rather artificial and rhetorical questions. But in early January 1776 they were vital and urgent, and *Common Sense* was written to answer them. There was open warfare between England and America, but though confidence in the English government had been severely eroded, the weight of opinion still favored restoration of the situation as it had been before 1764, a position arrived at not by argument so much as by recognition of the obvious sense of the matter, which was rooted in the deepest presuppositions of the time.

In the weeks when *Common Sense* was being written the future—even the very immediate future—was entirely obscure; the situation was malleable in the extreme. No one then could confidently say which course history would later declare to have been the right course to have followed. No one then could know who would later be seen to have been heroes and who weaklings or villains. No one then could know who would be the winners and who the losers.

But Paine was certain that he knew the answers to all these questions, and the immediate impact that *Common Sense* had was in large part simply the result of the pamphlet's ringing assertiveness, its shrill unwavering declaration that all the right was on the side of independence and all the wrong on the side of loyalty to Britain. History favored Paine, and so the pamphlet became prophetic. But in the strict context of the historical moment of its appearance, its assertiveness seemed to many to be more outrageous than prophetic, and rather ridiculous if not slightly insane.

All of this is part of the remarkable history of the pamphlet, part of the extraordinary impact it had upon contemporaries' awareness. Yet I do not think that, at this distance in time and in the context of what we now know about the causes of the Revolution, the question of its influence on the developing movement toward independence is the most useful question that can be asked. We know both too much and too little to determine the degree to which *Common Sense* precipitated the conclusion that Congress reached in early July. We can now depict in detail the stages by which Congress was led to vote for independence—who played what role and how the fundamental, difficult, and divisive problem was resolved. And the closer we look at the details of what happened in Congress in early 1776 the less important *Common Sense* appears to have been. It played a role in the background, no doubt; and many people, in Congress and out, had the memory of reading it as they accepted the final determination to move to independence. But, as John Adams noted, at least as many people were offended by the pamphlet as were persuaded by it—he himself later called it "a poor, ignorant, malicious, short-sighted, crapulous mass"—and we shall never know the proportions on either side with any precision.

What strikes one more forcefully now, at this distance in time, is something quite different from the question of the pamphlet's unmeasurable contribution to the movement toward independence. There is something extraordinary in this pamphlet—something bizarre, outsized, unique—quite aside from its strident appeal for independence, and that quality, which was recognized if not defined by contemporaries and which sets it off from the rest of the pamphlet literature of the Revolution, helps us understand, I believe, something essential in the Revolution as a whole. A more useful effort, it seems to me, than attempting to measure its influence on independence is to seek to isolate this special quality.

COMMON SENSE;

ADDRESSED TO THE

INHABITANTS

OF

AMERICA,

On the following interesting

SUBJECTS.

I. Of the Origin and Design of Government in general, with concise Remarks on the English Constitution.

II. Of Monarchy and Hereditary Succession.

III. Thoughts on the present State of American Affairs.

IV. Of the present Ability of America, with some miscellaneous Reflections.

Man knows no Master save creating HEAVEN,
Or those whom choice and common good ordain.
THOMSON.

PHILADELPHIA;
Printed, and Sold, by R. BELL, in Third-Street.
MDCCLXXVI.

Certainly the language is remarkable. For its prose alone, *Common Sense* would be a notable document—unique among the pamphlets of the American Revolution. Its phraseology is deeply involving—at times clever, at times outrageous, frequently startling in imagery and penetration—and becomes more vivid as the pamphlet progresses.

In the first substantive part of the pamphlet, ostensibly an essay on the principles of government in general and of the English constitution in particular, the ideas are relatively abstract but the imagery is concrete: "Government, like dress, is the badge of lost innocence; the palaces of kings are built upon the ruins of the bowers of paradise." As for the "so much boasted constitution of England," it was "noble for the dark and slavish times in which it was erected"; but that was not really so remarkable. Paine said, for "when the world was overrun with tyranny, the least remove therefrom was a glorious rescue." In fact, Paine wrote, the English constitution is "imperfect, subject to convulsions, and incapable of producing what it seems to promise," all of which could be "easily demonstrated" to anyone who could shake himself loose from the fetters of prejudice. For "as a man who is attached to a prostitute is unfitted to choose or judge of a wife, so any prepossession in favor of a rotten constitution of government will disable us from discerning a good one."

The imagery becomes arresting in Part 2, on monarchy and hereditary succession, institutions which together, Paine wrote, formed "the most prosperous invention the Devil ever set on foot for the promotion of idolatry." The heathens, who invented monarchy, at least had had the good sense to grant divinity only to their *dead* kings; "the Christian world has improved on the plan by doing the same to their living ones. How impious is the title of sacred majesty applied to a worm, who in the midst of his splendor is crumbling into dust!" Hereditary right is ridiculed by nature herself, which so frequently gives "mankind an *ass for a lion*."

What of the true origins of the present-day monarchs, so exalted by myth and supposedly sanctified by antiquity? In all probability, Paine wrote, the founder of any of the modern royal lines was "nothing better than the principal ruffian of some restless gang, whose savage manners or preeminance of subtility obtained him the title of chief among the plunderers; and who, by increasing in power and extending his depredations, overawed the quiet and defenseless to purchase their safety by frequent contributions." The English monarchs? "No man in his senses can say that their claim under William the Conqueror is a very honorable one. A French bastard, landing with an armed banditti and establishing himself king of England against the consent of the natives, is in plain terms a very paltry rascally original." Why should one even bother to explain the folly of hereditary right? It is said to provide continuity and hence to preserve a nation from civil wars. That, Paine said, is "the most barefaced falsity ever imposed upon mankind." English history alone disproves it. There had been, Paine confidently declared, "no less than eight civil wars and nineteen rebellions" since the Conquest. The fact is that everywhere hereditary monarchy has "laid . . . the world in blood and ashes." "In England a king hath little more to do than to make war and give away places; which in plain terms is to impoverish the nation and set it together by the ears. A pretty business indeed for a man to be allowed eight hundred thousand sterling a year for, and worshipped into the bargain!" People who are fools enough to believe the claptrap about monarchy, Paine wrote, should be allowed to do so without interference: "let them promiscuously worship the Ass and the Lion, and welcome."

But it is in the third section, "Thoughts on the Present State of American Affairs," that Paine's language becomes most effective and vivid. The emotional level is extremely high throughout these pages and the lyric passages even then must have seemed prophetic:

> The sun never shined on a cause of greater worth. . . . 'Tis not the concern of a day, a year, or an age; posterity are virtually involved in the contest, and will be more or less affected even to the end of time by the proceedings now. Now is the seedtime of continental union, faith, and honor. The least fracture now will be like a name engraved with the point of a pin on the tender rind of a young oak; the wound will enlarge with the tree, and posterity read it in full grown characters.

The arguments in this section, proving the necessity for American independence and the colonies' capacity to achieve it, are elaborately worked out, and they respond to all the objections to independence that Paine had heard. But through all of these pages of argumentation, the prophetic, lyric note of the opening paragraphs continues to be heard, and a sense of urgency keeps the tension high. "Everything that is right or reasonable," Paine writes, "pleads for separation. The blood of the slain, the weeping voice of nature cries, 'TIS TIME TO PART." *Now* is the time to act, he insists: "The present winter is worth an age if rightly employed, but if lost or neglected the whole continent will partake of the misfortune." The possibility of a peaceful conclusion to the controversy had vanished, "wherefore, since nothing but blows will do, for God's sake let us come to a final separation, and not leave the next generation to be cutting throats under the violated unmeaning names of parent and child." Not to act now would not eliminate the need for action, he wrote, but only postpone it to the next generation, which would clearly see that "a little more, a little farther, would have rendered this continent the glory of the earth." To talk of reconciliation "with those in whom our reason forbids us to have faith, and our affections, wounded through a thousand pores, instruct us to detest, is madness and folly." The earlier harmony was irrecoverable: "Can ye give to prostitution its former innocence? Neither can ye reconcile Britain and America. . . . As well can the lover forgive the ravisher of his mistress as the continent forgive the murders of Britain." And the section ends with Paine's greatest peroration:

O ye that love mankind! Ye that dare to oppose not only the tyranny but the tyrant, stand forth! Every spot of the old world is overrun with oppression. Freedom hath been hunted round the globe. Asia and Africa have long expelled her. Europe regards her like a stranger, and England hath given her warning to depart. O! receive the fugitive, and prepare in time an asylum for mankind.

In the pamphlet literature of the American Revolution there is nothing comparable to this passage for sheer emotional intensity and lyric appeal. Its vividness must have leapt out of the pages to readers used to greyer, more stolid prose.

But language does not explain itself. It is a reflection of deeper elements—qualities of mind, styles of thought, a writer's personal culture. There is something unique in the intellectual idiom of the pamphlet.

Common Sense, it must be said, is lacking in close rigor of argumentation. Again and again Paine's logic can be seen to be grossly deficient. His impatience with following through with his arguments at certain points becomes almost amusing. In the fourth and final section, for example, which is on America's ability to achieve and maintain independence, Paine argues that one of America's great advantages is that, unlike the corrupt European powers, it is free of public debt, a burden that was well known to carry with it all sorts of disabling social and political miseries. But then Paine recognizes that mounting a full-scale war and maintaining independence would inevitably force America to create a national debt. He thereupon proceeds to argue, in order, the following: 1) that *such* a debt would be "a glorious memento of our virtue"; 2) that even if it *were* a misery, it would be a cheap price to pay for independence and a new, free constitution—though not, for reasons that are not made entirely clear, a cheap price to pay for simply getting rid of the ministry responsible for all the trouble and returning the situation to what it was in 1764: "such a thought is unworthy a man of honor, and is the true characteristic of a narrow heart and a peddling politician." Having reached that point, he goes the whole way around to make the third point, which is that "no nation ought to be without a debt," though he had started with the idea that the absence of one was an advantage. But this new notion attracts him, and he begins to grasp the idea, which the later federalists would clearly see, that "a national debt is a national bond"; but then, having vaguely approached that idea, he skitters off to the curious thought that a national debt could not be a grievance so long as no interest had to be paid on it; and that in turn leads him into claiming that America could produce a navy twice the size of England's for 1/20th of the English national debt.

As I say, close logic, in these specific arguments, contributes nothing to the force of *Common Sense*. But the intellectual style of the pamphlet is extraordinarily impressive nevertheless, because of a more fundamental characteristic than consistency or cogency. The great intellectual force of *Common Sense* lay not in its close argumentation on specific points but in its reversal of the presumptions that underlay the arguments, a reversal that forced thoughtful readers to consider, not so much a point here and a conclusion there, but a wholly new way of looking at the entire range of problems involved. For beneath all of the explicit arguments and conclusions against independence, there were underlying, unspoken, even unconceptualized presuppositions, attitudes, and habits of thought that made it extremely difficult for the colonists to break with England and find in the prospect of an independent future the security and freedom they sought. The special intellectual quality of *Common Sense*, which goes a long way toward explaining its impact on contemporary readers, derives from its reversal of these underlying presumptions and its shifting of the established perspectives to the point where the whole received paradigm within which the Anglo-American controversy had until then proceeded came into question.

No one set of ideas was more deeply embedded in the British and the British-American mind than the notion, whose genealogy could be traced back to Polybius, that liberty could survive in a world of innately ambitious and selfish if not brutal men only where a balance of the contending forces was so institutionalized that no one contestant could monopolize the power of the state and rule without effective opposition. In its application to the Anglo-American world this general belief further presumed that the three main socioconstitutional contestants for power—the monarchy, the nobility, and the people—had an equal right to share in the struggle for power: these were the constituent elements of the political world. And most fundamental of all in this basic set of constitutional notions was the unspoken belief, upon which everything else rested, that complexity in government was good in itself since it made all the rest of the system possible, and that, conversely, simplicity and uncomplicated efficiency in the structure of government were evil in that they led to a monopolization of power, which could only result in brutal state autocracy.

Paine challenged this whole basic constitutional paradigm, and although his conclusions were rejected in America—the American state and national governments are of course built on precisely the ideas he opposed—the bland, automatic assumption that all of this made sense could no longer, after the appearance of *Common Sense*, be said to exist, and respect for certain points was permanently destroyed.

The entire set of received ideas on government, Paine wrote, was false. Complexity was not a virtue in government, he said—all that complexity accomplished was to make it impossible to tell where the faults lay when a system fell into disarray. The opposite, he said, was in fact true: "the more simple anything is, the less liable it is to be disordered and the easier repaired when disordered." Simplicity was embedded in nature itself, and if the British constitution had reversed the natural order of things, it had done so only to serve the unnatural purposes of the nobility and the monarchy, neither of which had a right to share in the power of the state. The nobility was scarcely even worth considering; it was nothing but the dead remains of an ancient "aristocratical tyranny" that had managed to survive under the cover of encrusting mythologies. The monarchical branch was a more serious matter, and Paine devoted pages of the pamphlet to attacking its claim to a share in the constitution.

As the inheritor of some thuggish ancestor's victory in battle, the "royal brute of Great Britain," as he called George III, was no less a ridiculous constitutional figure than his continental equivalents. For though by his constitutional position he was required to know the affairs of his realm thoroughly and to participate in them actively, by virtue of his exalted social position, entirely removed from everyday life—"distinguished like some new species"—he was forever barred from doing just that. In fact the modern kings of England did nothing at all, Paine wrote, but wage war and hand out gifts to their followers, all the rest of the world's work being handled by the Commons. Yet by virtue of the gifts the king had at his disposal, he corrupted the entire constitution, such as it was. The king's only competitor for power was the Commons, and this body he was able to buy off with the rewards of office and the intimidation of authority. The whole idea of balance in the British constitution was therefore a fraud, for "the *will* of the king is as much the *law* of the land in Britain as in France, with this difference, that instead of proceeding directly from his mouth, it is handed to the people under the formidable shape of an act of Parliament." Yet, was it not true that individuals were safer in England than in France? Yes, Paine said, they are, but not because of the supposed balance of the constitution: "the plain truth is that *it is wholly owing to the constitution of the people and not to the constitution of the government* that the crown is not as oppressive in England as in Turkey."

This was a very potent proposition, no matter how poorly the individual subarguments were presented, for it was well known that even in the best of times formal constitutional theory in England bore only a vague relation to the informal, ordinary operation of the government, and although penetrating minds like David Hume had attempted to reconceive the relationship so as to bring the two into somewhat closer accord, no one had tried to settle the matter by declaring that the whole notion of checks and balances in the English constitution was "farcical" and that two of the three components of the supposed balance had no rightful place in the constitutional forms at all. And no one—at least no one writing in America—had made so straightforward and unqualified a case for the virtues of republican government.

This was Paine's most important challenge to the received wisdom of the day, but it was only the first of a series. In passage after passage in *Common Sense* Paine laid bare one after another of the presuppositions of the day which had disposed the colonists, consciously or unconsciously, to resist independence, and by exposing these inner biases and holding them up to scorn he forced people to think the unthinkable, to ponder the supposedly self-evident, and thus to take the first step in bringing about a radical change.

So the question of independence had always been thought of in filial terms: the colonies had once been children, dependent for their lives on the parent state, but now they had matured, and the question was whether or not they were strong enough to survive and prosper alone in a world of warring states. This whole notion was wrong, Paine declared. On this, as on so many other points, Americans had been misled by "ancient prejudices and . . . superstition." England's supposedly protective nurturance of the colonies had only been a form of selfish economic aggrandizement; she would have nurtured Turkey from exactly the same motivations. The fact is, Paine declared, that the colonies had never needed England's protection; they had indeed suffered from it. They would have flourished far more if England had ignored them, for their prosperity had always been based on a commerce in the necessities of life, and that commerce would have flourished, and would continue to flourish, so long as "eating is the custom of Europe." What in fact England's maternal nurture had given America was a burdensome share of the quarrels of European states with whom America, independent of England, could have lived in harmony. War was endemic in Europe because of the stupidities of monarchical rivalries, and England's involvements had meant that America too was dragged into quarrels in which it had no stake whatever. It was a ridiculous situation even in military terms, for neutrality, Paine wrote, is "a safer convoy than a man of war." The whole concept of England's maternal role was rubbish, he wrote, and rubbish, moreover, that had tragically limited America's capacity to see the wider world as it was and to understand the important role America had in fact played in it and could play even more in the future.

> . . . the phrase *parent* or *mother country* hath been jesuitically adopted by the king and his parasites with a low papistical design of gaining an unfair bias on the credulous weakness of our minds. Europe, and not England, is the parent country of America. This new world hath been the asylum for the persecuted lovers of civil and religious liberty from *every part* of Europe. . . . we claim brotherhood with every European Chris-

tian, and triumph in the generosity of the sentiment. . . . Not one third of the inhabitants even of this province [Pennsylvania] are of English descent. Wherefore I reprobate the phrase of parent or mother country applied to England only, as being false, selfish, narrow, and ungenerous.

The question, then, of whether America had developed sufficiently under England's maternal nurture to be able to live independent of the parent state was mistaken in its premise and needed no answer. What was needed was freedom from the confining imagery of parent and child which had crippled the colonists' ability to see themselves and the world as they truly were.

So too Paine attacked the fears of independence not defensively, by putting down the doubts that had been voiced, but aggressively, by reshaping the premises on which those doubts had rested. It had been said that if left to themselves the colonies would destroy themselves in civil strife. The opposite was true, Paine replied. The civil strife that America had known had flowed from the connection with England and was a necessary and inescapable part of the colonial relationship. Similarly, it had been pointed out that there was no common government in America, and doubts had been expressed that there ever could be one; so Paine sketched one, based on the existing Continental Congress, which he claimed was so fairly representative of the 13 colonies that anyone who stirred up trouble "would have joined Lucifer in his revolt." In his projected state, people would worship not some "hardened, sullen-tempered Pharaoh" like George III, but law itself and the national constitution, "for as in absolute governments the king is law, so in free countries, the law *ought* to be KING." The question was not whether America could create a workable free constitution but how, in view of what had happened, it could afford not to.

So too it had been claimed that America was weak and could not survive in a war with a European power. Paine commented that only in America had nature created a perfect combination of limitless resources for naval construction and a vast coastal extension, with the result that America was not simply capable of self-defense at sea but was potentially the greatest naval power in the world—if it began to build its naval strength immediately, for in time the resources would diminish. So it was argued that America's population was too small to support an army: a grotesquely mistaken idea, Paine said. History proved that the larger the population the *smaller* and *weaker* the armies, for large populations bred prosperity and an excessive involvement in business affairs, both of which had destroyed the military power of nations in the past. The City of London, where England's commerce was centered, was the most cowardly community in the realm: "the rich are in general slaves to fear, and submit to courtly power with the trembling duplicity of a spaniel." In fact, he concluded, a nation's bravest deeds are always done in its youth. Not only was America now capable of sustaining a great military effort, but now was the *only* time it would *ever* be able to do so, for its commerce was sure to rise, its wealth to increase, and its anxiety for the safety of its property to become all-engrossing.

> The vast variety of interests, occasioned by an increase of trade and population, would create confusion. Colony would be against colony. Each being able, would scorn each other's assistance: and while the proud and foolish gloried in their little distinctions, the wise would lament that the union had not been formed before.

So on the major questions Paine performed a task more basic than arguing points in favor of independence (though he did that too); he shifted the premises of the questions and forced thoughtful readers to come at them from different angles of vision and hence to open for scrutiny what had previously been considered to be the firm premises of the controversy.

Written in arresting prose—at times wild and fierce prose, at times lyrical and inspirational but never flat and merely argumentative, and often deeply moving—and directed as a polemic not so much at the conclusions that opponents of independence had reached but at their premises, at their unspoken presumptions, and at their sense of what was obvious and what was not, *Common Sense* is a unique pamphlet in the literature of the Revolution. But none of this reaches its most important inner quality. There is something in the pamphlet that goes beyond both of these quite distinguishing characteristics, and while it is less susceptible to proof than the attributes I have already·discussed, it is perhaps the most important element of all. It relates to the social aspects of the Revolution.

Much ink has been spilled over the question of the degree to which the American Revolution was a social revolution, and it seems to me that certain points have now been well established. The American Revolution was not the result of intolerable social or economic conditions. The colonies were prosperous communities whose economic condition, recovering from the dislocations of the Seven Years' War, improved during the years when the controversy with England rose in intensity. Nor was the Revolution deliberately undertaken to recast the social order, to destroy the last remnants of the *ancien régime,* such as they were in America. And there were no "dysfunctions" building up that shaped a peculiarly revolutionary frame of mind in the colonies. The Anglo-American political community could have continued to function "dysfunctionally" for ages untold if certain problems had not arisen which were handled clumsily by an insensitive ministry supported by a political population frozen in glacial complacency, and if those problems had not stirred up the intense ideological sensibilities of the American people. Yet in an indirect way there was a social component in the Revolutionary movement, but it is subtle and latent, wound in, at times quite obscurely, among other elements, and difficult to grasp in itself. It finds its most forceful expression in the dilated prose of Paine's *Common Sense*.

The dominant tone of *Common Sense* is that of rage. It was written by an enraged man—not someone who had reasoned doubts about the English constitution and the related establishment in America, but someone who hated them both and who wished to strike back at them in a savage response. The verbal surface of the pamphlet is heated, and it burned into the consciousness of contemporaries because below it was the flaming conviction, not simply that England was corrupt and that America should declare its independence, but that the whole of organized society and government was stupid and cruel and that it survived only because the atrocities it systematically imposed on humanity had been papered over with a veneer of mythology and superstition that numbed the mind and kept people from rising against the evils that oppressed them.

The aim of almost every other notable pamphlet of the Revolution—pamphlets written by substantial lawyers, ministers, merchants, and planters—was to probe difficult, urgent, and controversial questions and make appropriate recommendations. The aim of *Common Sense* was to tear the world apart—the world as it was known and as it was constituted. *Common Sense* has nothing of the close logic, scholarship, and rational tone of the best of the American pamphlets. Paine was an ignoramus, both in ideas and in the practice of politics, next to Adams, Wilson, Jefferson, or Madison. He could not discipline his thoughts; they were sucked off continuously from the sketchy outline he apparently had in mind when he began the pamphlet into the boiling vortex of his emotions. And he had none of the hard, quizzical, grainy quality of mind that led Madison to probe the deepest questions of republicanism not as an ideal contrast to monarchical corruption but as an operating, practical, everyday process of government capable of containing within it the explosive forces of society. Paine's writing was not meant to probe unknown realities of a future way of life, or to convince, or to explain; it was meant to overwhelm and destroy. In this respect *Common Sense* bears comparison not with the writings of the other American pamphleteers but with those of Jonathan Swift. For Swift too had been a verbal killer in an age when pamphleteering was important to politics. But Swift's chief weapon had been a rapier as sharp as a razor and so pointed that it first entered its victim unfelt. Paine's writing has none of Swift's marvelously ironic subtlety, just as it has none of the American pamphleteers' learning and logic. Paine's language is violent, slashing, angry, indignant.

This inner voice of anger and indignation had been heard before in Georgian England, in quite special and peculiar forms. It is found in certain of the writings of the extreme leftwing libertarians; and it can be found too in the boiling denunciations of English corrup-

Hogarth's Bathos *repeats, in all its symbols, the idea of the apocalypse, the end of everything.*

tion that flowed from the pens of such would-be prophets as Dr. John Brown, whose sulfuric *Estimate of the Manners and Principles of the Times* created such a sensation in 1757. But its most vivid expression is not verbal but graphic: the paintings and engravings of William Hogarth, whose awareness of the world had taken shape in the same squalor of London's and the provinces' demimonde in which Paine had lived and in which he had struggled so unsuccessfully. In Paine's pamphlet all of these strains and sets of attitudes combine: the extreme leftwing political views that had developed during the English Civil War period as revolutionary republicanism and radical democracy and that had survived, though only underground, through the Glorious Revolution and Walpole's complacent regime; the prophetic sectarian moralism that flowed from seventeenth-century Puritan roots and that had been kept alive not in the semiestablished nonconformism of Presbyterians and Independents but in the militancy of the radical Baptists and the uncompromising Quakers whom Paine had known so well; and finally, and most important, the indignation and rage of the semidispossessed, living at the margins of respectable society and hanging precariously over the abyss of debtors prison, threatened at every turn with an irrecoverable descent into the hell that Hogarth painted so brilliantly and so compulsively in his savage morality tales—those dramatic "progresses" that depict with fiendish, almost insane intensity the passages people in Paine's circumstances took from marginal prosperity, hope, and decency, through scenes of seduction, cruelty, passion, and greed, into madness, disease, and a squalor that became cosmic and apocalyptic in Hogarth's superb late engraving entitled *The Bathos.*

These were English strains and English attitudes—just as *Common Sense* was an English pamphlet written on an American theme—and they were closer in spirit to the viciousness of the Parisian demimonde depicted in the salacious reportage of Restif de La Bretonne than to the Boston of the Adamses and the Philadelphia of Franklin. Yet for all the differences—which help explain why so many American radicals found *Common Sense* so outrageous and unacceptable—there are similarities too. In subdued form something of the same indignation and anger lurks around the edges and under the surface of the American Revolutionary movement. It is not the essential core of the Revolution, but it is an important part of it, and one of the most difficult aspects to depict. One catches a sense of it in John Adams' intense hatred of the Hutchinson–Oliver establishment in Boston, a hatred that any reader of Adams' diary can follow in innumerable blistering passages of that wonderful book, and that led to some of the main triggering events of the Revolution. It can be found too in the denunciations of English corruption that sprang so easily to the lips of the New England preachers, especially those most sunk in provincial remoteness and closest to the original fires of Puritanism which had once burned with equal intensity on both sides of the Atlantic. And it can be found in the resentment of otherwise secure and substantial Americans faced with the brutal arrogance and irrational authority of Crown officials appointed through the tortuous workings of a patronage system utterly remote from America and in no way reflective of the realities of American society.

Common Sense expresses all of this in a magnified form—a form that in its intensity no American could have devised. The pamphlet sparked into flame resentments that had smoldered within the American opposition to England for years, and brought into a single focus the lack of confidence in the whole European world that Americans had vaguely felt and the aspirations for a newer, freer, more open world, independent of England, which had not, until then, been freely expressed. *Common Sense* did not touch off the movement for a formal declaration of independence, and it did not create the Revolutionary leaders' determination to build a better world, more open to human aspirations, than had ever been known before. But it stimulated both; and it exposes in unnaturally vivid dilation the anger—born of resentment, frustraton, hurt, and fear—that is an impelling force in every transforming revolution.

Richard M. Ketchum
England's Vietnam: The American Revolution

Although so far in human experience history has never actually repeated itself, the folk belief that it often does so has considerable basis in fact. If things never occur exactly as they have in the past, they frequently follow patterns remarkably similar to ones in some bygone age. To the extent that we make ourselves aware of how our predecessors managed (or mismanaged) the problems of their times we can indeed learn from history. That the record shows that we seldom do so is only evidence of the value of the study of history.

In the following article Richard M. Ketchum points out some startling parallels between Great Britain's attitude toward the American Revolution and the attitude of the United States toward the war in Vietnam two centuries later. His essay was written in 1971 obviously with the hope that it would convince doubters that the Vietnamese involvement had been a mistake. The danger in using history in this way is that the writer may be tempted to distort the evidence to make it fit the argument, either by ignoring facts that do not strengthen the case or by giving undeserved weight to past events which at the time had little or no impact upon the course of history. Ketchum carefully avoids twisting facts; his essay is a sound and balanced account of how Britain came to the fateful decision to use force against the colonies and of why the British persisted so long in their fruitless effort to subdue them. His main purpose, in other words, was to throw light on the Revolution, not to propagandize for any current policy. Ketchum is an editor of *American Heritage* and the author of many books, including the *American Heritage Book of the Revolution*, and most recently, a biography of the humorist Will Rogers.

If it is true that those who cannot remember the past are condemned to repeat it, America's last three Presidents might have profited by examining the ghostly footsteps of America's last king before pursuing their adventure in Vietnam. As the United States concludes a decade of war in Southeast Asia, it is worth recalling the time, two centuries ago, when Britain faced the same agonizing problems in America that we have met in Vietnam. History seldom repeats itself exactly, and it would be a mistake to try to equate the ideologies or the motivating factors involved; but enough disturbing parallels may be drawn between those two distant events to make one wonder if the Messrs. Kennedy, Johnson, and Nixon had their ears closed while the class was studying the American Revolution.

Britain, on the eve of that war, was the greatest empire since Rome. Never before had she known such wealth and power; never had the future seemed so bright, the prospects so glowing. All, that is, except the spreading sore of discontent in the American colonies that, after festering for a decade and more, finally erupted in violence at Lexington and Concord on April 19, 1775. When news of the subsequent battle for Bunker Hill reached England that summer, George III and his ministers concluded that there was no alternative to using force to put down the insurrection. In the King's mind, at least, there was no longer any hope of reconciliation—nor did the idea appeal to him. He was determined to teach the rebellious colonials a lesson, and no doubts troubled him as to the righteousness of the course he had chosen. "I am not sorry that the line of conduct seems now chalked out," he had said even before fighting began; later he told his prime minister, Lord North, "I know I am doing my Duty and I can never wish to retract." And then, making acceptance of the war a matter of personal loyalty, "I wish nothing but good," he said, "therefore anyone who does not agree with me is a traitor and a scoundrel." Filled with high moral purpose and confidence, he was certain that "when once these rebels have felt a smart blow, they will submit . . ."

In British political and military circles there was general agreement that the war would be quickly and easily won. "Shall we be told," asked one of the King's men in Commons, "that [the Americans] can resist the powerful efforts of this nation?" Major John Pitcairn, writing home from Boston in March, 1775, said, "I am satisfied that one active campaign, a smart action, and burning two or three of the towns, will set everything to rights." The man who would direct the British navy during seven years of war, the unprincipled, inefficient Earl of Sandwich, rose in the House of Lords to express his opinion of the provincial fighting man. "Suppose the Colonies do abound in men," the First Lord of the Admiralty asked, "what does that signify? They are raw, undisciplined, cowardly men. I wish instead of forty of fifty thousand of these *brave* fellows they would produce in the field at least two hundred thousand; the more the better, the easier would be the conquest; if they did not run

THE AMERICAN RIFLE MEN.

The contempt with which most of the British viewed the American soldier is vividly shown in this contemporary caricature of the "creature."

away, they would starve themselves into compliance with our measures. . . ." And General James Murray, who had succeeded the great Wolfe in 1759 as commander in North America, called the native American "a very effeminate thing, very unfit for and very impatient of war." Between these estimates of the colonial militiaman and a belief that the might of Great Britain was invincible, there was a kind of arrogant optimism in official quarters when the conflict began.

"As there is not common sense in protracting a war of this sort," wrote Lord George Germain, the secretary for the American colonies, in September, 1775, "I should be for exerting the utmost force of this Kingdom to finish the rebellion in one campaign."

Optimism bred more optimism, arrogance more arrogance. One armchair strategist in the House of Commons, William Innes, outlined for the other members an elaborate scheme he had devised for the conduct of the war. First, he would remove the British troops from Boston, since that place was poorly situated for defense. Then, while the people of the Massachusetts Bay Colony were treated like the madmen they were and shut up by the navy, the army would move to one of the southern colonies, fortify itself in an impregnable position, and let the provincials attack if they pleased. The British could sally forth from this and other defensive enclaves at will, and eventually "success against one-half of America will pave the way to the conquest of the whole. . . ." What was more, Innes went on, it was "more than probable you may find men to recruit your army in America." There was a good possibility, in other words, that the British regulars would be replaced after a while by Americans who were loyal to their king, so that the army fighting the rebels would be Americanized, so to speak, and the Irish and English lads sent home. General James Robertson also believed that success lay in this scheme of Americanizing the combat force: "I never had an idea of subduing the Americans," he said, "I meant to assist the good Americans to subdue the bad."

This notion was important not only from the standpoint of the fighting, but in terms of administering the colonies once they were beaten; loyalists would take over the reins of government when the British pulled out, and loyalist militiamen would preserve order in the pacified colonies. No one knew, of course, how many "good" Americans there were; some thought they might make up half or more of the population. Shortly after arriving in the colonies in 1775, General William Howe, for one, was convinced that "the insurgents are very few, in comparison with the whole of the people."

Before taking the final steps into full-scale war, however, the King and his ministers had to be certain about one vitally important matter: they had to be able to count on the support of the English people. On several occasions in 1775 they were able to read the public pulse (that part of it, at least, that mattered) by observing certain important votes in Parliament. The King's address to both Houses on October 26, in which he announced plans to suppress the uprising in America, was followed by weeks of angry debate; but when the votes were counted, the North ministry's majority was overwhelming. Each vote indicated the full tide of anger that influenced the independent members, the country gentlemen who agreed that the colonials must be put in their place and taught a lesson. A bit out of touch with the news, highly principled, and content in the belief that the King and the ministry must be right, none of them seem to have asked what would be best for the empire; they simply went along with the vindictive measures that were being set in motion. Eloquent voices—those of Edmund Burke, Charles James Fox, the Earl of Chatham, John Wilkes, among others—were raised in opposition to the policies of the Crown, but as Burke said, ". . . it was almost in vain to contend, for the country gentlemen had abandoned their duty, and placed an implicit confidence in the Minister."

The words of sanity and moderation went unheeded because the men who spoke them were out of power and out of public favor; and each time the votes were tallied, the strong, silent, unquestioning majority prevailed. No one in any position of power in the government proposed, after the Battle of Bunker Hill, to halt the fighting in order to settle the differences; no one seriously contemplated conversations that might have led to peace. Instead the government—like so many governments before and since—took what appeared to be the easy way out and settled for war.

George III was determined to maintain his empire, intact and undiminished, and his greatest fear was that the loss of the American colonies would set off a reaction like a line of dominoes falling. Writing to Lord North in 1779, he called the contest with America "the most serious in which any country was ever engaged. It contains such a train of consequences that they must be examined to feel its real weight. . . . Independence is [the Americans'] object, which every man not willing to sacrifice every object to a momentary and inglorious peace must concur with me in thinking this country can never submit to. Should America succeed in that, the West Indies must follow, not in independence, but for their own interest they must become dependent on America. Ireland would soon follow, and this island reduced to itself, would be a poor island indeed."

Despite George's unalterable determination, strengthened by his domino theory; despite the wealth and might of the British empire; despite all the odds favoring a quick triumph, the problems facing the King and his ministers and the armed forces were formidable ones indeed. Surpassing all others in sheer magnitude was the immense distance between the mother country and the rebellious colonies. As Edmund Burke described the situation in his last, most eloquent appeal for conciliation, "Three thousand miles of ocean lie between you and them. No contrivance can prevent the effect of this distance in weakening government. Seas roll, and months pass, between the order and the execution; and the want of a speedy explanation of a single point is enough to defeat a whole system." Often the westerly passage took three months, and every soldier, every weapon, every button and gaiter and musket ball, every article of clothing and great quantities of food and even fuel, had to be shipped across those three thousand miles of the Atlantic. It was not only immensely costly and time consuming, but there was a terrifying wastefulness to it. Ships sank or were blown hundreds of miles off course, supplies spoiled, animals died en route. Worse yet, men died, and in substantial numbers: returns from regiments sent from the British Isles to the West Indies between 1776 and 1780 reveal that an average of 11 per cent of the troops was lost on these crossings.

Beyond the water lay the North American land mass, and it was an article of faith on the part of many a British military man that certain ruin lay in fighting an enemy on any large scale in that savage wilderness. In the House of Lords in November, 1775, the Duke of Richmond warned the peers to consult their geographies before turning their backs on a peaceful settlement. There was, he said, "one insuperable difficulty with which an army would have to struggle"—America abounded in vast rivers that provided natural barriers to the progress of troops; it was a country in which every bush might conceal an enemy, a land whose cultivated parts would be laid waste, so that "the army (if any army could march or subsist) would be obliged to draw all its provisions from Europe, and all its fresh meat from Smithfield market." The French, the mortal enemies of Great Britain, who had seen a good deal more of the North American wilds than the English had, were already laying plans to capitalize on the situation when the British army was bogged down there. In Paris, watchfully eyeing his adversary's every move, France's foreign minister, the Comte de Vergennes, predicted in July, 1775, that "it will be vain for the English to multiply their forces" in the colonies; "no longer can they bring that vast continent back to dependence by force of arms." Seven years later, as the war drew to a close, one of Rochambeau's aides told a friend of Charles James Fox: "No opinion was clearer than that though the people of America might be conquered by well disciplined European troops, the country of America was unconquerable."

Yet even in 1775 some thoughtful Englishmen doubted if the American people or their army could be defeated. Before the news of Bunker Hill arrived in London, the adjutant general declared that a plan to defeat the colonials militarily was "as wild an idea as ever controverted common sense," and the secretary-at-war, Lord Barrington, had similar reservations. As early as 1774 Barrington ventured the opinion that a war in the wilderness of North America would cost Britain far more than she could ever gain from it; that the size of the country and the colonials' familiarity with firearms would make victory questionable—or at best achievable only at the cost of enormous suffering; and finally if Britain should win such a contest, Barrington believed that the cost of maintaining the colonies in any state of subjection would be staggering. John Wilkes, taunting Lord North on this matter of military conquest, suggested that North—even if he rode out at the head of the entire English cavalry—would not venture ten miles into the countryside for fear of guerrilla fighters. "The Americans," Wilkes promised, "will dispute every inch of territory with you, every narrow pass, every strong defile, every Thermopylae, every Bunker's Hill."

It was left to the great William Pitt to provide the most stirring warning against fighting the Americans. Now Earl of Chatham, he was so crippled in mind and body that he rarely appeared in the House of Lords, but in May, 1777, he made the supreme effort, determined to raise his voice once again in behalf of conciliation. Supported on canes, his eyes flashing with the old fire and his beak-like face thrust forward belligerently, he warned the peers: "You cannot conquer the Americans. You talk of your numerous friends to annihilate the Congress, and of your powerful forces to disperse their army, but I might as well talk of driving them before me with this crutch. . . . You have been three years teaching them the art of war, and they are apt scholars. I will venture to tell your lordships that the American gentry will make officers enough fit to command the troops of all the European powers. What you have sent there are too many to make peace, too few to make war. You cannot make them respect you. You cannot make them wear your cloth. You will plant an invincible hatred in their breast against you . . ."

"My lords," he went on, "you have been the aggressors from the beginning. I say again, this country has been the aggressor. You have made descents upon their coasts. You have burnt their towns, plundered their country, made war upon the inhabitants, confiscated their property, proscribed and imprisoned their persons. . . . The people of America look upon Parliament as the authors of their miseries. Their affections are estranged from their sovereign. Let, then, reparation come from the hands that inflicted the injuries. Let conciliation succeed chastisement. . . ." But there was no persuading the majority; Chatham's appeal was rejected and the war went on unabated.

It began to appear, however, that destruction of the Continental Army—even if that goal could be achieved—might not be conclusive. After the disastrous campaign around Manhattan in 1776, George Washington had determined not to risk his army in a major engagement, and he began moving away from the European battle style in which two armies confronted each other head to head. His tactical method became that of the small, outweighed prizefighter who depends on his legs to keep him out of range of his opponent and who, when the bigger man begins to tire, darts in quickly to throw a quick punch, then retreats again. It was an approach to fighting described by Nathanael Greene, writing of the campaign in the South in 1780: "We fight, get beat, rise, and fight again." In fact, between January and September of the following year, Greene, short of money, troops, and supplies, won a major campaign without ever really winning a battle. The battle at Guilford Courthouse, which was won by the British, was typical of the results. As Horace Walpole observed, "Lord Cornwallis has conquered his troops out of shoes and provisions and himself out of troops."

There was, in the colonies, no great political center like Paris or London, whose loss might have been demoralizing to the Americans;

indeed, Boston, New York, and Philadelphia, the seat of government, were all held at one time or another by the British without irreparable damage to the rebel cause. The fragmented political and military structure of the colonies was often a help to the rebels, rather than a hindrance, for it meant that there was almost no chance of the enemy striking a single crushing blow. The difficulty, as General Frederick Haldimand, who succeeded Carleton in Canada, saw it, was the seemingly unending availability of colonial militiamen who rose up out of nowhere to fight in support of the nucleus of regular troops called the Continental Army. "It is not the number of troops Mr. Washington can spare from his army that is to be apprehended," Haldimand wrote, "it is the multitude of militia and men in arms ready to turn out at an hour's notice at the shew of a single regiment of Continental Troops. . . ." So long as the British were able to split up their forces and fan out over the countryside in relatively small units, they were fairly successful in putting down the irregulars' activities and cutting off their supplies; but the moment they had to concentrate again to fight the Continentals, guerrilla warfare burst out like so many brush fires on their flank and rear. No British regular could tell if an American was friend or foe, for loyalty to King George was easy to attest; and the man who was a farmer or merchant when a British battalion marched by his home was a militiaman as soon as it had passed by, ready to shoulder his musket when an emergency or an opportunity to confound the enemy arose.

Against an unnumberable supply of irregular forces the British could bring to bear only a fixed quantity of troops—however many, that is, they happened to have on the western side of the Atlantic Ocean at any given moment. Early in the war General James Murray had foreseen the difficulties that would undoubtedly arise. Writing to Lord Barrington, he warned that military conquest was no real answer. If the war proved to be a long one, their advantage in numbers would heavily favor the rebels, who could replace their losses while the British could not. Not only did every musket and grain of powder have to be shipped across the ocean; but if a man was killed or wounded, the only way to replace him was to send another man in full kit across the Atlantic. And troop transports were slow and small: three or four were required to move a single battalion.

During the summer of 1775 recruiting went badly in England and Ireland, for the war was not popular with a lot of the people who would have to fight it, and there were jobs to be had. It was evident that the only means of assembling a force large enough to suppress the rebellion in the one massive stroke that had been determined upon was to hire foreign troops. And immediately this word was out, the rapacious petty princes of Brunswick, Hesse-Cassel, and Waldeck, and the Margrave of Anspach-Bayreuth, generously offered up a number of their subjects—at a price—fully equipped and ready for duty, to serve His Majesty George III. Frederick the Great of Prussia, seeing the plan for what it was, announced that he would "make all the Hessian troops, marching through his dominions to America, pay the usual cattle tax, because, although human beings, they had been sold as beasts." But George III and the princes regarded it as a business deal, in the manner of such dubious alliances ever since: each foot soldier and trooper supplied by the Duke of Brunswick, for instance, was to be worth seven pounds, four shillings, fourpence halfpenny in levy money to his Most Serene Highness. Three wounded men were to count as one killed in action, and it was stipulated that a soldier killed in combat would be paid for at the same rate as levy money. In other words the life of a subject was worth precisely seven ponds, four shillings, fourpence halfpenny to the Duke.

As it turned out, the large army that was assembled in 1776 to strike a quick, overpowering blow that would put a sudden end to the rebellion proved—when that decisive victory never came to pass—to be a distinct liability, a hideously expensive and at times vulnerable weapon. In the indecisive hands of men like William Howe and Henry Clinton, who never seemed absolutely certain about what they should do or how they should do it, the great army rarely had an opportunity to realize its potential; yet, it remained a ponderous and insatiable consumer of supplies, food, and money.

The loyalists, on whom many Englishmen had placed such high hopes, proved a will-o'-the-wisp. Largely ignored by the policy makers early in the war despite their pleas for assistance, the loyalists were numerous enough but were neither well organized nor evenly distributed throughout the colonies. Where the optimists in Britain went wrong in thinking that loyalist strength would be an important factor was to imagine that anything like a majority of Americans *could* remain loyal to the Crown if they were not continuously supported and sustained by the mother country. Especially as the war went on, as opinions hardened, and as the possibility increased that the new government in America might actually survive, it was a very difficult matter to retain one's loyalty to the King unless friends and neighbors were of like mind and unless there was British force nearby to safeguard such a belief. Furthermore it proved almost impossible for the British command to satisfy the loyalists, who were bitterly angry over the persecution and physical violence and robbery they had to endure and who charged constantly that the British generals were too lax in their treatment of rebels.

While the problems of fighting the war in distant America mounted, Britain found herself unhappily confronted with the combination of circumstances the Foreign Office dreaded most: with her armies tied down, the great European maritime powers—France and Spain—vengeful and adventurous and undistracted by war in the Old World, formed a coalition against her. When the American war began, the risk of foreign intervention was regarded as minimal, and the decision to fight was made on the premise that victory would be early and complete and that the armed forces would be released before any threatening European power could take advantage of the situation. But as the war continued without any definite signs of American collapse, France and Spain seized the chance to embarrass and perhaps humiliate their old antagonist. At first they supported the rebels surreptitiously with shipments of weapons and other supplies; then, when the situation appeared more auspicious, France in particular furnished active support in the form of an army and a navy, with catastrophic results for Great Britain.

One fascinating might-have-been is what would have happened had the Opposition in Parliament been more powerful politically. It consisted, after all, of some of the most forceful and eloquent orators imaginable, men whose words still have the power to send shivers up the spine. Not simply vocal, they were highly intelligent men whose concern went beyond the injustice and inhumanity of war. They were quick to see that the personal liberty of the King's subjects was as much an issue in London as it was in the colonies, and they foresaw irreparable damage to the empire if the government followed its unthinking policy of coercion. Given a stronger power base, they might have headed off war or the ultimate disaster; had the government been in the hands of men like Chatham or Burke or their

This 1775 cartoon reflects the bitter feeling of those in Parliament who opposed the King and Lord North's ministry. While the colonies are in flames, a fat-faced North (lower left) is paying off a Member of Parliament who had sold his vote to the North ministry.

followers, some accommodation with America might conceivably have evolved from the various proposals for reconciliation. But the King and North had the votes in their pockets, and the antiwar Opposition failed because a majority that was largely indifferent to reason supported the North ministry until the bitter end came with Cornwallis' surrender. Time and again a member of the Opposition would rise to speak out against the war for one reason or another: "This country," the Earl of Shelburne protested, "already burdened much beyond its abilities, is now on the eve of groaning under new taxes, for the purpose of carrying on this cruel and destructive war." Or, from Dr. Franklin's friend David Hartley: "Every proposition for reconciliation has so constantly and uniformily been crushed by Administration, that I think they seem not even to wish for the appearance of justice. The law of force is that which they appeal to. . . ." Or, from Sir James Lowther, when he learned that the King had rejected an "Olive Branch Petition" from the provincials: "Why have we not peace with a people who, it is evident, desire peace with us?" Or this, from General Henry Seymour Conway, inviting Lord North to inform members of the House of Commons about his overall program: "I do not desire the detail; let us have general outline, to be able to judge of the probability of its success. It is indecent not to lay before the House some plan, or the outlines of a plan. . . . If [the] plan is conciliation, let us see it, that we may form some opinion of it; if it be hostility and coercion, I do repeat, that we have no cause for a minute's consideration; for I can with confidence pronounce, that the present military armament will never succeed." But all unavailing, year after year, as each appeal to reason and humanity fell on ears deafened by self-righteousness and minds hardened against change.

Although it might be said that the arguments raised by the Opposition did not change the course of the war, they nevertheless affected the manner in which it was conducted, which in turn led to the ultimate British defeat. Whether Lord North was uncertain of that silent majority's loyalty is difficult to determine, but it seems clear that he was sufficiently nervous about public support to decide that a bold policy which risked defeats was not for him. As a result, the war of the American Revolution was a limited war—limited from the standpoint of its objectives and the force with which Britain waged it.

In some respects the aspect of the struggle that may have had the greatest influence on the outcome was an intangible one. Until the outbreak of hostilities in 1775 no more than a small minority of the colonials had seriously contemplated independence, but after a year of war the situation was radically different. Now the mood was reflected in words such as these—instructions prepared by the county of Buckingham, in Virginia, for its delegates to a General Convention in Williamsburg: ". . . as far as your voices are admitted, you [will] cause a free and happy Constitution to be established, with a renunciation of the old, and so much thereof as has been found inconvenient and oppressive." That simple and powerful idea—renunciation of the old and its replacement with something new, independently conceived—was destined to sweep all obstacles before it. In Boston James Warren was writing the news of home to John Adams in Philadelphia and told him: "Your Declaration of Independence came on Saturday and diffused a general joy. Every one of us feels more important than ever; we now congratulate each other as Freemen." Such winds of change were strong, and by contrast all Britain had to offer was a return to the status quo. Indeed, it was difficult for the average Englishman to comprehend the appeal that personal freedom and independence held for a growing number of Americans. As William Innes put it in a debate in Commons, all the government had to do to put an end to the nonsense in the colonies was to "convince the lower class of those infatuated people that the imaginary liberty they are so eagerly pursuing is not by any means to be compared to that which the Constitution of this happy country already permits them to enjoy."

With everything to gain from victory and everything to lose by defeat, the Americans could follow Livy's advice, that "in desperate matters the boldest counsels are the safest." Frequently beaten and disheartened, inadequately trained and fed and clothed, they fought on against unreasonably long odds because of that slim hope of attaining a distant goal. And as they fought on, increasing with each passing year the possibility that independence might be achieved, the people of Britain finally lost the will to keep going.

In England the goal had not been high enough, while the cost was too high. There was nothing compelling about the limited objective of bringing the colonies back into the empire, nothing inspiring about punishing the rebels, nothing noble in proving that retribution awaited those who would change the nature of things.

After the war had been lost and the treaty of peace signed, Lord North looked back on the whole affair and sadly informed the members of the House of Commons where, in his opinion, the fault lay. With a few minor changes, it was a message as appropriate to America in 1971 as to Britain in 1783: "The American war," he said, "has been suggested to have been the war of the Crown, contrary to the wishes of the people. I deny it. It was the war of Parliament. There was not a step in it that had not the sanction of Parliament. It was the war of the people, for it was undertaken for the express purpose of maintaining the just rights of Parliament, or, in other words, of the people of Great Britain, over the dependencies of the empire. For this reason, it was popular at its commencement, and eagerly embraced by the people and Parliament. . . . Nor did it ever cease to be popular until a series of unparalleled disasters and calamities caused the people, wearied out with almost uninterrupted ill-success and misfortune, to call out as loudly for peace as they had formerly done for war."

Alden T. Vaughan
Shays' Rebellion

The American Revolution has been rightly praised for its essentially conservative character; for once, a people rose against an oppressive government without losing their respect for government itself, or for law. The American revolutionaries sought drastic change, but pursued it, as Jefferson put it in the Declaration of Independence, with "a decent respect to the opinions of mankind." However, the dislocations that the Revolution produced were severe, and in the years after Yorktown the young nation had its full share of social and economic problems, some of which threatened to destroy the respect of the people for legally established authority. Whether this was truly a "critical period" has long been debated; the current opinion of historians seems to be that conditions, in the main, were not as bad as they have sometimes been pictured. But the new national government did lack many important powers, and many of the state governments displayed insufficient will and confidence and thus failed to assume responsibility for governing with the force and determination that critical times require.

In this essay Professor Alden T. Vaughan of Columbia University describes the difficulties that plagued Massachusetts in the 1780's and produced what is known as Shays' Rebellion. How the fundamental conservatism and respect for democratic values of the citizens of Massachusetts eventually resolved this conflict is the theme of his narrative, although he also weighs the influence of the affair on the Constitutional Convention at Philadelphia, which followed closely upon it.

*O*CTOBER, 1786: "Are your people . . . mad?" thundered the usually calm George Washington to a Massachusetts correspondent. Recent events in the Bay State had convinced the General, who was living the life of a country squire at Mount Vernon, that the United States was "fast verging to anarchy and confusion!" Would the nation that had so recently humbled the British Empire now succumb to internal dissension and die in its infancy? To many Americans in the fall of 1786 it seemed quite possible, for while Washington was writing frantic notes to his friends, several thousand insurgents under the nominal leadership of a Revolutionary War veteran named Daniel Shays were closing courts with impunity, defying the state militia, and threatening to revamp the state government.

The uprising in Massachusetts was serious in itself, but more frightening was the prospect that it could spread to the other states. It had, in fact, already tainted Rhode Island, Vermont, and New Hampshire, and it showed some danger of infecting Connecticut and New York as well. By the spring of 1787, American spokesmen from Maine to Georgia were alarmed, Congress had been induced to raise troops for possible deployment against the rebels, and observers on both sides of the Atlantic voiced concern for the future of the nation. Even John Adams in London and Thomas Jefferson in Paris took time from their critical diplomatic duties to comment—the former, as might be expected, pessimistically; the latter with his usual optimism—on the causes and consequences of Shays' Rebellion. And well they might: the Massachusetts uprising of 1786–87 was to make a lasting contribution to the future of the United States by magnifying the demand for a stronger central government to replace the one created by the Articles of Confederation—a demand that reached fruition in the drafting and ratification of the Constitution in 1787–88. From the vantage point of the twentieth century, the rebellion of Daniel Shays stands—with the exception of the Civil War—as the nation's most famous and most important domestic revolt.

The root of the trouble in Massachusetts lay in the economic chaos that accompanied political independence. The successful war against Great Britain had left the thirteen former colonies free to rule themselves, but it had also left them without the commercial ties that had done so much to promote colonial prosperity. While American producers, merchants, and shippers scurried after new goods and new markets to replace the old, the ill effects of economic independence crept across the nation.

Of all the American states, perhaps none felt the postwar slump so grievously as did Massachusetts. Its $14 million debt was staggering, as was its shortage of specie. Bay Staters once again swapped wheat for shoes, and cordwood for help with the plowing. They suffered too from the ruinous inflation that afflicted the entire nation as the value of Continental currency fell in the three years after 1777 to a ridiculous low of four thousand dollars in paper money to one dollar in silver or gold. But in addition, Massachusetts caught the full brunt of

England's decision—vengeful, the Americans considered it—to curtail trade between the United States and the British West Indies. To New Englanders, more than half of whom lived in Massachusetts, the new British policy threatened economic disaster. Gone was their dominance of the carrying trade, gone the booms in shipbuilding, in distilling, in food and lumber exporting, and in the slave trade. Gone too was New England's chief source of hard cash, for the West Indies had been the one place with which New England merchants enjoyed a favorable balance of trade.

Most residents of Massachusetts were probably unaware of the seriousness of their plight until it came close to home. By the early 1780's the signs were unmistakable. Men in debt—and debt was epidemic in the late seventies and eighties—saw their farms confiscated by the state and sold for as little as a third of what they considered to be the true value. Others, less fortunate, found themselves in the dark and filthy county jails, waiting helplessly for sympathetic friends or embarrassed relatives to bail them out of debtors' prison. As the economic crisis worsened, a gloomy pessimism spread among the farmers and tradesmen in the central and western parts of the state.

The economic problems of Massachusetts were difficult, but probably not insoluble. At least they could have been lessened by a wise and considerate state government. Unfortunately for the Bay Staters, good government was as scarce as good money in the early 1780's. After creating a fundamentally sound framework of government in the state constitution of 1780, the voters of Massachusetts failed to staff it with farsighted and dedicated servants of the people. "Thieves, knaves, and robbers," snorted one disgruntled citizen. With mounting grievances and apathetic legislators, the people increasingly took matters into their own hands.

As early as February, 1782, trouble broke out in Pittsfield in the Berkshires, and before the year was over, mob actions had disrupted the tranquillity of several other towns in the western part of the state. The immediate target of the Pittsfield agitators was the local court, which they temporarily closed by barring the door to members of the bench. A court that did not sit could not process foreclosures, pass judgments on debts, or confiscate property for defaulted taxes. In April, violence broke out at Northampton, where a former Connecticut clergyman named Samuel Ely—branded by one early historian as "a vehement, brazen-faced declaimer, abounding in hypocritical pretensions to piety, and an industrious sower of discord"—led the attack on the judges. Ely harangued a Northampton crowd to "go to the woodpile and get clubs enough, and knock their grey wigs off, and send them out of the world in an instant." Ely was promptly arrested and sentenced to six months in prison, but a mob soon freed him from the Springfield jail. The ex-parson found refuge in Vermont.

Instead of recognizing the validity of such protests, the Massachusetts legislature countered with a temporary suspension of habeas corpus and imposed new and higher court costs as well. And while the government did bend to the extent of authorizing certain foodstuffs and lumber to be used in lieu of money, the net effect of its measures was to rub salt into wounds already smarting. Currency remained dear, foreclosures mounted, the shadow of debtors' prison continued to cast a pall, and the state's legal system remained unduly complicated and expensive. Many citizens of western Massachusetts now began to question the benefits of independence; a few even concluded that the patriot leaders of 1776 had deluded them, and cheers for King George III were heard once again in towns that a few years before had cursed his name. And unrest continued to spread. In May, 1783, a mob tried to prevent the opening of the spring session of the Hampshire County Court at Springfield.

Perhaps the major outbreak of 1786 would have occurred a year or so sooner had it not been for a fortuitous combination of events that made the years 1784 and 1785 relatively easy to bear. In 1784 came news that a final peace had been signed with England; in 1785 Massachusetts farmers enjoyed their best harvest in several years, while the legislature, in one of its conciliatory if vagrant moods, refrained from levying a state tax. Although tempers continued to simmer, no serious outbreaks marred the period from early 1783 to midsummer 1786.

The episodes of 1782–83 and those that followed held a particular appeal for veterans of the Revolution. Even more than their civilian neighbors, the former soldiers nursed grievances that they could attribute to incompetent, if not dishonest, government. They had left their farms and shops to fight the hated redcoats, but they could not even depend on the paltry sums their services had earned for them. Inflation had made their Continental currency almost worthless, and now the government set up by the Articles of Confederation was delaying payment of overdue wages and retracting its promises of lifetime pensions to officers.

One lesson of the Revolution not lost on the Massachusetts veterans was that in times of necessity the people could reform an insensitive government by force of arms, and many of them still had in their possession the weapons they had used so effectively against the British and Hessian troops. Old habits and old weapons increasingly took on new meaning to the men of Massachusetts as the economic and political crisis of the 1780's deepened. The veterans of the Bay State knew where to find leadership, too, for among those hard-pressed by the economic problems of the decade were many who had served as officers during the War for Independence.

By 1786 several of these officers had emerged as acknowledged leaders in their own localities, although not until the final stages of the rebellion would any single commander claim the allegiance of more than a few hundred men at most.

In the eastern part of the state the most prominent leader was Captain Job Shattuck of Groton, a veteran of the French and Indian War as well as of the Revolution. Now in his fifties, Shattuck had been protesting vehemently, and sometimes violently, since 1781. His principal lieutenant in Middlesex County was Nathan Smith of Shirley, a tough veteran of both wartime and peacetime conflict—with a patch over one eye as testimony to his involvement in the latter. It was the burly Smith who on one occasion gave his hearers the unhappy choice of joining his band or being run out of town.

Farther west the rebels looked to other leaders. In Springfield and neighboring towns it was to Luke Day, said by some to be "the master spirit of the insurrection." A former brevet major in the Continental Army, Day seems to have had the inclination as well as the experience necessary to command a rebellion. In the dismal eighties he was often found grumbling his discontent in West Springfield's Old Stebbin's Tavern or drilling his followers on the town common.

But it was not upon Shattuck or Smith or Day that the final leadership devolved, with its mixed portions of glory and infamy, but on Captain Daniel Shays of Pelham. In some respects Shays was an improbable leader for a popular revolt, for he seems to have been a reluctant rebel in the first place; as late as the fall of 1786 he insisted: "I at their head! I am not." And even after he had assumed command of the bulk of the rebel army, he expressed eagerness to accept a pardon. But at the same time, Shays had attributes that made him a likely prospect for gaining the loyalty of the insurgents. Unlike the others, Shays presented a calm moderation that inspired confidence and respect. He also had a penchant for military courtesy and protocol, a quality that would have undoubtedly been repugnant to the veterans if overdone, but one that was essential if the "mobbers," as they were often called, were to acquire the discipline and organization necessary to resist the forces of government.

Daniel Shays also attracted confidence through his impressive Revolutionary War record. Joining the Continental Army at the outbreak of hostilities, he fought bravely at Bunker Hill (where his courage earned him a promotion to sergeant), served under Ethan Allen at Ticonderoga, helped thwart Gentleman Johnny Burgoyne at Saratoga, and stormed Stony Point with Mad Anthony Wayne. For recruiting a company of volunteers in Massachusetts Shays ultimately received a commission as their captain, a position he seems to have filled adequately if not outstandingly. And before leaving the service, Shays suffered at least one wound in battle.

Shays resigned from the army in 1780 and turned his hand to farming in the small town of Pelham, a few miles east of the Connecticut River. There his popularity, undoubtedly enhanced by his military reputation, won him election to various local offices. At the same time, Shays learned at first hand the problems that can beset a returned veteran. He had already sold for cash the handsome ceremonial sword that the Marquis de Lafayette had presented to him in honor of the victory at Saratoga. On long winter evenings at Conkey's Tavern, Daniel Shays listened to his neighbors' tales of distress. In 1784 he was himself sued for a debt of twelve dollars; by 1786 he was deeply involved in the insurrection. Like so many other men in western and central Massachusetts, Shays had been maneuvered by events of the postwar period into actions that he would hardly have contemplated a few years earlier.

The relative calm that followed the outbreaks of 1782–83 was abruptly shattered in 1786. To make up for the low revenue of the previous year, the legislature in the spring of 1786 imposed unusually heavy poll and property taxes, amounting to one third of the total income of the people. In 1774 taxes had been fifteen cents per capita; in 1786 they leaped to $1.75—a hefty sum for heads of families in frontier areas where a skilled laborer earned thirty to fifty cents a day. Protested one poor cobbler, "The constable keeps at us for rates, rates, rates!" Besides, the new tax schedule was notorious for its inequity, placing heavy duties on land without regard to its value—a palpable discrimination against the poorer farmers. The new schedule also worked injury on the least affluent classes by seeking almost forty per cent of its revenue through a head tax, asking equal amounts from pauper and merchant prince. As court and jail records poignantly testify, many people in the central and western parts of the state could not pay both the new taxes and their old debts. Worcester County, for example, had four thousand suits for debt in 1785–86 (double the total of the preceding two years), and the number of persons imprisoned for debt jumped from seven to seventy-two during that period. In 1786 debtors outnumbered all other criminals in Worcester County prisons 3 to 1.

The new taxes would probably have caused considerable anger by themselves, but when added to old grievances they were sure to bring trouble. During the summer of 1786, conventions met in several western counties—in Worcester, in Hampshire, in Berkshire—and even as far east as Middlesex, only a few miles from Boston. From these quasi-legal meetings came resolutions to the Massachusetts legislature calling for a variety of reforms: reduction of court and lawyers' fees, reduction of salaries for state officials, issuance of paper money, removal of the state capital from Boston (where it was deemed too susceptible to the influence of eastern commercial interests), reduction of taxes, redistribution of the tax load, and many similar changes. A few protests called for still more drastic reforms, such as abolition of the state senate and curtailment of the governor's appointive power, while some petitioners insisted on a state-wide convention to amend the constitution of 1780, now barely six years old. But on the whole the petitions demanded evolution, not revolution. This was a tempered and healthy challenge to an administration that had shown itself insensitive and incompetent.

In the protests about the government, two categories of citizens were singled out for criticism by the petitioners. First were the merchants and professional men, who enjoyed an unfair advantage within the tax system. Second were the lawyers, who seemed to be conspiring with judges and creditors to force the debtor still further into obligation. Perhaps not all lawyers were so harshly judged, but the condemnation was certainly meant to apply to those whom John Adams called "the dirty dabblers in the law," men who often created more litigation than they resolved. In contrast to the turbulent days before the Revolution, the new era in Massachusetts did not find lawyers in the vanguard of the movement for reform.

But in one respect, at least, the 1780's bore resemblance to the years before Lexington: peaceful protest soon gave way to more forceful action. In late August, following a Hampshire County convention at Hatfield, a mob of 1,500 men "armed with guns, swords, and other deadly weapons, and with drums beating and fifes playing" took command of the county courthouse at Northampton and forced the judges of the Court of Common Pleas and General Sessions of the Peace to adjourn sine die. During the next few months, similar conventions with similar results took place in Middlesex, Bristol, and Worcester counties. By early fall, mobs armed with muskets or hickory clubs and often sporting sprigs of hemlock in their hats as a sign of allegiance to the rebel cause moved at will through the interior counties.

Farmers threatened with foreclosure seize a Massachusetts court, depicted in 1884 by the noted illustrator, Howard Pyle.

The rebels did not go unopposed. In each county there were some citizens who looked askance at the growing anarchy and did their best to thwart it. In Worcester, seat of Worcester County, Judge Artemas Ward showed the mettle of those who would not succumb to mob rule. When on the fifth of September two hundred armed men blocked his path to the courthouse, the aging but still impressive ex-general defied the bayonets that pierced his judicial robes and for two hours lectured the crowd on the dangers of anarchy and the meaning of treason. A heavy downpour finally silenced the judge, though not until he had intoned a timely plea that "the sun never shine on rebellion in Massachusetts." But neither rain nor words had got the judge and his colleagues into the courthouse.

Elsewhere the story was much the same: a few citizens tried to stem the tide of rebellion but in the end were swept aside. At Great Barrington, in Berkshire County, a mob of 800 stopped the court, broke open the jail and released its prisoners, and abused the judges who protested. At Springfield, Daniel Shays and Luke Day made sure that the courthouse doors remained shut, while at Concord, less than twenty miles from Boston, Job Shattuck, aided by Nathan Smith and his brother Sylvanus, prevented the sitting of the Middlesex County court. Only at Taunton, in Bristol County, did a sizable mob meet its match. There Chief Justice (and former general) David Cobb was ready with a field piece, thirty volunteers, and a determination to "sit as a judge or die as a general." The Bristol court met as scheduled.

Governor James Bowdoin and the legislature responded to the latest outbreaks with a confusing mixture of sternness, concession, and indecision. In early September, the Governor issued his first proclamation, condemning the mobbers' flirtation with "riot, anarchy and confusion." In October the legislature suspended habeas corpus, but it also authorized some categories of goods as legal tender for specified kinds of public and private debts, and it offered full pardon to all rebels who would take an oath of allegiance before the end of the year. Yet the government failed to find solutions to the major complaints. No significant reforms were made in court procedures, the tax load was not reduced, officials' salaries were not lowered, the capital was not moved, and no curbs were placed on lawyers' machinations.

As mob violence continued through the fall of 1786, spokesmen in the Bay State and elsewhere voiced a growing fear that the anarchy of Massachusetts might infect the entire nation. Several months earlier John Jay had predicted a crisis—"something I cannot foresee or conjecture. I am uneasy and apprehensive; more so than during the war." Now Secretary of War Henry Knox, Massachusetts statesman Rufus King, and others began to have similar apprehensions. They wrote frantic letters to one another, asking for news and predicting disaster. Abigail Adams, then in London, bristled at the "ignorant and wrestless desperadoes," while reports of the uprising helped prod her husband John into writing his ponderous *Defence of the Constitutions*. Even General Washington lost his equanimity. "[For] God's sake, tell me," he wrote to his former aide-de-camp, David Humphreys, in October, "what is the cause of all these commotions? Do they proceed from licentiousness, British influence disseminated by the tories, or real grievances which admit of redress? If the latter, why were they delayed 'till the public mind had been so much agitated? If the former, why are not the powers of Government tried at once?"

Fearful that the powers of state government would not be sufficient to thwart the rebellion, Governor Bowdoin and Secretary of War Knox hatched a scheme for employing federal troops should the need arise. Knox discussed the matter with Congress: the outcome was a call for 1,340 volunteers for the federal army (which then numbered only 700), most of them to be raised in Massachusetts and Connecticut. The additional troops were ostensibly to be used against the Indians of the Northwest, but in secret session Congress acknowledged the possibility that they might be sent instead against the self-styled "regulators" in New England, and that they might be needed to protect the federal arsenal in Springfield—a likely target for the rebellious veterans. Meanwhile the Massachusetts Council authorized a state army of 4,400 men and four regiments of artillery, to be drawn largely from the militia of the eastern counties.

Command of the state forces fell to Major General Benjamin Lincoln, a battle-tested veteran of the Revolution, and a man of tact and humanity as well as martial vigor. But before taking the field, Lincoln served a brief stint as fund-raiser for his own army, for the cost of a thirty-day campaign had been calculated at about £5,000, or about $20,000, and the impoverished state treasury could offer nothing but promises of eventual reimbursement to any who would lend cash to the government. In less than twenty-four hours General Lincoln collected contributions from 130 of Boston's wealthy citizens, including £250 from Governor Bowdoin.

By the time Lincoln's army was equipped for action, the rebellion was over in eastern Massachusetts. It had never been strong there, but in November of 1786 a mob tried to halt the Middlesex County court. This time the militia was alert. After a brief skirmish in which Job Shattuck received a crippling wound, the Groton leader and two of his lieutenants were captured. While Shattuck languished in the Boston jail, his followers drifted west to join other rebel groups.

The situation now grew alarming in Worcester, where the Supreme Court was scheduled to meet on December 5; by late November, mobs of armed men drifting into town had closed the Court of Common Pleas and made it obvious that no court could meet without an army to back it up. Local officials looked on helplessly. Even bold Sheriff Greenleaf, who offered to help alleviate the high court costs by hanging every rebel free of charge, was powerless in the face of such numbers, and he became a laughingstock to boot when he strode away from the courthouse one day unaware that someone had adorned his hat with the symbolic hemlock tuft.

At first the rebels at Worcester suffered from lack of a universally recognized leader. Then in early December Daniel Shays rode in from

Pelham, mounted on a white horse and followed by 350 men. He had not come to do battle if he could avoid it; to a friend he confided: "For God's sake, have matters settled peaceably: it was against my inclinations I undertook this business; importunity was used which I could not withstand, but I heartily wish it was well over." Still, as a showdown with the judges approached, Shays increasingly assumed the role of spokesman for the disparate forces. And it was just as well; with milling crowds of disgruntled veterans and a frightened and divided populace, violence might well have erupted. Instead, choosing wisdom as the better part of valor, the rebels put their energies into drafting a petition to the legislature for a redress of grievances and into several wordy defenses of their own actions. Violence was scrupulously avoided. And their immediate point, after all, had been won; the Worcester court gathered meekly in the Sun Tavern and adjourned until January 23. The insurgents then gave way before the more impressive force of winter blizzards and dispersed to the west. Friends of the rebels were not greatly heartened, however, for the basic grievances remained. Friends of the government rejoiced at the retreat of the rebels, and chanted:

> *Says sober Bill, "Well Shays has fled,*
> *And peace returns to bless our days!"*
> *"Indeed," cries Ned, "I always said*
> *He'd prove at last a* fall-back *Shays,*
> *And those turned over and undone*
> *Call him a worthless Shays, to run!"*

But Shays was only running to a new scene of action. The Hampshire County court, scheduled to meet in Springfield in late January, should be stopped. Besides, the federal arsenal in that town had the only cache of arms the rebels could hope to capture, and without weapons the rebellion must collapse.

General Lincoln was preparing to defend the January session of the Worcester court when news reached him of the crisis in Springfield. The arsenal there boasted a garrison of some 1,100 militia under General William Shepard, but surrounding the troops were three rebel forces: Daniel Shays commanded 1,200 men at Wilbraham, eight miles to the east; Eli Parson had 400 at Chicopee, three miles to the north; Luke Day led another 400 at West Springfield, just across the Connecticut River to the west. There was every reason to believe they could overwhelm Shepard's garrison if they were willing to risk some bloodshed. General Lincoln headed for Springfield on the double.

Had Shays and his cohorts carried out their original plan they would in all likelihood have had possession of the arsenal before Lincoln arrived with reinforcements. The attack had been set for January 25: Shays was to have led a frontal assault from the southeast while Day directed a flanking movement from the west. But at the last minute Day decided to wait until the twenty-sixth, and his note informing Shays of the change was intercepted by Shepard's men. When Shays moved forward on the afternoon of the twenty-fifth,

After Shays' followers were repulsed at the Springfield armory, as shown here, the rebellion quickly fell apart.

Shepard confidently grouped his full strength against the lone attack. But not much strength was needed. Shepard fired only three cannon shots. When two warning volleys failed to turn back the rebels, Shepard aimed the third into their midst. Three insurgents fell dead in the snow, a fourth lay mortally wounded. The remainder fled in confusion. It was a shattered band that Shays succeeded in regrouping a few miles from the scene of conflict.

At this point General Lincoln arrived and took position between Day and Shays. Both rebel armies at once broke camp and headed for safer territory—Day's men so hastily that they left pork and beans baking in their ovens and discarded knapsacks strewn along their route. The main force, under Shays, beat a rapid retreat to the northeast, passing through Ludlow, South Hadley, Amherst, and Pelham. Lincoln followed in close pursuit, moving overland after Shays, while General Shepard marched up the frozen Connecticut River to prevent a reunion of the rebel army's eastern and western wings.

At Hadley, General Lincoln halted his pursuit long enough to discuss surrender proposals with Shays. The rebel leader was willing to negotiate, but his insistence on an unconditional pardon for himself and his men was more than General Lincoln was authorized to grant. With no agreement likely, Shays suddenly shifted his men to the relative security of Petersham, a center of regulator sentiment which lay in terrain easier to defend. It was midwinter—an unusually cold and stormy winter—and deep snow blanketed the Connecticut Valley. Perhaps the militia would not bother to follow.

But Shays reckoned without General Lincoln. Ever since 1780, when he had surrendered Charleston, South Carolina, and its garrison of 5,400 men to the British in the most costly American defeat of the Revolution, Benjamin Lincoln had had to endure charges of cowardice and indecision. Although he had been officially exonerated, a few critics persisted; in a vigorous suppression of the Shaysites General Lincoln could perhaps fully restore himself in the public's esteem. With superb stamina and determination, Lincoln marched his men the thirty miles from Hadley to Petersham through a blinding snowstorm on the night of Saturday, February 3, arriving at Petersham early the next morning. Taken completely by surprise, the insurgents were routed: some 150 were captured; the rest, including Shays, escaped to the north. Lincoln then moved across the Connecticut River to disperse rebel nests in the Berkshires. By the end of February only scattered resistance remained. What the legislature had recently condemned as a ''horrid and unnatural Rebellion and War . . . traiterously raised and levied against this Commonwealth'' had come to an inglorious end.

While the militia crushed the remnants of rebellion, the state government drafted a series of regulations for punishing the insurgents. In mid-February, two weeks after Shays' dispersal at Petersham, it issued a stiff Disqualifying Act, offering pardons to privates and noncommissioned officers, but denying them for three years the right to vote, to serve on juries, and to be employed as schoolteachers, innkeepers, or liquor retailers. Massachusetts citizens would thus be shielded from the baneful influence of the Shaysites. Not included in the partial amnesty were the insurgent officers, citizens of other states who had joined the Massachusetts uprising, former state officers or members of the state legislature who had aided the rebels, and persons who had attended regulator conventions. Men in those categories would be tried for treason.

The government's vindictive measures aroused widespread protest, not only from those who had sympathized with the rebel cause but from many of its active opponents as well. General Lincoln, among others, believed that such harsh reprisals would further alienate the discontented, and he observed to General Washington that the disfranchisement of so many people would wholly deprive some towns of their representation in the legislature. New outbreaks, he argued, would then occur in areas that had no other way to voice their grievances. In token concession to its critics, the legislature in March, 1787, appointed a special commission of three men to determine the fate of rebels not covered by the Disqualifying Act. General Lincoln served on the commission, and under his moderating influence it eventually extended pardons to 790 persons. But in the meantime, county courts apprehended and tried whatever rebel leaders they could find. In Hampshire County, with Robert Treat Paine serving as prosecuting attorney, six men were sentenced to death and many others incurred fines or imprisonment. In Berkshire County eight men were sentenced to die for their part in the uprising .

Had the government of 1786–87 remained in office, more than a dozen lives would have been lost to the hangman, hundreds of other men would have suffered disqualifications, and the fundamental causes of Shays' Rebellion might have lingered on to trigger new outbreaks. But however strongly the regulators might complain of the legislative and judicial shortcomings of Massachusetts, they had cause to be thankful that its constitution required annual elections and that the franchise was broad enough to let popular sentiment determine the tenor of government. The result of the April election revealed the breadth and depth of the sympathy in which the regulators were held by the citizens and the extent of popular revulsion at the ineptitude of the government. In the gubernatorial contest, popular John Hancock, recently recovered from an illness that had caused him to resign the governorship early in 1785, overwhelmingly defeated Governor Bowdoin. Only 62 of the 222 members of the legislature and 11 members of the 24-man senate were returned to their seats. In some instances the voters chose men who had actively participated in the rebellion, including Josiah Whitney, who had recently served sixteen days in the Worcester jail.

Within the next few months the new legislature sharply mitigated both the causes of unrest and the punishments assigned to the rebels. It repealed the Disqualifying Act, reprieved all men under sentence of death—some on the very steps of the gallows—and by the following summer it had pardoned even Daniel Shays, though he and a few other leaders were still precluded from holding civil and military offices in the state. Equally important, it enacted long-range reforms—extending the law that permitted the use of certain personal and real property in payment of debts, imposing a lower and more equitable tax schedule, and releasing most debtors from prison.

Now in truth the rebellion was over. Peace, and soon prosperity, returned to the Massachusetts countryside. Differences of opinion still lingered, of course, as was made clear one Sunday when the church at Whately christened two infants—one named after Daniel Shays, the other after Benjamin Lincoln. But the Shaysites made no further trouble for Bay State authorities, and Daniel Shays, the reluctant leader, soon moved on to New York State, where he eked out a skimpy existence on his Revolutionary War pension until his death in 1825.

Americans of the 1780's drew various lessons from the affair in Massachusetts. Some, like Washington and Madison, appear to have misinterpreted the event and ascribed to the rebels a more drastic program than the majority of them had ever advocated. Others, like Mercy Warren, the lady historian, and Joseph Hawley, the Massachusetts patriot, detected the hand of Great Britain behind the uprising. Still others sensed that the true causes of Shays' Rebellion were local in origin and primarily the fault of the state government. Baron von Steuben had correctly surmised that "when a whole people complains . . . something must be wrong," while Thomas Jefferson, then American Minister to France, thought the rebellion of no dangerous importance and preferred to set it in a broader perspective than had most Americans. "We have had," wrote Jefferson, "13 states independent 11 years. There has been one rebellion. That comes to one rebellion in a century and a half for each state. What country before ever existed a century and a half without a rebellion? And what country can preserve its liberties if their rulers are not warned from time to time that the people preserve the spirit of resistance? . . . The tree of liberty must be refreshed from time to time with the blood of patriots and tyrants." But while observers were drawing these diverse conclusions from the episode in Massachusetts, an increasing number of Americans were concerned with how to make sure it would never happen again.

On May 25, 1787, less than four months after the rout at Petersham, the Constitutional Convention began its deliberations at Independence Hall, Philadelphia. Through a long hot summer the delegates proposed, argued, and compromised as they sought to construct a new and better form of government for the American nation. And among the knottiest problems they faced were several recently emphasized by Shays' Rebellion: problems of currency regulation, of debts and contracts, and of ways to thwart domestic insurrection. As the records of the federal Convention reveal, the recent uprising in Massachusetts lay heavily on the minds of the delegates. Although it is impossible to pinpoint the exact phrases in the final document that owed their wording to the fear of similar revolts, there is no doubt that the Constitution reflected the determination of the Founding Fathers to do all they could to prevent future rebellions and to make it easier for the new government to suppress them if they did occur. Significantly, the new polity forbade the states to issue paper money, strengthened the military powers of the executive branch, and authorized Congress to call up state militiamen to "suppress Insurrections" and enforce the laws of the land. Jefferson's first glimpse of the Constitution convinced him that "our Convention has been too much impressed by the insurrection of Massachusetts. . . ." Jefferson exaggerated, but it is clear that the movement for a stronger central government had gained immense momentum from the "horrid and unnatural Rebellion" of Daniel Shays.

By the summer of 1788 the requisite nine states had ratified the new Constitution, and in the following spring General Washington took the oath of office as President. In the prosperous and dynamic years that followed, the passions generated by the insurrection in Massachusetts were gradually extinguished. But the lesson and the impact of Shays' Rebellion are still with us. Because of it, important changes were made in the government of Massachusetts as well as in the government of the nation, changes that have stood the test of time. Perhaps this episode lends some ironic credence to Thomas Jefferson's suggestion that "the spirit of resistance to government is . . . valuable on certain occasions."

Henry Steele Commager

The Constitution: Was It an Economic Document?

When Charles A. Beard published *An Economic Interpretation of the Constitution* in 1913, in which he argued that the personal economic interests of the Founding Fathers played a major role in the shaping of the Constitution, he roused a furor, and incidentally triggered a rash of studies designed to show how importantly material interests had influenced people's behavior throughout our history. Beard's line of reasoning was never accepted by all scholars, but for a long generation his basic approach came close to dominating the writing of American history. In recent times, however, the Beardian economic interpretation has been subjected to devastating attack (almost line by line) by such historians as Robert E. Brown and Forrest McDonald.

In this essay Professor Henry Steele Commager of Amherst College takes a fresh look at this controversial subject, offering a thoughtful and objective evaluation of Beard's work and of the motives and actions of the Founding Fathers. Commager, a historian of wide-ranging interests, combines a detailed knowledge of constitutional history with a sensitive perception of the force of ideas in shaping events.

*B*y June 26, 1787, tempers in the Federal Convention were already growing short, for gentlemen had come to the explosive question of representation in the upper chamber. Two days later Franklin moved to invoke divine guidance, and his motion was shunted aside only because there was no money with which to pay a chaplain and the members were unprepared to appeal to Heaven without an intermediary. It was not surprising that when James Madison spoke of representation in the proposed legislature, he was conscious of the solemnity of the occasion. We are, he said, framing a system "which we wish to last for ages" and one that might "decide forever the fate of Republican Government."

It was an awful thought, and when, a few days later, Gouverneur Morris spoke to the same subject he felt the occasion a most solemn one; even the irrepressible Morris could be solemn. "He came here," he observed (so Madison noted),

> as a Representative of America; he flattered himself he came here in some degree as a Representative of the whole human race; for the whole human race will be affected by the proceedings of this Convention. He wished gentlemen to extend their views beyond the present moment of time; beyond the narrow limits . . . from which they derive their political origin. . . .
>
> Much has been said of the sentiments of the people. They were unknown. They could not be known. All that we can infer is that if the plan we recommend be reasonable & right; all who have reasonable minds and sound intentions will embrace it . . .

These were by no means occasional sentiments only. They were sentiments that occurred again and again throughout the whole of that long hot summer, until they received their final, eloquent expression from the aged Franklin in that comment on the rising, not the setting, sun. Even during the most acrimonious debates members were aware that they were framing a constitution for ages to come, that they were creating a model for people everywhere on the globe; there was a lively sense of responsibility and even of destiny. Nor can we now, as we contemplate that Constitution which is the oldest written national constitution, and that federal system which is one of the oldest and the most successful in history, regard these appeals to posterity as merely rhetorical.

That men are not always conscious either of what they do or of the motives that animate them is a familiar rather than a cynical observation. Some 45 years ago Charles A. Beard propounded an economic interpretation of the Constitution—an interpretation which submitted that the Constitution was *essentially* (that is a crucial word) an economic document—and that it was carried through the Convention and the state ratifying conventions by interested economic groups for economic reasons. "The Constitution," Mr. Beard concluded, "was essentially an economic document based upon the concept

*Independence Hall as it
appeared in an engraving done
just prior to the Revolution.*

that the fundamental private rights of property are anterior to
government and morally beyond the reach of popular majorities.''

At the time it was pronounced, that interpretation caused something of a sensation, and Mr. Beard was himself eventually to comment
with justifiable indignation on the meanness and the vehemence of the
attacks upon it—and him. Yet the remarkable thing about the economic interpretation is not the criticism it inspired but the support
it commanded. For within a few years it had established itself as the
new orthodoxy, and those who took exception to it were stamped
either as professional patriots—perhaps secret Sons or Daughters of
the Revolution—or naïve academicians who had never learned the
facts of economic life.

The attraction that the economic interpretation had for the generation of the twenties and thirties—and that it still exerts—is one of
the curiosities of our cultural history, but by no means an inexplicable
one. To a generation of materialists Beard's thesis made clear that the
stuff of history was material. To a generation disillusioned by the
exploitations of big business it discovered that the past, too, had been
ravaged by economic exploiters. To a generation that looked with
skeptical eyes upon the claims of Wilsonian idealism and all but
rejoiced in their frustration, it suggested that all earlier idealisms and
patriotisms—even the idealism and patriotism of the framers—had
been similarly flawed by selfishness and hypocrisy.

Yet may it not be said of *An Economic Interpretation of the Constitution* that it is not a conclusion but a point of departure? It

*Thomas Rossiter's view of
the signing of the Constitution was painted about 1850.*

explains a great deal about the forces that went into the making of the
Constitution, and a great deal, too, about the men who assembled in
Philadelphia in 1787, but it tells us extraordinarily little about the
document itself. And it tells us even less about the historical meaning
of that document.

What were the objects of the Federal Convention? The immediate
objects were to restore order; to strengthen the public credit; to
enable the United States to make satisfactory commercial treaties
and agreements; to provide conditions in which trade and commerce
could flourish; to facilitate management of the western lands and
of Indian affairs. All familiar enough. But what, in the light of
history, were the grand objects of the Convention? What was it that
gave Madison and Morris and Wilson and King and Washington
himself a sense of destiny?

There were two grand objects—objects inextricably interrelated.
The first was to solve the problem of federalism, that is, the problem
of the distribution of powers among governments. Upon the wisdom
with which members of the Convention distinguished between powers
of a general and powers of a local nature, and assigned these to their
appropriate governments, would depend the success or failure of
the new experiment.

But it was impossible for the children of the eighteenth century
to talk or think of powers without thinking of power, and this was a
healthy realism. No less troublesome—and more fundamental—than
the problem of the distribution of powers, was the problem of

sanctions. How were they to enforce the terms of the distribution and impose limits upon all the governments involved? It was one thing to work out the ideal distribution of general and local powers. It was another thing to see to it that the states abided by their obligations under the Articles of Union and that the national government respected the autonomy of states and liberty of individuals.

Those familiar with the Revolutionary era know that the second of these problems was more difficult than the first. Americans had learned how to limit government: the written constitutions, the bills of rights, the checks and balances. They had not yet learned (nor had anyone) how to "substitute the mild magistracy of the law for the cruel and violent magistracy of force." The phrase is Madison's.

Let us return to the *Economic Interpretation*. The correctness of Beard's analysis of the origins and backgrounds of the membership of the Convention, of the arguments in the Convention, and of the methods of assuring ratification, need not be debated. But these considerations are, in a sense, irrelevant and immaterial. For though they are designed to illuminate the document itself, in fact they illuminate only the processes of its manufacture.

The idea that property considerations were paramount in the minds of those assembled in Philadelphia is misleading and unsound and is borne out neither by the evidence of the debates in the Convention nor by the Constitution itself. The Constitution was not *essentially* an economic document. It was, and is, *essentially* a political document. It addresses itself to the great and fundamental question of the distribution of powers between governments. The Constitution was—and is—a document that attempts to provide sanctions behind that distribution; a document that sets up, through law, a standing rule to live by and provides legal machinery for the enforcement of that rule. These are political, not economic functions.

Not only were the principles that animated the framers political rather than economic; the solutions that they formulated to the great questions that confronted them were dictated by political, not by economic considerations.

Here are two fundamental challenges to the Beard interpretation: first, the Constitution is primarily a document in federalism; and second, the Constitution does not in fact confess or display the controlling influence of those who held that "the fundamental private rights of property are anterior to government and morally beyond the reach of popular majorities."

Let us look more closely at these two contentions. The first requires little elaboration or vindication, for it is clear to all students of the Revolutionary era that the one pervasive and over-branching problem of that generation was the problem of imperial organization. How to get the various parts of any empire to work together for common purposes? How to get central control—over war, for example, or commerce or money—without impairing local autonomy? How, on the other hand, preserve personal liberty and local self-government without impairing the effectiveness of the central government? This was one of the oldest problems in political science—as old as the history of the Greek city-states; as new as the recent debate over Federal aid to education or the Bricker amendment.

The British failed to solve the problem of imperial order; when pushed to the wall they had recourse to the hopelessly doctrinaire Declaratory Act, which was, in fact, a declaration of political bankruptcy; as Edmund Burke observed, no people is going to be argued into slavery. The Americans then took up the vexatious problem. The Articles of Confederation were satisfactory enough as far as the distribution of powers was concerned, but wholly wanting in sanctions. The absence of sanctions spelled the failure of the Articles—and this failure led to the Philadelphia Convention.

Now it will be readily conceded that many, if not most, of the questions connected with federalism were economic in character. Involved were such practical matters as taxation, the regulation of commerce, coinage, western lands, slavery, and so forth. The problem that presented itself to the framers was not whether goverment should exercise authority over such matters; it was *which* government should exercise such authority—and how should it be exercised?

There were, after all, no anarchists at the Federal Convention. Everyone agreed that *some* government had to have authority to tax, raise armies, regulate commerce, coin money, control contracts, enact bankruptcy legislation, regulate western territories, make treaties, and do all the things that government must do. But where should these authorities be lodged—with the state governments or with the national government they were about to erect, or with both?

This question was a political, not an economic, one. And the solution at which the framers arrived was based upon a sound understanding of politics, and need not be explained by reference to class attachments or security interests.

Certainly if the framers were concerned primarily or even largely with protecting property against popular majorities, they failed signally to carry out their purposes. It is at this point in our consideration of the *Economic Interpretation of the Constitution* that we need to employ what our literary friends call *explication du texte*. For the weakest link in the Beard interpretation is precisely the crucial one—the document itself. Mr. Beard makes amply clear that those who wrote the Constitution were members of the propertied classes,* and that many of them were personally involved in the out-

* "A majority of the members were lawyers by profession.

"Most of the members came from towns, on or near the coast, that is, from the regions in which personalty was largely concentrated.

"Not one member represented in his immediate personal economic interests the small farming or mechanic classes.

"The overwhelming majority of members, at least five-sixths, were immediately, directly, and personally interested in the outcome of their labors at Philadelphia, and were to a greater or less extent economic beneficiaries from the adoption of the Constitution."
Beard, *An Economic Interpretation of the Constitution.*

come of what they were about to do; he makes out a persuasive case that the division over the Constitution was along economic lines. What he does not make clear is how or where the Constitution itself reflects all these economic influences.

Much is made of the contract clause and the paper money clause of the Constitution. No state may impair the obligations of a contract—whatever those words mean, and they apparently did not mean to the framers quite what Chief Justice Marshall later said they meant in *Fletcher v. Peck* or *Dartmouth College v. Woodward*. No state may emit bills of credit or make anything but gold and silver coin legal tender in payment of debts.

These are formidable prohibitions, and clearly reflect the impatience of men of property with the malpractices of the states during the Confederation. Yet quite aside from what the states may or may not have done, who can doubt that these limitations upon the states followed a sound principle—the principle that control of coinage and money belonged to the central, not the local governments, and the principle that local jurisdictions should not be able to modify or overthrow contracts recognized throughout the Union?

What is most interesting in this connection is what is so often overlooked: that the framers did not write any comparable prohibitions upon the United States government. The United States was not forbidden to impair the obligation of its contracts, not at least in the Constitution as it came from the hands of its property-conscious framers. Possibly the Fifth Amendment may have squinted toward such a prohibition; we need not determine that now, for the Fifth Amendment was added by the *states* after the Constitution had been ratified. So, too, the emission of bills of credit and the making other than gold and silver legal tender were limitations on the states, but not on the national government. There was, in fact, a lively debate over the question of limiting the authority of the national government in the matter of bills of credit. When the question came up on August 16, Gouverneur Morris threatened that "The Monied interest will oppose the plan of Government, if paper emissions be not prohibited." In the end the Convention dropped out a specific authorization to emit bills of credit, but pointedly did not prohibit such action. Just where this left the situation troubled Chief Justice Chase's Court briefly three quarters of a century later; the Court recovered its balance, and the sovereign power of the government over money was not again *successfully* challenged.

Nor were there other specific limitations of an economic character upon the powers of the new government that was being erected on the ruins of the old. The framers properly gave the Congress power to regulate commerce with foreign nations and among the states. The term commerce—as Hamilton and Adair (and Crosskey, too!) have made clear—was broadly meant, and the grant of authority, too, was broad. The framers gave Congress the power to levy taxes and, again, wrote no limitations into the Constitution except as to the apportionment of direct taxes; it remained for the most conservative of Courts peachments of Officers of the United States; to all cases of Admiralty and Maritime Jurisdiction; to Controversies between two or more States, (⸺) between a State and citizens of another State, between citizens of different States, and between a State or the citizens thereof and foreign States, citizens or subjects. In cases of Impeachment, cases affecting Ambassadors, other Public Ministers and Consuls, and those in which a State shall be party, ⸺ In all the other cases beforementioned ⸺, with such exceptions and under such regulations as the Legislature shall make. The Legislature may assign any part of the jurisdiction abovementioned (except the trial of the President of the United States) in the manner and under the limitations which it shall think proper, to such Inferior Courts as it shall constitute from time to time.

Sect. 4. The trial of all criminal offences (except in cases of impeachments) shall be in the State where they shall be committed;

Sect. 5. Judgment, in cases of Impeachment, shall not extend further than to removal from office, and disqualification to hold and enjoy any office of honour, trust or profit under the United States. But the party convicted shall nevertheless be liable and subject to indictment, trial, judgment and punishment, according to law.

XII

No State shall coin money; nor grant letters of marque and reprisal; nor enter into any treaty, alliance, or confederation; nor grant any title of nobility.

XIII

No State, without the consent of the Legislature of the United States, shall lay imposts or duties on imports; nor keep troops or ships of war in time of peace; nor enter into any agreement or compact with another State, or with any foreign power; nor engage in any war, unless it shall be actually invaded by enemies, or the danger of invasion be so imminent, as not to admit of a delay, until the Legislature of the United States can be consulted.

XIIII

The citizens of each State shall be entitled to all privileges and immunities of citizens in the several States.

XV.

Any person charged with treason, felony, or ⸺ in any State, who shall flee from justice, and shall be found in any other State, shall, on demand of the Executive Power of the State from which he fled, be delivered up and removed to the State having jurisdiction of the offence.

XVI.

Full faith shall be given in each State to the acts ⸺, records, and judicial proceedings of ⸺ every other State.

XVII

XVII.

Washington's working copy of a printed draft of the Constitution indicates approval of federal control over coinage and duties in Articles XII and XIII.

to reverse itself, and common sense, and discover that the framers had intended to forbid an income tax! Today, organizations that invoke the very term "constitutional" are agitating for an amendment placing a quantitative limit upon income taxes that may be levied; fortunately, Madison's generation understood better the true nature of governmental power.

The framers gave Congress—in ambiguous terms, to be sure—authority to make "all needful Rules and Regulations respecting the Territory or other Property" of the United States, and provided that "new states may be admitted." These evasive phrases gave little hint of the heated debates in the Convention over western lands. Those who delight to find narrow and undemocratic sentiments in the breasts of the framers never cease to quote a Gouverneur Morris or an Elbridge Gerry on the dangers of the West, and it is possible to compile a horrid catalogue of such statements. But what is significant is not what framers said, but what they did. They did not place any limits upon the disposition of western territory, or establish any barriers against the admission of western states.

The fact is that we look in vain *in the Constitution itself* for any really effective guarantee for property or any effective barriers against what Beard calls "the reach of popular majorities."

It will be argued, however, that what the framers feared was the *states*, and that the specific prohibitions against state action, together with the broad transfer of economic powers from state to nation, were deemed sufficient guarantee against state attacks upon property. As for the national government, care was taken to make that sufficiently aristocratic, sufficiently the representative of the propertied classes, and sufficiently checked and limited so that it would not threaten basic property interests.

It is at this juncture that the familiar principle of limitation on governmental authority commands our attention. Granted the wisest distribution of powers among governments, what guarantee was there that power would be properly exercised? What guarantees were there against the abuse of power? What assurance was there that the large states would not ride roughshod over the small, that majorities would not crush minorities or minorities abuse majorities? What protection was there against mobs, demagogues, dangerous combinations of interests or of states? What protection was there for the commercial interest, the planter interest, the slave interest, the securities interests, the land speculator interests?

It was Madison who most clearly saw the real character of this problem and who formulated its solution. It was not that the people as such were dangerous; "The truth was," he said on July 11, "that all men having power ought to be distrusted to a certain degree." Long before Lord Acton coined the aphorism, the Revolutionary leaders had discovered that power corrupts. They understood, too, the drive for power on the part of individuals and groups. All this is familiar to students of *The Federalist*, No. 10. It should be familiar to students of the debates in Philadelphia, for there, too, Madison set forth his theory and supported it with a wealth of argument. Listen to him on one of the early days of the Convention, June 6, when he is discussing the way to avoid abuses of republican liberty—abuses which "prevailed in the largest as well as the smallest [states] . . ."

> . . . And were we not thence admonished [he continued] to enlarge the sphere as far as the nature of the Government would admit. This was the only defence against the inconveniences of democracy *consistent with the democratic form of Government* [our italics]. All civilized Societies would be divided into different Sects, Factions & interests, as they happened to consist of rich & poor, debtors and creditors, the landed, the manufacturing, the commercial interests, the inhabitants of this district or that district, the followers of this political leader or that political leader, the disciples of this religious Sect or that religious Sect. In all cases where a majority are united by a common interest or passion, the rights of the minority are in danger. . . . In a Republican Govt. the Majority if united have always an opportunity [to oppress the minority. What is the remedy?] The only remedy is to enlarge the sphere, & thereby divide the community into so great a number of interests & parties, that in the first place a majority will not be likely at the same moment to have a common interest separate from that of the whole or of the minority; and in the second place, that in case they should have such an interest, they may not be apt to unite in the pursuit of it. It was incumbent on us then to try this remedy, and . . . to frame a republican system on such a scale & in such a form as will controul all the evils which have been experienced.

This long quotation is wonderfully eloquent of the attitude of the most sagacious of the framers. Madison, Wilson, Mason, Franklin, as well as Gerry, Morris, Pinckney, and Hamilton feared power. They feared power whether exercised by a monarch, an aristocracy, an army, or a majority, and they were one in their determination to write into fundamental law limitations on the arbitrary exercise of that power. To assume, as Beard so commonly does, that the fear of the misuse of power by majorities was either peculiar to the Federalists or more ardent with them than with their opponents, is mistaken. Indeed it was rather the anti-Federalists who were most deeply disturbed by the prospect of majority rule; they, rather than the Federalists, were the "men of little faith." Thus it was John Lansing, Jr., of New York (he who left the Convention rather than have any part in its dangerous work) who said that "all free constitutions are formed with two views—to deter the governed from crime, and the governors from tyranny." And the ardent Patrick Henry, who led the attack on the Constitution in the Virginia Convention—and almost defeated it—complained not of too little democracy in that document, but too much.

The framers, to be sure, feared the powers of the majority, as they feared all power unless controlled. But they were insistent that, in the last analysis, there must be government by majority; even conservatives like Morris and Hamilton made this clear. Listen to Hamilton, for example, at the very close of the Convention. Elbridge Gerry, an opponent of the Constitution, had asked for a reconsideration of the provision for calling a constitutional convention, alleging that this opened the gate to a majority that could "bind the union to innovations that may subvert the State-Constitutions altogether." To this Hamilton replied that

> There was no greater evil in subjecting the people of the U.S. to the major voice than the people of a particular State. . . . It was equally desirable now that an easy mode should be established for supplying defects which will probably appear in the New System. . . . There could be no danger in giving this power, as the people would finally decide in the case.

. . . But we need not rely upon what men said; there it too much of making history by quotation anyway. Let us look rather at what men did. We can turn again to the Constitution itself. Granted the elaborate system of checks and balances: the separation of powers, the bicameral legislature, the executive veto, and so forth—checks found in the state constitutions as well, and in our own democratic era as in the earlier one—what provision did the framers make against majority tyranny? What provisions did they write into the Constitution against what Randolph called "democratic licentiousness"?

They granted equality of representation in the Senate. If this meant that conservative Delaware would have the same representation in the upper chamber as democratic Pennsylvania, it also meant that democratic Rhode Island would have the same representation as conservative South Carolina. But the decision for equality of representation was not dictated by considerations either economic or democratic, but rather by the recalcitrance of the small states. Indeed, though it is difficult to generalize here, on the whole it is true that it was the more ardent Federalists who favored proportional representation in both houses.

They elaborated a most complicated method of electing a Chief Executive, a method designed to prevent the easy expression of any majority will. Again the explanation is not simple. The fact was that the framers did not envision the possibility of direct votes for presidential candidates which would not conform to state lines and interests and thus lead to dissension and confusion. Some method, they thought, must be designated to overcome the force of state prejudices (or merely of parochialism) and get an election; the method they anticipated was a preliminary elimination contest by the electoral college and then eventual election by the House. This, said George Mason, was what would occur nineteen times out of twenty.* There is no

---

* It has happened twice: Jefferson vs. Burr (1801) and J. Q. Adams vs. Clay, Jackson, and Crawford (1825).

evidence in the debates that the complicated method finally hit upon for electing a President was designed either to frustrate popular majorities or to protect special economic interests; its purpose was to overcome state pride and particularism.

Senators and Presidents, then, would not be the creatures of democracy. But what guarantee was there that senators would be representatives of property interests, or that the President himself would recognize the "priority of property"? Most states had property qualifications for office holding, but there are none in the Federal Constitution. As far as the Constitution is concerned, the President, congressmen, and Supreme Court justices can all be paupers.

Both General Charles Cotesworth Pinckney and his young cousin Charles, of South Carolina, were worried about this. The latter proposed a property qualification of $100,000 (a tidy sum in those days) for the Presidency, half that for the judges, and substantial sums for members of Congress. Franklin rebuked him. He was distressed, he said, to hear anything "that tended to debase the spirit of the common people." More surprising was the rebuke from that stout conservative, John Dickinson. "He doubted," Madison reports, "the policy of interweaving into a Republican constitution a veneration for wealth. He had always understood that a veneration for poverty & virtue were the objects of republican encouragement." Pinckney's proposal was overwhelmingly rejected.

What of the members of the lower house? When Randolph opened "the main business" on May 29 he said the remedy for the crisis that men faced must be "the republican principle," and two days later members were discussing the fourth resolution, which provided for election to the lower house by the people. Roger Sherman of Connecticut thought that "the people should have as little to do as may be about the Government," and Gerry hastened to agree in words now well-worn from enthusiastic quotation that "The evils we experience flow from the excess of democracy." These voices were soon drowned out, however. Mason "argued strongly for an election . . . by the people. It was to be the grand depository of the democratic principle of the Govt." And the learned James Wilson, striking the note to which he was to recur again and again, made clear that he was for "raising the federal pyramid to a considerable altitude, and for that reason wished to give it as broad a basis as possible." He thought both branches of the legislature—and the President as well, for that matter—should be elected by the people. "The Legislature," he later observed, "ought to be the most exact transcript of the whole Society."

A further observation is unhappily relevant today. It was a maxim with John Adams that "where annual elections end, there tyranny begins," and the whole Revolutionary generation was committed to a frequent return to the source of authority. But the framers put into the Constitution no limits on the number of terms which Presidents or congressmen could serve. It was not that the question was ignored; it received elaborate attention. It was rather that the generation that wrote the Constitution was better grounded in political principles than is our own; that it did not confuse, as we so often do, quantitative and qualitative limitations; and that—in a curious way—it had more confidence in the intelligence and the good will of the people than we seem to have today. It is, in any event, our own generation that has the dubious distinction of writing into the Constitution the first quantitative limitation on the right of the majority to choose their President. It is not the generation of the framers that was undemocratic; it is our generation that is undemocratic.

It is relevant to note, too, that the Constitution contains no property qualification for voting. Most states, to be sure, had such qualifications—in general a freehold or its equivalent—and the Constitution assimilated such qualifications as states might establish. Yet the framers, whether for reasons practical or philosophical we need not determine, made no serious efforts to write any property qualifications for voting into the Constitution itself.

The question of popular control came up clearly in one other connection as well: the matter of ratification. Should the Constitution be ratified by state legislatures, or by conventions? The practical arguments for the two methods were nicely balanced. The decisive argument was not, however, one of expediency but of principle. "To the people with whom all power remains that has not been given up in the Constitutions derived from them" we must resort, said Mason. Madison put the matter on principle, too. "He considered the difference between a system founded on the Legislatures only, and one founded on the people, to be the true difference between a *league* or *treaty* and a *Constitution*." Ellsworth's motion to refer the Constitution to legislatures was defeated by a vote of eight to two, and the resolution to refer it to conventions passed with only Delaware in the negative.

Was the Constitution designed to place private property beyond the reach of majorities? If so, the framers did a very bad job. They failed to write into it the most elementary safeguards for property. They failed to write into it limitations on the tax power, or prohibitions against the abuse of the money power. They failed to provide for rule by those whom Adams was later to call the wise and the rich and the well-born. What they did succeed in doing was to create a system of checks and balances and adjustments and accommodations that would effectively prevent the suppression of most minorities by majorities. They took advantage of the complexity, the diversity, the pluralism, of American society and economy to encourage a balance of interests. They worked out sound and lasting political solutions to the problems of class, interest, section, race, religion, party.

Perhaps the most perspicacious comment on this whole question of the threat from turbulent popular majorities against property and order came, *mirabile dictu*, from the dashing young Charles Pinckney of South Carolina—he of the "lost" Pinckney Plan. On June 25 Pinckney made a major speech and thought it important enough to write out and give to Madison. The point of departure was the hackneyed one of the character of the second branch of the legislature, but the comments were an anticipation of De Tocqueville and Lord Bryce. We need not, Pinckney asserted, fear the rise of class conflicts in America, nor take precautions against them.

> The genius of the people, their mediocrity of situation & the prospects which are afforded their industry in a Country which must be a new one for centuries are unfavorable to the rapid distinction of ranks. . . . If equality is . . . the leading feature of the U. States [he asked], where then are the riches & wealth whose representation & protection is the peculiar province of this permanent body [the Senate]. Are they in the hands of the few who may be called rich; in the possession of less than a hundred citizens? certainly not. They are in the great body of the people . . . [There was no likelihood that a privileged body would ever develop in the United States, he added, either from the landed interest, the moneyed interest, or the mercantile.] Besides, Sir, I apprehend that on this point the policy of the U. States has been much mistaken. We have unwisely considered ourselves as the inhabitants of an old instead of a new country. We have adopted the maxims of a State full of people . . . The people of this country are not only very different from the inhabitants of any State we are acquainted with in the modern world; but I assert that their situation is distinct from either the people of Greece or of Rome . . . Our true situation appears to me to be this—a new extensive Country containing within itself the materials for forming a Government capable of extending to its citizens all the blessings of civil & religious liberty—capable of making them happy at home. This is the great end of Republican Establishments. . . .

Not a government cunningly contrived to protect the interests of property, but one capable of extending to its citizens the blessings of liberty and happiness—was that not, after all, what the framers created?

An early nineteenth-century allegory by John A. Woodside is symptomatic of the nationalistic fervor of the period. The triumphant seaman, his fetters broken, treads on England's crown and scepter.

Part Four

National Growing Pains

WE OWE ALLEGIANCE TO NO CROWN.

Henry Steele Commager
The Search for a Usable Past

One of the most remarkable things about the American nation, as Professor Commager points out in the following essay, is that it came into being before its people really had much sense of their common nationality. The word "American," used as a generalization for the common set of values and traditions possessed by the inhabitants of what is now the United States, did not exist before the middle of the eighteenth century, a mere generation before these inhabitants revolted against Great Britain and established the political organism called the United States. This was the case for a number of reasons, the most important probably being that most of the colonists came to America without much sense of psychological alienation from the mother country; they continued to think of themselves as Englishmen. Furthermore, the decentralized political structure imposed upon the colonies by Britain prevented for many decades the development of a general, or American, point of view: if settlers did not consider themselves primarily as Englishmen, they were likely to describe themselves as New Yorkers, Virginians, Pennsylvanians, and so on.

Thus, when the Revolution occurred and the nation was "born," it was necessary to create a national spirit, a sense of common identity. How this was accomplished is the theme of Commager's essay. This type of historical writing demands a well-stocked, imaginative mind, one that has ranged widely over the sources, exploring out-of-the-way as well as obvious records of the past. How well Commager fulfills these requirements is amply demonstrated in the following pages.

The United States was the first of the "new" nations. As the American colonies were the first to rebel against a European "mother country," so the American states were the first to create—we can use Lincoln's term, to bring forth—a new nation. Modern nationalism was inaugurated by the American, not the French, Revolution. But the new United States faced problems unknown to the new nations of nineteenth-century Europe—and twentieth. For in the Old World the nation came before the state; in America the state came before the nation. In the Old World nations grew out of well-prepared soil, built upon a foundation of history and traditions; in America the foundations were still to be laid, the seeds still to be planted, the traditions still to be formed.

The problem which confronted the new United States then was radically different from that which confronted, let us say, Belgium, Italy, Greece, or Germany in the nineteenth century, or Norway, Finland, Iceland, and Israel in the twentieth. These "new" states were already amply equipped with history, tradition, and memory—as well as with many of the other essential ingredients of nationalism except political independence. Of them it can be said that the nation was a product of history. But with the United States, history was rather a creation of the nation, and it is suggestive that in the New World the self-made nation was as familiar as the self-made man.

It is unnecessary to emphasize anything as familiar as the importance of history, tradition, and memory to successful nationalism. On this matter statesmen, historians, and philosophers of nationalism are all agreed. It was the very core of Edmund Burke's philosophy: the nation—society itself—is a partnership of past, present, and future; we (the English) "derive all we possess as an inheritance from our forefathers." It is indeed not merely the course of history but of nature itself. Thus Friedrich von Schlegel, trying to quicken a sense of nationalism in the Germans, urged that "nothing is so important as that the Germans . . . return to the course of their own language and poetry, and liberate from the old documents of their ancestral past that power of old, that noble spirit which . . . is sleeping in them." And Mazzini, in his struggle for the unification of Italy, was ever conscious that "the most important inspiration for nationalism is the awareness of past glories and past sufferings."

So, too, with the philosophers of nationalism, and the historians as well. Listen to Ernest Renan. In that famous lecture "What Is a Nation?" he emphasized "the common memories, sacrifices, glories, afflictions, and regrets," and submitted that the worthiest of all cults was "the cult of ancestors." So, too, with the hard-headed John Stuart Mill, across the Channel. "The strongest cause [for the feeling of nationality] is identity of political antecedents, the possession of a national history, and consequent community of recollections, collective pride and humiliation, pleasure and regret."

But if a historical past and a historical memory are indeed essential ingredients for a viable nationalism, what was the new United States to do in 1776, or in 1789, or for that matter at almost any time before the Civil War? How does a country without a past of her own acquire one, or how does she provide a substitute for it? Where could such a nation find the stuff for patriotism, for sentiment, for pride, for memory, for collective character? It was a question that came up very early, for Americans have always been somewhat uncomfortable about their lack of history and of antiquity, somewhat embarrassed about being historical *nouveaux riches.*

It was Henry James who put the question in most memorable form. I refer to the famous passage about the historical and intellectual environment in which the young Nathaniel Hawthorne found himself in 1840. It takes a great deal of history to make a little literature, said James, and how could Hawthorne make literature with a history so meager and so thin: "No state, in the European sense of the word, and indeed barely a specific national name. No sovereign, no court, no personal loyalty, no aristocracy, no church, no clergy, no army, no diplomatic service, no country gentlemen, no palaces, no castles, nor manors, nor old country houses, nor parsonages, nor thatched cottages, nor ivied ruins; no cathedrals, nor abbeys, nor little Norman churches; no great Universities, nor public schools, no Oxford nor Eton nor Harrow; no literature, no novels, no museums, no pictures, no political society, no sporting class—no Epsom nor Ascot!"

There is almost too much here; the indictment, as James himself remarked, is a lurid one, and he noted, too, with some satisfaction, that Hawthorne had not been wholly frustrated by the thinness of his materials—how he managed was, said James wryly, our private joke. It is suggestive that James' famous outburst was inspired by Hawthorne himself; he had, so he wrote, delighted in a place—his own dear native land—which had "no shadow, no antiquity, no mystery, no picturesque and gloomy wrong, nor anything but a commonplace prosperity, in broad and simple daylight, as is happily the case with my dear native land." It is worth dwelling on this for a moment, for this is from the author of *The Scarlet Letter,* and of *The House of Seven Gables,* and of a score of stories which did precisely dwell on shadows, antiquities, gloomy wrongs—witchcraft, for example. If a Hawthorne, who all his life felt it necessary to immerse himself in New England antiquities and inherited wrongs, could yet contrast his own dear native land with the Old World in these terms, think how unshadowed were the lives of most Americans—or how empty, if you want to adopt the James point of view.

A host of Americans had anticipated all this, but with different emphasis. Thus the poet Philip Freneau, introducing the abbé Robin's *New Travels in America:* "They who would saunter over half the Globe to copy the inscription on an antique column, to measure the altitude of a pyramid, or describe the ornaments on the Grand Seigneur's State Turban, will scarcely find anything in American Travels to gratify their taste. The works of art are there comparatively trivial and inconsiderable, the splendor of pageantry rather obscure, and consequently few or none but the admirers of simple Nature can either travel with pleasure themselves or read the travels of others with satisfaction, through this country." And half a century later James Fenimore Cooper, caught in that dilemma of New World innocence and Old World corruption so pervasive in the first century of our history, admitted that in America "there are no annals for the historian, no follies beyond the most vulgar and commonplace for the satirist; no manners for the dramatist; no obscure fictions for the writer of romance; no gross and hardy offenses against decorum for the moralist; nor any of the rich artificial auxiliaries of poetry."

But if there were "no annals for the historian," and if a historical past was necessary to nation-making, what were Americans to do?

Americans had, in fact, several courses open to them, and with characteristic self-confidence, took them all.

Over a century before the Revolution it had been observed of the Virginians that they had no need of ancestors, for they themselves were ancestors. The variations on this theme were infinite, but the theme was simple and familiar: that Americans had no need of a past because they were so sure of a future. Goethe had congratulated them on their good fortune in a famous but almost untranslatable poem: *Amerika, du hast es besser:* "no ruined castles, no venerable stones, no useless memories, no vain feuds [he said]. . . . May a kind providence preserve you from tales of knights and robber barons and ghosts."

Americans took up the refrain with enthusiasm. The romantic artist Thomas Cole observed that though American scenery was "destitute of the vestiges of antiquity" it had other features that were reassuring, for "American associations are not so much with the past as of the present and the future, and in looking over the uncultivated scene, the mind may travel far into futurity."

This theme runs like a red thread through early American literature and oratory, and finally connects itself triumphantly with Manifest Destiny. It began, appropriately enough, with Crèvecoeur: "I am sure I cannot be called a partial American when I say that the spectacle afforded by these pleasing scenes must be more entertaining and more philosophical than that which arises from beholding the musty ruins of Rome. Here everything would inspire the reflecting traveller with the most philanthropic ideas; his imagination, instead of submitting to the painful and useless retrospect of revolutions, desolations, and plagues, would, on the contrary, wisely spring forward to the anticipated fields of future cultivation and improvement, to the future extent of those generations which are to replenish and embellish this boundless continent." Washington Irving's friend and collaborator, James Paulding, entertained the same sentiment: "It is for the other nations to boast of what they have been, and, like garrulous age, muse over the history of their youthful exploits that only renders decrepitude more conspicuous. Ours is the more animating sentiment of hope, looking forward with prophetic eye."

Best of all is Cooper's John Cadwallader in *Notions of the Americans*, rebuking his travelling companion, the bachelor Count, for his unmanly longing for antiquity: "You complain of the absence of association to give its secret, and perhaps greatest charm which such a sight is capable of inspiring. You complain unjustly. The moral feeling with which a man of sentiment and knowledge looks upon the plains of your [Eastern] Hemisphere is connected with his recollections; here it should be mingled with his hopes. The same effort of the mind is as equal to the one as to the other.''

The habit of looking forward instead of back blended readily enough with Manifest Destiny. Thus John Louis O'Sullivan, who all but invented Manifest Destiny, dismissed the past in favor of the future: ''We have no interest in scenes of antiquity, only as lessons of avoidance of nearly all their examples. The expansive future is our arena. We are entering on its untrodden space with the truth of God in our minds, beneficent objects in our hearts, and with a clear conscience unsullied by the past. We are the nation of human progress, and who will, what can, set limits on our onward march? . . . The far-reaching, the boundless future will be the era of American greatness. . . .''

There was nothing surprising in Emerson's conclusion that America had no past. ''All,'' he said, ''has an outward and prospective look.'' For transcendentalism—the first genuine expression of the American temperament in philosophy, or New England's at least—was impatient with origins, put its confidence in inspiration, looked upon each day as a new epoch and each man as an Adam. It is difficult to exaggerate the impatience of the transcendentalists with the past. It was not so much that they were opposed to it as they found it irrelevant. And note that New England's major historians—Bancroft, Prescott, Ticknor, Motley, and Parkman—were all outside the mainstream of transcendentalism.

This was all very well, this confidence in the future. But it was, after all, pretty thin fare for nationalism to feed on at a time when other self-conscious nations were rejoicing in an ancient and romantic past. To be sure, the past became ancient and the future became present more rapidly in America than anywhere else: thus Thomas Jefferson could write from Paris in 1787 that much was to be said for keeping the ''good, old, venerable, fabrick'' of the six-year-old Articles of Confederation. And thus, too, John Randolph, in the Virginia ratifying convention, could ''take farewell of the Confederation, with reverential respect, as an old benefactor.''

Happily, there was a second formula to which Americans had recourse, and one no less convenient than the first: that America had, in fact, the most impressive of all pasts; *all* Europe was the American past. After all, we speak the tongue that Shakespeare spake—and for good measure, the tongues of Luther and Racine and Dante and Cervantes as well. Just because Americans had crossed the Atlantic Ocean did not mean that they had forfeited or repudiated their heritage. Americans enjoyed, in fact, the richest and most varied of all heritages. Other benighted peoples had only their past—the Danes a Danish, the Germans a German—but Americans had them all. Were we not in very truth a teeming nation of nations? Edward Everett asserted this as early as 1820: ''We suppose that in proportion to our population Lord Byron and Walter Scott are more read in America

than in England, nor do we see why we are not entitled to our full
share of all that credit which does not rest . . . in the person of the
author. . . ." Whitman made this the burden of "Thou Mother With
Thy Equal Brood":

Sail, sail thy best, ship of Democracy,
Of value is thy freight, 'tis not the Present only,
The Past is also stored in thee,
Thou holdest not the venture of thyself alone, not of the Western
*   Continent alone,*
Earth's résumé entire floats on thy keel O ship, is steadied by thy
*   spars, . . .*
Steer then with a good strong hand, and wary eye O helmsman,
*   thou carriest great companions,*
Venerable priestly Asia sails this day with thee,
And royal feudal Europe sails with thee.

All very well, but a risky business, this assimilation of the Old
World past. For could the Old World be trusted? Could the past be
trusted? We come here to one of the major themes of American
intellectual history, and one of the most troublesome of all the problems
in the creation of a usable past.

The theme of New World innocence and Old World corruption
emerged early, and persisted all through the nineteenth century: it is
a constant of American literature as of American politics, and if it no
longer haunts our literature, it still bedevils our politics and diplomacy.

How deeply they were shocked, these innocent Americans, by the
goings on in Europe! Benjamin Franklin, after a long residence in
England, could deprecate the notion of a reconciliation between the
Americans and the mother country on moral grounds: "I have not
heard what Objections were made to the Plan in the Congress, nor
would I make more than this one, that, when I consider the extreme
Corruption prevalent among all Orders of Men in this old rotten
State, and the glorious publick Virtue so predominant in our rising
Country, I cannot but apprehend more Mischief than Benefit from a
closer Union." Dr. Benjamin Rush, who had studied in Edinburgh
and in London, never ceased to preach the danger of contamination
from abroad. With Jefferson—surely the most cosmopolitan American
of his generation—New World innocence and Old World corruption
was almost an *idée fixe.* How illuminating, that famous letter to John
Banister about the education of his son. "Why send an American
youth to Europe for education? . . . Let us view the disadvantages.
. . . To enumerate them all, would require a volume. I will select a
few. If he goes to England, he learns drinking, horse racing, and boxing. These are the peculiarities of English education. The following
circumstances are common to education in that, and the other countries of Europe. He acquires a fondness for European luxury and dis-
sipation, and a contempt for the simplicity of his own country; he is
fascinated with the privileges of the European aristocrats and sees,
with abhorrence, the lovely equality which the poor enjoy with the

rich, in his own country; he contracts a partiality for aristocracy or monarchy; he forms foreign friendships which will never be useful to him . . . he is led, by the strongest of all the human passions, into a spirit for female intrigue, destructive of his own and others' happiness, or a passion for whores, destructive of his health, and, in both cases, learns to consider fidelity to the marriage bed as an ungentlemanly practice. . . . It appears to me, then, that an American coming to Europe for education, loses in his knowledge, in his morals, in his health, in his habits, and in his happiness. . . ."

The theme, and the arguments, persisted. Hezekiah Niles wrote on the eve of the War of 1812 that "the War, dreadful as it is, will not be without its benefits in . . . separating us from the *strumpet governments of Europe.*" It is the most persistent theme in American literature from Crèvecoeur to Tocqueville, from Hawthorne's *Marble Faun* to James' *Daisy Miller* and *Portrait of a Lady,* from *Innocents Abroad* to *The Sun Also Rises.* Something of its complexity and difficulty can be seen in the position of the expatriate. Here Americans long maintained a double standard; it was taken for granted not only that European immigrants to the United States give up their nationality and identify themselves with their adopted country, but that they do so exuberantly. But for Americans to give up their nationality and identify themselves with a foreign country was another matter.

Needless to say, there are philosophical and psychological implications here which we ignore at our peril. For this concept of New World innocence and Old World corruption encouraged that sense of being a people apart which nature herself had already sufficiently dramatized. How characteristic that Jefferson should have combined nature and morality in his first inaugural: "Kindly separated by nature from one quarter of the globe; too high-minded to endure the degradations of the others. . . ." To this day Americans are inclined to think that they are outside the stream of history, exempt from its burden.

But quite aside from the theme of Old World corruption, the availability of the European past was not a simple matter of chronological assimilation or absorption. It was available, to be sure, but only on limited terms. It was there more for purposes of contrast than for enrichment; it pointed the moral of American superiority, and adorned the tale of American escape from contamination. It was there, too, as a museum, a curio shop, and a moral playground. But for practical purposes it contributed little to the juices of American Life.

Americans had a third choice: They could use what they had. "We have not, like England and France, centuries of achievements and calamities to look back on," wrote the indefatigable diarist George Templeton Strong, "but being without the eras that belong to older nationalities—Anglo-Saxon, Carolingian, Hohenstaufen, Ghibelline, and so forth—we dwell on the details of our little all of historic life and venerate every trivial fact about our first settlers and colonial governors and revolutionary heroes." Not all Americans struck so modest a pose. All their past lacked, after all, was antiquity, and antiquity was relative; in any event, this meant that the American past was better authenticated than the European.

Nothing in the history of American nationalism is more impressive than the speed and the lavishness with which Americans provided themselves with a usable past: history, legends, symbols, paintings, sculpture, monuments, shrines, holy days, ballads, patriotic songs, heroes, and—with some difficulty—villains. Henry James speaks of Emerson dwelling for fifty years "within the undecorated walls of his youth." To Emerson they did not seem undecorated, for he embellished them with a profusion of historical association and of memory: the author of "Concord Hymn" was not unaware of the past.

Not every American, to be sure, was as deeply rooted as Emerson, but even to newcomers America soon ceased to be undecorated. Uncle Sam was quite as good as John Bull, and certainly more democratic. The bald eagle (Franklin sensibly preferred the turkey, but was overruled) did not compare badly with the British lion and was at least somewhat more at home in America than the lion in Britain. The Stars and Stripes, if it did not fall straight out of heaven like Denmark's *Dannebrog,* soon had its own mythology, and it had, besides, one inestimable advantage over all other flags, in that it provided an adjustable key to geography and a visible evidence of growth. Soon it provided the stuff for one of the greatest of all national songs—the tune difficult but the sentiments elevated—and one becoming to a free people. The Declaration of Independence was easier to understand than Magna Carta, and parts of it could be memorized and recited— as Magna Carta could not. In addition it had a Liberty Bell to toll its fame, which was something the British never thought of. There were no less than two national mottoes—*E pluribus unum,* selected, so appropriately, by Franklin, Jefferson, and John Adams, and *Novus ordo seclorum,* with their classical origins. There were no antiquities, but there were shrines: Plymouth Rock, of course, and Independence Hall and Bunker Hill and Mount Vernon and Monticello; eventually there was to be the Log Cabin in which Lincoln was born, as indestructible as the hull of the *Mayflower.*

These were some of the insignia, as it were, the ostentatious manifestations of the possession of a historical past. The stuff of that past was crowded and rich; it is still astonishing that Americans managed to fill their historical canvas so elaborately in so short a time. The colonial era provided a remote past: Pocahontas saving John Smith; the Pilgrims landing on the sandy coast of Plymouth, and celebrating the first Thanksgiving; Roger Williams fleeing through the wintry storms to Narragansett Bay; William Penn treating with the Indians; Deerfield going up in flames, its captives trekking through the snow to Canada; Franklin walking the streets of Philadelphia, munching those "three great puffy rolls" that came to be permanent props.

The Revolution proved a veritable cornucopia of heroic episodes and memories: Washington crossing the Delaware; Washington dwelling at Valley Forge; the signing of the Declaration; Captain Parker at Lexington Common: "If they mean to have a war, let it begin here!''; Prescott at Bunker Hill: "Don't fire until you see the

whites of their eyes!''; John Paul Jones closing with the *Serapis:*
''I have not yet begun to fight!''; Nathan Hale on the gallows: ''I only
regret that I have but one life to lose for my country''; Tom Paine
writing the first *Crisis* on the flat of a drum, by the flickering light of
campfires; George Rogers Clark wading through the flooded Wabash
bottom lands to capture Vincennes; Washington at Yorktown: ''The
World Turned Upside Down''; Washington, again, fumbling for his
glasses at Newburgh: ''I have grown gray in your service, and now
find myself growing blind''; Washington even in Heaven, not a
pagan Valhalla but a Christian Heaven, doubly authenticated by a
parson and a historian—one person to be sure—the incomparable
Parson Weems.

The War of 1812, for all its humiliations, made its own contributions to national pride. Americans conveniently forgot the humiliations
and recalled the glories: Captain Lawrence off Boston Harbor: ''Don't

*This painting of Washington's apotheosis was
done in China about 1800 by an unknown artist.*

give up the ship''; the *Constitution* riddling the *Guerrière;* Francis Scott Key peering through the night and the smoke to see if the flag was still there; Perry at Put-in-Bay: ''We have met the enemy and they are ours''; the hunters of Kentucky repulsing Pakenham—

> *There stood John Bull in Martial pomp*
> *But here was old Kentucky.*

No wonder Old Hickory went straight to the White House.

The West, too—not one West but many—provided a continuous flow of memories and experiences and came to be, especially for immigrants, a great common denominator. There was the West of the Indian; of Washington at Fort Necessity; the West of Daniel Boone; of Lewis and Clark; of the Santa Fe Trail and the Oregon Trail and the California Gold Rush; the West of the miner and the cowboy; the West of the Union Pacific trail and the other transcontinentals. ''If it be romance, if it be contrast, if it be heroism that we require,'' asked Robert Louis Stevenson, ''what was Troytown to this?'' What indeed?

And richest of all in its contribution to the storehouse of American memory was the Civil War, with its hero, Lincoln: it produced the best literature and the best songs of any modern war; it was packed with drama and with heroism. To one part of America it gave the common bond of defeat and tragedy, but a defeat that fed sentiment so powerful that it was metamorphosed into victory. It gave to the whole of America a dramatic sense of unity; to Negroes it associated national unity with freedom; and to all it gave the most appealing of national heroes, probably the only modern hero to rank with Alfred and Barbarossa and Joan of Arc. Certainly, of all modern heroes it is Lincoln who lends himself most readily to mythology; his birth humble and even mysterious; his youth gentle and simple; his speech pithy and wise; his wit homely and earthy; his counsels benign. He emerged briefly to save his nation and free the slaves, and died tragically as the lilacs bloomed; no wonder the poets and the myth-makers have exhausted themselves on this theme.

No less remarkable was the speed and comprehensiveness with which the new nation provided itself with an artistic record. From the beginning, to be sure, Americans had been fortunate in this realm; no other nation, it is safe to say, has had its entire history so abundantly recorded as the American, from the first contributions by Le Moyne and De Bry and John White to the realism of the Ash Can school of the early twentieth century. Never before in recorded history had anything excited the imagination like the discovery of the New World —O brave new world, O strange new world, new world that was Utopia and Paradise. Everything about it excited the explorers and conquerors: the Patagonian giants and the Amazons of Brazil and the pygmies of the Far North; the mountains that soared fifty miles into the clouds and the lakes as vast as continents and the caves of solid gold; the natives who were descended from the Chinese or the Jews or the Norwegians or the Welsh; the flora and fauna so strange they all but defied description. How to make clear the wonder and the terror of it all?

All the explorers were historians, to be sure; almost all of them were artists as well, and soon all Europe could share the wonder of those who had seen what men had never seen before. It was as if cartographers had given us maps of the voyages of the Phoenicians or of the Vikings; it was as if artists had pictured Hector and Agamemnon before the walls of Troy or Romulus founding the city that would bear his name, or Hengist and Horsa on the shores of Ebbsfleet!

Political independence brought with it artistic freedom, and an ardent preoccupation with the birth of the nation created the stirring political drama; the scenes of battle, lurid and triumphant; the Founding Fathers, grave, as became men occupying a sure place in history. In a generation when Franklin doubted the possibility and John Adams the propriety of art, a host of artists emerged, as if in defiance of counsels too sober; if they were not Rembrandts or Turners, they were better than anyone had any right to expect. It is not, however, their artistic merits that interest us, but their historical function. John Singleton Copley gave us a rich and crowded portrait gallery of colonial society in the process of becoming American—the merchants, the statesmen, the captains, and their ladies as well. John Trumbull regarded himself as the official painter of the Revolution and covered that chapter of history systematically though not comprehensively. Scarcely less impressive was the contribution of the versatile Charles Willson Peale, who left us a whole gallery of Founding Fathers as well as an academy of artistic sons, while the achievement of Gilbert Stuart in impressing on future generations his image of the Father of His Country is almost without parallel in the history of art. This school of artistic historians came to an end when its work was done, when it had provided posterity with artistic archives and monuments of its birth and its youth. Then the new nation, secure in the possession of an artistic record, could afford to indulge the romanticism of an Allston or a Cole, of the Hudson River school, or of genre painters like the puckish John Quidor—worthy companion to Washington Irving—or William Sidney Mount.

The celebration of independence and the founding of the republic was but one chapter in the history of the creation of an artistic image of the American past. Another school seized, almost instinctively, on the inexhaustible theme of the Indian and the winning of the West. Thus, while scores of American artists sailed for the Italian Arcadia, others, untrained, or trained in the irrelevant school of Düsseldorf, moved quite as confidently across the Alleghenies and on to the prairies and the plains and the mountains of the West. What a romantic group they were: the Swiss Carl Bodmer, who went with Prince Maximilian of Wied up the Missouri River in the early 1830's, and who gave us a crowded gallery of Sioux, Crees, Assiniboins, and Mandans; the indefatigable George Catlin with his hundreds of Indian portraits—surely the fullest artistic re-creation of the West before photography; Alfred Jacob Miller, who was the artist for Captain Stewart's explorations in the Far West and who sketched not only Indians but the landscape—Chimney Rock and Independence

Rock and the Tetons and the Wind River Mountains; the luckless John Mix Stanley, who was ubiquitous, from the lead mines of Galena to the Cherokee country, with Kearny on the Santa Fe Trail, one thousand miles by canoe up the Columbia, even to distant Hawaii—the work of a lifetime lost in the great Smithsonian fire of 1865.

Not all of these artists of the early West re-created the past for their own generation. Miller, for example, was not really known in his own day, nor was Stanley. Far more important in the creation of the popular image of America were two artist-ornithologists, Alexander Wilson and John James Audubon, who captured for all time the flora and fauna of America in its pastoral age. Wilson's nine-volume *American Ornithology* was perhaps the most ambitious work of science in the early republic. Soon came Audubon's *Birds of America,* less scientific than Wilson's *Ornithology* but more splendid, "the most magnificent monument" said Cuvier, "which art has ever raised to ornithology." And Audubon, of course, contributed more: his own extraordinary life and legend.

The sumptuous paintings of Wilson and Audubon reached the public only gradually, and in cheap reproductions. More effective was the impact of the almost forgotten school of panoramists. The hapless John Vanderlyn, who had dared display his nude *Ariadne* to an outraged public, introduced the panorama, in a specially built rotunda in New York's City Hall Park. But it was Versailles and Athens and Mexico which he chose to display; perhaps that is why he failed. His successors preferred to reveal America, and particularly the Father of Waters, which had the advantage of being almost the only object of nature longer than their paintings. One John Rowson Smith did a panorama of the Mississippi as early as 1844; when he displayed it at Saratoga Springs, New York, he took in twenty thousand dollars in six weeks. Soon there were a dozen rivals in the field: John Banvard, for example, who claimed that his Mississippi panorama was three miles long (actually it was only a quarter of a mile—a bad calculation, that). Poor John Stanley, who had so little luck with his Indian paintings, scored a tremendous success with a panorama of the *Western Wilds,* forty-two episodes, no less, requiring a minimum of two hours to view! Greatest of all the panoramists was Henry Lewis, who managed to cover almost three quarters of a mile of canvas with his paintings; his earnings from his great panorama enabled him to settle in Düsseldorf and learn to paint. Whatever their artistic merits, or demerits, the panoramas helped give a whole generation of Americans some feeling for the spaciousness and the beauty of the early West.

Writing in 1841, Emerson had lamented that "banks and tariffs, the newspaper and caucus, Methodism and Unitarianism, are flat and dull to dull people but rest on the same foundations of wonder as the town of Troy and the temple of Delphi. . . . Our logrolling, our stumps and their politics, our fisheries, our Negroes and Indians, our boasts and our repudiations . . . the northern trade, the southern planting, the western clearing, Oregon and Texas, are yet unsung. Yet America

is a poem in our eyes; its ample geography dazzles the imagination.''
Poets and artists had responded, but none had quite encompassed
American nature. Even Whitman and Winslow Homer could not
quite do that. For nature played a special role in American history and
in the process of creating a sense of history and a national consciousness. Since the seventeenth century, Europeans have not had to concern themselves energetically with the conquest of nature, for nature,
like history, was given. For Americans, on the other hand, the relationship to nature was more personal, and more complex. They had an
empty continent to settle and successive frontiers to conquer, and for
them nature had always played a twofold role: her ruggedness was a
challenge, and her richness a manifestation of divine favor. How
suggestive it is that for over two hundred years Europeans could not
make up their minds whether the New World was Paradise or an
accursed place, whether its natives were Noble Savages or degenerate
men without souls. But however nature was to be interpreted—and
by the nineteenth century the paradisiacal interpretation had
triumphed—it was, in a peculiar way, the great common denominator
and the great common experience. Virginians, Pilgrims, and Quakers
alike could rejoice in the abundance of nature, and generations of
pioneers, even those who were not *Mayflower* descendants or FFV's,
could cherish the common memory of hardship endured and overcome.

Because they had conquered nature, Americans came in time to
think that they had created it and to display toward it a proprietary
interest. The stupendous flow of Niagara, the luxuriance of the Blue-
grass, the power and majesty of the Father of Waters, the limitless
expanse of prairie and plain, the glory of the Rockies—all of these
came to be regarded as national attributes, and failure to appreciate
them, like failure to appreciate political attributes, an affront. How
interesting that from ''Swanee River'' to ''Ol' Man River'' songs
celebrating nature have usurped the place of formal patriotic music
—''Dixie,'' for example, or ''My Old Kentucky Home,'' or ''On the
Banks of the Wabash,'' or ''Home on the Range,'' or best of all,
''America, the Beautiful.''

And how interesting, too, that where in other countries topography
is local, in America it is national. In the Old World, plains, valleys,
and mountains belong to the people who happen to inhabit them,
but in America the whole country, ''from sea to shining sea,'' belongs
to the whole people. The Italians and Germans traditionally celebrate
their own cities, their particular churches or bridges; the English
write two-volume works on Fly-casting in the Dart, or Cricket in
Lower Slaughter, but until recently there has been little of this local
possessiveness about Americans. ''We have so much country that we
have no country at all,'' Hawthorne lamented back in 1837, but
Hawthorne was far from typical, and newcomers who could find little
satisfaction in the slums of New York or the coal mines of Pennsylvania
or the steel mills of Gary might yet rejoice in the Great Lakes and
Yosemite. Movement, especially westward movement, is an essential
ingredient in the American memory. When John F. Kennedy hit on

the slogan, "Get America moving," he touched a responsive chord.

The task of providing themselves with a historical past was peculiarly difficult for Americans because it was not something that could be taken for granted, as with most peoples, or arranged once and for all. It was something that had to be done over and over again, for each new wave of newcomers, and that had to be kept up to date, as it were, continually reinvigorated and modernized. Above all, it had to be a past which contained an ample supply of easily grasped common denominators for a heterogeneous people, English and German, Irish and Norse, white and black, gentile and Jew, Protestant, Mormon, and Catholic, old stock and newcomer. Almost inevitably the common denominators tended to be pictorial and symbolic: the Pilgrims and Valley Forge, Washington and Lincoln, cowboy and Indian, and along with them ideas and institutions like Democracy, Liberty, Equality, the American Dream, and the American Way of Life.

One consequence of this emphasis on the simple, the symbolic, and the ideological is that American patriotism tended to be more artificial, labored, and ostentatious than that of most Old World peoples. It was almost inevitably calculated and artificial: after all, the process of drawing the juices of tradition for a German boy newly arrived in America was very different from that for a French or an English lad at home, where everything could be taken for granted, or left to nature. Tradition in America had to be labored, for it was not born into the young; it did not fill the horizon, as the glory of Joan of Arc or the fame of Nelson filled the horizons of French and English boys and girls. The American past could not be absorbed from childhood on in the art and architecture of every town and village, in song and story and nursery rhyme, in novel and history, in the names of streets and squares and towns. Growing up in Pittsburgh or Chicago was a very different experience, historically, from growing up in London or Edinburgh, Paris or Rome. And patriotism probably had to be ostentatious; in any event, it is. Ostentation characterizes new wealth, and new loyalties as well. This is doubtless one reason there is so much emphasis on the overt observance of patriotism in America. Americans dedicate a large number of days to ceremonial patriotism: the Fourth of July, Memorial Day, Confederate Memorial Day, Veterans Day, Washington's Birthday, Lincoln's Birthday, Columbus Day, Loyalty Day, and many others, and for good measure many states have their own special holidays—Patriots' Day in Massachusetts or Texas Independence Day. Americans require children to "pledge allegiance to the flag," impose loyalty oaths for every conceivable occasion, and march in "I Am an American Day" parades, and there is no W. S. Gilbert to satirize what so many take with passionate seriousness. Perhaps nowhere else in the Western world is loyalty such a touchstone as in the United States, perhaps nowhere else are there so many organizations dedicated to fostering patriotism: the Daughters of the American Revolution, the Sons of the American Revolution, the Colonial Dames, the United Daughters of the Confederacy, the Americanism committees of the great veterans' organizations, and, more recently, the Minute Women.

The process of acquiring a usable past was immensely facilitated by two extraordinary circumstances. The first was the eagerness of almost all newcomers from every part of the globe to slough off their pasts and take on an American habit, an eagerness so avid and so pervasive that it made nonsense of the compunctions and fears of native Americans from Fisher Ames to Thomas Bailey Aldrich a century later. Perhaps no other society in the process of transforming itself into a nation had more co-operative material to work with. The American newcomer, as he told us over and over again, was under both moral and practical compulsions to achieve acceptance for himself and for his children by becoming completely American as rapidly and as thoroughly as possible. Crèvecoeur, who saw so much, saw this, and so too the magisterial Tocqueville, but it is a lesson that has had to be relearned in every generation.

That it was *possible* for newcomers to become American overnight was the second circumstance. The explanation here lies in large part in the high degree of literacy that obtained in America, even in the eighteenth century, and the tradition of literacy and of education that flourished in that and the next century. Schools proved, in the long run, the most effective agencies for the creation and the transmission of an American memory. If they did not deliberately inculcate Americanism, that was because they did not need to: Noah Webster's Spellers, McGuffey's many Readers, Jedidiah Morse's Geographies and Peter Parley's Histories—these and scores of books like them conjured up an American past and provided, for generations of children, the common denominators, the stories and songs and poems, the memories and symbols. And it was the children, in turn, who educated the parents, for America is the only country where, as a matter of course, it is assumed that each new generation is wiser and more sophisticated than the old, and where parents adopt the standards of their children rather than children adopting those of their parents. For newcomers too old for school, and too inflexible to learn from their children, the work of providing an American past was carried on by voluntary organizations which have always performed the most miscellaneous of social tasks: churches, political parties, labor unions, lyceums, fraternal and filiopietistic organizations, and so forth.

What this meant was that the sentiment of American nationalism was, to an extraordinary degree, a literary creation, and that the national memory was a literary and, in a sense, a contrived memory. The contrast here with the Old World is sharp. There the image of the past was conjured up and sustained by a thousand testimonials: folklore and folk song, the vernacular and the patois, church music and architecture, monuments, paintings and murals, the pageantry of the court and of popular feasts and holidays. To be sure, literature —poetry and drama and formal histories—came to play a role, but only when it was quarried from cultural foundations that went deep. In America the image of the past was largely the creation of the poets and the storytellers, and chiefly of the New England-New York group who flourished between the War of 1812 and the War for the Union, that group familiar to an earlier generation through the amiable game of Authors: Irving, Cooper, and Bryant; Longfellow, Hawthorne, and Whittier; Emerson, Lowell, and Holmes. These were the Founding Fathers of American literary nationalism, and their achievement was scarcely less remarkable than that of the Founding Fathers of political nationalism.

In a single generation these men of letters gave Americans the dramas, the characters, the settings, which were to instruct and delight succeeding generations: Uncas and Deerslayer and Long Tom Coffin; Rip Van Winkle and the Headless Horseman; Miles Standish, Paul Revere, Evangeline, and Hiawatha; Goodman Brown, the Grey Champion, and Hester Prynne, as well as the Salem Customs House, the House of Seven Gables, the Old Manse, and the Great Stone Face; Skipper Ireson and Concord Bridge and Old Ironsides and the One-Hoss Shay and Hosea Biglow with all his Yankee company.

Note that this image of the past which the literary Founding Fathers created and imposed upon Americans was very largely a New England image, and much that was most distinctive about American nationalism was to be conditioned by this circumstance. It meant that Americans on Iowa prairies or the plains of Texas would sing *"I love thy rocks and rills, thy woods and templed hills"* with no sense of incongruity; that Plymouth would supplant Jamestown as the birthplace of America; that Thanksgiving Day would be a New England holiday; that Paul Revere would be the winged horseman of American history and Concord Bridge the American equivalent of the Rubicon; that Boston's Statehouse would vindicate its claim—or Holmes'—to be the "hub of the solar system." If all this was hard on the South, southerners had only themselves to blame for their indifference to their own men of letters. The most familiar of southern symbols came from the North: Harriet Beecher Stowe of New England gave us Uncle Tom and Little Eva and Topsy and Eliza, while it was Stephen Foster of Pittsburgh who sentimentalized the Old South, and even "Dixie" had northern origins.

The literary task of creating a usable past was largely performed by 1865; after that date perhaps only Mark Twain, Bret Harte, and Louisa May Alcott added anything substantial to the treasure house of historical memories. This was, in perspective, the most significant achievement of American literature and one almost without parallel in the literature of any other country in a comparable period. How interesting that a people supposed to be indifferent to literature—supposed by some to have no literature—should depend so largely upon literature for the nourishment of its historical self-consciousness. Certainly the speed and effectiveness with which Americans rallied their resources to supply themselves with a historical past cannot but excite astonishment. And what a past it was—splendid, varied, romantic, and all but blameless, in which there were heroes but no villains, victories but no defeats—a past that was all prologue to the Rising Glory of America.

John A. Garraty
Marbury v. Madison

One of the most remarkable aspects of the Constitution of the United States (and the secret of its longevity) is its flexibility. A form of government designed to deal with the problems of a handful of farmers, merchants, and craftsmen scattered along a thousand miles of coastline, separated from one another by acres of forest and facing the trackless western wilderness, has endured with a minimum of changes through nearly two centuries, in which the nation has occupied a continental domain and become an urban-industrial behemoth.

A major reason for the flexibility of the Constitution has been the system of judicial review, which exists in the document largely by implication, but which has nonetheless functioned with enormous effectiveness. The following essay deals with one of the great landmarks in the development of the power of the Supreme Court to interpret the meaning of the Constitution and thus define the powers of both the federal government and the states. The case of *Marbury v. Madison,* like so many controversies that crucially affected the Constitution, was in itself of no importance. A minor federal official, deprived of his office by a technicality, was seeking redress from the Court. But in deciding his fate, the Court laid down a principle that altered the whole future of the country, shaping events that neither Marbury, nor Madison, nor the framers of the Constitution could possibly have anticipated.

*I*t was the evening of March 3, 1801, his last day in office, and President John Adams was in a black and bitter mood. Assailed by his enemies, betrayed by some of his most trusted friends, he and his Federalist party had gone down to defeat the previous November before the forces of Thomas Jefferson. His world seemed to have crumbled about his doughty shoulders.

Conservatives of Adams' persuasion were deeply convinced that Thomas Jefferson was a dangerous radical. He would, they thought, in the name of individual liberty and states' rights, import the worst excesses of the French Revolution, undermine the very foundations of American society, and bring the proud edifice of the national government, so laboriously erected under Washington and Adams, tumbling to the ground. Jefferson was a "visionary," Chief Justice Oliver Ellsworth had said. With him as President, "there would be no national energy." Ardent believers in a powerful central government like Secretary of State John Marshall feared that Jefferson would "sap the fundamental principles of government." Others went so far as to call him a "howling atheist."

Adams himself was not quite so disturbed as some, but he was deeply troubled. "What course is it we steer?" he had written despairingly to an old friend after the election. "To what harbor are we bound?" Now on the morrow Jefferson was to be inaugurated, and Adams was so disgruntled that he was unwilling to remain for the ceremonies, the first to be held in the new capital on the Potomac. At the moment, however, John Adams was still President of the United States, and not yet ready to abandon what he called "all virtuous exertion" in the pursuit of his duty. Sitting at his desk in the damp, drafty, still-unfinished sandstone mansion soon to be known as "the White House," he was writing his name on official papers in his large, quavering hand.

The documents he was signing were mostly commissions formally appointing various staunch Federalists to positions in the national judiciary, but the President did not consider his actions routine. On the contrary: he believed he was saving the republic itself. Jefferson was to be President and his Democratic-Republicans would control the Congress, but the courts, thank goodness, would be beyond his control: as soon as the extent of Jefferson's triumph was known, Adams had determined to make the judiciary a stronghold of Federalism. Responding enthusiastically to his request for expansion of the courts, the lame-duck Congress had established sixteen new circuit judgeships (and a host of marshals, attorneys, and clerks as well). It had also given Adams blanket authority to create as many justices of the peace for the new District of Columbia as he saw fit, and—to postpone the evil day when Jefferson would be able to put one of his sympathizers on the Supreme Court—it provided that when the next vacancy occurred, it should not be filled, thus reducing the Court from six justices to five. (The Constitution says nothing about the number of justices on the Court; its size is left to Congress. Originally six, the membership was enlarged to seven in 1807. The justices first numbered nine in 1837. Briefly during the Civil War the bench held ten; the number was set at seven again in 1866 and in 1869 returned to nine, where it has remained.)

In this same period between the election and the inauguration of the new President, Chief Justice Ellsworth, who was old and feeble, had resigned, and Adams had replaced him with Secretary of State Marshall. John Marshall was primarily a soldier and politician; he knew relatively little of the law. But he had a powerful mind, and, as Adams reflected, his "reading of the science" was "fresh in his head." He was also but forty-five years of age, and vigorous. Clearly a long life lay ahead of him, and a more forceful opponent of Jeffersonian principles would have been hard to find.

Marshall had been confirmed by the Senate on January 27, and without resigning as Secretary of State he had begun at once to help Adams strengthen the judicial branch of the government. They had worked rapidly, for time was short. The new courts were authorized by Congress on February 13; within two weeks Adams had submitted a full slate of officials for confirmation by the Senate. The new justices of the peace for the District of Columbia were authorized on February 27; within three days Adams had submitted for confirmation the names of no less than forty-two justices for the sparsely populated region. The Federalist Senate had done its part nobly, pushing through the various confirmations with great dispatch. Now, in the lamplight of his last night in Washington, John Adams was affixing his signature to the commissions of these "midnight justices," as the last-minute appointees were to become derisively known.

Working with his customary puritanical diligence, Adams completed his work by nine o'clock, and when he went off to bed for the last time as President of the United States, it was presumably with a clear conscience. The papers were carried to the State Department, where Secretary Marshall was to affix the Great Seal of the United States to each, and see to it that the commissions were then dispatched to the new appointees. But Marshall, a Virginian with something of the southerner's easygoing carelessness about detail, failed to complete this routine task.

All the important new circuit judgeships were taken care of, and most of the other appointments as well. But in the bustle of last-minute arrangements, the commissions of the new justices of the peace for the District of Columbia went astray. As a result of this trivial slip-up, and entirely without anyone's having planned it, a fundamental principle of the Constitution—affecting the lives of countless millions of future Americans—was to be established. Because *Secretary of State* Marshall made his last mistake, *Chief Justice* Marshall was soon to make one of the first—and in some respects the greatest—of his decisions.

It is still not entirely clear what happened to the missing commissions on the night of March 3. To help with the rush of work, Adams had borrowed two State Department clerks, Jacob Wagner and Daniel Brent. Brent prepared a list of the forty-two new justices and gave it to another clerk, who filled in the blank commissions. As fast as batches of these were made ready, Brent took them to Adams' office, where he turned them over to William Smith Shaw, the President's private secretary. After they were signed, Brent brought them back to the State Department, where Marshall was supposed to affix the Great Seal. Evidently he did seal these documents, but he did not trouble to make sure that they were delivered to the appointees. As he later said: "I did not send out the commissions because I apprehended such . . . to be completed when signed & sealed." Actually, he admitted, he would have sent them out in any case "but for the extreme hurry of the time & the absence of Mr. Wagner who had been called on by the President to act as his private secretary."

March 4 dawned and Jefferson, who apparently had not yet digested the significance of Adams' partisan appointments, prepared to take the oath of office and deliver his inaugural address. His mood, as the brilliant speech indicated, was friendly and conciliatory. He even asked Chief Justice Marshall, who administered the inaugural oath, to stay on briefly as Secretary of State while the new administration was getting established. That morning it would still have been possible to deliver the commissions. As a matter of fact, a few actually were delivered, although quite by chance.

Marshall's brother James (whom Adams had just made circuit judge for the District of Columbia) was disturbed by rumors that there was going to be a riot in Alexandria in connection with the inaugural festivities. Feeling the need of some justices of the peace in case trouble developed, he went to the State Department and personally picked up a number of the undelivered commissions. He signed a receipt for them, but "finding that he could not conveniently carry the whole," he returned several, crossing out the names of these from the receipt. Among the ones returned were those appointing William Harper and Robert Townsend Hooe. By failing to deliver these commissions, Judge James M. Marshall unknowingly enabled Harper and Hooe, obscure men, to win for themselves a small claim to legal immortality.

The new President was eager to mollify the Federalists, but when he realized the extent to which Adams had packed the judiciary with his "most ardent political enemies," he was indignant. Adams' behavior, he said at the time, was an "outrage on decency," and some years later, when passions had cooled a little, he wrote sorrowfully: "I can say with truth that one act of Mr. Adams' life, and one only, ever gave me a moment's personal displeasure. I did consider his last appointments to office as personally unkind." When he discovered the justice-of-the-peace commissions in the State Department, he decided at once not to allow them to be delivered.

James Madison, the Secretary of State, was not yet in Washington. Jefferson called in his Attorney General, a Massachusetts lawyer named Levi Lincoln, whom he had designated Acting Secretary. Giving Lincoln a new list of justices of the peace, he told him to put them "into a general commission" and notify the men of their selection.

Thomas Jefferson,
by Gilbert Stuart.

In truth, Jefferson acted with remarkable forbearance. He reduced the number of justices to thirty, fifteen for the federal District, fifteen for Alexandria County. But only seven of his appointees were his own men; the rest he chose from among the forty-two names originally submitted by Adams. Lincoln prepared two general commissions, one for each area, and notified the appointees. Then, almost certainly, he destroyed the original commissions signed by Adams.

For some time thereafter Jefferson did very little about the way Adams had packed the judiciary. Indeed, despite his much-criticized remark that office holders seldom die and never resign, he dismissed relatively few persons from the government service. For example, the State Department clerks, Wagner and Brent, were permitted to keep their jobs. The new President learned quickly how hard it was to institute basic changes in a going organization. "The great machine of society" could not easily be moved, he admitted, adding that it was impossible "to advance the notions of a whole people suddenly to ideal right." Soon some of his more impatient supporters, like John Randolph of Roanoke, were grumbling about the President's moderation.

But Jefferson was merely biding his time. Within a month of the inauguration he conferred with Madison at Monticello and made the basic decision to try to abolish the new system of circuit courts. Aside from removing the newly appointed marshals and attorneys, who served at the pleasure of the Chief Executive, little could be done until the new Congress met in December. Then, however, he struck. In his first annual message he urged the "contemplation" by Congress of the

Judiciary Act of 1801. To direct the lawmakers' thinking, he submitted a statistical report showing how few cases the federal courts had been called upon to deal with since 1789. In January, 1802, a repeal bill was introduced; after long debate it passed early in March, thus abolishing the jobs of the new circuit judges.

Some of those deposed petitioned Congress for "relief," but their plea was coldly rejected. Since these men had been appointed for life, the Federalists claimed that the repeal act was unconstitutional, but to prevent the Supreme Court from quickly so declaring, Congress passed another bill abolishing the June term of the Court and setting the second Monday of February, 1803, for its next session. By that time, the Jeffersonians reasoned, the old system would be dead beyond resurrection.

This powerful assault on the courts thoroughly alarmed the conservative Federalists; to them the foundations of stable government seemed threatened if the "independence" of the judiciary could be thus destroyed. No one was more disturbed than the new Chief Justice, John Marshall, nor was anyone better equipped by temperament and intellect to resist it. Headstrong but shrewd, contemptuous of detail and of abstractions but a powerful logician, he detested Jefferson (to whom he was distantly related), and the President fully returned his dislike.

In the developing conflict Marshall operated at a disadvantage that in modern times a Chief Justice would not have to face. The Supreme Court had none of the prestige and little of the accepted authority it now possesses. Few cases had come before it, and few of these were of any great importance. Before appointing Marshall, Adams had offered the Chief Justiceship to John Jay, the first man to hold the post, as an appointee of President Washington. Jay had resigned from the Court in 1795 to become governor of New York. He refused the reappointment, saying that the Court lacked "energy, weight, and dignity." A prominent newspaper of the day referred to the Chief Justiceship, with considerable truth, as a "sinecure." One of the reasons Marshall had accepted the post was his belief that it would afford him ample leisure for writing the biography of his hero, George Washington. Indeed, in the grandiose plans for the new capital, no thought had been given to housing the Supreme Court, so that when Marshall took office in 1801 the justices had to meet in the office of the clerk of the Senate, a small room on the first floor of what is now the north wing of the Capitol.

Nevertheless, Marshall struck out at every opportunity against the power and authority of the new President; but the opportunities were pitifully few. In one case, he refused to allow a presidential message to be read into the record on the ground that this would bring the President into the Court, in violation of the principle of separation of powers. In another, he ruled that Jefferson's decision in a prize case involving an American privateer was illegal. But these were matters of small importance.

When he tried to move more boldly, his colleagues would not sustain him. He was ready to declare the judicial repeal act unconstitutional, but none of the deposed circuit court judges would bring a case to court. Marshall also tried to persuade his associates that it was unconstitutional for Supreme Court justices to ride the circuit, as they were forced again to do by the abolishment of the lower courts. But although they agreed with his legal reasoning, they refused to go along —because, they said, years of acquiescence in the practice lent sanction to the old law requiring it. Thus frustrated, Marshall was eager for any chance to attack his enemy, and when a case that was to be known as *Marbury v. Madison* came before the Court in December, 1801, he took it up with gusto.

William Marbury, a forty-one-year-old Washingtonian, was one of the justices of the peace for the District of Columbia whose commissions Jefferson had held up. Originally from Annapolis, he had moved to Washington to work as an aide to the first Secretary of the Navy, Benjamin Stoddert. It was probably his service to this staunch Federalist that earned him the appointment by Adams. Together with one Dennis Ramsay and Messrs. Harper and Hooe, whose commissions James Marshall had *almost* delivered, Marbury was asking the Court to issue an order (a writ of mandamus) requiring Secretary of State Madison to hand over their "missing" commissions. Marshall willingly assumed jurisdiction and issued an order calling upon Madison to show cause at the next term of the Supreme Court why such a writ should not be issued. Here clearly was an opportunity to get at the President through one of his chief agents, to assert the authority of the Court over the executive branch of the government.

This small controversy quickly became a matter of great moment both to the administration and to Marshall. The decision to do away with the June term of the Court was made in part to give Madison more time before having to deal with Marshall's order. The abolition of the circuit courts and the postponement of the next Supreme Court session to February, 1803, made Marshall even more determined to use the Marbury case to attack Jefferson. Of course Marshall was personally and embarrassingly involved in this case, since his carelessness was the cause of its very existence. He ought to have disqualified himself, but his fighting spirit was aroused, and he was in no mood to back out.

On the other hand, the Jeffersonians used every conceivable means to obstruct judicial investigation of executive affairs. Madison ignored Marshall's order. When Marbury and Ramsay called on the Secretary to inquire whether their commissions had been duly signed (Hooe and Harper could count on the testimony of James Marshall to prove that theirs had been attended to), Madison gave them no satisfactory answer. When they asked to *see* the documents, Madison referred them to the clerk, Jacob Wagner. He, in turn, would only say that the commissions were not then in the State Department files.

Unless the plaintiffs could prove that Adams had appointed them, their case would collapse. Frustrated at the State Department, they turned to the Senate for help. A friendly senator introduced a motion calling upon the Secretary of the Senate to produce the record of the action in executive session on their nominations. But the motion was defeated, after an angry debate, on January 31, 1803. Thus, tempers were hot when the Court finally met on February 9 to deal with the case.

In addition to Marshall, only Justices Bushrod Washington (a nephew of the first President) and Samuel Chase were on the bench, and the Chief Justice dominated the proceedings. The almost childishly obstructive tactics of administration witnesses were no match for his fair but forthright management of the hearing. The plaintiffs' lawyer was Charles Lee, an able advocate and brother of "Light-Horse Harry" Lee; he had served as Attorney General under both Washington and Adams. He was a close friend of Marshall, and his dislike of Jefferson had been magnified by the repeal of the Judiciary Act of 1801, for he was another of the circuit court judges whose "midnight" appointments repeal had cancelled.

Lee's task was to prove that the commissions had been completed by Adams and Marshall, and to demonstrate that the Court had authority to compel Madison to issue them. He summoned Wagner and Brent, and when they objected to being sworn because "they were clerks in the Department of State, and not bound to disclose any facts relating to the business or transactions in the office," Lee argued that in addition to their "confidential" duties as agents of the President, the Secretary and his deputies had duties "of a public nature" delegated to them by Congress. They must testify about these public matters just as, in a suit involving property, a clerk in the land office could be compelled to state whether or not a particular land patent was on file.

Marshall agreed, and ordered the clerks to testify. They then disclosed many of the details of what had gone on in the presidential mansion and in the State Department on the evening of March 3, 1801, but they claimed to be unsure of what had become of the plaintiffs' commissions.

Next Lee called Attorney General Levi Lincoln. He too objected strenuously to testifying. He demanded that Lee submit his questions in writing so that he might consider carefully his obligations both to the Court and to the President before making up his mind. He also suggested that it might be necessary for him to exercise his constitutional right (under the Fifth Amendment) to refuse to give evidence that might, as he put it, "criminate" him. Lee then wrote out four questions. After studying them, Lincoln asked to be excused from answering, but the justices ruled against him. Still hesitant, the Attorney General asked for time to consider his position further, and Marshall agreed to an overnight adjournment.

The next day, the tenth of February, Lincoln offered to answer all Lee's questions but the last: What had he done with the commissions? He had seen "a considerable number of commissions" signed and sealed, but could not remember—he claimed—whether the plaintiffs' were among them. He did not know if Madison had ever seen these documents, but was certain that *he* had not given them to the Secretary. On the basis of this last statement, Marshall ruled that the embarrass-

John Marshall,
by Chester Harding.

ing question as to what Lincoln had done with the commissions was irrelevant; he excused Lincoln from answering it.

Despite these reluctant witnesses, Lee was able to show conclusively through affidavits submitted by another clerk and by James Marshall that the commissions had been signed and sealed. In his closing argument he stressed the significance of the case as a test of the principle of judicial independence. "The emoluments or the dignity of the office," he said, "are no objects with the applicants." This was undoubtedly true; the positions were unimportant, and two years of the five-year terms had already expired. As Jefferson later pointed out, the controversy itself had become "a moot case" by 1803. But Marshall saw it as a last-ditch fight against an administration campaign to make lackeys of all federal judges, while Jefferson looked at it as an attempt by the Federalist-dominated judiciary to usurp the power of the executive.

In this controversy over principle, Marshall and the Federalists were of necessity the aggressors. The administration boycotted the hearings. After Lee's summation, no government spokesman came forward to argue the other side, Attorney General Lincoln coldly announcing that he "had received no instructions to appear." With his control over Congress, Jefferson was content to wait for Marshall to act. If he overreached himself, the Chief Justice could be impeached. If he backed down, the already trifling prestige of his Court would be further reduced.

Marshall had acted throughout with characteristic boldness; quite possibly it was he who had persuaded the four aggrieved justices of the peace to press their suit in the first place. But now his combative temperament seemed to have driven him too far. As he considered the Marbury case after the close of the hearings, he must have realized this himself, for he was indeed in a fearful predicament. However sound his logic and just his cause, he was on very dangerous ground. Both political partisanship and his sense of justice prompted him to issue the writ sought by Marbury and his fellows, but what effect would the mandamus produce? Madison almost certainly would ignore it, and Jefferson would back him up. No power but public opinion could make the executive department obey an order of the Court. Since Jefferson was riding the crest of a wave of popularity, to issue the writ would be a futile act of defiance; it might even trigger impeachment proceedings against Marshall that, if successful, would destroy him and reduce the Court to servility.

Yet what was the alternative? To find against the petitioners would be to abandon all principle and surrender abjectly to Jefferson. This a man of Marshall's character could simply not consider. Either horn of the dilemma threatened utter disaster; that it was disaster essentially of his own making could only make the Chief Justice's discomfiture the more complete.

But at some point between the close of the hearings on February 14 and the announcement of his decision on the twenty-fourth, Marshall found a way out. It was an inspired solution, surely the cleverest of his long career. It provided a perfect escape from the dilemma, which probably explains why he was able to persuade the associate justices to agree to it despite the fact that it was based on the most questionable legal logic. The issue, Marshall saw, involved a conflict between the Court and the President, the problem being how to check the President without exposing the Court to his might. Marshall's solution was to state vigorously the justice of the plaintiffs' cause and to condemn the action of the Chief Executive, but to deny the Court's power to provide the plaintiffs with relief.

Marbury and his associates were legally entitled to their commissions, Marshall announced. In withholding them Madison was acting "in plain violation" of the law of the land. But the Supreme Court could not issue a writ of mandamus, because the provision of the Judiciary Act of 1789 authorizing the Court to issue such writs was unconstitutional. In other words, Congress did not have the legal right to give that power to the Court.

So far as it concerned the Judiciary Act, modern commentators agree that Marshall's decision was based on a very weak legal argument. Section 13 of the Act of 1789 stated that the Supreme Court could issue the writ to "persons holding office under the authority of the United States." This law had been framed by experts thoroughly familiar with the Constitution, including William Paterson, one of Marshall's associate justices. The Court had issued the writ in earlier cases without questioning Section 13 for a moment. But Marshall now claimed that the Court could not issue a mandamus except in cases that came to it *on appeal* from a lower court, since the Constitution, he said, granted original jurisdiction to the Court only in certain specified cases—those "affecting ambassadors, other public ministers and consuls, and those in which a state shall be a party." The Marbury case had *originated* in the Supreme Court; since it did not involve a diplomat or a state, any law that gave the Court the right to decide it was unauthorized.

This was shaky reasoning because the Constitution does not necessarily *limit* the Supreme Court's original jurisdiction to the cases it specifies. And even accepting Marshall's narrow view of the constitutional provision, his decision had a major weakness. As the Court's principal chronicler, Charles Warren, has written, "It seems plain, at the present time, that it would have been possible for Marshall, if he had been so inclined, to have construed the language of [Section 13 of the Act of 1789] which authorized writs of mandamus, in such a manner as to have enabled him to escape the necessity of declaring the section unconstitutional."

Marshall was on more solid ground when he went on to argue cogently the theory that "the constitution controls any legislative act repugnant to it," which he called "one of the fundamental principles of our society." The Constitution is "the *supreme* law of the land," he emphasized. Since it is the "duty of the judicial department to say what the law is," the Supreme Court must overturn any law of Congress that violates the Constitution. "A law repugnant to the Constitution," he concluded flatly, "is void." By this reasoning, Section 13 of the Act of 1789 simply ceased to exist, and without it the Court could not issue the writ of mandamus. By thus denying himself authority, Marshall found the means to flay his enemies without exposing himself to their wrath.

Although this was the first time the Court had declared an act of Congress unconstitutional, its right to do so had not been seriously challenged by most authorities. Even Jefferson accepted the principle, claiming only that the executive as well as the judiciary could decide questions of constitutionality. Jefferson was furious over what he called the "twistifications" of Marshall's gratuitous opinion in *Marbury v. Madison,* but his anger was directed at the Chief Justice's stinging criticisms of his behavior, not at the constitutional doctrine Marshall had enunciated.

Even in 1803, the idea of judicial review, which Professor E. S. Corwin has called "the most distinctive feature of the American constitutional system," had had a long history in America. The concept of natural law (the belief that certain principles of right and justice transcend the laws of mere men) was thoroughly established in American thinking. It is seen, for example, in Jefferson's statement in the immortal Declaration that men "are endowed by their Creator" with "unalienable" rights. Although not a direct precedent for Marshall's decision, the colonial practice of "disallowance," whereby various laws had been ruled void on the ground that local legislatures had exceeded their powers in passing them, illustrates the American belief that there is a limit to legislative power and that courts may say when it has been overstepped.

More specifically, Lord Coke, England's chief justice under James I, had declared early in the seventeenth century that "the common law will controul acts of Parliament." One of the American Revolution's chief statesmen and legal apologists, James Otis, had drawn upon this argument a century and a half later in his famous denunciation of the Writs of Assistance. And in the 1780's, courts in New Jersey, New York, Rhode Island, and North Carolina had exercised judicial review over the acts of local legislatures. The debates at the Constitutional Convention and some of the Federalist Papers (especially No. 78) indicated that most of the Founding Fathers accepted the idea of judicial review as already established. The Supreme Court, in fact, had considered the constitutionality of a law of Congress before— when it upheld a federal tax law in 1796—and it had encountered little questioning of its right to do so. All these precedents—when taken together with the fact that the section of the Act of 1789 nullified by Marshall's decision was of minor importance—explain why no one paid much attention to this part of the decision.

Thus the "Case of the Missing Commissions" passed into history, seemingly a fracas of but slight significance. When it was over, Marbury and his colleagues returned to the obscurity whence they had arisen.* In the partisan struggle for power between Marshall and Jefferson, the incident was of secondary importance. The real showdown came later—in the impeachment proceedings against Justice Chase and the treason trial of Aaron Burr. In the long run, Marshall won his fight to preserve the independence and integrity of the federal judiciary, but generally speaking, the courts have not been able to exert as much influence over the appointive and dismissal powers of the President as Marshall had hoped to win for them in *Marbury v. Madison*. Even the enunciation of the Supreme Court's power to void acts of Congress wrought no immediate change in American life. Indeed, it was more than half a century before another was overturned.

Nevertheless, this trivial squabble over a few petty political plums was of vital importance for later American history. For with the expansion of the federal government into new areas of activity in more recent times, the power of the Supreme Court to nullify acts of Congress has been repeatedly employed, with profound effects. At various times legislation concerning the income tax, child labor, wages and hours, and many other aspects of our social, economic, and political life have been thrown out by the Court, and always, in the last analysis, its right to do so has depended upon the decision John Marshall handed down to escape from a dilemma of his own making.

---

*What happened to Marbury? According to his descendants, he became president of a Georgetown bank in 1814, reared a family, and died, uncommissioned, in 1835.

Irving Brant

Madison and the War of 1812

Historians, as Irving Brant writes in this essay, should "appraise," not "acquit or indict." That duty is often difficult to fulfill, especially for political historians, who deal with controversial issues and with men who were subject to sharp partisan attacks and showered with equally distorting praise by their contemporaries. This essay is an excellent example of how a good historian tries to solve the problem of stripping away the blanket of prejudice that so often surrounds a subject.

The War of 1812, which might well have been avoided and which had no official results, has frequently been seen as a comic, and sometimes as a tragic, blunder. President James Madison has, with equal frequency, been denounced and laughed at for his management of the conflict. Brant, author or a multivolume life of Madison noted for its meticulous research and its generally favorable interpretation of the man, seeks here to rehabilitate Madison's reputation as a wartime President and to demonstrate that the war was neither purposeless nor inconclusive. How well he succeeded in doing so is an open question. Like most biographers, his long years of study led him to become so absorbed in his subject that he took on Madison's point of view almost completely; in redressing the balance he may well in this case have tipped it in the opposite direction. Nevertheless, Brant always supports his argument with hard evidence. His essay reads like a lawyer's brief, but like a good brief it bristles with facts and references to authorities. Although not every reader will accept all of Brant's conclusions, no one, having read the essay, can again see President Madison as a weak-willed, ineffective old man overwhelmed by events.

*O*f all the major events in American history, the War of 1812 is least known to the most people. Its naval glories are exploited in popular narrative. Its military failures, formerly glossed over, are emphasized by more objective historians with something akin to pleasure. Least known of all is the part taken by President Madison, who by virtue of the Constitution was commander in chief of the Armed Forces, charged with the duty of "making" the war that Congress "declared."

Through the years, however, a picture of James Madison has been built up by the brushes or palette knives of historians and popular word-artists. He appears as a pacifistic little man overshadowed by the ample figure of his wife, Dolley; a great political philosopher overwhelmed by the responsibilities of a war into which he was projected, at the age of sixty-one, against his will and with no capacity for executive leadership.

The purpose of this article is to appraise, not to acquit or indict. But in the case of Madison, the adverse preconceptions are embedded so deeply that they stand in the way of a fair appraisal. Historians have rejected the Federalist charge that he carried the United States into war to help Napoleon master the Old World. But with few exceptions they have treated him as the dupe of the French Emperor, tricked into war with England by the apparent repeal by the French of the Berlin and Milan Decrees at a time when both countries were despoiling American commerce. As for his conduct of the war, Madison has received little credit for victories and plenty of blame for misfortunes. Finally, the Treaty of Ghent satisfied none of the grievances cited in the declaration of war, and the one decisive military victory—that of General Andrew Jackson at New Orleans—was won two weeks after the signing of the peace treaty. It all adds up to the picture of a useless and costly conflict, saved by mere luck from being a disaster, and coming to an inconclusive end.

"Everybody knew" in 1812, just as everybody "knows" today, that Madison was timid, hesitant, ruled by stronger men. Everybody knew it, that is, except the foreign diplomats who were sent to overawe him. "Curt, spiteful, passionate," France's Louis Turreau called him. "Madison is now as obstinate as a mule," wrote England's "Copenhagen" Jackson (the Francis James Jackson who in 1807 had burned Denmark's capital) just before the President kicked him out of the country. Turreau's friendlier successor, Louis Sérurier, heard that the Chief of State was ruled by his Cabinet. He waited several months before he wrote to Paris: "Mr. Madison governs by himself."

Expelling an obnoxious minister was a civilian job. But how could Madison be anything of a war leader when "everybody knew" that he had been kicked into the war by Clay, Calhoun, Grundy, and other congressional War Hawks? There were certain things that "everybody" did not know. They did not know that in March, 1809, two weeks after he became President, Madison authorized British Minister David M. Erskine to inform his government that if she would relax her Orders in Council, he would ask Congress "to enter upon immediate measures of hostility against France.''

They did not know of a simultaneous notice to France that if she ceased her commercial aggressions and Great Britian did not, "the President of the United States will advise to an immediate war with the latter.'' Neither Congress nor the public ever learned that when President Madison proclaimed nonintercourse with England on November 2, 1810, he informed General Turreau that continued interference with American trade by England "will necessarily lead to war"—as it did. The 1809 offer to join England against France brought gasps of astonishment in Congress when Madison revealed it in asking for the declaration of war against England. It brought no gasps of any sort from writers of history. It didn't fit their conception of Madison, so they disposed of it by silence.

England first, then France, was Madison's schedule of redress. In August, 1812, the moment he was notified that England had repealed her Orders in Council, he offered to settle the one remaining issue— impressment of seamen—by informal agreement. At the same time he wrote to his minister in Paris that if England made peace and France failed to repair American wrongs, war would be declared against France as soon as Congress convened, and that if England did not make peace he might even recommend a double war. Joel Barlow was directed to show that letter to the French government. As a result, Barlow was called to Poland to confer with Napoleon in the field and complete a treaty, but Napoleon's defeat at Berezina intervened, and Barlow died of pneumonia near Cracow on his way back to Paris. Madison's letter has been in print for nearly a hundred years, ignored even by historians who knew that it was described in the French foreign office as an ultimatum of war.

The same Federalist editors who jeered at "poor Madison" in 1812 denounced him as a dictator in 1814. They were free to do so. Open sedition and silent resistance forced the United States to fight the war with one arm—New England—tied behind her back. That was more crippling than incompetent generals, raw militia, and an empty treasury. Yet the President rejected every counsel that would have narrowed the constitutional liberties of those who gave vocal aid to the enemy. They would hang themselves, he said, and they did. Among all the words of praise addressed to him when he left office, he may have felt keenest pride in those of the Citizens' Committee of Washington:

> Power and national glory, sir, have often before been acquired by the sword; but rarely without the sacrifice of civil or political liberty. When we reflect that this sword was drawn under your guidance, we cannot resist offering you our own as well as a nation's thanks for the vigilance . . . the energy . . . and the safety with which you have wielded an armed force of 50,000 men . . . without infringing a political, civil or religious right.

It takes time, of course, for people to accept a portrait after a hundred years of caricature. At the risk of being abrupt, let us turn

*James Madison was Jefferson's
Secretary of State when
Gilbert Stuart did this portrait.*

to Madison's actions as war leader. Expecting hostilities with England, why did he not call for adequate preparations? He did, but in Congress a vote for taxes was looked on as political suicide. Madison's first action in national defense was to lay up most of President Jefferson's little gunboats as wasteful of men and money in proportion to gunpower and to order laid-up frigates refitted. Congress cut the requested appropriation and stopped the work. In September, 1811, Sérurier told his government that the President was stimulating a nationwide debate on the question of whether it suited the Republic to have a navy, and if so, should it not be "such as can make the American flag respected"? The proposition had to be presented "in this questioning and deferential form," said the Minister, to avoid exciting state jealousy of federal power.

At the ensuing session of Congress the administration asked for twelve seventy-four-gun ships and ten new frigates, and the repair or reconstruction of six of the ten existing frigates. The new construction was voted down and the reconditioning limited to three ships.

To prepare for the land war, which would have to be fought either on American or Canadian soil, the President wanted a quick build-up of military forces. Then, if the expected bad news came from England, the troops would be ready to march on weakly defended Montreal and Quebec before reinforcements could cross the ocean.

With an authorized personnel of ten thousand, the Army had only about four thousand. The President asked that the old regiments be filled up, that ten thousand additional regulars be recruited, and that provision be made for fifty thousand volunteers. Senator William Branch Giles of Virginia, leader of the anti-Madison Democrats, shook the roof as he decried these puny measures. He demanded thirty-five thousand regulars and five-year enlistments, making it necessary to build a large and costly officer corps before men could be recruited.

"The efforts of General [Senator Samuel] Smith and of Mr. Giles of Virginia," British Minister Augustus J. Foster reported, "have been added to those of the Federalists as a means to overthrow Mr. Madison and his administration." Congress talked most of the winter and Giles won. The bill for fifty thousand volunteers occasioned a lengthy constitutional harangue and a decision for state-appointed officers. The result, many believed, would be a militia that could refuse to go onto foreign soil. Skeptically, Madison signed the bills for the regulars and the volunteers.

His skepticism had warrant. On June 8 the number of recruits was estimated at five thousand, and there were few unbalky volunteers except in the West.

With England unyielding, the President on March 31 notified the House Committee on Foreign Relations that he was ready to ask for a shipping embargo—a prelude to war. But "the Executive will not take upon itself the responsibility of declaring that we are prepared for war." Congress must make the final decision with its eyes open. Four days later it did so, the embargo taking effect on April 4.

By that time, military and naval decisions were crowding in upon the Executive. In those fields, two stories are told which carry the suggestion that Madison was stupid, or at least indecisive. The fact that they are still in circulation proves that some writers have been a trifle credulous. One story says that the President decided to make an untrained civilian, Henry Clay, supreme military commander but was dissuaded by his Cabinet. The other is that Madison made up his mind to keep the American Navy tied up for harbor defense, but reversed himself on the pleas of Navy Captains Charles Stewart and William Bainbridge.

The story of the abortive appointment of Henry Clay reached full and rounded form in Calvin Colton's 1857 biography of Clay. It can be traced backward in print and manuscript, diminishing as it recedes —back to Colonel Isaac Cole's recollection, in 1838, of what he once heard from General John Mason, back to Mason's memory of what he was told by his brother-in-law, General Ben Howard. And that was: a group of Clay's friends suggested Clay's appointment to President Madison, who "assented to their opinion of [Clay's] fitness, etc., but said he could not be spared out of Congress." That was the molehill out of which the mountain grew.

The naval history was no third-hand, dry-land scuttlebutt. It came from Captain Stewart himself. As Stewart published the story in 1845, he and Captain Bainbridge went to the Navy Department on June 21, 1812, three days after the declaration of war, to solicit commands at sea. They were told by Secretary Paul Hamilton that the President and Cabinet had decided to keep the ships tied up. They protested, and the argument was continued before the President, who agreed with the captains but gave way to the Cabinet at a special meeting called that evening. Bainbridge and Stewart thereupon drafted a joint letter to the President, who overruled the Cabinet and ordered the Navy into action. Capping Stewart's story was his account of a great naval ball in the following December to which a courier brought news of Captain Stephen Decatur's victory over the frigate *Macedonian*. Whereupon President Madison told the assembled guests that if it had not been for Bainbridge and Stewart, the warships never would have gone to sea.

All rather convincing, unless you happen to know that Madison did not attend that December ball, that on June 23 Bainbridge wrote from Boston (he was not in Washington at all at the time) asking for a fighting command, and that all major warships ready for action were ordered to sea on the day war was declared. Stewart did not invent his 1845 story. It arose out of his muddled recollection and grandiose enlargement of a discussion held at the White House in February, 1812, some months before the declaration of war, in which the President sided with the captains against the Secretary of the Navy. Congress had just rejected the administration's request for twenty-two new warships. The captains, arguing with Hamilton, conceded that even if an American vessel were victorious it might, without reinforcements, be overwhelmed and captured by the enemy. To which Madison replied: "It is victories we want; if you give us them and lose your ships afterwards, they can be replaced by others."

The February discussion between the captains and the President was prophetic. For when Madison made his next request for greater sea power, in the closing weeks of 1812, it was dramatized by the *Constitution*'s victory over the *Guerrière* in August, the capture of the *Macedonian* by the *United States* in October, and especially by the gallant exploit of the sloop *Wasp*, which ran into exactly the kind of trouble Stewart and Bainbridge had predicted. Victorious over the *Frolic*, the *Wasp* was unable to hoist a sail when a lumbering British seventy-four came along and took both victor and prize to Bermuda. Captain Stewart, in this campaign for funds, furnished Secretary Hamilton with the technical arguments that helped persuade Congress to authorize four ships of the line, four heavy frigates, and as many sloops of war.

In one critical area the issue of naval power could not wait until the war began. In March, 1812, Stewart was called to Washington and offered a yet-uncreated command on the Great Lakes, controlled then by a few British armed vessels. The President intended to ask Congress for money to build a fleet; in the meantime enough would be scraped up for an eighteen-gun brig. Stewart refused; he was a deep-sea man.

The matter was given a new turn by Governor William Hull of Michigan Territory, a veteran of the Revolution. Offered a commission as brigadier general, he urged the building of lake squadrons. But with Stewart rejecting the command and Congress hostile to naval construction, Hull assured the President that he could lead an army across the Detroit River and down the north shore of Lake Erie to the Niagara River. That would restrain the northwestern Indians, deliver much of upper Canada into American hands, and win control of the lakes in less time and at less cost than building a fleet.

A Detroit campaign was being forced on the government anyway. Early operations against Montreal were made impossible by the dearth of regulars and the refusal of New England governors to furnish militia for federal service. On the other hand, western volunteers were so eager to break up the British-Indian alliance, Clay and others reported, that inaction might chill their spirit. Madison accepted Hull's promise of lake control by land action and thereby made the biggest strategic error of the war.

The appointment of Hull was a major blunder, but hardly a foreseeable one. Thirty years of peace with the Army almost non-existent forced the President to choose his generals either from aging Revolutionary veterans with fighting experience and reputation, or from young regimental officers who had never seen action. Among the veterans called back, Hull had an unsurpassed Revolutionary record. Even Federalist editors applauded Madison's selection.

Hull commanded twenty-five hundred confident Kentuckians, Ohioans, regulars, and Michigan territorials. He crossed into Canada on July 12, 1812, skirmished with the vastly outnumbered enemy, and retreated to Fort Detroit. There, on August 16, without firing a shot, without consulting his officers, he surrendered his entire army to General Isaac Brock, who was advancing at the head of 330 British regulars and 400 Canadian militiamen, with several hundred Indians whooping in the woods.

Hull's claim that he was short of supplies was categorically denied by his officers but avidly accepted by the Federalist press, with a resultant impact on historians. His most startling assertion was that he had only one day's supply of powder. When he made the same remark to Sir George Prevost, the British commander handed him "the return of the large supply found in the fort; it did not create a blush." Those were the words of British Adjutant General Edward Baynes. Hull's actions, wrote another member of Prevost's staff, "stamp him either for a coward or a traitor." With such comments coming from the captors, it seems just a trifle severe to blame the surrender on either the President or the War Department.

Suppose, instead, we find out how the President reacted to the disaster. New land forces, he said, could be counted on to redeem the country's honor. The immediate necessity was to speed up the building of warships to gain control of the lakes—a method that would have been adopted at the outset "if the easy conquest of them by land held out to us [by Hull] had not misled our calculations." The strength of his feeling was recorded by Richard Rush, who wrote to John Adams the following June: "I know the President to be so convinced upon this subject that I heard him say last fall if the British build thirty frigates upon [the lakes] we ought to build forty."

Madison's insistence produced the warships with which Commodore Perry defeated and captured the British squadron on Lake Erie in September, 1813, changing the whole complexion of the war. He ordered the building of ship after ship on Lake Ontario. Superiority swung back and forth on that lake like reversing winds, but neither side could force a decision because each had protected bases—the British at York (now Toronto) and Kingston, the Americans at Sackets Harbor—to retire to when the other was ahead.

Far more important and more critical was the state of affairs in 1814 on Lake Champlain, the great sluice that opened a supply route northward to Montreal and southward to the Hudson River valley. By summer, more than twenty thousand seasoned veterans of the Peninsular War, released for transatlantic service by Napoleon's downfall, were crowding onto British transports bound for Canada, Chesapeake Bay, and New Orleans. On Lake Champlain, the American ship *Saratoga* was launched thirty-five days after the laying of her keel. Sailors were in short supply both there and on Lake Ontario. Madison ordered the crews filled up with soldiers and told the protesting Secretary of War that naval efficiency was essential even for land operations.

Then came news that the enemy was building a new vessel on Lake Champlain, the *Confiance,* far more powerful than the twenty-six-gun *Saratoga.* Loss of the lake might still be averted, Captain Thomas Macdonough believed, by the swifter building of a light brig. Navy Secretary William Jones, though far more vigorous and capable than his predecessor, said the limit of available funds had been reached.

Madison ordered the ship built anyhow. Its keel had been laid when Jones again drew back. "God knows where the money is to come from," he wrote. The President reaffirmed the order and obtained a pledge of the utmost speed. On July 15 the timbers of the twenty-gun *Eagle* were still standing in the forest. The vessel was launched on August 11 and furnished the margin of power that changed sure defeat into a victory which resounded from Washington to Ghent.

"The battle of Lake Champlain, more than any other incident of the War of 1812, merits the epithet 'decisive,'" wrote the distinguished naval historian Alfred Thayer Mahan many years later. Within earshot of the battle, many of them within sight, nearly fourteen thousand of Wellington's battle-hardened soldiers waited for the Royal Navy to open the way to Albany and New York. When the British fleet surrendered, the army of invasion marched back to Canada and never returned.

In naval affairs, Madison could rely on officers unsurpassed anywhere in the world for knowledge and ability. In army matters he had to learn by hard experience. His first Secretary of War, William Eustis, was a Massachusetts medical man of bustling energy who bore a tremendous load of work in a War Department consisting of himself and eight clerks. Eustis, even in the opinion of some congressmen who wanted him fired, outperformed what anybody had a right to expect in equipping the Army as war approached. But he had no more than a civilian's knowledge of military operations, did little to systematize the nation's defenses, and seemed unable to recognize incompetence in field officers before it was demonstrated in battle. The President shared this last fault. When Adjutant General Baynes visited Major General Henry Dearborn under a flag of truce, he saw at a glance that the

American commander lacked energy. Neither Madison nor Eustis sensed this, and the President couldn't see the deficiencies of Eustis. His resignation, after failures on the Niagara front followed the Hull catastrophe, was a concession to public opinion.

Brigadier General John Armstrong, who succeeded Eustis, was notorious for political intrigue but had enough of a military reputation to warrant his selection. The President chose him reluctantly, after Secretary of State James Monroe and Senator William Harris Crawford had refused the place.

During the next year and a half, until the burning of Washington forced him to resign, Armstrong performed his work with one eye on the war and the other on the 1816 presidential race. His good and bad traits showed up at once but not in equal measure. He drove the competent Andrew Jackson to fury and disobedience with a brusque, unappreciative dismissal of his temporary Tennessee volunteers in a distant wilderness. He removed the incompetent General Dearborn with a note even more callous. Both men wrote to the President, Jackson boiling with indignation, Dearborn heartbroken. Madison forced Armstrong to make amends to Jackson. He himself consoled Dearborn but affirmed the removal.

Armstrong's strategy to gain the presidential nomination paralleled that of his rival, James Monroe. Each hoped to be made a lieutenant general and win the war. Monroe's chance vanished when Armstrong took the War Department. Armstrong's opportunity seemed to open when the President, in June of 1813, was stricken with an almost fatal illness followed by several months' convalescence in Virginia. Freed of effective presidential supervision, Armstrong went north under the pretense of making an inspection trip and did not come back until Christmas. During the interval he assumed personal direction of a two-pronged campaign against Montreal, failed to co-ordinate the mishandled offensive movements, and ducked away to Albany to watch the approaching double fiasco as a detached observer.

Personal ambition and laziness turned Armstrong's strategic ideas, even when sound, into flashy gambits, without the preparation or drive required to follow through. Two weeks before the event that drove him out of office, he received a written rebuke from Madison that would have pierced the hide of a rhinoceros—though it did not penetrate his—for secretly exercising powers delegated by Congress to the President, ordering military operations without consultation, suppressing letters intended for the President, accepting the resignation of General William Henry Harrison without authority, and posing to Harrison's successor as the bestower of the appointment.

Nevertheless, Armstrong possessed capabilities that, combined with Madison's ability to thwart their misuse, gave a new look to the American Army. Both men recognized youthful talent, and Armstrong was ruthless enough to get rid of old incompetents.

Zebulon Pike, promoted to brigadier general, was killed in winning his first victory. Jacob Brown and George Izard, lately raised to the same rank, stood out in the Montreal campaign in contrast to their soon-to-be-ousted commanders, Major Generals James Wilkinson and Wade Hampton. Shining talents were displayed by Colonels E. P. Gaines and Winfield Scott; solid performance by Alexander Macomb, T. A. Smith, E. W. Ripley. Every one of these eight men was recommended by Armstrong for promotion, with the exception of Brown. He advised the President that for major generals, not a moment should be lost in promoting Brigadiers Izard and Thomas Flournoy.

Flournoy, a nobody at New Orleans! His promotion, by making Andrew Jackson his subordinate instead of his superior, would have knocked Jackson straight out of the military service—if not into apoplexy. But it also would have barricaded the upward path of Brown —the man most likely to stand in Armstrong's way if Armstrong succeeded in establishing the grade of lieutenant general—by filling all the major-generalships allowed by law.

The President nominated Izard—*and Brown*. It could almost be said that at that moment the Battle of New Orleans was won, although Jackson's appointment as major general still awaited a future vacancy. Also, the leadership was established that retrieved American prestige in the 1814 battles of the Niagara peninsula and helped persuade England that the time was ripe for peace.

The location of that Niagara campaign, illogical because of its limited objective, resulted from troop movements made by Armstrong without consulting the President. To remedy that feature, the Secretary sent a proposal to Madison at Montpelier that Brown's army bypass the peninsula and swing around Lake Ontario to Burlington and York. Madison imposed the same restriction that was to be recognized a hundred years later by Admiral Mahan: control of the lake must first be won to prevent the landing of an army in the American rear. The civilian commander in chief was learning the art of war. By a succession of decisions affecting strength, strategy, and leadership on Lake Champlain, at New Orleans, and on the Niagara front— overruling his subordinates in every instance—Madison went far to determine the outcome.

In spite of their conflicts over appointments, Armstrong and the President worked effectively together in a fundamental regeneration of the military command. On the day war was declared the United States Army had eight generals, most of them just appointed. Their average age was sixty years. Two years later all of them were out of service or assigned to quiescence. In the first half of 1814 nine generals were appointed or promoted—their average age was thirty-six— and these men turned raw American recruits into disciplined soldiers. When the war ended they had just begun to fight.

These redeeming events of 1814 are obscured in popular narrative and even in histories by the burning of Washington and the miserable failure of its defenders. For that occurrence President Madison bore an inescapable responsibility: constitutionally, he was commander in chief; physically, he was in Washington when the enemy approached. Why did he not foresee the attack; why didn't he guard against it?

The burning of Washington in 1814 by the British is the subject of this highly dramatized contemporary engraving.

The answer to the first question accentuates the second. On May 24, after reading a British proclamation calling for a general uprising of southern slaves, the President wrote to Armstrong that this presaged a campaign of ruthless devastation in which the national capital could not fail to be "a favorite target." On July 1, without dissent but with skepticism concerning the danger (so wrote Navy Secretary William Jones), the Cabinet approved Madison's proposal that ten thousand militiamen be drawn out to help guard the Washington-Baltimore area. When Brigadier General William H. Winder wished to summon them, Secretary Armstrong (the chief skeptic) made the fatal reply that the best mode of using militia "was upon the spur of the occasion." Nevertheless, the power and responsibility belonged to the President, and his own recorded foresight called for vigorous defensive measures. He intervened again and again, to overcome Armstrong's sloth and skepticism, but never forced action on a large enough scale.

Almost in another world is the popular word-picture of the Madisons at this time. It is a composite of Dolley saving the portrait of George Washington as the enemy approached, and of the President—as depicted by the scurrilous (and anonymous) versifier of "The Bladensburg Races"—galloping in terrified flight forty miles into Maryland.

The rhapsodic glee with which the versifier danced in the ashes of the Capitol and White House may not impeach his veracity, but his figurative observation post hardly matched the physical one of Sérurier, who had a panoramic view from the unmenaced Octagon House. The President, Sérurier wrote to Talleyrand two days before the battle, "has just gone to the camp to encourage, by his presence, the army to defend the capital." Madison returned to the White House from the actual battlefield (where Congreve rockets fell near him) after Dolley left the house. He remained there, the French minister said, until after the Georgetown and Washington militia streamed by in confused flight toward Frederick. The manner of his departure as described by Sérurier would be of little moment except that it emphasizes still further how different Madison's character was from the one history has bestowed on him:

> It was then, my lord, that the President, who, in the midst of all this disorder, had displayed to stop it a firmness and constancy worthy of a better success . . . coolly mounted his horse, accompanied by some friends, and slowly gained the bridge that separates Washington from Virginia.

By the time the news of the burning of Washington reached London, the bellicosity and bad temper that had given rise to Admiral Alexander Cochrane's "treat 'em rough" instructions were things of the past. War weariness in England, fresh dangers emerging in chaotic Europe, and the sharp improvement in the American position, strength, and morale in the north, all helped produce a sudden reversal of British policy at Ghent. Peace was signed the day before Christmas, and the fighting ended on January 8, 1815, when two thousand British soldiers—a third of the entire assaulting army—fell dead or wounded at New Orleans.

The Treaty of Ghent left things as they were. Did the war itself leave them unchanged? Impressment and the Orders in Council both vanished before the treaty was signed. European peace removed them as immediate future hazards. If the war had lifted American prestige, no treaty was needed to abolish them forever. By that measurement the New Orleans victory was climax, not epilogue. In 1815, Justice Joseph Story weighed the results of the war and found them massive:

> Never did a country occupy more lofty ground; we have stood the contest, single-handed, against the conqueror of Europe; and we are at peace, with all our blushing victories thick crowding on us. If I do not much mistake, we shall attain to a very high character abroad as well as crush domestic faction.

Domestic faction was crushed in the next election. Those who would fix the time at which the country attained international stature might ask themselves: Could there have been a Monroe Doctrine in 1823 without the War of 1812? It was under President James Madison that the struggling young republic won an equal position among the free nations of the world, and began its long climb to leadership.

Bray Hammond

Was Jackson Wise to Dismantle the Bank?

The conflict waged by President Andrew Jackson against the Second Bank of the United States, one of the most dramatic political confrontations in American history, has produced over the years a wide variety of reactions. Jackson's Whig enemies presented him as a ruthless, dictatorial ignoramus striking out at the Bank in order to increase his own power; his friends described him as a noble crusader destroying the "monster," a monopolistic economic colossus that was extracting profits for its wealthy stockholders from "the people's money." In later years historians tended to accept one or the other of these views, usually without much understanding of the financial questions around which the "bank war" raged.

This was the situation when the late Bray Hammond, then a retired governor of the Federal Reserve Board, wrote the following essay. In the 1940's a liberal young historian, Arthur M. Schlesinger, Jr., had published *The Age of Jackson,* a widely read book which took an extremely pro-Jackson position in the controversy. Hammond, whose knowledge of banking and finance enabled him to grasp and explain the issues involved, disagreed with Schlesinger's interpretation. His researches also led to the uncovering of a great deal of new evidence about the attitudes and actions of Nicholas Biddle, president of the Bank, and of many of the state bankers who opposed him. Although the subject, like nearly all important historical questions, is still being debated, Hammond's thesis represents the dominant view at the present time.

Relief, sir!'' interrupted the President. "Come not to me, sir! Go to the monster. It is folly, sir, to talk to Andrew Jackson. The government will not bow to the monster. . . . Andrew Jackson yet lives to put his foot upon the head of the monster and crush him to the dust.''

The monster, "a hydra of corruption,'' was known also as the Second Bank of the United States, chartered by Congress in 1816 as depository of the federal government, which was its principal stockholder and customer. The words were reported by a committee which called on President Jackson in the spring of 1834 to complain because he and Secretary of the Treasury Roger Taney had removed the federal deposits from the federal depository into what the Jacksonians called "selected banks" and others called "pet banks." The President was disgusted with the committee.

"Andrew Jackson," he exclaimed in the third person as before, "would never recharter that monster of corruption. Sooner than live in a country where such a power prevailed, he would seek an asylum in the wilds of Arabia."

In effect, he had already put his foot on the monster and crushed him in the dust. He had done so by vetoing a new charter for the Bank and removing the federal accounts from its books. So long as the federal Bank had the federal accounts, it had been regulator of the currency and of credit in general. Its power to regulate had derived from the fact that the federal Treasury was the largest single transactor in the economy and the largest bank depositor. Receiving the checks and notes of local banks deposited with it by government collectors of revenue, it had had constantly to come back on the local banks for settlements of the amounts which the checks and notes called for. It had had to do so because it made those amounts immediately available to the Treasury, wherever desired. Since settlement by the local banks was in specie, i.e. silver and gold coin, the pressure for settlement automatically regulated local bank lending; for the more the local banks lent, the larger the amount of their notes and checks in use and the larger the sums they had to settle in specie. This loss of specie reduced their power to lend.

All this had made the federal Bank the regulator not alone of the currency but of bank lending in general, the restraint it had exerted being fully as effective as that of the twelve Federal Reserve Banks at present, though by a different process. With its life now limited to two more years and the government accounts removed from its books, it was already crushed but still writhing.

The Jacksonian attack on the Bank is an affair respecting which posterity seems to have come to an opinion that is half hero worship and half discernment. In the words of Professor William G. Sumner, the affair was a struggle "between the democracy and the money power." Viewed in that light, Jackson's victory was a grand thing. But Sumner also observed—this was three quarters of a century ago— that since Jackson's victory the currency, which previously had owned no superior in the world, had never again been so good. More

Jackson slays the Bank, "the hydra of corruption," assisted by Van Buren (center) and a popular cartoon character of the day (right). Bank President Biddle is in the top hat.

recently Professor Lester V. Chandler, granting the Bank's imperfections, has said that its abolition without replacement by something to take over its functions was a "major blunder" which "ushered in a generation of banking anarchy and monetary disorder." So the affair stands, a triumph and a blunder.

During Andrew Jackson's lifetime three things had begun to alter prodigiously the economic life of Americans. These were steam, credit, and natural resources.

Steam had been lifting the lids of pots for thousands of years, and for a century or so it had been lifting water from coal mines. But only in recent years had it been turning spindles, propelling ships, drawing trains of cars, and multiplying incredibly the productive powers of man. For thousands of years money had been lent, but in most people's minds debt had signified distress—as it still did in Andrew Jackson's. Only now was its productive power, long known to merchants as a means of making one sum of money do the work of several, becoming popularly recognized by enterprising men for projects which required larger sums than could be assembled in coin. For three centuries or more America's resources had been crudely surmised, but only now were their variety, abundance, and accessibility becoming practical realities. And it was the union of these three, steam, credit, and natural resources, that was now turning Anglo-Saxon America from the modest agrarian interests that had preoccupied her for two centuries of European settlement to the dazzling possibilities of industrial exploitation.

In the presence of these possibilities, the democracy was becoming transformed from one that was Jeffersonian and agrarian to one that was financial and industrial. But it was still a democracy: its recruits were still men born and reared on farms, its vocabulary was still Jeffersonian, and its basic conceptions changed insensibly from the libertarianism of agrarians to that of *laissez faire*. When Andrew Jackson became President in 1829, boys born in log cabins were already becoming businessmen but with no notion of surrendering as bankers and manufacturers the freedom they might have enjoyed as farmers.

There followed a century of exploitation from which America emerged with the most wealthy and powerful economy there is, with her people the best fed, the best housed, the best clothed, and the best equipped on earth. But the loss and waste have long been apparent. The battle was only for the strong, and millions who lived in the midst of wealth never got to touch it. The age of the Robber Barons was scarcely a golden age. It was scarcely what Thomas Jefferson desired.

It could scarcely have been what Andrew Jackson desired either, for his ideals were more or less Jeffersonian by common inheritance, and the abuse of credit was one of the things he abominated. Yet no man ever did more to encourage the abuse of credit than he. For the one agency able to exert some restraint on credit was the federal Bank. In destroying it, he let speculation loose. Though a hard-money devotee who hated banks and wanted no money but coin, he fostered the formation of swarms of banks and endowed the country with a filthy and depreciated paper currency which he believed to be unsound and unconstitutional and from which the Civil War delivered it in the Administration of Abraham Lincoln thirty years later.

This, of course, was not Andrew Jackson's fault, unless one believes he would have done what he did had his advisers been different. Though a resolute and decisive person, he also relied on his friends. He had his official cabinet, largely selected for political expediency, and he had his "kitchen cabinet" for informal counsel. Of those advisers most influential with him, all but two were either businessmen or closely associated with the business world. The two exceptions were Major William B. Lewis, a planter and neighbor from Tennessee who came to live with him in the White House; and James K. Polk, also of Tennessee, later President of the United States. These two, with Jackson himself, constituted the agrarian element in the Jacksonian Administration. Several of the others, however, were agrarian in the sense that they had started as poor farm boys.

Martin Van Buren, probably the ablest of Jackson's political associates, was a lawyer whose investments had made him rich. Amos Kendall, the ablest in a business and administrative sense, later made the telegraph one of the greatest of American business enterprises and himself a man of wealth. He provided the Jacksonians their watchword, ''The world is governed too much.'' He said ''our countrymen are beginning to demand'' that the government be content with ''protecting their persons and property, leaving them to direct their labor and capital as they please, within the moral law; getting rich or remaining poor as may result from their own management or fortune.'' Kendall's views may be sound, but they are not what one expects to hear from the democracy when struggling with the money power.

Roger Taney, later Chief Justice, never got rich, but he liked banks and was a modest investor in bank stock. ''There is perhaps no business,'' he said as Jackson's secretary of the treasury, ''which yields a profit so certain and liberal as the business of banking and exchange; and it is proper that it should be open as far as practicable to the most free competition and its advantages shared by all classes of society.'' His own bank in Baltimore was one of the first of the pets in which he deposited government money.

David Henshaw, Jacksonian boss of Massachusetts, was a banker and industrialist whose advice in practical matters had direct influence in Washington. Henshaw projected a Jacksonian bank to take the place of the existing institution but to be bigger. (A similar project was got up by friends of Van Buren in New York and one of the two was mentioned favorably by Jackson in his veto message as a possible alternative to the existing United States Bank.) Samuel Ingham, Jackson's first secretary of the treasury, was a paper manufacturer in Pennsylvania and later a banker in New Jersey. Churchill C. Cambreleng, congressional leader of the attack on the Bank, was a New York businessman and former agent of John Jacob Astor. These are not all of the Jacksonians who were intent on the federal Bank's destruction, but they are typical.

There was a very cogent reason why these businessmen and their class generally wanted to kill the Bank of the United States. It interfered with easy money; it kept the state banks from lending as freely as they might otherwise and businessmen from borrowing.

New York, for example, was now the financial and commercial center of the country and its largest city, which Philadelphia formerly had been. The customs duties collected at its wharves and paid by its businessmen were far the largest of any American port, and customs duties were then the principal source of federal income. These duties were paid by New York businessmen with checks on New York banks. These checks were deposited by the federal collectors in the New York office of the Bank of the United States, whose headquarters were in Philadelphia and a majority of whose directors were Philadelphia businessmen. This, Amos Kendall observed, was a ''wrong done to New York in depriving her of her natural advantages.''

It was not merely a matter of prestige. As already noted, the United States Bank, receiving the checks of the New York businessmen, made the funds at once available to the secretary of the treasury. The Bank had therefore to call on the New York banks for the funds the checks represented. This meant that the New York banks, in order to pay the federal Bank, had to draw down their reserves; which meant that they had less money to lend; which meant that the New York businessmen could not borrow as freely and cheaply as they might otherwise. All this because their money had gone to Philadelphia.

Actually the situation was not so bad as my simplified account makes it appear. For one thing, the goods imported at New York were sold elsewhere in the country, and more money came to New York in payment for them than went out of the city in duties paid the government. But I have described it in the bald, one-sided terms that appealed to the local politicians and to the businessmen prone to grumbling because money was not so easy as they would like. There was truth in what they said, but less than they made out.

New York's grievance was special because her customs receipts were so large and went to a vanquished rival. Otherwise the federal Bank's pressure on the local banks—all of which were state banks—was felt in some degree through the country at large. Wherever money was paid to a federal agency—for postage, for fines, for lands, for excise, for import duties—money was drawn from the local banks into the federal Bank. The flow of funds did not drain the local banks empty and leave them nothing to do, though they and the states' rights politicians talked as if that were the case. The federal Bank was simply their principal single creditor.

And though private business brought more money to New York and other commercial centers than it took away, the federal government took more away than it brought. For its largest payments were made elsewhere—to naval stations, army posts, Indian agents, owners of the public debt, largely foreign, and civilians in the government service throughout the country. In the normal flow of money payments from hand to hand in the economy, those to the federal government and consequently to the federal Bank were so large and conspicuous that the state banks involved in making them were disagreeably conscious of their size and frequency.

These banks, of course, were mostly eastern and urban rather than western and rural, because it was in eastern cities that the federal government received most of its income. Accordingly, it was in the eastern business centers, Boston, New York, Baltimore, and Charleston, that resentment against Philadelphia and the federal Bank was strongest. This resentment was intensified by the fact that the federal Bank's branch offices were also competitors for private business in these and other cities, which the present Federal Reserve Banks, very wisely, are not.

General Jackson's accession to the presidency afforded an opportunity to put an end to the federal Bank. Its charter would expire in seven years. The question of renewal was to be settled in that interval. Jackson was popular and politically powerful. His background and principles were agrarian. An attack on the Bank by him would be an attack "by the democracy on the money power." It would have, therefore, every political advantage.

The realities behind these words, however, were not what the words implied. The democracy till very recently had been agrarian because most of the population was agricultural. But the promoters of the assault on the Bank were neither agrarian in their current interests nor representative of what democracy implied.

In the western and rural regions, which were the most democratic in a traditional sense, dislike of the federal Bank persisted, though by 1829 it had less to feed on than formerly. Years before, under incompetent managers, the Bank had lent unwisely in the West, had been forced to harsh measures of self-preservation, and had made itself hated, with the help, as usual, of the state banks and states' rights politicians. But the West needed money, and though the Bank never provided enough it did provide some, and in the absence of new offenses disfavor had palpably subsided by the time Jackson became President.

There were also, in the same regions, vestiges or more of the traditional agrarian conviction that all banks were evil. This principle was still staunchly held by Andrew Jackson. He hated all banks, did so through a long life, and said so time after time. He thought they all violated the Constitution. But he was led by the men around him to focus his aversion on the federal Bank, which being the biggest must be the worst and whose regulatory pressure on the state banks must obviously be the oppression to be expected from a great, soulless corporation.

However, not all agrarian leaders went along with him. For many years the more intelligent had discriminated in favor of the federal Bank, recognizing that its operations reduced the tendency to inflation which, as a hard-money party, the agrarians deplored. Altogether, it was no longer to be expected that the agrarian democracy would initiate a vigorous attack on the federal Bank, though it was certainly to be expected that such an attack would receive very general agrarian support.

It was in the cities and within the business world that both the attack on the Bank and its defense would be principally conducted. For there the Bank had its strongest enemies and its strongest friends. Its friends were the more conservative houses that had dominated the old business world but had only a minor part in the new. It was a distinguished part, however, and influential. This influence, which arose from prestige and substantial wealth, combined with the strength which the federal Bank derived from the federal accounts to constitute what may tritely be called a "money power." But it was a disciplined, conservative money power and just what the economy needed.

But it was no longer *the* money power. It was rivaled, as Philadelphia was by New York, by the newer, more vigorous, more aggressive, and more democratic part of the business world.

The businessmen comprising the latter were a quite different lot from the old. The Industrial Revolution required more men to finance, to man, and manage its railways, factories, and other enterprises than the old business world, comprising a few rich merchants, could possibly provide. The Industrial Revolution was set to absorb the greater part of the population.

Yet when the new recruits, who yesterday were mechanics and farmers, offered themselves not only as laborers but as managers, owners, and entrepreneurs requiring capital, they met a response that was not always respectful. There was still the smell of the barnyard on their boots, and their hands were better adapted to hammer and nails than to quills and ink. The aristocrats were amused. They were also chary of lending to such borrowers; whereupon farmers' and mechanics' banks began to be set up. These banks found themselves hindered by the older banks and by the federal Bank. They and their borrowers were furious. They resisted the federal Bank in suits, encouraged by sympathetic states' rights politicians, and found themselves blocked by the federal courts.

Nor were their grievances merely material. They disliked being snubbed. Even when they became wealthy themselves, they still railed at "the capitalists" and "the aristocrats," as David Henshaw of Massachusetts did, meaning the old families, the Appletons and Lawrences whom he named, the business counterparts of the political figures that the Jacksonian revolution had replaced. Henshaw and his fellow Jacksonian leaders were full of virtue, rancor, and democracy. Their struggle was not merely to make money but to demonstrate what they already asserted, that they were as good as anyone, or more so. In their denunciation of the federal Bank, one finds them calling it again and again "an aristocracy" and its proprietors, other than the federal government, "aristocrats."

The Jacksonians, as distinct from Jackson himself, wanted a world where *laissez faire* prevailed; where, as Amos Kendall said, everyone would be free to get rich; where, as Roger Taney said, the benefits of banks would be open to all classes; where, as the enterprising exploiters of the land unanimously demanded, credit would be easy. To be sure, relatively few would be rich, and a good many already settling into an urban industrial class were beginning to realize it. But that consideration did not count with the Jacksonian leaders. They wanted a new order; they achieved the age of the Robber Barons.

The attack on the old order took the form of an attack on the federal Bank for a number of reasons which may be summed up in political expediency. A factor in the success of the attack was that the president of the Bank, Nicholas Biddle, was the pampered scion of capitalists and aristocrats. He was born to wealth and prominence. He was elegant, literary, intellectual, witty, and conscious of his own merits. When at the age of 37 he became head of the largest moneyed corporation in the world he was wholly without practical experience. In his new duties he had to rely on brains, self-confidence, and hard work. With these he did extraordinarily well. He had a remarkable grasp of productive and financial interrelations in the economy. The policies he formulated were sound. His management of the Bank, despite his inexperience, was efficient. His great weakness was naïveté, born of his ignorance of strife . . . .

Nicholas Biddle's response to the Jacksonian attack was inept. He was slow in recognizing that an attack was being made and ignored the warnings of his more astute friends. He expected the public to be moved by careful and learned explanations of what the Bank did. He broadcast copies of Jackson's veto message, one of the most popular and effective documents in American political history, with the expectation that people in general would agree with him that it was a piece of hollow demagogy. He entered a match for which he had no aptitude, impelled by a quixotic sense of duty and an inability to let his work be derogated. He engaged in a knock-down-drag-out fight with a group of experts as relentless as any American politics has ever known. The picture he presents is that of Little Lord Fauntleroy, lace on his shirt and good in his heart, running into those rough boys down the alley.

In his proper technical responsibilities Nicholas Biddle was a competent central banker performing a highly useful and beneficial task. It is a pity he had to be interrupted, both for him and for the economy. For him it meant demoralization. He lost track of what was going on in the Bank, he made blundering mistakes, he talked big. These things his opponents used tellingly against him. He turned from able direction of the central banking process to the hazardous business of making money, of which he knew nothing and for which his only knack lay in an enthusiastic appraisal of America's great economic future. In the end his Bank of the United States broke, he lost his fortune, he was tried on criminal charges (but released on a technicality), and he died a broken man.

This was personal misfortune, undeserved and severe. The more important victim was the American people. For with destruction of the United States Bank there was removed from an overexcitable economy the influence most effective in moderating its booms and depressions.

Andrew Jackson had vetoed recharter in 1832 and transferred the federal accounts to the pet banks in 1833 and 1834. The Bank's federal charter expired in 1836, though Nicholas Biddle obtained a charter from Pennsylvania and continued the organization as a state bank. The period was one of boom. Then in 1837 there was panic, all the banks in the country suspended, prices fell, and business collapsed. It was all Andrew Jackson's fault, his opponents declared, for killing the federal Bank. This was too generous. Jackson was not to blame for everything. The crisis was world-wide and induced by many forces. It would have happened anyway. Yet certainly Jackson's destruction of the Bank did not help. Instead it worsened the collapse. Had the Bank been allowed to continue the salutary performance of the years immediately preceding the attack upon it, and had it been supported rather than undermined by the Administration, the wild inflation which culminated in the collapse would have been curbed and the disaster diminished. Such a course would have been consistent with Jackson's convictions and professions. Instead he smote the Bank fatally at the moment of its best performance and in the course of trends against which it was needed most. Thereby he gave unhindered play to the speculation and inflation that he was always denouncing.

To a susceptible people the prospect was intoxicating. A continent abounding in varied resources and favorable to the maintenance of an immense population in the utmost comfort spread before the gaze of an energetic, ambitious, and clever race of men, who to exploit its wealth had two new instruments of miraculous potency: steam and credit. They rushed forward into the bright prospect, trampling, suffering, succeeding, failing. There was nothing to restrain them. For about a century the big rush lasted. Now it is over. And in a more critical mood we note that a number of things are missing or have gone wrong.

That critical mood was known to others than Jackson. Emerson, Hawthorne, and Thoreau felt it. So did an older and more experienced contemporary of theirs, Albert Gallatin, friend and aide in the past to Thomas Jefferson, and now president of a New York bank but loyal to Jeffersonian ideals.

"The energy of this nation," he wrote to an old friend toward the end of Andrew Jackson's Administration, "is not to be controlled; it is at present exclusively applied to the acquisition of wealth and to improvements of stupendous magnitude. Whatever has that tendency, and of course an immoderate expansion of credit, receives favor. The apparent prosperity and the progress of cultivation, population, commerce, and improvement are beyond expectation. But it seems to me as if general demoralization was the consequence; I doubt whether general happiness is increased; and I would have preferred a gradual, slower, and more secure progress. I am, however, an old man, and the young generation has a right to govern itself. . . ."

In these last words, Mr. Gallatin was echoing the remark of Thomas Jefferson that "the world belongs to the living." Neither Gallatin nor Jefferson, however, thought it should be stripped by the living. Yet nothing but the inadequacy of their powers seems to have kept those nineteenth-century generations from stripping it. And perhaps nothing else could.

But to the extent that credit multiplies man's economic powers, curbs upon credit extension are a means of conservation, and an important means. The Bank of the United States was such a means. Its career was short and it had imperfections. Nevertheless it worked. The evidence is in the protest of the bankers and entrepreneurs, the lenders and the borrowers, against its restraints. Their outcry against the oppressor was heard, and Andrew Jackson hurried to their rescue. Had he not, some other way of stopping its conservative and steadying influence could doubtless have been found. The appetite for credit is avid, as Andrew Jackson knew in his day and might have foretold for ours. But because he never meant to serve it, the credit for what happened goes rather to the clever advisers who led the old hero to the monster's lair and dutifully held his hat while he stamped on its head and crushed it in the dust.

Meanwhile, the new money power had curled up securely in Wall Street, where it has been at home ever since.

William Sidney Mount was a founder of the American school of genre art. In The Rustic Dance *(1830, detail), he portrayed antebellum society with lighthearted candor.*

Part Five
Antebellum Society

Bernard A. Weisberger
Religion on the Frontier

The following essay illustrates how exotic and colorful historical material can be presented in all its vigor without the historian surrendering his obligation to analyze and explain the significance of the subject he is describing. Indeed, in this case the discussion of the "meaning" of a backwoods revivalism adds greatly to the verisimilitude of the strange events themselves. Portraits of the emotionally charged religious camp meetings of the nineteenth-century frontier easily degenerate into caricature. Bernard A. Weisberger studiously avoids this trap both by showing that the meetings were complex affairs (to which many kinds of people, driven by differing urges, came) and by pointing out the rational bases for the meetings and the emotional excesses they generated. He takes a relatively narrow subject, frontier religion, and relates it to a wide range of larger questions: American democracy; east-west conflicts; the nature of nationalism; human nature itself.

Dr. Weisberger, formerly a professor of history at Chicago, Rochester, and other universities, is currently devoting himself full time to historical research and writing. Among his books are *They Gathered at the River,* a study of revivalism, *The American Newspaperman,* and *The New Industrial Society.*

Т he Great Revival in the West, or the Kentucky Revival of 1800, as it was sometimes called, was a landmark in American history. It was not some accidental outburst of religious hysteria that crackled through the clearings. Rather, it was one of many answers to a question on which America's destiny hung during Thomas Jefferson's Presidency. Which way would the West go? It was filling up fast in 1800, and yet it still remained isolated behind the mountain barriers, only thinly linked to the nation by a cranky, awkward, and dangerous transportation "system" of trails and rivers. Could it be held within the bounds of American institutions as they had developed over 175 colonial years? Would its raw energies pull it into some new orbit—say, an independent confederation? Or, if it stayed in the Union, would it send representatives swarming back eastward to crush old patterns under the weight of numbers?

No group asked this question more anxiously than eastern clergymen. For, in 1800, they saw that their particular pattern was being abandoned on the frontier. From Kentucky, Tennessee, the western Carolinas, and Virginia, reports came back of a world that was shaggy, vicious, and churchless. The hard-living men and women of the forest clearings were not raising temples to God. Their morals (to eastern eyes) were parlous. Corn liquor flowed freely; marriages were celebrated long after children had arrived; gun and rope settled far too many legal disputes. The West was crowded with Sabbath-breakers and profane swearers, thieves, murderers, and blasphemers, with neither courts of law nor public opinion to raise a rebuke. The whole region seemed "hair-hung and breeze-shaken" over Hell's vault. And this was a matter of life-or-death seriousness to the churches. It was clear even then that America's future lay beyond the mountains. And if the West grew up Godless, then the entire nation would one day turn from His ways, to its destruction. It was no wonder that pious folk of the seaboard dug into their pocketbooks to scrape up funds for "home missionary" societies aimed at paying the way of parsons traveling westward. Or that church assemblies warned of crises ahead and called for special days of fasting, humiliation, and prayer for the West.

Yet, for a fact, the easterners were wrong. They misjudged their pioneers. Western people wanted and needed the church just as badly as the church needed their support for survival. Religion had a part to play in the hard-driven lives of the frontier settlers. It was more than a mere foundation for morality. It offered the hope of a bright future, shining beyond the dirt-floored, hog-and-hominy present. It offered an emotional outlet for lives ringed with inhibition. It was a social thing, too, furnishing occasions on which to lay aside axe and gun and skillet and gather with neighbors, to sing, to weep, to pray, or simply to talk with others. The West had to have religion—but religion of its own special kind. The West was not "lost" in 1800, but on the verge of being saved. Only it was going to be saved the same way it did everything else: on its own individualistic terms.

The East found this hard to understand. The East had trouble taking stock of such a man as the father of the western revival, James McGready. McGready was an angular, black-eyed Scotch-Irishman, born on the Pennsylvania frontier. He came of a hard-working and pious stock that had filled the western stretches of the Colonies in the sixty years before the Revolution. McGready was true to the spirit of his Highland Calvinistic ancestors, who worked, prayed, and fought heartily. He grew to adolescence without becoming a swearer, drinker, or Sabbath-breaker, which made him something of a God-fearing rarity among frontier youth. So his family sent him to a private school conducted by a minister, where he wrestled with Scripture in the morning and did farm chores in the afternoon for his "tuition." In 1788, he was licensed to preach, and came down to western North Carolina's Guilford County, where his family had moved. Thus, McGready was a product of western Presbyterianism.

That was important. In the 1790's, the religious picture in the United States already showed considerable (and characteristic) variety. Episcopalianism was solidly rooted among the landed gentry of the South. The Dutch Reformed Church carried on the heritage established when the flag of Holland flapped over New York. Various shoots of Lutheranism pushed up out of the soil of German settlements. Baptism and Methodism were small but growing faiths. There were little wedges in the pie of church membership labeled "Quaker," "Catholic," and "Jewish." A few bold souls called themselves Deists. A few more were on the way to becoming Unitarians. American worship wore a coat of many colors. But in New England and the mid-Atlantic states, the Presbyterian and Congregational bodies were unquestionably in the forefront. Both were rooted in the preceding century's Puritanism. Both officially believed in "predestination" and "limited election"—God had chosen a few individuals to be saved from general damnation, and the list, made up from the beginning of eternity, was unchangeable. These chosen "saints" were born in sin, but in His own way God would convert them to holiness during their lifetimes. Meanwhile, the laws of God must be interpreted and explained to mankind. In order to do this, the Presbyterians and Congregationalists had raised up colleges to train their ministers, the most famous among them by 1800 being Harvard, Yale, and Princeton. Graduates of these schools thundered of Jehovah's wrath to their congregations in two-hour sermons rich with samples of their learning. During the week they warmed their study chairs ten hours a day, writing black-bound volumes of theology.

Religion of this sort lacked appeal for the Scotch-Irish migrants pushing into the frontier regions. They were Presbyterians in name. But their wild surroundings did something to them. They came to resent authority—whether exercised by excise collectors, land speculators, lawyers, or, finally, ministers. What was more, they wanted a little stronger assurance of salvation than a strict reading of limited election gave them. There was a need, in this fur-capped, bewhiskered Christian world, for more promise in life, and more passion too. Learned lectures might do for townspeople, but not for pioneers.

Among common folk, both East *and* West, a ferment of resentment against the "aristocratic" notion of election was at work. In the 1740's it had exploded in a revival called the Great Awakening. Baptist, Presbyterian, Congregationalist, Anglican, and Dutch-Reformed Christians were caught up in a common whirlwind of handclapping, shouting, and hosannaing. A good many new leaders, and a number of unpleasant schisms, had risen out of this storm. And in western Pennsylvania, revival-minded Presbyterians had founded a number of little academies to train their preachers. Derisively dubbed "log colleges" by the learned, they took the name proudly. Their graduates were short on Greek and exegesis but long on zeal. When the Great Awakening sputtered out before the Revolution, these colleges remained, helping to keep the sparks alive. Now, with the new nation established, the fire was ready to blaze again. McGready, himself a log-college graduate, was one of the first to blow on it.

McGready got to grips with the powers of darkness in North Carolina without wasting any time. He began to preach against the "formality and deadness" of the local churches. Besides that, he

*Anabaptists of Hudson Falls, New York, attend
a convert's immersion in the Hudson River.*

demanded some concrete testimony of good living from his flock, and the particular evidence he asked for was highly exacting. The new preacher insisted that strong drink was a slippery path to Hell. In Guilford County this did not sit well. Frontiersmen saw no harm in lightening a hard life with a dram or two, and they wanted no lectures on the subject from men of the cloth. In point of fact, there was no cloth. Pioneer ministers wore buckskin, and took their turn with the next man at hoeing corn or splitting kindling. McGready got nowhere—at least nowhere in North Carolina. After a futile battle, he left to seek a more promising future in Kentucky—some said by request of the congregation.

In Kentucky, circumstances were riper for him. Despite eastern concern, a new Christian community was taking shape in that rugged, bear-and-savage-haunted wilderness province, where crude living went along with high dreaming. It was a community ready to be stirred into life, and McGready was the man to seize the stick. In Logan County, in the southwestern part of the state—a region well-known for unre-generate doings—he had three small congregations: at Red River, Gasper River, and Muddy River. He began to preach to these con-gregations, and he did not deal with such recondite matters as the doctrines contained in Matthew, or their applications. Instead he would "so describe Heaven" that his listeners would "see its glories and long to be there." Then he went on to "array hell and its horrors" so that the wicked would "tremble and quake, imagining a lake of fire and brimstone yawning to overwhelm them." With that brim-stone smoking away in the background, McGready struck for bedrock. The whole point of Christianity, for him, was in the conversion of sinners to saints assured of eternal bliss. His question of questions was dagger-sharp: "If I were converted, would I feel it and know it?" A McGready parishioner was not going to be allowed to rest in self-satisfaction merely because he attended worship and avoided the grosser forms of indecency.

Under such spurring, results began to show among the faithful. In 1799, during a service at Gasper River, many fell to the ground and lay "powerless, groaning, praying and crying for mercy." Women began to scream. Big, tough men sobbed like hysterical children. What could explain this? Simply the fact that belly-deep fear was taking over. For it is well to remember that in those days conversion was the *only* token of salvation. No matter how young one was, no matter how blameless a life he had led, until the moment of transformation one was a sinner, bound for torment. If death stepped in before conversion was completed, babes and grandsires alike sank screaming into a lake of burning pitch—a lake that was not metaphorical, not symbolical, but *real* and eternal. And death on the frontier was always around the corner—in the unexpected arrow, the milk sickness, the carelessly felled tree, the leap of the wounded grizzly. Frontiersmen bottled up their fear. It was the price of sanity and survival. But when a religious service provided an acceptable excuse for breaking down the barriers, it was no wonder that men shivered and wept.

After shaking up the dry bones of the Gasper River settlement, McGready moved on in June of 1800 to Red River. He meant to hold a sacramental service, at the end of which church members would take the Lord's Supper together. What he got was something more uncontrolled. In a meetinghouse of undressed logs McGready shared his pulpit with three other Presbyterian ministers. A Methodist preacher was also present. That was not unusual. Frontier preachers were a small band. They knew each other well. A service was a social occasion, and therefore a treat, and several ministers often took part in order to draw it out.

The Presbyterian shepherds did their preaching, and what they said has not come down to us, but they must have dragged a harrow through the congregation's feelings. When John McGee, the Methodist, arose, an awesome hush had fallen on the house. McGee faced a problem. The Methodists were relative newcomers to America, officially on the scene only since 1766. They were frowned on by more established groups, mainly because they gave emotion free rein in their worship. It was not unusual at a Methodist meeting for women to faint, men to shout in strange tongues, and the minister himself to windmill his arms and bawl himself red-faced. For the more formal Presbyterians, such conduct was out of bounds. McGee knew this, and wanted to mind his ecclesiastical manners. But he knew a ripe audience when he saw one, too, and after an apparent debate with himself, he made his move. Rising, he shouted that everyone in the house should submit to "the Lord Omnipotent." Then he began to bounce from backless bench to backless bench, pleading, crying, shouting, shaking, and exhorting, "with all possible energy and ecstasy."

That broke the dam. The sinners of Red River had spent a lonely winter with pent-up terrors gnawing at them. McGee's appeal was irresistible. In a moment the floor was "covered with the slain; their screams for mercy pierced the heavens." Cursers, duelers, whiskey-swillers, and cardplayers lay next to little children of ten and eleven, rolling and crying in "agonies of distress" for salvation. It was a remarkable performance for a region "destitute of religion." When it was through, a new harvest of souls had been gathered for the Lord.

Word of the Red River meeting whisked through the territory. When McGready got to Muddy River, his next congregation, new scenes of excitement were enacted. During the meeting, sinners prayed and cried for mercy once again, and some of them, overwhelmed by feeling, bolted from the house and rushed in agony into the woods. Their cries and sobs could be heard ringing through the surrounding trees. And when this meeting had yielded up its quota of saved, the Kentucky Revival was not only a fact, but a well-known one. McGready announced another sacramental meeting for Gasper River, and before long, dozens, perhaps hundreds, of Kentuckians who did not belong to his district were threading the trails on their way to the service. Some came as far as a hundred miles, a hard week's trip in the back country. In wagons, on horseback, and on foot came the leather-shirted men, rifles balanced on their shoulders, and their pinched-looking, tired women, all looking for blessed assurance and a washing away of their sins.

At Gasper River, history was made. The cabins of the neighborhood could not hold the influx of visitors, so the newcomers came prepared to camp out. They brought tents—some of them—and cold pork, roasted hens, slabs of corn bread, and perhaps a little whiskey to hold them up through the rigors of a long vigil. The Gasper River meetinghouse was too small for the crowd, so the men got out their educated axes, and in a while the clop-clop of tree-felling formed an overture to the services. Split-log benches were dragged into place outdoors, and the worshipers adjourned to God's first temple. What was taking place was an outdoor religious exercise, meant to last two or three days, among people who camped on the spot. This was the camp meeting. Some claimed that Gasper River sheltered the very first of them. That claim has been challenged in the court of historical inquiry. But whether it stands up or not, the Gasper River meeting was something new in worship. It took its form from its western surroundings. Outsiders were a long time in understanding it, because they saw its crude outside and not its passionate heart.

The outside was raw enough. Once again McGready exhorted, and once again sinners fell prostrate to the ground. Night came on; inside the meetinghouse, candlelight threw grotesque, waving shadows on the walls. Outside, the darkness deepened the sense of mystery and of eternity's nearness. Preachers grew hoarse and exhausted, but insatiable worshipers gathered in knots to pray together, and to relieve their feelings by telling each other of "the sweet wonders which they saw in Christ." Hour followed hour, into dawn. For people who had to rise (and generally retire) with the sun each day of their lives, this alone was enough to make the meeting memorable for the rest of their lives. Lightheaded and hollow-eyed, the "mourners," or unconverted, listened alternately to threats of sulphur and promises of bliss, from Saturday until Monday. On Tuesday, after three throbbing days, they broke it up. Forty-five had professed salvation. Satan had gotten a thorough gouging.

Now the tide of camp-meeting revivalism began to roll northward. One of the visitors at the Logan County meetings was a young Presbyterian clergyman whose life was something of a copy of McGready's. Barton Warren Stone too had learned on the frontier to revere God Almighty and to farm well. He too had studied religion in a log college. But more than this, he was one of McGready's own converts, having fallen under the power of the older man's oratory in North Carolina. Stone liked what he observed in Logan County, and he took McGready's preaching methods and the camp-meeting idea back to his own congregations in Bourbon County, well to the north and east. Soon he too had imitators, among them Richard McNemar, who had small Presbyterian charges across the river in Ohio.

But it was Stone himself who touched off the monster camp meeting of the region's history. He set a sacramental service for August 6, 1801, at Cane Ridge, not far from the city of Lexington. Some unde-

*With the help of the Word, and sometimes of
the bottle, frontier camp meetings went on for
days and reaped rich harvests of converts.*

finable current of excitement running from cabin to cabin brought out every Kentuckian who could drop his earthly concerns and move, by horseflesh or shoe leather, toward the campground. Later on, some people estimated that 25,000 were on hand, but that figure is almost too fantastic for belief. In 1800, Kentucky had only a quarter of a million residents, and Lexington, the largest town, numbered under two thousand. But even a crowd of three or four thousand would have overwhelmed anything in the previous experience of the settlers.

Whatever the actual number, there was a sight to dazzle the eyes of the ministers who had come. Technically the meeting was Presbyterian, but Baptist and Methodist parsons had come along, and there was room for them, because no one man could hope to reach such a mob. Preaching stands built of logs were set up outdoors. One man remembered a typical scene—a crowd spilling out of the doors of the one meetinghouse, where two Presbyterian ministers were alternately holding forth, and three other groups scattered within a radius of a hundred yards. One cluster of sinners was gathered at the feet of a Presbyterian preacher, another gave ear to a Methodist exhorter, and lastly, a knot of Negroes was attending on the words of some orator of their own race. All over the campground, individual speakers had gathered little audiences to hear of *their* experiences. One observer said that there were as many as three hundred of these laymen "testifying."

So Cane Ridge was not really a meeting, but a series of meetings that gathered and broke up without any recognizable order. One Methodist brother who could not find a free preaching-stand ventured up the slanting trunk of a partly fallen tree. He found a flat spot, fifteen feet off the ground, and he spoke from this vantage point while a friend on the ground held up an umbrella on a long pole to shelter him from the weather. Within a few moments, this clergyman claimed, he had gathered an audience of thousands. Undoubtedly they stayed until lured away by some fresh address from a stump or the tail of a wagon. For the crowds were without form as they collected, listened, shouted "Amen!" and "Hallelujah!" and drifted off to find neighbors or refreshments or more preaching. The din can only be guessed at. The guilty were groaning and sometimes screaming at the top of their lungs, and those who felt that they were saved were clapping their hands, shouting hymns, and generally noising out their exultation. There were always hecklers at the meetings too, and some of them were no doubt shouting irreverent remarks at the faithful. Crying children added their bit, and tethered horses and oxen stamped, bawled, and whinnied to make the dissonance complete. Someone said that the meeting sounded from afar like the roar of Niagara. At night the campfires threw weird shadow-patterns of trees across the scene, and the whole moving, resounding gathering appeared to be tossing on the waves of some invisible storm. As if to etch the experience into men's memories, there were real rainstorms, and the drenched participants were thrown into fresh waves of screaming as thunder and lightning crashed around them.

All in all, a memorable enough episode. And yet still stranger things happened to put the brand of the Lord's sponsorship on Cane Ridge's mass excitement. Overwhelmed with their sensations, some men and women lay rigid and stiff on the ground for hours in a kind of catalepsy. One "blasphemer" who had come to scoff at the proceedings tumbled from his saddle unconscious and remained so for a day and a half. There was something incredibly compelling in what was going on. One remembered testimony came from a reasonably hardheaded young man named James Finley. Later in life Finley became a Methodist preacher, but in 1801 he was, except for a better-than-average education, a typical frontiersman. He had a small farm, a new wife, and a vigorous love of hunting. He had come to the Cane Ridge meeting out of curiosity, but as he looked on, he was taken with an uncontrollable trembling and feelings of suffocation. He left the campground, found a log tavern, and put away a glass of brandy to steady his nerves. But they were beyond steadying. All the way home he kept breaking out in irrational fits of laughter or tears. Many a spirit, returning from Cane Ridge, must have been moved in the same near-hysterical way.

A holy frenzy seemed to have taken hold of the West. Throughout the frontier communities, the ecstasy of conversion overflowed into the nervous system. At Cane Ridge, and at a hundred subsequent meetings, the worshipers behaved in ways that would be unbelievable if there were not plenty of good testimony to their truth. Some got the "jerks," a spasmodic twitching of the entire body. They were a fearful thing to behold. Some victims hopped from place to place like bouncing balls. Sometimes heads snapped from side to side so rapidly that faces became a blur, and handkerchiefs whipped off women's heads. One preacher saw women taken with the jerks at table, so that teacups went flying from their hands to splash against log walls. Churchmen disagreed about the meaning of these symptoms. Were they signs of conversion? Or demonstrations of the Lord's power, meant to convince doubters? Peter Cartwright, a famous evangelist of a slightly later era, believed the latter. He told of a skeptic at one of his meetings who was taken with the jerks and in a particularly vicious spasm snapped his neck. He died, a witness to the judgment of Omnipotence but gasping out to the last his "cursing and bitterness." Besides the jerks, there were strange seizures in which those at prayer broke into uncontrollable guffaws or intoned weird and wordless melodies or barked like dogs.

It was wild and shaggy, and very much a part of life in the clearings. Westerners wanted to feel religion in their bones. In their tough and violent lives intellectual exercises had no place, but howls and leaps were something that men who were "half-horse and half-alligator" understood. It was natural for the frontier to get religion with a mighty roar. Any other way would not have seemed homelike to people who, half in fun and half in sheer defensiveness, loved their brag, bluster, and bluff.

Yet there was something deeper than mere excitement underneath it all. Something fundamental was taking place, some kind of genuine religious revolution, bearing a made-in-America stamp. The East was unhappy with it. For one thing, camp-meeting wildness grated on the nerves of the educated clergy. All of this jigging and howling looked more like the work of Satan than of God. There were ugly rumors too, about unsanctified activities at the meetings. Some candidates for salvation showed up with cigars between their teeth. Despite official condemnation, liquor flowed free and white-hot on the outskirts of the gatherings. It might be that corn did more than its share in justifying God's ways to man. Then there were stories that would not down which told how, in the shadows around the clearing, excited men and women were carried away in the hysteria and, as the catch phrase had it, "begot more souls than were saved" at the meeting. All these tales might have had some partial truth, yet in themselves they did not prove much about frontier religion. As it happened, a part of every camp-meeting audience apparently consisted of loafers and rowdies who came for the show and who were quite capable of any sin that a Presbyterian college graduate was likely to imagine.

Yet it was not the unscrubbed vigor of the meetings that really bothered conservatives in the Presbyterian Church. Their fundamental problem was in adjusting themselves and their faith to a new kind of democratic urge. Enemies of the revivals did not like the success of emotional preaching. What would happen to learning, and all that learning stood for, if a leather-lunged countryman with a gift for lurid word pictures could be a champion salvationist? And what would happen—what *had* happened—to the doctrine of election when the revival preacher shouted "Repent!" at overwrought thousands, seeming to say that any Tom, Dick, or Harry who felt moved by the Spirit might be receiving the promise of eternal bliss? Would mob enthusiasm replace God's careful winnowing of the flock to choose His lambs? The whole orderly scheme of life on earth, symbolized by a powerful church, an educated ministry, and a strait and narrow gate of salvation, stood in peril.

Nor were the conservatives wrong. In truth, when the McGreadys and Stones struck at "deadness" and "mechanical worship" in the older churches, they were going beyond theology. They were hitting out at a view of things that gave a plain and unlettered man little chance for a say in spiritual affairs. A church run by skilled theologians was apt to set rules that puzzled simple minds. A church which held that many were called, but few chosen, *was* aristocratic in a sense. The congregations of the western evangelists did not care for rules, particularly rules that were not immediately plain to anyone. In their view, the Bible alone was straightforward enough. Neither would they stand for anything resembling aristocracy, whatever form it might take. They wanted cheap land and the vote, and they were getting these things. They wanted salvation as well—or at least free and easy access to it—and they were bound to have that too. If longer-established congregations and their leaders back east did not like that notion, the time for a parting of the ways was at hand. In politics, such a parting is known as a revolution; in religion, it is schism. Neither word frightened the western revivalists very much.

The trouble did not take long to develop. In McGready's territory, a new Cumberland Presbytery, or subgroup, was organized in 1801. Before long it was in a battle with the Kentucky Synod, the next highest administrative body in the hierarchy. The specific issue was the licensing of certain "uneducated" candidates for the ministry. The root question was revivalism. The battle finally went up to the General Assembly, for Presbyterians a sort of combined Congress and Supreme Court. In 1809 the offending revivalistic presbytery was dissolved. Promptly, most of its congregations banded themselves into the separate Cumberland Presbyterian Church. Meanwhile, Barton Stone, Richard McNemar, and other members of the northern Kentucky wing of camp-meeting Presbyterianism were also in trouble. They founded a splinter group known as the "New Lights," and the Kentucky Synod, as might have been foreseen, lost little time in putting the New Lights out, via heresy proceedings. Next, they formed an independent Springfield Presbytery. But like all radicals, they found it easier to keep going than to apply the brakes. In 1804 the Springfield Presbytery fell apart. Stone and some of his friends joined with others in a new body, shorn of titles and formality, which carried the magnificently simple name of the Christian Church. Later on, Stone went over to the followers of Thomas and Alexander Campbell, who called themselves Disciples of Christ. Richard McNemar, after various spiritual adventures, became a Shaker. Thus, ten years after Cane Ridge, the score was depressing for Presbyterians. Revivalism had brought on innumerable arguments, split off whole presbyteries, and sent ministers and congregations flying into the arms of at least four other church groups. That splintering was a stronger indictment than any conservative could have invented to bring against Cane Ridge, or against its western child, the camp meeting.

A dead end appeared to have been reached. But it was only a second-act curtain. In the first act, religion in the West, given up for lost, had been saved by revivalism. In the second, grown strong and rambunctious, it had quarreled with its eastern parents. Now the time was at hand for a third-act resolution of the drama. Both sides would have to back down and compromise. For the lesson of history was already plain. In religious matters, as in all matters, East and West, metropolis and frontier, were not really warring opposites. Each nourished the other, and each had an impact on the other. Whatever emerged as "American" would carry some of the imprint of both, or it would perish.

On the part of the West, the retreat consisted of taming the camp meeting. Oddly enough, it was not the Presbyterians who did that. By 1812 or so, they had drawn back from it, afraid of its explosive qualities. But the Methodists were in an excellent position to make use of revivalism and all its trappings. They had, at that time at least, no educated conservative wing. They welcomed zealous backwood preachers, even if they were grammatically deficient. In fact, they worked such men into their organization and sent them, under the name of "circuit-riders," traveling tirelessly on horseback to every lonely settlement that the wilderness spawned. The result was that the Methodists were soon far in the lead in evangelizing the frontier. They did not have to worry about the claims of limited election either. Their formal theology did not recognize it. With a plain-spoken and far-reaching ministry freely offering salvation to all true believers, Methodism needed only some kind of official harvest season to count and bind together the converts. The camp meeting was the perfect answer. By 1811, the Methodists had held four or five hundred of them throughout the country; by 1820, they had held a thousand—by far the majority of all such gatherings in the nation.

But these meetings were not replicas of Cane Ridge. They were combed, washed, and made respectable. Permanent sites were picked, regular dates chosen, and preachers and flocks given ample time to prepare. When meeting time came, the arriving worshipers in their wagons were efficiently taken in charge, told where to park their vehicles and pasture their teams, and given a spot for their tents. Orderly rows of these tents surrounded a preaching area equipped with sturdy benches and preaching stands. The effect was something like that of a formal bivouac just before a general's inspection. Tight scheduling kept the worship moving according to plan—dawn prayers, eight o'clock sermons, eleven o'clock sermons, dinner breaks, afternoon prayers and sermons, meals again, and candlelight services. Years of experience tightened the schedules, and camp-meeting manuals embodied the fruits of practice. Regular hymns replaced the discordant bawling of the primitive era. Things took on a generally homelike look. There were Methodist ladies who did not hesitate to bring their best feather beds to spread in the tents, and meals tended to be planned and ample affairs. Hams, turkeys, gravies, biscuits, preserves, and melons produced contented worshipers and happy memories.

There were new rules to cope with disorderliness as well. Candles, lamps, and torches fixed to trees kept the area well lit and discouraged young converts from amorous ways. Guards patrolled the circumference of the camp, and heroic if sometimes losing battles were fought to keep whiskey out. In such almost decorous surroundings jerks, barks, dances and trances became infrequent and finally nonexistent.

Not that there was a total lack of enthusiasm. Hymns were still yelled and stamped as much as sung. Nor was it out of bounds for the audience to pepper the sermon with ejaculations of "Amen!" and "Glory!" Outsiders were still shocked by some things they saw. But they did not realize how far improvement had gone.

Eastern churchmen had to back down somewhat, too. Gradually, tentatively, they picked up the revival and made it part of their religious life. In small eastern towns it became regularized into an annual season of "ingathering," like the harvest or the election. Yet it could not be contained within neat, white-painted meetinghouses. Under the "sivilized" clothing, the tattered form of Twain's Pap Finn persisted. Certain things were taken for granted after a time.

The doctrine of election was bypassed and, in practice, allowed to wither away.

Moreover, a new kind of religious leader, the popular evangelist, took the stage. Men like Charles G. Finney in the 1830's, Dwight L. Moody in the 1870's, and Billy Sunday in the decade just preceding the First World War flashed into national prominence. Their meetings overflowed church buildings and spilled into convention halls, auditoriums, and specially built "tabernacles." As it happened, these men came from lay ranks into preaching. Finney was a lawyer, Moody a shoe salesman, and Sunday a baseball player. They spoke down-to-earth language to their massed listeners, reduced the Bible to basic axioms, and drew their parables from the courtroom, the market, and the barnyard. They made salvation the only goal of their service, and at the meeting's end they beckoned the penitents forward to acknowledge the receipt of grace. In short, they carried on the camp-meeting tradition. By the closing years of the nineteenth century, however, the old campgrounds for the most part were slowly abandoned. Growing cities swallowed them up, and rapid transportation destroyed the original reason for the prolonged camp-out. But the meetings were not dead. Mass revivalism had moved them indoors and made them a permanent part of American Protestantism.

All of this cost something in religious depth, religious learning, religious dignity. Yet there was not much choice. The American churches lacked the support of an all-powerful state or of age-old traditions. They had to move with the times. That is why their history is so checkered with schismatic movements—symptoms of the struggle to get in step with the parade. Hence, if the West in 1800 could not ignore religion, the rest of the country, in succeeding years, could not ignore the western notion of religion. One student of the camp meeting has said that it flourished "side by side with the militia muster, with the cabin raising and the political barbecue." That was true, and those institutions were already worked deeply into the American grain by 1840. They reflected a spirit of democracy, optimism, and impatience that would sweep us across a continent, sweep us into industrialism, sweep us into a civil war. That spirit demanded some religious expression, some promise of a millennium in which all could share.

The camp meeting was part of that religious expression, part of the whole revival system that channeled American impulses into churchgoing ways. In the home of the brave, piety was organized so that Satan got no breathing spells. Neither, for that matter, did anyone else.

Elaine Kendall
The Education of Women

The great contemporary interest in the position of women in American society has led to many historical investigations in an attempt to throw light on how the current situation came to be. Much of this work has centered around the long struggle of feminists to obtain equal treatment before the law: the vote, equal pay for equal work, even such basic rights as that of married women to own property in their own names and to make wills without their husbands' approval. But historical attention has also been focused on other aspects of women's place—on such interesting questions as family structure and function in different periods, and, as in the following essay, on female education. The author, Elaine Kendall, traces the history of how girls were educated in America from colonial times to the middle of the nineteenth century. This is a story of progress, but of limited progress, one that helps explain both the strength of the feminists' demands for reform and the slowness with which these demands were achieved. Kendall is the author of a history of women's education, appropriately titled, as readers of her essay here will understand, *Peculiar Institutions*.

*C*ould I have died a martyr in the cause, and thus ensured its success, I could have blessed the faggot and hugged the stake.'' The cause was state support for female education, the would-be Saint Joan was Emma Willard, and the rhetorical standards of the 1820's were lofty and impassioned. The most militant feminists rarely scale such heights today. For one thing, dogged effort has finally reduced the supply of grand injustices; and today's preference for less florid metaphor has deprived the movement of such dramatic images. Comparatively speaking, the rest of the struggle is a downhill run, leading straight to twenty-four-hour day-care centers, revised and updated forms of marriage, free access to the executive suite, and rows of ''Ms's'' on Senate office doors. Glorying in our headway, we easily forget that leverage comes with literacy, and literacy for women is a relative novelty.

Long before the Revolution, American males already had Harvard, Yale, and Princeton, as well as a full range of other educational institutions—grammar schools, academies, seminaries, and numerous smaller colleges. American girls had only their mother's knee. By 1818, the year in which Emma Willard first introduced her *Plan for the Improvement of Female Education*, the gap was almost as wide as ever. Public schooling was a local option, quite whimsically interpreted. The towns could provide as much or as little as they wished, extending or restricting attendance as they saw fit. Ms. Willard presented her novel proposals to the New York State legislature, which dealt with the question by putting it repeatedly at the bottom of the agenda until the session was safely over. Lavish tributes to Mother's Knee filled the halls of Albany. In the opinion of the senators, M.'s K. not only outshone our men's colleges but also Oxford, Cambridge, and Heidelberg as an institution of female edification. Despite the support of De Witt Clinton, John Adams, and Thomas Jefferson, it was three more years—when a building and grounds were offered independently by the town of Troy—before the Willard Seminary actually got under way. The academy still flourishes and claims to ''mark the beginning of higher education for women in the United States.'' Since that is not precisely the same as being the first such school and the rival contenders have either vanished or metamorphosed into other sorts of institutions entirely, there is no reason to dispute it. The pre-Revolutionary South did have a few early convents, including one at New Orleans that was established by the Ursuline order in 1727 and taught religion, needlework, and something of what was called basic skills. Other religious groups, particularly the Moravians and Quakers, supported female seminaries during the eighteenth century, but these places did not really attempt to offer advanced education—a commodity for which there was little market in an era when girls were unwelcome in elementary schools. A few New England clergymen opened small academies for girls during the first decade of the nineteenth century, but these noble and well-intentioned efforts were ephemeral, never outlasting their founders.

Emma Willard.

Until Emma Willard succeeded in extracting that bit of real estate from Troy, public and private support for such ventures was virtually nonexistent.

Some few ambitious and determined girls did succeed in learning to read and write in colonial America, but hardly ever at public expense and certainly not in comfort. Their number was pitifully small, and those who gained more than the rudiments of literacy would hardly have crowded a saltbox parlor. . . .

As the grip of Puritanism gradually relaxed, the image of a learned female improved infinitesimally. She was no longer regarded as a disorderly person or a heretic but merely as a nuisance to her husband, family, and friends. A sensible woman soon found ways to conceal her little store of knowledge or, if hints of it should accidentally slip out, to disparage or apologize for it. Abigail Adams, whose wistful letters show a continuing interest in women's education, described her own with a demurely rhymed disclaimer:

The little learning I have gained
Is all from simple nature drained.

In fact, the wife of John Adams was entirely self-educated. She disciplined herself to plod doggedly through works of ancient history whenever her household duties permitted, being careful to do so in the privacy of her boudoir. In her letters she deplored the fact that it was still customary to "ridicule female learning" and even in the "best families" to deny girls more than the barest rudiments.

The prevailing colonial feeling toward female education was still so unanimously negative that it was not always thought necessary to mention it. Sometimes this turned out to be a boon. A few villages, in their haste to establish schools for boys, neglected to specify that only males would be admitted. From the beginning they wrote their charters rather carelessly, using the loose generic term "children." This loophole was nearly always blocked as soon as the risks became apparent, but in the interim period of grace girls were occasionally able to pick up a few crumbs of knowledge. They did so by sitting outside the schoolhouse or on its steps, eavesdropping on the boys' recitations. More rarely, girls were tolerated in the rear of the schoolhouse behind a curtain, in a kind of makeshift seraglio. This Levantine arrangement, however, was soon abandoned as inapproprate to the time and place, and the attendance requirements were made unambiguous. New England winters and Cape Cod architecture being what they are, the amount of learning that one could have acquired by these systems was necessarily scanty. Still it was judged excessive. The female scholars in the yard and on the stairs seemed to suffer disproportionately from pleurisy and other respiratory ailments. Further proof of the divine attitude toward the educating of women was not sought. Girls were excluded for their own good, as well as to ensure the future of the Colonies.

After the Revolution the atmosphere in the New England states did become considerably more lenient. Here and there a town council might vote to allow girls inside the school building from five to seven in the morning, from six to eight at night, or, in a few very liberal communities, during the few weeks in summer when the boys were at work in the fields or shipyards. This was a giant step forward and would have been epochal if teachers had always appeared at these awkward times. Unfortunately the girls often had to muddle through on their own without benefit of faculty. The enlightened trend, moreover, was far from general. In 1792 the town of Wellesley, Massachusetts, voted "not to be at any expense for schooling girls," and similarly worded bylaws were quite usual throughout the northern states until the 1820's. In the southern Colonies, where distances between the great estates delayed the beginnings of any public schooling even longer, wealthy planters often imported tutors to instruct their sons in academic subjects. If they could afford the additional luxury, they might also engage singing and dancing masters for the daughters, who were not expected to share their brothers' more arduous lessons. In a pleasant little memoir of the South, *Colonial Days and Dames*, Anne Wharton, a descendant of Thomas Jefferson, noted that "very little from books was thought necessary for a girl. She was trained to domestic matters . . . the accomplishments of the day . . . to play upon the harpischord or spinet, and to work impossible dragons and roses upon canvas."

Although the odds against a girl's gaining more than the sketchiest training during this era seem to have been overwhelming, there were some remarkable exceptions. The undiscouraged few included Emma Willard herself; Catherine and Harriet Beecher, the clergyman's daughters, who established an early academy at Hartford; and Mary Lyon, who founded the college that began in 1837 as Mount Holyoke Seminary. Usually, however, the tentative and halfhearted experiments permitted by the New England towns served only to give aid and comfort to the opposition. They seemed to show that the female mind was not inclined to scholarship and the female body was not strong enough to withstand exposure—*literal* exposure, in many cases—to it. By 1830 or so primary education had been grudgingly extended to girls almost everywhere, but it was nearly impossible to find anyone who dared champion any further risks. Boston had actually opened a girls' high school in 1826 only to abolish it two years later. . . .

Public schools obviously were not the only route to learning or most female American children up through colonial times would have been doomed to total ignorance. Fathers, especially clergymen fathers, would often drill their daughters in the Bible and sometimes teach them to read and do simple sums as well. Nothing that enhanced an understanding of the Scriptures could be entirely bad, and arithmetic was considered useful in case a woman were to find herself the sole support of her children. Brothers would sometimes lend or hand down their old school books, and fond uncles might help a favorite and clever niece with her sums. The boys' tutor was often amenable to a pretty sister's pleas for lessons. For those girls not fortunate enough to be the daughters of foresighted New England parsons or wealthy tobacco and cotton factors, most colonial towns provided dame schools. These catered to boys as well as to girls of various ages. They offered a supplement to the curriculum at Mother's Knee, but only just. Because these schools were kept by women who had acquired their own learning haphazardly, the education they offered was motley at best. The solitary teacher could impart no more than she herself knew, and that rarely exceeded the alphabet, the shorter catechism, sewing, knitting, some numbers, and perhaps a recipe for baked beans and brown bread. The actual academic function of these early American institutions seems to have been somewhat exaggerated and romanticized by historians. Dame schools were really no more than small businesses, managed by impoverished women who looked after neighborhood children and saw to it that idle little hands did not make work for the devil. The fees (tuition is too grand a word) were tiny, with threepence a week per child about par. That sum could hardly have paid for a single hornbook for the entire class. The dame school itself was an English idea, transplanted almost intact to the Colonies. Several seem to have been under way by the end of the seventeenth century. . . .

As the country became more affluent, schoolkeeping gradually began to attract more ambitious types. Older girls were still being excluded from the town seminaries and in many places from the grammar schools as well. A great many people quickly realized that there was money to be made by teaching the children of the new middle class and that they could sell their services for far more than pennies. No special accreditation or qualification was required, and there was no competition from the state. Toward the end of the eighteenth century and at the beginning of the nineteenth, platoons of self-styled professors invaded American towns and cities, promising to instruct both sexes and all ages in every known art, science, air, and grace. These projects were popularly known as adventure schools, a phrase that has a pleasant modern ring to it, suggesting open classrooms, free electives, and individual attention.

That, however, is deceptive. The people who ran such schools were usually adventurers in the not very admirable sense of the word: unscrupulous, self-serving, and of doubtful origins and attainments. Many simply equipped themselves with false diplomas and titles from foreign universities and set up shop. The schools continued to operate only as long as they turned a profit. When enrollment dropped, interest waned, or fraud became obvious, the establishment would simply fold and the proprietors move to another town for a fresh start. The newer territories were particularly alluring to the worst of these entrepreneurs, since their reputations could neither precede nor follow them there. A new name, a new prospectus, an ad in the gazette, and they were in business again until scandal or mismanagement obliged them to move on. Such "schools" were not devised for the particular benefit of girls; but because they were independent commercial enterprises, no solvent person was turned away. Thousands of young women did take advantage of the new opportunity and were, in many cases, taken advantage of in return. For boys the adventure schools were an alternative to the strict classicism and religiosity of the academies and seminaries, but for girls they were the only educational possibility between the dame school and marriage.

There was little effort to devise a planned or coherent course of study, though elaborately decorated certificates were awarded upon completion of a series of lessons. The scholar could buy whatever he or she fancied from a mind-bending list. One could take needlework at one place, languages at another, dancing or "ouranology" at a third. (It was a pompous era, and no one was fonder of polysyllables than the professors. Ouranology was sky-watching, but it sounded impressive.) There were no minimum or maximum course requirements, though the schoolmasters naturally made every effort to stock the same subjects offered by the competition, in order to reduce the incidence of school-hopping. . . .

Many of the adventure schools hedged their financial risks by functioning as a combination store and educational institution, selling fancywork, "very good Orange-Oyl," sweetmeats, sewing notions, painted china, and candles along with lessons in dancing, foreign languages, geography, penmanship, and spelling. Usually they were mama-and-papa affairs, with the wife instructing girls in "curious works" and the husband concentrating upon "higher studies." Curious works covered a great deal of ground—the making of artificial fruits and flowers, the "raising of paste," enamelling, japanning, quilting, fancy embroidery, and in at least one recorded case "flowering on catgut," an intriguing accomplishment that has passed into total oblivion, leaving no surviving examples.

The adventure schools advertised heavily in newspapers and journals of the period, often in terms indicating that teaching was not an especially prestigious profession. One Thomas Carroll took several columns in a May, 1765, issue of the New York *Mercury* to announce a curriculum that would have taxed the entire faculty of Harvard and then proceeded to explain that he "was not under the necessity of coming here to teach, he had views of living more happy, but some unforeseen and unexpected events have happened since his arrival here . . . ," thus reducing this Renaissance paragon to schoolkeeping and his lady to teaching French knots and quilting.

While they lasted adventure schools attempted to offer something for everyone, including adults, and came in all forms, sizes, and price ranges. They met anywhere and everywhere: "at the Back of Mr. Benson's Brew-House," in rented halls, in borrowed parlors, at inns, and from time to time in barns or open fields. The adventurer was usually available for private lessons as well, making house calls "with the utmost discretion," especially in the case of questionable studies like dancing or French verbs. The entire physical plant usually fitted into a carpetbag. . . .

The pretentious and empty promises of the adventure schools eventually aroused considerable criticism. Americans may not yet have appreciated the value of female education, but they seem always to have known the value of a dollar. It was not long before the public realized that flowering on catgut was not so useful an accomplishment for their daughters as ciphering or reading. The more marginal operators began to melt away, and those schoolmasters who hung on were obliged to devote more attention to practical subjects and eliminate many of the patent absurdities. . . .

Certain religious groups, particularly the Moravians and the

Quakers, had always eschewed frippery and pioneered in the more realistic education of women. Friends' schools were organized as soon as the size and prosperity of the settlements permitted them. This training emphasized housewifery but did include the fundamentals of literacy. Many of the earliest eighteenth-century Quaker primary schools were co-educational, though access to them was limited to the immediate community. Because these were concentrated in the Philadelphia area, girls born in Pennsylvania had a much better chance of acquiring some education than their contemporaries elsewhere. The Moravians (who also settled in the southeastern states) quickly recognized the general lack of facilities in the rest of the Colonies and offered boarding arrangements in a few of their schools. The student body soon included intrepid and homesick girls from New England and even the West Indies. These institutions were purposeful and rather solemn, the antithesis of superficiality. The Moravians insisted upon communal household chores as well as domestic skills, and in the eighteenth century these obligations could be onerous; dusting, sweeping, spinning, carding, and weaving came before embroidery and hemstitching. These homely lessons were enlivened by rhymes celebrating the pleasure of honest work. Examples survive in the seminary archives and supply a hint of the uplifting atmosphere:

> I've spun seven cuts, dear companions allow
> That I am yet little, and know not right how;
>
> Mine twenty and four, which I finished with joy,
> And my hands and my feet did willing employ.

Though the teaching sisters in these sectarian schools seem to have been kind and patient, the life was rigorous and strictly ordered, a distinct and not always popular alternative to pleasant afternoons with easygoing adventure masters. In an era when education for women was still widely regarded as a luxury for the upper classes, the appeal of the pioneering religious seminaries tended to be somewhat narrow. If a family happened to be sufficiently well-off to think of educating their girls, the tendency was to make fine ladies of them. As a result there were many young women who could carry a tune but not a number, who could model a passable wax apple but couldn't read a recipe, who had memorized the language of flowers but had only the vaguest grasp of English grammar. There seemed to be no middle ground between the austerities of the religious schools and the hollow frivolities offered by commercial ventures. Alternatives did not really exist until the 1820's, when the earliest tentative attempts were made to found independent academies and seminaries.

Catherine and Harriet Beecher, who were among the first to open a school designed to bridge the gulf, believed almost as strongly as the Moravians in the importance of domestic economy. They were, however, obliged by public demand to include a long list of dainty accomplishments in their Hartford curriculum. Many girls continued to regard the new secular seminaries as they had the adventure schools —as rival shops where they could browse or buy at will, dropping in and out at any time they chose. To the despair of the well-intentioned founders few students ever stayed to complete the course at any one place. Parents judged a school as if it were a buffet table, evaluating it by the number and variety of subjects displayed. In writing later of the difficult beginnings of the Hartford Seminary, Catherine Beecher said that "all was perpetual haste, imperfection, irregularity, and the merely mechanical commitment of words to memory, without any chance for imparting clear and connected ideas in a single branch of knowledge. The review of those days is like the memory of a troubled and distracting dream."

Public opinion about the education of girls continued to be sharply (if never clearly) divided until after the Civil War. Those who pioneered in the field were at the mercy of socially ambitious and ambivalent parents, confused and unevenly prepared students, and constantly shifting social attitudes. In sudden and disconcerting switches "the friends" of women's education often turned out to be less than wholehearted in their advocacy. Benjamin Rush, whose *Thoughts Upon Female Education*, written in 1787, influenced and inspired Emma Willard, Mary Lyon, and the Beecher sisters, later admitted that his thoughtful considerations had finally left him "not enthusiastical upon the subject." Even at his best, Rush sounds no more than tepid; American ladies, he wrote, "should be qualified to a certain degree by a peculiar and suitable education to concur in instructing their sons in the principles of liberty and government." During her long editorship of *Godey's Lady's Book* Sarah Josepha Hale welcomed every new female seminary and academy but faithfully reminded her readers that the sanctity of the home came first: ". . . on what does social well-being rest but in our homes . . . ?" "Oh, spare our homes!" was a constant refrain, this chorus coming from the September, 1856, issue. *Godey's Lady's Book* reflects the pervasive nineteenth-century fear that the educated woman might be a threat to the established and symbiotic pattern of American family life. The totally ignorant woman, on the other hand, was something of an embarrassment to the new nation. The country was inundated by visiting European journalists during this period, and they invariably commented upon the dullness of our social life and the disappointing vacuity of the sweet-faced girls and handsome matrons they met. Though Americans themselves seemed to feel safer with a bore than with a bluestocking, they were forced to give the matter some worried thought.

"If all our girls become philosophers," the critics asked, "who will darn our stockings and cook the meals?" It was widely, if somewhat irrationally, assumed that a maiden who had learned continental stichery upon fine lawn might heave to and sew up a shirt if necessary, but few men believed that a woman who had once tasted the heady delights of Shakespeare's plays would ever have dinner ready on time— or at all.

The founders of female seminaries were obliged to cater to this unease by modifying their plans and their pronouncements accordingly. The solid academic subjects were so generally thought irrelevant for "housewives and helpmates" that it was usually necessary to disguise them as something more palatable. The Beechers taught their girls chemistry at Hartford but were careful to assure parents and prospective husbands that its principles were applicable in the kitchen. The study of mathematics could be justified by its usefulness in running a household. Eventually the educators grew more daring, recommending geology as a means toward understanding the Deluge and other Biblical mysteries and suggesting geography and even history as suitable because these studies would "enlarge women's sphere of thought, rendering them more interesting as companions to men of science." There is, however, little evidence that many were converted to this extreme point of view. The average nineteenth-century American man was not at all keen on chat with an interesting companion, preferring a wife like the one in the popular jingle *"who never learnt the art of schooling/Untamed with the itch of ruling."* The cliché of the period was "woman's sphere." The phrase was so frequently repeated that it acquires almost physical qualities. Woman's Sphere—the nineteenth-century woman was fixed and sealed within it like a model ship inside a bottle. To tamper with the arrangement was to risk ruining a complex and fragile structure that had been painstakingly assembled over the course of two centuries. Just one ill-considered jolt might make matchwood of the entire apparatus.

In 1812 the anonymous author of *Sketches of the History, Genius, and Disposition of the Fair Sex* wrote that women are "born for a life of uniformity and dependence. . . . Were it in your power to give them genius, it would be almost always a useless and very often a dangerous present. It would, in general, make them regret the station which Providence has assigned them, or have recourse to unjustifiable ways to get from it." The writer identified himself only as a "friend of the sex" (not actually specifying which one).

This century's feminists may rage at and revel in such quotes, but the nineteenth-century educators were forced to live with this attitude and work within and around it. In order to gain any public or private support for women's secondary schools they had to prove that a woman would not desert her husband and children as soon as she could write a legible sentence or recite a theorem. That fear was genuine, and the old arguments resurfaced again and again. What about Saint Paul's injunction? What about the sanctity of the home? What about the health of the future mothers of the race? What about supper?

Advocates of secondary education for women, therefore, became consummate politicians, theologians, hygienists, and, when necessary, apologists. "It is desirable," wrote Mary Lyon in 1834 of her Mount Holyoke Female Seminary project, "that the plans relating to the subject should not seem to originate with us but with benevolent *gentlemen*. If the object should excite attention there is danger that

13

HORIZONTAL BAR.

14

THE TRIANGLE.

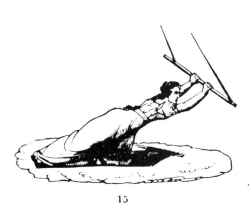

15

STOOPING FORWARD.

16

BENDING BACKWARD.

A series of genteel exercises for genteel young ladies from Godey's Lady's Book. *How the young ladies managed to perform much, if any, serious exercise swathed in those voluminous skirts remains something of a mystery.*

many good men will fear the effect on society of so much female influence and what they will call female greatness." New and subtle counterarguments were presented with great delicacy. God had entrusted the tender minds of children to women; therefore women were morally obliged to teach. The home would be a holier place if the chatelaine understood religious principles and could explain them. The founders of Abbot Academy proclaimed that "to form the immortal mind to habits suited to an immortal being, and to instill principles of conduct and form the character for an immortal destiny, shall be subordinate to no other care." All that harping on immortality went down smoothly in the evangelistic atmosphere of the 1820's. A thick coating of religion was applied to every new educational venture. The parents of prospective students were assured that their daughters would not only study religion in class but would have twice-daily periods of silent meditation, frequent revival meetings, and a Sunday that included all of these. In reading the early seminary catalogues, one finds it hard to see where secular studies could have fit in at all. To the religious guarantees were appended promises of careful attention to health. The educators lost no time in adding the new science of calisthenics to their curricula. They had the medical records of their students compared to that of the public at large and published the gratifying results in newspapers and magazines. Domestic work was also to be required of girls who attended the new seminaries, partly for economy's sake but mainly so that they would not forget their ultimate destiny.

All of this was calming and persuasive, but nothing was so effective as simple economics. By the 1830's most states had begun a program of primary public education. As the West followed suit the need for teachers became acute and desperate. Men were not attracted to the profession because the pay was wretched, the living conditions were lonely, and the status of a schoolmaster was negligible if not downright laughable. Saint Paul was revised, updated, and finally reversed. He had not, after all, envisioned the one-room schoolhouses of the American prairies, the wages of three dollars a month, or the practice of "boarding around."

Within an astonishingly short time fears for female health subsided. The first women teachers proved amazingly durable, able to withstand every rigor of frontier life. In a letter to her former headmistress one alumna of the Hartford Seminary described accommodations out west:

I board where there are eight children, and the parents, and only two rooms in the house. I must do as the family do about washing, as there is but one basin, and no place to go to wash but out the door. I have not enjoyed the luxury of either lamp or candle, their only light being a cup of grease with a rag for a wick. Evening is my only time to write, but this kind of light makes such a disagreeable smoke and smell, I cannot bear it, and do without light, except the fire. I occupy a room with three of the children and a niece who boards here. The other room serves as a kitchen, parlor, and bedroom for the rest of the family. . . .

Other graduates were just as stoical and often no more comfortable:

> I board with a physician, and the house has only two rooms. One serves as kitchen, eating, and sitting room; the other, where I lodge, serves also as the doctor's office, and there is no time, night or day, when I am not liable to interruption.
>
> My school embraces both sexes, and all ages from five to seventeen, and not one can read intelligibly. They have no idea of the proprieties of the schoolroom or of study. . . . My furniture consists now of . . . benches, a single board put up against the side of the room for a writing desk, a few bricks for andirons, and a stick of wood for shovel and tongs.

These letters were collected by Catherine Beecher in her book *True Remedy for the Wrongs of Women,* which advanced the cause of women's education by showing the worthwhile uses to which it could be put. Delighted with the early results, several states quickly set up committees to consider training women teachers on a larger scale. Their findings were favorable, though couched in oddly ambiguous language. New York's group reported that women seemed to be "endued with peculiar faculties" for the occupation. "While man's nature is rough, stern, impatient, ambitious, hers is gentle, tender, enduring, unaspiring." That was most encouraging, but the gentlemen also generously acknowledged that "the habits of female teachers are better and their morals purer; they are much more apt to be content with, and continue in, the occupation of teaching." A Michigan report stated in 1842 that "an elementary school, where the rudiments of an English education only are taught, such as reading, spelling, writing, and the outlines barely of geography, arithmetic, and grammar, requires a female of practical common sense with amiable and winning manners, a patient spirit, and a tolerable knowledge of the springs of human action. A female thus qualified, carrying with her into the schoolroom the gentle influences of her sex, will do more to inculcate right morals and prepare the youthful intellect for the severer discipline of its after years, than the most accomplished and learned male teacher." Far from objecting to these rather condescending statements, the founders of the struggling seminaries were more than happy to hear them. Even the miserable wages offered to teachers could be regarded as an advantage, since they provided the single most effective argument for more female academies. "But where are we to raise such an army of teachers as are required for this great work?" asked Catherine Beecher in the same book that contained the letters from her ex-students. "Not from the sex which finds it so much more honorable, easy, and lucrative, to enter the many roads to wealth and honor open in this land. . . . It is WOMAN who is to come [forth] at this emergency, and meet the demand—woman, whom experience and testimony have shown to be the best, as well as the cheapest guardian and teacher of childhood, in the school as well as the nursery."

Teaching became a woman's profession by default and by rationalization. Clergymen and theologians suddenly had nothing but praise for women teachers. God must have meant them to teach because he made them so good at it. They would work for a half or a third of the salary demanded by a man. What, after all, was a schoolroom but an extension of the home, woman's natural sphere? And if females had to have schools of their own to prepare them for this holy mission, then so be it. Future American generations must not be allowed to suffer for want of instruction when a Troy, Hartford, or Mount Holyoke girl asked no more than three dollars a month, safe escort to the boondocks, and a candle of her own.

Lewis Mumford
Ralph Waldo Emerson

Too often historians treat great individuals of the past only as reflections of their times, and draft from their lives and beliefs social blueprints or designs for the construction of large generalizations. All people, of course, are products of their surroundings; their ways of looking at the world, their basic values, even their language are to a large degree imposed upon them by the particular time and place in which they live. And the study of such persons and their careers is indeed a fruitful way to approach the study of their world. Nevertheless, the truly great are not merely reflections of a special *Zeitgeist,* and as biographers from the earliest times have recognized, their lives are important to later generations as examples, as inspiration, and for a dozen other didactic purposes. Such was the life of Ralph Waldo Emerson, as Lewis Mumford so well demonstrates in this essay.

Emerson was surely a product of early nineteenth-century American culture, as many lesser historians have noted, and Mumford reminds us of this. But Mumford does not place any special importance on this "typical" Emerson; instead he portrays the unique genius of Emerson and uses his life to throw light not so much on the nineteenth century as on the twentieth. To write history in this way demands not only a great subject but a great author. Lewis Mumford, best known as an architectural critic, has over a long and richly productive career established his own claim to greatness, both through his trenchant analyses of modern urban society and through his remarkable historical works, such as *The Brown Decades, The City in History,* and his biography of Herman Melville.

The first twenty-five years of Ralph Waldo Emerson's life —from 1803 to 1828—were a struggle for bodily survival. He was threatened with the lethal disease of his day, tuberculosis, which two of his three younger brothers finally succumbed to; and he was poor. His father, minister of Boston's First Unitarian Church, died when he was eight, and the Emerson family lived in genteel penury, so poor that Emerson was forced to share a greatcoat with a brother during the grim Boston winters. Soon after marrying, his father had reported: "We are poor and cold and have little meal, and little wood, and little meat; but thank God, courage enough."

Armed with this family fortitude, Emerson, like his younger brothers, managed to get a Harvard education; and in the end the discipline of poverty underwrote his independence. By merely external pressures he could not be bullied or bribed. The fact that the outer world gave him so little during his growing period fostered his habit of living from within. But there his widowed mother had set him a good example: even in their neediest days, she withdrew for an hour after breakfast from the cares of the household, to meditate behind a closed door.

"A man must thank his defects," Emerson wrote in "Fate," "and stand in some terror of his talents." His original defects were a poor constitution, low vitality, shyness and awkwardness in company, a lack of outward warmth and responsiveness. It took him half a lifetime to compensate for these defects, if not entirely to overcome them, in acts of hospitality and friendly service and secret generosity. These acts touched not only those he loved, like Thomas Carlyle, Henry Thoreau, or Bronson Alcott, but passing strangers. Happily, Emerson's courtly manners softened his remoteness; and to the very end, as Walt Whitman noted on a final visit to him, he bore a cheerful and intelligent face, such a face as Emerson regarded as the ultimate proof and justification of culture.

If some of Emerson's essays, like those on Love and on Friendship, seem a little too toplofty, a little too rarefied, this is perhaps because during his early years he could survive only by keeping his actual environment—that bed of nails—at a distance, and countering it with ideal possibilities that existed only in his mind. His immunity to pain and grief, or at least his reluctance to give vent to them, was not a mark of stolid optimism; it was rather a psychological nerve block that enabled him to get on with his true work: his daily reading of nature and culture and the human soul, for the sake of catching some new illumination; for, as he noted in 1861, "A rush of thoughts is the only conceivable prosperity that can come to me." Fortunately, after his first marriage, in 1829, Emerson's economic circumstances improved, though he never escaped the pressure of supporting a large household.

The dividing line in Emerson's intellectual development was his first trip to Europe, in 1833; for he returned from this adventure, despite its physical ordeals, in robust health, with the old threat of tuberculosis overcome, and a kind of inner toughness that enabled him later, as a lecturer, to withstand the most gruelling journeys into the West, in crowded canal-boats, in sordid inhospitable taverns, over jolting icy roads; crossing the Mississippi on foot in the depth of winter, sometimes reaching his destination more dead than alive. To have endured these vulgar indignities, to have survived these misadventures, without a groan of self-pity, marks Emerson's iron discipline. Such a character could (as he put it) afford to write "Whim" over his door.

The first trip to Europe was an attempt to overcome two crises in Emerson's life. The personal crisis was occasioned by the death (in 1831) of his first wife, Ellen Tucker: a lovely, quietly impish, impassioned spirit, who had awakened an ardor and a love that he found himself unable adequately to express. ("I do not wish to hear of your prospects," she had said when Emerson had begun to preface a declaration of love with a summary of modest material expectations.) Her going left an empty niche in his life that his second wife, Lydia Jackson, a maturer woman, could never fill. It was surely with Ellen in mind that he wrote, in 1840: "I finish this morning transcribing my old essay on Love, but I see well its inadequateness. I, cold because I am hot—cold at the surface only, as a sort of guard and compensation for the fluid tenderness of the core—have much more experience than I have written there, more than I will, more than I can write."

Ellen's death was Emerson's first direct encounter with grief and desolation; and it was followed in a few years by the premature deaths of two younger brothers, one of whom, Charles Chauncy, he always regarded as having talent superior to his own. Even before this, some sobering premonition had made him write, on being engaged to Ellen, that he was "now as happy as it is safe in life to be."

The other crisis was a religious one, occasioned by his abandoning the calling he had struggled during the eighteen twenties to fit himself for: that of a duly qualified clergyman in the Unitarian Church. He had approached the duties of a minister with some repulsion for the homely routines of visitation, comfort for the dying, and moral suasion, with all their intrusive intimacies. But still more, he had come to realize that the God he had found in his consciousness had little need for either the dogmas or the rituals of an established church: even the Christ that moved him was not a God come to earth, but a singular being who had demonstrated while on earth the secret by which any man might become godlike. Emerson broke with his congregation at the Second Church of Boston over a single issue: his unwillingness to celebrate the Lord's Supper. But that break widened during the next decade into a total rejection of the church's whole institutional life and its claims to a unique revelation.

This parting of the ways removed the economic prop of Emerson's life and made it necessary for him to find an alternative mode of getting a living: that of a lecturer at the new lyceums that were springing up all over the country. For Emerson the lecture hall had become the living church of his day, spreading a many-tongued gospel that was destined to replace the "cant and snuffle of a dead Christianity."

This photograph of the aging Emerson captures with remarkable clarity his philosophy of self-reliance and courage.

Emerson's lectures, in reality soliloquies spoken aloud, were little different in texture from the notes in his Journals, where many parts of them were first recorded as scattered items.

In shaking himself loose from the Unitarian Church, Emerson had found his true vocation: that of being Emerson. This new mode of preaching turned out to be another blessing in disguise, for without the direct, face-to-face contact with mixed audiences of everyday people, in every part of the country except the South, Emerson would have lacked his sense of the more expansive and masculine America one associates with Audubon and Lincoln. New Englander that he was, he respected the uncouth vigor of the pioneers. And when Emerson met

President Lincoln face to face, Lincoln reminded him of what he had said about Kentuckians in an Illinois lecture: "A Kentuckian seems to say by his air and manners, 'Here am I; if you don't like me, the worse for you.'"

Emerson's difficulties did not come to an end with his marriage to Lidian—as he re-named his second wife—in 1835, and his settling down in a commodious house, surrounded by a few acres of usable land at the edge of Concord: for if he had a good garden, productive pear trees, willing servants, a tender and devoted wife, he all too soon had the shattering experience of losing his five-year-old son Waldo to scarlet fever, that son whose angelic qualities had won free access to Emerson's otherwise inviolate study. Well had he written earlier to his spiritual monitor, Aunt Mary Moody Emerson: "He has seen but half the Universe who has never been shown the house of pain." Even in the serene years before little Waldo's death Emerson had faced, no less than Herman Melville did, the evils that dog the human condition: "Now, for near five years," he wrote in 1840, "I have been indulged by the gracious Heaven in my long holiday in this goodly house of mine, entertaining and entertained by so many worthy and gifted friends, and all this time poor Nancy Barron, the mad-woman, has been screaming herself hoarse at the Poor-house across the brook and I still hear her whenever I open my window."

In the middle years, between 1835 and 1865, Emerson did the bulk of his work: the little book on Nature; the two trenchant series of essays—in every way his central work; the book on English Traits; the sometimes crabbed but authentic poems, rough-skinned, tart, like his own winter pears; and those maturer reflections on the Conduct of Life, which at least one contemporary thought more "pungent and piercing" than anything he had written before. During those same middle years, despite Emerson's original need for solitude, despite his resolute effort to free his days for communion with nature and his own mind, he took on all the demands of daily life. On settling in Concord, he accepted the ancient office of hogreeve—in charge of stray pigs; and as a husband and father, as a householder, a lyceum lecturer, and an editor of the *Dial*, he bore cheerfully, or if pressed, stoically, the duties of domestic and civic life. What he often characterized as his "indolence" was his need between whiles to recoup his energies for thought.

Whatever Emerson's reluctance to leave his study, his involvement in the political and social issues of his time, from the forties on, grew deeper: in the crises that culminated in the Civil War, his moral commitment was not only firm but passionate. Witness his protest to President Martin Van Buren over the scandalous chicane practiced by the federal government against the Cherokee Indians, his denunciation of slavery and the Fugitive Slave Law, his contempt for his one-time hero, Daniel Webster, the chief sponsor of that law; and not least his scalding attacks upon the infamous Mexican War, the Vietnam of his day, in his "Ode" inscribed to William Henry Channing.

In his mature years the aloof, self-contained, self-sufficient Emerson gave to society some of the allegiance he had once given too exclusively to solitude. For this was not only the period of his great friendships, with Carlyle, Arthur Hugh Clough, Bronson Alcott, Thoreau, Margaret Fuller, but also of the relaxing sociabilities of the Saturday Club, with its monthly luncheon meeting at the Parker House in Boston. There a more congenial Emerson appeared, one who horrified the elder Henry James by drinking wine and by covering his diffidence in company by smoking a cigar—as if a disembodied angel could enjoy a cigar!

By 1865 Emerson's main written work, with the exception of a few poems, was done; and when the war was over, his lecturing tapered off too, though he would still at intervals struggle painfully through old lectures, handicapped by lapses of memory, but sustained by sympathetic and indulgent audiences. Ironically, one of the last lectures he gave was on Memory—a lecture in which he redressed his original overemphasis upon the fresh and the newborn while dismissing the past: "Life only avails, not the having lived." Now he realized, belatedly, that the American, in the raw confidence of youth, had forgotten too much: that memory was "the thread on which the beads of man are strung, making the personal identity which is necessary to moral action. Without it all life and thought are an unrelated succession." He had lived long enough to realize, at last, that the "having lived" availed too.

Since Emerson still has much to give us—not because his method or his mood reflects that of our own times, but because it is so defiantly the opposite—there is no need to gloze over his deficiencies. His coldness and remoteness were almost constitutional qualities: they are hardly more a subject for reproach than his sloping shoulders, his narrow frame, his long nose. He himself "thought it a good remark" that "I always seemed to be on stilts. . . . Most of the persons whom I see in my own house, I see across a gulf, I cannot go to them nor they come to me."

With this coldness went, it would seem, not a failure of love—far from it—but a lack of strong sexual ardor. As late as the age of thirty-one, he could dismiss Boccaccio because he represented only the pleasure of appetite, "which only at rare intervals, a few times in a lifetime, are intense." Even by the standards of Puritan New England, that was a startling statement. The celebrations of sex in Walt Whitman's *Leaves of Grass* served, doubtless unconsciously, to fill in this omission in Emerson, whom Whitman revered as his master. But for all this quantitative lack of energy, Emerson had boxed the compass of life in a sense that none of his great American contemporaries had done: even sexually he was more mature than the fastidious but adolescent Thoreau, or the amative but unmarried Whitman. The sweet Emersonian smile, as on an archaic Greek face, was the witness of a complete, fully manifested life: he was "all there." And his work, though seemingly in fragments, was equally complete.

Perhaps one of the reasons for the pallid impression that Emerson left on a later generation is that he himself in his last fifteen years gradually faded out of the picture, ceasing after 1870 even to have the impulse to post in his Journals such stray thoughts as perhaps flickered through his mind. Yet no one could have met the disturbances of senescence with more smiling tranquillity, with more equable resignation. A little later, no longer able even to edit his unpublished papers, he left that task to his trusted friend, James Elliot Cabot, and his daughter, Ellen. Like a winter apple, still ruddy though mealy-ripe, he clung to the tree, safe from the worms and the wasps. When his thoughts no longer made sense, he had the sense to be silent. But the halo remained gay and bright; and today, against the addled counsels, the insensate threats, the artful, self-induced psychoses of our age, that halo has become gayer and brighter than ever, for it radiates from a poised and finely balanced personality. The sense of Emerson's luminous presence—that is what the reader will find on every page.

To understand the peculiar gifts of Emerson and the quality of his mind, one must realize that he was, primarily, neither a philosopher nor a didactic writer, still less a scholar or a scientist, but a poet: one who used the materials of other arts and disciplines to provide colors for his own palette. He did not regard himself as a great poet, but whatever he was, he told a friend, was of poet all through; yet he qualified this modestly, in another place, by saying that he was only half a poet. Yes; half a poet, if one thinks only of his verses: but what a half! Emerson nevertheless was a major poet, if one realizes that all his thought underwent a poetic transformation: an intensification, a distillation, a penetration that again and again would be crystallized in a perfect paragraph or poem. Emerson the poet remains present everywhere in his work, for all his thought is by its nature metaphoric and evocative, meant to excite a corresponding resonance directly in the reader's mind.

As a writer, Emerson stands on the level of the great essayists he admired—Michel de Montaigne and Francis Bacon: he has the same wide range of interests, the same sharp perceptions, the same gift for reducing a whole chapter of experience to a single sentence; and in addition, he has a crystalline freshness all his own, as of cool water bubbling upward from an underground spring. Though, like Montaigne, he ceaselessly read and often quoted old authors, he presents even old thoughts as if he were perceiving them anew and asking what, after all, they mean here and now.

If any one essay might be singled out to reveal Emerson's peculiar virtue and character as an American, it would probably be that on Self-Reliance; for there he spoke with the unmistakable voice of New World man, opening up and exploring a virgin continent of the mind, testing himself against nature, and finding out how much past knowledge and equipment he might need in order to survive and prosper.

In ''Self-Reliance'' Emerson established, better than anyone else had yet done, the central trait of the American character, at the moment when it became conscious of its special nature and its potential destiny. This sense was expressed in art by the aesthetic doctrines of the sculptor Horatio Greenough; in the novel by Cooper, Hawthorne, and Melville; in moral philosophy by Thoreau; in poetry by Whitman, as later in philosophy by William James and John Dewey; and it was not by accident that the most original of American architects, who bore indubitably the New World stamp, Frank Lloyd Wright, was more deeply devoted to Emerson than to any other writer. Emerson saw that if his country was to have free cultural intercourse with other countries, it must first have a character of its own. He realized that even the swagger and crudity of the Kentuckian or the Hoosier were better than a subservient colonialism that sought only to ape traditional Old World forms that had outlived their uses, or to keep up with the passing fashions of Paris and London.

This was the note Emerson struck repeatedly in *Nature,* in "Self-Reliance," and again in "The American Scholar." But neither Emerson nor those who were truly influenced by him could be trapped for long by an ingrowing provincial isolationism. If they had left Europe behind them, it was to take not only America but the whole world as their spiritual province. Before Whitman had composed his "Salut au Monde" and his "Passage to India," Emerson had made that same salute and traced the same passage himself, the latter with the aid of a small library of Oriental classics that some English friends had brought over to Concord. So deeply did Emerson immerse himself in the religion and philosophy of that elder Old World that some Hindus have taken his poem "Brahma," one of a half dozen perfect poems he wrote, as a true expression of the essential Hindu spirit.

So, when Emerson had swept away all the battered furniture and dusty heirlooms of the past, it was not for the purpose of conducting a miserable existence in an empty, cold, desolate chamber decorated only by a national flag, but in order to make better use of the space, and to provide it with more adequate furnishings. Some of the old belongings would come back again, not because they were old and respectable, but because they were still imperishably new. His "Away with the Dead!" meant "Hail to the Living!" He knew better than most that by regrouping old words one brings forth new thoughts. Past, present, and future, near and far, fused in his consciousness. "A true man belongs to no other time and place, but is the center of things." By the same token, once self-reliance was established, one might give and take aid freely, profiting the more by society because one was no longer dependent upon it.

Partly as a result of his temperamental remoteness and insulation, Emerson was more at home with Plato or Shakespeare than with his own contemporaries. As a young man he was an overcaptious critic even of those writers he admired, like Wordsworth, William Savage Landor, or Goethe. Most current novels seemed to him trivial and superficial: Jane Austen, Dickens, Thackeray, even Hawthorne, did not engage him. But he realized that Thoreau wrote an even meatier prose than his own, and almost alone he dared at once to acclaim Whitman's *Leaves of Grass* as the original work that it was. Yet it is not as a critic of literature that one turns to Emerson: he was primarily a critic of life, and he had a capacity to face bitter realities that his contemporaries flinched from.

"Great men, great nations," Emerson wrote, "have not been boasters and buffoons, but perceivers of the terror of life, and have manned themselves to face it." And again in the same essay on Fate he observed:

> We must see that the world is rough and surly, and will not mind drowning a man or a woman, but swallows your ship like a grain of dust. . . . The diseases, the elements, fortune, gravity, lightning, respect no persons. The way of Providence is a little rude. . . . The forms of the shark, the *labrus*, the jaw of the sea-wolf paved with crushing teeth, the weapons of the grampus and other warriors hidden in the sea, are hints of ferocity in the interiors of nature. Let us not deny it up and down. Providence has a wild, rough, incalculable road to its end, and it is of no use to try to whitewash its huge, mixed instrumentalities, or to dress up that terrific benefactor in the clean shirt and white neckcloth of a student in divinity.

Did Herman Melville ever indict the nature of things in harsher terms?

Yet there was a difference between Emerson and the Melville of *Moby Dick* and *Pierre*, not only in their respective visions of evil, but in their attitude as to how it should be treated. "What can we do in dark hours?" Emerson asked. And he answered: "We can abstain. In the bright hours we can impart." This is perhaps Emerson's final justification for his reserves, his inhibitions, his silences: he did not deny the existence of evil and pain, still less hide them from himself, but he answered them as his father had done when facing starvation: "We have, thank God, courage enough." If there is any central lesson to be learned from Emerson's thought, it is the lesson of heroism: *have courage!* And he might have drily added, looking around him at the screaming madwoman, the corrupt politicians, the whip-happy slavemongers, "You will need it."

Just because Emerson rejected none of the offices of the mind, he was, within the compass of his own experience, full of fresh perceptions, and he anticipated vividly, sometimes by a generation, sometimes by a whole century, the more studious efforts and discoveries of other men. As early as 1832 Emerson wrote: "Dreams and Beasts are two keys by which we are to find out the secrets of our own nature. All mystics use them. They are like comparative anatomy. They test objects; or we may say, that must be a good theory of the universe, that theory will bring a commanding claim to confidence, which explains these phenomena." The theory of Beasts is Darwin and evolution; the theory of Dreams is Freud and the unconscious. In Emerson, neither of these interests was haphazard or the result of a lucky stab. From the currents of evolutionary doctrine that flowed through the nineteenth century, after Buffon and Lamarck, Emerson realized in poetic phrase, well before Darwin, that "striving to be man, the worm mounts through all the spires of form." Man's life in nature includes every aspect of nature, however formidable, not only those that flatter or comfort man; yet nature, coming into consciousness in man, discloses purposes and ideal ends that transcend all previous evolutionary experience.

But if the theory of Beasts, that is, man's linkages with all organic nature, was important, this was tied up in Emerson's mind with that other mystery still to be penetrated, the mystery of Dreams; and in taking dreams seriously, not least his own, Emerson was well in advance of the thinkers of his own day who had, since the time of Descartes, regarded the inner life as the special province of religion. In this matter, Emerson was a better naturalist than most of his scientific contemporaries: he accepted dreams as a natural phenomenon which had some significance for man's own development. The fact that Emerson regarded sex, too, as one of the mysteries that needed further investigation—though he confined this recognition to his Journals— only shows how central, and in a sense how faithful to natural revelation, his essential thought was.

Emerson's attaching importance to beasts, dreams, and sex was an example of his devotion to the truths available to him through self-revelations rather than books, and this was connected with an even more central faith in the reality of God's presence and influence, disclosed in every manifestation of life. He would have nothing of the doctrine that supposed that revelation was something that happened long ago, was "given and gone, as if God were dead." God was tremendously alive for Emerson, as were the soul and the oversoul, the first immediate and individual, the second general and universal. This god was not the god of the churches; and it is only now, perhaps, that we can begin to see what Emerson was really talking about when he used the orthodox term "God" to express his new perception.

"There is a power above and behind us," wrote Emerson, "and we are the channel of its communication." If I am not deceived, Emerson had realized that a direct access to the unconscious was as important in opening one's eyes to reality as the pageant of the outer world—or even more important, since the unconscious bore within it the whole experience of the race, from the time before consciousness itself had emerged.

Emerson himself linked the experience of God with the operation of the unconscious, sometimes in so many words, as when he observed: "Blessed is the child; the unconscious is ever the act of God himself. Nobody can reflect upon his unconscious period; or any particular word or act in it, with regret or contempt." Or again, "The central fact is the super-human intelligence, pouring into us from the unknown fountain, to be received with religious awe and defended from any mixture of our will." When Emerson says, "Dare to love God without mediator or veil," he is saying, "Dare to respect and embrace and live openly with your unconscious."

In this poetic discovery of the role of the unconscious Emerson was not alone: the same discovery was made by Hawthorne and Melville, and this served as a secret link between those two souls, though as yet there was no name for the unconscious except the ancient one that Emerson loyally clung to: God. But as more than one religion had testified, this God has an almost equal counterpart and antagonist, Satan, whose exalted energies Milton and Blake had contemplated even before Melville had baptized Moby Dick in the name of the Devil. Through the exploration of dreams, fantasies, and psychal disorders that has gone on for the last half century and more, we now realize that both versions of the unconscious are true: this polarity plays an essential role in human creativity. Emerson's unconscious is mainly the luminous one, out of which love and brotherhood and justice and truth are born; while Melville's is the dark one, from which come forth murderous hate, satanic pride, insensate destruction—or demonic revelation. Neither version is to be trusted as an expression of cosmic and human potentialities without the other: but only when the luminous god gains the upper hand can life prosper.

At first, Emerson did not realize this ambivalent quality of the unconscious: when he was young, his private revelations were apparently so angelic and so well disciplined that he trusted them absolutely. Even in middle life he had said jauntily, in reply to an older friend who asked how he could be sure that his confident new revelation might not come from below rather than from above, "If I am the Devil's child, I will live then from the Devil." This was all very well as a youthful act of defiant integrity: but it is no answer if it happens that the Devil's disciple is not a staid, well-bred, firmly moralized young man, needing to discard his moral braces, but a Hitler or a Stalin, heeding every sadistic impulse and magnifying all the possibilities for human iniquity.

In later life Emerson corrected his youthful bias: he fervently blessed the yoke of men's opinions which he had once forsworn. In his poem "Grace," Emerson even thanked his "preventing God" for the defenses he had set around him: "example, custom, fear, occasion slow"—scorned bondmen who had served as parapet, keeping him from "the roaring gulf below." This again is one of those occasions when those who gauge Emerson's mind by this or that isolated expression fail to correct the momentary aberration by the full report of his life.

All this, and more, one will find in Emerson. But there is no use looking in his work for a closely ordered philosophic system; and to make Emerson into a mere Transcendentalist, as many have done, is to show little insight into either the scope or the depth of his thought, for he transcended Transcendentalism as decisively as he protested against Protestantism and dematerialized Materialism. The nearest Emerson ever came to presenting his philosophy as a unity was in his first work on Nature, where he laid out the four chief categories of his thought—commodity, beauty, language, and discipline. But if that were his sole credential as a seminal thinker, it would hardly meet his own criteria; for he kept on contemplating a more adequate expression of his metaphysics in a natural history of the mind, a work whose belated publication as an essay did not fulfill the hopes he had long nourished.

The fact is that Emerson's abortive efforts to produce a coherent philosophy were untrue to his own system-shattering openness. His mission was to examine crumbling foundations, to condemn unsound structures, to clear the site of lumber, to quarry new materials—not to instruct the would-be builders, nor to design a new structure. Repeatedly Emerson told Carlyle that he had no talent for construction. But what Emerson regarded as a defect was perhaps his essential virtue: his unwillingness to deny a truth because it was inconsistent in appearance or in logic with other equally reputable truths. What he retained, through this constitutional ineptitude, was a readiness to examine and even anticipate incredible new discoveries that system-mongers could not open the door to without acknowledging the insufficiency of their systems. George Edward Woodberry, an unsympathetic critic, said that in studying Emerson "one is reminded of the early sages of Greece." Precisely: for in both cases this originality and imperfection marked the embryonic expression of a new culture.

Such a description places Emerson's mind in its proper social setting: it does justice to his intellectual nakedness, his bright innocence, his sparkling richness of potentialities. Unburdened by past encrustations, untrammelled by future constraints, he was free to move in any direction. Emerson's, in short, was the most liberated mind that the West had produced in several centuries: as liberated as Shakespeare's. If Emerson "has no philosophy" it is because, like Shakespeare, his philosophy is as large as life, and cannot be reduced to an articulated skeleton without forfeiting its life.

"The day will come," Emerson prophesied, "when no badge or uniform or star will be worn." That day has not yet dawned; indeed, in our status-conscious, caste-bound America it seems further away now than ever. No such ungraded, fully individuated society as yet exists anywhere. So perhaps the high value of Emerson's thought for the present generation lies not only in the way it anticipated or marched ahead of the special discoveries of our time, as in the place it gave to the unconscious and the prerational processes of the mind, but even more in the way it radically differs from our current assumptions and challenges our practices: our conformity, our timidity, our docility —or those fashionable negative images of these same traits, our mindless anarchies, our drug-excited audacities, our aimless violence.

Certainly Emerson's America is not our present America: it is rather an older yet more youthful America, part achieved reality, part hopeful ideal, which we have lost. It is in Emerson's mind, more fully even than in Jefferson's, Whitman's, Thoreau's, or Lincoln's mind, that we can measure all that we have disowned or buried, and may, if we go further in the same direction, lose forever. And it is by entering Emerson's mind once more that we may recover at least a portion of our lost heritage, and gain courage—"courage enough!" —to seek a better life.

David J. Rothman
Poverty in America

The anomaly of the existence of poverty in the United States, by far the richest nation in the world, has been the subject of much recent discussion. As generally understood, it has been seen as one of the unfortunate results of the Industrial Revolution, its roots traced back particularly to the burgeoning of cities in the late nineteenth century, with their sweatshops and slums. Public concern about the poor has been strong at certain times, at others much less so. Books like Jacob Riis' *How the Other Half Lives* (1890) and Michael Harrington's *The Other America* (1963) have stimulated the interest and compassion of millions, and so have periods of acute economic distress, such as the Great Depression of the 1930's. But during other periods, unfortunately, the subject of poverty has been neglected, although the poor themselves remained.

One result of the recent interest in the poverty question has been an increase in the study of poverty in America by historians. These researches have shown that poverty has existed in America since colonial times and that industrialization has only made the problem more serious and more paradoxical. One of the leading students of the subject is David J. Rothman of Columbia University, who has approached the problem as part of his work on the history of how all sorts of disadvantaged and deviant persons—the insane, the criminal, the feebleminded, as well as the poor—have been cared for or punished since colonial times. His book, *The Discovery of the Asylum,* covers the story down to the Civil War; together with his wife, Sheila, he is currently working on the more recent period. In this essay Rothman discusses how and why the "care" of the poor changed in the early nineteenth century.

*F*rom the opening decades of the nineteenth century to our own day, Americans' persistent efforts to understand the causes and conditions of poverty have fixed upon the word "paradox." Writing in 1822, the managers of one early reform organization, the Society for the Prevention of Pauperism, puzzled over the existence of poverty in the new Republic. "Our territory is so expansive, its soil so prolific," they exclaimed, our institutions so "free and equal," and our citizens so blessed with "ample scope for industry and enterprise," that surely "pauperism would be foreign to our country." Instead, to their dismay and wonderment they confronted the "strange paradox that pauperism, as a practical evil, should be known among us." A century and a half later a Presidential commission appointed to study essentially the same problem expressed equal wonderment. Its report, aptly entitled *Poverty amid Plenty: The American Paradox*, tried to explain why, in a nation as prosperous as ours, twenty-five million people had to "eke out a bare existence under deplorable conditions." Thus, for most of our national history a mood of genuine perplexity has characterized our view of poverty. And not surprisingly, this perspective has almost always led commentators to mix charges and countercharges, to censure some and exonerate others for the problem. From the Jacksonian period to the present a number of critics have faulted the poor themselves, citing their supposed immorality and recklessness. Others have blamed the economy, pointing to its failure to sustain high wages and full employment. Still others have focused on the charities and state programs that attempt to alleviate need, insisting that they have so amply rewarded the poor as to trap them in their poverty. But despite the variety of responses, all these observers share the premise that poverty amid plenty ought not to exist, that the paradox must be solved.

Yet, this notion is a comparatively modern one. Americans in the colonial period adopted a very different stance toward dependency. They were calm and complacent, not prone to allocate blame for poverty or to design programs for its eradication. From their perspective, need was a natural and inevitable part of social organization. This was the lesson that they learned in their churches. Poverty, according to eighteenth-century Protestant clergymen, was even a blessing. The poor were always to be with us, in America as elsewhere; but rather than lament a tragic fact of human existence, they praised it as a God-given opportunity for men to do good. Relieving the needy, explained the Boston clergyman Samuel Cooper in 1753, was the highest Christian virtue: "It ennobles our nature, charity conforms us to the Son of God himself." Benevolence justified the pursuit of wealth, for without benevolence men would grow "sensual, profane, and insolent, unjust and unrighteous." It was senseless to expect that poverty would disappear, given its essential place in God's order. Most clerics, it is true, conceded that a few unworthy beggars might be scattered here and there among the needy. But they advised parishioners not to devote much energy to this dis-

Vol. II.—No. 56.]   NEW YORK, SATURDAY, JANUARY 23, 1858.   [Price Five Cents.

IN THE BITTER COLD.

This tear-jerking, sentimental- ized scene of a poor woman and her children evicted from their home appeared on the cover of Harper's Weekly, *January 23, 1858. It shows another, softer side of the ambivalent American attitude toward the poor then and now.*

tinction. It would be foolhardy, said Samuel Seabury in 1788, to let the "idle and even intemperate . . . suffer before our eyes. . . . [For] what if God were to refuse his mercy to those of us who do not deserve it?"

The secular definitions of society also encouraged a broad accept- ance of the poor. Eighteenth-century Americans conceived of a well- ordered society as hierarchical, with each level enjoying its special privileges and obligations: some men would be rich and powerful; others low, mean, and in subjection. This interpretation made the poor a permanent fixture, integral to the community. They were to respect those above them, pay all due deference, and, in return, receive assistance in time of need. If townsmen made no effort to eliminate poverty, at least they did not ignore, harshly punish, or isolate the poor.

Another element that encouraged the colonists' tolerance for poverty and yet set limits to this sentiment was a sharp differentia- tion between the town resident and nonresident, between the insider and the outsider. Townsmen relieved a neighbor's need without sus- picion but showed little compassion for the plight of the stranger. Whether the outsider was an honest and poor man or a petty thief, the response was to move him beyond the town limits as quickly as possible. In part, the insularity of eighteenth-century settlements reflected English traditions; Elizabethan poor laws, for example, made relief the exclusive responsibility of each parish. But more important, localism suited New World conditions. Colonists were necessarily bound together by strong ties, and among other things they relied on each other to safeguard the community. In an era when the few constables who patrolled the streets at night were old men incapable of apprehending a criminal, insularity was a major element in keeping order. A townsmen who committed an offense could be whipped or fined or, worse, shamed before his neighbors by being displayed in the stocks. But outsiders were much less easy to control, especially when they were penniless and away from people who knew them. Propertyless strangers not only would increase poor-relief expenditures but also would threaten public security.

The day-to-day treatment of the poor reflected these attitudes. Officials relieved neighbors quickly and without elaborate investigation, supporting them at home where possible or, when their disabilities were too great, in relatives' or friends' households. The dependent townsman remained within the community, not forced to enter such an institution as the almshouse; in fact, before 1820 few towns bothered to build a poorhouse. To counter the danger of outsiders, communities enforced stringent settlement laws, establishing property requirements for those who would enter and reside in the town. Transients—vagrants, poor but healthy strangers, nonresident widows with children, or unwed mothers—were moved out of town as quickly as possible. The boundaries were guarded with all the care that sentries give an international frontier.

Americans' understanding and response to poverty underwent a revolution in the Jacksonian era. Beginning in the 1820's and increasingly thereafter, observers defined poverty as both unnatural in the New World and capable of being eradicated. Colonial complacency gave way to a reform movement in which a heightened suspicion of the poor went hand in hand with the promise of improvement.

The spread of the ideas of the Enlightenment throughout the nation encouraged this change. The prospect of boundless progress wore away the grim determinism of Calvinist doctrines, so that men no longer believed that misery and want were permanent to society. As popular thinking became increasingly secular, God's will or the inherent depravity of man no longer seemed a satisfactory explanation for the differences in social conditions. So, too, republican enthusiasm enhanced the prospect of progress. In the aftermath of the Revolution, Americans believed that their Republic would accomplish goals that corrupt European monarchies had missed. An obvious target for action was poverty, an evil that had to exist where aristocrats oppressed peasants but not where men were equal, resources were abundant, and labor scarce.

It was also impossible in Jacksonian America to maintain colonial localism and insularity. Men were now moving all the time, westward to the virgin territories or into the burgeoning cities of New York, Boston, and Philadelphia. A system of poor relief that attempted to distinguish between the neighbor and the stranger was no longer feasible when men picked up stakes on hearing rumors of more fertile land ahead or of new opportunities in growing urban centers.

At the same time, citizens' close identification with their particular community was giving way to a wider view. Now one did not belong exclusively to the town but to the state and nation as well.

But while such considerations increased Americans' willingness to eradicate poverty, they also encouraged a harsh and suspicious view of the poor. Observers concluded that because of New World wealth no one ought to be poor, and therefore those actually in need had themselves to blame in some degree. The first page of a typical tract on relief divided dependents into two categories: the poor, that is, the worthy but unfortunate, and paupers, the unworthy idlers. But by page 4 of the pamphlet the distinction fell away, and the discussion of poverty centered almost exclusively on the corrupted. After an extensive tour of eastern cities, a Philadelphia investigatory committee in 1827 unhesitantly reported that it was "vice" that had created "here and everywhere, by far the greater part of the poor." The answer to the paradox of poverty reached by New York's Society for the Prevention of Pauperism in 1821 was that "the paupers of this city are, for the most part . . . depraved and vicious, and require support because they are so." The poor had become objects, not neighbors; people to be acted upon, to be improved, manipulated, elevated, and reformed.

These new ideas and social conditions prompted the almshouse movement. In the Jacksonian period cities and towns eagerly and rapidly constructed special institutions to confine all of the needy, devoting the bulk of public-relief funds to this enterprise. The proponents of the program were a mixed lot, in Boston ranging from the city's mayor, Josiah Quincy, and its most prominent doctor, Walter Channing, to its noted Unitarian clergyman, Joseph Tuckerman. But they all agreed on certain essentials. Surely the poor were partly to blame for their own misery, having succumbed to the vice of idleness or intemperance. Yet, these critics vigorously insisted, they were not inherently depraved but rather were the victims of the numerous temptations set before them by society. Who else but the towns licensed the grog shops and allowed gambling halls and dens of iniquity to flourish? And who else but the towns supported the poor at home, giving them the wherewithal to subsist without working, the opportunity to languish in vice? Of all methods for supporting the needy, proclaimed Mayor Quincy in 1821, ". . . the most wasteful, the most expensive, and most injurious to their morals, and destructive of their industrious habits, is that of supply in their own families." Therefore, reformers concluded, to eliminate poverty the poor had to be isolated from temptation and forced to acquire habits of industry and labor. This grandiose task they assigned to the almshouse.

The hopes for the program appeared in the designs for New York's and Boston's relief systems. The poor, regardless of their moral standing or work history or residence, would receive aid only within an almshouse. Once inside this institution, they would learn

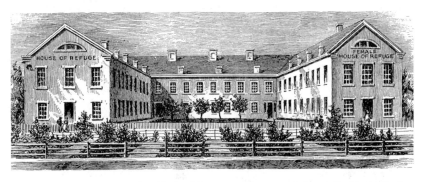

A tidy-looking poorhouse, euphemistically called a "House of Refuge," in New York City, 1832. The separation of the sexes seems indicated by the sign on the right wing.

order, discipline, and habits of work, the very traits the community had neglected to teach. The routine was to be precise and rigorous. An early morning bell would awaken the inmates, and another bell would signal the time for breakfast. They would go to their assigned seats at long mess tables, eat their meal, and then head for the workshop. There would be no drinking, loafing, or gambling; only honest living and steady labor. As Dr. Walter Channing told a group of Boston philanthropists in 1843, the almshouse was "a place where the tempted are removed from the means of their sin, and where the indolent [man], while he is usefully and industriously employed . . . by a regular course of life . . . is prepared for a better career when restored to liberty again." The poor, after completing this regimen, would return to society girded as in an armor against temptation, ready to earn their keep.

The almshouse, however, never fulfilled its founders' expectations. For one, its managers, generally recruited from the ranks of petty shopkeepers and small farmers, were ill trained to run an institution. For another, almost all of the inmates were not ablebodied loafers but the very old and decrepit and the very young. The routine that reformers had devised applied badly, and few were able to perform steady labor. So in short order the almshouse degenerated into a custodial institution, characteristically overcrowded, in sad disrepair, lacking all internal discipline and order, and cruel and punitive in its methods. A committee conducting a state-wide survey in New York reported in 1857: "The great mass of the poor houses are most disgraceful memorials of the public charity. Common domestic animals are usually more humanely provided for than the paupers in some of these institutions."

Yet, despite the terrible gap between reformers' ideology and institutional reality, almshouses not only persisted but proliferated in the last half of the nineteenth century.

Arnold Welles

Samuel Slater Imports a Revolution

The transition of the United States from an agricultural to a predominantly industrial nation was one of the most important, and by the end of the period, most obvious developments of the nineteenth century. When Washington became President there was not a true factory in the entire country; when Theodore Roosevelt became President the United States was already the leading industrial nation of the world. Industrialization and the factory system are not absolutely synonymous terms, but factories are the basic structures in which the industrial process operates most effectively. And Samuel Slater, a young English immigrant, was the man who designed and built the first factory in America. What Slater did, a remarkable personal story as well as one of the key events in the economic and social history of the United States, is told in this essay by one of his great-great-grandsons, Arnold Welles, a successful businessman who is also a fine historian.

*F*eats of memory, particularly of the kind of memory derided as "photographic"—for all the cornucopias of wealth they sometimes pour over television contestants—are looked down on in modern times, but they have their role in history. Consider, for example, the story of Samuel Slater. It would be impolite to call him a spy, for he would not have considered himself one. Furthermore, he was a man of peace. Yet in his own time this cotton spinner's apprentice achieved with his prodigious memory an effect as great as or greater than any successful military espionage has brought about in our own. For he successfully transplanted the infant Industrial Revolution, which was in many ways an English monopoly, across an ocean to a new country.

To understand Slater's feat, one must look back to the economic situation of England and America in the days directly after the Colonies had achieved their independence. If Britain no longer ruled her former colonies, she clung tenaciously to her trade with them. Thanks to her flourishing new textile industry, she was able to sell large quantities of cotton goods in the United States at prices so low there was little incentive left for making cloth over here by the old-fashioned hand methods. To maintain this favorable dependency as long as possible, England went to fantastic lengths to guard the secrets that had mechanized her cotton industry, and so effective were these measures that America might well have continued solely as an agricultural nation for years, had it not been for Samuel Slater.

Slater was born in 1768 on his family's property, Holly House, in Derbyshire, England. His father, William Slater, was an educated, independent farmer and timber merchant, the close friend and neighbor of Jedediah Strutt, successively farmer, textile manufacturer, and partner of England's famous inventor, Sir Richard Arkwright, whose spinning frame had revolutionized the manufacture of cotton yarn. Three years after Samuel Slater's birth, Strutt had financed Arkwright's factory at Cromford—the world's earliest authentic cotton mill—where water power replaced humans and animals in moving the machinery, and where the whole operation of spinning yarn could be accomplished for the first time automatically under one roof. Within five years Arkwright's mills were employing over 5,000 workers, and England's factory system was launched.

It was in this atmosphere of industrial revolution that young Slater grew up. He showed signs of his future mechanical bent at a tender age by making himself a polished steel spindle with which to help wind worsted for his mother, and whenever he had the chance, he would walk over to nearby Cromford or Belper on the Derwent River to see the cotton mills which Strutt and Arkwright owned. In 1782 Strutt began to erect a large hosiery factory at Milford, a mile from the Slater property, and he asked William Slater's permission to engage his eldest son as clerk. Slater, who had noticed the ability and inclinations of his younger son, Samuel, recommended him instead, observing that he not only "wrote well and was good at figures" but was also of a decided mechanical bent.

Thus, at the age of fourteen, Samuel Slater went to live and work with Strutt. When William Slater died shortly afterward, in 1783, young Samuel Slater signed his own indenture to learn cotton spinning as an apprentice in Strutt's factory until the age of 21.

During the early days of his term the boy became so engrossed in the business that he would go for six months without seeing his family, despite the fact that they lived only a mile away, and he would frequently spend his only free day, Sunday, experimenting alone on machinery. In those days millowners had to build all their own machinery, and Slater acquired valuable experience in its design, as well as its operation, and in the processes of spinning yarn. Even before completing his term of indenture he was made superintendent of Strutt's new hosiery mill.

But Slater had become concerned about the chances for an independent career in England. Arkwright's patents having expired, factories had sprung up everywhere, and Slater could see that to launch out on his own he would need more and more capital to stay ahead of the technical improvements constantly taking place. His attention had been drawn to the United States by an article in a Philadelphia paper saying that a bounty of £100 had been granted by the Pennsylvania legislature to a man who had designed a textile machine. Young Slater made up his mind that he would go to the United States and introduce the Arkwright methods there. As his first step, even before his term with Strutt expired, Slater obtained his employer's permission to supervise the erection of the new cotton works Arkwright was then starting, and from this experience he gained valuable knowledge for the future.

There were, it was true, grave risks to consider. Britain still strictly forbade the export of textile machinery or the designs for it. With France entering a period of revolution which might unsettle the economy of the Old World, it was even more important that the large American market be safeguarded for British commerce. As a result, the Arkwright machines and techniques were nowhere in use in America at the time, and various attempts—in Pennsylvania, Massachusetts, Connecticut, Maryland, and South Carolina—to produce satisfactory cotton textiles had borne little fruit. Without Arkwright's inventions it was impossible to make cotton yarn strong enough for the warps needed in hand-loom weaving.

Enterprising Yankees undertook all kinds of ingenious attempts to smuggle out modern machines or drawings. Even the American minister to France was involved in some of them: machinery would be quietly purchased in England, dismantled, and sent in pieces to our Paris legation for transshipment to the United States in boxes labeled "glassware" or "farm implements." British agents and the Royal Navy managed to intercept almost all such shipments, however, and skilled workers who attempted to slip away with drawings or models were apprehended on the high seas and brought back. Passengers leaving England for American ports were thoroughly searched by customs agents before boarding ship.

This portrait of an eminently successful Samuel Slater includes in the background a view of his first cotton-spinning mill.

Slater knew of these handicaps and determined to take along nothing in writing save his indenture papers. . . . But he was carrying with him in a very remarkable memory the complete details of a modern cotton mill.

After a passage of 66 days, Slater's ship reached New York. He had originally intended to go to Philadelphia, but when he learned of the existence of the New York Manufacturing Company on Vesey Street in downtown Manhattan, he showed his indenture and got a job there instead. The company had recently been organized to make yarns and cloth, but the yarn was linen and the machinery, hand-operated, was copied from antiquated English models. This was a far cry from the factories Slater had supervised in Derbyshire.

Fortunately, about this time, the newcomer happened to meet the captain of a packet sailing between New York and Providence, Rhode Island, and from him learned of the interest in textile manufacturing shown by a wealthy, retired merchant of Providence, Moses Brown, later to become one of the founders of Brown University. A converted Quaker and a man of large imagination and business acumen, Brown had invested considerable cash in two rough, hand-operated spinning frames and a crude carding machine as well as in a couple of obsolete "jennies." But all his attempts to produce cotton yarns had ended in failure, and he could find little use for his expensive machinery. Such was the situation when he received a letter from Slater:

SIR,—

New York, December 2d, 1789

A few days ago I was informed that you wanted a manager of *cotton spinning*, etc., in which business I flatter myself that I can give the greatest satisfaction, in making machinery, making good yarn, either for *stockings* or *twist*, as any that is made in England; as I have had opportunity, and an oversight of Sir Richard Arkwright's works, and in Mr. Strutt's mill upwards of eight years. If you are not provided for, should be glad to serve you; though I am in the New York manufactory, and have been for three weeks since I arrived from England. But we have but *one card, two machines*, two spinning jennies, which I think are not worth using. *My intention* is to erect a *perpetual card and spinning*. (Meaning the Arkwright patents). If you please to drop a line respecting the amount of encouragement you wish to give, by favor of Captain Brown, you will much oblige, sir, your most obedient humble servant.

SAMUEL SLATER

N.B.—Please to direct to me at No. 37, Golden Hill, New York.

Slater's letter fired the shrewd Quaker's imagination, and he hastened to reply, declaring that he and his associates were "destitute of a person acquainted with water-frame spinning" and offering Slater all the profits from successful operation of their machinery over and above interest on the capital invested and depreciation charges. His invitation concluded: "If the present situation does not come up to what thou wishes, and, from thy knowledge of the business, can be ascertained of the advantages of the mills, so as to induce thee to come and work ours, and have the *credit* as well as the advantage of perfecting the first water-mill in America, we should be glad to engage thy care so long as they can be made profitable to both, and we can agree."

Tempted and flattered, and assuming that the Providence operation needed only an experienced overseer to make it a success, Slater decided to accept. He took a boat in January, 1790, reached Providence on the eighteenth of the month, and immediately called on Moses Brown.

The two men were in striking contrast. Slater, only 21, was nearly six feet tall and powerfully built, with ruddy complexion and fair hair. Moses Brown, in his soft, broad-brimmed Quaker hat, was well past middle age, of small stature, with a pair of bright, bespectacled eyes set in a benevolent face framed by flowing gray locks. Satisfied from a glance at the Strutt indenture that his young caller was bona fide, Brown took Slater in a sleigh to the little hamlet of Pawtucket, a community consisting of a dozen or so cottages on both sides of the Blackstone River, just outside Providence. They stopped at a small clothier's shop on the river's bank, close by a bridge which linked Rhode Island and Massachusetts. Here was assembled Brown's ill-assorted machinery.

Slater took one look and shook his head, his disappointment obvious.

Compared to Strutt's splendid mill this was almost a caricature. He spoke bluntly: "These will not do; they are good for nothing in their present condition, nor can they be made to answer." Brown urged him to reconsider, to give the machines a try, but the young Englishman was not to be persuaded. At last, in desperation, the old merchant threw Slater a challenge:

"Thee said thee could make machinery. Why not do it?"

Reluctantly, Slater finally agreed to build a new mill, using such parts of the old as would answer, but only on one condition: that Brown provide a trusted mechanic to make the machinery which Slater would design and that the man be put under bond neither to disclose the nature of the work nor to copy it.

"If I don't make as good yarn as they do in England," Slater declared, "I will have nothing for my services, but will throw the whole of what I have attempted over the bridge!" Brown agreed, arranging in addition to pay Slater's living expenses.

Then the old merchant took his visitor to the cottage of Oziel Wilkinson, an ingenious ironmaster, with whom Slater could board. Wilkinson, also a Quaker, operated a small anchor forge using water power from the river, and there he turned out ships' chandlery, shovels, scythes, and other tools. As the young Englishman entered the Wilkinson home, his host's younger daughter shyly scampered out of sight, but Hannah, the elder, lingered in the doorway to look at the stranger. Slater fell in love with her. (Within two years they would be married, and Hannah Slater would later acquire fame in her own right as the discoverer of cotton sewing thread, which she first produced from the fine yarns her husband manufactured.) In the Wilkinson household young Slater found new parents who helped him overcome his homesickness and encouraged him in the first difficult months.

Part of that winter he spent experimenting with Moses Brown's crude carding machine, and he was able to improve the quality of cotton fleece it turned out. This, when spun by hand on the jennies, produced a better yarn, but one which was still too weak and uneven to be used as warp in the hand-weaving of cloth. Slater was downhearted; he realized that he must build everything from scratch.

The rest of the winter he spent assembling the necessary materials for constructing the Arkwright machines and processes. He lacked even the tools with which to make the complicated equipment, and he was forced to make many of them himself before any building could commence. Furthermore, without models to copy, he had to work out his own computations for all measurements. One of the most ingenious elements of the Arkwright inventions was the variation in speeds of various parts of the machines. Mathematical tables for these were not available anywhere save in England; Slater had to rely on his own extraordinary memory. Nevertheless, by April, 1790, he was ready to sign a firm partnership agreement to build two carding machines, a drawing and roving frame, and two spinning frames, all to be run automatically by water power. He was to receive one dollar a day as wages, half-ownership in the machinery he built, and, in addition, one half of the mill's net profits after it was in operation. Moses Brown had turned over the supervision of his textile investments to William Almy, his son-in-law, and Smith Brown, his cousin, and these two men became Slater's new partners.

Now, behind shuttered windows in the little clothier's building on the riverbank, young Slater began to design the first successful cotton mill in America. As he drew the plans with chalk on wood, Sylvanus Brown, an experienced local wheelwright, cut out the parts from sturdy oak and fastened them together with wooden dowels. Young David Wilkinson, Slater's future brother-in-law and like his father a skilled ironworker, forged shafts for the spindles, rollers for the frames, and teeth in the cards which Pliny Earle, of Leicester, Massachusetts, prepared for the carding machines. Before iron gearwheels and card rims could be made, Slater and Wilkinson had to go to Mansfield, Massachusetts, to find suitable castings. By autumn, working sixteen hours a day, Slater had more than fulfilled his agreement: he had built not two but three carding machines, as well as the drawing and roving frame and the two spinning frames. At last he was ready for a trial.

Taking up a handful of raw cotton, Slater fed it into the carding machine, cranked by hand for the occasion by an elderly Negro. This engine was one of the most important elements of the Arkwright system, for in it the raw cotton was pulled across leather cards studded with small iron teeth which drew out and straightened the fibers, laid them side by side, and formed them into a long, narrow fleece called an "end," or "sliver." This was then placed on the drawing and roving frame to be further stretched, smoothed, and then twisted before being spun into yarn on the spinning frame. Before the cotton was run through the cards, the fibers lay in every direction, and it was essential that the carding be successful if the "end" was to be suitable for the subsequent steps. But when Slater fed the test cotton into his machine it only piled up on the cards. . . .

After a number of sleepless nights, Slater determined that the trouble arose from a faulty translation of his design into reality, for Pliny Earle had never before made cards of that description. Slater decided that the teeth stood too far apart, and that under pressure of the raw cotton they fell back from their proper places instead of standing firm and combing the cotton as it moved past. He pointed out the defect to Earle, and together, using a discarded piece of grindstone, they beat the teeth into the correct shape. Another test was made and the machine worked satisfactorily.

The final stage was now at hand. Almost a year had passed in preparation for this moment. Would the machinery operate automatically by water power? That was the miracle of the Arkwright techniques, which gave them their name, "perpetual spinning." A connection was made to the small water wheel which had been used by the clothier in whose little shop Slater's new machinery now stood. It was deep winter, and the Blackstone River was frozen over, so that Slater was obliged to crawl down and break up the ice around the wheel. When the wheel turned over, his machinery began to hum.

On December 20, 1790, Samuel Slater's mill produced the first cotton yarn ever made automatically in America. It was strong and of good quality, suitable for sheetings and other types of heavy cotton goods; soon Slater was turning out yarn fine enough to be woven into shirtings, checks, ginghams, and stockings, all of which had until then been imported from Europe. Good cotton cloth woven at home from English yarn had cost from forty to fifty cents per yard, but soon Slater brought the cost down as low as nine cents. For the remainder of that first winter, unable to get anyone else to do the job, Slater spent two or three hours each morning before breakfast breaking the river ice to start the water wheel. Daily it left him soaking wet and numb from exposure; his health was affected for the rest of his life.

The little mill started with four employees, but by the end of one month Slater had nine hands at work, most of them children. In this he was following the practice in England, where entire families were employed in the mills. Early English millowners had found children more agile and dexterous than adults, their quick fingers and small hands tending the moving parts more easily. Slater, like other pioneer millowners dealing with small working forces, was able to maintain a paternalistic attitude toward the young persons in his charge; until the coming of the factory system and absentee ownership, child labor was not the evil it later became. Slater introduced a number of social customs he had learned in the Arkwright and Strutt mills. For his workers he built the first Sunday school in New England and there provided instruction in reading, writing, and arithmetic, as well as in religion. Later he promoted common day schools for his mill hands, often paying the teachers' wages out of his own pocket.

About 1812 an unknown artist portrayed Slater's first mill, on Rhode Island's Blackstone River.

Proudly Slater sent a sample of his yarn back to Strutt in Derbyshire, who pronounced it excellent. Yet Americans hesitated to use it, preferring traditional hand-spun linen yarn or machine-made cotton yarn imported from England. Within four months Moses Brown was writing to the owners of a little factory in Beverly, Massachusetts, run by a relative, proposing a joint petition to Congress: Why not raise the duties on imported cotton goods? Some of the proceeds could be given to southern cotton farmers as a bounty for upgrading their raw cotton, and some could be presented to the infant textile industry as a subsidy.

Next, Brown arranged to transmit to Alexander Hamilton, secretary of the treasury and already known as a supporter of industry, a sample of Slater's yarn and of the first cotton check made from it, along with various suggestions for encouraging the new textile manufacturers. He reported to Hamilton that within a year machinery and mills could be erected to supply enough yarn for the entire nation. Two months later, when Hamilton presented to Congress his famous *Report on Manufactures*, he mentioned "the manufactory at Providence [which] has the merit of being the first in introducing into the United States the celebrated cotton mill."

By the end of their first ten months of operations, Almy, Brown & Slater had sold almost 8,000 yards of cloth produced by home weavers from their yarns. After twenty months the factory was turning out more yarn than the weavers in its immediate vicinity could use; a surplus of 2,000 pounds had piled up. Desperately, Moses Brown appealed to Slater, "Thee must shut down thy gates or thee will spin all my farms into cotton yarn."

It was at this point that the full force of Slater's revolutionary processes began to become apparent. To dispose of their surplus the partners began to employ agents in Salem, New York, Baltimore, and Philadelphia, and so encouraging were the sales that it became obvious to them that their potential market was enormous. In 1791, therefore, they closed the little mill and built nearby a more efficient factory designed to accommodate all the processes of yarn manufacturing under one roof. It was opened in 1793. (Now the Old Slater Mill Museum, the building still stands today.)

As of December, 1792, the partners' ledgers had shown a credit in Slater's name of £882, representing his share of the proceeds from the sale of yarn spun by his mill. From then on both he and the infant industry he had helped to create prospered rapidly. The factory was no longer a neighborhood affair but sought its markets in a wider world. When the War of 1812 had ended, there were 165 mills in Rhode Island, Massachusetts, and Connecticut alone, many of them started by former employees of Slater who had gone into business for themselves. By this time Slater, too, had branched out; he owned at least seven mills, either outright or in partnership. An important mill town in Rhode Island already bore the name of Slatersville. Around three new cotton, woolen, and thread mills which he built in Massachusetts, a new textile center sprang up which became the town of

Webster. Later, his far-reaching enterprise carried him to Amoskeag Falls on the Merrimac River; in 1822 he bought an interest in a small mill already established there, and in 1826 erected a new mill which became the famous Amoskeag Manufacturing Company, hub of an even greater textile center—Manchester, New Hampshire.

President James Monroe had come to Pawtucket in 1817 to visit the "Old Mill," which was then the largest cotton mill in the nation, containing 5,170 spindles. It had started with 72. Slater himself conducted his distinguished visitor through the factory and proudly showed him his original spinning frame, still running after 27 years. Some years later another President, Andrew Jackson, visited Pawtucket, and when he was told that Slater was confined to his house by rheumatism brought on from that first winter of breaking the ice on the Blackstone, Old Hickory went to pay his respects to the invalid. Courteously addressing Slater as "the Father of American Manufactures," General Jackson said:

"I understand you taught us how to spin, so as to rival Great Britain in her manufactures; you set all these thousands of spindles to work, which I have been delighted in viewing, and which have made so many happy, by a lucrative employment."

Slater thanked his visitor politely and with the dry wit for which he was well known replied:

"Yes, Sir, I suppose that I gave out the psalm, and they have been singing to the tune ever since."

By the time he died in 1835, Slater had become generally recognized as the country's leading textile industrialist. The industry he had founded 45 years earlier had shown phenomenal growth. In 1790 the estimated value of all American manufactured goods barely exceeded $20,000,000, and the domestic cotton crop was about 2,000,000 pounds. By 1835 cotton manufactured goods alone were valued in excess of $47,000,000, and that single industry was consuming almost 80,000,000 pounds of cotton annually. Few men in our history have lived to see such tremendous economic changes wrought in one lifetime by their own efforts.

The social changes which Samuel Slater witnessed and helped to further were even more far-reaching. When he arrived in 1789 America was a nation of small farmers and artisans. By the time he died, and to a considerable extent because of his accomplishments, many artisans had become mill hands.

Three years after Slater's mill began operations, a young Yale graduate named Eli Whitney, visiting a Georgia plantation, devised the cotton gin, and this, in combination with English cotton mills and American ones like Slater's in New England, enormously stimulated the cotton economy (and the slave-labor system) of the South. Simultaneously, and paradoxically, Slater and Whitney helped fasten on the North an industrial economy which would defeat the South when the long-standing economic conflict between the two sections flared out at last in civil war.

Carl N. Degler

There Was Another South

To uncover the meaning of complicated historical events, historians search for generalizations; they sift through the clutter of fact and opinion that makes up the sources and locate the common elements that show us the significance of the past. On the other hand, the process of generalization requires the discarding of "atypical" and "irrelevant" material, although what is put aside is obviously part of history too. The historian's constant problem is to find true generalizations without distorting truth. The broader his generalizations, the more likely they are to ignore part of the reality being described, yet the more the historian qualifies his conclusions in the interest of complete accuracy, the less meaningful his conclusions become.

In this essay, which deals with southern attitudes before, during, and immediately after the Civil War, Professor Carl N. Degler of Stanford University examines some important but overly broad generalizations. He shows with a convincing array of evidence that historians who write about "the South" and even about southern attitudes toward slavery and race relations before 1860 as though a common point of view pervaded the region are missing a large part of the story. His intention, however, is not to destroy the old generalizations or to supplant them with completely different ones. Rather his argument points up the complexity of history, which is one of its fascinations. From his account the reader can extract newer generalizations, less simple but more convincing since they conform to a large generalization about human nature, namely that in any large group uniformity of opinion is impossible.

*T*he stereotype of the South is as tenacious as it is familiar: a traditionally rebellious region which has made a dogma of states' rights and a religious order of the Democratic party. Here indeed is a monotonous and unchanging tapestry, with a pattern of magnolia blossoms, Spanish moss, and the inevitable old plantations running ceaselessly from border to border. To this depiction of almost willful backwardness, add the dark motif of the Negro problem, a few threads of poor white, and the picture is complete.

Such is the mythical image, and a highly inaccurate one it is, for the South is a region of immense variety. Its sprawling landscape ranges from the startlingly red soil of Virginia and North Carolina to the black, sticky clay of the Delta; from the wild and primitive mountain forests of eastern Kentucky to the lush, junglelike swamps of southern Louisiana; from the high, dry, wind-swept plains of the Texas Panhandle to the humid tidelands of the South Carolina coast. An environment so diverse can be expected to produce social and political differences to match, and in fact, it always has.

Today, with the South in ferment, we have come to recognize increasingly the wide variety of attitudes that exist in the region. But this denial of the southern stereotype is a relatively new development, even among historians. For too long the history of the region has been regarded as a kind of unbroken plain of uniform opinion. This is especially true of what has been written about the years before the Civil War; a belief in states' rights, the legality of secession, and the rightfulness of slavery has been accepted almost without question as typical of southern thought. In a sense, such catch phrases do represent what many southerners have believed; but at the same time there were many others who both denied the legality of secession and denounced slavery. It is time this "other South" was better known.

Let us begin with the story of those southerners who so cherished the Union that they refused to accept the doctrine of nullification and secession. They included not only humble farmers and remote mountain men, but some of the greatest names in the history of the South; their devotion to the Union was tested in several bitter clashes with states' righters during the ante-bellum decades. The first of these contests came over the question of the high protective tariffs which many southerners felt would hurt the cotton trade; the arguments advanced at the beginning set forth the basic lines of debate that were followed thereafter. South Carolina's *Exposition and Protest* of 1828, which John C. Calhoun wrote secretly in opposition to the tariff passed that year, embodied the classic defense of state sovereignty. In the *Exposition,* Calhoun contended that nullification of federal legislation by a state and even secession were constitutional—a doctrine rejected by many prominent southerners in 1828 and after.

Foremost among them was former President James Madison, the reputed "father of the Constitution." As a Jeffersonian in politics and a Virginian by birth and heritage, Madison was no friend of the protective tariff, and certainly not of the monstrous one of 1828, which had been promulgated by the Jacksonian faction in Congress in an effort to discredit the Adams administration. But he could not accept even that politically inspired tariff as sufficient reason for nullification. Indeed, he could not accept the constitutional doctrine of nullification on any grounds. It is worthwhile to consider briefly Madison's views on nullification, because virtually all subsequent southern defenses of the Union followed his line of thought; at the time, no man in the South carried more authority on the meaning and interpretation of the Constitution than the venerable Virginian, who celebrated his eightieth birthday in 1830, and was the last surviving signer of that document.

Many political leaders sought his views all through the tariff crisis of 1828–33, and to all of them Madison reiterated the same conclusions. The United States was a "mixed government" in which the states were supreme in some areas and the federal government in others. In the event of conflict between them, the Supreme Court was the intended arbiter under the Constitution; the Court, Madison wrote, was "so constituted as to be impartial as it could be made by the mode of appointment and responsibility of the judges."

If confidence were lacking in the objectivity of the judges, Madison continued, then there were further remedies: the impeachment of offending officials, election of a new government, or amendments to the Constitution. But neither nullification nor secession was legal, he tirelessly pointed out. Of course, if tyrannized sufficiently, a state could invoke its natural right to overthrow its oppressor; but that was a right of revolution, and not a constitutional right as Calhoun and his followers maintained.

As a southern Unionist, Madison did not stand alone, either at the time of the nullification crisis or later. In Calhoun's own state, in fact, the Unionists were a powerful and eloquent minority. Hugh S. Legare (pronounced Legree, curiously enough), Charleston aristocrat, intellectual, and one-time editor of the *Southern Review*, distinguished himself in defense of the Union, vigorously opposing Calhoun during the heated debates in Charleston in 1832. (Eleven years later, as United States Attorney General, Legare again differed with the majority of southerners when he offered the official opinion that free Negroes in the United States enjoyed the same civil rights as white men.)

James Petigru and Joel Poinsett (who, as minister to Mexico, gave his name to the Poinsettia) were two other prominent Charlestonians who would not accept the doctrine that a state could constitutionally withdraw from the Union. Unlike Legare and Poinsett, Petigru lived long enough to fight nullification and secession in South Carolina until that state left the Union. (When asked by a stranger in December, 1860, where the insane asylum was, he contemptuously pointed to the building where the secession convention was meeting.)

Andrew Jackson is often ignored by those who conceive of the South as a monolith of states' rights and secession. A Carolinian by birth and a Tennessean by choice, Jackson acted as an outspoken advocate of the Union when he threatened South Carolina with overwhelming force in the crisis of 1832–33. Jackson's fervently nationalistic proclamation

Charleston Unionist James Louis Petigru, by Thomas Sully.

to the people of the dissident state was at once a closely reasoned re-statement of the Madisonian view that the United States was a "mixed government," and a highly emotional panegyric to the Union. Though there can be no question of Jackson's wholehearted acceptance of every patriotic syllable in that proclamation, it comes as no surprise to those acquainted with the limited literary abilities of Old Hickory that its composition was the work of an adviser. That adviser, it is worth noting, was a southerner, Secretary of State Edward Livingston of Louisiana.

There were few things on which Henry Clay of Kentucky and Andrew Jackson could agree, but the indissolubility of the Union was one of them. Clay never concurred with those southern leaders who accepted Calhoun's position that a state could nullify national legislation or secede from the Union. As a matter of fact, Henry Clay's Whig party was probably the most important stronghold of pro-Union sentiment in the ante-bellum South. Unlike the Democratic party, the Whigs never succumbed, in defending slavery, to the all-encompassing states' rights doctrine. Instead, they identified themselves with the national bank, internal improvements, the tariff, and opposition to the "tyranny" of Andrew Jackson. Despite the "unsouthern" sound of these principles to modern ears, the Whig party was both powerful and popular, capable of winning elections in any southern state. In the heyday of the Whigs, a solidly Democratic South was still unimaginable.

In 1846, the attempt of antislavery forces to prohibit slavery in the vast areas about to be acquired as a result of the Mexican War precipitated another bitter sectional struggle. But as much as they might support the "peculiar institution," the southern Whigs stood firm against Calhoun's efforts to commit the whole South to a states' rights position that once more threatened the existence of the Union. When, in 1849,

The daguerreotype of Henry Clay (left) dates from the late 1840's. Clay devoted himself to preserving the Union from the curse of "Secession Fever," as depicted in the contemporary newspaper cartoon at right.

Calhoun invited southern Congressmen to join his Southern Rights movement in order to strengthen resistance against northern demands, forty of the eighty-eight he approached refused to sign the call. Almost all of them were Whigs.

Throughout the Deep South in the state elections of 1851, Unionist Democrats and Whigs combined to stop the incipient secessionist movement in its tracks. In Georgia, Howell Cobb, the Unionist candidate for governor, received 56,261 votes to 37,472 for his opponent, a prominent Southern Rights man; in the legislature the Unionists captured 101 of the 127 seats. After the same election the congressional delegation of Alabama consisted of two secessionists and five Union supporters. In the Calhoun stronghold of Mississippi, where Jefferson Davis was the best-known spokesman for the Southern Rights movement, Davis was defeated for the governorship, 28,738 to 27,729, by his Unionist opponent, Henry S. Foote. Even in fire-eating South Carolina itself, the anti-Calhoun forces won overwhelmingly, 25,045 to 17,710.

By the time of the Kansas-Nebraska Act of 1854, the Whig party had all but disappeared, the victim of a widening sectional schism. Bereft of its traditional political organization, southern Unionism was, for the time, almost voiceless, but it was not dead. In the election of 1860, it reappeared in the shape of the Constitutional Union party. Its candidate was John Bell of Tennessee, an old-line Whig and staunch Unionist who, in order to prevent disruption of the nation, made his platform the Union itself. That year, in a four-party race, the Constitutional Unionists were the effective second party to the southern Democrats; for Stephen A. Douglas, the candidate of the northern Democrats, received few votes outside the border states, and Lincoln was not even on a ballot in ten of the fifteen slave states.

Deaf Man—I have got the Secession Fever, and it is making me deaf.

The Constitutional Unionists gave the dominant Democratic party a hot fight in every southern state. Of the upper southern states, Virginia, Kentucky, and Tennessee went to Bell outright, while Maryland gave him forty-five per cent and North Carolina forty-seven per cent of their votes.

Bell's showing in the Deep South was not as strong as in the upper South, but it nonetheless demonstrated that those southerners still willing to be counted for the Union were a large minority in almost all of the states. From the whole South, Bell received forty per cent of the popular vote to southern Democrat Breckinridge's forty-five.

A clear indication of the continuity of Unionism from the days of the Whigs to the election of 1860 is that Bell's support in the Deep South centered in the same general areas where the Whigs had been most powerful in the 1840's. Many of the delta counties along the Mississippi River—in Arkansas, Mississippi, and Louisiana—which were always strongholds of Whiggery, went for Bell. Whig votes had always been conspicuous in the black belt counties of central Alabama and Georgia, and so were Bell's in 1860.

Surprisingly enough, the wealthy, slaveholding counties of the South were more often Whig than Democratic in the years before the war. Ever since the days of Jackson, the Democracy had been predominantly the party of the small planter and non-slaveholder. Regardless of the serious threat to slavery posed by the Republican party in 1860, many slaveholders could still not bring themselves to violate their traditional political allegiances and vote for a Democratic candidate identified with states' rights.

A further test of southern Unionism was provided in the election of delegates to the state secession conventions in the winter of 1860–61. Unfortunately, the voting figures do not tell us as much as we would like to know. To most southerners at the time, the issue was not simply the Union versus the right of a state to secede; more often it was whether secession was expedient, with little thought about its constitutionality. Therefore, those delegates who favored a course other than immediate secession did not necessarily support the Union under all and every circumstance.

Nevertheless, these voting returns make clear that even on the verge of secession, tens of thousands in all the states of the Deep South were still opposed to a break with the Union. In Alabama, for example, 28,200 voted against immediate secession to 35,700 for; furthermore, one third of the delegates to the convention refused to sign the secession ordinance because it would not be submitted to the people. In Georgia, 37,123 were against secession to 50,243 in favor; in Louisiana the Unionists were an even larger minority: 17,296 against secession, 20,448 for. In Texas, despite much intimidation of Unionists, twenty-two per cent of the voters still opposed secession.

Before Sumter was fired upon and Lincoln called for volunteers, the states of the upper South refused to join the seceding states. Early in 1861, the people of Tennessee voted against having a secession convention, 68,282 to 59,449; the vote of the people of Arkansas against secession in February, 1861, was 22,000 to 17,000. North Carolina, in a popular vote, also turned down a call for a secession convention. As late as April 4, the Virginia convention voted down a proposal to draw up an ordinance of secession by an almost two-to-one majority. Even after Sumter, when the upper South states did secede, it is clear that loyalty to the Union was still a powerful sentiment.

Throughout the war southern Unionists were active in opposition to the Confederacy. Areas of strong Unionist feeling, like eastern Tennessee, western Virginia, northern Alabama, and the mountain counties of Arkansas, quickly come to mind. In eastern Tennessee, for example, Unionist sentiment was so widespread and deep-felt that for a large part of the war, the courts of the Confederacy in that area could not function without military support and not always even then. After the war broke out, Charles Galloway, a staunch Unionist who had opposed secession in Arkansas, led two companies of his fellow southerners to Springfield, Missouri, where they were mustered into the Union Army. Galloway then led his men back to Arkansas to fight the Confederates. Some 48,000 white southern Unionists, it has been estimated, served voluntarily in the Army of the United States. In northern Alabama and Georgia in 1863 and after, peace societies, replete with secret grips, passwords and elaborate security precautions, worked to encourage desertion from the Confederate Army.

A recent study of the Southern Claims Commission provides the most explicit and detailed evidence of the character of southern Unionism during the war. The commission was set up by the United States government at the end of hostilities in order to reimburse those southerners who had sustained certain kinds of property losses because of their loyalty to the Union. (Only actual material losses incurred by loyal southerners in behalf of the Union armies were to be honored;

acts of charity or mercy, or losses occasioned by Confederate action, for example, were not included.) Since all claimants first had to offer ironclad proof of loyalty before their losses could even be considered, those who did file claims may well be taken as the hard core of southern Unionism. There must have been thousands more who, because they lacked the opportunity or the substance to help the Union armies, went uncounted. Still others may not have been able to meet the high standards set for proof of loyalty, though their devotion to the Union was unquestioned. Under these circumstances, 22,298 claimants is an impressive number.

One of the striking facts that emerges from a study of the records of the commission is the great number of southern Unionists who were people of substance. The total amount of the claims was $22.5 million, and 701 claims were for losses of $10,000 or more—a very substantial sum in the 1860's. The wealthy claimants were mainly planters, owners of great plantations and large numbers of slaves. Despite their wealth, or perhaps because of it, they stood with the Union when the storm of secession broke upon them—though to do so often meant obloquy and harassment at the very least, and not infrequently confiscation of property and personal danger.

Southern Unionism also played its part in the complicated history of Reconstruction. Tennessee, for example, probably escaped radical congressional Reconstruction because of the large number of Unionists in the state. William "Parson" Brownlow, an old Whig and Unionist turned Republican, was able to gain control of the state after the war, and under his leadership Tennessee managed to avoid the military occupation that was the retribution visited upon its more recalcitrant neighbors.

In Louisiana, the first Republican governor, Michael Hahn, was also a lifelong Unionist, though originally a Democrat; he had opposed secession and during the war had refused to take a pledge of loyalty to the Confederacy. About a third of the members of the Mississippi legislature during Reconstruction were so-called scalawags; but far from being the disreputable persons usually associated with that label, most of them were actually respectable former Whig Unionists turned Republican.

This shift in allegiance from Whig to Republican—by no means a rarity in the Reconstruction South—is not so strange when it is recalled that Lincoln, the first Republican President, was once a confirmed Whig. Indeed, to many former southern Whigs it must have seemed that the Republican party—the party of business, national authority, sound money, and internal improvements—was a most fortunate reincarnation of Henry Clay's old organization. And now that slavery was no more, it seemed that southerners could once again divide politically as their interests dictated.

The opportunity, however, proved to be short-lived, for to resist effectively the excesses of the Radicals during Reconstruction, all southerners of consequence became Democrats as a matter of necessity. But though they may have been Democrats in name, in principles they were Whigs, and as such worked quite easily with northern Republicans to end Reconstruction and to bring new railroads and industry to the South in the 1880's.

Most Americans assume that between 1830 and 1860 all southerners favored slavery. This is not so. In the earlier years of the Republic, the great Virginians had not defended the institution but only excused it as an undeniable evil that was exceptionally difficult to eradicate. It was not until the 1830's that it began to be widely upheld as something to be proud of, a positive good. Here too, as in the nullification controversy, Calhoun's thought dominated the southern mind. He had been among the first prominent southerners to shake off the sense of guilt over slavery and to proclaim it a "great moral revolution." At the same time, however, many men and women in the South continued to doubt the utility, the wisdom, and the justice of slavery. These, too, constituted another South.

Although there were some southerners who opposed slavery for reasons of Christian ethics, many more decried it for economic and political reasons. Cassius Marcellus Clay of Kentucky, a cousin of the more famous Henry, was prominent among those who abominated slavery because it retarded the economic growth of the South. The son of a wealthy slaveholder, Clay was educated at Yale, where his future is supposed to have been decided by hearing William Lloyd Garrison present an abolitionist lecture. Regardless of the cause for Clay's subsequent antislavery views, he emancipated his slaves in 1833, soon after his graduation, and devoted himself to ridding his state of slavery. Despite his proclaimed hostile sentiments on the subject, Clay gained a large following in state and national politics.

Cassius Marcellus Clay, cousin of Henry, objected to slavery on economic grounds.

The nature of Clay's objections to slavery were made clear in a speech he delivered before the Kentucky legislature in 1841:

Gentlemen would import slaves "to clear up the forests of the Green River country." Take one day's ride from this capital and then go and tell them what you have seen. Tell them that you have looked upon the once most lovely and fertile lands that nature ever formed; and have seen it in fifty years worn to the rock . . . tell them of the depopulation of the country and the consequent ruin of the towns and villages; tell them that the white Kentuckian has been driven out by slaves, by the unequal competition of unpaid labor; tell them that the mass of our people are uneducated; tell them that you have heard the children of white Kentuckians crying for bread, whilst the children of the African was [sic] clothed, and fed, and laughed! And then ask them if they will have blacks to fell their forests.

The troublesome race question effectively prevented some anti-slavery southerners from taking any concrete steps to end slavery; others saw a threat in the possibility of a large free Negro population. To many, the return of former slaves to Africa seemed the necessary first step in any movement toward emancipation. Cassius Clay was both more radical and more realistic. He recognized that colonization was as illusory a solution to the evils of slavery and the Negro problem as it actually proved to be; many more Negroes were born each year than could possibly be sent to Liberia in a generation. Instead, Clay boldly advocated gradual emancipation, with the owners of the slaves being compensated by the state.

Hinton Rowan Helper is better known today as an antislavery southerner than Clay, though the latter was certainly the more prominent at the time. Helper was the son of a poor North Carolina farmer; with the publication of his book, *The Impending Crisis of the South,* in 1857, he became a nationally known figure. In an effort to demonstrate the material and cultural backwardness of the slave states, Helper brought together statistics from the Census of 1850 —compiled by that most indefatigable southern publicist, J. D. B. De Bow, and therefore unimpeachable in southern eyes—to show that in number of libraries, newspapers, and schools, as well as in wealth, manufactures, population, and commerce, the North far outdistanced the South. Helper pointed out that even in agriculture, the vaunted specialty of Dixie, northern production exceeded southern. Almost contemptuously, he observed that the value of the Cotton Kingdom's chief staple was surpassed by that of the North's lowly hay crop. The cause for all these discrepancies, Helper contended, was slavery.

Helper's indictment of slavery was sufficiently telling to arouse violent southern attacks. He also serves to illustrate the variety of motives underlying the southern antislavery movement. He was more disturbed about what slavery did to the poor white man than about what it did to the Negro. Many antislavery men felt the same, but

Helper went further; his concern for the white man was coupled with an almost pathological hatred of the black.

Not its economic disadvantages, but its essential incompatibility with the genius of America, was the more compelling argument against slavery for some southerners. The great Virginians of the eighteenth century—men like Washington, Marshall, Patrick Henry, Madison, Jefferson, and Monroe—all felt that it somehow contradicted their ideal of a new republic of freemen. Echoes of this view were heard by Frederick Law Olmsted when he traveled through the back country of the South in the 1850's. One mountain dweller told Olmsted that he "was afraid that there was many a man who had gone to the bad world, who wouldn't have gone if he hadn't had any slaves."

Though less moralistic in his conclusions, Henry Clay was of much the same opinion. "I am no friend to slavery," he wrote to an Alabaman in 1838. "I think it is an evil; but I believe it better that slaves should remain slaves than to be set loose as free men among us . . ." For Clay, as for many antislavery southerners, it was difficult to believe that emancipated Negroes and whites could live together peacefully in the same country. This deep-seated belief in the incompatibility of the two races constituted the great dilemma in the minds of antislavery southerners; often it paralyzed all action.

The effects of this dilemma were certainly evident in the course of the remarkable debate on slavery in the Virginia legislature in 1832.

The event which precipitated it was a brief but violent uprising of slaves in Southampton County on August 21, 1831. Led by Nat Turner, a slave preacher given to visions and prophecies, the insurrectionists deliberately killed some sixty white people, mainly women and children. But even the rapidity and efficiency with which the might of the white man had been mobilized against the runaway slaves did not assuage the fear that surged through the minds of southerners everywhere. And so it was that on January 11, 1832, there began one of the most searching debates on slavery ever held by the elected representatives of a slaveholding people. For two weeks the venerable institution was subjected to the frankest kind of criticism.

Three quarters of the members of the House of Delegates held slaves, yet more than half of that body spoke out against the institution in one fashion or another. In analyzing the statements and the notes of the members, one historian concluded that 60 of the 134 delegates were consistently antislavery, working for legislation that would eventually terminate Negro bondage in Virginia. Twelve more, whom he calls the compromisers, were antislavery in belief, but were not prepared to vote for any measure which would, at that time, commit the state to emancipation. It was this latter group, in league with the sixty or so defenders of the *status quo*, who defeated the efforts to initiate gradual emancipation in 1832.

Though individual opponents of slavery remained in the South right up to the Civil War, it is impossible to ascertain their numbers. However, a glimpse into the mind of one such southerner has been afforded by the publication of the diary of Mary Minor Blackford.

Mrs. Blackford lived in Fredericksburg, Virginia, across the street from a slave trader's house, a location which permitted her to see slavery at its worst. And it was slavery as a moral evil rather than as an economic fallacy which troubled her: how could people otherwise good and humane, kind and Christian, hold fellow human beings in bondage? For unlike some northern abolitionists, she knew slave owners too well to think them innately evil. Her answer was not surprising: material self-interest morally blinded them.

The tragedy of the South's history was woven into the fabric of Mary Minor Blackford's life. Despite her long opposition to slavery, she proudly saw five of her sons serve in the Confederate Army. Yet with its defeat, she could still write early in 1866: "A New Era has dawned since I last wrote in this book. Slavery has been abolished!!!"

Other individual opponents of slavery in the South could be cited, but perhaps it would be best to close by mentioning an antislavery organization. The American Colonization Society, founded in 1817 by southern and northern antislavery men, always included prominent southerners among its leaders. In the course of its half century of operations, the society managed to send more than six thousand Negroes to its African colony in Liberia.

The society was strongest in the South; indeed, it was anathema to the New England and middle western abolitionists. Though it is true that antislavery was never a popular cause in the South, it was never a dead one, either, so long as thousands of southerners refused to view slavery as anything but an evil for their region.

As we have seen, the South was even less united on nullification and secession than it was on the question of slavery. In fact, it is now clear that if a majority of southerners ever did support secession— and there is real doubt on this—it was never a big majority, and it was not achieved until the very eve of the Civil War. In short, the South, rather than being a monolith of undivided opinion, was not even of one mind on the two most vital issues of the thirty years that led up to the war.

*Quite innocent of war, these
Confederate volunteers struck
bold poses before the First
Battle of Bull Run in 1861.*

Part Six

Civil War and Reconstruction

Allan Nevins
The Needless Conflict

The qualities that made Allan Nevins such an excellent example of the scholar-historian writing for a broad audience are all illustrated in this story of the tragic events that occurred in Kansas in the decade before the Civil War. Scholarship, a powerful narrative style, historical imagination, sound judgment, and a deep understanding of the fallible human beings whose story he tells combine to make this essay a model for future historians.

Nevins believed that the troubles in Kansas resulting from the opening up of that territory to slavery under the Kansas-Nebraska Act, troubles which, as he says, were central to the events that led to secession, could have been avoided. He does not hesitate to place the blame for what happened on the shoulders of particular individuals. Yet unlike some of the historians who have seen the Civil War as caused by "a blundering generation," Nevins was not an apologist for the South. He condemned slavery flatly and believed that it had to be destroyed.

Nevins was a professor of history at Columbia University. Among the dozens of books that he produced in his long career was his eight-volume *Ordeal of the Union*.

When James Buchanan, standing in a homespun suit before cheering crowds, took the oath of office on March 4, 1857, he seemed confident that the issues before the nation could be readily settled. He spoke about an army road to California, use of the Treasury surplus to pay all the national debt, and proper guardianship of the public lands. In Kansas, he declared, the path ahead was clear. The simple logical rule that the will of the people should determine the institutions of a territory had brought in sight a happy settlement. The inhabitants would declare for or against slavery as they pleased. Opinions differed as to the proper time for making such a decision; but Buchanan thought that "the appropriate period will be when the number of actual residents in the Territory shall justify the formation of a constitution with a view to its admission as a State." He trusted that the long strife between North and South was nearing its end, and that the sectional party which had almost elected Frémont would die a natural death.

Two days after the inaugural Buchanan took deep satisfaction in a decision by the Supreme Court of which he had improper foreknowledge: the Dred Scott decision handed down by Chief Justice Taney. Its vital element, so far as the nation's destiny was concerned, was the ruling that the Missouri Compromise restriction, by which slavery had been excluded north of the 36° 30' line, was void; that on the contrary, every territory was open to slavery. Not merely was Congress without power to legislate *against* slavery, but by implication it should act to protect it. Much of the northern press denounced the decision fervently. But the country was prosperous; it was clear that time and political action might change the Supreme Court, bringing a new decision; and the explosion of wrath proved brief.

Buchanan had seen his view sustained; slavery might freely enter any territory, the inhabitants of which could not decide whether to keep it or drop it until they wrote their first constitution. In theory, the highway to national peace was as traversible as the Lancaster turnpike. To be sure, Kansas was rent between two bitter parties, proslavery and antislavery; from the moment Stephen A. Douglas' Kansas-Nebraska Act had thrown open the West to popular sovereignty three years earlier, it had been a theater of unrelenting conflict. Popular sovereignty had simply failed to work. In the spring of 1855 about five thousand invading Missourians, swamping the polls, had given Kansas a fanatically proslavery legislature which the free-soil settlers flatly refused to recognize. That fall a free-soil convention in Topeka had adopted a constitution which the slavery men in turn flatly rejected. Some bloody fighting had ensued. But could not all this be thrust into the past?

In theory, the President might now send out an impartial new governor; and if the people wanted statehood, an election might be held for a new constitutional convention. Then the voters could give the nation its sixteenth slave state or its seventeenth free state— everybody behaving quietly and reasonably. Serenity would prevail. Actually, the idea that the people of Kansas, so violently aroused, would show quiet reason, was about as tenable as the idea that Europeans would begin settling boundary quarrels by a quiet game of chess. Behind the two Kansas parties were grim southerners and determined northerners. "Slavery will now yield a greater profit in Kansas," trumpeted a southern propagandist in *De Bow's Review*, "either to hire out or cultivate the soil, than any other place." He wanted proslavery squatters. Meanwhile, Yankees were subsidizing their own settlers. "I know people," said Emerson in a speech, "who are making haste to reduce their expenses and pay their debts . . . to save and earn for the benefit of Kansas emigrants."

Nor was reason in Kansas the only need. Impartiality in Congress, courage in the presidential chair, were also required. The stage was dressed for a brief, fateful melodrama, which more than anything else was to fix the position of James Buchanan and Stephen A. Douglas in history, was to shape the circumstances under which Lincoln made his first national reputation, and was to have more potency than any other single event in deciding whether North and South should remain brothers or fly at each other's throats. That melodrama was entitled "Lecompton." Douglas was to go to his grave believing that, had Buchanan played an honest, resolute part in it, rebellion would have been killed in its incipiency. The role that Buchanan did play may be counted one of the signal failures of American statesmanship.

To hold that the Civil War could not have been averted by wise, firm, and timely action is to concede too much to determinism in history. Winston Churchill said that the Second World War should be called "The Unnecessary War"; the same term might as justly be applied to our Civil War. Passionate unreason among large sections of the population was one ingredient in the broth of conflict. Accident, fortuity, fate, or sheer bad luck (these terms are interchangeable) was another; John Brown's raid, so malign in its effects on opinion, North and South, might justly be termed an accident. Nothing in the logic of forces or events required so crazy an act. But beyond these ingredients lies the further element of wretched leadership. Had the United States possessed three farseeing, imaginative, and resolute Presidents instead of Fillmore, Pierce, and Buchanan, the war might have been postponed until time and economic forces killed its roots. Buchanan was the weakest of the three, and the Lecompton affair lights up his incompetence like a play of lightning across a nocturnal storm front.

The melodrama had two stages, one in faraway, thinly settled Kansas, burning hot in summer, bitter cold in winter, and, though reputedly rich, really so poor that settlers were soon on the brink of starvation. Here the most curious fact was the disparity between the mean actors and the great results they effected. A handful of ignorant, reckless, semi-drunken settlers on the southern side, led by a few desperadoes of politics—the delegates of the Lecompton Constitutional Convention—actually had the power to make or mar the nation. The other stage was Washington. The participants here, representing great interests and ideas, had at least a dignity worthy of the scene and the consequences of their action. James Buchanan faced three main groups holding three divergent views of the sectional problem.

The proslavery group (that is, Robert Toombs, Alexander H. Stephens, Jefferson Davis, John Slidell, David Atchison, and many more) demanded that slavery be allowed to expand freely within the territories; soon they were asking also that such expansion be given federal protection against any hostile local action. This stand involved the principle that slavery was morally right, and socially and economically a positive good. Reverdy Johnson of Maryland, in the Dred Scott case, had vehemently argued the beneficence of slavery.

The popular sovereignty group, led by Douglas and particularly strong among northwestern Democrats, maintained that in any territory the issue of slavery or free soil should be determined *at all times* by the settlers therein. Douglas modified the Dred Scott doctrine: local police legislation and action, he said, could exclude slavery even before state-making took place. He sternly rejected the demand for federal protection against such action. His popular sovereignty view implied indifference to or rejection of any moral test of slavery. Whether the institution was socially and economically good or bad depended mainly on climate and soil, and moral ideas were irrelevant. He did not care whether slavery was voted up or voted down; the right to a fair vote was the all-important matter.

The free-soil group, led by Seward and Chase, but soon to find its best voice in Lincoln, held that slavery should be excluded from all territories present or future. They insisted that slavery was morally wrong, had been condemned as such by the Fathers, and was increasingly outlawed by the march of world civilization. It might be argued that the free-soil contention was superfluous, in that climate and aridity forbade a further extension of slavery anyhow. But in Lincoln's eyes this did not touch the heart of the matter. It might or might not be expansible. (Already it existed in Delaware and Missouri, and Cuba and Mexico might be conquered for it.) What was important was for America to accept the fact that, being morally wrong and socially an anachronism, it *ought* not to expand; it *ought* to be put in the way of ultimate eradication. Lincoln was a planner. Once the country accepted nonexpansion, it would thereby accept the idea of ultimate extinction. This crisis met and passed, it could sit down and decide when and how, in God's good time and with suitable compensation to slaveholders it might be ended.

The Buchanan who faced these three warring groups was victim of the mistaken belief among American politicians (like Pierce, Benjamin Harrison, and Warren G. Harding, for example) that it is better to be a poor President than to stick to honorable but lesser posts. He would have made a respectable diplomat or decent Cabinet officer under a really strong President. Sixty-six in 1857, the obese bachelor felt all his years. He had wound his devious way up through a succession of offices without once showing a flash of inspiration or an ounce of grim courage. James K. Polk had accurately characterized

Hedged in by his own circumspection and vacillation, President Buchanan was ill-equipped to surmount the growing national crisis.

him as an old woman—"It is one of his weaknesses that he takes on and magnifies small matters into great and undeserved importance." His principal characteristic was irresolution. "Even among close friends," remarked a southern senator, "he very rarely expressed his opinions at all upon disputed questions, except in language especially marked with a cautious circumspection almost amounting to timidity."

He was industrious, capable, and tactful, a well-read Christian gentleman; he had acquired from forty years of public life a rich fund of experience. But he was pedestrian, humorless, calculating, and pliable. He never made a witty remark, never wrote a memorable sentence, and never showed a touch of distinction. Above all (and this was the source of his irresolution) he had no strong convictions. Associating all his life with southern leaders in Washington, this Pennsylvanian leaned toward their views, but he never disclosed a deep adherence to any principle. Like other weak men, he could be stubborn; still oftener, he could show a petulant irascibility when events pushed him into a corner. And like other timid men, he would sometimes flare out in a sudden burst of anger, directed not against enemies who could hurt him but against friends or neutrals who would not. As the sectional crisis deepened, it became his dominant hope to stumble through it, somehow, and anyhow, so as to leave office with

Buchanan ran head on into Douglas, the "Little Giant." Convinced that he had "made" Buchanan President, Douglas vowed he would "unmake" him.

the Union yet intact. His successor could bear the storm.

This was the President who had to deal, in Kansas and Washington, with men of fierce conviction, stern courage and, all too often, ruthless methods.

In Kansas the proslavery leaders were determined to strike boldly and unscrupulously for a slave state. They maintained close communications with such southern chieftains in Washington as Senator Slidell, Speaker James L. Orr, and Howell Cobb and Jacob Thompson, Buchanan's secretaries of the Treasury and the Interior. Having gained control of the territorial legislature, they meant to keep and use this mastery. Just before Buchanan became President they passed a bill for a constitutional convention—and a more unfair measure was never put on paper. Nearly all county officers, selected not by popular vote but by the dishonestly chosen legislature, were proslavery men. The bill provided that the sheriffs and their deputies should in March, 1857, register the white residents; that the probate judges should then take from the sheriffs complete lists of qualified voters; and that the county commissioners should finally choose election judges.

Everyone knew that a heavy majority of the Kansas settlers were antislavery. Many, even of the southerners, who had migrated thither opposed the "peculiar institution" as retrogressive and crippling in character. Everybody also knew that Kansas, with hardly thirty thousand people, burdened with debts, and unsupplied with fit roads, schools, or courthouses, was not yet ready for statehood; it still needed the federal government's care. Most Kansans refused to recognize the "bogus" legislature. Yet this legislature was forcing a premature convention, and taking steps to see that the election of delegates was controlled by sheriffs, judges, and county commissioners who were mainly proslavery Democrats. Governor John W. Geary, himself a Democrat appointed by Pierce, indignantly vetoed the bill. But the legislature immediately repassed it over Geary's veto; and when threats against his life increased until citizens laid bets that he would be assassinated within forty days, he resigned in alarm and posted east to apprise the country of imminent perils.

Along the way to Washington, Geary paused to warn the press that a packed convention was about to drag fettered Kansas before Congress with a slavery constitution. This convention would have a free hand, for the bill just passed made no provision for a popular vote on the instrument. Indeed, one legislator admitted that the plan was to avoid popular submission, for he proposed inserting a clause to guard against the possibility that Congress might return the constitution for a referendum. Thus, commented the *Missouri Democrat*, "the felon legislature has provided as effectually for getting the desired result as Louis Napoleon did for getting himself elected Emperor." All this was an ironic commentary on Douglas' maxim: "Let the voice of the people rule."

And Douglas, watching the reckless course of the Kansas legislators with alarm, saw that his principles and his political future were at stake. When his Kansas-Nebraska Act was passed, he had given the North his solemn promise that a free, full, and fair election would decide the future of the two territories. No fraud, no sharp practice, no browbeating would be sanctioned; every male white citizen should have use of the ballot box. He had notified the South that Kansas was almost certain to be free soil. Now he professed confidence that President Buchanan would never permit a breach of fair procedure. He joined Buchanan in persuading one of the nation's ablest men, former Secretary of the Treasury Robert J. Walker, to go out to Kansas in Geary's place as governor. Douglas knew that if he consented to a betrayal of popular sovereignty he would be ruined forever politically in his own state of Illinois.

For a brief space in the spring of 1857 Buchanan seemed to stand firm. In his instructions to Governor Walker he engaged that the new constitution would be laid before the people; and "they must be protected in the exercise of their right of voting for or against that instrument, and the fair expression of the popular will must not be interrupted by fraud or violence."

It is not strange that the rash proslavery gamesters in Kansas prosecuted their designs despite all Buchanan's fair words and Walker's desperate efforts to stay them. They knew that with four fifths of the people already against them, and the odds growing greater every year, only brazen trickery could effect their end. They were aware that the South, which believed that a fair division would give Kansas to slavery and Nebraska to freedom, expected them to stand firm. They were egged on by the two reckless southern Cabinet members, Howell Cobb and Thompson, who sent an agent, H. L. Martin of Mississippi, out to the Kansas convention. This gathering in Lecompton, with 48 of the 60 members hailing from slave states, was the shabbiest conclave of its kind ever held on American soil. One of Buchanan's Kansas correspondents wrote that he had not supposed such a wild set could be found. The *Kansas News* termed them a body of "broken-down political hacks, demagogues, fire-eaters, perjurers, ruffians, ballot-box stuffers, and loafers." But before it broke up with the shout, "Now, boys, let's come and take a drink!" it had written a constitution.

This constitution, the work of a totally unrepresentative body, was a devious repudiation of all the principles Buchanan and Douglas had laid down. Although it contained numerous controversial provisions, such as a limitation of banking to one institution and a bar against free Negroes, the main document was not to be submitted to general vote at all. A nominal reference of the great cardinal question was indeed provided. Voters might cast their ballots for the "constitution with slavery" or the "constitution without slavery." But when closely examined this was seen to be actually a piece of chicanery. Whichever form was adopted, the 200 slaves in Kansas would remain, with a constitutional guarantee against interference. Whenever the proslavery party in Kansas could get control of the legislature, they might open the door wide for more slaves. The rigged convention had put its handiwork before the people with a rigged choice: "Heads I win, tails you lose."

Would Buchanan lay this impudent contrivance before Congress, and ask it to vote the admission of Kansas as a state? Or would he contemptuously spurn it? An intrepid man would not have hesitated an instant to take the honest course; he would not have needed the indignant outcry of the northern press, the outraged roar of Douglas, to inspirit him. But Buchanan quailed before the storm of passion into which proslavery extremists had worked themselves.

The hot blood of the South was now up. That section, grossly misinformed upon events in Kansas, believed that *it* was being cheated. The northern freesoilers had vowed that no new slave state (save by a partition of Texas) should ever be admitted. Southerners thought that in pursuance of this resolve, the Yankees had made unscrupulous use of their wealth and numbers to lay hands on Kansas. Did the North think itself entitled to every piece on the board—to take Kansas as well as California, Minnesota, Iowa, Nebraska, Oregon—to give southerners nothing? The Lecompton delegates, from this point of view, were dauntless champions of a wronged section. What if they did use sharp tactics? That was but a necessary response to northern arrogance. Jefferson Davis declared that his section trembled under a sense of insecurity. "You have made it a political war. We are on the defensive. How far are you to push us?" Sharp threats of secession and battle mingled with the southern denunciations. "Sir," Senator Alfred Iverson of Georgia was soon to assert, "I believe that the time will come when the slave States will be compelled, in vindication of their rights, interests, and honor, to separate from the free States, and erect an independent confederacy; and I am not sure, sir, that the time is not at hand."

Three southern members of the Cabinet, Cobb, Thompson, and John B. Floyd, had taken the measure of Buchanan's pusillanimity. They, with one northern sympathizer, Jeremiah Black, and several White House habitués like John Slidell of Louisiana, constituted a virtual Directory exercising control over the tremulous President. They played on Buchanan's fierce partisan hatred of Republicans, and his jealous dislike of Douglas. They played also on his legalistic cast of mind; after all, the Lecompton constitution was a legal instrument by a legal convention—outwardly. Above all, they played on his fears, his morbid sensitiveness, and his responsiveness to immediate pressures. They could do this the more easily because the threats of disruption and violence were real. Henry S. Foote, a former senator from Mississippi and an enemy of Jefferson Davis, who saw Lecompton in its true light and hurried to Washington to advise the President, writes:

"It was unfortunately of no avail that these efforts to reassure Mr. Buchanan were at that time essayed by myself and others; he had already become thoroughly *panic-stricken;* the howlings of the bulldog of secession had fairly frightened him out of his wits, and he ingloriously resolved to yield without further resistance to the decrial and villification to which he had been so acrimoniously subjected."

And the well-informed Washington correspondent of the New Orleans *Picayune* a little later told just how aggressively the Chief Executive was bludgeoned into submission:

"The President was informed in November, 1857, that the States of Alabama, Mississippi, and South Carolina, and perhaps others, would hold conventions and secede from the Union if the Lecompton Constitution, which established slavery, should not be accepted by Congress. The reason was that these States, supposing that the South had been cheated out of Kansas, were, whether right or wrong, determined to revolt. The President believed this. Senator Hunter, of Virginia, to my knowledge, believed it. Many other eminent men did, and perhaps not without reason."

Buchanan, without imagination as without nerve, began to yield to this southern storm in midsummer, and by November, 1857, he was surrendering completely. When Congress met in December his message upheld the Lecompton Constitution with a tissue of false and evasive statements. Seldom in American history has a chief magistrate made a greater error, or missed a larger opportunity. The astute secretary of his predecessor, Franklin Pierce, wrote: "I had considerable hopes of Mr. Buchanan—I really thought he was a statesman—but

I have now come to the settled conclusion that he is just the damndest old fool that has ever occupied the presidential chair. He has deliberately walked overboard with his eyes open—let him drown, for he must.''

As Buchanan shrank from the lists, Douglas entered them with that *gaudium certaminis* which was one of his greatest qualities. The finest chapters of his life, his last great contests for the Union, were opening. Obviously he would have had to act under political necessity even if deaf to principle, for had he let popular sovereignty be torn to pieces, Illinois would not have sent him back to the Senate the following year; but he was not the man to turn his back on principle. His struggle against Lecompton was an exhibition of iron determination. The drama of that battle has given it an almost unique place in the record of our party controversies.

"By God, sir!" he exclaimed, "I made James Buchanan, and by God, sir, I will unmake him!" Friends told him that the southern Democrats meant to ruin him. "I have taken a through ticket," rejoined Douglas, "and checked my baggage." He lost no time in facing Buchanan in the White House and denouncing the Lecompton policy. When the President reminded him how Jackson had crushed two party rebels, he was ready with a stinging retort. Douglas was not to be overawed by a man he despised as a weakling. "Mr. President," he snorted, "I wish you to remember that General Jackson is dead."

As for the southern leaders, Douglas' scorn for the extremists who had coerced Buchanan was unbounded. He told the Washington correspondent of the Chicago *Journal* that he had begun his fight as a contest against a single bad measure. But his blow at Lecompton was a blow against slavery extension, and he at once had the whole "slave power" down on him like a pack of wolves. He added: "In making the fight against this power, I was enabled to stand off and view the men with whom I had been acting; I was ashamed I had ever been caught in such company; they are a set of unprincipled demagogues, bent upon perpetuating slavery, and by the exercise of that unequal and unfair power, to control the government or break up the Union; and I intend to prevent their doing either.''

After a long, close, and acrid contest, on April 1, 1858, Lecompton was defeated. A coalition of Republicans, Douglasite Democrats, and Know-Nothings struck down the fraudulent constitution in the House, 120 to 112. When the vote was announced, a wild cheer rolled through the galleries. Old Francis P. Blair, Jackson's friend, carried the news to the dying Thomas Hart Benton, who had been intensely aroused by the crisis. Benton could barely speak, but his exultation was unbounded. "In energetic whispers," records Blair, "he told his visitor that the same men who had sought to destroy the republic in 1850 were at the bottom of this accursed Lecompton business. Among the greatest of his consolations in dying was the consciousness that the House of Representatives had baffled these treasonable schemes and put the heels of the people on the neck of the traitors.''

The Administration covered its retreat by a hastily concocted measure, the English Bill, under which Kansas was kept waiting on the doorstep—sure in the end to enter a free state. The Kansas plotters, the Cobb-Thompson-Floyd clique in the Cabinet, and Buchanan had all been worsted. But the damage had been done. Southern secessionists had gained fresh strength and greater boldness from their success in coercing the Administration.

The Lecompton struggle left a varied and interesting set of after-effects. It lifted Stephen A. Douglas to a new plane; he had been a fighting Democratic strategist, but now he became a true national leader, thinking far less of party and more of country. It sharpened the issues which that summer and fall were to form the staple of the memorable Lincoln-Douglas debates in Illinois. At the same time, it deepened the schism which had been growing for some years between southern Democrats and northwestern Democrats, and helped pave the way to that disruption of the party which preceded and facilitated the disruption of the nation. It planted new seeds of dissension in Kansas—seeds which resulted in fresh conflicts between Kansas free-soilers or jayhawkers on one side and Missouri invaders or border ruffians on the other, and in a spirit of border lawlessness which was to give the Civil War some of its darkest pages. The Lecompton battle discredited Buchanan in the eyes of most decent northerners, strengthened southern conviction of his weakness, and left the Administration materially and morally weaker in dealing with the problems of the

Armed and disorderly border ruffians from Missouri head for Lawrence, Kansas, determined to win the entire territory for slaveholders.

next two and a half critical years.

For the full measure of Buchanan's failure, however, we must go deeper. Had he shown the courage that to an Adams, a Jackson, a Polk, or a Cleveland would have been second nature, the courage that springs from a deep integrity, he might have done the republic an immeasurable service by grappling with disunion when it was yet weak and unprepared. Ex-Senator Foote wrote later that he knew well that a scheme for destroying the Union "had long been on foot in the South." He knew that its leaders "were only waiting for the enfeebling of the Democratic Party in the North, and the general triumph of Free-soilism as a consequence thereof, to alarm the whole South into acquiescence in their policy." Buchanan's support of the unwise and corrupt Lecompton constitution thus played into the plotters' hands.

The same view was taken yet more emphatically by Douglas. He had inside information in 1857, he later told the Senate, that four states were threatening Buchanan with secession. Had that threat been met in the right Jacksonian spirit, had the bluff been called—for the four states were unprepared for secession and war—the leaders of the movement would have been utterly discredited. Their conspiracy would have collapsed, and they would have been so routed and humiliated in 1857 that the Democratic party schism in 1860 might never have taken place, and if it had, secession in 1861 would have been impossible.

The roots of the Civil War of course go deep; they go back beyond Douglas' impetuous Kansas-Nebraska Bill, back beyond the Mexican War, back beyond the Missouri Compromise. But the last good chance of averting secession and civil strife was perhaps lost in 1857. Even Zachary Taylor in 1850 had made it plain before his sudden death that he would use force, if necessary, to crush the secessionist tendencies which that year became so dangerous. A similar display of principle and resolution seven years later might well have left the disunionist chieftains of the Deep South so weakened in prestige that Yancey and his fellow plotters would have been helpless. The lessons of this failure in statesmanship, so plain to Douglas, ought not to be forgotten. The greatest mistake a nation can make is to put at its helm a man so pliable and unprincipled that he will palter with a clean-cut and momentous issue.

Bruce Catton
Soldiering in the Civil War

Surely one of the most "popular" of American historians is Bruce Catton, editor emeritus of *American Heritage* magazine, whose books about the Civil War have been read and enjoyed by hundreds of thousands of persons. Yet Catton is also among the most scholarly of historians; his work is based on meticulous research in archives and old attics, and his analyses of events and men have been widely praised by Civil War scholars.

One of the reasons for Catton's success has been his ability to understand the Civil War both in broad strategic terms and also as a very human conflict, full of tragedy, bravery, and humor. In this essay he draws a graphic portrait of the ordinary soldier, Union and Confederate. From dozens of anecdotes and small details one gathers a general impression, vivid yet with a sense of its universal applicability, of what it was like to fight in that epic struggle. At the same time—and it is one of the infallible marks of a good historian—Catton sees the "G.I." of the 1860's from a modern perspective and is thus able to explain why he acted and believed as he did.

The volunteer soldier in the American Civil War used a clumsy muzzle-loading rifle, lived chiefly on salt pork and hardtack, and retained to the very end a loose-jointed, informal attitude toward the army with which he had cast his lot. But despite all of the surface differences, he was at bottom blood brother to the G.I. Joe of modern days.

Which is to say that he was basically, and incurably, a civilian in arms. A volunteer, he was still a soldier because he had to be one, and he lived for the day when he could leave the army forever. His attitude toward discipline, toward his officers, and toward the whole spit-and-polish concept of military existence was essentially one of careless tolerance. He refused to hate his enemies—indeed, he often got along with them much better than with some of his own comrades—and his indoctrination was often so imperfect that what was sometimes despairingly said of the American soldier in World War II would apply equally to him: he seemed to be fighting chiefly so that he could some day get back to Mom's cooking.

What really set the Civil War soldier apart was the fact that he came from a less sophisticated society. He was no starry-eyed innocent, to be sure—or, if he was, the army quickly took care of that—but the America of the 1860's was less highly developed than modern America. It lacked the ineffable advantages of radio, television, and moving pictures. It was still essentially a rural nation; it had growing cities, but they were smaller and somehow less urban than today's cities; a much greater percentage of the population lived on farms or in country towns and villages than is the case now, and there was more of a backwoods, hay-seed-in-the-hair flavor to the people who came from them.

For example: every war finds some ardent youngsters who want to enlist despite the fact that they are under the military age limit of eighteen. Such a lad today simply goes to the recruiting station, swears that he is eighteen, and signs up. The lad of the 1860's saw it a little differently. He could not swear that he was eighteen when he was only sixteen; in his innocent way, he felt that to lie to his own government was just plain wrong. But he worked out a little dodge that got him into the army anyway. He would take a bit of paper, scribble the number *18* on it, and put it in the sole of his shoe. Then, when the recruiting officer asked him how old he was, he could truthfully say: "I am *over* eighteen." That was a common happening, early in the Civil War; one cannot possibly imagine it being tried today.

Similarly, the drill sergeants repeatedly found that among the raw recruits there were men so abysmally untaught that they did not know left from right, and hence could not step off on the left foot as all soldiers should. To teach these lads how to march, the sergeants would tie a wisp of hay to the left foot and a wisp of straw to the right; then, setting the men to march, they would chant, "Hay-foot, straw-foot, hay-foot, straw-foot"—and so on, until everybody had caught on. A common name for a green recruit in those days was "strawfoot."

On the drill field, when a squad was getting basic training, the men were as likely as not to intone a little rhythmic chant as they tramped across the sod—thus:

March! March! March old soldier march!
Hayfoot, strawfoot,
Belly-full of bean soup—
March old soldier march!

Because of his unsophistication, the ordinary soldier in the Civil War, North and South alike, usually joined up with very romantic ideas about soldiering. Army life rubbed the romance off just as rapidly then as it does now, but at the start every volunteer went into the army thinking that he was heading off to high adventure. Under everything else, he enlisted because he thought army life was going to be fun, and usually it took quite a few weeks in camp to disabuse him of this strange notion. Right at the start, soldiering had an almost idyllic quality; if this quality faded rapidly, the memory of it remained through all the rest of life.

Early days in camp simply cemented the idea. An Illinois recruit, writing home from training camp, confessed: "It is fun to lie around, face unwashed, hair uncombed, shirt unbuttoned and everything un-everythinged. It sure beats clerking." Another Illinois boy confessed: "I don't see why people will stay at home when they can get to soldier-ing. A year of it is worth getting shot for to any man." And a Massa-chusetts boy, recalling the early days of army life, wrote that "Our drill, as I remember it, consisted largely of running around the Old Westbury town hall, yelling like Devils and firing at an imaginary foe." One of the commonest discoveries that comes from a reading of Civil War diaries is that the chief worry, in training camp, was a fear that the war would be over before the ardent young recruits could get into it. It is only fair to say that most of the diarists looked back on this innocent worry, a year or so afterward, with rueful amusement.

There was a regiment recruited in northern Pennsylvania in 1861 —13th Pennsylvania Reserves officially, known to the rest of the Union Army as the Bucktails because the rookies decorated their caps with strips of fur from the carcass of a deer that was hanging in front of a butcher shop near their camp—and in mid-spring these youthful soldiers were ordered to rendezvous at Harrisburg. So they marched cross-country (along a road known today as the Bucktail Trail) to the north branch of the Susquehanna, where they built rafts. One raft, for the colonel, was made oversized with a stable; the colonel's horse had to ride, too. Then the Bucktails floated down the river, singing and firing their muskets and having a gay old time, camping out along the bank at night, and finally they got to Harrisburg; and they served through the worst of the war, getting badly shot up and losing most of their men to Confederate bullets, but they never forgot the picnic air of those first days of army life, when they drifted down a river through the forests, with a song in the air and the bright light of ad-venture shining just ahead. Men do not go to war that way nowadays.

A haunting face from a lost generation: Georgia
Private Edwin Jennison, killed at Malvern Hill.

Discipline in those early regiments was pretty sketchy. The big catch was that most regiments were recruited locally—in one town, or one county, or in one part of a city—and everybody more or less knew everybody else. Particularly, the privates knew their officers—most of whom were elected to their jobs by the enlisted men—and they never saw any sense in being formal with them. Within reasonable limits, the Civil War private was willing to do what his company commander told him to do, but he saw little point in carrying it to extremes.

So an Indiana soldier wrote: "We had enlisted to put down the Rebellion, and had no patience with the red-tape tomfoolery of the regular service. The boys recognized no superiors, except in the line of legitimate duty. Shoulder straps waived, a private was ready at the drop of a hat to thrash his commander—a thing that occurred more than once." A New York regiment, drilling on a hot parade ground, heard a private address his company commander thus: "Say, Tom, let's quit this darn foolin' around and go over to the sutler's and get a drink." There was very little of the "Captain, sir" business in those armies. If a company or regimental officer got anything especial in the way of obedience, he got it because the enlisted men recognized him as a natural leader and superior and not just because he had a commission signed by Abraham Lincoln.

Odd rivalries developed between regiments. (It should be noted that the Civil War soldier's first loyalty went usually to his regiment, just as a navy man's loyalty goes to his ship; he liked to believe that his regiment was better than all others, and he would fight for it, any time and anywhere.) The army legends of those days tell of a Manhattan regiment, camped near Washington, whose nearest neighbor was a regiment from Brooklyn, with which the Manhattanites nursed a deep rivalry. Neither regiment had a chaplain; and there came to the Manhattan colonel one day a minister, who volunteered to hold religious services for the men in the ranks.

The colonel doubted that this would be a good idea. His men, he said, were rather irreligious, not to say godless, and he feared they would not give the reverend gentleman a respectful hearing. But the minister said he would take his chances; after all, he had just held services with the Brooklyn regiment, and the men there had been very quiet and devout. That was enough for the colonel. What the Brooklyn regiment could do, his regiment could do. He ordered the men paraded for divine worship, announcing that any man who talked, laughed, or even coughed would be summarily court-martialed.

So the clergyman held services, and everyone was attentive. At the end of the sermon, the minister asked if any of his hearers would care to step forward and make public profession of faith; in the Brooklyn regiment, he said, fourteen men had done this. Instantly the New York colonel was on his feet.

"Adjutant!" he bellowed. "We're not going to let that damn Brooklyn regiment beat us at anything. Detail twenty men and have them baptized at once!"

Each regiment seemed to have its own mythology, tales which may have been false but which, by their mere existence, reflected faithfully certain aspects of army life. The 48th New York, for instance, was said to have an unusually large number of ministers in its ranks, serving not as chaplains but as combat soldiers. The 48th, fairly early in the war, found itself posted in a swamp along the South Carolina coast, toiling mightily in semitropical heat, amid clouds of mosquitoes, to build fortifications, and it was noted that all hands became excessively profane, including the one-time clergymen. A visiting general, watching the regiment at work one day, recalled the legend and asked the regiment's lieutenant colonel if he himself was a minister in private life.

"Well, no, General," said the officer apologetically. "I can't say that I was a regularly ordained minister. I was just one of these —— —— local preachers."

Another story was hung on this same 48th New York. A Confederate ironclad gunboat was supposed to be ready to steam through channels in the swamp and attack the 48th's outposts, and elaborate plans were made to trap it with obstructions in the channel, a tangle of ropes to snarl the propellers, and so on. But it occurred to the colonel that even if the gunboat was trapped the soldiers could not get into it; it was sheathed in iron, all its ports would be closed, and men with axes could never chop their way into it. Then the colonel had an inspiration. Remembering that many of his men had been recruited from the less savory districts of New York City, he paraded the regiment and (according to legend) announced:

"Now men, you've been in this cursed swamp for two weeks—up to your ears in mud, no fun, no glory and blessed poor pay. Here's a chance. Let every man who has had experience as a cracksman or a safeblower step to the front." To the last man, the regiment marched forward four paces and came expectantly to attention.

Not unlike this was the reputation of the 6th New York, which contained so many Bowery toughs that the rest of the army said a man had to be able to show that he had done time in prison in order to get into the regiment. It was about to leave for the South, and the colonel gave his men an inspirational talk. They were going, he said, to a land of wealthy plantation owners, where each Southerner had riches of which he could be despoiled; and he took out his own gold watch and held it up for all to see, remarking that any deserving soldier could easily get one like it, once they got down to plantationland. Half an hour later, wishing to see what time it was, he felt for his watch . . . and it was gone.

If the Civil War army spun queer tales about itself, it had to face a reality which, in all of its aspects, was singularly unpleasant. One of the worst aspects had to do with food.

From first to last, the Civil War armies enlisted no men as cooks, and there were no cooks' and bakers' schools to help matters. Often enough, when in camp, a company would simply be issued a quantity of provisions—flour, pork, beans, potatoes, and so on—and invited to prepare the stuff as best it could. Half a dozen men would form a mess, members would take turns with the cooking, and everybody had to eat what these amateurs prepared or go hungry. Later in the war, each company commander would usually detail two men to act as cooks for the company, and if either of the two happened to know anything about cooking the company was in luck. One army legend held that company officers usually detailed the least valuable soldiers to this job, on the theory that they would do less harm in the cook shack than anywhere else. One soldier, writing after the war, asserted flatly: "A company cook is a most peculiar being; he generally knows less about cooking than any other man in the company. Not being able to learn the drill, and too dirty to appear on inspection, he is sent to the cook house to get him out of the ranks."

When an army was on the march, the ration issue usually consisted of salt pork, hardtack, and coffee. (In the Confederate Army the coffee was often missing, and the hardtack was frequently replaced by corn bread; often enough the meal was not sifted, and stray bits of cob would appear in it.) The hardtack was good enough, if fresh, which was not always the case; with age it usually got infested with weevils, and veterans remarked that it was better to eat it in the dark.

In the Union Army, most of the time, the soldier could supplement his rations (if he had money) by buying extras from the sutler—the latter being a civilian merchant licensed to accompany the army, functioning somewhat as the regular post exchange functions nowadays. The sutler charged high prices and specialized in indigestibles like pies, canned lobster salad, and so on; and it was noted that men who patronized him regularly came down with stomach upsets. The Confederate Army had few sutlers, which helps to explain why the hungry Confederates were so delighted when they could capture a Yankee camp: to seize a sutler's tent meant high living for the captors, and the men in Lee's army were furious when, in the 1864 campaign, they learned that General Grant had ordered the Union Army to move without sutlers. Johnny Reb felt that Grant was really taking an unfair advantage by cutting off this possible source of supply.

If Civil War cooking arrangements were impromptu and imperfect, the same applied to its hospital system. The surgeons, usually, were good men by the standards of that day—which were low since no one on earth knew anything about germs or about how wounds became infected, and antisepsis in the operating room was a concept that had not yet come into existence; it is common to read of a surgeon whetting his scalpel on the sole of his shoe just before operating. But the hospital attendants, stretcher-bearers, and the like were chosen just as the company cooks were chosen; that is, they were detailed from the ranks, and the average officer selected the most worthless men he had simply because he wanted to get rid of men who could not be counted on in combat. As a result, sick or wounded men often got atrocious care.

A result of all of this—coupled with the fact that many men enlisted without being given any medical examinations—was that every Civil War regiment suffered a constant wastage from sickness. On paper, a regiment was supposed to have a strength ranging between 960 and 1,040 men; actually, no regiment ever got to the battlefield with anything like that strength, and since there was no established system for sending in replacements a veteran regiment that could muster 350 enlisted men present for duty was considered pretty solid. From first to last, approximately twice as many Civil War soldiers died of disease—typhoid, dysentery, and pneumonia were the great killers—as died in action; and in addition to those who died a great many more got medical discharges.

In its wisdom, the Northern government set up a number of base hospitals in Northern states, far from the battle fronts, on the theory that a man recovering from wounds or sickness would recuperate better back home. Unfortunately, the hospitals thus established were under local control, and the men in them were no longer under the orders of their own regiments or armies. As a result, thousands of men who were sent north for convalescence never returned to the army. Many were detailed for light work at the hospitals, and in these details they stayed because nobody had the authority to extract them and send them back to duty. Others, recovering their health, simply went home and stayed there. They were answerable to the hospital authorities, not to the army command, and the hospital authorities rarely cared very much whether they returned to duty or not. The whole system was ideally designed to make desertion easy.

On top of all of this, many men had very little understanding of the requirements of military discipline. A homesick boy often saw nothing wrong in leaving the army and going home to see the folks for a time. A man from a farm might slip off to go home and put in a crop. In neither case would the man look on himself as a deserter; he meant to return, he figured he would get back in time for any fighting that would take place, and in his own mind he was innocent of any wrong-doing. But in many cases the date of return would be postponed from week to week; the man might end as a deserter, even though he had not intended to be one when he left.

A drawing of Confederate soldiers carousing in camp typifies the casual discipline of both Northern and Southern soldiers.

*Combat artist Alfred Waud made this
sketch of the results of a foraging expedition by Northern troops in Virginia.*

This merely reflected the loose discipline that prevailed in Civil
War armies, which in turn reflected the underlying civilian-minded-
ness that pervaded the rank and file. The behavior of Northern armies
on the march in Southern territory reflected the same thing—and, in
the end, had a profound effect on the institution of chattel slavery.

Armies of occupation always tend to bear down hard on civilian
property in enemy territory. Union armies in the Civil War, being
imperfectly disciplined to begin with—and suffering, furthermore,
from a highly defective rationing system—bore down with especial
fervor. Chickens, hams, cornfields, anything edible that might be found
on a Southern plantation, looked like fair game, and the loose fringe
of stragglers that always trailed around the edges of a moving Union
army looted with a fine disregard for civilian property rights.

This was made all the more pointed by the fact that the average
Northern soldier, poorly indoctrinated though he was, had strong
feelings about the evils of secession. To his mind, the Southerners who
sought to set up a nation of their own were in rebellion against the
best government mankind had ever known. Being rebels, they had
forfeited their rights; if evil things happened to them that (as the
average Northern soldier saw it) was no more than just retribution.
This meant that even when the army command tried earnestly to
prevent looting and individual foraging the officers at company and
regimental levels seldom tried very hard to carry out the high command's orders.

William Tecumseh Sherman has come down in history as the very archetype of the Northern soldier who believed in pillage and looting; yet during the first years of the war Sherman resorted to all manner of ferocious punishments to keep his men from despoiling Southern property. He had looters tied up by the thumbs, ordered courts-martial, issued any number of stern orders—and all to very little effect. Long before he adopted the practice of commandeering or destroying Southern property as a war measure, his soldiers were practicing it against his will, partly because discipline was poor and partly because they saw nothing wrong with it.

It was common for a Union colonel, as his regiment made camp in a Southern state, to address his men, pointing to a nearby farm, and say: "Now, boys, that barn is full of nice fat pigs and chickens. I don't want to see any of you take any of them"—whereupon he would fold his arms and look sternly in the opposite direction. It was also common for a regimental commander to read, on parade, some ukase from higher authority forbidding foraging, and then to wink solemnly—a clear hint that he did not expect anyone to take the order seriously. One colonel, punishing some men who had robbed a chicken house, said angrily: "Boys, I want you to understand that I am not punishing you for stealing but for getting caught at it."

It is more than a century since that war was fought, and things look a little different now than they looked at the time. At this distance, it may be possible to look indulgently on the wholesale foraging in which Union armies indulged; to the Southern farmers who bore the brunt of it, the business looked very ugly indeed. Many a Southern family saw the foodstuffs needed for the winter swept away in an hour by grinning hoodlums who did not need and could not use a quarter of what they took. Among the foragers there were many lawless characters who took watches, jewels, and any other valuables they could find; it is recorded that a squad would now and then carry a piano out to the lawn, take it apart, and use the wires to hang pots and pans over the campfire. . . . The Civil War was really romantic only at a considerable distance.

Underneath his feeling that it was good to add chickens and hams to the army ration, and his belief that civilians in a state of secession could expect no better fate, the Union soldier also came to believe that to destroy Southern property was to help win the war. Under orders, he tore up railroads and burned warehouses; it was not long before he realized that anything that damaged the Confederate economy weakened the Confederate war effort, so he rationalized his looting and foraging by arguing that it was a step in breaking the Southern will to resist. It is at this point that the institution of human slavery enters the picture.

Most Northern soldiers had very little feeling against slavery as such, and very little sympathy for the Negro himself. They thought they were fighting to save the Union, not to end slavery, and except for New England troops most Union regiments contained very little abolition sentiment. Nevertheless, the soldiers moved energetically and effectively to destroy slavery, not because they especially intended to

Winslow Homer's sketch of Union troops on the firing line portrays the kind of mass formations vulnerable to the Civil War's improved weaponry.

but simply because they were out to do all the damage they could do. They were operating against Southern property—and the most obvious, important, and easily removable property of all was the slave. To help the slaves get away from the plantation was, clearly, to weaken Southern productive capacity, which in turn weakened Confederate armies. Hence the Union soldier, wherever he went, took the peculiar institution apart, chattel by chattel.

As a result, slavery had been fatally weakened long before the war itself came to an end. The mere act of fighting the war killed it. Of all institutions on earth, the institution of human slavery was the one least adapted to survive a war. It could not survive the presence of loose-jointed, heavy-handed armies of occupation. It may hardly be too much too say that the mere act of taking up arms in slavery's defense doomed slavery.

Above and beyond everything else, of course, the business of the Civil War soldier was to fight. He fought with weapons that look very crude to modern eyes, and he moved by an outmoded system of tactics, but the price he paid when he got into action was just as high as the price modern soldiers pay despite the almost infinite development of firepower since the 1860's.

Standard infantry weapon in the Civil War was the rifled Springfield—a muzzle-loader firing a conical lead bullet, usually of .54 caliber.

To load was rather laborious, and it took a good man to get off more than two shots a minute. The weapon had a range of nearly a mile, and its "effective range"—that is, the range at which it would hit often enough to make infantry fire truly effective—was figured at about 250 yards. Compared with a modern Garand, the old muzzle-loader is no better than a museum piece; but compared with all previous weapons—the weapons on which infantry tactics in the 1860's were still based—it was a fearfully destructive and efficient piece.

For the infantry of that day still moved and fought in formations dictated in the old days of smoothbore muskets, whose effective range was no more than 100 yards and which were wildly inaccurate at any distance. Armies using those weapons attacked in solid mass formations, the men standing, literally, elbow to elbow. They could get from effective range to hand-to-hand fighting in a very short time, and if they had a proper numerical advantage over the defensive line they could come to grips without losing too many men along the way. But in the Civil War the conditions had changed radically; men would be hit while the rival lines were still half a mile apart, and to advance in mass was simply to invite wholesale destruction. Tactics had not yet been adjusted to the new rifles; as a result, Civil War attacks could be fearfully costly, and when the defenders dug entrenchments and got some protection—as the men learned to do, very quickly—a direct frontal assault could be little better than a form of mass suicide.

It took the high command a long time to revise tactics to meet this changed situation, and Civil War battles ran up dreadful casualty lists. For an army to lose 25 per cent of its numbers in a major battle was by no means uncommon, and in some fights—the Confederate army at Gettysburg is an outstanding example—the percentage of loss ran close to one third of the total number engaged. Individual units were sometimes nearly wiped out. Some of the Union and Confederate regiments that fought at Gettysburg lost up to 80 per cent of their numbers; a regiment with such losses was usually wrecked, as an effective fighting force, for the rest of the war.

The point of all of which is that the discipline which took the Civil War soldier into action, while it may have been very sketchy by modern standards, was nevertheless highly effective on the field of battle. Any armies that could go through such battles as Antietam, Stone's River, Franklin or Chickamauga and come back for more had very little to learn about the business of fighting.

Perhaps the Confederate General D. H. Hill said it, once and for all. The battle of Malvern Hill, fought on the Virginia peninsula early in the summer of 1862, finished the famous Seven Days campaign, in which George B. McClellan's Army of the Potomac was driven back from in front of Richmond by Robert E. Lee's Army of Northern Virginia. At Malvern Hill, McClellan's men fought a rear-guard action—a bitter, confused fight which came at the end of a solid week of wearing, costly battles and forced marches. Federal artillery wrecked the Confederate assault columns, and at the end of the day Hill looked out over the battlefield, strewn with dead and wounded boys. Shaking his head, and reflecting on the valor in attack and in defense which the two armies had displayed, Hill never forgot about this. Looking back on it, long after the war was over, he declared, in substance:

"Give me Confederate infantry and Yankee artillery and I'll whip the world!"

James G. Randall and R.N. Current

How Lincoln Would Have Rebuilt the Union

What would Lincoln have done after the Civil War had he not been assassinated? The sainthood that his foul murder brought to him distorted for decades his actual views. He was pictured as both the Great Emancipator of the blacks and as the binder of the nation's wounds, the man who, "with malice toward none," would have treated the former slaveholders with Christlike compassion. That he could not have been both an ardent champion of Negro rights and the forgiving friend of the former rebels eventually became clear, but a full understanding of his attitudes was only slowly uncovered by historians.

One of the historians who did most to throw light on Lincoln's policies was the late James G. Randall, whose four-volume *Lincoln the President* is a model of lucid and painstaking scholarship. When Randall died before completing the last volume of this work, Richard N. Current, now professor of history at the University of North Carolina at Greensboro, took on the task of finishing it. In the following essay Randall and Current discuss Lincoln's approach to reconstructing the Union. As they admit, no one can say with total assurance how Lincoln would have acted if he had not been killed, or what the result would have been. But they demonstrate beyond argument that his policy was carefully thought out and based on close observation of conditions in the South.

In his annual message to Congress, delivered in December of 1863 in fulfillment of the provision of the Constitution requiring that the President shall "give to the Congress Information of the State of the Union," Lincoln addressed himself to the question of reconstruction. He did not deal in quibbles or generalities, but came up with a plan. Anyone who knew Lincoln would have known that his design for a restored Union would not be hateful and vindictive. It would not rule out the very spirit of reunion. His view had never been narrowly sectional. Born in the Southern state of Kentucky of Virginia-born parents, moving thence to Indiana and Illinois, he was part of that transit of culture by which Southern characteristics, human types, and thought patterns had taken hold in the West and Northwest. Though he was antislavery and of course antisecession, he was never anti-Southern.

He had said in his first inaugural: "Physically we cannot separate," and on various later occasions he had returned to this theme. As he wrote in his annual message of December 1, 1862, to "separate our common country into two nations" was to him intolerable. The people of the greater interior, he urged, "will not ask where a line of separation shall be, but will vow rather that there shall be no such line." The situation as he saw it, in "all its adaptations and aptitudes . . . demands union and abhors separation." It would ere long "force reunion, however much of blood and treasure the separation might cost."

Thus Lincoln's fundamental adherence to an unbroken Union was the point of departure for his reconstruction program. One could find, in the earlier part of his presidency, other indications bearing upon restoration. In an important letter to General G. F. Shepley, military governor of Louisiana (November 21, 1862), he advised strongly against what came to be known as "carpetbagger" policy. He did not want "Federal officers not citizens of Louisiana" to seek election as congressmen from that state. On this his language was emphatic: he considered it "disgusting and outrageous . . . to send a parcel of Northern men here as representatives, elected, as it would be understood (and perhaps really so), at the point of the bayonet."

While in this manner disallowing the idea of importing Northern politicians into a Southern state as pseudo-representatives in Congress, he also repudiated the opposite policy of Fernando Wood of New York which would accept Southerners in Congress prematurely—that is, before resistance to the United States was ended and loyalty assured. To mention another point, he had, in considering the formation of the new state of West Virginia, expressed his view that, in the pattern of the Union, only those who were loyal—i. e., who adhered to the United States—could be regarded as competent voters.

To these points—the indispensable Union, loyalty, and the unwisdom of carpetbaggism—one must add Lincoln's fundamental policy of emancipation and his non-vindictiveness in the matter of confiscation. Taking these factors together the historian has, before December, 1863, the ingredients of the President's reunion program.

In announcing that program on December 8, 1863, Lincoln issued two documents: a proclamation, and a message to Congress. In his proclamation, having the force of law, he set forth the conditions of a general pardon and the terms of restoring a Southern state to the Union. In his accompanying message he commented upon his plan, telling more fully what was in his mind and defending his course by reason and persuasion. The offer of pardon (with stated exceptions) and restoration of rights (except as to slaves) was given to anyone in a seceded state who would take and keep a simple oath. Phrased by the President, this oath constituted a solemn pledge to support the Constitution of the United States "and the union of the States thereunder." The oath-taker would also swear to abide by and faithfully support all the acts of Congress and all the proclamations of the President relating to slaves unless repealed, modified, or declared void by the Supreme Court.

So much for the oath, with pardon and restoration of rights. The next element in the proclamation was re-establishment of a state government. This again was intended to be simple and practical. Whenever, in a seceded state, a number not less than one tenth of those voting in 1860, should re-establish a republican government, such a government, according to Lincoln's proclamation, would "be recognized as the true government of the State."

Turning from the proclamation to the simultaneous message, we find Lincoln setting forth the reasons and conditions of his policy. In this he addressed himself to various questions that he knew would arise. What about the oath? Why the ten per cent? What about state laws touching freedmen? Why preserve the state as it was? How about state boundaries? Why was the President assuming the power of reconstruction as an executive function? He started with the obvious unwisdom and absurdity of protecting a revived state government constructed from the disloyal element. It was essential to have a test "so as to build only from the sound." He wanted that test to be liberal and to include "sworn recantation of . . . former unsoundness." As for laws and proclamations against slavery, they could not be abandoned. Retaining so far as possible the existing political framework in the state, as Lincoln saw it, would "save labor, and avoid confusion." He did not, of course, mean by this that the system in any state was to be permanently frozen for the future in unchangeable form.

As to the specific formula of ten per cent, he said little; yet his simile of a rallying point held the key. The important object was to get a movement started. Acceptance of an initial electorate of ten per cent did not signify that Lincoln was favoring minority rule. It was not his thought that any minority should usurp the rights of the majority. Within his pattern of loyalty, Union, non-dictatorial government, and emancipation, he was putting the formation of any new state government in the hands of the loyal people of the state. Government by the people was to him fundamental, but as a practical matter some loyal nucleus was essential; else time would pass, precious time, and nothing would be done.

In J.E. Baker's 1864 cartoon,
Andrew Johnson, who was
a tailor as a young man, and
Lincoln, the railsplitter,
labor to reunite the Union.

The whole situation, of course, was abnormal. All beginnings, or re-beginnings, are difficult, especially rebuilding after or during a war, taking up the shattered pieces of a disrupted social and political order and putting them partly together so that ultimately they could be fully restored. Lincoln was willing to accept informality in order to accomplish the main practical purpose which he considered imperative. He was unwilling to throw away the cause while futilely waiting for perfection. Reconstruction, as he saw it, was a matter of stages. His "ten per cent plan" was easy to criticize. Yet it was the first step.

Lincoln would take his first step in the most available manner. A few states could be rebuilt and restored. This was to be done during the war, indeed as an important factor in waging and ending the war. Let people see that Lincoln did not intend an ugly and vindictive policy, and Southerners themselves, the President hoped, would set their own houses in order. Let one or two states do this; they would serve as examples for others as the armies advanced and national authority was extended. In time of war, prepare for peace, was Lincoln's thought. On the other hand, let the months pass, and let the Southern people witness only carpetbaggism, Federal occupation, and a repressive attitude as to the future, and victory itself would lose much of its value. It was Lincoln's intent that policy associated with victory should envisage willing loyalty while leaving free play for self government.

Lincoln's plan of reunion was greeted with a mixed response. The Washington *Chronicle,* regarded as a Lincoln "organ," naturally praised the President's announcement. The editor noted that the President gave out his statement in a setting of military and naval success: our armies victorious, our navy in control of Southern coasts, our cause strengthened by increased friendship of foreign nations. His generous offering of pardon was interpreted by the *Chronicle* as evidence of his kindness and sympathy toward the people of the South.

An English gentleman friendly to the United States wrote: "We have just received the news of President Lincoln's message, accompanied with his amnesty; also the message of . . . [Jefferson] Davis. The two documents coming together are doing an immense amount of good for the right cause."

It is doubtful how many readers made the comparison of the two messages, but those who did must have noted a marked difference of tone. In general spirit Lincoln's message of December 8, 1863, was notable for its absence of war-engendered hatred toward the South, ending as it did on the note of "freedom disenthralled." In appealing for reunion the President was holding out the hand for genuine renewal of friendly relations. This attitude, however, was not reciprocated by the Confederate President. Though perhaps the comparison should not be overstressed, one finds quite the opposite note in the message (December 7, 1863) of Jefferson Davis to his Congress. After a depressing account of Confederate military reverses and of discouraging condition in foreign affairs and finance, the Southern Executive threw in bitter denunciations of the "barbarous policy" and "savage ferocity" of "our enemies." At one point he referred to them as "hardened by crime." (There were, of course, those in the North, though not Lincoln, who were saying equally hateful things of the South.) That enemy, wrote Davis, refused "even to listen to proposals . . . [of peace] of recognizing the impassable gulf which divides us." This expression, the orthodox attitude of Confederate officialdom, must be remembered along with Lincoln's other problems. If anyone doubted why the President, in his reconstruction plans and his wariness toward "peace negotiations," realized the hopelessness of expecting high Confederate officials to consider a peaceable restoration of the Union, the reading of this message of Davis would have been enough to dispel such doubt.

It was obvious from the start that the President's plan would not have smooth sailing, but on several fronts steps were taken to make it known and put it into operation. Army officers were instructed to take copies of the proclamation and distribute them so as to reach soldiers and inhabitants within Confederate-held territory. Aid and protection was to be extended to those who would declare loyalty. On the occasion of raids into enemy territory a number of men were to be detailed "for the purpose of distributing the proclamation broadcast among rebel soldiers and people, and in the highways and byways."

On the legal or prosecuting front the effect of the pardon policy was explained in an instruction from the office of the attorney general of the United States to district attorneys throughout the country. It was made known that the "President's pardon of a person guilty of . . . rebellion . . . [would] relieve that person for the penalties" of that crime. District attorneys were therefore directed to discontinue proceedings in United States courts whenever the accused should take the oath and comply with the stated conditions.

Such a statement would make it appear that the transition from a kind of rebellious guilt to complete relief from penalty was easy, automatic, and practically instantaneous, but it soon became evident that the matter was not so simple as that. Lincoln found that he had to make a distinction in applying his offer of pardon in return for the oath. What about Confederate soldiers held by Union authorities as prisoners of war? On this point the President issued a letter clarifying the proclamation, declaring that his pardon did not apply to men in custody or on parole as prisoners of war. It did apply, he explained, to persons yet at large (i.e., free from arrest) who would come forward and take the oath. It was also explained that those excluded from the general amnesty could apply to the President for clemency and their cases would have due consideration.

What it amounted to was that Lincoln himself was generous in the application of his pardon both to soldiers and civilians, and the same was true of the attorney general's office; but army officers were not prepared, in return for the oath, to deliver prisoners nor give up penalties for offences of various sorts, such as violation of rules of war. No one statement applies. Some enemies held as prisoners, on establishing loyalty, were discharged from custody by the President on assurance of good faith by three congressmen. This showed, as in many cases, that Lincoln's general rules were subject to individual exceptions.

With a scorn of fine-spun theories and an urgent wish to get ahead with the job of reconstruction, the President proceeded, so far as possible, to make restoration a reality whenever, and as soon as, any reasonable opportunity offered in the seceded South.

In Lincoln's plan of reconstruction the effort in Louisiana was of vital importance. From the time that New Orleans fell to Union arms on May 1, 1862, the President saw, in terms of Federal occupation, an early opportunity to make reconstruction a wartime reality. Let Louisiana be restored, he thought, let this be done in a reasonable manner with Washington approval, let it be seen that the plan would work, and other states would follow. To go into all the details of the Louisiana story, treating its complications month by month, would be a tedious process. It will be convenient to reduce this elaborate Louisiana story to four successive phases:

First Phase in Louisiana: Military Rule Under Butler and Shepley. The first phase was that of army rule under General B. F. Butler. Immediate adjustments were of course necessary from the moment when New Orleans, largest city of the South, together with a large portion of Louisiana, came under the Union flag. Governmental officials in the occupied region, including merely local functionaries in city or parish, were now under Federal authority—not in terms of any deliberation as to procedure by Congress or the Executive, but simply by the fortunes of war. Where men in local office stood ready to co-operate with the occupying power, they had a good chance of being retained; if un-cooperative, they were dismissed. For a time the mayor and council of New Orleans were continued in office subject to General Butler's authority with some relaxation of military pressure, but this situation did not last long. Within a month the mayor was deposed and imprisoned, and George F. Shepley, acting closely with Butler, took over mayoral functions. Then in June, 1862, Shepley became military governor of Louisiana; soon afterward he had the rank of brigadier general.

This was military occupation, and of course it was intended only as a temporary condition. It amounted to martial law which has been defined as the will of the military commander; this meant that the sometimes eccentric will of General Butler was paramount. If nothing offered in the form of a re-established and recognized state government, the abnormal and temporary regime would continue.

It thus came about that Federal rule in Louisiana, the first step toward what Lincoln regarded as restoration of loyalty and normal conditions, got off to a bad start. The name of "Beast Butler" became a hated byword in the South, with far-reaching complications in Federal-Confederate relations; it came as a considerable relief when President Lincoln removed him from his Louisiana command on December 16, 1862. His successor, as commander of the military forces stationed in Louisiana and Texas, was Major General Nathaniel P. Banks, with Shepley retaining his position as "military governor of Louisiana."

Under Butler little or nothing had been done toward wartime governmental reconstruction in the state, but this problem, dear to Lincoln's heart, was tackled under the President's urging during the Banks-Shepley regime.

A careful study of these matters reveals a problem as to top executive leadership locally applied—that is, the difficulty of achieving effectiveness in a particular area in terms of policy developed in Washington. Lincoln was President; he was the Chief; he made the appointments and formed decisions; presumably he would choose men to put his policies into operation. Yet so unpredictable were events and so complicated was the situation as to politicians' maneuvers that those who supposedly should have carried out Lincoln's purposes promoted their own factional and contrary schemes in such manner as to jeopardize the President's best laid plans.

George F. Shepley was a case in point. He had been a Maine Democrat, an appointee of Pierce and later of Buchanan as district attorney, and a supporter of Douglas in 1860. These factors in his background did not militate against him in Lincoln's view—the President often appointed Democrats—nor should they have been a drawback to successful service in Louisiana's reconstruction. There was, however, the further fact that Shepley became a Butlerite and a Radical; remaining after Butler's removal, he played the Radical game at a time when it was hoped that a more Lincolnian policy would be inaugurated. Thus Shepley stood as an obstacle to Lincoln's efforts to allay factionalism and to promote speedy and liberal restoration.

Toward the end of the Butler-Shepley period an election was held within the Union lines on December 3, 1862, for members of Congress from Louisiana. Two men of different outlook were elected: B. F. Flanders from New Hampshire, who was to become an instrument of the Radical faction; and Michael Hahn, a citizen of Louisiana born in Bavaria, who was more in tune with Lincoln's purposes. When the question of admitting these gentlemen as members of the House of Representatives was brought before that body (February 9, 1863) a species of dog fight ensued, a forerunner of the rough treatment in store for Lincoln's whole reunion program. Few were ready for frontal attack and sidestepping was more in evidence; the result was confusion, unrelated motions, and postponement. Finally, on February 17, 1863, the House voted, 92 to 44, to seat Flanders and Hahn. By that time that particular Congress, the Thirty-seventh, was about to pass out of existence.

Second Phase: Shepley and Durant versus Banks. In the next phase, while Banks was in top command in Louisiana with Shepley as military governor—i. e., governor as to civil affairs under military authority—certain groups in the state got to work, though at cross purposes, to seize control of the process of state remaking. It turned out to be a period of bickering and futility, a time of bitter disappointment to the President. Taking over the rebuilding task and attempting to do it in his own way, Governor Shepley proceeded to make a registry of voters, appointing T. J. Durant, a Radical like himself, as commissioner of registration. An oath of allegiance was required (this was before the presidentially prescribed oath of December 8, 1863) and the registration of whites who would take the oath was ordered. It was Durant's idea that ten loyal men in a parish, if no more could be registered, would be a sufficient basis for an election. This was a period when Banks was preoccupied with military command in the Port Hudson and Texas areas, while Shepley was also absent from Louisiana, spending a large part of the summer of 1863 in Washington. Lincoln approved the Shepley-Durant registration and wanted it pushed.

The President was trying to keep himself in the background, to avoid seeming to dictate, and to let things work themselves out as a Louisiana movement. Yet he soon found that a jurisdictional dispute or confusion as to control was spoiling everything. Shepley as military governor and Durant, his appointee, were claiming "that they were exclusively charged with the work of reconstruction in Louisiana," while Banks had "not felt authorized to interfere" with them. In a letter of December 16, 1863, Banks advised the President that he was "only in partial command," adding: "There are not less than *four* distinct governments here claiming . . . independent powers based upon instructions received directly from Washington, and recognizing no other authority than their own."

Though this unfortunate situation was due in large part to the activities of Radical groups, another factor may have been a bit of inadvertence on the part of the burdened President: he had supposed all the time that Banks was in chief command but had not made that point sufficiently clear. He now wrote a strong letter to Banks (December 24, 1863) with a fourfold repetition of the main theme: You are master. The President was seriously annoyed at the frustration and delay. Shepley, he wrote, was to "assist" Banks, not to "thwart" him. The desirable object, of course, was to have unity among pro-Union men and leaders, but a serious obstacle to such unity was the attitude of Shepley and his considerable faction. It became increasingly apparent that these Radicals were unwilling to co-operate with the man whom Lincoln had placed in chief authority and whom he had plainly designated as "master." Treating delay and factionalism as if things of the past, Lincoln wrote to Banks: "Give us a free State reorganization of Louisiana in the shortest possible time."

Third Phase: The Louisiana Constitution of 1864. Under Lincoln's spurring Banks went into action. In January and February of 1864 he issued proclamations for two kinds of elections: an election for governor under the old Louisiana constitution of 1853, and an election of delegates to a convention to make a new state constitution. In his proclamations, copies of which he sent to the President, Banks declared that officials then to be chosen were to govern unless they tried to change Federal statutes as to slavery. Voters were required to take the oath of allegiance to the United States.

Lincoln continued to prod and encourage. Proceed "with all possible dispatch," wrote the President. "Frame orders, and fix times and places for this and that. . . ." Recognition of the death of slavery in Louisiana was causing less difficulty than might have been expected. While the planter class wanted to keep the institution, they were in the minority; the majority of the people were ready to accept emancipation.

Both of the elections were a success from the standpoint of Banks and of Lincoln. Not that Lincoln considered the outcome perfect, but the whole point of Lincoln's policy was that he was not expecting perfection. He wanted steps to be taken, a "free" government set up; modifications and improvements could come later. The vote for state officials was held on February 22, 1864. In a total of 11,411 votes (over a fourth of the normal peacetime vote of Louisiana) Michael Hahn, the moderate Union candidate acceptable to Banks and Lincoln, received 6,183 votes and was elected; Flanders, candidate of the anti-Banks

Radical element, received 2,232 votes; J. Q. A. Fellows, nominated by the proslavery conservatives, received the disturbingly large vote of 2,996.

Next came the problem of constitution remaking. By Banks's proclamation an election was held on March 28, 1864, by which delegates were chosen (not a distinguished lot, but they represented the people rather than officials or politicians) to form a new instrument of government. From April to July the convention labored. Among its main acts was to abolish slavery by a vote of seventy to sixteen. Negro suffrage, then a new question and a difficult one, came harder. After voting it down, the convention reconsidered; it then "empowered" the legislature to grant the vote to colored persons; by the constitution it was provided that a militia be enrolled without distinction of color.

On September 5, 1864, the people of Louisiana voted to ratify the constitution (6,836–1,566); members of Congress were then chosen by popular election, after which the legislature set up under the new constitution chose two senators. If and when these men should be admitted by Congress—a big "if"—reconstruction for Louisiana, so far as essential political structure was concerned, would be complete. In the matter of preliminary steps—shaping up the situation so that Congress could act—the work of the executive branch for this pivotal state was done.

Fourth Phase: Trouble in Congress. Much water was to pass over the mill before one could know what Congress would do as to admitting Louisiana according to Lincoln's plan. The Radical clique in Louisiana had opposed the measures taken in 1864 looking toward a new state government. This element made a break with the Lincoln Administration, denounced the new constitution as null and void, and proceeded to make their influence felt in Congress. The Radical element in Congress was working strongly against Lincoln's program in any case, and it was no surprise that the decision of the solons at Washington concerning Louisiana reorganization was negative. A long period of Federal occupation and troublous abnormality was to ensue. There were a number of uneasy years after Lincoln's death before the state was, one should not say restored, but outfitted with a carpetbag government. After that there was to be further delay—nearly a decade—before that unworkable carpetbag regime collapsed.

As in Louisiana, so in other regions of the Confederate South, Lincoln did his best to promote reorganization measures so that state governments could supersede Federal military rule, but wartime conditions made for obstruction and progress was slow. In Tennessee, where secession had been strongly resisted and where Union victories came in February and April of 1862, it might have seemed that a choice opportunity was offered for early restoration of civil government under unionist auspices. The pro-Confederate regime in Tennessee was brief; it extended only from May 7, 1861 (legislative ratification of the military league with the Confederacy) to March 3, 1862, when Lincoln appointed Andrew Johnson military governor of the state, a period of ten months.

Johnson's attitude had been demonstrated by "violent opposition to slavery and secession" and by retention of his seat in the United States Senate. His unionism was unassailable, but he could only perform the functions of civil government on an emergency basis and Lincoln's hopes for instituting a more permanent and regular regime were repeatedly deferred. There was heavy fighting in 1862 and 1863. Guerrilla warfare, raids by Forrest, agitation among discordant pro-Union elements, puzzlement as to what was "regular" by the old code of the state (nothing could be strictly regular in those war times), lack of popular interest when elections were held, complications as to soldier voting and military influence, divided leadership as between Nashville and Washington—these were among the factors that caused continual delay.

Not until February, 1865, was an election held in Tennessee which had importance in terms of popular voting for fundamental state reorganization. After that there loomed, as always, the serious obstacle of congressional opposition. Tennessee was not to be admitted to the Union until 1866. Yet as early as September 11, 1863, Lincoln had written to Governor Johnson: "All Tennessee is now clear of armed insurrectionists." Insisting that "Not a moment should be lost" in "reinaugurating a loyal State government," the President insisted, as in Louisiana, that prudent steps be taken without delay. Discretion was left with Johnson and "co-operating friends" as to ways and means, with the presidential injunction that the reinauguration should not be allowed to slip into the hands of enemies of the Union, "driving its friends . . . into political exile." "It must not be so," wrote Lincoln. "You must have it otherwise."

In September, 1863, Andrew Johnson said to his people: "Here lies your State; a sick man in his bed, emaciated and exhausted . . . unable to walk alone. The physician comes. Don't quarrel about antecedents, but administer to his wants . . . as quickly as possible. . . . This is no . . . metaphysical question. It is a plain, common sense matter, and there is nothing in the way but obstinacy." Johnson's simile of the sick man and his suggestion as to the ineptness of those administering to him could have covered a great deal more territory than Tennessee.

Events of 1863 and early 1864 in Arkansas proceeded with little difficulty so far as that commonwealth itself was concerned. It was a sparsely settled state, with 435,000 inhabitants in 1860, of whom 111,115 were slaves. Illinois, of comparable area, had nearly four times the population. It was chiefly in the southeastern part, in the plantation area near the Mississippi River, that slaveholding was concentrated. Throughout most of the state there were few slaves, in the northern portion hardly any. People of the Ozark mountain region had little in common with the few cotton-growing magnates. To the vast majority of the people the abolition of slavery would produce no serious re-ordering of their lives and economy.

The state had avoided secession until swept away by the post-Sumter excitement; when secession was adopted it was done reluctantly. Even after secession, considerable Union sentiment remained.

According to a contemporary account, pertaining to the situation in 1863, "Citizens of distinction came forward to advocate the Union cause; among others, Brig.-Gen. E. W. Gantt, of the Confederate army, once held as a prisoner of war." The shift of General Gantt from Confederate to Union allegiance was, as he said, part of a popular movement; Union sentiment, he noted, was "manifesting itself on all sides and by every indication." For many who were of like mind with Gantt the open declaration of loyalty to the Federal government, especially after the Confederate surrender of Vicksburg, came naturally. It was like snapping out of an abnormal situation.

Military events provided a considerable impulse toward Union reorganization, especially the Union victories at Vicksburg and Port Hudson, and the Helena-Little Rock expedition of General Frederick Steele, U. S. A., against Sterling Price, C. S. A., which resulted in Confederate evacuation of Little Rock on September 10, 1863. With this Confederate reverse a large part of the state was brought under Union control.

Lincoln kept in touch with Arkansas affairs, notifying General Steele that he, as in the case of Banks in Louisiana, was "master" of the reorganization process. "Some single mind," wrote the President, "must be master, else there will be no agreement in anything." He had ample reason to realize the truth of this statement.

The pattern of the Arkansas movement reveals much as to Lincoln's plan in practical operation. Sentiment developed in meetings, with Union resolutions, in large parts of the state. Delegates were chosen in such meetings (by no more and no less authority than is usual in such popular movements under the stress of abnormal conditions) for a "convention" designed to make a new regime constitutional and legal. Lincoln encouraged the holding of the convention, welcoming it as a fulfillment of his plan as announced in December, 1863. On January 20, 1864, he indicated that the reorganization emanated from citizens of Arkansas petitioning for an election, and directed Steele to "order an election immediately" for March 28, 1864. When, on counting the votes for a Union-minded governor and for changes in the state constitution, the number should reach or exceed 5,406 (that being ten per cent of the Arkansas vote of 1860), Lincoln directed that the governor thus chosen should be declared qualified and that he should assume his duties under the modified state constitution. (As a minor detail, when it was found that the Union convention in Arkansas was planning the election for March 14, not March 28, the President quickly acquiesced in the convention plan.)

In the President's mind a milestone had been reached in Arkansas affairs with that election of March 14. By an overwhelming majority (12,179 to 226) the voters, having qualified by taking the Federal oath of allegiance, approved those changes in the state constitution which abolished slavery, declared secession void, and repudiated the Confederate debt. Isaac Murphy, already installed as provisional governor by the convention, was now elected governor by "more than double what the President had required." On April 11 the new state government under the modified constitution was inaugurated at Little Rock. The reconstructed legislature chose senators (William M. Fishbach and Elisha Baxter); three members of Congress had already been chosen in the March election.

Obstruction in House and Senate prevented the admission of these representatives and senators, and for long years Arkansas remained outside the pale so far as Congress was concerned. Lincoln's view, however, both as to practical matters and as to his own function in promoting them, was shown in his executive measures to get these important steps taken, and in his advice to Steele (June 29, 1864) that, despite congressional refusal to give these solons their seats at Washington, the new state government should have "the same support and protection that you would [have given] if the members had been admitted, because in no event . . . can this do any harm, while it will be the best you can do toward suppressing the rebellion."

A different type of situation presented itself in Florida, where the reconstruction effort was of a minor sort. Military accomplishment, so evident in Louisiana, Tennessee, and Arkansas, was lacking in this detached area, which was off the main line of strategy and unpromising as a field in which to commit any considerable body of troops. Aside from holding a few coastal points and maintaining the blockade, the United States paid little attention to the region of the St. John's, the St. Mary's, and the Suwannee. The only sizable engagement in the state during the war was the ill-starred "battle of Olustee," in the northeast corner, a short distance inward from Jacksonville, where a minor Union force under General Truman Seymour, U. S. A., was defeated by somewhat superior numbers, with advantage of defensive position, under General Joseph Finegan, C. S. A. This engagement, February 20, 1864, was the futile anticlimax of an army-navy expedition of Seymour, a subordinate of General Quincy A. Gillmore who was in command of the "Department of the South" with headquarters at Hilton Head, S. C.

Under these circumstances, though Union sentiment was held to be widespread in the state, the small-scale efforts to restore Florida were subject to the taunt that their motive was to give a plausible basis for sending pro-Lincoln delegates to the coming Republican convention; even the Seymour expedition was derided as a feature of the political campaign of 1864.

From Lincoln's standpoint the approach to reconstruction in Florida was like that in other Southern areas. On January 13, 1864, he wrote Gillmore advising that the general was to be "master" if differences should arise; in this letter the President urged that restoration be pushed "in the most speedy way possible," and that it be done within the range of the December proclamation. To handle some of the details John Hay was sent to Florida "with some blank-books [for recording oaths] and other blanks, to aid in the reconstruction." This trip of Hay's (February-March 1864) was not a brilliant success and the sum-total of the Florida gesture for reconstruction was far from impressive. Florida's "delegates," chosen by a few in Jacksonville, did turn up at the Republican convention in June, 1864, but not until after the war did the commonwealth proceed to the making of a new state constitution within the range of the Union; readmission to the Union—i.e., inauguration of carpetbag government—occurred in 1868; restoration of home rule—the throwing off of Radical Republican control—was deferred to 1877.

Small though it was, there was more in the Union effort in Florida than at first met the eye. One could treat the Seymour, or Gillmore-Seymour, expedition of 1864 as a sorry military enterprise, or as a disappointing phase of Lincoln's reconstruction plan, but in a realistic study one needs to enlarge the scope of inquiry. The episode must also be viewed in its relation to such subjects as the use of Negro troops (in which there was creditable performance), maneuvers in the pro-Chase sense, the opening of trade, and what has been called "carpetbag imperialism." In a detailed study George Winston Smith has pointed out that grandiose schemes or experiments were conjured up in connection with the Florida effort. There was, for example, the "extravagant plan" of Eli Thayer of Kansas emigrant fame—a well-intentioned plan to set up "soldier-colonists" and create model communities on the most approved New England pattern. The plan reached "only the blueprint stage," but it reveals much as to Yankee enterprise in the deep South. There was also injected into the wartime Florida scene the "machinations" of Lyman K. Stickney, "the most notorious of the early Florida carpetbaggers," who operated under Secretary Chase in the enforcement of a congressional act for collecting the Federal direct tax in the South. This law, writes Smith, was a "move to confiscate the real property of southern landholders" and was so administered as to become "an instrument of predatory corruption in Florida."

These factors need to be borne in mind in judging Lincoln's approach to reconstruction. It was a complicated problem of many facets, with idealistic motives combined with profit-seeking greed. Lincoln tried to keep restoration on the main track and keep it unmarred, but it was part of the history of the time—the prelude to the "Gilded Age"—that debased and uninspiring maneuvers would creep in. Florida was only an example. When one remembers such influences, he can realize with fuller force the significance of Lincoln's rejection of the whole drive and tendency toward carpetbaggism.

. . . In Lincoln's planning for a restored Union he kept his eye constantly on a highly important factor, that of unionism in the South. Of course it could have been said by critics that Lincoln was not bothering with the opposition, that he was requiring an oath of Union allegiance as a prerequisite for the right to vote on any state reorganization, and that he was thus stacking the cards in his favor, working only with friends of the Union. This seemed the more striking because of his willingness to depend on a Union-minded minimum of ten per cent (of 1860 voters) for the initial steps of reconstruction.

Yet on closer study it will be seen that success for any reunion movement was dependent upon popular support in the state. Always at some point there had to be an election, a popular choice of a constitutional convention to remake the state constitution, and a vote for state officials and members of Congress. People who voted in these initial elections had to take the Union oath; but no one was to be coerced into taking it, and if the number of oath-takers was too insignificant, the plan would not get very far. Lincoln was starting with a loyal minority, but the quality and extent of that minority was never unimportant. Furthermore, the President was planning for peace, for the long years ahead after the war ended.

At all times the President felt assured that his plan would work for the whole South. He could hardly have proceeded with such confidence unless he genuinely believed that unionists in the South were, for the long run and for normal times, in the majority. In fact the validity of Lincoln's basic political philosophy depended upon self rule by the people. To impose a government upon an unwilling state— even a benevolent government—would have been contrary to this fundamental philosophy. There was a risk involved in Lincoln's scheme but it was a calculated risk. When there would come the hazard of an election, that would not merely mean that people should vote because of having sworn allegiance. It meant that such allegiance was expected to prove justified in the type of government set up, the working out of labor adjustment, the choice of well disposed officials, the installing of honest government, and the like.

If these things went wrong even after the initial steps had been taken in compliance with the President's plan, the broad policy would fail. Lincoln's feeling of assurance that it would not fail must have been based on more than wishful thinking. It is therefore of importance to look into the matter and find the basis for this assurance—in other words, to discover some of the evidences of unionism in the South which were known to the President. To give the whole body of such evidence is obviously impracticable, but a few items may be mentioned with the understanding that they were typical of a large and impressive total.

There was the element of war-weariness in the South; people were sick and tired of the continued slaughter. A captured Union general, the famous Neal Dow, wrote to Lincoln from Libby Prison, Richmond, on November 12, 1863: ". . . I have seen much of Rebeldom, behind the curtain, and have talked with a great many soldiers, conscripts, deserters, officers, and citizens. The result of all is, to my mind, that . . . the masses are heartily . . . anxious for its [the war's] close on any terms. . . ." He went on to mention numerous Confederate desertions, soldier infirmities, general debility, the worthlessness of conscripts, depreciation of the currency, flour at $125 a barrel, and "everything in the provision line . . . [bearing] a corresponding price."

In Virginia the attitude of intelligent and patriotic unionists was typified by Alexander H. H. Stuart. Though not active against secession during the war, he had been fundamentally opposed to it as inexpedient. Stuart defined his wartime attitudes as follows:

"During the war, I abstained from all participation in public affairs, except on two or three occasions when I was called to address public meetings to urge contributions for the relief of the suffering soldiers and the prisoners going to as well as returning from the North.

"My age relieved me from the obligation to render military service, and all the assistance I gave to the Confederate cause was by feeding the hungry and clothing the naked and nursing the sick Confederate soldiers, and making myself and urging others to make liberal donations for their relief."

Another prominent Virginia unionist was the distinguished lawyer John Minor Botts. He had strongly opposed Southern Democratic disunionists, and, though disapproving also of abolitionists, had given support to the efforts of John Quincy Adams in the matter of anti-slavery petitions presented to Congress. When Lincoln was a Whig member of Congress from Illinois, Botts was a Whig member from Virginia (1847-49); indeed many of his views were similar to Lincoln's. Both in 1850 and in 1860 he was an earnest opponent of secession, his opposition to Jefferson Davis and to Governor Henry Wise of Virgina being especially marked. He greatly regretted the secession of his state in 1860, which he had tried to prevent. During the war he was so far out of sympathy with the Confederate government that he was arrested and confined for some months in jail. For the most part, however, he spent the war years in retirement. His later career showed the steadfastness of his Union loyalty.

The fact that certain Southern areas had never left the Union was, of course, significant. That was true of Kentucky. It was remarked that the mountainous districts of that border state were "with very few exceptions . . . thoroughly union." The same observer noted derisively that in the central part of the state "most of the large slave holders, . . . the gamblers . . . all the decayed chivalry . . . all the fast & fashionable ones & nearly all the original Breckinridge Democrats are bitter to secessionists."

Unionist voices were audible throughout the unhappy South. A clear sign of the times in Louisiana was the editorial of the *True Delta* of New Orleans (February 5, 1864) praising Lincoln, comparing him to Washington and Jackson, and favoring his re-election. In Mississippi a local judge wrote: "I have *first, last and all the time*, been a Union man." Secession, he reported, had been put over without the people understanding what was involved. In another report from Mississippi it was indicated that there were "thousands . . . who desire most ardently the restoration of the United States."

In North Carolina peace movements were rife and it was reported early in 1864 that troops from the Old North State were deserting rapidly and extensively from the Confederate service. In the previous year a group of North Carolina citizens had presented a petition to the President, asking him to "order an election day for this district for the purpose of electing a representative for the next Congress." These petitioners represented themselves as "loyal to the Constitution of our country anxious that it should be perpetuated."

As to Alabama it was predicted that if the question of returning to the Union were submitted to a vote, the people would "vote aye, *five to one*." The President was given the following assurance: "Could you know how deep and universal is the returning love for the union among the people of Ala & Geo you would discharge your great responsibilities with a hymn of joy in your heart."

These evidences, and more of the same, were available to Lincoln. Since his day further material has come to light tending to reveal the extent of Union sentiment in seceded states. Naturally, men and women of Union sympathies in the South found existing conditions difficult for any expression of loyalty in active, organized form. Yet their restricted attitude was significant as they maintained a kind of passive resistance, avoided voluntary measures against the government at Washington, opposed the Confederate draft, carried provisions and medicines to Union soldiers, contributed money for the welfare of blue-coats, attended boys in hospitals, and performed other friendly acts for Federal troops. Such acts incurred persecution, and the Southern unionist moved often in an atmosphere of scorn and hostility not unaccompanied by threats and acts of personal violence. Of course, in various respects he was compelled to act against his will when it was a matter of serving as conscript, subscribing to a Confederate loan, contributing cotton, paying taxes, or performing labor. Since Southern wartime history has been largely remembered and recorded in Confederate terms, these details are still somewhat obscure; at least their full force is not generally recognized.

No history of Lincoln, however, can ignore them. His reports from the South were a vital element in policy making. When he made his broad appeal in December, 1863, offering pardon, prescribing his simple oath, and opening the way for new state governments by genuine Southern effort looking toward peace with freedom and union, he had reason to know, at least in large part, the kind of support and fulfillment upon which he could count. His sense of his own function as leader was strengthened by his realization that Southern unionism did not signify willingness to accept the program and regime of congressional Radicals. On the contrary, such union-mindedness was oriented in Lincolnian terms. In taking on the responsibility of launching and promoting reconstruction, Lincoln saw an opportunity which needed to be seized while its most fruitful results were yet possible. . . .

The many-sided problem of reconstruction was a subject of continual debate in the North from 1863 on. After reaching a furious pitch in the summer of 1864, the debate had been toned down during the final weeks of the presidential campaign, to be renewed fitfully and shrilly as the final military victory approached. Lee's surrender brought the issue to a climax again. Then, temporarily at least, Lincoln and the Radicals found themselves even farther apart than before.

For a while, in early April, 1865, he seemed willing to readmit the Southern states on terms more generous than those he had announced in his ten per cent plan and in his amnesty proclamation of December, 1863. But the Radicals were prepared to demand terms even more rigorous than those they had embodied in the Wade-Davis bill, which Lincoln had refused to sign in July, 1864.

With a new sense of urgency the Radicals began to consult with one another and to speak out. On the day after Appomattox, in Washington, General Butler made a speech in which he recommended, on the one hand, that the leaders of the rebellion should be disfranchised and disqualified for public office and, on the other, that the masses including the Negroes should be given immediately all the rights of citizenship. The next evening, in Baltimore on court duty, Chief Justice Chase dined with Henry Winter Davis and other Maryland Radicals, then wrote a letter to the President. "It will be, hereafter, counted equally a crime and a folly," Chase said, "if the colored loyalists of the rebel states shall be left to the control of restored rebels, not likely, in that case, to be either wise or just, until taught both wisdom and justice by new calamities."

That same evening, April 11, Lincoln made his own, last contribution to the public debate when he addressed the crowd gathered on the White House grounds. After a few congratulatory words on Grant's recent victory, he proceeded to defend at some length his own reconstruction view.

The problem, as he saw it, was essentially one of re-establishing the national authority throughout the South. This problem was complicated by the fact that there was, in the South, "no authorized organ" to treat with. "Nor is it a small additional embarrassment that we, the loyal people, differ among ourselves as to the mode, manner, and means of reconstruction." He had been criticized, he said, because he did not seem to have a fixed opinion on the question "whether the seceded States, so called," were "in the Union or out of it." He dismissed that question as "a merely pernicious abstraction" and went on to declare: "We all agree that the seceded States, so called, are out of their proper practical relation with the Union; and that the sole object of the government, civil and military, in regard to those States is to again get them into that proper practical relation."

He had been criticized also for setting up and sustaining the new state government of Louisiana, which rested on the support of only ten per cent of the voters and did not give the franchise to the colored man. He confessed that the Louisiana government would be better if it rested on a larger electorate including the votes of Negroes—at least "the very intelligent" and those who had served as soldiers. "Concede that the new government of Louisiana is only to what it should be as the egg is to the fowl, we shall sooner have the fowl by hatching the egg than by smashing it?" The loyalists of the South would be encouraged and the Negroes themselves would be better off, Lincoln argued, if Louisiana were quickly readmitted to the Union. An additional ratification would be gained for the Thirteenth Amendment, the adoption of which would be "unquestioned and unquestionable" only if it were ratified by three fourths of *all* the states.

What Lincoln said of Louisiana, he applied also to the other states of the South. "And yet so great peculiarities pertain to each state; and such important and sudden changes occur in the same state; and, withal, so new and unprecedented is the whole case, that no exclusive, and inflexible plan can safely be prescribed as to details and collatterals.'' (Virginia was not mentioned.) In concluding, Lincoln said enigmatically that it might become his duty ''to make some new announcement to the people of the South. I am considering, and shall not fail to act, when satisfied that action will be proper.''

In Washington and throughout the country the speech aroused much speculation about Lincoln's undisclosed intentions, and it provoked mixed feelings about his general approach to reconstruction. The editor of the Philadelphia *Public Ledger* noted that the President had indicated his ''feelings and wishes'' rather than his ''fixed opinions,'' then commended him for his lack of ''passion or malignancy'' toward the late rebels. The Washington correspondent of the Cincinnati *Gazette* believed that Lincoln's position was generally approved except among the Radical Republicans, who were saying that the rebel leaders must be punished and the rebel states subjected to ''preliminary training'' before being restored to their rights as members of the Union. ''The desire of the people for a settlement—speedy and final—upon the easiest possible terms, will, it is believed, sustain the President in his policy foreshadowed in his speech.''

Whatever the people might have approved, it was again made clear to Lincoln, when the Cabinet met on the morning of April 14 (with General Grant present), that some of his own advisers would not approve a settlement upon easy terms. Secretary Stanton came to the meeting with a project for military occupation as a preliminary step toward the reorganization of the Southern states, Virginia and North Carolina to be combined in a single military district. Secretary Welles objected to this arrangement on the grounds that it would destroy the individuality of the separate states. The President sustained Welles's objection but did not completely repudiate Stanton's plan. Instead, he suggested that Stanton revise it so as to deal with Virginia and North Carolina separately, and that he provide copies of the revised plan for the members of the Cabinet at their next meeting.

Before the Cabinet meeting adjourned, Lincoln said he was glad that Congress was not in session. The House and the Senate, he was aware, had the unquestioned right to accept or reject new members from the Southern states; he himself had nothing to do with that. Still, he believed, the President had the power to recognize and deal with the state governments themselves. He could collect taxes in the South, see that the mails were delivered there, and appoint Federal officials (though his appointments would have to be confirmed, of course, by the Senate). He knew that the congressional Radicals did not agree with him, but they were not in session to make official objection, and he could act to establish and recognize the new state governments before Congress met in December. He did not intend to call a special session before that time, as he told the Speaker of the House, Schuyler Colfax, later on the day of that final Cabinet meeting, as he was leaving to go to Ford's Theater.

When, in December, 1865, the regular session of Congress finally began, Andrew Johnson had been President for nearly eight months. At first, in the days of terror following Lincoln's assassination, Johnson talked like a good Radical. He also acted like one when he ordered the arrest of Jefferson Davis and other Confederate leaders on the charge of complicity in the assassination. But Johnson and the Radicals soon disagreed on reconstruction. During the summer he succeeded in the restoration of state governments according to a plan which required them only to abolish slavery, retract their ordinances of secession, and repudiate their debts accumulated in the Confederate cause. In December the Radicals in Congress refused to seat the Senators and Representatives from these restored states. After checking Johnson's program, the Radicals proceeded to undo it, while impeaching the President. Eventually they carried through their own program of military occupation, similar to the one Stanton had proposed at the Cabinet meeting of April 14, and they undertook to transfer political power from the old master class to the freedmen, as Chase and other Radicals long had advocated.

Whether Lincoln, if he had lived, would have done as Johnson did, is hard to say. Certainly Lincoln would not have hounded Jefferson Davis or other Confederate officials (but, then, the presupposition here is that there would have been no assassination to seem to justify it). To his Cabinet in April he had indicated his hope that there would be no persecution, no bloody work, with respect to any of the late enemy. "None need expect he would take any part in hanging or killing those men, even the worst of them," Welles paraphrased him. "Frighten them out of the country, open the gates, let down the bars, scare them off, said he, throwing up his hands as if scaring sheep."

As for the restoration of state governments, it is impossible to guess confidently what Lincoln would have done or tried to do, since the very essence of his planning was to have no fixed and uniform plan, and since he appeared to be changing his mind on some points shortly before he died. In the states already being reconstructed under his program of December, 1863, he doubtless would have continued to support that program, as he did to the last. In other states he might have tried other expedients.

Whether, if Lincoln had lived and had proceeded along Johnson's lines, he would have succeeded any better than Johnson, is another "iffy" question, impossible to answer. It seems likely that, with his superior talent for political management, Lincoln would have avoided the worst of Johnson's clashes with Congress. Yet he could scarcely have escaped the conflict itself, unless he had conceded much more to the Radicals than Johnson did.

Another poser is the question whether Lincoln's approach to peace, if he had lived and had carried it through, would have advanced the Negro toward equal citizenship more surely than did the Radical program, which degenerated into a rather cynical use of the Negro for party advantage. One is entitled to believe that Lincoln's policy would have been better in the long run for Negroes as well as for Southern whites and for the nation as a whole.

David Herbert Donald
Why They Impeached Andrew Johnson

The story of Presidential Reconstruction begun by Randall and Current in the last essay is completed in this one by David Herbert Donald, Charles Warren Professor of American History at Harvard University. Lincoln's approach to restoring the Union was cautious, practical, thoughtful—humane in every sense of the word. Because of his assassination, however, the evaluation of his policy has to be a study in the might-have-beens of history. The Reconstruction policy of his successor, Andrew Johnson, superficially similar to Lincoln's, was reckless, impractical, emotional, and politically absurd. While historians have differed in evaluating his purposes, they have been in unanimous agreement that his management of the problem was inept and that his policy was a total failure.

Professor Donald's essay provides an extended character study of Johnson, and it is not an attractive portrait. Donald believes that Johnson "threw away a magnificent opportunity" to smooth and speed the return of the Confederate states to a harmonious place in the Union. But he also shows how difficult Johnson's task was and to how great an extent southern white opinion was set against the full acceptance of Negro equality. Donald, a former student of James G. Randall, is best known for his revision and expansion of Randall's *The Civil War and Reconstruction,* and for his own Pulitzer Prize winning biography of the Massachusetts senator, *Charles Sumner.*

Reconstruction after the Civil War posed some of the most discouraging problems that have ever faced American statesmen. The South was prostrate. Its defeated soldiers straggled homeward through a countryside desolated by war. Southern soil was untilled and exhausted; southern factories and railroads were worn out. The four billion dollars of southern capital invested in Negro slaves was wiped out by advancing Union armies, "the most stupendous act of sequestration in the history of Anglo-American jurisprudence." The white inhabitants of eleven states had somehow to be reclaimed from rebellion and restored to a firm loyalty to the United States. Their four million former slaves had simultaneously to be guided into a proper use of their new-found freedom.

For the victorious Union government there was no time for reflection. Immediate decisions had to be made. Thousands of destitute whites and Negroes had to be fed before long-range plans of rebuilding the southern economy could be drafted. Some kind of government had to be established in these former Confederate states, to preserve order and to direct the work of restoration.

A score of intricate questions must be answered: Should the defeated southerners be punished or pardoned? How should genuinely loyal southern Unionists be rewarded? What was to be the social, economic, and political status of the now free Negroes? What civil rights did they have? Ought they to have the ballot? Should they be given a freehold of property? Was Reconstruction to be controlled by the national government, or should the southern states work out their own salvation? If the federal government supervised the process, should the President or the Congress be in control?

Intricate as were the problems, in early April, 1865, they did not seem insuperable. President Abraham Lincoln was winning the peace as he had already won the war. He was careful to keep every detail of Reconstruction in his own hands; unwilling to be committed to any "exclusive, and inflexible plan," he was working out a pragmatic program of restoration not, perhaps, entirely satisfactory to any group, but reasonably acceptable to all sections. With his enormous prestige as commander of the victorious North and as victor in the 1864 election, he was able to promise freedom to the Negro, charity to the southern white, security to the North.

The blighting of these auspicious beginnings is one of the saddest stories in American history. The reconciliation of the sections, which seemed so imminent in 1865, was delayed for more than ten years. Northern magnanimity toward a fallen foe curdled into bitter distrust. Southern whites rejected moderate leaders, and inveterate racists spoke for the new South. The Negro, after serving as a political pawn for a decade, was relegated to a second-class citizenship, from which he is yet struggling to emerge. Rarely has democratic government so completely failed as during the Reconstruction decade.

The responsibility for this collapse of American statesmanship is, of course, complex. History is not a tale of deep-dyed villains or pure-as-snow heroes. Part of the blame must fall upon ex-Confederates who refused to recognize that the war was over: part upon freedmen who confused liberty with license and the ballot box with the lunch pail; part upon northern antislavery extremists who identified patriotism with loyalty to the Republican party; part upon the land speculators, treasury grafters, and railroad promoters who were unwilling to have a genuine peace lest it end their looting of the public till.

Yet these divisive forces were not bound to triumph. Their success was due to the failure of constructive statesmanship that could channel the magnanimous feelings shared by most Americans into a positive program of reconstruction. President Andrew Johnson was called upon for positive leadership, and he did not meet the challenge.

Andrew Johnson's greatest weakness was his insensitivity to public opinion. In contrast to Lincoln, who said, "Public opinion in this country is everything," Johnson made a career of battling the popular will. A poor white, a runaway tailor's apprentice, a self-educated Tennessee politician, Johnson was a living defiance to the dominant southern belief that leadership belonged to the plantation aristocracy.

As senator from Tennessee, he defied the sentiment of his section in 1861 and refused to join the secessionist movement. When Lincoln later appointed him military governor of occupied Tennessee, Johnson found Nashville "a furnace of treason," but he braved social ostracism and threats of assassination and discharged his duties with boldness and efficiency.

Such a man was temperamentally unable to understand the northern mood in 1865, much less to yield to it. For four years the northern people had been whipped into wartime frenzy by propaganda tales of Confederate atrocities. The assassination of Lincoln by a southern sympathizer confirmed their belief in southern brutality and heartlessness. Few northerners felt vindictive toward the South, but most felt that the rebellion they had crushed must never rise again. Johnson ignored this postwar psychosis gripping the North and plunged ahead with his program of rapidly restoring the southern states to the Union. In May, 1865, without any previous preparation of public opinion, he issued a proclamation of amnesty, granting forgiveness to nearly all the millions of former rebels and welcoming them back into peaceful fraternity. Some few Confederate leaders were excluded from his general amnesty, but even they could secure pardon by special petition. For weeks the White House corridors were thronged with ex-Confederate statesmen and former southern generals who daily received presidential forgiveness.

Ignoring public opinion by pardoning the former Confederates, Johnson actually entrusted the formation of new governments in the South to them. The provisional governments established by the President proceeded, with a good deal of reluctance, to rescind their secession ordinances, to abolish slavery, and to repudiate the Confederate debt. Then, with far more enthusiasm, they turned to electing governors, representatives, and senators. By December, 1865, the southern states had their delegations in Washington waiting for admission by Congress. Alexander H. Stephens, once vice president of the Con-

A Harper's Weekly *cartoon depicts Johnson (left) and Thaddeus Stevens as engineers committed to a collision course.*

federacy, was chosen senator from Georgia; not one of the North Carolina delegation could take a loyalty oath; and all of South Carolina's congressmen had "either held office under the Confederate States, or been in the army, or countenanced in some way the Rebellion."

Johnson himself was appalled, "There seems in many of the elections something like defiance, which is all out of place at this time." Yet on December 5 he strongly urged the Congress to seat these southern representatives "and thereby complete the work of reconstruction." But the southern states were omitted from the roll call.

Such open defiance of northern opinion was dangerous under the best of circumstances, but in Johnson's case it was little more than suicidal. The President seemed not to realize the weakness of his position. He was the representative of no major interest and had no genuine political following. He had been considered for the vice presidency in 1864 because, as a southerner and a former slaveholder, he could lend plausibility to the Republican pretension that the old parties were dead and that Lincoln was the nominee of a new, nonsectional National Union party.

A political accident, the new Vice President did little to endear himself to his countrymen. At Lincoln's second inauguration Johnson appeared before the Senate in an obviously inebriated state and made a long, intemperate harangue about his plebeian origins and his hard-won success. President, Cabinet, and senators were humiliated by the shameful display, and Charles Sumner felt that "the Senate should call upon him to resign." Historians now know that Andrew Johnson was not a heavy drinker. At the time of his inaugural display, he was just recovering from a severe attack of typhoid fever. Feeling ill just before he entered the Senate chamber, he asked for some liquor to steady his nerves, and either his weakened condition or abnormal sensitivity to alcohol betrayed him.

Lincoln reassured Republicans who were worried over the affair: "I have known Andy for many years; he made a bad slip the other day, but you need not be scared. Andy ain't a drunkard." Never again was Andrew Johnson seen under the influence of alcohol, but his reformation came too late. His performance on March 4, 1865, seriously undermined his political usefulness and permitted his opponents to discredit him as a pothouse politician. Johnson was catapulted into the presidency by John Wilkes Booth's bullet. From the outset his position was weak, but it was not necessarily untenable. The President's chronic lack of discretion made it so. Where common sense dictated that a chief executive in so disadvantageous a position should act with great caution, Johnson proceeded to imitate Old Hickory, Andrew Jackson, his political idol. If Congress crossed his will, he did not hesitate to defy it. Was he not "the Tribune of the People"?

Sure of his rectitude, Johnson was indifferent to prudence. He never learned that the President of the United States cannot afford to be a quarreler. Apprenticed in the rough-and-tumble politics of frontier Tennessee, where orators exchanged violent personalities, crude humor, and bitter denunciations, Johnson continued to make stump speeches from the White House. All too often he spoke extemporaneously, and he permitted hecklers in his audience to draw from him angry charges against his critics.

On Washington's birthday in 1866, against the advice of his more sober advisers, the President made an impromptu address to justify his Reconstruction policy. "I fought traitors and treason in the South," he told the crowd; "now when I turn around, and at the other end of the line find men—I care not by what name you call them— who will stand opposed to the restoration of the Union of these States, I am free to say to you that I am still in the field."

During the "great applause" which followed, a nameless voice shouted, "Give us the names at the other end. . . . Who are they?"

"You ask me who they are," Johnson retorted. "I say Thaddeus Stevens of Pennsylvania is one; I say Mr. Sumner is another; and Wendell Phillips is another." Applause urged him to continue. "Are those who want to destroy our institutions . . . not satisfied with the blood that has been shed? . . . Does not the blood of Lincoln appease the vengeance and wrath of the opponents of this government?"

The President's remarks were as untrue as they were impolitic. Not only was it manifestly false to assert that the leading Republican in the House and the most conspicuous Republican in the Senate were opposed to "the fundamental principles of this government" or that they had been responsible for Lincoln's assassination; it was incredible political folly to impute such actions to men with whom the President had to work daily. But Andrew Johnson never learned that the President of the United States must function as a party leader.

There was a temperamental coldness about this plain-featured, grave man that kept him from easy, intimate relations with even his political supporters. His massive head, dark, luxuriant hair, deep-set and piercing eyes, and cleft square chin seemed to Charles Dickens to indicate "courage, watchfulness, and certainly strength of purpose," but his was a grim face, with "no genial sunlight in it." The coldness and reserve that marked Johnson's public associations doubtless stemmed from a deep-seated feeling of insecurity; this self-educated tailor whose wife had taught him how to write could never expose himself by letting down his guard and relaxing.

Johnson knew none of the arts of managing men, and he seemed unaware that face-saving is important for a politician. When he became President, Johnson was besieged by advisers of all political complexions. To each he listened gravely and non-committally, raising no questions and by his silence seeming to give consent. With Radical Senator Sumner, already intent upon giving the freedmen both homesteads and the ballot, he had repeated interviews during the first month of his presidency. "His manner has been excellent, & even sympathetic," Sumner reported triumphantly. With Chief Justice Salmon P. Chase, Sumner urged Johnson to support immediate Negro suffrage and found the President was "well-disposed, & sees the rights & necessities of the case." In the middle of May, 1865, Sumner reassured a Republican caucus that the President was a true Radical; he had listened repeatedly to the Senator and had told him "there is no difference between us." Before the end of the month the rug was pulled from under Sumner's feet. Johnson issued his proclamation for the reconstruction of North Carolina, making no provisions for Negro suffrage. Sumner first learned about it through the newspapers.

While he was making up his mind, Johnson appeared silently receptive to all ideas; when he had made a decision, his mind was immovably closed, and he defended his course with all the obstinacy of a weak man. In December, alarmed by Johnson's Reconstruction proclamations, Sumner again sought an interview with the President. "No longer sympathetic, or even kindly," Sumner found, "he was harsh, petulant, and unreasonable." The Senator was depressed by Johnson's "prejudice, ignorance, and perversity" on the Negro suffrage issue. Far from listening amiably to Sumner's argument that the South was still torn by violence and not yet ready for readmission, Johnson attacked him with cheap analogies. "Are there no murders in Massachusetts?" the President asked.

"Unhappily yes," Sumner replied, "sometimes."

"Are there no assaults in Boston? Do not men there sometimes knock each other down, so that the police is obliged to interfere?",

"Unhappily yes."

"Would you consent that Massachusetts, on this account, should be excluded from Congress?" Johnson triumphantly queried. In the excitement the President unconsciously used Sumner's hat, which the Senator had placed on the floor beside his chair, as a spittoon!

Had Johnson been as resolute in action as he was in argument, he might conceivably have carried much of his party with him on his Reconstruction program. Promptness, publicity, and persuasion could have created a presidential following. Instead Johnson boggled. Though he talked boastfully of "kicking out" officers who failed to support his plan, he was slow to act. His own Cabinet, from the very beginning, contained members who disagreed with him, and his secretary of war, Edwin M. Stanton, was openly in league with the Republican elements most hostile to the President. For more than two years he impotently hoped that Stanton would resign; then in 1867, after Congress had passed the Tenure of Office Act, he tried to oust the Secretary. This belated firmness, against the letter of the law, led directly to Johnson's impeachment trial.

Instead of working with his party leaders and building up political support among Republicans, Johnson in 1866 undertook to organize his friends into a new party. In August a convention of white southerners, northern Democrats, moderate Republicans, and presidential appointees assembled in Philadelphia to endorse Johnson's policy. Union General Darius Couch of Massachusetts marched arm in arm down the convention aisle with Governor James L. Orr of South Carolina, to symbolize the states reunited under Johnson's rule. The convention produced fervid oratory, a dignified statement of principles —but not much else. Like most third-party reformist movements it lacked local support and grass-roots organization.

Johnson himself was unable to breathe life into his stillborn third party. Deciding to take his case to the people, he accepted an invitation to speak at a great Chicago memorial honoring Stephen A. Douglas. When his special train left Washington on August 28 for a "swing around the circle," the President was accompanied by a few Cabinet members who shared his views and by the war heroes Grant and Farragut.

At first all went well. There were some calculated political snubs to the President, but he managed at Philadelphia, New York, and Albany to present his ideas soberly and cogently to the people. But Johnson's friends were worried lest his tongue again get out of control. "In all frankness," a senator wrote him, do not "allow the excitement of the moment to draw from you any *extemporaneous speeches.*"

At St. Louis, when a Radical voice shouted that Johnson was a "Judas," the President flamed up in rage. "There was a Judas and he was one of the twelve apostles," he retorted. ". . . The twelve apostles had a Christ. . . . If I have played the Judas, who has been my Christ that I have played the Judas with? Was it Thad Stevens? Was it Wendell Phillips? Was it Charles Sumner?" Over mingled hisses and applause, he shouted, "These are the men that stop and compare themselves with the Saviour; and everybody that differs with them . . . is to be denounced as a Judas."

Johnson had played into his enemies' hands. His Radical foes denounced him as a "trickster," a "culprit," a man "touched with insanity, corrupted with lust, stimulated with drink." More serious in consequence was the reaction of northern moderates, such as James Russell Lowell, who wrote, "What an anti-Johnson lecturer we have in Johnson! Sumner has been right about the *cuss* from the first. . . ."

The fall elections were an overwhelming repudiation of the President and his Reconstruction policy.

Johnson's want of political sagacity strengthened the very elements in the Republican party which he most feared. In 1865 the Republicans had no clearly defined attitude toward Reconstruction. Moderates like Gideon Welles and Orville Browning wanted to see the southern states restored with a minimum of restrictions; Radicals like Sumner and Stevens demanded that the entire southern social system be revolutionized. Some Republicans were passionately concerned with the plight of the freedmen; others were more interested in maintaining the high tariff and land grant legislation enacted during the war. Many thought mostly of keeping themselves in office, and many genuinely believed, with Sumner, that "the Republican party, in its objects, is identical with country and with mankind." These diverse elements came slowly to adopt the idea of harsh Reconstruction, but Johnson's stubborn persistency in his policy left them no alternative. Every step the President took seemed to provide "a new encouragement to (1) the rebels at the South, (2) the Democrats at the North and (3) the discontented elements everywhere." Not many Republicans would agree with Sumner that Johnson's program was "a defiance to God and Truth," but there was genuine concern that the victory won by the war was being frittered away.

The provisional governments established by the President in the South seemed to be dubiously loyal. They were reluctant to rescind their secession ordinances and to repudiate the Confederate debt, and they chose high-ranking ex-Confederates to represent them in Congress. Northerners were even more alarmed when these southern governments began to legislate upon the Negro's civil rights. Some laws were necessary—in order to give former slaves the right to marry, to hold property, to sue and be sued, and the like—but the Johnson legislatures went far beyond these immediate needs. South Carolina, for example, enacted that no Negro could pursue the trade "of an artisan, mechanic, or shopkeeper, or any other trade or employment besides that of husbandry" without a special license. Alabama provided that "any stubborn or refractory servants" or "servants who loiter away their time" should be fined $50 and, if they could not pay, be hired out for six months' labor. Mississippi ordered that every Negro under eighteen years of age who was an orphan or not supported by his parents must be apprenticed to some white person, preferably the former owner of the slave. Such southern laws indicated a determination to keep the Negro in a state of peonage.

It was impossible to expect a newly emancipated race to be content with such a limping freedom. The thousands of Negroes who had served in the Union armies and had helped conquer their former Confederate masters were not willing to abandon their new-found liberty. In rural areas southern whites kept these Negroes under control through the Ku Klux Klan. But in southern cities white hegemony was less secure, and racial friction erupted in mob violence. In May, 1866, a quarrel between a Memphis Negro and a white teamster led to a riot in which the

JOHNSON'S LOVE FOR THE SOLDIER.

Black Soldier—Massa, I come for my Bounty of $300, under the bill signed by President Johnson.

Johnson Paymaster, All right, my brave man, here is your money.

White Soldier— I come for the EXTRA bounty of $100 which Congress voted to me.

Johnson Paymaster, I am very sorry, but the President says the brave black troops must be paid first.

This cartoon is an example of the virulence of the attacks on Johnson by his enemies.

city police and the poor whites raided the Negro quarters and burned and killed promiscuously. Far more serious was the disturbance in New Orleans two months later. The Republican party in Louisiana was split into pro-Johnson conservatives and Negro suffrage advocates. The latter group determined to hold a constitutional convention, of dubious legality, in New Orleans, in order to secure the ballot for the freedmen and the offices for themselves. Through imbecility in the War Department, the Federal troops occupying the city were left without orders, and the mayor of New Orleans, strongly opposed to Negro equality, had the responsibility for preserving order. There were acts of provocation on both sides, and finally, on July 30, a procession of Negroes marching toward the convention hall was attacked.

"A shot was fired . . . by a policeman, or some colored man in the procession," General Philip Sheridan reported. "This led to other shots, and a rush after the procession. On arrival at the front of the Institute [where the convention met], there was some throwing of brick-bats by both sides. The police . . . were vigorously marched to the scene of disorder. The procession entered the Institute with the flag, about six or eight remaining outside. A row occurred between a policeman and one of these colored men, and a shot was again fired by one of the parties, which led to an indiscriminate firing on the building, through the windows, by the policemen.

"This had been going on for a short time, when a white flag was displayed from the windows of the Institute, whereupon the firing ceased and the police rushed into the building. . . . The policemen opened an indiscriminate fire upon the audience until they had emptied their revolvers, when they retired, and those inside barricaded the doors. The door was broken in, and the firing again commenced when many of the colored and white people either escaped out of the door, or were passed out by the policemen inside, but as they came out, the policemen who formed the circle nearest the building fired upon them, and they were again fired upon by the citizens that formed the outer circle.''

Thirty-seven Negroes and three of their white friends were killed; 119 Negroes and seventeen of their white sympathizers were wounded. Of their assailants, ten were wounded and but one killed. President Johnson was, of course, horrified by these outbreaks, but the Memphis and New Orleans riots, together with the Black Codes, afforded a devastating illustration of how the President's policy actually operated. The southern states, it was clear, were not going to protect the Negroes' basic rights. They were only grudgingly going to accept the results of the war. Yet, with Johnson's blessing, these same states were expecting a stronger voice in Congress than ever. Before 1860, southern representation in Congress had been based upon the white population plus three fifths of the slaves; now the Negroes, though not permitted to vote, were to be counted like all other citizens, and southern states would be entitled to at least nine additional congressmen. Joining with the northern Copperheads, the southerners could easily regain at the next presidential election all that had been lost on the Civil War battlefield.

It was this political exigency, not misguided sentimentality nor vindictiveness, which united Republicans in opposition to the President.

Johnson's defenders have pictured Radical Reconstruction as the work of a fanatical minority, led by Sumner and Stevens, who drove their reluctant colleagues into adopting coercive measures against the South. In fact, every major piece of Radical legislation was adopted by the nearly unanimous vote of the entire Republican membership of Congress. Andrew Johnson had left them no other choice. Because he insisted upon rushing Confederate-dominated states back into the Union, Republicans moved to disqualify Confederate leaders under the Fourteenth Amendment. When, through Johnson's urging, the southern states rejected that amendment, the Republicans in Congress unwillingly came to see Negro suffrage as the only counterweight against Democratic majorities in the South. With the Reconstruction Acts of 1867 the way was open for a true Radical program toward the South, harsh and thorough.

Andrew Johnson became a cipher in the White House, futilely disapproving bills which were promptly passed over his veto. Through his failure to reckon with public opinion, his unwillingness to recognize his weak position, his inability to functon as a party leader, he had sacrificed all influence with the party which had elected him and had turned over its control to Radicals vindictively opposed to his policies. In March, 1868, Andrew Johnson was summoned before the Senate of the United States to be tried on eleven accusations of high crimes and misdemeanors. By a narrow margin the Senate failed to convict him, and historians have dismissed the charges as flimsy and false. Yet perhaps before the bar of history itself Andrew Johnson must be impeached with an even graver charge—that through political ineptitude he threw away a magnificent opportunity.

W9-AGK-037

INSIGHT GUIDE
PUERTO RICO

Discovery CHANNEL

APA PUBLICATIONS
Part of the Langenscheidt Publishing Group

Editorial
Project Editor
Barbara Balletto
Managing Editor
Lesley Gordon
Editorial Director
Brian Bell

Distribution

UK & Ireland
GeoCenter International Ltd
The Viables Centre , Harrow Way
Basingstoke, Hants RG22 4BJ
Fax: (44) 1256-817988

United States
Langenscheidt Publishers, Inc.
46–35 54th Road, Maspeth, NY 11378
Fax: (718) 784-0640

Canada
Prologue Inc.
1650 Lionel Bertrand Blvd., Boisbriand
Québec, Canada J7H 1N7
Tel: (450) 434-0306. Fax: (450) 434-2627

Australia & New Zealand
Hema Maps Pty. Ltd.
24 Allgas Street, Slacks Creek 4127
Brisbane, Australia
Tel: (61) 7 3290 0322. Fax: (61) 7 3290 0478

Worldwide
**Apa Publications GmbH & Co.
Verlag KG (Singapore branch)**
38 Joo Koon Road, Singapore 628990
Tel: (65) 865-1600. Fax: (65) 861-6438

Printing

Insight Print Services (Pte) Ltd
38 Joo Koon Road, Singapore 628990
Tel: (65) 865-1600. Fax: (65) 861-6438

©1999 Apa Publications GmbH & Co.
Verlag KG (Singapore branch)
All Rights Reserved

First Edition 1987
Third Edition 1999

CONTACTING THE EDITORS
Although every effort is made to
provide accurate information, we
live in a fast-changing world and
would appreciate it if readers
would call our attention to any
errors or outdated information
that may occur by writing to us:
**Insight Guides, P.O. Box 7910,
London SE1 1WE, England.
Fax: (44 171) 403-0290.
insight@apaguide.demon.co.uk**

NO part of this book may be reproduced,
stored in a retrieval system or transmitted
in any form or means electronic, mechanical, photocopying, recording or otherwise, without prior written permission of
Apa Publications. Brief text quotations
with use of photographs are exempted
for book review purposes only. Information has been obtained from sources
believed to be reliable, but its accuracy
and completeness, and the opinions
based thereon, are not guaranteed.

This guidebook combines the
interests and enthusiasms of
two of the world's best known
information providers: Insight
Guides, whose titles have set the
standard for visual travel guides
since 1970, and Discovery Channel, the world's premier source
of nonfiction television
programming.

Insight Guides' edi-
tors provide practical
advice and general
understanding about a
place's history, culture,
institutions and people.
Discovery Channel and
its extensive web site,

www. discovery.com, help millions
of viewers explore their world from
the comfort of their own home and
also encourage them to explore it
firsthand.

In this, the third edition of the
guide, we take you all around
this island-nation and look at the
elements that have given
the country its interesting
"cultural confusion": Spanish architecture, African-
influenced music and
dance, Caribbean cuisine
with a distinctively Puerto
Rican flair. Discover the
island's equally diverse
landscape – dense moun-

EXPLORE YOUR WORLD

Discovery CHANNEL

tainous tropical forests, azure Caribbean oceans, arid flatlands and the rugged *cordillera*.

How to use this book

The book is carefully structured to convey an understanding of Puerto Rico and its culture and to guide readers through its sights and attractions:
◆ The Features section, with a yellow color bar, covers the country's history and culture in lively authoritative essays written by specialists.
◆ The Places section, with a blue bar, provides full details of all the sights and areas worth

seeing. The chief places of interest are coordinated by number with specially drawn maps.
◆ The Travel Tips listings section, with an orange bar, at the back of the book, offers a convenient point of reference for information on travel, accommodation, restaurants and other practical aspects of the country. Information may be located quickly using the index printed on the back cover flap, which also serves as a handy bookmark.

The contributors

This new edition, which builds on the earlier editions edited by **Christopher Caldwell**, **Tad Ames** and **Larry Luxner**, was edited by **Barbara Balletto** (who was happy to see her many years of "schoolgirl Spanish" finally be of practical use), assisted by managing editor **Lesley Gordon**.

The principal updater of this edition was **Gerry Tobin**, a Hato Rey resident who for many years served as an editor and writer for the *San Juan Star*. As well as updating the Travel Tips, he refined the original text written by a team including Luxner, Caldwell, **Sarah Ellison Caldwell**, **Webster** and **Robert Stone**, **Angelo Lopez**, **Adam Cherson**, **Kathleen O'Connell**, **Hanne-Maria Maijala**, **Eleanora Abreau Jimenez** and **Susan Hambleton**.

The principal photographers were **Bill Wassman**, **Tony Arruza**, **Robert Fried** and **Bob Krist**. Proofreading and indexing were undertaken by **Laura Hicks**, and the final touches were added by **Rachel Parsons** and **Sylvia Suddes** at Insight Guides' editorial office.

Map Legend

— · ··	International Boundary
— • —	National Park/Reserve
— — —	Ferry Route
✈ ✈	Airport: International/ Regional
🚌	Bus Station
Ⓟ	Parking
❶	Tourist Information
✉	Post Office
✝ ✝	Church/Ruins
†	Monastery
☾	Mosque
✡	Synagogue
⚔ 🏰	Castle/Ruins
∴	Archeological Site
∩	Cave
🗿	Statue/Monument
★	Place of Interest

The main places of interest in the Places section are coordinated by number with a full-colour map (e.g. ❶), and a symbol at the top of every right-hand page tells you where to find the map.

CONTENTS

Maps

Puerto Rico **112**

Old San Juan **116**

Metropolitan
San Juan **140**

Northeast **156**

Southeast **168**

North **176**

West **196**

Mayagüez **198**

South **215**

Ponce **216**

Cordillera Central **232**

Isla de Vieques
& Isla de Culebra **248**

Isla Mona **253**

Inside front cover: Puerto Rico
Inside back cover: Old San Juan

Introduction

A Heady Mix.......................... **15**

History

Decisive Dates **20**
Beginnings........................... **23**
The Spanish Settlers **27**
Self Rule and the
    United States................... **37**
Modern Times **45**

Features

People and Society............... **57**
Language............................. **69**
Puerto Rican Cuisine **75**
Island Art **83**
Rhythm of the Tropics **93**
A Sporting Life **101**

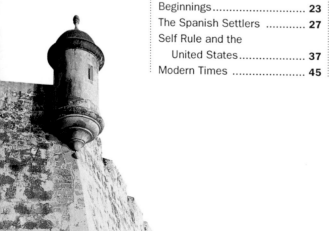

Plaza Colón in
the heart of
Old San Juan.

Travel Tips

Getting Acquainted .. **258**
Planning the Trip **259**
Practical Tips **260**
Getting Around **262**
Where to Stay **263**
Where to Eat **268**
Culture **272**
Nightlife **273**
Festivals **274**
Outdoor Activities ... **274**
Shopping **276**
Language **277**
Further Reading **282**

◆ **Full Travel Tips index
is on page 257**

Insight on ...

Festivals **64**
Folk Art **88**
Rum **150**
Flora **208**

Information panels

Drug Country **48**
Arecibo Observatory **182**
Tuna Territory...................... **200**
Ponce Art Museum................**222**

Places

Introduction **111**
Old San Juan **119**
Metropolitan San Juan **139**
Northeast **155**
Southeast **167**
North............................... **175**
The West **195**
The South **213**
Cordillera Central **231**
Outer Islands **247**

A HEADY MIX

Interesting history, colorful culture, breathtaking scenery and distinctive rhythms make Puerto Rico truly a "rich port"

Although the island was originally called *San Juan Bautista* – St John the Baptist – by Christopher Columbus when he discovered it in 1493, it was Ponce de León, the island's first governor, who enthusiastically gave the entire country the name of what was then just the capital: *Puerto Rico*, meaning "rich port". And it's no wonder, for Puerto Rico is indeed "rich" in many ways. What was once Spain's most important military outpost in the Caribbean has blossomed into not only a marvellous place to live and work for some 3.8 million people with an unparalleled passion for life, but also an "out-of-this-world" vacation destination – an exotic land spiced with romance and adventure.

The island of Puerto Rico is 100 miles (160 km) long and just 32 miles (51 km) from north to south; if it were to be flattened, however, it would be three times that size thanks to large areas of densely-forested mountains. This topography concentrates the population in a few very dense urban centers, where car ownership is the sixth highest in the world. Meanwhile, up in the mountains, rural life prevails; time ticks by virtually unnoticed, and farming is carried out using the same methods as five centuries ago.

As a result of its varied landscape, the island has three different kinds of weather: a tropical climate on the beaches of the north coast; endless rains in the lush forests of the mountainous center; and a dry, arid heat along the southern coast. In fact, some people say that weather is born in Puerto Rico.

Puerto Rico overflows with traces of its past: in primitive carvings, in architecture, in cuisine and even in farming techniques. Yet, at the same time, the island has kept up with progress – as its designer stores, art galleries, symphony concerts, floor shows and championship golf courses all attest.

Cultural cocktail

In Puerto Rico, everyone comes from somewhere else. Although the Taíno population had all but vanished within a few years of Spanish colonization, a few poor Spanish farmers intermarried with some remaining Amerindians. Few of these, known as *jíbaros*, remain today, but their cultural imprint survives. Later, African slaves arrived to work on the sugar plantations, as well as other Caribbean islanders seeking jobs. Spanish loyalists sought refuge here, fleeing Simón Bolívar's independence movement in South America.

The French also flocked to Puerto Rico, leaving behind various upheavals in Louisiana and Haiti. Even farmers from Scotland and Ireland in search of a better life ended up on the island,

PRECEDING PAGES: Playa Mar Chiquita, near Arecibo; the Cabo Rojo lighthouse; Fuerte San Cristóbal, San Juan; San Cristóbal Canyon.
LEFT: colorful character taking a stroll in Old San Juan.

hoping to benefit from its rich sugar-cane economy. Chinese workers came to build roads in the 1800s; they were followed by Italians, Germans and even Lebanese. In 1898, it was American expatriates who sought the island as a home. If ever there was a cultural cocktail, Puerto Rico is it.

Although English is spoken well, Spanish is predominant – but it, too, is a mix, with many words borrowed from both the pre-Columbian Amerindian tongue and modern-day English.

After the struggles of independence, and power tussles with the Dutch and the English, Puerto Rico eventually arrived at a strange but fruitful relationship with the United States. Puerto Ricans have citizen status and can travel freely to and from the mainland; there's no such thing as a Puerto Rican passport. Oddly, they can't vote in US presidential elections, but they *can* vote in the Democratic and Republican primaries – hence presidential candidates sometimes campaign here. A resident commissioner is elected to the US House of Representatives by Puerto Ricans, but although he has a voice he has no vote on legislative matters.

Without question, the relationship with the United States is vital for Puerto Rico's economy: many US corporations have bases on the island, and 2½ million Puerto Ricans spend their working lives on the mainland. Nevertheless, the island likes to keep its distance: in repeated referendums Puerto Ricans have voted against becoming America's 51st state.

Island spirits

Although Puerto Rico is predominantly Roman Catholic, its Christianity is blended with some Taíno and African traditions, and some say it is spiritualism – once banned by Spanish colonial rulers – that is the country's true religion, for it flourishes in many pockets of the island. Spiritualists believe that *jípia*, or spirits of the dead, sleep by day and roam the island at night, searching for wild fruit to eat. Even today, modern homes will have a bowl of bright plastic fruit in the kitchen to appease the spirits.

You may spot children wearing bead charm bracelets to guard against the "evil eye"; to look on another person or person's possessions covetously may lead to sickness or even death, according to believers. Indeed, spiritualism figures in the day-to-day activities of many islanders – through healing, folk medicine and even food. Spiritualist literature can be found throughout the island.

Saints are relied upon to keep the hurricanes away – not always successfully: witness the devastation caused in 1998 by Hurricane Georges, just one of many such storms to plow across Puerto Rico over the centuries. Every town has a patron saint, and *santos*, carved religious figures, are in every home to protect the family. The family unit is still key to local life, with Sunday picnics on the beaches a traditional pastime.

Puerto Rico is an enigmatic, spiritual, magical destination, where the familiar mixes completely naturally with the exotic. This most distinctive, heady mix is examined, explored, and celebrated, in the following pages.   ❑

RIGHT: *vejigante* fiesta mask dancer.

Decisive Dates

ANCIENT TIMES

4500 BC Archaic Indians arrive in Puerto Rico, probably from Venezuela's Rio Orinoco delta.
AD 200–700 Igneri people inhabit the island.
800–1500 Taíno Indian civilization flourishes.

AGE OF EXPLORERS

1493 Columbus lands near Aguadilla, claiming the island for Spain.
1508 Juan Ponce de León establishes first settlement at Caparra.

1510 King of Spain appoints Ponce de León governor of San Juan Bautista, as Puerto Rico is then known.
1516 Entrepreneurs construct the island's first *ingenio* – a factory in which raw cane is ground, boiled and reduced to sugar crystals.
1520s Island officially called Puerto Rico.
1521 Ponce de León dies in Florida: Caparra settlement moved Caparra to present-day Old San Juan.
1530 Casa Blanca, Puerto Rico's first real defensive edifice, is completed.
1531 Puerto Rico sends its first sugar exports to Spain.
1532 Army begins building La Fortaleza.
1539 Spaniards begin construction of El Morro fortress.

1580s Governor Diego Menéndez de Valdes improves the island's military preparedness by constructing new fortresses and refurbishing others.
1598 Ginger replaces sugar as Puerto Rico's main cash crop; influenza epidemic wipes out most of the able-bodied population of San Juan.
1625 Dutch captain Boudewijn Hendrikszoon lays siege to San Juan; retreats after only a month.
1630s–1640s King Philip IV of Spain realizes his plan to fortify the entire city of San Juan: seven fortresses were linked by a line of stone walls.
1765 Spain sends Alejandro O'Reilly to probe illicit island trade; population estimated at 45,000.
1797 British forces under General Abercromby try to take San Juan; they retreat only a few weeks later.
1812 Spain grants conditional citizenship to island residents.
1813–18 Puerto Rican trade grows to eight times its previous level.
1823 Miguel de la Torres appointed governor.
1824 King of Spain concedes the right of Puerto Rican ports to harbor non-Spanish merchant ships.
185 Ramón Emeterio Betances is exiled for his criticism of the colonial authorities.
1868 *Grito de Lares* revolt marks beginning of the *independentista* movement.
1887 Luis Muñoz Rivera becomes one of the founders of the Autonomist Party.
1897 Spain declares Puerto Rico an autonomous territory; Muñoz Rivera is appointed Secretary of State and Chief of the Cabinet.

ENTER THE US

1898 Spanish-American War; US troops land at Guánica, ending Puerto Rico's autonomy and bringing the island under American jurisdiction.
1899 Hurricane San Ciriaco devastates sugar and coffee industry.
1900 Foraker Act formalizes Puerto Rico's colonial status.
1904 Luis Muñoz Rivera becomes a founder of the Unionist Party.
1910 Muñoz Rivera elected Resident Commissioner to the US House of Representatives.
1917 Jones Act extends US citizenship to Puerto Ricans; labor leader Pablo Iglesias is elected to the new Senate.
1922 Nationalist Party is founded.
1936 Two Nationalist gunmen shoot and kill San Juan's police chief.

LEFT: Juan Ponce de León.
RIGHT: Luis Muñoz Marín.

1937 Twenty Nationalist protesters are killed by police in the "Ponce Massacre".

1938 Luis Muñoz Marín, only son of Luis Muñoz Rivera, forms the Popular Democratic Party.

1942 Puerto Rico Industrial Development Company established.

POST-WORLD WAR II

1946 Jesús Piñero, appointed by President Truman, becomes the first native governor in the island's history.

1948 Muñoz Marín takes office as the first freely elected governor of Puerto Rico.

1950 Nationalists try to kill President Truman in Washington, and stir up revolt at home.

1952 Puerto Rico becomes a US commonwealth on July 25.

1954 Nationalists open fire in the US House of Representatives, wounding five Congressmen.

MODERN TIMES

1960s Operation Bootstrap in full swing.

1964 Muñoz Marín resigns from political office.

1967 More than 60 percent of voters choose to retain commonwealth status in islandwide plebiscite.

1975 Igneri and pre-Taíno ruins found at Tibes, north of Ponce.

1978 Police kill two young *independentistas*, sparking the Cerro Maravilla scandal.

1985 Governor Rafael Hernández Colón links Section 936 benefits to President Reagan's CBI program, preserving the benefits, provided that Puerto Rico funds development projects of $100 million a year in various Caribbean islands.

1986 A New Year's Eve fire at the Dupont Plaza Hotel kills 97; arsonists are blamed.

1989 Hurricane Hugo hits the island, inflicting heavy damage on Vieques and Culebra.

1991 Hernández Colón abolishes English as one of Puerto Rico's two official languages.

1992 Pedro Rosselló, after his election as governor, restores English as an official language.

1993 In a November status plebiscite, voters elect to retain commonwealth status; five days later, Puerto Rico celebrates 500th anniversary of the island's discovery by Columbus.

1996 Governor Pedro Rosselló is re-elected for another four-year term. Carlos Romero-Barceló re-elected as the Resident Commissioner in Washington, DC.

1998 Hurricane Georges wreaks havoc on the island. A third plebiscite is held to determine Puerto Rico's status; voters reject statehood once again. ❏

A BEGINNER'S GUIDE TO PUERTO RICAN POLITICS

Contrary to popular belief, Puerto Rico's No. 1 sport isn't baseball – it's politics. No matter where you go, you'll find any number of people enthusiastically discussing and arguing about the political situation. The pros and cons of statehood, commonwealth and independence – as well as the activities of politicians – dominate most conversations. Puerto Rican voters exceed 60 percent participation at every election, a figure so high it is not found anywhere else in the world.

There basically are five "players": the National Republican Party, the Popular Democratic Party, the New Progressive Party, the Independence Party, and the Communist Party which has a much smaller following than the other four.

The Independence Party, obviously, is pushing for independence. It is vocal and highly visible and receives a lot of press coverage and attention – but not a lot of votes (less than 3 percent in the 1998 plebiscite to determine the island's status). A closer battle is fought between those groups who want statehood (mainly the New Progressive Party) and the proponents of commonwealth (the Popular Democratic Party).

So now sit back, sip your *cerveza* (beer) and enjoy the lively banter. You'll even be permitted to join in.

BEGINNINGS

By the time the Spanish came, the native peoples had created a sophisticated culture with ingenious farming techniques and fine handicrafts

Within a year of his triumphant return to Spain with news of his discoveries, Columbus set sail across the Atlantic on a second voyage to the New World. When he discovered Puerto Rico on this 1493 trip, he found plenty of Taíno (and Arawak) Indians already occupying the island.

It has not yet been conclusively determined how or when the Taínos arrived, but much has been learned by the discovery at Loíza of a limestone cave containing artifacts of the early people. Carbon-dating reveals that the island has been occupied since the 1st century AD, and shells fashioned into gouging tools for use in the manufacture of dug-out canoes suggest that the first Indians rowed over from Venezuela, where similar relics have been recovered. There was unquestionably steady communication and trade between the Caribbean islands. In his journal Columbus describes a Taínos canoe which seated three men abreast and 70 to 80 in all. "A barge could not keep up with them in rowing," he wrote, "because they go with incredible speed, and with these canoes they navigate among these islands."

A stratified society

Part of a well-defined Indian culture that extended throughout the Antilles, the Taínos in Puerto Rico lived in a rigidly stratified society. A great king lived on the island of Hispaniola, and district *caciques* – chiefs – governed the districts of Puerto Rico, which the Indians called *Borinquen* – "Island of the Brave Lord". Each district had a centrally located capital village where the *cacique* resided. As in medieval Europe, heredity determined status within society, which comprised *nitaínos*, or nobles who advised the *caciques* and enjoyed certain privileges; commoners; and *naborías*, or slaves.

Taíno villages ranged in size from a couple of hundred to a couple of thousand people. The Indians spent most of their time out-of-doors,

yet they did build large bell-shaped thatched houses in which as many as 40 family members slept. These were built around a large open space reserved for public ceremonies and for *batey,* which the Spanish referred to as *pelota* – a ball game. The house of the *cacique* was the largest in town and always fronted on this pub-

lic square. At Tibes, in Ponce, an Indian village has been reconstructed from ancient ruins.

The Taínos believed in a polytheistic order of creation. Yocahú, the Supreme Creator, commanded all the gods, the earth and its creatures. The angry god of the winds, Juracán, invoked the eponymous hurricanes. In the central square, the Indians observed religious worship and participated in ceremonial dances. Ceramic icons and clay idols displayed in anthropological museums are evidence of the religious past. South of Arecibo, at the 13-acre (5-hectare) Caguana Indian Ceremonial Park, used for religious purposes eight centuries ago, there are stone monoliths, 10 *batey* balls and other artifacts.

LEFT: ancient Taino stones at Caguana.
RIGHT: mask at Tibes Ceremonial Park.

Traces of Taíno agriculture remain in Puerto Rico. Their ingenious method of sowing a variety of plants in earthen mounds called *conducos* is still employed by some farmers. The *conduco* system mitigated the problems of water distribution: water-intensive crops were placed at the bottom and those requiring good drainage at the top. Cassava bread, the staple of the Taíno diet, was made by grating and draining the root, which the Indians formed into loaves and baked. They also relied heavily upon yams –sweet *batates* and unsweet *ages* – and among the plants the early settlers sent back to Spain were maize, beans, squash and peanuts. Using *macanas* – stout double broad-swords still used by Puerto Rican farmers – and pointed sticks, the Taínos cleared the thick woods and sowed their fields. Various sources of animal protein supplemented the starchy diet: fish and sometimes pigeon or parrot.

A golden age

In the time left over from farming, fishing and bagging small game, the Taínos developed various handicrafts. Early Spanish settlers in the region greatly admired the Indian woodwork: dishes, basins, bowls and boxes. Most prized of all were the ornate *duhos,* carved wooden thrones used by the *caciques.* The Great Taíno Cacique made a gift of a dozen of these to the Spanish Crown in the 1490s. Indian weavers used cotton and other fibrous plants to make colorfully dyed clothing, belts and hammocks. But the handicraft that aroused greatest excitement among the Spanish was the gold jewelry that the Indians wore as rings in their ears and noses. They neither mined nor panned for gold. When the Spaniards, smitten with desire for the precious metal, coaxed the natives into leading them to their sources, they were taken to beaches where gold nuggets from the ocean floor occasionally washed ashore.

Recent findings have shed more light on these indigenous peoples. The Institute of Puerto Rican Culture has amassed large collections of stones, pottery, tools and skeletal remains. Archeologists are deciphering information from ongoing digs. In Old San Juan, El Museo del Indio's artifacts and indigenous exhibits, together with a miniature model of a Taíno village on display at Casa Blanca, give some insight into the way of life of the early people in the Old City. ❏

RIGHT: Taíno rock carvings near Cayey.

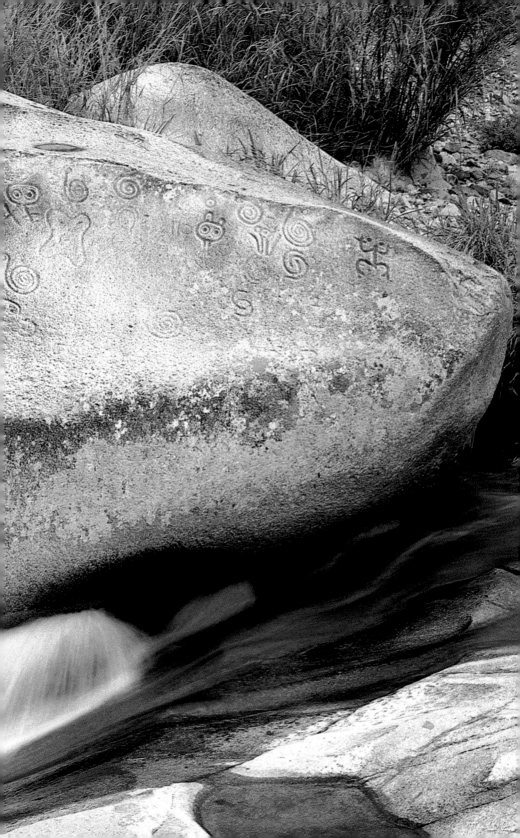

THE SPANISH SETTLERS

At first the Spanish treated the Taíno population well. But soon the natives were enslaved as their invaders lusted for gold. Then came the trade wars

Fifteen years passed between the time of Columbus's discovery of the island of Borinquen on November 19, 1493, and serious attempts to settle it. The adventurer to the New World came across the island by chance during his second voyage while he was trying to reach Hispaniola. Renaming it San Juan Bautista, Columbus claimed it for the Spanish crown and promptly departed. From 1493 until 1508, the approximately 30,000 Taínos living on the island enjoyed a period of benevolent neglect: from time to time, Spaniards sailed to San Juan from Hispaniola seeking to barter with local people for food. These encounters were always very friendly.

Enticing gold

One of the Spaniards who visited the island was Juan Ponce de León. The natives' ornaments and trinkets of gold caught Ponce de León's eye. He felt sure that the area was rich in gold, and he secretly scouted the southern coast for sites for mines. In the early summer of 1508 Ponce de León and the Spanish governor of the Caribbean, Nicolas de Ovando, signed a clandestine agreement which granted Ponce de León rights to mine the island on the condition that he would yield two-thirds to the king. Secrecy was of utmost importance: Christopher Columbus's son, Diego Colón, had inherited the rights to exploit the island, but his family's megalomaniacal desire for wealth had proved dangerous in the past. Physical abuse, dissolution of tribes and families and starvation of the Indians on Hispaniola had been followed by rebellion and bloodshed.

In July 1508, Ponce de León and a band of 50 men – among them Luis de Añasco, the namesake of the river and village – set off for the island of San Juan Bautista. As they sailed eastward along the northern coast, they made friendly contact with the Indians, and Agueybaná, the head *cacique* of the island, provided

---

LEFT: Ponce de León, Puerto Rico's first governor.
RIGHT: Diego Colón and a bust of his famous father.

Ponce de León with an entry which ensured safe passage for him and his crew. Finally, after six long weeks of searching, the intrepid explorers sighted a suitable site for settlement. In a valley several miles inland on an arm of the Bayamon river, Ponce de León founded the island's first European town, *Caparra* (a word

that might be translated as "blossoming"). In official documents, it was referred to as *Ciudad de Puerto Rico*.

Relations between the Indians and the Europeans proceeded swimmingly. Panning the river beds produced enough gold to persuade Ponce de León that the island merited permanent settlement. He had hoped for a small, strictly controlled group of Spaniards to live and work among the Indians without committing abuses or arousing hostility. However, as soon as King Ferdinand caught wind of Puerto Rico's excellent prospects he directed a number of family friends there. Meanwhile, Diego Colón also entered the scene. Incensed that Ponce de León had grabbed the island for himself, he granted titles to two of his father's supporters – Cristóbal Sotomayor and Miguel Díaz – and subsidized their establishment on the island. San Juan Bautista was now destined to suffer what Ponce de León had tried to avoid. By a colonial ordinance called a *repartimiento* one of Colón's men enslaved 5,500 Indians, ostensibly in order to convert them to Christianity but in reality to press them into labor.

The enslaved natives were divided and placed "under the protection" of 48 *hidalgos* (minor aristocracy, from *hijo de algo*, meaning "son of a somebody"). A combination of feu-

Indigenous resistance

During the winter of 1511, violence erupted, and guerrilla warfare soon spread through the island. Ponce de León responded immediately. Within a few days of the initial outburst he and his captains had captured nearly 200 Indians, whom they subsequently sold into slavery, branding them on the face with the king's first initial. By June, peace once again reigned.

For a few years, the search for Puerto Rican gold continued at the expense of the Indians' freedom and until 1540, when the sources dried up, San Juan Bautista remained one of the New World's foremost suppliers of gold to Spain. To

dalism and capitalism, this was the *encomienda* system, and it was employed throughout Spain's 16h-century New World empire. Across the northern coast the Spanish opened mines and panning operations, all supported by the free labor of the natives. The king appointed Ponce de León governor in 1510 but did not empower him to relinquish the *repartimiento*. The mining business proliferated, though there was so much competition for gold that the few who profited were men like Ponce de León, who made their fortunes selling food and supplies to the miners. Moreover, not even Ponce de León could check the Spanish settlers' abuse of the Indians, especially in the remote western end of the island.

assuage the wounded sensibilities of Juan Ponce de León for stripping his office down to little more than a title, King Ferdinand gave him permission to explore the virgin peninsula northwest of the Antilles which the Spanish called *La Florida*.

As people continued to immigrate to the island of San Juan Bautista they brought new commercial enterprises. The days when *hidalgos* left their homeland to strike it rich in New World gold mines were gone. Gradually, the settlers turned to agriculture. Land was plentiful and easy to come by, water was abundant and the climate mild. Labor posed a problem at first, for the Indians had disappeared quickly after the institution of the *repartimiento*. Epidemics of European diseases had swept through the communities of enslaved Indians, devastating the population. Those Indians who escaped fled into the mountainous interior or across the sea to join the tribes of coastal South America. However, West African blacks, imported by Portuguese slavers and supplied by the Spanish crown, provided an affordable replacement.

Peasant roots

Two sorts of farm developed. Some islanders, denied political and social status because they were *mestizos* (the progeny of a white and an

on the island) were chiefly interested in profit. After experimenting with a variety of crops, including ginger and tobacco, they finally settled on sugar as the most dependable and profitable cash crop. It was relatively new to Europeans, but their sweet tooth appeared to be insatiable.

In 1516 entrepreneurs constructed the island's first *ingenio* – a factory in which raw cane is ground, boiled and reduced to sugar crystals. A decade and a half later, Puerto Rico sent its first sugar exports to Spain. Ferdinand's successor, Holy Roman Emperor Charles V, was so encouraged by it that he provided a

Indian or black), were unable to obtain large land grants and credit. They resorted to subsistence farming and on their tiny plots raised cassava, corn, vegetables, fruit, rice and a few cattle. Generally, *mestizos* cleared fields in inland regions that would not compete with the large coastal plantations. Puerto Rico's sizeable peasant class blossomed from the seeds of these 16th-century subsistence farmers.

In addition there were, of course, owners of large plantations. Usually of purely European ancestry, these immigrants and Creoles (born

LEFT: the arrival of Christopher Columbus.
ABOVE: slave labor created the plantations.

number of technicians and loans for the industry's growth. Peripheral industries burgeoned as well: demand for timber to fuel the *ingenios* and food to fuel the laborers soared, and where sugar is processed, so inevitably is rum produced. Determined to squeeze all the profit possible out of their sugar-cane, the Spanish settlers built distilleries soon after harvesting the first sugar crop.

By 1550, there were 10 active *ingenios* on the island, but the restrictive policies of the mercantilist King Philip II led to a crash in it during the 1580s. Eventually it recovered, but throughout Puerto Rico's history sugar would be not only one of the island's pre-eminent products but also one of its most troubled industries.

Horses and husbandry

After the collapse of the sugar trade, ginger emerged as the most successful product, and despite edicts from the monarch – who preferred the cultivation of sugar – it flourished until the market bottomed out through a surplus. Animal husbandry was another lucrative industry. The armies that conquered Peru, Central America and Florida rode Puerto Rican horses, and island *hatos* (cattle ranches) supplied the local garrisons with meat.

THE MIGHTY LION

Born around 1460 in San Servos, Spain, Don Juan Ponce de León is known essentially for three things: the discovery of what is now Florida, the conquering and governing of Puerto Rico, and his never-ending search for the mythical Fountain of Youth. Historians believe he sought not only the age-restorative waters but also gold and silver thought to be at the site of the fountain. He explored many regions including the Bahamas and Bimini in his quest, but a poisoned arrow shot into his stomach brought his explorations to an abrupt halt. His epitaph, by poet and historian Juan de Castellanos, reads "Here lie the bones of a Lion/mightier in deeds than in name."

The possibility of foreign aggression remained a constant threat. By the 1520s, the economic and strategic promise of the island – now officially called *Puerto Rico* – had become apparent. Moreover, the individual with the clearest sense of Puerto Rico's potential and importance was gone. Juan Ponce de León had been fatally wounded in an encounter with Florida Indians in 1521; his remains are interred in the Metropolitan Cathedral of San Juan. Without a leader close to the Spanish king, defensive measures were hard to obtain.

In the year of Ponce de León's burial, the colonialists transferred the capital city from the site chosen by him to a large natural bay to the north, renaming it San Juan. Mosquitoes had plagued settlers incessantly in the old riverbank town, and the site proved too small to support increased river traffic as agriculture and industry developed.

Advantageous as the new location was for shipping, it left the people vulnerable to foreign invaders. In the 16th and 17th centuries the French, English and Dutch dedicated themselves to unseating the powerful Habsburg monarchs both at home and abroad. As part of this campaign, they launched attack after attack on Spanish salients in the New World. Many of these attacks were carried out by privateers.

Fortifications

Encouraged by rumors of impending assault by French war vessels, San Juan officials in 1522 initiated the construction of the port's first garrison. The wooden structure had not been completed before they realized it would be insufficient in the face of an attack. The island's first real defensive edifice was not completed until 1530, when descendants of Ponce de León built a house of stone, the Casa Blanca, designed to provide a refuge for colonialists in the face of foreign aggression. The house still stands in Old San Juan. But not even the Casa Blanca fulfilled the defensive needs of the settlement, particularly given the expected large-scale population growth. Two years later, the army began building La Fortaleza, sometimes known as Santa Catalina. Today it houses the offices of the governor of Puerto Rico, and it holds the distinction of being the oldest executive mansion in the Western Hemisphere.

The Fortaleza did little to supplement the defenses already provided by the Casa Blanca.

Before it had been completed, army officers informed the crown that it had been built in "a poor place" and begged the appropriation of funds for another fortress. El Castillo de San Felipe del Morro (or, simply, El Morro) was the product of their entreaties. Placed on the rocky tip of the San Juan Peninsula, the fortification, which was finished in the 1540s, did much to assuage the fears of the northern capital's residents.

But Puerto Ricans had more to be concerned with than the French alone. The celebrated "sea dogs" of Queen Elizabeth, Francis Drake and Captain John Hawkins, forcibly seized dozens

colonial policy in the Western Hemisphere, conferred upon the governor the title of Captain-General and directed him to improve the island's military preparedness. Governor Diego Menéndez de Valdes exercised tremendous initiative during the 1580s. A number of fortresses were constructed during his tenure, including El Boquerón and Santa Elena in San Juan. Menéndez ordered the refurbishing of the land bridge La Puente de San Antonio – now La Puente de San Geronimo – and the strengthening of La Fortaleza. He also requisitioned artillery and ammunition, expanding the troop count from 50 to 209 men.

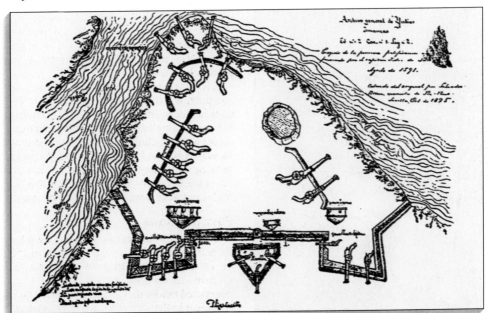

of Spanish cargo ships traveling between the Antilles and Spain. In 1585, open war broke out between the two nations. England's well-known defeat of the Spanish Invincible Armada in 1588 left Spain permanently disabled as a naval power.

More defenses

Towards the end of the 16th century, Puerto Rico received cursory attention. The Council of the Indies, the bureaucracy that oversaw the enforcement and administration of Spanish

Menéndez stepped in just in the nick of time. A string of English assaults launched with the intention of capturing Puerto Rico was thwarted, thanks to sturdy defenses. A historic confrontation in the autumn of 1594 resulted in an English defeat. During one of these battles a cannonball shot through the side of Francis Drake's ship and mortally wounded John Hawkins, who was with Drake in his cabin. Drake was forced to retreat.

Yet the English would not give up. While the Spanish king nearly doubled – to 409 – the number of troops at the San Juan garrison of El Morro, the veteran sea warrior George Clifford, third Earl of Cumberland, secretly

LEFT: foreign navies were a constant threat, hence the heavy fortifications at El Morro (**ABOVE**).

planned an assault. He was aided by an influenza epidemic in 1598, which wiped out most of the able-bodied population of San Juan. As a result, the city was seriously unprepared for the imminent attack.

Influenza's revenge

From a point 80 miles (129 km) east of the capital, Cumberland's troops marched toward San Juan in June, easily taking fortifications as they proceeded. On July 1, the defenders who had been forced to hole up in El Morro surrendered the town. But the same scourge which had weakened the Puerto Ricans now struck the

English conquerors. More than 400 English soldiers died of influenza within six weeks. The Puerto Ricans promptly availed themselves of the British state of weakness. Refusing to acknowledge Cumberland's authority, they engaged relentlessly in skirmishes on the outskirts of the town. On August 27, Cumberland withdrew from the island, destroying two plantations in his wake.

Next the Dutch entered the picture. Determined to bring Spanish dominance of the Caribbean to an end, they commissioned Boudewijn Hendrikszoon to take over the island. Hendrikszoon's fleet of eight vessels arrived in San Juan harbor on September 24,

1625. In the course of the next three days the Dutch slowly advanced, forcing a Spanish retreat into El Morro.

The siege of San Juan lasted a month. Finally, the courageous captains Juan de Amezquita and Andres Botello led surprise attacks on the Dutch trenches on October 22. The next 10 days of battle left the Dutch fleet severely damaged – one ship destroyed and the troops depleted. The island was confirmed as a Spanish domain.

In the 1630s and 1640s, King Philip IV of Spain realized his plan to fortify the entire city of San Juan: seven fortresses were linked by a line of stone walls. The natives were inducted into the provincial district militia.

In control

Having seen off the English and the Dutch, the island was now relatively safe from invaders, and attention was turned to the problem of establishing a strong economic base. But, as a Spanish colony, Puerto Rico was allowed to keep open only one port – San Juan – and was barred from trading with non-Spanish powers. These strictures seriously limited the chances for economic growth.

In the mid-16th century, when the influx of African slaves diminished, Britain threatened Spain on the high seas, and when non-Spanish producers in the West Indies developed more efficient sugar production, the sugar industry collapsed. Virtually nothing was exported in the 1560s and 1570s. In 1572 there was not a single ship in the harbor, and there was a seven-year span in which no European vessels docked at San Juan at all.

The Spanish crown, wishing to convert Puerto Rico into a defensive salient, instituted an assistance program called the *situado*. According to this plan, Puerto Rico was to receive from Mexico 2½ million *maravedies* annually – a substantial sum. Although the *situado* was fraught with problems – such as privateers repeatedly intercepting the money in transit – the erratic delivery of bullion from Mexico kept the island afloat until independent economic development began.

Smugglers all

Ironically, what turned the flagging island economy around was the circumvention of the Spanish mercantilist policies that had been the cause of Puerto Rico's problems to begin with. Refused permanent concessions by the crown, the planters and merchants on Puerto Rico engaged increasingly in illicit foreign trade. Local produce – sugar, livestock, tobacco – was exchanged for slaves, staples, tools and other manufactured goods. By the mid-17th century almost everyone, from clerical authorities to soldiers, from friars to peasants, was involved in smuggling. The coastal towns of Aguada, Arecibo, Cabo Rojo and Fajardo grew into busy centers of illicit international trade.

Word of the proliferation of contraband activity and privateering in Puerto Rico eventually got back to Spain. Recognizing that the island's problems were critical, the king sent a commissioner, Alejandro O'Reilly, to evaluate the state of Puerto Rico. O'Reilly's report of 1765 was remarkably comprehensive and perspicacious. He reckoned the island's population had reached about 45,000: 40,000 free men and 5,000 slaves. Most of the urban inhabitants lived in northeastern coastal towns and earned their livelihood through smuggling and black-market trade. Smuggling was so prevalent that O'Reilly could report extensively on prices, supply, demand and distribution.

In 1765, a Spanish council met to review O'Reilly's report and to formulate a solution to the Puerto Rican problem. Recognizing the need for a stronger enforcement agent to curb contraband trade, Spain more than doubled the *situado* and installed Don Miguel de Muesas as governor. He was instructed to create a sturdy domestic economy. By building bridges and roads, by strengthening defenses, and by improving public education he hoped to promote agricultural prosperity and domestic self-sufficiency.

Despite the ability with which O'Reilly pleaded Puerto Rico's case, Spain continued to see the development of the island's economy as secondary to its importance as the first naval fortification in the New World empire. Further, a population boom – largely attributable to immigration – had more than tripled the number of residents on the island by the turn of the century.

Meanwhile, Great Britain had its eye on Puerto Rico and was showing a readiness to acquire it. In 1797, after Napoleonic France and

Spain had declared war on Britain, a British fleet of 60 vessels manned by 9,000 troops under the command of General Abercromby landed at Boca de Cangrejos. On April 17, they took Santurce and quickly laid siege to the walled capital. Militia detachments from around the island arrived and launched a counter-attack. Abercromby ordered a retreat on May 1.

Shifting control

Napoleon's invasion of Spain in 1808 sent shock waves through the empire and led to a complete reorganization of colonial rule. As control over the transatlantic territories became

weakened, several countries in the Americas won independence from Spain. A provisional assembly called the *Cortes* was convened in Spain to rule in the name of the deposed King Ferdinand VII. Fearing that Puerto Rican separatists who sympathized with the rebellious colonialists in South and Central America – Mexico and Venezuela particularly – would instigate revolutions at home, the *Cortes* invited Puerto Rico to send a delegation to Cádiz in 1809.

An island Creole by the name of Ramón Power Giralt went as the colony's emissary and was elected vice-president of the assembly. He pushed for reforms designed to ameliorate the

LEFT: relics at Casa Blanca, Puerto Rico's first fort. **RIGHT:** the patron saint of sailors.

social and economic ills of the island. Puerto Ricans gained status as Spanish citizens; tariffs on machinery and tools were dropped; a university was founded, and measures were taken to improve island industry. The *Cortes* disbanded in 1814 when Napoleon retreated and King Ferdinand VII returned to the throne. But the king, wary of the independence fever pervading the colonies, left in place a fair number of Power Giralt's reforms in a *cédula de gracias* (royal decree) granted in 1815.

During the 10 years from 1795, trade between the United States and the Spanish West Indies grew by a factor of six. Household

goods, food and, to a minor extent, slaves were supplied by the United States in exchange for West Indian staples such as sugar, coffee, rum and spices. In 1803 Puerto Rico sent 263,000 pounds of sugar to the United States, and the amount exported grew yearly. In 1807 the US president, Thomas Jefferson, placed an embargo on all trade with the Spanish West Indies, which cut exports by more than half, but after Napoleon Bonaparte's invasion of the Iberian peninsula Jefferson lifted the embargo.

Not long after it was lifted, new difficulties floated into Puerto Rican harbors. Trying to respond to the threat Napoleon's armies posed on Spain's borders, the Spanish governor

called upon its colonies to ship an extraordinary supply of resources which could be used to outfit and maintain its own troops. With most profitable products going to Spain, Puerto Rico's economy suffered. And added to all these woes was the War of 1812 between Great Britain and the United States. The British blockade of the North American coast severely hampered American trade. Puerto Rico, by then one of the major suppliers of sugar to America, had nowhere to turn.

Increasing independence

The recovery following this tumultuous period included tremendous growth in the island economy. Power Giralt's economic reforms remained in place and, for the first time since their institution, began to have a real effect. Not only was trade with the wealthy United States permitted, but the tariffs were also decreased significantly. The *cédula de gracias* declared by Ferdinand VII in 1815 ended the Spanish trade monopoly in Puerto Rico by permitting trade with other countries. However, according to the dictates of the king, only Spanish vessels were allowed to carry on the exports. Once again, the colonial governors took exception to Spanish policy. Disobeying the king's orders, they gave right of entry to ships regardless of their origins. Also, under a civil intendancy plan instituted by Power Giralt, an independent official was appointed to oversee financial affairs, rather than their being left in the hands of the governor. Alejandro Ramírez Blanco filled the post first. During his tenure he opened several ports, abolished superfluous taxes, and increased the export of cattle.

Between 1813 and 1818 Puerto Rican trade grew to eight times its previous level, and in 1824 the king finally relinquished the last vestiges of mercantilism, conceding the right of Puerto Rican ports to harbor non-Spanish merchant ships. The future of the Puerto Rican economy became clear to many. Spain was neither a reliable nor a tremendously profitable trading partner, and the more Puerto Rico moved away from its dependence on the mother country, the faster its economy would develop. ❏

LEFT: the US flag flies prominently outside the University of Puerto Rico.
RIGHT: slave market in Puerto Rico.

SELF RULE AND THE UNITED STATES

"It wasn't much of a war, but it was all the war there was," said Teddy Roosevelt.

Even so, the Spanish-American War marked a turning point for Puerto Rico

In 1820 the population of Puerto Rico was estimated at 150,000. By 1900 it had mushroomed to about a million. The character of society had changed drastically; for the first time, agitators for Puerto Rican autonomy were vocal and posed a serious threat to the Spanish government. Increasingly, the royally appointed governor and the army would be identified as impediments to the achievement of Puerto Rican independence. In 1820 Pedro Dubois had scarcely initiated a recruitment program when he was discovered by the government. The governor incarcerated Dubois at El Morro and had him executed before a firing squad.

Three years after the Dubois incident, another event in the struggle for autonomy took place. After the restoration of Ferdinand to the throne in 1814, a series of governors with absolute power ruled Puerto Rico. On the first day of 1820, an army commander declared the liberal reformist constitution of 1812 to be still in effect. One by one officials of various districts joined him. The already weak king, hoping to avoid an all-out revolution, had to concede, and decided to resurrect the *Cortes,* disbanded in 1814. José María Quiñones went as the representative from Puerto Rico in 1823. He submitted a plan to introduce more autonomy to the island colonies, particularly in the administration of domestic affairs.

The *Cortes* approved the Quiñones proposal, but its intentions fell to pieces before it could see them through. In 1823 the constitutional government of Spain collapsed. The king returned to absolute power and appointed the first of 14 governors of Puerto Rico who exercised unlimited authority over the colony, collectively staging a 42-year reign of oppression and virtual martial law.

The first of these dictators was Miguel de la Torres. Hanging on to the governorship for 15 years, Torres imposed a 10 o'clock curfew and

established the *visita* – an island-wide inspection network that allowed him to keep abreast of activity in the colony and maintain tight security. Although Torres's reign was oppressive, it had some benefits. He took control of the country's development, built roads and bridges and brought in huge numbers of black

BETANCES.

slaves to foster sugar production, contributing significantly to the lasting development of the local economy.

Subversive beards

In 1838 a group of separatists led by Buenaventura Quiñones plotted a putsch. Word of the conspiracy leaked out and several of the participants were executed; the others were exiled. Declaring beards subversive, the new governor banned the wearing of facial hair. Subsequent governors passed laws aimed at the suppression of blacks (following the historic slave rebellion on Martinique) and instituted the *libreta* laws which required all inhabitants of

LEFT: battling in the Spanish-American War.
RIGHT: a "subversive beard", Dr Ramón Emeterio Betances spoke out against the authorities.

Puerto Rico to carry passbooks and restricted unauthorized movement. It was a troubled time for the beautiful island; between 1848 and 1867, seven consecutive military dictators governed the island, taking advantage of the institutions put into place by the Torres administration. To add to the colony's misery, in the 1850s a cholera epidemic swept across the island, claiming the lives of 30,000. Ramón Emeterío Betances, a doctor renowned for his efforts against the epidemic, was exiled in 1856 for his criticism of the colonial authorities.

Intimidated by the growing separatist fervor in Puerto Rico and Cuba, and by the Dominican

1870s under the aegis of the Puerto Rican Revolutionary Committee. Covert satellite organizations formed in villages and towns across Puerto Rico, centering around Mayagüez. On September 23, 1868, several hundred men congregated at a farm outside the northwestern mountain town of Lares. Marching under a banner that read *Libertad o Muerte. Viva Puerto Rico Libre. Año 1868* ("Liberty or Death. Long Live Free Puerto Rico. Year 1868") they took the town and arrested its officials. They elected a provisional president and proclaimed the Republic of Puerto Rico. The Republic would be short-lived. Troops sent by the governor met

Revolution in 1862, the crown of Spain invited Puerto Rico and Cuba in 1865 to draft a colonial constitution in the form of a "Special Law of the Indies". The documents which emerged called for the abolition of slavery, freedom of the press and speech, and independence on a commonwealth basis. While the crown dragged its feet in granting these concessions, in Puerto Rico the angry governor, José María Marchessi, exiled several leading reformists, including the recently returned Betances. Fleeing to New York, they joined with other separatist Puerto Ricans and Cubans.

From New York the autonomists directed the independence movement during the 1860s and

the rebel front at San Sebastián and won an easy victory. Within six weeks the echoes of the "Grito de Lares" – "the Shout of Lares" – had died completely, although it has retained lasting symbolic importance in the Puerto Rican independence movement.

Brief independence

Puerto Rico did enjoy a brief flash of autonomy in 1897. The Autonomist Party voted to fuse with the monarchist Liberal Party of Spain after forming a pact with its leader, Mateo Sagasta, which guaranteed Puerto Rican autonomy if the Liberals came to power. On the assassination of the Spanish prime minister

Sagasta became Spain's leader; he immediately declared Puerto Rico an autonomous state.

Adopting a two-chamber constitutional republican form of government, as agreed with Sagasta, the Puerto Ricans elected a lower house of assembly and half of the delegates to the upper house. The governor was still appointed by Spain, but his power was carefully restricted. The new government assumed power in July 1898. Later that month General Nelson A. Miles of the United States landed on the

LAST PRIZE?

When the US "won" Puerto Rico, only an eighth of the population was literate, and only one out of 14 children was in school.

ABOVE: 19th-century Spanish currency.

southern coast with an army of 16,000 men. It was the beginning of the Spanish-American War and the end of short-lived Puerto Rican autonomy.

The US steps in

"It wasn't much of a war, but it was all the war there was," Teddy Roosevelt reflected on the Spanish-American War. On August 31, 1898, Spain surrendered. The Puerto Rico campaign had lasted only two weeks, the whole war less than four months. General Miles tried to assuage the inhabitants' anxiety about annexation

as a United States protectorate, however, telling them: "We have come ... to promote your prosperity and to bestow upon you the immunities and blessing of the liberal institutions of our government." His assurances did not pacify everyone. Emeterío Betances, now aging, issued a warning to his fellow Puerto Ricans: "If Puerto Rico does not act fast, it will be an American colony forever."

On December 10, 1898, the Treaty of Paris, which settled the final terms of Spain's surrender, was signed. In addition to a large reparations payment, the United States won Puerto Rico and the Philippines from Spain, but Puerto Rico wasn't exactly a grand prize at the time. Its population had reached about a million. A third were blacks and mulattoes who generally had little capital or land. Two percent of the population owned more than two-thirds of the agricultural land, yet 60 percent of the land owned was mortgaged at high interest rates.

It ain't over till it's over

The United States set up a military government, and Puerto Rico was placed under the charge of the War Department. Assuming a hard-headed approach to underdevelopment and a lagging economy, the first three governors-general enjoyed almost dictatorial power. They introduced American currency, suspended defaulted mortgages and promoted trade with the United States. They improved public health, reformed tax laws and overhauled local government.

But to many Puerto Ricans, autonomy was still vital. A leading autonomist leader, Luis Muñoz Rivera, organized a new party in an attempt to reach a compromise between the separatists and the United States government. The Federal Party and its ally, the new Republican Party, advocated cooperation with the United States, especially in commercial matters, full civil rights and an autonomous civilian government. But not even the conciliatory approach Muñoz Rivera endorsed satisfied the McKinley administration. The colonial governor-general, George W. Davis, reported to the president that "the people generally have no conception of political rights combined with political responsibilities."

As if political turmoil were not enough, Mother Nature interfered in the form of Hurricane San Ciriaco in 1899. Three thousand people lost their lives, and the damage to property was immense. The hurricane devastated the vital sugar and coffee crops and left a fourth of the island's inhabitants without homes. The US Congress awarded only $200,000 to the island in relief payments.

Puerto Rico faced an unhappy future. The economy was on the brink of collapse, the hostilities with inept American administrators continued, and there were the apparently insurmountable difficulties of illiteracy and poverty. Things began to look up in 1900, when the Secretary of War, Elihu Root, proposed a program

culturally and economically if its bonds with the United States were to strengthen.

Puerto Rico looms large in recent American history. It was the first non-continental US territory and served as the test case for the formation and implementation of colonial policy.

Special interest groups in the United States polarized into two lobbies. The agricultural contingent, fearing competition from Puerto Rican producers whose labor costs were lower, allied with racists who dreaded the influx of the "Latin race" which would result from granting American citizenship to Puerto Ricans. And as proof of Benjamin Franklin's observation

for the gradual introduction of autonomy for Puerto Ricans which President McKinley endorsed. However, though Puerto Rico was suddenly closer to autonomy than it had been since before the Spanish-American War, the path to home rule was not clear yet.

The big debate

For the next 48 years, Puerto Rico and the US had a strange colonial-protectorate relationship. While it was widely acknowledged that the latter possessed enormous wealth from which the former stood to benefit, Puerto Ricans also feared that Betances' prediction would come true – that Puerto Rico would be swallowed up

that politics makes strange bedfellows, these opponents of the administration's Puerto Rican colonial plan found themselves under the blankets with liberal Democrats who opposed imperialism of any sort.

The burgeoning of a colony

With the passing in 1900 of the Foraker Act (*see box on facing page*), Puerto Rico took on a new colonial status, but reception of the Act could have been better. An immediate challenge

ABOVE: US and Puerto Rican flags fly harmoniously over Fuerte San Cristóbal.
RIGHT: American medical officers at Coamo Springs.

to its constitutional legality brought it before the Supreme Court of the United States where the majority declared that constitutionality was not applicable in an "unincorporated entity" like Puerto Rico. Dissenting Chief Justice Fuller wrote that it left Puerto Rico "a disembodied shade in an intermediate state of ambiguous existence".

Reluctant US citizens

On the eve of the United States entry into World War I in 1917, President Wilson approved the Jones-Shafroth Act granting US citizenship to all Puerto Ricans. This Act affronted many Puerto Rican statesmen. For years they had pressed for a break from the US and now, in blatant contradiction of their demands, Congress was drawing them in even more. Muñoz Rivera, the Resident Commissioner, had beseeched Congress to hold a plebiscite – but to no avail. The "Catch-22" of Puerto Rico's relationship with the US had emerged full-blown. The more political maturity the colony showed, the more fervently nationalists agitated for independence. The more hostile to the US the colony seemed to American lawmakers, the more reluctant they were to give any ground.

THE FORAKER ACT

On April 2, 1900, US President McKinley signed a civil law that established a civilian government in Puerto Rico. Although officially known as the Organic Act of 1900, it was more commonly referred to as the Foraker Act for its sponsor, Charles Benson Foraker.

The new government had a presidentially appointed governor, an Executive Council comprising both Americans and Puerto Ricans, and a House of Delegates with 35 elected members. There was also a judicial system with a Supreme Court. All federal laws of the United States were to be in effect on the island. In addition, a Resident Commissioner chosen by the Puerto Rican people would speak for the colony in the House of Representatives, but have no vote. The first civil governor of the island under the Act was Charles H. Allen, inaugurated on May 1, 1900, in San Juan.

An initial 15-percent tariff was imposed on all imports to and exports from the United States, and the revenues would be used to benefit Puerto Rico. Free trade was promised after two years. The colonial government would determine its own taxation programs and oversee the insular treasury. Ownership of large estates by American corporations was discouraged by prohibiting businesses to carry on agriculture on more than 500 acres. However, this clause was rarely enforced and capital-rich firms from the US moved in.

During this period of antagonism between Puerto Rico and the US, the economy and the population grew rapidly. Efforts to combat poor health care and disease had resulted in a precipitous drop in the death rate. Meanwhile, employment increased, production skyrocketed, and government revenues rose. Big US corporations pocketed most of the profits from this growth, and their sway with Congress assured them of continued wealth. The average Puerto Rican family earned between $150 and $200 a year; many *jíbaros* had sold their own little farms to work for farm estates and factories.

Pablo Iglesias, a disciple of Samuel Gompers,

one of the great fathers of American trade unions, led the move to organize Puerto Rican laborers. By 1909 the labor movement, organized under Iglesias' leadership as the Free Federation, identified itself with the labor union movement in the US. It even assumed the task of Americanizing Puerto Rico. "The labor movement in Porto [sic] Rico," Iglesias wrote, "has no doubt been, and is, the most efficient and safest way of conveying the sentiments and feelings of the American people to the hearts of the people of Porto Rico." A 1914 cigar strike and then a 1915 cane strike brought useful publicity. Iglesias was elected to the new Senate of Puerto Rico in 1917.

Trouble-shooting

The Great Depression of the 1930s nearly undid Puerto Rico. Two hurricanes accompanied the collapse of the economy – San Felipe in 1928 and San Cipriano in 1932 – destroying millions of dollars' worth of property and crops. Starvation and disease took a heavy toll on the population during the Depression. Across the island, haggard, demoralized people waited in long queues for inadequate government food handouts. But out of the poverty and deprivation, a new voice emerged.

It belonged to Pedro Albizu Campos, a former US Army officer and a graduate of Harvard Law School. He was of a generation of Puerto Ricans who were children at the time of the United States' takeover. Equipped with a great understanding of the American system, he used it to become a leader of militant revolutionaries. Albizu Campos's accusation was that (according to both American foreign policy and international law) the United States' claims on Puerto Rico were in fact illegal, since Puerto Rico was already autonomous at the time of occupation.

The strength and seriousness of Albizu Campos's Nationalist organization were made abundantly clear on February 23, 1936. Two of his followers, Hiram Rosado and Elías Beauchamp, shot and killed the chief of police of San Juan. The assassins were arrested and summarily beaten to death, and Albizu Campos and seven key party members were imprisoned in the Federal Prison in Georgia.

A year later, however, the party was still strong. Denied a permit to hold a demonstration in the town of Ponce, a group of Albizu Campos's followers dressed in black shirts assembled to march on March 21, 1937. As the procession moved forward to the tune of *La Borinqueña* – the Puerto Rican anthem – a shot rang out. The origin of the gunfire has never been determined, but within moments police and marchers were exchanging bullets. Twenty people were killed and another hundred wounded in the panic-stricken crossfire that subsequently ensued. The governor called the affair "a riot"; the American Civil Liberties Union labeled it "a massacre". The event is still remembered today as *La Massacre de Ponce*. ❏

LEFT: the Puerto Rican national crest.
RIGHT: sugar-cane harvest near Guayama.

MODERN TIMES

Colony or commonwealth? Or independent state? Luis Muñoz Marín helped
decide the issue with the innovative "Operation Bootstrap"

The United States began to export Puerto Rico's share of the New Deal in 1933, but it was not a winning hand. President Franklin Roosevelt sent a string of appointees to the Governor's Mansion in San Juan, but their efforts proved inadequate and aggravating to many Puerto Ricans. Then, from amidst the crumbling political parties, a brilliant star in Puerto Rico's history appeared.

Luis Muñoz Marín, son of the celebrated statesman Luis Muñoz Rivera, had served in government since 1932 and had used his charm and connections with the American political elite to bring attention to the plight of the colony. In 1938, young Muñoz Marín founded the Partido Democratico Popular (PDP), running on the slogan "Bread, Land and Liberty", and adopting the *pava* – the broad-brimmed straw hat worn by *jíbaros* – as the party symbol. In 1940, the *populares* took over half the total seats in the upper and lower Houses.

A people's governor

Muñoz Marín, elected leader of the Senate, decided to try to work with the new governor to achieve recovery. The appointee, Rexford Guy Tugwell, was refreshingly different from his predecessors. Able to speak Spanish and evincing a genuine compassion for the Puerto Ricans, he seemed promising. Muñoz Marín's good faith paid off. By improving the distribution of relief resources and by proposing a plan for long-term economic development contingent upon continued union with the United States, Muñoz Marín convinced Tugwell that Puerto Rico was finally ready to assume the responsibility of electing its own governor.

As a first step, the United States appointed Puerto Rico's resident commissioner, Jesús Piñero, to the post. In 1946 Piñero became the first native governor in the island's history. Simultaneously, the United States

unveiled plans for the popular election of Puerto Rico's governor, demonstrating new confidence in the colony.

The people elected Muñoz Marín, of course. In 1948 he took office as the first popularly elected governor and put forward his proposal for turning Puerto Rico into an *Estado Libre*

Puerto Rico

PUERTO RICO WANTS YOU

Asociado – an associated free state. Learning from the newly independent Philippines, where instant autonomy had crippled economic and social progress, the US delayed endorsing Muñoz Marín's plan.

However, in 1950, President Truman approved Public Law 600, the Puerto Rican Commonwealth Bill. It provided for a plebiscite in which voters would decide whether to remain a colony or assume status as a commonwealth. As the latter, Puerto Rico would draft its own constitution, though the US Congress would retain "paramount power." In June 1951, Puerto Ricans voted three to one in favor of the commonwealth.

LEFT: tuna plant, Mayagüez. Industries such as this boomed under Operation Bootstrap.
RIGHT: Uncle Sam's daughter.

Two disturbing events punctuated the otherwise smooth transition to commonwealth status. On the very day that President Truman signed Public Law 600, a group of armed Nationalists marched on the Governor's Mansion, La Fortaleza. In a brief skirmish a policeman and four Nationalists were gunned down. Simultaneously, outbursts in five other towns including Ponce and Arecibo left over a hundred casualties, including 27 dead. The violence extended beyond Puerto Rican shores. Two Puerto Ricans from New York traveled to Washington and made an attempt on the president's life a month later. In March 1954, four

Puerto Rican Nationalists, shouting *"Viva Puerto Rico Libre!"*, fired into the House of Representatives from the visitors' gallery, wounding five Congressmen.

Muñoz Marín resigned from political office in 1964 but his party remained in power. In 1966 a commission determined that commonwealth, statehood and independence all deserved consideration. Seven months later the PDP, pushing for a decision, passed a bill mandating a plebiscite. Muñoz Marín re-entered the fray in support of continuing as a commonwealth. He argued that Puerto Rico had been placed fourth in the worldwide rate of economic progress only due to its relationship with the

US. Further, he claimed, statehood could easily bring an end to the independent culture of Puerto Rico. His arguments held sway; two-thirds of the ballots in 1967 were cast for commonwealth status.

Muñoz Marín had long ago recognized that the key to averting future economic catastrophe lay in avoiding a dependence on agriculture. Relying heavily on one or two crops left Puerto Rico subject to too many risks: weather, foreign production and interest rates. The government established the Puerto Rican Industrial Development Corporation in 1942 to oversee the development of government-sponsored manufacturing. When the state plans floundered, the administration canceled the program and initiated a new plan, known as Operation Bootstrap.

Aimed at developing an economy based on rum, tourism and industry, the program sent dozens of public relations agents to the mainland on promotional tours. An advertising campaign extolled the virtues of the Puerto Rican climate, geography, economy and people.

During the early years of Operation Bootstrap, jobs in manufacturing quadrupled to over 20,000, but between 1950 and 1954 over 100,000 Puerto Ricans moved to the mainland in order to take advantage of the post-war labor market. In New York, Puerto Ricans became the archetypal Latinos, later celebrated in Bernstein's *West Side Story*, the film version of which starred the Puerto Rican actress Rita Moreno.

A slowdown followed the resumption of peace, but in 1955 manufacturing contributed more to the economy than agriculture for the first time ever.

Operation Serenity

As a complement to Operation Bootstrap, the government instituted a program entitled "Operation Serenity", which had the uplifting of the arts as its objective. Programs to promote music and art were administered by the Institute of Puerto Rican Culture. The thinking at the time was that "man cannot live by bread alone". Poster-making got its start at the Department of Community Education, where serigraph and lithograph techniques were developed. Puerto

LEFT: Luis Muñoz Marín, Puerto Rico's brilliant political star and the first popularly elected governor.
RIGHT: Rita Moreno in *West Side Story*.

Rico's newfound skill of poster-making promoted government instructional films and art exhibits, and portrayed local history. A large group of artists and filmmakers were able to develop their skills through the Community Education programs.

Today, the production of Puerto Rico's imaginative posters goes back to those days in the 1950s when the islanders began to pick themselves up from their meager conditions.

Tax holiday

Operation Bootstrap later evolved into Section 936, a clause in the US Internal Revenue Code that partially exempted manufacturers from having to pay federal income tax on profits earned by their subsidiaries located in Puerto Rico. Thanks to 936, some 2,000 factories now operate throughout the island, churning out everything from Microsoft floppy disks to Star Kist tuna, all for the huge American market.

In 1985, when Section 936 was threatened by Congressional budget-cutters, former governor Rafael Hernández Colón came up with a novel approach to save it: he offered to link 936 to President Reagan's Caribbean Basin Initiative, a trade program designed to help

POPULAR CULTURE: A PUERTO RICAN HALL OF FAME

Rita Moreno's fiery performance in the 1961 film of *West Side Story* not only made her a household name around the globe, it also set the stage for a string of Puerto Ricans to make their mark on popular culture. José Ferrer and Raul Juliá also enjoyed much success in the world of film, while television – particularly American TV – became the medium of choice for journalist Geraldo Rivera, *CHiPs* star Erik Estrada (born in New York to Puerto Rican parents) and Ricky Martin of *General Hospital* fame.

Celebrities on the music scene have included José Feliciano and salsa singer Tony Vega. The ever popular Tito Puente continues to wow international audiences with his form of latin jazz. A classically trained percussionist, Puente is also an accomplished composer.

Puerto Rico has also had its share of household names when it comes to sport world. Topping this list is baseball Hall-of-Famer Roberto Clemente, with other baseball greats including Hiram Bithorn (the first Puerto Rican to play in the major leagues), Orlando Cepeda and Roberto Alomar.

Achieving fame for his prowess in the ring was boxer Hector "Macho" Camacho, while jockey Angel Cordero Jr was well known in horse-racing circles. The world of golf, too, has its famous Puerto Rican: Juan "Chichi" Rodríguez remains a popular figure on the Seniors Tour in the US.

Drug Country

Mention Caribbean drug exports, and most people are likely to think of *ganja* being smuggled out on leaky boats, or vials of cocaine tucked into airplane carry-on luggage. In Puerto Rico, however, drugmaking generally means the manufacturing of pharmaceuticals – the legal kind – for large-scale shipment to the United States and other countries.

Drugs, in fact, are very big business here. Some $6 billion worth of medications are produced and exported every year, making pharmaceuticals the

island's most important industry and accounting for more than a quarter of its gross domestic product. More than 100 drug companies have plants in Puerto Rico, including just about every pharmaceutical firm on the Fortune 500 list. And they churn out thousands of products, from Anacin (for headache relief) to Zantac (an over-the-counter ulcer medication).

In addition, a dizzying variety of prescription tranquilizers, anti-hypertensives, cardiovascular drugs and birth-control pills also carry the "Made in Puerto Rico" label.

All are manufactured here because of the now defunct Section 936, a job-creating clause of the United States Internal Revenue Code. For years,

this complicated law exempted companies from paying federal income tax on profits generated by their Puerto Rican operations. Although the law is no more, its benefits for companies already here continue until the year 2006.

Abbott Laboratories has spent $200 million – the largest single expansion in Puerto Rican history – on enlarging its bulk pharmaceutical operation in Barceloneta, west of San Juan. Abbott manufactures nutritional, pharmaceutical, diagnostic, chemical and agricultural products on the island.

In 1997, ICN Pharmaceuticals acquired Roche's pharmaceutical product line and bought its modern manufacturing plant in Humacao. Other companies include American Home Products Corp., Bristol-Myers Squibb Co., Eli Lilly Industries and Johnson & Johnson.

Beside the drugs, companies also manufacture health-care products such as intravenous solutions, blood-pressure kits and thermometers on the island. Puerto Rico's largest private employer is Baxter Healthcare Corp., which has 6,000 workers in nine factories and three service centers.

One of the first drugmakers to set up shop here was Searle & Co., which in 1969 established a huge factory in Caguas. By the mid-1980s, the island had surpassed New Jersey in US drug production and was well on its way to becoming the pharmaceutical capital of the world.

Today, modern, state-of-the-art drug factories can be found just about everywhere in Puerto Rico, even in remote mountain towns like Maricao and Jayuya. The industry seems most prevalent, however, in Carolina (in the Metropolitan San Juan area), and in the Arecibo-Barceloneta-Manatí strip along Puerto Rico's northern coast.

Hidden behind high fences, island drug factories generally have the greenest lawns anywhere, thanks to careful landscaping and rich chemical effluents in the wastewater. Their workers are well-paid, often earning as much as $10 an hour – the highest average manufacturing wage of any industry in Puerto Rico.

Some towns are almost entirely dependent on these companies – and on the jobs and business they generate. In Humacao, for example – in addition to the Roche/ICN manufacturing plant – Medtronic of Minneapolis assembles pacemakers, Sandoz of Switzerland makes Ex-Lax, and Syntex of Panama produces birth-control pills – all within 10 minutes of each other. ❏

LEFT: pharmaceutical production in Caguas.

the struggling economies of Central America and the Caribbean. As a result of the deal, 936 was rescued, and Puerto Rico agreed to fund at least $100 million worth of development projects a year in selected CBI beneficiary nations.

Yet in the end, all the lobbying in the world was not enough to save 936: 1997 budget cuts eventually brought it down, thus eliminating the tax benefits to mainland companies of operating on the island.

US subsidies and direct manufacturing in-

are 1½ million cars on the island, almost one for every two inhabitants, and fuel consumption is half of the Caribbean total.

On the other hand, Puerto Rico is plagued with overpopulation, high unemployment, water contamination, deforestation, a high incidence of Aids and a frightening number of serious crimes. Around 800 murders are committed every year on the island, making it one of the most violent places in the Caribbean outside Haiti. Sociologists blame many of the problems on

> **GREAT STRIDES**
>
> Today, Puerto Rico has an 89 percent literacy rate – a big improvement over 1898, when only an eighth of the population could read.

vestment have given Puerto Rico a per-capita income of around $7,000. Though this is far less than the poorest US state, Mississippi, it tops most other Caribbean islands and outranks anywhere in Latin America. Puerto Rico, in fact, has one of the highest standards of living in the Caribbean.

Prosperity is measured in other ways in this region. Houses here are all built of concrete now, unlike most other Caribbean islands. Virtually every Puerto Rican family owns a TV set; nearly all enjoy telephone services; there

---

ABOVE: a well-thought-out political statement on a hidden wall.

the identity crisis caused by Puerto Rico's unsure political status.

Under commonwealth status, Puerto Ricans are exempt from US federal income tax, though they do pay personal income taxes to their own government, and are subjected to the US Army draft. Proportionately more Puerto Ricans died in Vietnam – all having been sent there by a president for whom they could not vote. In 1986 a Puerto Rican pilot was shot down in an air raid against Libya's Colonel Qadaffi. In 1993 the first casualty in Somalia was Puerto Rican.

Because Puerto Rico is not an independent nation, there is no Puerto Rican passport, and travel to the US mainland is unrestricted. Some 2½ million now live in *los Estados*, about half of them in New York City. These *Neoyorkinos*, however, still maintain close links with their homeland.

Although island residents cannot vote in US presidential elections, they *can* vote in the Democratic and Republican primaries, which is why presidential candidates sometimes campaign here. Puerto Ricans also elect a resident commissioner to the US House of Representatives who has a voice – but no vote – on legislative matters.

Two parties are fighting to change that. The

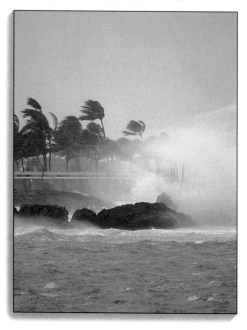

Partido Nuevo Progressivo (PNP), founded in 1968, wants to make Puerto Rico the 51st state. This, the party claims, would rapidly give the island economic parity with the rest of the US, though it wants to keep sufficient sovereignty to participate separately in the Olympics and the Miss Universe contest.

At the other end of the spectrum is the Partido Independentista Puertorriqueño (PIP). The PIP dreams of a republic free of US influence. These *independentistas* make lots of headlines, but they rarely win more than 5 percent of the island votes.

A third party, the Partido Democratico Popular (PDP), favors continued commonwealth

status and sees both statehood and independence as potential economic and social disasters. A plebiscite in 1993 showed a narrow majority opposed to statehood, with the majority preferring the status quo.

The controversy continued in 1998, which marked the 100th anniversary of the US occupation of Puerto Rico. In December, another plebiscite saw about 51 percent voting for the fifth alternative on the ballot – "None of the Above" – narrowly defeating the 46 percent who opted for statehood. Less than 3 percent favoured independence. It seems that the status problem is destined to remain unresolved – and an ever-volatile, endlessly discussed issue – for some time to come.

Weather woes

Hurricanes and tropical storms have played a major role in island life ever since San Ciriaco struck in 1899. Almost 100 years later, in 1998, Puerto Rico sustained huge losses as Hurricane Georges swept from east to west, wreaking havoc throughout every area of the island. The death toll was 12, but widespread loss of both the natural environment and man-made structures will ensure replanting and rebuilding for years to come. It was estimated that 400,000 trees were either lost or severely damaged, and about 80,000 homes were destroyed.

When Georges struck, the island had just recovered from four hurricanes that caused great devastation: Hugo in 1989, Luis and Marilyn in 1995 and Hortense in 1997. Before Georges, the last hurricane to traverse the entire island was San Felipe in 1927.

Immediately after Georges' swath of destruction, Puerto Rico was declared a disaster area by US President Bill Clinton and his wife, Hillary Rodham Clinton, who visited the island to assess the devastation. The estimated loss in property was $2 billion. The US Congress allocated $74 million in emergency funds to help in the recovery. Federal Emergency Management Agency officials were on hand within days to help residents to recoup their property losses, but the sting of Georges will linger on well into the 21st century. ❑

ABOVE: prelude to disaster: waves crash on the rocks near San Juan as Hurricane Georges draws near.
RIGHT: one of Puerto Rico's major attractions is its golf courses, like Las Palmas near Humacao.

PEOPLE AND SOCIETY

Nearly everyone comes from somewhere else. But the wide range of ethnic types

has forged a proud and dynamic Hispanic culture

There is a song, one among many, which stands as the most evocative of what it means to live in the paradise which is Puerto Rico. If it does not exist in fact – there is squalor amid the great natural beauty, a certain sadness amid the promise – this paradise exists in the heart.

Written by José Manuel Rivera, *Mi Tierra Borincana* extols with deceptive simplicity the reasons to endure the *tapones* (traffic jams) in San Juan, the ineptitude of certain bureaucracies, and even the preciousness of certain resources – water in particular – which Continentals (non-Puerto Ricans from the mainland who come to live here) too often take for granted or with impatience.

"How beautiful it is, to live in this dreamland! And how beautiful it is to be the master of the *coquí's* song!" as the song says. "What an advantage it is to reap the coffee of this great gift!"

In a certain sense the lyrics are themselves an illusion, yet in another they're very real. For while life on the island for natives and immigrants alike is not what it was 20 or even 10 years ago – there is more crime and unemployment in the bigger cities; its working class works harder for what seems to be less and less – its lure, for those who truly love Puerto Rico, is not diminished.

Living anywhere within the commonwealth requires a balance of cleverness, common sense, and hard realism for Puerto Ricans and Continentals alike. Opulence is hardly uncommon among those who can afford it – in the wealthier suburbs of San Juan, for example, a modest-looking three-bedroom house with a small yard can cost upwards of $200,000 – but even so the display of wealth isn't encouraged.

Look beyond the suntanned tourists enjoying the sunshine on the beaches, the glass-fronted modern buildings of Metropolitan San Juan and the coastal factories, and you'll see the attraction of what remains: a Caribbean countryside of small, colorful towns filled with locals – always ready with a smile and a greeting – chatting peacefully in the plaza, selling

their produce at roadside stands or taking a stroll in the night air.

The Puerto Rican people are a friendly and passionate lot, vivacious and expressive in their conversations – and their dancing. Music and food are two essential elements which the people – young and old – use to help them celebrate life to the fullest.

Sense of pleasure

What's important here is a sense of belonging, acquired largely through willing readjustment to Puerto Rico's pace. The practice of businesses closing for a long lunchtime *siesta* isn't as prevalent as it used to be, due mostly to the

PRECEDING PAGES: Spanish colonial house, Guayama; loading plantains.
LEFT: a typical smiling Puerto Rican welcome.
RIGHT: costumed children on parade in Old San Juan during the Carnival.

increasing use of air-conditioning, but it still happens. And the attitude behind it is certainly quite a healthy one. It's an attitude which sees work not as an end in itself, but merely as a means to fund subsequent enjoyment.

Weekends are taken very seriously, and major holidays, especially Christmas, even more so. In the United States, Christmas lasts perhaps a week; on the island the celebrations begin in late November and don't stop until mid-January.

In addition to Christmas Day, Puerto Ricans

the last glasses of *coquíto* (a mix of milk, rum, vanilla and cinnamon) consumed.

Local produce

Though the University of Puerto Rico's ambitious School of Agriculture continues to experiment with ways of growing the kinds of produce which now have to be imported, fruits and vegetables which are almost ubiquitously common in the States are usually hard to find.

And yet, who needs apples when there are still trucks along almost every major road sell-

> ### RELIGIOUS TIES
>
> Some 85 percent of Puerto Ricans are member of the Roman Catholic Church.

celebrate Three Kings' Day, or Epiphany, on January 6. Following tradition, local children cut grass (to feed the Wise Men's camels), put it in boxes and place them under their beds on January 5, just before they go to sleep. The next morning, the grass is gone and gifts have been left in its place – much to the delight of the youngsters throughout the island.

During this long holiday period, it's presumed by residents that there will be company, people coming from far away to visit or just neighbors stopping by from roughly December 15 (also the official start of the tourist season, which ends on April 15 of the following year) until the last *pasteles* (tamales) are eaten and

ing native oranges – *chinas* ("chee-nas") – at a few dollars for a big bag? Despite the incursion of a horde of mainland products of dubious nutritional repute, *comida Criolla* is still the food of the day in most households.

It's heavy food, rich with an invigorating assortment of beans, from *arroz con habichuelas* (rice with either small pink beans or kidney beans) and *arroz con gandules* (pigeon peas) to *lechón asado* (whole roast suckling pig) prepared almost exclusively for holidays and large family gatherings, and its counterpart, *perníl* (fresh picnic ham in most Stateside butcher shops and supermarkets). Both are seasoned with *adóbo*, a thick, fragrant paste of garlic, vinegar, peppercorns, and parsley or oregano.

Strangely, for a place with so much marine bounty – its waters are full of grouper, yellow-tail, spiny lobster, squid, sea snail, conch and shark – native Puerto Ricans prefer chicken and pork. However, red snapper, shrimp (*camarones*) and *langosta* (lobster) are enjoyed by the locals, as is salt cod – known as *bacalao* – which is a staple. Seafood lovers will find plenty of good restaurants to choose from, as well as local *fondas*, where specialties such as *mofongo relleno* (battered spiced plantain) with *mariscos* (seafood) are firm favorites. The most

for the ratio of motor vehicles to people; nearly one for every two inhabitants – is there any indication that anyone is in a hurry. Here, assertive driving is considered an asset.

Automobiles are bought for either practical-ity or show, and those who buy for show know they're taking risks. Amazingly, Puerto Rico consumes half the gasoline in the Caribbean, even though it is more expensive here than on the US mainland. The island's poverty has been a sad and consistent fact of life. It explains in part the decorative but restrictive iron grillwork known as *rejas*, found on almost every middle- and upper-class home.

popular local snacks include *alcapurrias*, meat or crab fritters, (*see also "Puerto Rican Cuisine", page 75*).

Siestas, cars and crime

With or without the benefits of a *siesta*, quality eating, still done mostly during the lunch hour, tends to make the pace of transacting business a little slower: even, perhaps, more sensible. Only behind the wheels of the island's 1½ million cars – Puerto Rico ranks sixth in the world

Sadly, violent crime, and that includes every-thing from carjacking to murder, plagues Puerto Rico like never before. On December 31 each year, local newspapers announce a new high in the annual homicide tally. Surveys consistently show voters are far more con-cerned about increasing crime than political status or anything else. The violence is blamed largely on drugs – as is the island's severe Aids epidemic. Politicians haven't found solutions to any of these problems, but in the mid-1990s the government did increase the number of police officers, put harsher prison sentences into force for drug dealers, and carry out an increasing number of drugs and arms raids.

LEFT: shooting craps at a San Juan casino.
ABOVE: goat salesmen at a local flea market take shelter from the rain.

Barrios and barriers

In the meantime, wealthier Puerto Ricans are protecting themselves from crime by closing their neighborhoods to outsiders. Today, many of San Juan's best *urbanizaciones* – Parkville, Caparra Heights and Torrimar, to name a few – are islands unto themselves; the streets leading to them are barricaded with electronic gates that open only to residents and approved visitors. The closed neighborhoods, unheard of 10 years ago, have sparked debates over the legality of such practices. Until the crime rate comes down, however, they are sure to continue.

Puerto Rico's ills may also be attributed to

sheer overpopulation. Because of traditionally high birth rates and medical advances that caused the death rate to plummet shortly after the Spanish-American War, Puerto Rico's population jumped to about a million by 1900, and now stands at around 3.8 million. This gives the island a population density of nearly 1,100 per square mile (425 per sq km), among the world's highest. Only Bangladesh, the Maldives, Barbados, Taiwan, South Korea and the city-states of Hong Kong and Singapore are more crowded. Indeed, if it weren't for the safety valve that allows Puerto Ricans unrestricted travel to the American mainland, the island might have 5 million people today.

For administrative purposes, Puerto Rico is divided into 78 municipalities. They range in size from Arecibo and Ponce, with more than 100 square miles (260 sq km), to 6-square-mile (15-sq.-km) Cataño. Population-wise, the largest *municipio* is San Juan, with more than 430,000 people; the smallest is offshore Culebra, with only 2,000.

Driving in Puerto Rico is on the right-hand side, unlike in the nearby Virgin Islands, where motorists drive on the left. Adding to the confusion is the fact that the island adheres half-heartedly to the metric system, which means that all distances are posted in kilometers, and gasoline is sold by the liter. Nevertheless, temperatures are still given in Fahrenheit rather than Celsius, and speed-limit signs are still in miles per hour (in order to accommodate the speedometers of American-made cars). This is unlikely to change as long as Puerto Rico remains under the US flag.

Español sí, inglés no!

A far more contentious issue is the language debate. For 90 years the island had two official languages, Spanish and English. Then, in 1991, former Governor Rafael Hernández Colón – citing Puerto Rico's "cultural heritage" – abolished English as an official language. This won him Spain's Prince of Asturias award and praise from the *independentistas*, but sparked an outcry from many local educators and business people. The controversy heated up further when Hernández Colón's pro-statehood successor, Pedro Rosselló, took office in January 1993. One of the first things he did was restore English's official status, making Puerto Rico once again bilingual.

Regardless of the law, fewer than a fourth of Puerto Ricans are completely bilingual; outside the big cities you will need a few basic words of Spanish to get around.

Puerto Rico is a place of which it can truly be said everyone comes from somewhere else. There are the traces of Taíno and Carib blood left in the fine, high cheekbones and caught in the depths of the deep and beautiful eyes of many of those whose families have lived on the island for generations. In the town of Loíza, in fact, the evidence of the island's slave-trading days is impossible to ignore. There are women with skin the color of *café con leche* – the strong coffee with hot milk which is a staple on every breakfast table – whose tightly curly hair is naturally auburn, and children with liquid blue eyes and blond hair whose faces are exotically beautiful, thanks to any number of forebears – traders, pirates, artisans, slaves and colonists.

Patriotism

Despite all varieties of political difference, pride is universal and strong. Though US flags fly alongside all Puerto Rican flags in public places (by law), and, schoolchildren sing *The Star Spangled Banner* before *La Bor-*

THE LONE STAR

Although officially adopted in 1952, Puerto Rico's flag was first used in 1895; its "lone star" was the "guide of the patriots".

Fajardo, Vieques and Culebra have a well-honed sense of humor towards its less-than-pristine equipment. It might take two hours. It might take six. *Así es la vida.* That's life.

There is, however, determination beneath that patience. The attitude of many toward the US Navy, which maintains a major base at Sabana Seca and conducts maneuvers in and around the island's waters, ranges from conspicuously faint affection to undisguised resentment.

This was especially acute in 1970, when

inqueña, the island's own beautiful anthem, being Puerto Rican always comes first. This isn't without its paradoxical side. The people who've chosen to live here, Puerto Ricans and Continentals alike, love the island intensely yet know that many things are far from perfect. That's where patience, cleverness and common sense come into play.

The Ports Authority (Autoridad de Puertos), for example, is the only municipal agency which consistently makes a profit. Yet those who rely on the ferries it operates between

LEFT: selling oysters.
ABOVE: family party on Flamenco Beach, Culebra.

Culebrans were kept off Flamenco Beach – as they had been for decades – during practice bombing runs.

"Enough," said 2,000 people all at once. The red flag went up to keep people off the beach; the majority of the population headed straight for it, loaded with picnic coolers. They were going to picnic until the Navy stopped its target runs so close to their beach. Three years later, the Navy finally agreed to leave Flamenco Beach alone.

Continentals who relocate to the bigger cities and their environs learn very quickly from their neighbors how to be practical. It's unwise, and downright foolish in some places, to flaunt

wealth with fancy cars and grand houses filled with expensive possessions. To grow too attached to property is almost to court losing it.

As a result, and in no small way a fortunate one, what the island's residents really cherish are the things which have no price tags: family, friends and the pleasure, challenging as it can be, of living here. Even the tradition of family, however, has changed, moving from the old extended collection of various uncles, aunts and grandparents to a more nuclear one.

Puerto Rico's national anthem expresses it best. Unlike other nations' songs, which speak glowingly of military might and triumph over adversaries, *La Borinqueña* is a celebration of a reality which is at the same time an ideal:

> *The land of Borinquen,*
> *where I was born*
> *is a flowering garden*
> *of exquisite magic.*
>
> *A sky, always clear,*
> *serves as its canopy,*
> *and sings calm lullabies*
> *to the waves at its feet.*
>
> *When Columbus came*
> *to its beaches,*
> *he exclaimed full of admiration*
> *Oh! Oh! Oh!*
>
> *This is the beautiful land*
> *I've been looking for;*
> *it's Borinquen, the daughter,*
> *the daughter of the sea and the sun,*
> *the sea and the sun.*

Puerto Rico is a place where beauty co-exists on occasions with squalor; a place where politics and poetry very often merge; a place where its most celebrated leaders, among them Luis Llorens Torres and Luis Muñoz Marín, were also poets.

There is poverty, certainly, a chronic ache to those who love their island. But art flourishes here too, with the craftworkers, the musicians, the composers, the playwrights and painters and sculptors and actors. It gives Puerto Rico's beauty a face which is proud yet edged in sadness, exotic yet utterly recognizable. ❑

LEFT: street party during the San Sebastián festival.

A LAND OF FANTASTIC FESTIVALS

Puerto Ricans express their zest for life through a succession of exuberant celebrations. Many have their origins in the island's strong Catholicism

No matter where or when you go, Puerto Ricans always seem to be celebrating some-thing – be it a saint's feast day or a cultural tradition. First and foremost are the *fiestas patronales*, or patron saint festivals, during which each town honors the area's patron saint. Incredibly, there are 78 of these, beginning on January 6 and continuing straight through December 12, and the festivities at each last 10 days. So, in theory, you can party your way around the island non-stop.

And this isn't even taking into consideration the *other* festivals, which all celebrate something, no matter how insignificant it may seem.

In April, for instance, Juana Díaz hosts the Maví Festival, which honors *maví*, a fermented drink made from the bark of the ironwood tree.

With farming being a dominant occupation, harvest festivals abound. Yauco and Maricao both have Coffee Harvest Festivals in February, while the picturesque western town of San Germán marks the end of the island's sugar harvest in April with an appropriate celebration.

If you have to choose, three of the best festivals are the Carnival in Ponce (February), where the *vejigante* masks were first created; Loíza's *fiesta* of Santiago Apóstol (July) and the Hatillo Masks Festival (December).

All feature music, dancing, ornate masks and costumes, games, religious processions, shows, parades, much drink and food, food, food. It's hard not to join in the dancing, and to forget about the diet.

◁ **ROYALTY FOR A DAY**
San Juan's Children's Parade at Carnival time is a kid's dream come true.

△ **ANYTHING GOES**
Parades feature costumed marchers, bands, floats – and generally anyone who wants to tag along.

◁ SPIRIT CHASERS

Garishly dressed masked *vejigantes* roam the streets during the island's *fiestas patronales* to chase away evil spirits.

△ BEJEWELED BEAUTIES

Festival time shows off the country's attractive ladies – and there are many. Puerto Rico has proudly produced two Miss Universes.

◁ TIME TO DANCE

An essential element of *any* festival is music and dance. Folk dances include the *bomba*, of pure African origin, and the *plena*, which blends elements from the island's many cultures.

THE CATHOLIC CONNECTION

With all the colorful costumes and riotous behavior, it is easy to forget that many of Puerto Rico's festivals – particularly the *fiestas patronales* – have religious roots. Religious candle processions (such as the one above, during the capital's San Juan Bautista festival) with statues, or *santos*, often kick things off, and many Masses are held throughout each festival.

Puerto Rico is strongly Catholic, with many convents, monasteries and even one or two shrines where the Virgin Mary has appeared to the faithful. But this Catholicism has, over the years, been blended – like everything else in Puerto Rico – with animist elements of African and Taíno origin. Some of the elements are simple superstition: at midnight during the San Juan Bautista festival on June 24, thousands fill the beaches and walk backward into the sea (or nearest body of water – even a pool will do!) three times to renew good luck for the coming year. Beach parties, together with the usual dancing and music, round off the occasion.

THE LANGUAGE OF PUERTO RICO

Although English and Spanish are both designated "official" languages,
it's español that rules the heart – and tongue – of most Puerto Ricans

Even before Columbus's fleet "discovered" the island in 1493, Puerto Rico was in a state of cultural unrest. Invading Carib tribes from South America were threatening the native Arawaks, as they had many other cultures throughout the Caribbean. When the local Arawaks met the invading Caribs, what language was created? The Arawak name for the island, Borinquen, is still used (*La Borinqueña* is the Puerto Rican national anthem), and the Caribs live on in the word Caribbean. Many Puerto Rican municipalities go by their pre-Columbian names, for example Caguas, Arecibo, Mayagüez, Yauco and Guaynabo. The Arawaks feared the god Juracán, while we fear hurricanes. And the *hamacas* in which the early Indians slept are just as popular today under the name of hammocks.

If the Arawaks welcomed the Spaniards as a strategy to ward off the Caribs, they miscalculated. A wave of Spaniards swept across the island. Eventually there came battle and disease, which obliterated the native Arawak population. Then came sex, producing the first Puerto Ricans and the first men who could claim to speak a truly Puerto Rican Spanish. The Spanish of the earliest Puerto Ricans, like that of their modern descendants, can be said to reflect either a pronunciational sloppiness or an Arawak love of diphthongs. For example, Spanish words which end in *ado* are pronounced as if the *d* were silent. Humacao is an Arawak name, but *pescao* will get you fish anywhere on the island. A good stew is an *asopao*, but if your *fiao* (credit) isn't good enough, you won't be served one in any restaurant.

Puerto Rico's first Africans were brought as slaves, mostly from west-central Africa. They brought with them another language; they also had many musical instruments, including the drums, and countless customs and attitudes which have found their way into the lives of

everyone. The *baquine*, a festival of mourning for the death of an infant, is a ritual of African origin, and is usually the scene of a great deal of rum, dancing and *lechón asado* (roast suckling pig). By the mid-19th century, the Africans made up a fifth of the population, and such customs penetrated Puerto Rican society.

Integration of the races has worked smoothly in Puerto Rico, and it is said that *él que no tiene dinga tiene mandinga*, a phrase which attributes some amount of African ancestry to virtually all Puerto Ricans. The Mandinga were one of the more populous of the West African tribes, brought to Puerto Rico to harvest sugarcane, coffee and tobacco.

The farmers of those crops, black, white and *mestizo*, gradually became the Puerto Rican *jíbaros*. The most famous record of the *jíbaro* was written by Manuel A. Alonso, a doctor whose writings fit into the Latin American literary movement known as *costumbrismo*. In 1849, his book *El Gíbaro* was published in

---

PRECEDING PAGES: talking it over at El Combate.
LEFT: hanging out in Arecibo.
RIGHT: street talk in Calle San José.

Barcelona, and in it there are invaluable accounts of a *jíbaro* wedding, dances and cockfights, Christmas celebrations and the arrival of the magic lantern in the hills. Equally important is the portrait of mid-19th-century *jíbaro* speech patterns. In Alonso's verses we can hear the *jíbaro* dialect in its purest form. He mentions foods such as *lechón asado, toytiyas* (tortillas) and *maví* (a drink made from tree bark).

For all the eccentricities of the Puerto Rican tongue, it is important to remember that the language of the island is Spanish, albeit a Spanish heavily influenced by other nationalities, and that Puerto Rican Spanish shares many oddi-

ties with the Spanish of its Caribbean neighbors – such as *seseo*, by which *s* sounds are muted, and sometimes disappear altogether, at the end of syllables. Matches are *loh fohforoh* rather than *los fosforos* and *graciah* means thanks. *Yeismo* is another confusing variation; this involves pronouncing the Spanish *ll* and *y* sounds as English *js*, so as to render a word like *Luquillo*, the island's most popular beach, as "Look here, Joe." Let's not forget the truncation of words with terminal *e* sounds, like *noch'*. In Puerto Rico, go into a coffee shop for a cup of *café con lech'*.

Those who live in Puerto Rico also practice an important non-verbal language in everyday

dealings. For example, a twitch of the nose usually means, "What is that?". Both hands raised palms front means "Wait a minute", and when an individual tweaks his or her cheek it means "I like that". A movement akin to washing of the hands means "It's done".

Spanish spoken here

The granting of United States citizenship to Puerto Ricans in 1917 signaled the advent of English as the first Germanic language to become part of the Puerto Rican dialect. The startling result of this last infusion is Spanglish, a colloquial Spanish which may be as familiar to a North American as it is to a Spaniard. Spanglish consists not only of a shared vocabulary but also of the terse sentence construction characteristic of English. The first penetration of English into Puerto Rican Spanish seems to have come from English labels on consumer products.

Indeed, men still sit at bars nursing *un scotch* while their children look on, chewing *chicletes*. The introduction of American commerce was no less confounding in other ways. When the first American cash registers were introduced in San Juan's grocery and department stores, a whole generation stood paralyzed at checkout counters when the "No Sale" tab, marking the end of the transaction, flipped up. *No Sale* in Spanish translates as "Do not leave".

Spanglish truly entered its heyday only with the mass migration of Puerto Ricans to the United States in the 1940s. This exodus created a generation of so-called *Neoyorkinos*, who returned to their native island with the baffling customs and speech patterns of the streets of New York. Or they would send letters home with news, and, if they had no money, they would send the letter *ciodí* (cash on delivery).

Letters to the Cordillera would have to be transported by *el trucke*. Perhaps there would be bad news, that a son had been *bosteado* by the *policías* for dealing in *los drogues*. More often it was just idle chatter, discussions of the decisions of the world *líders*, or of how a brother had won a pool game by sinking the important eight ball in the corner *poquete*.

Puerto Ricans love pool, but if Puerto Rico and the Spanglish language have an official sport it has to be *el béisbol*, or baseball. Everyone knows that Roberto Clemente (from Carolina) and Orlando Cepeda (from Santurce) were

Puerto Rico's greatest hitters of *jonrones* and *dobles* (home-runs and doubles). Most Puerto Ricans would say their ballplayers were *wilson*, meaning "very good". Some things have remained little changed, though. Dollars are sometimes called *dolares*, but more often *pesos*. Quarters are *pesetas*, nickels *vellones* and pennies *centavos*.

Language means more in Puerto Rico than just about anything else. Most Puerto Ricans fear the loss of the language through the influence of other cultures, especially if the island were to become a state. One of the first questions a Puerto Rican asks of a visitor is "*Habla*

RAYMOND: *Cómo estamos, broki?* (How we doin', brother?)
PAPO: *Na' mas se me estallo la tabla.* (I just cracked my surfboard.)
RAYMOND: *Qué chavienda!* (What a drag!)
PAPO: *Estuve gufeando en un tubo y fua! se me fue la tabla contra esas rocas por ahi.* (I was goofing around in a tube, when, boom! my board flies into those rocks over there.)
RAYMOND: *Ea rayo!* (Gee whiz!)
PAPO: *Ay, pero mira a esa jeba. Vamos a rapiar.* (Oh, will you look at this babe. Let's rap.)
RAYMOND: *Oye, guapa, ven aca un momento.* (Hey, cutey, come here a minute.)

español?" If the visitor responds positively, then he or she is taken into the fold graciously.

Spicy talk

Puerto Rico's beaches have been the stage for dialogs in many languages, but none are as spicy as those you'll hear on the beach at Piñones between two *playeros* when the midwinter swells are up:
PAPO: *Oye, 'mano, que pasa?* (Hey brother, what's happening?)

MARTA: *No seas cafre o te rompo el coco.* (Don't be rude or I'll break your head).
PAPO: *De dónde tu eres?* (Where you from?)
MARTA: *De Guaynabo y a tí que te importa?* (Guaynabo, and what do you care?)
PAPO: *A ver si quieres pon pa' San Juan.* (To see if you'd like a lift to San Juan.)
MARTA: *Bueno, vale.* (Well, okay.)
PAPO: *Cógelo suave, Raymond.* (Take it easy, Raymond.)

Having such a rich and vibrant oral tradition, Puerto Ricans love good conversation, and, with at least four linguistic families from which to draw, enjoy a speech that is all at once cryptic and colorful. ❑

LEFT: Añasco men exchange the day's news.
RIGHT: the Friday flea market in San Sebastián is the scene of many a lively conversation.

PUERTO RICAN CUISINE

Junk food is threatening to squeeze out local dishes. But you can still find tasty concoctions from Taíno roots, African flavors and Spanish traditions

Carib and Spanish destruction of Puerto Rico's native Taíno tribes, for all its ruthlessness, was far from complete. It has been said that Puerto Rican society today reflects its African and Indian origins more than its Spanish ones, and there is much truth in that. Non-Spanish ways live on in customs, rituals, language and all aspects of life, and one can see in many facial features the unfamiliar expression of the Taínos, a race otherwise lost to us forever. But nowhere is the Taíno influence more visible, or more welcome, than in Puerto Rican cuisine, one of the great culinary amalgams of our hemisphere.

Imagine a Taíno man – call him Otoao and set his caste at *naboría*, one of the higher agricultural castes in the Taíno hierarchy – rising one sunny morning after having won a glorious victory the previous day over the invading Caribs. This victory was cause for an *areyto,* the Taíno ritual which either preceded or followed any happening of even the remotest importance. Births, deaths, victories, defeats ... it's *areyto* time. *Areytos*, like other socio-religious Taíno festivals, required intricate preparations for whatever food and drink was to be served, and, as a *naboría*, Otoao was in charge of hunting and fishing for the tribe.

Not that Otoao's wife Tai had it terribly easy. As a *naboría* woman (a woman's caste was determined by that of her husband), Tai was responsible for the cultivation and harvesting of the fields (*conucos*) as well as the preparation of the meals. These were elaborate, and the Taínos managed to get an astounding range of food on the banquet table.

The menu that evening included roast *jutías* (early guinea pigs) seasoned with sweet red chilli peppers, fried fish in corn oil, fresh shellfish and a variety of freshly harvested vegetables. Among the vegetables were *yautías* (starchy tubers similar to potatoes and yams),

corn yams, cassava and the same small red chili peppers used to season the *jutías*. Bread was *casabe*, a mixture of puréed cassava and water cooked between two hot rocks. For dessert, the Taínos had fresh fruit picked from the extensive variety available throughout the island. The culmination of the celebration was the

drinking of an alcoholic beverage made from fermented corn juice.

This activity was accompanied by the ceremonial inhalation of hallucinogenic fumes thought to make the warriors fitter for battle. The Taínos made hallucinogens of many sorts, the most common of which used the hanging, bell-shaped flowers of the *campana* tree to make a potent and mind-bending tea.

Most of the dietary staples of the Taínos survive in the Puerto Rican cuisine of today, albeit some in altered form. Puerto Rican cooking is now an amalgam of Taíno, Spanish and African traditions. Much of this intermingling took place early in the island's history, with

PRECEDING PAGES: an island favorite, roast suckling pig (*lechón asado*). **LEFT:** picking green peppers. **RIGHT:** a display of Puerto Rican cuisine.

Spanish colonists incorporating a variety of their own ingredients and techniques into the native cuisine, most of which were found to blend surprisingly well. A tremendous addition to this culinary mélange was made by the Africans brought as slaves shortly thereafter.

African tradition is responsible for what is perhaps the greatest achievement in Caribbean cooking – the combination of strikingly contrasting flavors which in other culinary traditions would be considered unblendable. One of these savory concoctions is *piñon*: ripe plantains layered between well-seasoned ground beef and almost invariably served with rice.

Surprisingly, many of the agricultural staples which look indigenous to the island were actually brought to Puerto Rico from other parts of the world. Among the great variety of crops imported were coffee, sugar-cane, coconuts, bananas, plantains, oranges and other citrus fruits, ginger and other spices, onions, potatoes, tomatoes, garlic and much more. These products, in combination with those already present, were to mold what was to become the Puerto Rican culinary tradition.

It is ironic that among these imports are several for which Puerto Rico was to become renowned. Puerto Rican coffee, for example,

Food from around the world

As different ingredients and cooking techniques were introduced to the island by its early settlers, a local culinary tradition began to take shape. Most important of the early imports were the Spanish cattle, sheep, pigs, goats and other grillable creatures, which the islanders had never tasted but took to with zeal. Along with the animals came an almost infinite number of vegetables, fruits and spices from the farthest reaches of Spain's vast colonial empire. A subtler, but no less important, influence on the Puerto Rican food supply was the introduction of European farming methods and agricultural equipment.

especially that from the region around Yauco, was long considered by Europeans the best coffee one could get in the world. And the plantain, arguably the most popular staple in Puerto Rican cuisine, is something of a national symbol – almost as the leek is to the Welsh. A man who is admired for his honesty and lack of pretension is said to have on him the *mancha del plátano*, or "stain of the plantain".

Myths and misconceptions

Puerto Rican cuisine is as eclectic as it is varied. Local food has earned a reputation it most decidedly does not deserve for being hot, fiery and spicy. In actuality, although it is prepared with a multiplicity of richly varied spices and condiments, Puerto Ricans tend to season their food more subtly than one might imagine. The base of a majority of native dishes is the *sofrito*, an aromatic and well-seasoned sauce made from puréed tomatoes, onions, garlic, green peppers, sweet red chili peppers, coriander, anatto seeds and a fairly arbitrary handful of other spices. This *sofrito* adds a zesty taste to stews, rices, stewed beans and a variety of other dishes, but only the blandest of palates would consider it to be piquant.

Native Caribbean flavors are evident in the majority of Puerto Rican recipes. The most

Social traditions of old

Puerto Ricans have very successfully kept alive not only the culinary but also many of the social traditions of their Taíno forebears. Christmas time on the island is not complete without rice, *gandules* (pigeon peas), *lechón asado* (roast suckling pig), *pasteles* (tamales made from plantains and *yautías* filled with a flavorful meat stuffing) and, as dessert, a *majarete* made with rice flour, coconut milk, grated coconut pulp, sugar and spices. During Lent, seafood dishes include the traditional *serenata*: codfish in a vinaigrette sauce served with tomatoes, onions, avocados and boiled tubers.

popular dinner dishes are stewed meats, rice and beans, and an enormous selection of fritters. Rice dominates many local main courses; expect a big heap with *arroz con pollo* (chicken – or another meat – served with rice cooked in coconut milk). Popular desserts include *flan* (custard), made of cheese, coconut or vanilla; and *guava con queso* (candied fruit slices with cheese). Fruit in general is popular and plentiful, and includes mango, papaya, passion fruit, bananas, breadfruit, pineapples and grapefruit.

LEFT: street corner temptations.
ABOVE: Puerto Rico has many fine restaurants, such as La Mallorquina in Old San Juan.

Though Puerto Rico is far too small to have many truly regional cuisines, a number of dishes are limited to particular areas of the island. For example, seafood dishes tend to be accompanied by *sorrullos* (corn fritters) in most of the restaurants on the south coast, from Salinas to Cabo Rojo. The same is true of the great variety of fritters available in the food shacks of Luquillo, a most rewarding 30-minute trip from San Juan for anyone interested in local cuisine. Bayamón and its environs offers a truly unusual snack in *chicharrón*, a sort of massive pork-scratching sold on the highways in and out of the city. It's definitely an acquired taste, but once you've acquired it, you'll understand why there are so many hefty individuals wandering the streets.

The island offers a great variety of restaurants for tourists and local consumers. Typical restaurants serving local food are only rarely luxurious or expensive. In fact, among Puerto Ricans, a rule of thumb applies that the shabbier the establishment, the better the food. The best native creations are found at modest little local *fondas*, where the prices are as reasonable as the food is distinguished. In a *fonda*, you can pick up a generous plate of rice and beans, *biftec criollo* (steak), *tostones* (fried plantains), salad, a can of beer and dessert for about $8. If

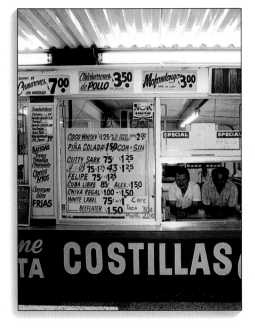

you can afford to splurge the extra 60¢, you can pick up one of the better cups of coffee you will have in your life. At the low end of the economic scale are delicious sandwiches made with a mixture of red meats, cheeses, tomatoes and other ingredients. Among the most popular are *cubanos* and *media noches*. The *cubano* consists of pork loin, ham and Swiss cheese on *pan de agua* (similar to French bread), while the *media noche* is smaller and uses egg bread. At the pricey end of the scale is *asopao*, probably Puerto Rico's most widely loved native dish. This thick stew can be made with chicken, pork or fish, and is invariably worth every penny one pays for it.

International cuisine

In addition to restaurants serving up traditional fare, you'll find a large assortment of places in which to savor food from different countries. Puerto Rico has become a proving ground for all sorts of global cuisine. Chinese food has practically become a staple, with fast-order restaurants found everywhere. Spanish restaurants, too, abound. The Puerto Rican "bakery" is usually Spanish in style and includes a wide assortment of delicacies from Spain and South America. The famous Cuban sandwich is very popular, as are Spanish omelettes – a thick pie-like arrangement of eggs, potatoes and onions.

Italian food, however, is probably consumed more than any other type. Pizza parlors can be seen everywhere, and home delivery is very common. German specialties are limited to a few choice restaurants, but Mexican eateries run hot and heavy in the San Juan metropolitan area. (Traditional Puerto Rican food lacks the hot spices of Mexico, but islanders still tend to indulge in the torrid fare at times.)

Even Thai and Japanese restaurants can be found, and *sushi* is gaining in popularity. One supermarket even prepares *sushi* to go.

If "gourmet" international food is not your style, rest assured that eateries serving hamburgers, hot dogs, crispy fried chicken and other exceptional "junk food" are ubiquitous throughout the island. Fast-food restaurants have become a way of life in the large population centers. There are more Burger Kings than you can shake a French fry at. If that doesn't appeal, then try McDonald's, KFC, Wendy's, Flamers, Church's Chicken, Pizza Hut … the list is endless. Many of these establishments have added a bit of Puerto Rican flavor. You can order a "Sandwich Criollo" at Burger King – a breakfast treat consisting of ham, egg and cheese on a local bun – or order a pizza with *chorizo* (Puerto Rican sausage).

The franchise fast-food boom has played another significant role in motivating local eateries to dispense varieties of food such as plantain fritters, stuffed potatoes and seafood salad, while employing novel merchandising techniques. Advertising for these establishments has become a billion-dollar industry in itself.

LEFT: everything under the sun, ready and waiting.
RIGHT: *fonda* food – plain, simple and filling.

Making it on your own

Armchair connoisseurs who will never go to Puerto Rico and live far enough from New York City to be completely unable to procure a pre-cooked Puerto Rican delicacy will be happy to find that the stuff is fairly easy to cook – once one gets the correct ingredients.

Here's a recipe for *mofongo*, a hearty, typically Puerto Rican plantain dish that makes a first-rate luncheon or dinner.

Mofongo abreu
Ingredients:
3 green plantains (plus vegetable oil for frying)

The influences on Puerto Rican cuisine are nothing if not international. Those familiar with Jewish cooking will recognize the first way of cooking *mofongo* as somewhat similar to putting matzoh balls in chicken stock. If, therefore, you worry that *mofongo* will be nothing new, do try it with *carnecita*:

Carnecita
Ingredients:
2 lbs. pork (the leaner the better)
2 recipes *adobo* (see below)
Cut pork into one-inch cubes. Marinate in *adobo* 24 hours. Fry in olive oil. Serve with *mofongo*.

¼ cup olive oil
1½ tsp. salt
½ cup grated pork rind
2–3 cloves garlic
Cut plantains into sections (about six pieces each). Fry in vegetable oil until slightly browned. Drain off oil. Mix with other ingredients, using – if you want to be really Puerto Rican about the whole thing – a mortar and pestle. Shape into balls and serve in chicken stock. Chicken soup's okay, but chicken stock is the real thing. Otherwise, shape the stuff into hamburger-shaped patties and serve with *carnecita* (see the following recipe), both dishes will provide a rewarding change of pace.

Adobo
Ingredients (enough for 2 lbs. of meat):
¾ tsp. salt
⅛ tsp. ground pepper
¼ tsp. ground oregano
1 pressed medium garlic clove
1 tbsp. olive oil (optional)
1 tsp. vinegar (optional)
Stir all this up well. Slather it on the *carnecita* and forget about it for a day or so. Fry it all up, eat it with *mofongo*, and you'll realize it is a tasty concoction indeed. It just might make you want to head down to this Spanish-speaking, Caribbean island and sample the full range of a truly unusual cuisine. ❑

ISLAND ART

It's the range that surprises. Flamboyant modern painting sits alongside remarkable folk art and a vast Taíno legacy of ancient art

Be warned that Puerto Rico's art scene offers delights to the mind and senses as meaningful and alluring as those of its landscape. This may mean entering a room of carved religious figures (*santos*) in the middle of a bustling city and finding yourself enveloped in their holy silence; or wandering into a museum or gallery in Old San Juan, only to find yourself as taken by a beautifully landscaped 17th-century courtyard as by what you see on the walls; or talking to a local artist or scholar and finding that his passion for the island and its craftsmen is yours.

To be sure, there are frustrations. In San Juan the problem centers around a glut of a good thing; finding the best is often a confusing task, with charlatans working next to some of the great artists of the day. Difficulties out on the island are more logistical, with many of Puerto Rico's fascinating local museums hiding in outbuildings on the edges of towns. But even the most cursory foray into the island's artistic past and present will be rewarding.

Museum isle

The Institute of Puerto Rican Culture, located in the Dominican Convent in Old San Juan, owns a vast amount of the island's cultural inheritance, and can guide you to almost anything you fancy. The nearby Museo de Arte also holds a vast array of local work. Old San Juan itself is particularly fortunate as an artistic center; beside its nine museums, it has a dozen contemporary art galleries, a few co-operatives and craft shops of all descriptions.

If buying art interests you as much as just looking at it, Old San Juan is certainly the spot to begin your shopping spree. You'll find pre-Columbian pieces at Galería Los Arcos, and prints as well as paintings at Botello, Coabey,

PRECEDING PAGES: sculptor Jan D'Esopo relaxes amidst her creations.
LEFT: street artist in Old San Juan.
RIGHT: carved religious figures (*santos*) were an early art form.

Labiosa and Marrozini. In Santurce, Casa Candina is a charming gallery in a beautiful and quiet hacienda. It's not only the island's center for ceramic arts but also the site of many important art shows and exhibitions.

The museum of the University of Puerto Rico in Río Piedras, San Juan, exhibits only a fifth of

its collection, but that small proportion is of absolutely top quality, from pre-Columbian art right up to the strongest and respected painters of the present day.

But the last word on Puerto Rican art must go to the Ponce Art Museum, envisioned by former Governor Luis Ferré and executed by architect Edward Durrell Stone. Here, in a series of dramatically sunlit hexagonal rooms, art reflects the full range of the drama of human life. From the simplest of faces in Jan van Eyck's *Salvator Mundi* to an overpopulated *Fall of the Rebel Angels* to Rossetti's wonderfully confrontational *Daughters of King Lear*, you'll find it impossible not to be moved. Go out of your way to get there and you will not be disappointed. (*See also page 222.*)

Art for heart's sake

Many of Puerto Rico's greatest achievements have been in the folk arts, and these retain a broad appeal (*see pages 88–89*). Most notable are the Puerto Rican *santos*, arguably the island's greatest contribution to the plastic arts. These wooden religious idols, evoking an uncanny spiritual quiet, vary greatly in size and shape. The Baroque detail of the earliest pieces reflects both their period origins and the tastes of a Spanish clientèle. But as Puerto Rico began

Ancient art

The Caguana Indian Ceremonial Ballpark near Utuado gives haunting echoes of pre-Columbian life and culture. Here, early Taíno Indians played *batey*, a more civilized version of the balancing game favored by Mexico's Mayans, in which one had to keep a small ball suspended in the air for long periods of time, hitting it only with shoulders, head and ankles. This version is only "more civilized" on the strength of the fact that the early Taínos were not sacrificed to the gods if they dropped the ball, as their Mexican counterparts were. The dolmen-like stones surrounding the *bateyes*, or

to develop a stronger sense of colonial identity, as well as an artisan tradition, *santeros* began to carve figures of a striking simplicity.

The proof of the healing powers of *santos* is said to be attested to by the presence of *milagros* ("miracles"), small silver appendages in shapes of parts of the body. These were donated by people who had prayed to particular saints for intercession in healing parts of the body. You can find such *santos* in the Cristo Chapel in Old San Juan. Though *santos* by the great masters are difficult to come by, there's hardly a home on the island where you won't find at least one *santo* of some sort, greatly revered and passed on from generation to generation.

playing spaces, show great feeling for the ideal spatial relationship between art and nature.

Similar evidence of the vast Taíno legacy is found at the University Museum in Río Piedras, which holds the cultural heritage of the island. Recent digs have been especially abundant in discoveries, some of them dazzling in quality. Amid the expected – amulets, potsherds, tools – are some baffling curiosities, like stone collars: great solid yokes at once regal and unwearable. In one intriguing case concerning Puerto Rico's early Taíno, men bend and sway together in entranced harmony. In another are two partially exposed skeletons, a few broken possessions at their sides.

For all the diversity of Puerto Rico's many cultural traditions, it was not until the 18th century that the island produced its first major artist in the Western tradition: José Campeche (1752–1809). In spite of never having left the island and having been exposed to European painting only through prints, Campeche still managed to create paintings of mastery. His religious works show a weakness for sentimentality, with their glut of *putti* and pastel clouds, but the inner peace which Campeche succeeds in displaying in his main holy figures dispels all doubt as to his stature as a truly inspired and talented artist.

A more accessible painter, and something of a local hero in Puerto Rico, is Francisco Oller (1833–1917). His work is housed in all three main sources: the Institute and the museums at Ponce and Río Piedras. To this day, the extent of his influence on Puerto Rican painting is immeasurable.

Unlike Campeche, Oller lived and traveled abroad throughout his life. He studied under Courbet, was an intimate of both Pissarro and Cézanne, painted European royalty, and yet remained loyal to – and fiercely proud of – his island homeland. He was a Realist with Impressionist ideas, able to paint gorgeously everything

There are two such masterpieces in the Ponce Museum, but it is in a formal portrait which hangs in the Institute of Puerto Rican Culture that one sees Campeche at the height of his powers. The eponymous *Governor Ustauriz* stands in a magnificent room, with sunlight entering from behind. In his left hand are the first plans to pave the streets of San Juan; outside in the distance are men laboring busily to make his dream into a reality. It is truly a triumphant picture.

he saw. He was adept at all genres: portraits, still lifes and landscapes – such as *Hacienda Aurora*, resonating with the vibrant colors of Puerto Rico which are just as much in evidence today.

A piece of work which defies reproduction is Oller's *El Velorio* (The Wake). An enormous painting, it covers an entire wall in the University of Puerto Rico Museum at Río Piedras and illuminates the common man's universe in a fashion that recalls the work of Breughel. Here people laugh, cry, drink, sing and dance about, while on a lace-covered table an almost forgotten, stone-white dead child lies strewn with flowers.

Oller's legacy to Puerto Rican painters has

LEFT: the Centro de Bellas Artes in Santurce.
ABOVE: artwork on display in a gallery at the Tibes Indian Ceremonial Park near Ponce.

been one not only of technique but also of theme. Since his time, island painters have taken an overwhelming pride in Puerto Rico's diverse populace and landscape. Miguel Pou and Ramon Frade were among the earliest to follow Oller's lead, doing some spectacular genre work in the early part of this century.

At the Institute, Frade's painting *The Jíbaro* is a splendid homage to Puerto Rico's country farmers. Shyly surveying us with a bunch of plantains in his arms, this tiny old fellow appears to be a giant, with the land miniatured at his feet and his head haloed by a cloud.

The 1940s saw a rise in printmaking, which

has left that medium one of the most vibrant in Puerto Rico to this day. Funded by the government, printmaking projects lured a slew of fine artists, many of whom are still active. Of particular note are Rafael Tufiño, Antonio Martorell, José Rosa and Lorenzo Homar. Posters by Ramón Power illustrate some of the clarity and strength from which the best of Puerto Rican artists continue to draw. Examples of prints and paintings by talented local artists can be seen at, among other places, the Graphic Arts Museum in Old San Juan, which is upstairs in the Casa de los Contrafuertes on Calle San Sebastían.

Over the past 30 years, almost all Puerto Rican artists have studied abroad, and the consequence has been a broadening and an increasingly avant-garde range of artistic attitudes. Some artists have remained abroad, like Rafael Ferrer, whose work is as popular in New York as it is in San Juan.

Others have returned to work and teach, producing an art with a distinctively Puerto Rican flavor. Myrna Baez falls into this category, her canvases interweaving past and present, inner and outer space. Her *Homage to Vermeer* shows a lone figure in an interior surrealistically touched by landscape. Reflectively, she seems to have loosed a phantom of tropical hubris as she opens the drawer of a nearby table.

The large fraternity of Puerto Rico's artists shows reverence and sensibility for the island and its people. Color plays an integral part in style and technique. The art of Augusto Marín, Angel Botello, Myrna Baez and Mari Mater O'Neill can be obtained in Puerto Rico and in New York auction houses for hefty prices. Examples of Puerto Rico's stellar paintings may sell for as high as $100,000 each.

Rafael Tufiño's woodcut ink prints tell the story of Puerto Rican life at mid-century. A group of Tufiño's pictures can be seen at the Tourism Company's headquarters in Old San Juan. Luis Cajiga paints dazzling flamboyant trees and humble *piragua* vendors. Jorge Zeno's and Sylvia Blanco's imaginative techniques are good examples of surrealistic art, while John Balosi's sculptures and paintings of horses are treasured for their originality. Noemi Ruiz, Nicky Quijano, Juan Ramón Velasquez, Jaime Suárez and Susan Espinosa portray a wide range of island life on canvas and in sculpture.

Viewing opportunities

Gallery nights, when many of Puerto Rico's young artists are discovered, are held in Old San Juan on the first Tuesday of each month from 6–9 pm. Two of the country's leading art galleries can be found on Calle de Cristo in Old San Juan: Galería Botélo and Galería Palomas.

Another excellent occasion to get more than a taste of local talent is at the San Juan Biennial Graphic Art Exhibition, which covers the spectrum of imaginative techniques and styles of Caribbean artists. ❏

LEFT: grand stairway at the Ponce Art Museum.
RIGHT: detail of Myrna Baez's *Homage to Vermeer.*

FOLK ART WITH A FLAVOR ALL ITS OWN

Many of Puerto Rico's handicrafts have evolved out of necessity, and focus on function as well as form, but some of it is just plain fun...

Puerto Rico's most exquisite form of "folk art" actually borders on "fine art": *santos*, the carved religious figures that have been produced here since the 1500s. (*See page 84.*) But over the centuries, the country's folk art has expanded into many other areas, with today's artisans producing a great variety of paintings, non-religious sculpture, jewelry and many other more quirky – and collectible – artifacts.

Usually bursting with bright colors, Puerto Rican folk art has an almost childlike quality. Many times folk artists base their themes on the nature around them: roosters, iguanas, and the tiny *coquis* (tree frogs) are frequently depicted.

Old San Juan is the best place to see – and purchase – local folk art. The Institute of Puerto Rican Culture (in the Dominican Convent) is a great source of information about the country's arts and crafts, but buyers should head for the two weekend craft markets – one on Plaza de la Dársena in front of Pier 1 (11am–10pm) and the other in Paseo de la Princesa (noon–8pm). Just before Christmas each year, the Bacardi Artisans Festival, held on the distillery grounds, features more than 100 booths displaying everything from stone necklaces to musical flutes.

◁ **EXPERT HANDS**
Bobbins flying, a lady from Moca keeps alive the 500-year-old craft of making *mundillo*, or tatted fabric.

◁ **HOME FOR SALE**
A craftsman proudly displays his intricate model of an island home at the San Sebastián Hammock Festival.

SCARY ART: *VEJIGANTE* MASKS

△ **ESSENTIAL ART**
Music is an integral part of life to a Puerto Rican, and the *cuatro* guitar – skillfully crafted by local artisans – plays an important role.

An unusual – and popular – form of folk art in Puerto Rico is the grotesque, colorfully painted masks that are one of the highlights of the island's many festivals. Artisans (such as the *ponceño* above) have been producing the horned, spike-toothed, speckled *papier mâché* creations for centuries – some historians believe the practice dates back to ancient Taínos; others link it to medieval Spain or tribal Africa. Traditionally the masks were black, red and yellow – symbolic of hellfire and damnation. Brightly costumed *vejigantes* don the masks and roam the streets at carnival time, in an attempt to scare sinners back into the church. Ponce and Loíza are the island's mask-making centers; their carnivals provide a chance to see masks in action.

◁ **THE ART OF RELAXING**
Dating back to Taíno times, hammock-making remains a favorite pastime of the islanders – perhaps second only to actually lying in them!

△ **FOLK FRESCOS**
When it comes to artistic expression, any wall will do. Puerto Rico is full of small buildings adorned with colorful scenes of local life.

RHYTHM OF THE TROPICS

Salsa is king, but the sounds range from the percussion of traditional instruments

to the classical music encouraged by Pablo Casals, who made his home here

Just before he died, the world-renowned Argentinian composer Alberto Ginastera visited Puerto Rico in order to attend the world première of one of his works commissioned by the Pablo Casals Festival. During an interview at the Caribe Hilton, Mr Ginastera's thoughts turned to the song of the *coquí*, the tiny frog that is found only in Puerto Rico and is famous for its persistent and ubiquitous nocturnal calls. "It is the only natural song that I know of," said Mr Ginastera, "which is formed of a perfect seventh." The *coquí* sings a two-note song – "co ... kee!" – and these two notes are a perfect seventh apart. It should come, therefore, as no surprise that the island's natural sounds have their unique man-made counterpart. The music of Puerto Rico is salsa.

From settlement to salsa

Puerto Ricans have always excelled in music, and the somewhat haphazard course of the island's history has given it a multitude of traditions from which to build a distinctively Puerto Rican sound. The earliest settlers were as enthusiastic about their music as any Spaniards; but, deprived of their native string instruments, found themselves in the position of having to create their own. As a result, there are at least half-a-dozen string instruments native to the island, about which more will be said below.

In the absence of many tonal instruments, the settlers made do with percussive ones, which are ready at-hand in the various gourds, woods, shoots and beans native to this land. The arrival of West African slaves, who brought with them a well-developed and long history of percussion-based music, accelerated this trend.

Even now, Puerto Ricans are very adept at making music with whatever happens to be within grabbing distance. No one *owns* a musi-

cal composition in Puerto Rico, as one does in other countries. Play a Puerto Rican a piano tune he likes in a bar room or café, and you won't believe your ears when you hear the rhythmic sounds he gets out of a spoon, a wood block, a bead necklace or even his knuckles on the table.

No lack of formality

To be fair, there is a somewhat formalized genre of this very type of music. It's collectively called *bomba y plena*, but the two are completely different types of music that are coupled with dance. Together, they are the most popular forms of folk music in Puerto Rico.

The *bomba* is purely African in origin and came over with the black slaves who were forced to work on the country's sugar plantations. It's essentially a marriage of drumming and dancing: one egging the other on in a rhythmic competition of sorts. The northeastern town of Loíza is a particularly good place to experience a typical *bomba*.

PRECEDING PAGES: the highly acclaimed Puerto Rico Symphony Orchestra.
LEFT: folk music figures prominently in island life.
RIGHT: drumming out a *bomba* beat.

Plena, on the other hand, is a blend of elements from the island's many cultures – even ancient Taíno – and generally involves a handful of musicians creating different rhythms on an amazing variety of hand-held percussion instruments. Some resemble hand-held tympanis, some Irish *bodhrans*, some tambourines. Many of them are homemade, and have become a type of "folk art" of sorts, as well as functional instruments. The custom of *plena* originated in Ponce, but today you can hear its distinctive sounds at any patron saint's festival and occasionally at Plaza de Armas or Plaza de la Dársena in Old San Juan.

Traditional music is still performed widely, especially during holidays and festivals. At family parties and get-togethers, there are usually guitarists, *güiro* (gourd) players and pianists playing the long-established music of the people – particularly such standards as *Flores Negros* and *Somos Novios*. Television and radio stations showcase popular singers and groups, such as Chucho Avellanet, Danny Rivera, Ednita Nazario, Lucesita Benitez and Nydia Caro. The "Tropical Salsa" renditions of balladeers Chayanne, Ricky Martin and Marc Anthony command large audiences at concerts held in Hiram Bithorn Stadium, Bellas Artes, or at town plazas.

"Jíbaro Jazz" became the rage in the 1990s, with *cuatro* player Pedro Guzman – who combines traditional country style with modern jazz techniques – one of the major stars. Mexico's popular music also has a strong influence in contemporary tastes.

Classical sounds, too

This is not to neglect the achievements of this small island in the more traditional forms. It is a haven for the opera, and has its own company; Justino Díaz, the island's finest male vocalist, has impressed critics from New York to Milan, and Puerto Rico's "Renaissance Man", composer Jack Delano, has made his mark on the classical scene.

The Puerto Rico Ballet Company stages classics as well as original local productions at the Center for Performing Arts (Bellas Artes) in Santurce, while the Puerto Rico Symphony Orchestra – despite being relatively young – is probably the best in the Caribbean, and has premièred works by some of Latin America's finest composers, many of them at San Juan's Casals Festival, the Caribbean's most celebrated cultural event, held for two weeks in June each year (exact dates vary). The orchestra and the Children's Chorus have drawn much attention internationally.

It is Pablo Casals who, more than any other Puerto Rican resident, is responsible for the upsurge of interest and proficiency in classical performance in Puerto Rico in recent years. Born in Catalonia in 1876 of a Puerto Rican mother, Casals was recognized almost before World War I as one of the greatest cellists of his era. After leaving Spain in 1936 as a protest against the Spanish Civil War, he settled in the French Pyrenees, where the first Casals Festival was held in 1950. He visited his mother's homeland in 1956, and spent the final years of his life in Puerto Rico.

In 1957, at the invitation of Governor Luis Muñoz Marín, he founded the Puerto Rican Casals Festival, which must rank as the greatest cultural event in the Antilles, and a formidable one even by world standards. In later years, Casals went on to form the Puerto Rico Symphony Orchestra and the Puerto Rico Conservatory of Music. On his death at the age of 97 in 1973, he considered himself a Puerto Rican; his countrymen consider him one of their national heroes.

Rhythm of the tropics

Salsa is what happens when Afro-Caribbean music meets big-band jazz. Its roots may be found in the early explorations of Puerto Rican Tito Puente and Cuban musicians in New York City clubs following World War II. After serving three years in the United States Navy, Puente studied percussion at the prestigious Julliard School on New York's West Side. He was soon playing and composing for top band-leaders such as Machito and Pupi Campo, and he quickly proceeded to establish his own orchestra. Puente's Latin Jazz Ensemble continues to delight audiences throughout the world.

> **SPICY SAUCE**
>
> *Salsa* literally translates as "sauce": in a musical sense, the "sauce" that makes parties happen.

In an interview in *Latin US* magazine, Puente was asked to define salsa. "As you know, salsa in Spanish means 'sauce', and we use it mostly as a condiment for our foods," he said. "Salsa in general is all our fast Latin music put together: the merengue, the rumba, the mambo, the cha-cha, the guaguanco, boogaloo, all of it is salsa … in Latin music, we have many different types of rhythms, such as ballads (boleros), rancheros, tangos, and, of course, salsa."

The salsa band is usually composed of a lead vocalist and chorus, a piano, a bass, a horn section and a heavy assortment of percussion instruments (bongos, conga, maracas, *güiros*, timbales, claves, and the ever-present cowbell – a *jíbaro* touch). The overall effect is mesmerizing; the rhythm contagious. It is unquestionably highly danceable music.

Salsa (the center of which is now thought to have shifted *back* to Puerto Rico from New York) has firmly placed the island on the map of popular music, with more and more young *salseros* getting in on the act every day – and not just in Puerto Rico. Says Puente, "It's totally unexpected to see Belgians, Swedes, Finns and Danes swing to the Latin Beat... the bands there are playing more salsa than we are." Indeed, one of the most popular international salsa bands isn't even Puerto Rican – it's Orchestra de la Luz, which, despite its name, is Japanese.

LEFT: Puerto Rican folk music is almost inevitably accompanied by lively dance.
RIGHT: Tito Puente, often referred to as the "king" of Puerto Rican salsa.

A musical evolution

Puerto Rican music has evolved into the salsa beat; music has played a crucial role in Puerto Rican society and culture for as long as there have been Puerto Ricans. During Spanish rule, the *danza* was the chief form of entertainment for the *criollo* aristocracy; it reached its high point in the late 19th century when Morel Campos and other masters gave it a popularity that resounded back to Spain. This highly stylized tradition of music and its accompanying dance movements are preserved by several local

ensembles in Puerto Rico. The *danza* is characterized by a string orchestra, woodwinds, and a formal ambience. *La Borinqueña*, the Puerto Rican national anthem, is a *danza*.

A more popular and widely practiced Puerto Rican musical tradition is the *aquinaldo*, a song performed around the Christmas and Three Kings holiday, usually in the form of an *asalto*. The *asalto* is a charming tradition which dates back to the 19th century, and perhaps earlier. It goes along with the unrestrained partying of the holiday season. It is customary at an *asalto* to feast on *lechón asado* (roast suckling pig), *yucca* (a local potato-like root), *arroz con pollo* (chicken with rice), *gandules* (local peas) and *palos de ron* (well, okay, so they have some rum). Following the feast, a group of noisy celebrants stumbles from house to house, waking the residents and singing *aquinaldos*. The members of each household are expected to join the *asalto* as it moves throughout the surrounding neighborhood. Recordings of these genial songs are available as performed by a *parranda* or *trulla*, which is any professional group of *aquinaldo* singers.

The *décima*

The *décima* is arguably the most appealing form of traditional Puerto Rican music. It is the

Star performers

In contemporary Puerto Rico, salsa is king, but who is the King of Salsa? No one really agrees, but lists generally include Willie Colón, Panamanian singer-turned-politician Rubén Blades, the late Hector Lavoe, El Gran Combo de Puerto Rico and the Fania All-Stars.

Puerto Rico's biggest salsa star is Gilberto Santa Rosa (a protégé of Willie Rosario), affectionately known as "Gilbertito". In addition to salsa, merengue groups from the nearby Dominican Republic have become very popular. In fact, it is the preferred dance music at many Puerto Rican parties. Some locals, led by

vehicle through which the *jíbaro* expresses his joys and frustrations; it is the poetry of the Puerto Rican soul. Instrumentation for the *décima* consists of a number of three-, four- and six-stringed instruments (called appropriately the *tres, cuatro* and *seis*); a minimal rhythm is kept up by claves or the *güiro*.

The trademark of the *décima* is verbal improvisation. Often, two singers will alternate stanzas, trying to outboast each other with rhyming tales of luscious fruit, pretty women or physical prowess. The verbal jousting is significantly fueled by the audience. The similarity between the traditional *décima* and the more modern verbal duelling of today's rap DJs is striking.

Olga Tañon, have been able to cash in on the fast-paced merengue sound with albums and concert appearances.

Local salsa musicians in Cuba and Puerto Rico compete for the most infectious melodies, but it is said the latter are more avant-garde. The pre-pubescent vote favors Menudo; young *puertorriqueños* have probably stained more fanmag photos of Menudo with tears than men have stained tissues during shows by the "Queen of Salsa", Isabel Chacón. But that's a book in itself. Whatever the individual's taste, salsa continues as one of the hottest forms of popular music in the world.

Willie Colón and his band have produced some

of the most inspired salsa to date. The album *Siembra*, a collaboration with Rubén Blades, is easily one of the hottest discs around. The songs on *Siembra* show the rhythmic complexity which is at the core of salsa, as well as the thematic motifs which tie all of salsa together.

Like the *plena* singers of old, today's salsa vocalists often tell a story filled with satire or a social commentary. *Pedro Navaja*, for example, tells the story of a street tough and his inevitable demise. Blades croons the final verse, describing the scene after a gunfight:

And believe me people, although there was noise, nobody came out. There were no busy-

to choose this emotive theme for a musical starting point.

Colón's talent sparkles in other collaborative efforts. His 1977 recording with Celia Cruz, entitled *Only They Could Have Made This Album*, is a superb example of salsa's African roots. The songs from *Pun Pun Catalu*, *Rinkinkalla*, and *Burundanga* make use of African linguistic and musical references. *Burundanga* is an outgrowth of the music of *santería*, the Afro-Caribbean religious cult.

Of the bands, El Gran Combo (de Puerto Rico) has had great success since the early 1960s, probably owing to its songs' optimism

bodies, no questions asked, and nobody cried. Only a drunk bumped into the two bodies, and picked up the revolver, the knife and the dollars and marched off; and stumbling, he went on his way singing off-tune the chorus that I bring you that gives the message of my song. Life gives you surprises, surprises will give you life, Oh, God!

He who lives by violence dies by violence; Colón and Blades are not the first salsa singers

LEFT: dancing to a modern beat at Condado's Peggy Sue disco.
ABOVE: the "town character" struts his stuff at the San Sebastián Hammock Festival.

and enthusiasm. It has great musical talent, a good sense of humor, and a massive popular following.

The road to a better future (like Puerto Rican Spanish) is not always easy to follow, and the song *Resignación* suggests an amusing relief for the "estress" of making a fulfilling life for one's self:

Tell me Mr Psychiatrist, what should I do?/I've lost my friends and my woman, too./I'm going to prescribe "bothers me not" potion/Along with an ointment and salve of "and so what"/And if you know English and things continue ugly/Take five pills of "I don't care". ❏

A SPORTING LIFE

Baseball and basketball were early imports from the US and now

American football is bidding for a slice of the action

When the first ball was thrown in the Taíno *batey*, sport was born in Puerto Rico. All that remains of this early interest in sport are the ruins of the Taíno game courts south of Arecibo at the Caguana Ceremonial Ballpark and the Tibes Indian Ceremonial Park near Ponce, where early people played a game much like soccer.

Today, baseball games have replaced the Taíno diversion. The 20th century brought a wealth of action to Puerto Rico, but it all started with America's National Pastime, which became the island's most popular sport. It's not surprising, since the climate enables baseball to be played virtually every day of the year.

The amateur leagues set up their schedules so that there are games on most days or nights. The Winter League, which includes many professional ballplayers from the minor and major leagues, slates its games from October to January. Teams represent San Juan, Santurce, Bayamon, Caguas, Arecibo, Ponce and Mayagüez. In January, the Caribbean Series is held, with teams representing Puerto Rico, the Dominican Republic, Venezuela and Mexico. The game has produced such luminaries as Roberto Clemente, Orlando Cepeda and Rubén Gomez, with the 1990s stars including Roberto Alomar, Sandy Alomar, Juan "Igor" Gonzalez, Ivan "Pudge" Rodriguez and Carlos Baerga.

A new favorite

Although baseball has been the sport most identified with Puerto Rico, it has actually been replaced in popularity by basketball. This sport draws more interest because of the island team's success in international competitions such as the Olympics and the Pan-American Games. Puerto Rican teams have even given the powerful US entries a run for their money. The Superior Basketball League fields 16 teams in Aguada, Aibonito, Arecibo, Bayamon, Car-

olina, Caguas, Coamo, Fajardo, Guayama, Guaynabo, Isabela, Mayagüez, Morovis, Ponce, Quebradillas and San Germán. The season runs from late May to early September. A second semi-pro league, Liga Puertorriqueño, represents other towns around the island. Most basketball games in Puerto Rico are played

indoors, either in large gymnasiums or in specially built structures called *canchas*. In the yearly Central America-Caribbean Games, island basketball teams have dominated such countries as Panama, Colombia and Mexico.

International competition has become so important that the majority of Puerto Ricans prefer to have their own representation rather than to be part of the US teams. This option of Puerto Rican representation in the Games, as well as participation in world beauty contests, is considered to be one of the arguments against statehood status.

Puerto Rico has produced a large group of champion boxers, tennis players, golfers – and

---

PRECEDING PAGES: underwater treasures.

LEFT: windsurfer sets sail.

RIGHT: aspiring Roberto Clementes.

even a horse that won the Kentucky Derby, Bold Forbes. Horse racing draws great interest around the island, even though there is only one race track – El Comandante in Canovanas. Offtrack betting agencies in every town are usually filled with bettors on racing days, which are every day except Tuesday and Saturday.

Puerto Rico's boxers have won gold medals in international competition. Professional pugilists have held champion status in virtually every weight category except heavyweight. Boxing enthusiasts acknowledge

DUFFER'S DELIGHT

Puerto Rico's ample 12 golfing facilities include a total of 16 golf courses – all within two hours of each other.

Golf is a natural for the island, with championship courses mostly at the resorts. Public courses are available at reasonable rates in Punta Borinquen, Aguirre and Buchanan. All hotel courses are available at higher rates. Puerto Rico's most famous golfer, Juan "Chichi" Rodriguez, plays on the Seniors Tour in the United States.

Watersports of all types feature naturally at the coast and on inland waterways. Boating marinas are plentiful and include locations in Isla Grande, Boca de Cangrejos, Fajardo, Ponce

and revere the accomplishments of José "Chegui" Torres, who held the light heavyweight title back in the 60s. Featherweight Wilfredo Gomez and Welterweight Wilfredo Benitez were champions, as was Middleweight José "Chapo" Rosario.

For the net set, tennis courts abound around the island, especially at the hotels and resorts. The public may use the facilities for a fee. A few internationally known netters have emerged from the local courts, such as Charlie Pasarell and Gigi Fernandez. For aspiring champions or just for recreation, the Baldrich Tennis Club in Hato Rey provides 10 regulation courts for use at a nominal cost.

and Mayagüez. Surfing has become a way of life in areas like Rincón, where international events have been held. Windsurfing is a natural choice for the waters of the Atlantic and the Caribbean. On any given day, the colorful sails flash by. Ocean kayaking has gained popularity in recent times, with kayaks for rent on the placid Condado Lagoon. On the beaches, racquetball, volleyball and even touch football attract large crowds.

Anglers can indulge in all types of fishing, although deep-sea fishing is particularly ideal, with billfish plentiful a few miles from shore. Marlin as heavy as 500 lbs (227 kg) have been reeled in. The record marlin catch of 604 lbs

(274 kg) is held by Carmina Mendez Miller, a retired broadcaster, who stands less than 5 ft (1½ meters) tall.

American influence

American football has been catching on slowly, with the advent of cable television bringing more interest in the game. Pee Wee Football, however, has been popular for 28 consecutive years, with a yearly participation of more than 500 boys and a few girls. High school football has been relegated to private schools, as an effort to bring the game to public schools failed in the 1980s. There are semi-pro teams com-

schools have teams of either or both sports. The Puerto Rico volleyball team has competed internationally. Other ball sports, such as stickball and handball, draw enthusiasts, with special events occasionally held at the parks and hotels.

Motor racing also enjoys wide interest. Races at Salinas Speedway in the south are held during the year. Car racing shows are brought in from around the world for presentation at Hiram Bithorn Stadium in Hato Rey.

Puerto Rico's gun clubs are not to be outdone. Members take part in international events. The P.R. Gun Club is located on Isla de Cabras, where the Police Department keeps its

peting in Río Piedras, Manatí, Bayamon and Condado. Attendance at these games is free. Sports bars provide a full complement of National Football League games on TV during the season. Shannan's Pub in Río Piedras shows all of Sunday's games with the help of two satellite dishes and a dozen TV receivers. And cable TV brings college and pro games into homes weekly during the season.

Soccer and volleyball are popular sports at the park courts and on the beaches. Most high

armory. Shotguns can be heard popping off during the weekly sessions of skeet shooting.

The grand San Blas Half-Marathon, held in the Coamo area every year, draws hundreds of contestants from around the world. Often the event is won by runners from Kenya. The 13-mile (21-km) race brings thousands of spectators to the south.

Unquestionably, the islanders' interest in a wide variety of sports is growing at an accelerating pace. And it's a far cry from the Taíno games of ancient times: modern technology, such as computerization and electronic communication, promises new dimensions to the already booming field.   ❑

LEFT: taking to the fairways on one of the island's lush golf courses.
ABOVE: surfer "soul arches" at "Wilderness", Ramey.

PLACES

A detailed guide to the entire island, with principal sites clearly cross-referenced by number to the maps

Puerto Rico? That's beaches, right, and *paradores,* and old Spanish forts tossed in with a few frosty rum drinks? Well, yes and no. You won't want to miss Old San Juan's colorful streets, or the chance to stand on El Morro's walls, looking out into the Atlantic at the ghosts of 16th-century British invaders, and you certainly shouldn't leave the island without tasting a *piña colada* – but there are far more places to see and understand than those fringed with surf and sand.

We've started this section of the book in Puerto Rico's most populous area, San Juan. Old San Juan, an eight-block area on a small peninsula, harks back to the 1500s, while only a few miles away, in Hato Rey and Río Piedras, modern commerce is being conducted in sleek steel-and-glass corporate offices.

If metropolitan San Juan is the most humanly populated area of the island, then the northeast is the most geographically populated. The range of terrain in the region, from beaches to dense rainforest to secluded islands, is staggering. Here, too, you'll find the island's best beach and some of the finest yachting.

As you head west from San Juan, exploration of the northern part of the island reveals one of the largest cave networks in the Western hemisphere, as well as the oddly-scaled karst mountain region. Limestone formations rise above the island's most historic cities – Arecibo, Lares, San Sebastián.

The western reaches of Puerto Rico feature beautiful beaches, surfers' paradises and towns worth discovering, such as metropolitan Mayagüez and architecturally rich San Germán.

In the south of the island, you'll realize fully the relaxed pace of life in Puerto Rico. There's Ponce, a pearl of a city, on the coast, but if you're tired of the urban hustle you'll never be at a loss to find a quiet place to sit in the sun.

The heart of the island is its spine, the Cordillera Central. Here, the Ruta Panoramica will take the adventurous driver from one end of the range to the other, affording spectacular views all the while.

But don't let the island's boundaries stop your explorations: off its shores lie three other islands with charms all their own: Vieques, Culebra and Mona. ❑

PRECEDING PAGES: San Juan skyline at dusk; ancient and modern at the Old Casino in San Juan; boats on the quay, San Juan Yacht Club.
LEFT: Playa las Palmas, Punta la Galiena.

A T L A N T I C

Pta Aguacate Jacinto
Pta Agujereada
Punta Borinquen
(Antigua Base Ramey)
Pta Borinquen
San Antonio
Feliciano
Bahía de
Aguadilla
Aguadilla
Palmar
Centro
Colosó
Cuba
Capá
Isabela
112
Mora
Quebradillas
San Antonio
Aceitunas
La Casa
de Piedra
Matojillo
Cordillera Jaicoa
Guajataca
Forest Reserve
112
Sabrinas
Pta
Jobos
Piedra
Gorda
Mt Zumamon
Lake
Guajataca

Pta
Peñón Hatillo
Camuy
Alcántarilla
Espiet
La Pica
La Cuesta
San Pedro
Rafael Capó
Pta
Maracayo
Camizales
22
Lechuga
Domínguito
Bajadero
Allende
Pta
las Tunas
La Marina
San Luis
Animas
22
Imbery
Palmas
Altas
La Boca
Barceloneta
Pta
Manatí
Playa Pu
Manatí
Beg
Cot
San José

Arecibo
Cueva del Indio

Manatí
Búfalo
149
Pa

Pta Higüero
119
Aguada
Centro Puntas
Pta Cadena
115
Cadena
La Tres
Hermanos
2
Anasco
Josefa
109
119
San Sebastián
119
Perchas
Tabonuco
128
Arecibo
Observatory
Bayaney
Tanamá
Bosque Estatal
de Río Abajo
Montaña
Montebello
Florida
Baraho
10
Dos Bocas
Lago
Dos Bocas
Area Recreativa
Río Abajo
Cerro Gordo
Ha
La Cordillera
149
149

Rincón
Córcega
Bahía
de Añasco
Mani
Playa del Mar
Pta Algarrobo
115
Mayagüez
La Corza
120
Grande
de Añasco
Las Marías
124
Lares
Ángeles
111
Lago
Caonillas
Utuado
Perchas
110
111
988
Jayuya
140
Los Tres Picachos
1205
149
1000
Toro Ne
Forest F

Bahía de
Mayagüez
Pta Guanajibo
Bahía Bramadero
Cerrillo
2
Sabalos
Rosario
Conde Avila
Joyuda
Delicias
Pta Ostiones
Puerto Real
Pta Boca Prieta
Las Vegas
120
Mariaco
105
Finca
Montañas de Urayan
Maricao
Forest Reserve
San
Agustín
103
La Ratina
Hormigueros
San
Germán
Cordillera
Alta
Villa Pérez
135
Los Rábanos
Guilarte
Forest Reserve
761
Monte Guilarte
1205
889
Guilarte
Forest Reserve
1044
129
939
Adjuntas
La Pica
Vivi Arriba
Cerro de Punta
1338
(Puntita)
Toro Negro
Forest Reserve
Guaraguao
Martueño
Santo
Domingo
Peñuelas
140
144
139
1183
Cerro Maravilla
Margarita
Maragüez
Corral
Viejo
139
Centr
Villal
Collores
150
Guay
Juana Díaz

Pta Guaniquilla
Bahía de Boquerón
Pta Melones
El Combate
Pta Aguila
Bahía Salinas
Pta Jagüey
Guaniquilla
100
Cabo
Rojo
102
Cuatro
Caminos
Lajas
Palmarejo
Llanos
117
Boquerón
Boquerón
Nature Reserve
Corozo
Bosque Estatal
de Boquerón
Pta Tocón
Isla
Guayacán
121
La Plata
Bosque Estatal
de Susúa
116
Parguera
Isla
Magueyes
Guánica
Forest Reserve
Ensenada
Salinas
Pta Brea
116
Negrón Torres
Palomas
Laguna
de Guánica
Guánica
Los Indios
Indios
Playa de
Tamarindo
Cayos de
Caña Gorda
Playa de
Guayanilla
Cayo
María Langa
Yauco
132
Tallaboa
Alta
Guayanilla
Tallaboa
Pashillo
Bajo
Coto Laurel
Santo
Pashillo
Bajo
2
10
Ponce
1
Boca
Chica
Pta
Cuchara
Pta
Carenero
Pta
Cabullones
14
Aguilita
149
El Allen
(US Navy)
52
132
Coabey
Cerro de Punta
140
10
Pta
Cortad
Vel
Cayo Berberia

Cayo Morrillito
Caja
de Mue

Dominican Republic

C A R I B B E A N

Puerto Rico

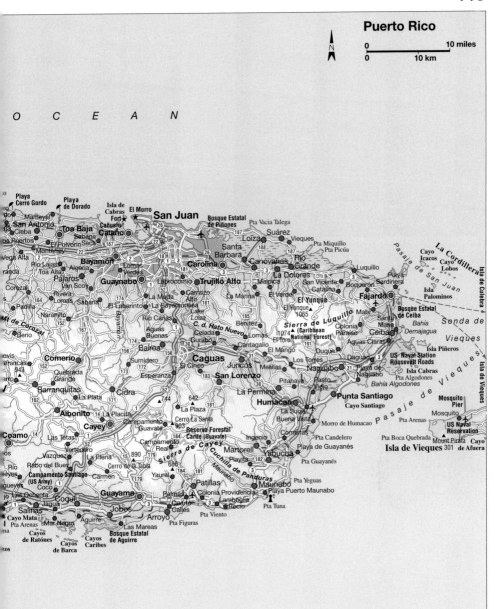

0 ─────────── 10 miles
0 ─────────── 10 km

Punta del Morro

Port of San Juan Lighthouse

City Walls (Murallas de San Juan)

El Morro
31

Bastion de San Antonio

32 SAN JUAN CEMETERY

Bateria San Fernando

Calle del Morro

Bastion de Santa Rosa

CEMENTERIO DE SANTA MARIA MAGDALENA DE PAZZIE

Bastion de Santa Elena

Bastion de Santo Domingo

35 La Perla

Calle Lucila Silva

Bastion de Las Animas

Escuela de Artes Plásticas

Calle Norzagaray

Plaza del Quinto Centenario

Dominican Convent, Institute of Puerto Rican Culture

Museo de Arte e **36** Historia de San Juan

City Walls (Murallas de San Juan)
18

Calle de las Monjas

Cuartel de Ballajá, Museo de las Américas **27** **29**

Totem Telurico **28**

23

26 San José

C. Virtud

Casa de las Contrafuertes, Pharmacy Museum

Calle San

Detensa de la

C. de Beneficiencia

Antiguo Asilo de Beneficienca **30**

Plaza San José

22 **24** Museo Pablo Casals

Calle Cruz

C. San Sebastián

Iglesia Metodista

Calle Sol

Dios de Pentecostal

Casa Blanca **33**

Casa Rosa **34**

Calle Sol

El Gran Convento

Calle del Cristo

Calle San José

Museo del Indio **25**

Calle

Bastion de San Augustin

La Rogativa **20**

Caleta de las Monjas

15

Calle Hospital

City Hall (Alcaldía)

San Juan Gate **16**

Caleta de San Juan

San Juan Cathedral **14**

7

Plaza de Armas **8**

Museo Felisa Rincón de Gautier **21**

Recinto Oeste

Calle R. Cordero

Calle Fortaleza

Santa

La Fortaleza **9**

Palacio Rojo

Centro Nacional de Artes Populares y Artesanías **13**

Casa del Libro **12**

11

Calle Tetuan

Calle Cruz

Calle

Rec

Siervas de Marin

PARQUE DE LAS PALOMAS

10

Cristo Chapel (Capilla de Cristo)

La Princesa **19**

Bastion de Las Palmas

City Wall **18**

Bastion Sant Jus

17

Paseo de la Princesa

Calle Presidio

Bahía de San Juan

Trolley Terminal

US Customs House (Edificio de Aduana)

Calle Puntillo

El Arsenal

Calle Puntillo

US Coast Guard

La Punt

Old San Juan

0 — 200 yds
0 — 200 m

N

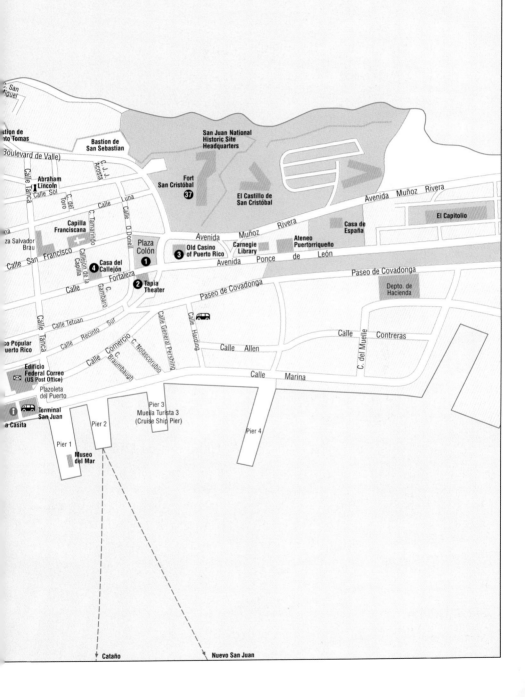

ATLANTIC OCEAN

San Juan National
Historic Site
Headquarters

Bastion de
San Sebastian

C. San
riguel

stion de
to Tomas

Boulevard de Valle)

Fort
San Cristóbal

37

Calle Tanca

Abraham
Lincoln

Calle Sol

C. del
Toro

C. J. J.
Acosta

Calle

Luna

Calle O.Donell

El Castillo de
San Cristóbal

Avenida   Muñoz   Rivera

El Capitolio

Capilla
Franciscana

C. Tamarindo

Avenida   Muñoz   Rivera

Casa de
España

za Salvador
Brau

Calle San Francisco

Callejón de la
Capilla

Plaza
Colón

1

Old Casino
of Puerto Rico

3

Carnegie
Library

Ateneo
Puertorriqueño

Casa del
Callejón

4

Fortaleza

C.
Gambaro

Calle

2 Tapia
Theater

Avenida   Ponce   de   León

Paseo de Covadonga

Calle Tanca

Calle Tetuan

Calle Recinto   Sur

Calle   Comercio

C. Notascorubio

Calle General Pershing

Calle Harding

Paseo de Covadonga

Depto. de
Hacienda

co Popular
uerto Rico

Calle

C. C.
Braumbaugh)

Calle   Allen

Calle   Contreras

C. del Muelle

Edificio
Federal Correo
(US Post Office)

Plazoleta
del Puerto

Calle   Marina

Terminal
San Juan

a Casita

Pier 1

Museo
del Mar

Pier 2

Pier 3
Muella Turista 3
(Cruise Ship Pier)

Pier 4

Cataño

Nuevo San Juan

OLD SAN JUAN

There's a wealth of architectural treasures in this oldest of American cities. Fortunately, many of them aren't swamped by the hordes of cruise-ship tourists

Map on pages 116–7

San Juan

N o matter how much history is crammed within the cobblestoned streets of Old San Juan, no matter how seductive the pastel-and-wrought-iron Spanish colonial houses may seem, no matter how chock-to-the-brim with opportunities for socializing and partying this city may be, it is something altogether more spiritual that attracts Puerto Ricans and overseas visitors alike to San Juan.

There is something in the place that traps travelers and forces them to move at the old city's pace. If you've rushed through Old San Juan, you certainly have not been there. Get a good pair of walking shoes and ramble; a car is as much a liability as it is an asset here, anyway.

This oldest of American cities has iron streets, filled in with *adoquines*, or blocks of slag, from the lowland smelting mills of Spain's 16th-century empire. (The stones were brought over by the Spanish and used as ballast for their ships.) It has two of the most invulnerable forts ever constructed, which are connected by walls that circle a peninsula, and some of the finest restaurants and bars in the Caribbean. And the city is full of art galleries.

It is also full of some of the loudest tourists you'll meet anywhere. If you are one of them, please adjust the volume. If you aren't, it might be mentioned at this point that even within its tiny area, Old San Juan has an endless supply of undiscovered attractions to enjoy. These are what lead second-time visitors to call for a taxi to Old San Juan as soon as they step off the plane at Luis Muñoz Marín International Airport.

PRECEDING PAGES: strolling along one of Old San Juan's many-hued streets. **LEFT:** colonial style in Old San Juan. **BELOW:** monument to Christopher Columbus in Plaza Colón.

Into the city

As Puerto Rico's Spanish history begins with Columbus, an exploration of Old San Juan could naturally begin in the **Plaza Colón ❶**, or Columbus Square, a quadrangle built around a commemorative statue of the explorer. It is here that the high-speed, heavily trafficked *avenidas* Ponce de León and Muñoz Rivera give way to the narrow and scarcely navigable grid that is Old San Juan. If you're without a car this will be your last stop on the municipal bus, or *público*. If you are driving, you should now start looking for a place to park.

Located at the southeastern corner of the Old San Juan quadrant, Plaza Colón is an ideal spot for fanning out on a walking tour of the city. The square itself offers a good introductory stroll. On its south side is the **Tapia Theater ❷**, a tasteful, ochre, hacienda-like structure dating from 1826 and beautifully restored in the mid-1970s (box office open Mon–Fri, 9am–4pm; tel: 722-0407).

For all its other cultural achievements, Puerto Rico has produced very little theater of note; Alejandro

TIP

A good way to get around the old city is by using the free small yellow buses that go to El Morro and Fuerte San Cristóbal (and points between the two), which run every 5–8 minutes from 7.30am to 7.30pm, reducing in frequency later in the evening. Stops (*paradas*) are marked.

BELOW: view of Old San Juan from just offshore.

Tapia y Rivera (1826–82), after whom the theater is named, is the earliest and perhaps most notable exception. Today the theater premières plays by contemporary international dramatists. Across the street from the theater on the plaza's eastern side is the **Old Casino of Puerto Rico ❸**, built shortly after Puerto Rico became a US colony early in the 20th century but harking back architecturally to the Spanish reign.

Ironically, if somewhat predictably, the path most tourists take into Old San Juan is the least characteristic of the city. **Calle Fortaleza** is, at least for three blocks, as cluttered with souvenir shops, jewelry shops and shoe stores as any place in the city. Fortunately, Calle Fortaleza is just as crowded with architectural wonders. The first right along the street is **Callejón de la Capilla**, a romantic, lantern-lit alley-way that arcs uphill to Calle San Francisco.

At the corner of Fortaleza and Callejón de la Capilla, the **Casa del Callejón ❹**, an 18th-century residence, houses two charming museums – one dedicated to colonial architecture and the other to the Puerto Rican family – but in 1999 both were closed indefinitely for restoration.

Continuing on Calle Fortaleza, you can turn right on Calle Tanca for a bit of relaxation in the sloping Plaza Salvador Brau, or make a left down Calle Tanca towards the piers of San Juan Port. Nearby at the waterfront, **Plazoleta de San Juan** teems with eager visitors who purchase souvenirs and folk art from local artisans.

Most ports which serve a large number of cruise ships end up looking rather like jungles of cranes and heavy machinery. San Juan, which takes more cruise traffic than any other port in the Caribbean, is an exception. The port not only benefits from the tastefulness of its more utilitarian maritime buildings (the

pink, mock-colonial **US Customs House** ❺ is a good example of this) but actually boasts a beautiful cityscape as well.

The waterfront has become even more attractive now that the ambitious $120-million **Frente Portuario** complex is finished. This Mediterranean-style mega-project offers 200 condominium apartments across three buildings, the 242-room Wyndham Hotel and Casino, two office towers, a 603-space parking garage and 110,000 sq. ft (10,200 sq. meters) of retail space.

Frente Portuario, designed to ensure that it blends in with the rest of Old San Juan, features picturesque cobblestone-like paved boulevards lined with wrought-iron lamps and red-tiled roofs. Visitors can browse through art galleries, eateries and boutiques.

The government has already spent $100 million on renovating half a dozen cruise-ship ports along the waterfront. Some of the world's largest cruise ships, including Royal Caribbean Line's *Monarch of the Seas* and its twin sister, *Sovereign of the Seas*, regularly call here. From Pier 2 you can also take the ferry to Cataño, home of the Bacardi rum distillery. At 50 cents a passenger, this ferry is truly one of Puerto Rico's great bargains.

Plaza de Hostos is an oasis of shade in a square full of *adoquines*. Named after the 19th-century scholar, it provides a haven for sunburnt tourists and locals alike; the square must be the dominoes capital of the Caribbean. Looming over the plaza is the original office of the **Banco Popular de Puerto Rico** ❻, which is surely one of the great modern architectural triumphs of the Caribbean region. This brawny, 10-story edifice, built in the mid-1930s, is a fine example of Art Deco. Heavy cameo eagles brood over the impressive main entrance, which is lettered in sans-serif gilt intaglio. Elongated windows with

Map on pages 116–7

The Spanish flavor of Old San Juan's architecture is evident from any angle.

BELOW: the old city is full of romantic little side streets.

prominent pastel mullions run the full height of a faintly apsidal façade. The bank, which celebrated its centennial in 1993, presents various exhibits of historical interest during the year.

The area is particularly fortunate in its culinary offerings. **Calle Recinto Sur** has a number of first-rate restaurants, ranging from Yukiyu (Japanese) to Al Dente (Italian).

Whether approaching uphill on Calle Cruz from Plaza de Hostos, or via Calle Fortaleza from Plaza Colón, almost all travelers pass through the workaday heart of Old San Juan, centering around the **City Hall** (Alcaldía) ❼ (open Mon–Fri; closed pub. hols; tel: 724-7171) and the adjacent **Plaza de Armas ❽**. City Hall was designed to be a replica of Madrid's. What works in Europe seems rather somber for the Antilles, but it is an attractive building nonetheless, one whose charms are enhanced by the fact that small businesses operate within the same arch-covered block as the local government.

The plaza, originally known as Plaza Mayor, is no less historic. Built in 1521, it was the first square in the newly established city. It also served, in the days before soldiers were permanently billeted in San Juan, as the training field for Spanish soldiers sent out from Europe in order to defend the island – hence its current name. Stone paving of the plaza began in 1840, but it was completely remodeled in the late 1980s.

Nonetheless, the main streets along the Plaza de Armas have the unpretentious likeability of a business district, rather than the imposing sense of history of much of Old San Juan. **Calle San Francisco** is a friendly mix of tourist shops and government buildings, while the part of Calle Fortaleza just south of the plaza is an engaging few blocks of restaurants and department stores.

The City Hall, or Alcaldía, was built in stages from 1604 to 1789 and underwent extensive alterations in 1841. Tours can be arranged by appointment.

BELOW: the broad, open Plaza de Armas was remodeled in the 20th century.

La Fortaleza

Calle Fortaleza grows more dignified as it approaches **La Fortaleza ❾** itself (open Mon–Fri; closed pub. hols; tel: 721-7000, ext. 2211). This chalk-white wonder of a fortress is the oldest continuously inhabited executive mansion in the Western Hemisphere. Its construction began in 1532 and was completed in 1540, and it serves to this day as the residence of the Governor of Puerto Rico. It is an architectural wonder, but strategically it was always inadequate. This was apparent even to the Spanish architects, who decided that the nubby peninsula on which La Fortaleza was being built did not command enough of San Juan Bay to protect completely against invasion from the sea. Accordingly, construction of the massive fort at the tip of the San Juan Peninsula – El Morro – began in the 1540s.

The 1588 sinking of the Spanish Armada made the West Indian possessions of the Spanish Crown more vulnerable than ever, with the result that even more Puerto Rican colonists clamored for greater fortification. By 1595, Queen Elizabeth I had dispatched Sir Francis Drake, whose ambitions included not only a great bounty of gold but all the Spanish lands of the New World as well. Drake arrived in San Juan in late November of that year. He stopped across the bay at Isla de Cabras, and launched several dozen ships from there. Ten would never go back to England, and a total of 400 English sailors would rest forever beneath San Juan harbor. Drake's own cabin was torn apart by a mortar shell during the invasion.

Perhaps the Spanish grew complacent after the first thwarted invasion of their colonial capital, for in June 1598 the Duke of Cumberland was able to land a force of about 1,000 men in the area of Puerta de Tierra, and then march

Map on pages 116–7

TIP

Guided tours of the public areas of La Fortaleza (in English every hour; in Spanish every half hour) depart from the small plaza next to the building.

BELOW: bright bougainvillea at La Fortaleza border a serene view over the bay.

Campeche paintings and a gold-and-silver altar can be seen through the Cristo Chapel's glass doors.

on to San Juan. The 400 Spanish soldiers defending the city were suffering from tropical diseases but put up valiant resistance, enduring a 15-day siege inside El Morro before capitulating. The English flag flew over the walls of La Fortaleza. The British were hounded by Spanish colonists almost immediately, but it was less Spanish resistance than British *lack* of resistance to the same disease that led them to give in. In a matter of several weeks after the invasion, Cumberland sailed for home, having lost over 400 men, to leave San Juan to recover in peace for another 27 years.

The year 1625 saw the final occupation of La Fortaleza during colonial times. A Dutch fleet under the command of Boudewijn Hendrikszoon swiftly moved into San Juan Bay and set up a beachhead between El Morro and La Fortaleza. The Dutch burned much of the city to the ground, including a large portion of La Fortaleza. Reconstruction began in 1640; the building was expanded in 1800 and 1846.

Romantic road

Calle del Cristo (Christ's Street) is the most alluring of Old San Juan's thoroughfares, an intoxicating avenue of sights and sounds, of romance and history. Running from a point high above San Juan Bay, Calle del Cristo arches to an even higher perch above San Juan's Atlantic shore, where El Morro looks sternly out to sea. It can claim Old San Juan's most popular park, most under-rated museum and most famous chapel.

This adventure in *adoquines* begins at the **Parque de las Palomas** (Pigeon Park) **❿**, a part of the city walls which thousands of pigeons have made their home. Fabulous views of San Juan Bay and the distant suburbs of Bayamón

BELOW: children frolic with feathered friends in Parque de las Palomas.

ARCHITECTURE IN THE OLD CITY

From an architectural standpoint, La Fortaleza really captures the essence of all of Old San Juan: it is an amazing blend of building styles through the ages, from its 16th-century core to its 19th-century façade. La Fortaleza and El Morro – both World Heritage Sites – are perhaps the most outstanding, but throughout the streets of the old city are fine examples of medieval, Gothic, baroque, neo-classical and even Arabian architecture. Most buildings are in excellent condition, partly owing to the painstaking efforts of those who restored them (who worked from many original plans and used, whenever possible, original materials, like *ausubo*, or ironwood, beams) and partly because Old San Juan's sandstone walls and fortresses prevented any modern expansion.

There are some 400 historically important structures in this part of the Puerto Rican capital city, some of which are considered to be the finest examples of Spanish colonial architecture in the New World. Those of particular note include San Juan Cathedral, with a baroque façade but medieval core; San José Church, the only truly Gothic structure under the US flag; and the Dominican Convent, a 16th-century white building that now houses the Institute of Culture.

and Guaynabo make Parque de las Palomas a popular spot for lovers and an even more popular spot for aspiring ones.

Building with love

Love almost certainly played a decisive part in the construction of the quaint **Cristo Chapel** or Capilla del Cristo ⑪ (open Tues, 10am–3.30pm; free). Romantic legend has it that, during an 18th-century horse-race, one of two competing riders failed to make a left turn onto Calle Tetuán and plummeted over the cliffs, seemingly to his death. When he survived, astounded locals constructed a chapel to commemorate Christ's intercession.

Others claim that the race was really a duel over a comely young woman between two chivalrous *enamorados*. One fell to his death, and the chapel was built both to commemorate the tragedy and to block off Calle del Cristo to prevent such a mishap from ever occurring again.

The peninsula stretching below the Cristo Chapel is known as **La Puntilla**. Today it accommodates a few official buildings, a modern condominium complex and a large parking lot.

A short walk up Calle del Cristo on the right is one of Puerto Rico's most enchanting and least-known museums. The **Casa del Libro** ⑫ (open Tues–Sat, 11am–4.30pm; closed pub. hols; free) is a breezy, parqueted sanctuary which is dedicated to the history of books and printing. Within its walls are nearly 5,000 rare sketches, illustrations and ancient manuscripts, as well as work by local artists and illustrators. Two of the museum's most prized possessions are royal mandates, signed in 1493 by Ferdinand and Isabella of Spain, concerning the provisioning of the fleet of Columbus for his second voyage, which resulted in

Map on pages 116–7

TIP

You can get many discounts and special offers on historic site tours, folklore shows, lodgings, meals and more by joining Puerto Rico's LeLoLai VIP program for a small fee. Phone 723-3135 for more information.

BELOW: dusk settles on Calle del Cristo, with the Cristo Chapel providing a romantic backdrop.

the discovery of Puerto Rico. Another precious work is one of only six known copies of the first printing of the Third Part of the *Summa* of St Thomas Aquinas, dating from 1477.

In front of San Juan Cathedral stands a gnarled tree – a living gesture of international friendship from dozens of North and South American nations.

Next door, the **Centro Nacional de Artes Populares y Artesanías** or Popular Arts and Crafts Center (open Mon–Sat, 9am–5pm), run by the Institute of Puerto Rican Culture, houses a collection of paintings from the 18th century to the present. A variety of island crafts are also displayed and offered for sale at the shop inside.

If you build up an appetite exploring this oldest and best-known street of the old city, don't worry: half a dozen eateries crowd this end of Calle del Cristo. In addition, any aesthetic overdose one suffers on the south part of the street can be cured with a bracing *piña colada* in one of the bars on the north side. A plaque around the corner on Calle Fortaleza claims that a bar which once occupied the site of what is now a jewelry store was the birthplace of the *piña colada* in 1963. According to long-time imbibers, however, the coconut, pineapple and rum drink was concocted well before then.

A cathedral and a convent

Ascending Cristo Street, even the most skeptical of travelers will begin to see what he or she came to San Juan for. On the right, usually bathed in sunlight in the afternoon, is **San Juan Cathedral** (open daily, 8.30am–4pm; free), a fabulous beige-and-white structure that must count among the most important houses of worship in the west. It was built in 1540 and carefully restored in the 19th and 20th centuries, and the beauty of its exterior is immediately perceptible. Three tiers of white pilasters and arches mount to a simple cross at the

BELOW: the much-photographed cupolas of San Juan Cathedral.

Map
on pages
116–7

cathedral's pinnacle. The three brick-red and white cupolas atop the building are among San Juan's most photogenic objects, and must themselves lure many visitors to the island each year.

But the interior of the cathedral is not as easy to appreciate for anyone who thinks of cathedrals primarily in their French, German or British incarnations. For one thing, the floor is of black parquet, which seems to belie the solemnity of the building. The brown and ochre *trompe l'oeil* ceiling is pretty, but it appears too close to the worshipper's eye. The cathedral really needs several visits but will in time reward the most discerning.

Among the highlights of the cathedral are **Ponce de León's marble tomb**, with an understated virgin warrior glancing down at the body and the red script of the epitaph, and the glittering blue statue of **La Virgen de Providencia**, Puerto Rico's patroness, located nearby. A relic of San Pio, a Roman martyr, is in a glass case containing a macabre plaster figure of the saint, to the rear of the altar. There's another such effigy, of a prostrate Jesus, in the **Chapel of Souls in Purgatory**, which is in the cathedral's right nave.

Directly across Calle del Cristo from the cathedral is **El Gran Convento** ⓯, established in 1651 as a convent for Carmelite nuns, San Juan's first. When the nuns moved to Santurce in the early part of this century, the convent fell into disrepair. Its most recent restoration took place in 1996, when private investors turned it into the five-star, 100-room luxury Gran Hotel. They also added a casino – much to the anger of the nuns, who argued that slot machines were a sacrilege to the memory of their sisters buried underneath. Though very few of the fixtures are originals, all the interior decor fits in harmoniously with the concept of a nunnery-turned-hotel.

BELOW: religious crafts for sale in the old city.

History aside, San Juan natives view their city as a place to have fun.

BELOW: modern sculpture in an ancient city: dramatic lines of La Rogativa.

One block away, the **Center for Advanced Studies** – originally built in 1842 as a religious school for young men – houses a fine library of the Caribbean and Puerto Rico. Besides its academic value, the center can be a haven for weary tourists and locals alike.

Steps and statues

Across Cristo from San Juan Cathedral, between the fork of two of San Juan's oldest and most pleasant *adoquine* streets, lies the lush **Plazuela de las Monjas** (Nuns' Square), a perfect spot for an urban picnic. The square looks out not only on the cathedral and El Gran Convento but also on the **Casa Cabildo**, San Juan's original City Hall, which now houses an interior design company.

A walk down **Caleta San Juan** will take you to the massive wooden **San Juan Gate** ⓰, built in 1639 and the only one of three original portals remaining. Sailors weary of their voyages used to moor their ships in San Juan Bay, ferry themselves ashore, enter through the gate, and walk to prayer services via Caleta San Juan, which describes a conveniently straight line between the gates and the main altar of the cathedral.

Through the gate is **Paseo de la Princesa** ⓱, a romantic bayfront promenade that skirts the **Old City Wall** ⓲, or *muralla*. Built of sandstone from 1635 to 1641, it measures up to 20 feet (6 metres) in thickness and at one time completely surrounded the colonial city, guarding it against enemy attacks. Along the *paseo* – an immaculate, landscaped pedestrian boulevard facing the sea – are various statues, a large fountain, and kiosk vendors selling everything from cotton candy to *guarapo de caña* (sugar-cane juice). Various family activities, such as concerts and children's theater, are scheduled here on many weekends.

The old **La Princesa ⑲** jail (open Mon–Sat, 9am–4pm), midway along the promenade, now houses the Tourism Company, an art gallery and a museum featuring the actual jail cells used centuries ago.

Continuing up Recinto del Oeste, past more examples of fine colonial architecture, one reaches a modern sculpture, **La Rogativa ⑳**, showing the bishop of San Juan followed by three torch-bearing women, which commemorates the failure of an English siege of the city in 1797. The legend runs that General Sir Ralph Abercromby led a fleet of British ships to take San Juan in a rapid, all-out assault by land and sea. When this plan failed, Abercromby ordered a naval blockade, which lasted two weeks, while the residents of San Juan began to suffer from dysentery, losing hope of the arrival of Spanish reinforcements from the inland settlements. The governor called for a *rogativa*, or divine entreaty, to the saints Ursula and Catherine. All the women of San Juan marched through the town carrying torches, to the accompaniment of loud ringing of tocsins. Abercromby, believing reinforcements had arrived, quit San Juan, never to return.

A short walk down Recinto del Oeste brings you to **El Museo Felisa Rincón de Gautier ㉑** (open Mon–Fri, 9am–4pm; free). This little museum is the former home of Felisa Rincón de Gautier, or "Dona Fela", one of San Juan's most popular mayors, who led the city from 1946 to 1968 and was noted for her flamboyant style. The home-turned-museum contains many items belonging to the late Dona Fela, including her impressive collection of hand fans – as well as a film clip from the 1950s which shows the mayor bringing a plane-load of snow to the island from New York so that the children of San Juan could have a snowball fight.

Map on pages 116–7

From Paseo de la Princesa the waters of San Juan Bay look enticing – but they are considered too polluted here for swimming. The more adventurous locals and visitors, however, do often swim to the right of the big pier outside the San Juan Gate.

BELOW: bustling street market in Plaza San José.

The walk back to the cathedral on **Caleta de las Monjas** is full of surprises, chief among them the "step streets" leading up to the left toward *calles* Sol and San Sebastián. At the top of the first, **Escalinata de las Monjas**, is the old Palace of the Bishop of San Juan. The second, **Calle de Hospitál**, is a favorite of artists and photographers.

With all the historical legacy San Juan offers, it's sometimes easy to forget to view the city as its natives view it: a place to have fun. **Calle San Sebastián** is perhaps the pre-eminent place in the old city to do just that. Perpendicular to the top of Calle del Cristo, it's a place of museums and old homes whose many bars and spacious plaza make it a mecca for *sanjuanero* youth.

Plaza San José  is the focal point of the street, paved with rosy Spanish conglomerate around a statue of Ponce de León made from English cannons melted down after the first invasion. The plaza draws hundreds of partying teenagers on warm weekend evenings, and hundreds of fun-loving tourists throughout the year.

San Juan's **Dominican Convent** ❷ (open Mon–Sat, 9am–5pm) dominates the plaza. Built in 1523, this mammoth, white, elegantly domed structure has seen as much history as any building on the island, having housed both English and Dutch occupying forces over the centuries.

The convent now houses the music and book store of the **Institute of Puerto Rican Culture**, the body which more than any other has been responsible for the renaissance in Puerto Rican scholarship and art over the last several years. Under its auspices the parts of the convent not used for office space have been converted to cultural use. A beautiful indoor patio is the scene of many concerts and plays, and it now serves as the focus for the magnificent San Juan Museum of History and Art. The old convent library has been restored to its original 16th-century decor.

Museum spin-offs

A whole complex of museums has sprung up around the Dominican Convent. The **Museo Pablo Casals** ❷ (open Tues–Sat, 9.30am–5.30pm), which abuts the convent, is a petite, gray, two-story townhouse storing memorabilia of the legendary cellist who moved to Puerto Rico in 1957 and lived here until his death in 1973. It includes manuscripts, instruments, texts of his speeches to the United Nations, and a collection of cassettes of his music which can be heard on request. A Casals arts festival takes place every year.

Other interesting visits to consider in the Dominican Convent area include the **Museo del Indio** ❷ (open Tues–Sat, 9am–4pm; free), which concentrates on the indigenous cultures of Puerto Rico, and the small scientific **Museum of Pharmacy** (open Wed–Sun, 9am–4.30pm) on the ground floor of the 18th-century Casa de los Contrafuertes.

Next to the Convent is the stunning and unusual **San José Church** ❷. Built shortly after the convent in the 1530s, San José is the second oldest church in the western hemisphere; only San Juan Cathedral, a half-block down the street, is older. The Gothic architecture of the structure is a true rarity; only the Spanish arrived in the New World early enough to

TIP

If your feet need a break, consider a ride on a *calesa* (horse-drawn carriage) reminiscent of old colonial days. The carriages are based just off Pier 1 at the San Juan Harbor front. Night rides are particularly enchanting.

BELOW: the Puerto Rican flag proudly displayed in a San Juan doorway.

build Gothic churches, and only a handful exist today. The interior of San José certainly has far more charm than that of the nearby cathedral.

A wooden crucifix of the mid-16th century, donated by Ponce de León, is one of the highlights, as is the 15th-century altar brought from Cadíz. In addition, the great Puerto Rican painter José Campeche is buried here.

Across from the Plaza San José is the **Cuartel de Ballajá** ㉗, built as a hospital, and later home to Spanish troops. This structure was the centerpiece of the restoration of Old San Juan in time for the 500th anniversary in 1992 of Columbus's arrival in the New World. A black granite tablet inscribed in Spanish offers maps of the area and tells how the building was restored.

Directly in front is the three-level **Plaza del Quinto Centenario** ㉘, which looks out over the Atlantic. Dominating this plaza, at the center of an eight-pointed pavement design, is the controversial **Totem Telurico**, a terracotta (some say phallic) sculpture by local artist Jaime Suárez that symbolizes the blending of Taíno, African and Spanish cultures. Nearby is a fountain with 100 jets of water; it is supposed to symbolize five centuries of Puerto Rican history.

On Ballajá's second floor is the **Museo de las Américas** ㉙ (open Tues–Fri 10am–4pm, Sat–Sun 11am–5pm), which provides an overview of cultural development in the New World. Among its colorful exhibit of crafts in the Americas are a replica of a country chapel and an exhibit on Haitian voodoo.

Across the plaza from the Cuartel de Ballajá, along unmarked Calle Beneficiencia, is the stately **Antiguo Asilo de Beneficienca**, or Old Home for the Poor ㉚ (galleries open Wed–Sun, 9am–4.30pm). The building, constructed in the 1840s to house the destitute, today serves as headquarters for the Puerto Rican Institute of Culture.

Map on pages 116–7

After Ponce de León's death in Cuba in 1521, his body was brought to Puerto Rico and laid to rest in San José Church, where his descendants worshipped. Later, in 1908, the body was moved to San Juan Cathedral.

BELOW: ancient and modern come together again: a US Coast Guard helicopter flies over El Morro.

The Port of San Juan Lighthouse sits at the highest point of El Morro and marks the channel entrance to San Juan Harbor.

BELOW: entrance to El Morro.

Climb the stairs, go through an ornate foyer and enter the room to your left. Here you'll find an impressive exhibit on the Taíno artifacts. On your right is a small exhibit of Puerto Rican religious statues. Two huge interior courtyards are used for various cultural activities; surrounding them are the institute's main administration offices.

The Spanish colonists considered San Juan chiefly as a military stronghold, and held military architecture as their first priority. It is not surprising, then, that contemporary *sanjuaneros* are proudest of the breathtaking forts, unique in the western world, that their antecedents left them.

El Morro

El Castillo San Felipe del Morro, simply known as **El Morro** ❸ (open daily, 9am–5pm), features a maze of secret access tunnels, dungeons, lookouts, ramps, barracks and vaults. Declared a World Heritage Site by the United Nations, El Morro falls under the auspices of the US National Park Service. Free tours, in English and Spanish, are given daily.

This, the larger of the city's two forts, commands San Juan Bay with six levels of gun emplacements and walls that tower 140 feet (43 meters) over the Atlantic. Its guns were capable of aiming at any ship within El Morro's field of vision, no matter the distance, and the walls themselves, connected with the system that circles Old San Juan, are 20 feet (6 meters) thick.

The fort's first battery was completed in the 1540s, but it was not until 1589, when Juan Bautista Antonelli arrived with a team of other Spanish military engineers to begin raising a true bulwark along the edge of the peninsula, that the fort was completed. When Sir Francis Drake attacked in 1595 he was

roundly repulsed, but Cumberland's land attack from the Condado succeeded in piercing El Morro's still vulnerable rear approach.

The English held the fort for three months, until dysentery took the lives of nearly half their men. It would be the last time El Morro would fall, even holding out against the Dutch siege of 1625 and the American gunnery fire which rained upon it during the Spanish-American War of 1898.

Today, visitors appreciate El Morro (which means "headland" in Spanish) more for its breathtaking views and architecture than for the protection it gives them. The approach to the fort is over a vast, 27-acre (11-hectare) parkland, once the former drill square for the soldiers and currently a haven for kite-flyers and strolling lovers. A gravel path through the green leads over a moat and into the massive structure, crossing El Morro's main courtyard with its beautiful yellow walls and white archways. Here are a souvenir shop and a museum, both of which are useful in orienting the traveler to the fort's layout and long history.

The massive archway facing over San Juan Bay on the west side of the courtyard is the entrance to what looks like the longest skateboard run in the world: a huge, stone, step-flanked ramp leading to the lower ramparts. This is the most popular of the fort's various sections, affording views of the surf crashing below, and profiling the fort from the ocean side, as its invaders saw it.

Back on the upper level of El Morro, a left turn through the courtyard patio leads to another ramp, this one twisting rightward toward the **Port of San Juan Lighthouse**, which was destroyed by an American mortar shell during the Spanish-American War but later restored.

San Juan Cemetery ㉜, considered by many to be the most picturesque resting-place for old bones in the world, sits on a broad, grassy hummock of land

Map on pages 116–7

The lovely rounded garitas, or sentry boxes, that line the walls of San Juan's forts serve as Puerto Rico's official symbol. But be warned: they are very secluded, and as the city is short on public restrooms, they are occasionally quite malodorous.

BELOW: San Juan Cemetery glimpsed through El Morro's stone walls.

Map
on pages
116–7

Playwright Oscar Wilde immortalized La Perla in his study of slum-life, La Vida.

BELOW: view of La Perla and El Morro from San Cristóbal.
RIGHT: Puerto Rico's most famous silhouette: El Morro fort in Old San Juan.

tucked between El Morro's walls and the pounding surf. Its highlight is a tiny, 19th-century circular chapel, set among the bleached-white gravestones.

Abutting El Morro's grounds, the **Casa Blanca** ❸ (open Tues–Sun, 9am–noon, 1–4.30pm) is the oldest house in Puerto Rico, having been built for Ponce de León in 1521. Used in the years preceding the construction of La Fortaleza as a shelter against the attacks of savage Carib tribes, it was owned by the conquistador's family until the late 18th century and is now a museum of 16th- and 17th-century family life, with an ethnographic section. The nearby **Casa Rosa** ❸ (also referred to as Casa Rosada) is a lovely pink building overlooking the bay and serves as a day-care center for government employees' children.

La Perla

A glance down the beachfront from El Morro will show one the most bizarre and colorful coastal cityscapes imaginable. One- and two-story shacks, seemingly piled one on top of another, crowd the coastline all the way from El Morro to San Cristóbal, running along the battlements which formerly connected the two castles. This is **La Perla** ❸, the so-called "world's prettiest slum". Set against the backdrop of an aquamarine Atlantic, it looks at first glance delightful, but even the toughest of San Juan residents will warn tourists against drugs, violence and a general lawlessness which are rampant in this otherwise charming neighborhood. Along Norzagaray Street, the **Museo de Arte e Historia de San Juan** ❸ beckons visitors for a look at the way the city was back then (open Mon–Fri, 8am–4pm).

Though overshadowed by its more famous neighbor to the west, **Fuerte San Cristóbal** ❸ (open daily, 9am–5pm) makes as fascinating a trip as El Morro. What El Morro achieved with brute force, San Cristóbal achieved with much more subtlety. It sits 150 feet (45 meters) above the ocean waves, reflects the best of 17th-century military architectural thought, and has a fascinating network of tunnels that was used both for transporting artillery and for ambushing luckless invaders.

The fort was completed in 1678 as a means of staving off land attacks on San Juan, like the English one under Cumberland, made to capture El Morro in 1595. But the fort as it is known today is the product of the acumen of two Irishmen, "Wild Geese" who had fled from the Orange monarchy and were in the employ of the Spanish army.

Alejandro O'Reilly and Tomas O'Daly designed a system of battlements and sub-forts that ensured that no one could take Fuerte San Cristóbal without taking all of its ramparts first. No one ever did. The first shot of the Spanish-American War was fired from San Cristóbal's walls.

Frequent guided tours explain how San Cristóbal's unique system of defense worked, and also point out some of the fort's big attractions, like the "**Devil's Sentry Box**", a *garita* at the end of a long tunnel that runs to the waterline. Views from the battlements are outstandingly spectacular, particularly in the direction *sanjuaneros* describe as "towards Puerto Rico": Condado, Hato Rey and El Yunque. ❑

METROPOLITAN SAN JUAN

*Condado, Punta las Marias and Isla Verde have fine beaches,
Santurce is a genuine marketplace, Hato Rey is a major
finance center, and Bayamón has a maverick quality*

Map,
page 140

I t's easy to try to relegate **Puerto de Tierra** ❶ to the status of a sort of
verdant buffer zone between San Juan's body and its soul, separating as it
does the brawn of Santurce from the historical grandeur and romance of Old
San Juan. But Puerto Rico's greatest allure must often be sought out, and so
it is with Puerto de Tierra. The word means "gateway of land", but Puerto de
Tierra is a gateway in more ways than just the narrow literal sense.

Beachfront capitol

Commanding a fabulous view of beach and blue water, straddled by Puerto de
Tierra's two main thoroughfares, **El Capitolio** ❷, Puerto Rico's Capitol building, serves as centerpiece to the whole peninsula. Designed by Puerto Rican architect Rafael Carmoega and constructed between 1925 and 1929, El Capitolio
is a grand, white classical structure resembling the Capitol building in Washington, on a rather smaller scale but with wonderful ocean views.

The large rotunda, the last part of the building to be completed, features four
corner sections done in Venetian mosaic with gold, silver and bronze, depicting
some of the most important events in Puerto Rico's history. In the very center
of the dome is a lovely stained-glass rendering of Puerto Rico's seal. Near the
main entrance is the original Constitution of Puerto
Rico, signed in 1952 and brought back to the island in
1992 after spending nearly five years in a Washington
restoration laboratory.

PRECEDING PAGES:
San Juan and
Condado at sunset.
LEFT: El Capitolio,
Puerto de Tierra.
BELOW: relaxing in
Muñoz Rivera Park.

Nearby are a number of other buildings which,
though less imposing, are no less beautiful. The ornate
Casa de España ❸, just down the hill towards Old
San Juan from El Capitolio, is a blue-tiled, four-
towered edifice built in 1935 and paid for by the
Spanish expatriate community. Once a popular gathering spot for local gentlemen, it now serves as the
site for cultural events. Of interest inside are the tiled
painting of Don Quixote and, on the second floor, the
Salon de Los Espejos (Mirror Room) with its painted
wooden ceiling.

Down Avenida Ponce de León is the lovely
Archives and General Library of Puerto Rico
(open by appointment). Pedestals and pilasters support a graceful pediment and throw a skeleton of white
against a lovely sun-washed yellow. Now run by the
Institute of Puerto Rican Culture, the General Library
lives up to the standards the Institute has set for its
other buildings, with tessellation of red stone, delicate chandeliers and fine furniture. There's also a
small chapel on the first floor. If this seems out of
place in a library, it is because the building, built in
1877 as the last major Spanish architectural effort on
the island, was originally designed as a hospital.

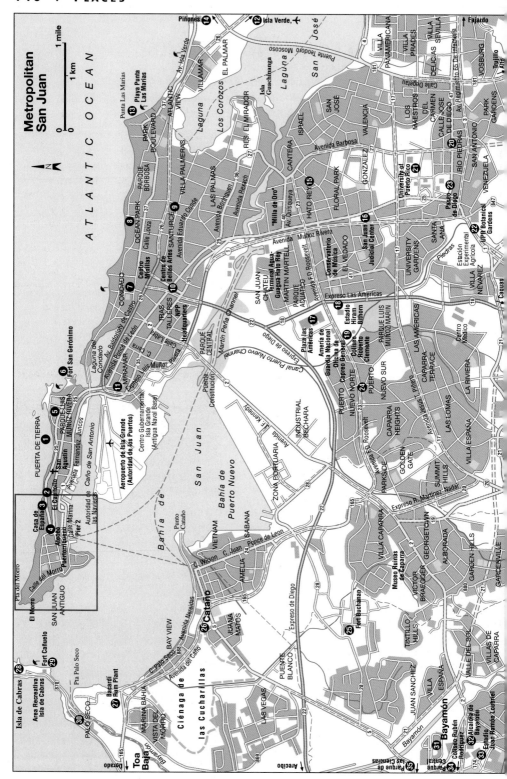

Another landmark along the boulevard is the **Ateneo Puertorriqueno** , which promotes cultural activity through conferences, lectures, films and the like. Next door is the **Carnegie Library**, established by the Carnegie Foundation and now run by the Department of Education. Further east, **Parque Luis Muñoz Rivera ❺**, with its Peace Pavilion, was dedicated in 1991 by Nobel Peace Prize-winner and former Costa Rican President Oscar Arias.

Map, page 140

The **Caribe Hilton** sits on several acres of beautifully landscaped grass and sand, overlooking a little beach-lined cove that stretches to Condado. The hotel played an important role in the industrialization of the island, as the many companies that set up shop from the 1950s onwards used the Caribe Hilton as an initial base for their executives. It closed its doors in March 1999 for a major refurbishment – including the addition of a vast shopping complex – but planned its reopening in time to see in the millennium.

The Caribe Hilton also has a historical asset in **Fort San Gerónimo ❻**, a small but crucial element of the old Spanish fortifications which stymied a British invasion of the region in 1797. The military museum inside (open Mon–Fri, 9am–4.30pm) is entertaining and worthwhile.

Within view of the Hilton stands the Art Deco **Normandie Hotel**, which first opened in 1942 and was designed to resemble the famous French ocean liner of the same name.

The Condado beaches are said to be the best in the city. Snorkeling is good, and water sports equipment can be hired. But it is not advisable to walk along the beaches at night.

Condado

"Condado" **❼** in Spanish means "county", and many Puerto Ricans still refer to the glittering strip of land between the Condado lagoon and the Atlantic Ocean as "*the* Condado". If the appellation is meant to convey anything rustic or sleepy about this part of town, it grossly misses the mark. A trip across the Puente San Gerónimo from Puerto de Tierra takes one out of history and into the tourist zone where gambling, dining, drinking and dancing are the main activities of the evening.

Ashford Avenue, Condado's main thoroughfare, looks as though it is desperately trying to run for election as the sixth borough of New York City, or perhaps as an annex of Miami Beach. In a large measure, it succeeds. Its miles of beachfront are lined with chic boutiques, banks, restaurants and – most conspicuously – hotels.

Hotels are, of course, of varying quality in Condado, but the town's lodgings seldom dip very far below the "luxury" rating. The casinos aren't exclusive; non-hotel patrons are welcome at the tables, as long as they bring their wallets. Restaurants, both hotel-affiliated and otherwise, tend to be of good quality. There's a price to pay for quality in Condado, and it is a high one. Some of the restaurants in town are almost legendary – for both their food and their prices – but are worth it for the experience.

The Condado area is constantly changing; old hotels are being knocked down and replaced by newer, bigger, more modern ones, or – as is the case with the venerable Condado Beach Hotel, constructed by the Vanderbilt family in 1919 – converted into up-market condominiums.

BELOW: catching the sun on Condado Beach.

Hot stuff: spicy Caribbean sauces are a good buy and a tasty – albeit temporary – reminder of a trip to Puerto Rico.

BELOW: shooting pool in Condado.

To go to the beach in Condado implies more than taking the sun and riding the waves. People-watching is the chief popular pastime, and there is certainly a fine variety to watch. The water here is warm and unpolluted. The Condado strip of sand, by the way, is the first beach east of San Juan which the Department of Natural Resources considers "swimmable". One unfortunate consideration for swimming and body-watching buffs who are just visiting Condado and don't have hotel rooms is that the wall of hotels lining the beach has made access somewhat difficult in spots. Remember that none of the beachfront is privately owned – all the beaches in Puerto Rico are public – but the big hotels aren't going to go out of their way to show anyone the easy route to the beach. The determined visitor, of course, will usually find the way.

Ocean Park

Heading east on Ashford Avenue, past the Marriott Hotel and the Radisson Ambassador, one approaches **Ocean Park** ❽, Condado's wild and woolly eastern fringe. Here, the houses become smaller and more spread out, and the beaches grow less crowded.

This is one of the more scenic of San Juan's beachfront panoramas, with views stretching from the palm-lined point at Boca de Cangrejos to the bright-white high-rise wall of Ashford Avenue's hotels. After a swim and perhaps a look at one of the longest and most varied stretches of Puerto Rico's north coast, retire to **Kassalta's**, an oasis of fine (and reasonably priced) native cuisine in a desert of kitsch. In this famous cafeteria/bakery/delicatessen you'll find all the San Juan newspapers, a range of Puerto Rican delicacies unmatched on the island and a fresh cup of local coffee that will electrify you.

South of Condado

A knot of highways and main roads, **Santurce** connects the more touristy and, admittedly, more picturesque areas of the metropolis. It can't claim a seacoast; in fact, one could almost define the area as the set of neighborhoods one encounters moving south from more fashionable Condado and Ocean Park. It hasn't the history of Old San Juan, having been founded only about a century ago as a fashionable suburb. But Santurce does have manifold charms of its own, making it well worth a visit for those few visitors who are prepared to make the effort.

Map, page 140

Love, not money

Santurce is considered by most to be the heart of San Juan, and not just in the sense that it's the source of the city's main traffic arteries. At a time when most cities in the world have razed their most charming business districts, Santurce survives as a true marketplace. The quaintest manifestation of this ethic is in the **Plaza del Mercado** on Calle Canals, where vendors bargain over and sell fruits, vegetables, spices and meat.

While many *sanjuaneros* come to work in Santurce, a surprising proportion come to eat. The area has long been host to many of the island's most elegant restaurants, but its most appealing establishments are often little *fondas*, as low on price as they are on pretentiousness. The arts thrive in Santurce as well, and the construction in 1981 of the attractive **Centro de Bellas Artes** , at the corner of *avenidas* Ponce de Léon and José de Diego, has brought the neighborhood a new share in San Juan's cultural wealth with its 1,800-seat Festival Hall, 760-seat Drama Hall and 210-seat Experimental Theater.

TIP

If you fancy seeing a film in English while in Puerto Rico, your best bet is in Santurce. Try the UA Paramount; Metro 1, 2, 3; or Fine Arts Cinema – all on Avenida Ponce de León.

BELOW: San Juan's Isla Verde Beach.

Back on the western edge of Santurce, closest to Old San Juan, is **Miramar** , one of the most charming and paradoxical of the suburbs in the metropolitan area, where lovely tree-lined avenues of pretty modern residences abut one of the island's sleazier red-light districts.

Airport beach

Almost everyone arrives in Puerto Rico at Luis Muñoz Marín International Airport in **Isla Verde** ⑫. Technically part of the municipality of Carolina, this San Juan suburb takes on a look of affluence that few areas as close to such booming noise, annoying traffic snarls and transient lifestyle possess – big, chalk-white blocks of high-income apartment houses choke one of the most beautiful beachfronts on the island, giving Isla Verde one of the most Miami-Beachesque aspects this side of … well, Miami Beach.

Isla Verde is very rich, but hardly anyone in Puerto Rico would disagree that it has never quite got over being an airport town. It's a bit dull. The usual airport businesses – car-rental agencies, vinyl cocktail lounges and the like – have overrun the place, and most of the residents of the area are either retired or doing their best to pretend they are. Part of the problem is, of course, location; suburbs separate Isla Verde from the historical charms of the older parts of San Juan, while water separates it from the charms of Piñones.

Riding the waves

This is not, however, to count Isla Verde as being utterly without its charms. The beaches of **Punta las Marias** ⑬ and **Isla Verde** stretch for over a mile, with white sand from the end of the beach at Ocean Park to the lovely coral

In the narrow strip of land beyond Isla Verde, between the sea and the airport, is Avenida Boca de Cangrejos, where many quioscos – semi-permanent trucks – sell barbecued specialties including fish and batter-fried vegetables.

BELOW: selecting watches at Cartier in Condado.

Map,
page 140

eefs at Boca de Cangrejos. The surf here is formidable, especially in winter, and the area known as **Piñones** ⓮ is among the most popular hangouts for young people throughout the year. And when the surf is up, and young bodies are working up a thirst riding the waves, those huge white hotels can seem very welcoming indeed.

Hato Rey

It's odd that, in so many of the great cities of the world, financial brawn and bohemian asceticism have shared the same neighborhoods. Opposites attract: New York's arty districts of Tribeca and Soho rub shoulders with Wall Street; the City of London is surrounded by universities and galleries. San Juan follows this rule to an unusual degree. Here, **Hato Rey** ⓯, the undisputed business and high-finance capital of the Caribbean, abuts – and often intermingles with – **Río Piedras**, the home of the University of Puerto Rico.

The Golden Mile

Most of the money in the Antilles is filtered through a group of institutions clustered on a section of Expreso Luis Muñoz Rivera in Hato Rey known as **The Golden Mile**. Though Operation Bootstrap certainly contributed to Puerto Rico's importance as a financial center, the recent emergence of Hato Rey as a mecca for banks and corporations owes a great deal to a long-standing Puerto Rican commitment to banking.

Everyone who visits San Juan should head down to Hato Rey, if only to see the intriguing modern architecture. Particularly interesting is the **Banco de Santander Building** – which, with its reflecting plate-glass arching from

BELOW: "The Golden Mile" – Hato Rey's financial district.

an austere concrete shaft, looks something like a giant refrigerator. Hato Rey is also home to the headquarters of **Banco Popular de Puerto Rico**, which is the island's oldest and largest bank. Law and order is carried out at the **San Juan Judicial Center** , where visitors may want to witness a criminal court case – Puerto Rican style.

Enrique Adsuar González, a respected commentator on local custom, has mentioned that the sight of Hato Rey businessmen walking the streets in Wall Street-cut woollen winter suits in 90-degree weather is one of the great ironies of contemporary Puerto Rican life.

Hato Rey has also become something of a culinary capital, if in a modest and basic way. One can't expect gourmet food in restaurants which cater solely to men who will lose their jobs if they go for an extra course, but solid Puerto Rican fare is to be had here for prices one wouldn't mind paying in the Cordillera.

A mile west of the business district on Route 23 (Avenida Franklin Delano Roosevelt) are some of Puerto Rico's more adventurous recent structures. The first, on the north side of the highway, is **Plaza Las Américas** (open Mon–Thurs and Sat, 9.30am–6pm; Fri to 9.30pm), the largest shopping mall in the Caribbean. Locals flock here to stroll amid its fountains and flowered walks and to buy everything from *guayaberas* (traditional Puerto Rican shirts) to guava juice. Across the highway to the south is the **Estadio Hiram Bithorn**, an odd, hyper-modern stadium, which is the site for a variety of sporting and cultural events – including the start of the baseball season in November each year. Neighboring **Coliseo Roberto Clemente** also hosts a number of major events, sporting and otherwise.

The largest J.C. Penney in the world is located in Plaza Las Américas; it has 350,000 sq. feet (32,500 sq m) of shopping space.

BELOW: Hato Rey's Estadio Hiram Bithorn, named after one of many Puerto Rican baseball greats.

Río Piedras

Perhaps Hato Rey maintains its humanity due only to the humanizing influence of the university town of **Río Piedras** ⓴ to the south. Within the shortest of walks, concrete and plate-glass give way to cobbled paths and flower gardens. With its 25,000 students and distinguished faculty from all parts of the world, the **University of Puerto Rico (UPR)** ㉑ is certainly unique in the American university community. Among those who've taught here have been Juan Ramón Jiménez, Pablo Casals and Arturo Morales Carrión.

The Jiménez Room, located on campus, contains a large collection of the poet's personal effects. The octagonal clock-tower, which soars out of the palms at one side of the campus, has become something of a symbol for Río Piedras.

The highlight of any visit to Río Piedras, however, must be the **Botanical Gardens** ㉒ at UPR's Agricultural Experimental Station, a mile south of the university and reachable by following the signs after turning off at the intersection of Muñoz Rivera and Route 847. Hundreds of varieties of tropical and semi-tropical plants, including many from Australia and Africa, make up one of the most extensive parks of its type in the world. The gardens comprise 200 acres (80 hectares). Suffice it to say that it's hard to imagine a botanical garden landscaped as imaginatively or as subtly as this one. Ponds, lilies, ferns and ubiquitous *yautía* compete for attention with an exceptional orchid garden.

Río Piedras is not, however, all ivory towers and ivied lanes. Its **Paseo de Diego** ㉓ is the largest pedestrian market in San Juan, with all the haggling, gesticulation and frenzy of an Arab *souk*.

Just west of here, off the Expreso Las Américas, is the fine **Centro Médico** (Medical Center), where the world-class Cardiovascular Center of Puerto Rico

Map, page 140

More than 700 cruise ships arrive every year at the Port of San Juan, the busiest ocean terminal in the West Indies.

LEFT: the Botanical Gardens.
BELOW: the university clock-tower.

and the Caribbean is to be found. Here, thousands of open-heart and bypass surgeries have been performed successfully.

Heading west on Avenida Franklin Delano Roosevelt, past Plaza Las Américas, stop at La Ceiba in **Puerto Nuevo** ㉔, a bakery or *panaderia* offering coffee, sandwiches, pastries and delicacies imported from Spain. Further up the road, **Fort Buchanan** ㉕ billets elements of the US Army, which hosts a number of community activities during the year, including Pee Wee Football.

Cataño

Crossing from San Juan on the Cataño Ferry allows excellent views of wind swept San Juan Bay. **Cataño** ㉖ itself is by no means a picturesque town. It is haphazard, almost shadeless, and utterly without charm in its shopping areas. It does, however, have a beachfront area and unrivaled views of Old San Juan.

It also has rum. In the most remote corners of the world, people who have no idea where Puerto Rico is nevertheless know the name Bacardi (for family members it's Bacardí). That they automatically associate it with Puerto Rico is all the more surprising, considering that Bacardi isn't the island's only rum, or even its best. Yet few tourists visit Puerto Rico without making a pilgrimage to the sprawling **Bacardi Rum Plant** ㉗, 5 minutes west on Route 165.

The company offers free bilingual tours of its Cataño distillery every 20 minutes (Mon–Sat, 9–10.30am and 12–4pm). The tour begins on the first floor, then goes up to the fifth floor for an exhibit of Bacardi products, and finally down to the second floor, where the production process is explained. From the distillery – which has a capacity of 100,000 gallons a day and is the largest rum distillery in the world – tourists are taken by trolley to the Bacardi

TIP

If you're planning on taking a tour of the Bacardi distillery, try to go there on a weekday when the bottling line is in production.

BELOW: bottling rum at Bacardi.

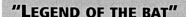

"LEGEND OF THE BAT"

The next time you pick up a bottle of Bacardi rum, take note of the bat on the label. When Don Facundo Bacardi experimented with the rum-making process in his tiny shed in Cuba back in the 1800s, colonies of fruit bats hung over his head and watched the proceedings with interest. The wine merchant and importer ended up inventing a whole new process, distilled his very first bottle of rum and never looked back. For the Bacardi family, the bat became a symbol of good luck, prosperity and tradition – and was made the Bacardi corporate symbol in 1862. Business was so good that Don Facundo quickly expanded it; by 1936 the family had decided to open a distillery in Puerto Rico.

In 1959, Fidel Castro came to power in Cuba. Shortly after, the Communists confiscated the family's extensive holdings – worth an estimated $76 million at the time – and the Bacardis were forced to shift production to Puerto Rico, Bermuda, the Bahamas and elsewhere. Today, Bacardi is truly a global empire, with plants in more than a dozen countries. Through a web of companies that include Bacardi Corporation, Bacardi & Company, Bacardi Limited and half a dozen others, the empire now accounts for 75 percent of US, and 50 percent of all the world's, rum consumption.

family museum, and finally to the visitors' pavilion, where free *piña coladas* are waiting. Here visitors can stroll around the spacious Bacardi grounds, which look across the bay to Old San Juan.

Map, page 140

Seafood center

Just north of Cataño, at the end of a pine-flecked spit of land, is **Isla de Cabras** ㉘, now a recreational area and hangout for local fishermen. The island originally housed the long-range artillery of **Fort Cañuelo** ㉙, built in 1608. In later centuries it served as a leper colony. Cabras also boasts a beautiful – but unswimmable – beach. Hedonists should head further west on Route 165; across Ensenada de Boca Vieja, **Punta Salinas** is flanked by two of the prettiest beaches in the area.

South of Cabras and bathed in the warm aroma of Bacardi's molasses, **Palo Seco** ㉚, though not in Cataño proper, lures most of Cataño's visitors with its seafood. An almost unbroken string of restaurants, many named after local pirate Roberto Cofresí, runs parallel to the ocean.

Every December the Bacardi Artisans Fair is held on the distillery grounds; more than 125 Puerto Rican artisans exhibit and sell the best of their work, and much other family-style entertainment is on offer.

Cowboy town

To the south of Cataño is **Bayamón** ㉛, whose inhabitants are referred to as *vaqueros* or "cowboys". This is due to a sort of maverick quality that has put the city in friendly opposition to others on the island.

Founded in 1509 by a group of settlers led by Ponce de León, Bayamón labors under the stereotype of a sort of glorified shopping mall. It is a place where the antiquated *fincas* and plantations of an older Puerto Rico are set in sharp juxtaposition to some of the most innovative civic architecture. Bayamón has been fastidious about retaining its regional customs and cuisine. Along almost every road leading into the city are *bayamoneses* food vendors selling roast chicken, bread, and the most legendary of all local treats – the *chicharrón*, a tart mix of pork and spice baked into a tough, bread mass. (Male visitors should know that *chicharrón* has a connotation which makes it inadvisable to ask local women if they would like to have a taste.)

The first sight of Bayamón is the eight-story **Alcaldía de Bayamón** ㉜, which spans five lanes of highway. Built in 1978 of concrete, glass and steel, it is the only building so suspended in the Caribbean.

Across the highway is the **Estadio Juan Ramón Loubriel** ㉝, an attractive modern baseball stadium. On the same side of the highway, the **Parque Central** ㉞ is also dedicated to recreation, with historical and cultural displays. Nearby, in the placid **Paseo Barbosa**, numerous shops are ranged about the restored 19th-century house of Barbosa.

Bayamón native Francisco Oller was Puerto Rico's greatest artist; his work is at the **Museo Francisco Oller** in the Old Alcaldía at Calle Degetau, 2. And not far from here, on Route 167, is the **Parque de las Ciencias** ㉟ (open Wed–Fri, 9am–4pm; weekends and pub. hols 10am–6pm). Much more than just a science museum, this is actually a major complex of seven themed museums and a zoo. ❏

BELOW: antique locomotive in Bayamón's Parque Central.

RUM: HOLDING ITS OWN IN THE SPIRITS WORLD

As Puerto Rico is the world's leading producer of rum, it's no surprise that's the national drink – but few realize its versatility and broad range of flavors

It's Christopher Columbus who can be thanked for the fine Caribbean rums today, because he happened to bring some sugar cane with him on his second voyage to the New World in 1493. It wasn't long before large cane plantations sprang up to meet the growing world demand for sugar. But the Spanish settlers discovered that sugar wasn't the only profitable substance produced from cane when they found that its by-product, molasses, fermented naturally.

Not satisfied with the flavor and proof of this "molasses wine" (which Puerto Ricans used to enjoy as a beverage called *aguardiente* or *madilla*), the Spaniards distilled it, filtering out impurities and increasing the concentration of alcohol. Rum was born.

There are four essential steps in the making of rum: fermentation, distillation, aging and blending. Aging is most commonly done in used bourbon barrels made of white American oak. Puerto Rican law states that rum must age untouched for at least one year; there are, in fact, rigid standards for every step of the rum-making process.

Puerto Rican rum is distinguished from other Caribbean rums by its light body and smooth flavor. Its premium-aged rum competes admirably in the upper end of the spirits world and is said to have a broader range of flavors than single malt Scotch.

▷ **A DRINK OF MANY COLORS**
Rum can be a light, dry white (a suitable replacement for gin or vodka in cocktails), smooth amber (often mixed with cola and hot drinks), or mellow gold ("on the rocks").

△ **RUM GARDEN**
The island is full of inviting places to relax and sample the national drink in some of its many guises. Tired of *piña coladas*? Then try the planter's punch.

▷ **MODERN METHODS**
Stainless-steel stills are said to give the cleanest rum and are the most widely used. Premium-age rums are distilled in copper to bring out more aroma and flavor.

THE ROLLS-ROYCE OF RUMS?

If you think rum is only good for fancy cocktails, think again. Gold, premium-aged rums can, at the very least, be a suitable substitute for whiskey: consumed straight or on the rocks. At their best, gold – or *añejos* – rums rank right up there with the finest Cognac. There is more than one *añejo* out there, of course – Bacardi has its "Gold Reserve"; Serralles has "El Dorado". But many rum connoisseurs point to Ron del Barrilito, who *only* makes premium-aged rums, as a real leader in the field with its unblended three-year-old Two-Star and blended six- to ten-year-old Three-Star – both coming in at 86 percent proof. Only 10 minutes away from the ultra-modern Bacardi facility in San Juan, Barrilito rum is produced on a 200-year-old family farm called Hacienda Santa Ana. Instead of using white American oak bourbon barrels for aging like most rums, Pedro Fernandez – who developed Ron del Barrilito – used only sherry casks, and this practice continues to this day. So put away those paper umbrellas and get out your snifter: these are rums to be savored.

▽ **COCKTAIL, ANYONE?**
No Puerto Rican bartender worth his salt doesn't have some sort of favorite rum concoction up his sleeve; rum is amazingly versatile.

△ **SWEET SUCCESS**
Spanish settlers planted sugar cane on the island in 1515, later discovering how to turn a sugar by-product, molasses, into rum.

▷ **CARIBBEAN CLASSIC**
Reputedly invented in Puerto Rico, the *piña colada* remains a favorite rum libation. It's made with cream of coconut, white rum and pineapple juice.

THE NORTHEAST

Map, page 156

Loíza is a center of authentic African culture, El Yunque is a protected rainforest, Luquillo is arguably the island's finest beach, and Icanos is the most popular cay

San Juan

I f someone arriving in Puerto Rico with the inexcusable intention of spending only a few days here were to hire a guide and ask to be shown as much as possible of the island, he or she would be driven directly east from San Juan. It is not that the northeastern corner of the island contains all the island's attractions; that would be impossible. It is only that the variety of landscapes and societies – none of them farther than 45 minutes from San Juan – is astonishing. The ease with which one can move from one landscape to another, which bears no resemblance to the previous one, will make even the crassest traveler feel that he or she is cheating.

Nowhere are the island's contrasts more shocking than on Route 187 just east of San Juan. Here, the highway that links the metropolis with the Caribbean's most modern international airport passes over a bridge and heads for **Boca de Cangrejos** ("Crabmouth") ❶, as exotic a spot as one will find within 20 minutes of any major city in the world. Perhaps at first appearance it is Puerto Rico at its most typically Latin American (read "Third World"), but the ricketiness is deceptive. The flocks of sheep and herds of cows in the area belong to the residents of nearby settlements around the *municipio* of Loíza. The shacks on the beach are not residences by any stretch of the imagination, rather seaside food emporia. Boca de Cangrejos is where *sanjuaneros* retreat for a *coco frío* – ice-cold coconut milk, which is served in its own shell.

Grove diggers

Long beaches under luxuriant pine groves are what draw visitors to Boca de Cangrejos. Surfers are the most devoted of such partisans, and can be seen riding the waves at the part of the beach called **Los Aviones** ("The Airplanes") after the flights from Isla Verde that roar over all day.

It's advisable to stay away from **Piñones** ❷ when the beach is deserted, which seldom happens. Those who crave company tend to stick to the extreme eastern and western ends of the beach, where the finest views of the Santurce skyline are to be had.

Piñones grows more eerie, rustic and beautiful as one moves east. At its farthest point from San Juan is **Vacia Talega Beach** ❸, a breathtaking finger of rock capped by palms and carved into strange formations by eons of surf.

Beyond the swamps

Few towns in Puerto Rico balance natural beauty and cultural achievement as gracefully or as charmingly as Loíza Aldea. Just 6 miles (10 km) east of metropolitan San Juan, predominantly black **Loíza** ❹ (population 29,000) has maintained its separateness from the

PRECEDING PAGES: setting moon over El Yunque. **LEFT:** La Mina Falls, El Yunque. **BELOW:** mask maker in Loíza.

50 varieties of fern, more than 20 kinds of orchid and some 240 types of tree are just some of the fantastic flora to be found in El Yunque.

capital thanks to a cluster of natural barriers. Puerto Rico's largest mangrove swamp, the massive and mysterious woodland of **Torrecilla Baja ❺**, sits smack between the two communities, and can be traversed via the coastal Route 187, which goes through Piñones and crosses the **Río Grande de Loíza ❻**, Puerto Rico's widest, roughest and only navigable river.

Loíza is arguably among the purest centers of true African culture in the Western world. It was settled in the 16th century by black slaves sent by the Spanish crown to mine a rich gold deposit in the area. When the gold ran out they became cane-cutters and, when slavery was abolished in 1873, many black residents turned to this agricultural economy.

They learned Spanish and became Catholics, but in the subsequent fusion of African culture with Spanish and Indian, the African certainly won out. Such influence is most visible during the Fiesta de Santiago Apostól, when the people of Loíza gather to praise Saint James, patron of the town. The week-long celebration commences each July 25, when citizens dress in ceremonial costumes strikingly and significantly similar to those of the Yoruba tribe of West Africa, from whom many of Puerto Rico's black peoples are descended. Participants include masqueraders, ghouls and *viejos* (old men), and the making of costumes for the ceremonial rites is ordered by a social hierarchy which is quite alien to Latin America.

The most distinctive festival attire, however, belongs to the *vejigantes*, most of them young men, who dress in garish costumes and parade through the streets. Their religious purpose is generally taken to be that of frightening the lapsed back into the Christian faith, though they can be just as much a source of celebration and mirth. Most true *vejigante* masks are made from coconuts or

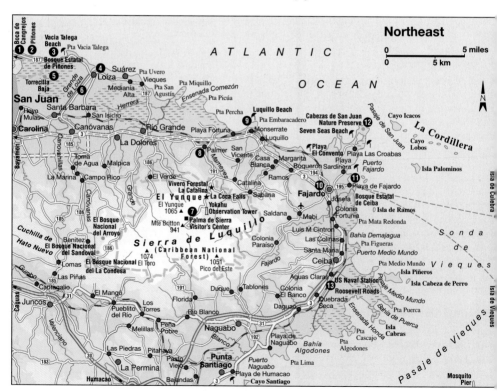

other gourds carved into grimaces like those of the most sinister jack-o'-lanterns. At times aluminum foil is used to make a mask's teeth look even more eerie.

Map, page 156

El Yunque rainforest

As you continue east, a turn-off at the town of Palmer points towards El Yunque, the rainforest that attracts many visitors to the island.

The only tropical forest in the USA's National Park system, and the only part of Puerto Rico administered by the US Department of Agriculture, the **Caribbean National Forest**, known to practically everybody as **El Yunque ❼** – named after the good Taíno spirit Yukiyú – is home to all the mystery and wonder that comes in the color green. These 28,000 acres (11,000 hectares) of bucking mountain at the highest part of the Sierra de Luquillo offer one of the island's most extreme climates, and the most extreme of its ecosystems as well.

Showers and towers

To begin with, there is the rain. The massive, low-lying, purplish-black clouds one sees moving across the Atlantic onto Puerto Rico's northeast coast dump most of their cargo when they hit the northern flank of the Sierra de Luquillo, with the result that this is far and away the rainiest section of Puerto Rico.

El Yunque gets upwards of 240 inches (600 cm) of rain annually – put in more alarming terms, this is 100 billion gallons per year. However, rain does not bother the hundreds of different animal species that make El Yunque their home, among them 26 endemic to the forest. Puerto Rico's most familiar animals are here, like the mellifluous tree frog known as the *coquí*. But more exotic ones are here as well, like the colorful but endangered Puerto

Literally millions of the tiny coquí *tree frogs – which have become somewhat of a Puerto Rican "symbol" – make El Yunque their home. They are nocturnal and endemic to the island; their distinctive cry of "koh-KEE" gave them their name.*

BELOW: mist settles into the rainforest.

TIP

It is wise to allow at least a day to fully appreciate El Yunque. If you're planning on hiking, the staff at El Yunque Catalina Field Office (tel: 887-2875) can provide hiking route information and, with notice, can help plan overnight treks into the forest.

BELOW: the El Portal Tropical Forest Center provides much information about the rainforest.

Rican parrot, and the rare Puerto Rican boa, the island's largest snake, which can grow up to 7 feet (2 meters) long.

Looking out at all the palm trees, ferns and other plant life crowding the road, it's hard to believe that Hurricane Hugo nearly wiped out this paradise on September 18, 1989. The storm's 200-mph (320-kph) winds left a path of destruction extending from the eastern fringes of San Juan to the offshore islands of Vieques and Culebra.

Yet Hugo may have done El Yunque a favor. Ecologists say that the hurricane removed the canopy of darkness created by taller trees, giving smaller plant life a chance to flourish.

Driving rain

However alluring the upper reaches of El Yunque, most people will see it only by automobile. The most popular and varied route leads south from the town of **Palmer ❸**, known in Spanish as Mameyes, along Route 191. Palmer is a tiny, haunting town, one which seems all the more so for its striking contrast to the 45-minute drive from San Juan, which carries you through glittering, modern industrial and commercial landscapes. Nonetheless, Palmer is admirably uncommercialized and untouristy for a park entrance.

Route 191 used to lead straight through the park to Naguabo, but a landslide which damaged roads on the southern edge of the park about 20 years ago has never been cleared; a gate now blocks access to the damaged part of the road at Km 13.5. But despite the damage, and despite the fact that Puerto Rico's hiking enthusiasts will tell you that you have to get up *into* the woods to appreciate them, Route 191 provides a sterling introduction to the park.

Another good introduction – which really should be a required pre-hike stop – is provided at the new **El Portal Tropical Forest Center** (open daily) within the park. Here, visitors can learn about the unique beauty and history of El Yunque and the forest environment through interpretive displays, discussions and a 30-minute documentary film. Patios provide a place to relax and admire the superb view.

Map, page 156

Attractive falls

Rising gradually, Route 191 hits one of El Yunque's premier attractions at a bend in the road scant kilometers into the park. **La Coca Falls**, at Km 8.2, is a blurry cascade of ice-gray river rushing down a wall of beautiful moss-covered stones. Though the park service claims most of the water in El Yunque to be perfectly potable, and although you'll almost certainly see people drinking from the stream, do exercise caution here, as anywhere in the mountains, as Puerto Rico has a number of river snails which produce "*schisto*" (*schistosoma*), a bacterium causing the highly dangerous liver disease bilharzia.

El Yunque's second great waterfall, **La Mina**, is just off the road a mile (2 km) ahead. Unfortunately, it's invisible from 191 and can be reached most easily from the Palo Colorado Recreation Site at Km 12. On your way there, you'll pass the **Palma de Sierra Visitors' Center**, an invaluable source of information on hiking trails and outdoor camping.

The island's road network traverses a surprising amount of its sometimes rugged terrain.

Hoofing it through the highlands

The landslides on Route 191 have left El Yunque much less accessible by car. Of the many hiking attractions of the place, a few are especially recommended.

BELOW: forester enjoys a breather in the rainforest.

THE MANY FACES OF THE FOREST

One would think that a forest is full of pretty much the same types of tree, but in fact a place like El Yunque – with an intensity characteristic of Puerto Rico's sub-climates – offers a startling diversity of vegetation and "forest types". Most widespread is the Tabonuco forest, which ranges around the warmer, drier parts of the park at altitudes of under 2,000 feet (600 meters). Higher up is the Colorado forest, which is mossy and somewhat more tropical than the Tabonuco. Although taking up less than a fifth of El Yunque's territory, the reserve's pine forest is the "rainforest" that gives the area its reputation. Perhaps this is because its beauty is so unexpected and almost unnatural; perhaps it's because Route 191, which most tourists take through El Yunque, never gets above 2,500 feet (760 meters), where the pine forest stops.

Sierra palms, which account for most of the sub-climate's vegetation, can grow in very slippery and unstable soil. Thus they can be found in the most dramatic locations: half-submerged in riverbeds or jutting from cliffsides. Areas above the pine forest are even more bizarre and fascinating, but are less visited. This area of dwarf pine and moss covers less than 1,000 acres (400 hectares) and gets the full brunt of the island's sometimes intense weather.

Mountain flora adds a touch of color in the rainforest.

The **Tradewinds National Recreation Trail**, known as El Toro to Puerto Ricans, is the island's longest nature trail, at about 8 miles (13 km). Commencing a few hundred meters beyond the gate on Route 191, it tends to be rather a trail out of the park, bypassing all of El Yunque's "big" attractions, but it does have the advantage of taking one through all the major ecosystems and vegetation types of the forest. The **Big Tree Trail**, leaving from the first parking lot along Route 191, gives one a good bird's-eye view of La Mina falls before meeting the road again at a well-situated camping site.

Perhaps most spectacular of all is the **El Yunque Trail**, which leaves the Palma de Sierra Visitors' Center for three of the most spectacular vistas in the park. To get to **Los Picachos Lookout Tower**, carry straight on; a left 2½-miles (4 km) down the trail takes you, after a southern detour of less than 350 feet (100 meters), along a dirt road to the **Mount Britton Lookout Tower**, perhaps the park's crowning glory. A turn left just before reaching Los Picachos brings you to the lookout tower at **Pico El Yunque** and the fabulous vistas at the remote **El Yunque Rock**.

The best beach

While it's true that there's plenty to see in Puerto Rico's northeast, few informed visitors get to see any of the area's attractions without first making at least a day's detour to what many consider the island's finest beach. Shimmering **Luquillo** 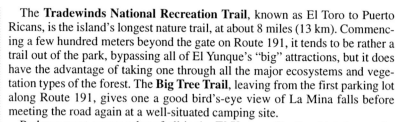 is just 35 minutes east of San Juan on Route 3, which, in travelers' terms, is about the same time it would take one to get to lovely but arduous El Yunque or Fajardo's mob scene, and about half the time it would take to get to Humacao. The only liability of a trip to Luquillo is that it is overcrowded, especially at weekends.

BELOW: Puerto Rico's finest beach, Luquillo.

Mountains to the sea

Even those not terribly enthusiastic about beaches will find it hard to ignore Luquillo's appeal. This beautiful, bleach-white town is tucked cozily between dark Atlantic waters and Puerto Rico's most imposing mountain chain, the Sierra de Luquillo, from which the town draws its name. There are few more dramatic sights on the island than that of the whitecaps of the shoreline glistening in summer sunlight while the peaks of the El Yunque rainforest just inland are suffused in purple thunder clouds. Occasionally, some of the rain intended for the forest does fall on Luquillo, and quite often the beach is under heavy cloud cover.

Luquillo is listed officially as being 2¼ miles (3.5 km) long, but it is actually linked to two other swimmable beaches – *playas* **San Miguel** and **El Convento** – which are every bit as lovely and almost as deserted, and stretch nearly to Las Cabezas de San Juan, at the far northeastern end of the island, making it ideal walking territory.

Luquillo is also the premier beachside food emporium on Puerto Rico; a seemingly endless string of *friquitines*, or kiosks – numbered from one to 65 – sells delectably rich local seafood specialties and a variety of alcoholic and soft drinks.

Two-faced town

To some, the town of **Fajardo** , the next sizeable destination beyond Luquillo, is merely an overcluttered dockfront town, ranking third behind Brindisi, Italy, and Hyannis, Massachusetts, in the "Grim Ferry Ports of the World". To others it is an eminently glamorous resort, a charming community, gateway to a handful of fabulous islands and home of the finest sailing in the Caribbean.

The first major town along Puerto Rico's northeast coast, Fajardo remains a mecca for yachting enthusiasts. Originally a small fishing and agricultural village, in the late 1700s it became a popular supply port for many pirate and contraband vessels. The town itself, a hodge-podge of clothing, furniture, and video stores, will appear somewhat unprepossessing to most visitors compared with the area's natural attractions – the calm, clear waters and cays and coral reefs of Vieques Sound.

Playa de Fajardo , a waterfront community at the east end of the town, is the docking-place for the ferries headed to Culebra, Vieques and a small island marina nearby. Next to the ferry terminal is the pink stucco **US Post Office/Customs House** and one of Fajardo's few hotels. Seven Seas, a public beach where one can camp with permission (tel: 722-1551), provides time out for enjoying Puerto Rico's attractions. Short walks offer access to secluded beaches.

Just north of Fajardo, two condominium high-rises, architectural anomalies here, loom over the small fishing village of **Playa Sardinera**. Hundreds of fancy motorboats and yachts of all descriptions crowd the two waterfront marinas nearby. Local fishermen line the beach in the middle of the village with boats and tents; they supply the half-dozen expensive local seafood restaurants. A road over the hill passes a comfortable guesthouse and the lavish **El Con-**

Don't let the Puerto Rican nickname for the residents of Fajardo – cariduros, meaning "the hard-faced ones" – put you off; the people here are very friendly.

BELOW: many trails criss-cross El Yunque.

(Map, page 156)

TIP

A tour of Las Cabezas de San Juan is well worthwhile. There are four each day (three in the morning and one in the afternoon) and there is an admission charge of US$5 for adults and US$2 for children.

BELOW: a local hazard! Iguanas frequent the El Conquistador golf course.

quistador Resort & Country Club. With 918 rooms and more than 2,000 employees, El Conquistador is now Puerto Rico's largest resort. It's also one of the most expensive.

First built in 1960s, the resort was abandoned at one point and later turned into a Maharishi university that soon went bankrupt. Today it is spread among five distinct themed areas, with Moorish and Spanish architecture featured throughout. Guests can even take a ferry to Palomino Island, where the hotel maintains its own private beach and grill.

The road continues on to **Playa Soroco**, a long, narrow stretch of crisp white-sand beach whose clean, shallow waters make it a favorite among locals. At the leftmost point of Soroco, a dirt road leads to **Playa El Convento**, an isolated beach stretching for miles.

Nearby, right off Route 987, is the **Las Cabezas de San Juan Nature Preserve ⑫** (open to groups Wed–Thur, to general public Fri–Sun only by reservation; tel: 722 5882, or 860-2560 on weekends), an environmental paradise that encompasses 316 acres (128 hectares) of some of the Caribbean's most stunning landscape. Admission to the preserve is by guided tour only.

Considering the park's beauty, it's surprising that so few tourists spend time here. One can observe nearly all of Puerto Rico's natural habitats – coral reefs, thalassia beds, sandy and rocky beaches, lagoons, a dry forest and a mangrove forest.

Another important attraction at Cabezas de San Juan is the lighthouse, known simply as "El Faro". Built in 1880, this pristine white neo-classical structure with black trim is one of only two operational lighthouses on the island. The view from Las Cabezas de San Juan is head-spinning. As you look back toward the heart of Puerto Rico, El Yunque towers over the island. In the

other direction a chain of cays ranges like enticing stepping stones to the islands of Culebra and Saint Thomas.

The dozens of cays and islands off Fajardo provide Puerto Rico's best boating. A protective reef stretching from Cabezas de San Juan to Culebra and beyond keeps the waters calm, while swift Atlantic tradewinds make for great sailing. Charter a yacht from one of Fajardo's marinas and spend the day sailing, sunbathing and snorkeling.

Icanos

Icacos, the largest and most popular cay, offers a narrow stretch of bone-white beach, making it a nice spot for picnicking or even camping. Two rows of wooden posts from an abandoned dock march into the water, and, just beyond, a coral underworld descends to the sandy bottom 20 feet (6 meters) below. The beach is certainly warm and comfortable, but all the action is around the reefs: elkhorn, staghorn, brain, star and other corals host legions of underwater plant and animal life.

Other popular cays, somewhat less readily accessible, include **Culebrita**, **Cayos Lobos** (wolves), **Diablo** (devil), **Palominos** (doves) and **Palominitos** (take a wild guess). These and many smaller cays are ripe for underwater exploration among coral, caverns and tunnels.

Just south of Fajardo, one of the largest naval bases in the world, **Roosevelt Roads** ⓭, occupies about a quarter of Puerto Rico's eastern coastline. Headquarters of the US Caribbean Naval Forces, this Reserve Center is a training base, and provides peace-time support services to the various branches of the US Navy. The nearest town to Roosevelt Roads is **Ceiba**, founded in 1838. ❑

Map, page 156

BELOW: pretty plaza in Fajardo.

THE SOUTHEAST

*Palmas del Mar is a busy resort, Cayo Santiago is strictly for
the monkeys, there are quiet beaches near Punta Tuna,
and towns such as Patillas and Arroyo are down-to-earth*

**Map,
page 168**

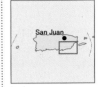

San Juan

The southeastern section of Puerto Rico – thought by many to be one of the prettiest parts of the island – has the interesting characteristic of having some of the most heavily developed as well as some of the least developed parts of the country. It is largely residential and quiet, blessed by the pleasant Caribbean tradewinds that blow steadily in this region all year, stabilizing the weather. During the "rainy" season, from about May to September, the southeast may get some 9 inches (23 cm) of rain a month, while during the December to April "dry" season, monthly rainfall averages 3 to 5 inches (5 to 12 cm).

A major town in the region is **Humacao ❶**, which, although a first-rate industrial center, does have its charms. Previously subsisting off agriculture, Humacao now aspires to being a first-rate resort town, which it is on the way to achieving; several tourist resorts, golf courses and beaches are among its attractions. The restored **Casa Roig Museum** (open Wed–Fri and Sun 10am–4pm), the former home of a wealthy sugar-cane land-owner, is worth a visit if you are stopping in the town. Only a 45-minute drive from San Juan via Route 30, Humacao is within 2 miles (3 km) of some of the most dazzling beachfront that Vieques Sound has to offer. Add to that its convenience as a starting-point for excursions in the southeast, and it becomes a place that has to be taken seriously as a holiday resort.

The best way to begin a beach tour of this part of the island is to head north to **Playa Humacao ❷**, probably the best-equipped public beach on the island. It boasts not only miles of bright sand, and a handful of offshore cays, but also a veritable arcade of lockers, refreshment stands and other amenities. The beach benefits from its size, drawing heavily enough from local and tourist groups alike to ensure that there's always something going on, if only a pickup volleyball game: join in.

Halfway down the eastern coast and a 10-minute drive south from Humacao is **Palmas del Mar ❸**, Puerto Rico's largest vacation resort. The self-appointed "New American Riviera", this 2,700-acre (1,100-hectare) holiday heaven comprises just about everything but a monorail: 20 tennis courts ("Is there a court available?" "No, sir, not 'til Thursday."), a gorgeous beachfront golf course, riding stables, fine beaches, deep-sea fishing, eight restaurants, numerous bars, an ice cream shop and so on. Palmas del Mar has proved itself popular among both families and conventioneers.

Monkey business

A little less than a mile off the coast of Playa Humacao lies a 39-acre (16 hectare) island that few people have had the opportunity to visit. This place,

PRECEDING PAGES:
colorful resident at
a Puerto Rican
resort.
LEFT: horsing
around at the
seaside.
BELOW: enjoying a
swim at Palmas
del Mar.

Brilliant red-blossomed flame trees dot the south-eastern countryside.

Cayo Santiago ❹, is home to approximately 700 rhesus monkeys. With a grant from Columbia University, the animals were brought from India to Puerto Rico in 1938 for research into primate behavior. Never before had such a social troupe of monkeys been transported into the Western world and placed in semi-natural conditions. Despite the comfortable climate and undisturbed environment of Cayo Santiago, many experts remained skeptical on the question of whether the primates could survive and breed.

For two years, tuberculosis scourged the colony. Then, during World War II, grant money ran out and the monkeys faced the threat of starvation. Townspeople from nearby Playa de Humacao supported the colony by taking bananas, coconuts and other available foods out to the island several times each week for the duration of the war.

Today the island is administered by the University of Puerto Rico, and scientists from the Caribbean Primate Research Center there spend many, many hours studying the behavioral patterns of these fascinating creatures.

Due to the ongoing scientific research and possible health hazards (and the fact that rhesus monkeys have large canine teeth and at times can be very aggressive), visitors are not allowed on the island. However, there are various sightseeing boats that can take visitors relatively close to the island, where they can snorkel and get a closer glimpse of the frisky primates (with the help of binoculars in most cases). Check at the Palmas del Mar marina.

Cane-sugar center

From Humacao to **Yabucoa** ❺ (a native Indian term meaning "Place of the Yucca Trees"), rolling hills, semi-tropical forests, sugar-cane fields and cow

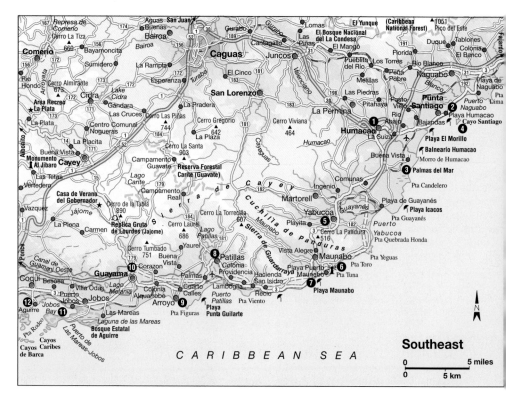

Southeast

CARIBBEAN SEA

0   5 miles
0   5 km

Map, page 168

pastures highlight an exceedingly pleasant drive. Just before reaching Yabucoa – also known as "The Sugar Town" – Route 3 passes the **Roig Sugar Mill**, a rusty piece of antiquity which is one of the few survivors of the southeast's agricultural economy, which unfortunately has gone belly-up. Also of interest in the area is **Hacienda Lucia**, an old sugar plantation.

Yabucoa marks the beginning of an industrial circuit that continues southwestward. Taking advantage of low-wage labor and liberal tax laws, oil refineries, pharmaceutical companies, textile manufacturers and industrial chemical plants border the smaller towns all the way down the coast.

Leaving Yabucoa, Route 901 takes you on a scenic drive southward (part of the Ruta Panoramica) through arid coastal headlands which form part of the Cuchilla de Pandura mountains.

The Festival del Azúcar *(Sugar Festival) is held in Yabucoa each May – one of half a dozen festivals held in the town throughout the year.*

Ghost beach

A few kilometers away from town along the **Balneario Lucia** shore, abandoned seafood restaurants indicate that, at one point, this spot was believed to have potential as a popular bathing retreat. Now, it's a ghost beach; few bother with it. Rows of planted coconut palm trees grow in awkwardly misshapen directions along the beach. The trunks of these trees are wrapped with sheet metal, apparently to prevent rats from climbing them.

The rats, apparently, have joy-riding in mind. According to a native writer: "When there are no such bands, rats with a penchant for primitive piloting climb the trunks, nibble a hole in the coconuts, lap out the milk, crawl through the hole into the nut, gnaw off the stem and sit inside the shell as it makes its break-neck descent to the ground …"

BELOW: hazy day at Punta Tuna.

Map, page 168

Route 901 curves upward into a series of hills overlooking rugged shoreline and an expanse of the Caribbean Sea, with the island of Vieques viewed through a haze in the distance.

Down to Punta Tuna

The road descends from the hills to **Punta Tuna** ❻, where one of Puerto Rico's two active lighthouses rests. Built in the 1890s by Spain, the lighthouse is now run by the US Coast Guard. Adjacent to Punta Tuna, a little-known beach ranks among the nicest on the southeastern coast.

Farther down the road, on the opposite side of Punta Tuna, another good beach arches more than a kilometer around tiny **Puerto Maunabo** ❼. Pack a lunch in the morning before setting out from Yabucoa. A lunch break on one of these lovely beaches is the perfect interlude on this circular trip; camping is also allowed.

The Ruta Panoramica continues past the town of Maunabo and winds up a narrow road past cliffside houses and damp verdure over the Cuchilla de Pandura and back to Yabucoa.

Unspoilt corner

You can tell you're in the southeastern corner of Puerto Rico when the local residents stop having marketing preconceptions about their part of the island. This place is not karstic or dry or cosmopolitan. Nonetheless, it's Puerto Rican landscape at its least spoiled.

With what some consider its sister city, **Patillas** ❽, **Arroyo** ❾ is one of the most down-to-earth of Puerto Rican towns. The landscape surrounding the city is fetching, if unspectacular – it's a reedy, bushy sort of place. The beaches by both towns are uncrowded and pleasant, and the weather generally makes lazing on them even more secure a prospect than in the immediate neighborhood of San Juan. The **Embalse de Patillas**, a short drive up Route 184 from that city, makes a fine place for a lakeside picnic on the way into the Cordillera. There are a number of restaurants in the Patillas–Maunabo area that sell good, cheap food.

Guayama ❿ borders on **Jobos Bay** ⓫, one of the finest protected shallow-water areas on the island. Ichthyologists (fish enthusiasts) and ornithologists will love the area – several species of Puerto Rican birds unseen elsewhere on the island frequent the place, and fish are well-served by the bay's healthy quantity of micro-organisms.

The fishing is good everywhere, but legal only outside protected waters. This means you need a boat, but boating is a very popular pastime in Jobos Bay, and *ponceños* frequently include the area in daytrips that depart from Caja de Muertos.

Also bordering on Jobos Bay is **Aguirre** ⓬. The Aguirre sugar mill ruled the area when sugar was king early in the 20th century. The complex produced most of the sugar that was exported around the world from the island. Families were raised on the plantation, which was virtually an enclosed community. Today, the fields and machinery lie still. ❑

Samuel Morse, inventor of the Morse code, visited Arroyo in 1848 and personally installed the local telegraph line. The town's main street, Calle Morse, is named in his honor.

BELOW: catching some rays in Guayama.
RIGHT: tuning up for a big performance.

THE NORTH

Dorado has upscale attractions, Playa de Vega Baja is a popular beach, Arecibo has a renowned observatory, and San Sebastián is a good base for exploring the remarkable karst country

Map, pages 176–7

Driving west from San Juan on Route 2, as the landscape opens up a bit and the first hills begin to rise, the first-time visitor may begin to feel he or she has left the metropolis and is about to penetrate Puerto Rico's fabled countryside. That is, until you hit sprawling, congested Bayamón; then you begin to wonder if the big cities will ever stop. They stop in **Dorado ❶**, 10 miles (16 km) west of San Juan, the first town which can claim to be out from under its shadow.

Dorado's a pleasant, quiet, unassuming little town. You'll miss it if you stay on the highway, and may have to look twice for it even if you take the detour on Route 165, which leaves Route 2 and runs north across emerald marshlands before looping back to Dorado.

The hospitable hamlet of **Toa Baja ❷** signals the turn-off. If Dorado is unassuming, Toa Baja is positively diffident, though it is full of charms which belie the quiet. Dividing Toa Baja from Dorado itself is the sluggish **Río de la Plata**, whose grassy banks and meandering course would remind you of some of the more timeless parts of rural England were it not for the clayey river bed which has turned the stream's waters a rugged brick red.

Dorado follows Route 165 loosely on both sides. No cross streets slow traffic enough to draw attention to the small main plaza by the roadside, and the town's businesses are admirably free of gaudy billboards and other "Welcome to..." bric-a-brac. "Urban" Dorado is just clean, slow-paced and friendly, and a disproportionate number of its business establishments – bakeries, bars, juice stands – have camaraderie as their *raison d'être*.

Of particular interest here are the historical Catholic church and **La Casa del Rey**, a former Spanish garrison. Both were built in 1823, the year the town was founded; the latter was restored in 1978 by the Institute of Puerto Rican Culture and is now a museum.

But Dorado is not all culture. Its beaches are inviting and easily accessible via the *guaguas* (buses) that leave from near the town plaza. A mile northwest of town, through a spinney of mangroves and a bone-white graveyard on Route 693, is the irresistibly lovely beach at **Playa Dorado Sardinera**, and also nearby is **El Ojo Del Buey** (The Ox's Eye), a seaside recreational area that takes its name from a large rock bearing an amazing resemblance to the head of an ox.

Dorado's luxury hotels, the Hyatt Dorado Beach and the Hyatt Regency Cerromar, are its double crowning glory. The adjoining beachfront resorts host celebrities and dignitaries from around the world as well as the local trade. Membership in the hotel can be had for a large fee. On the beaches, golf courses, tennis courts, restaurants and casinos, Puerto Rico residents mingle with the well-heeled visitors all year

PRECEDING PAGES: moto-cross racing in San Sebastián. **LEFT:** Caribbean sunset. **BELOW:** cheerful northerner.

Pineapples are just one of the many agricultural products of the fertile north; they're often sold at roadside kiosks in the region.

round. Many locals take advantage of special weekend rates and bring the whole family for some resort relaxation.

The Dorado Beach Hotel was originally a Rockresort, owned by Laurance Rockefeller, who bought the property from Clara Livingston, Puerto Rico's first woman pilot and head of the Air Civil Defense, in the 1950s. The Livingston family came to Puerto Rico from New York in 1905. It operated a grapefruit and coconut plantation here until 1954, when Clara, the last of the family, sold the property to Rockefeller. Visit Su Casa, one of the Dorado Beach restaurants, which originally was Livingston's plantation home.

There are four championship golf courses here, at one time administered by Juan "Chichi" Rodríguez. Two of the courses are considered among the best 25 created by golf course architect Robert Trent Jones. The par-5, 5,540-yard 13th hole at Dorado Beach's par-75 East course is ranked by Jack Nicklaus as one of the top ten holes in the world and is known for its water challenges. Green fees are *not* cheap – even for Hyatt guests.

The Cerromar features the world's longest freshwater swimming pool: in effect a "river pool", which recreates a winding tropical stream, complete with waterfalls, slides and an in-water bar. It takes 15 minutes to float from one end of the pool to the other in its riverlike current.

Popular beachfront

Further west, a fast, 35-minute drive from San Juan on Routes 2 and 686, **Playa de Vega Baja ❸** is one of the most popular of San Juan's metropolitan beachfronts, and is dotted with cabins belonging to the local residents. It benefits not only from spectacular juxtapositions of sand and sea, but also from lush and

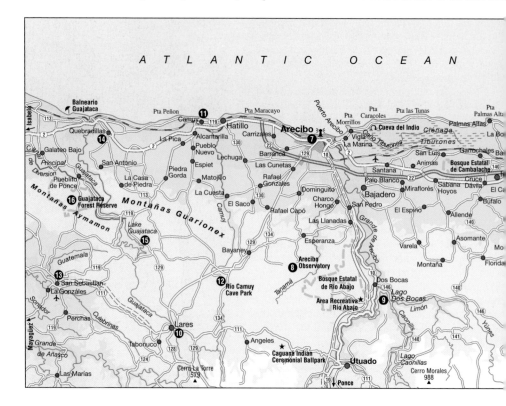

unusual surrounding countryside. The beach itself draws most attention for its weird and haunting rock formations, which are actually a string of coral islands running parallel to the seashore for 2,500 feet (760 meters), from the palm-lined cove of **Boca del Cibuco** to craggy **Punta Puerto Nuevo**. This odd, almost unique formation has sheltered most of Vega Baja while causing its western end to resemble at times a sort of preternaturally large jacuzzi.

The nearby town of Vega Baja has grown into a fairly modern and uniform Puerto Rican municipality. The town does have a sense of humor about its reputation as something of a hokey place. An official town bulletin offers not only the usual information on town history and famous residents but also a tongue-in-cheek roster of *Personajes típicos de Vega Baja*. These include the tallest man, the drunk, the beggar and the basketball fan.

A town that can parody itself so remorselessly deserves a visit, but not so much as the surrounding countryside does. Vega Baja sits in the middle of the fertile coastal flatlands west of San Juan. Visitors will be rewarded with long vistas over canefields and marshes, and an array of deciduous foliage: most impressive in an island full of tropical trees.

Further west along the coast, and accessible by Route 686, which runs near the bottom of it, is **Playa Tortuguero**, the largest and most palm-lined of the beaches. Half a mile inland, **Laguna Tortuguero ❹**, while not officially a nature reserve, provides a haven for bird life.

Continuing west, the **Manatí ❺** area has produced most of the island's pineapple products. Here Puerto Rico's famous Lotus pineapple juice is canned under the supervision of the Land Administration. Vendors offer fresh pineapples along the road (Route 2). The sweet, Spanish Red variety goes into the

Map, pages 176–7

The nickname for those who live in Vega Baja is "melao-melao", meaning "molasses-molasses", because of the large quantities of molasses produced here.

BELOW: Cerromar Beach Hotel, Dorado.

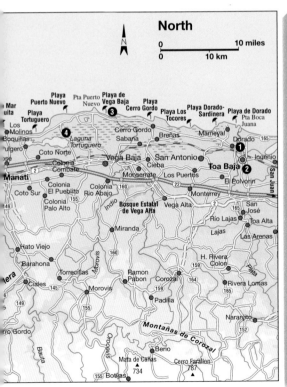

100 percent juice. No water is added. A short drive from town takes you to **Playa Mar Chiquita** ❻, an unusual beach in that the surf comes pounding through the high rocks to produce a most dramatic effect. The rocks enclose an oval lagoon that makes for excellent swimming.

Arecibo

TIP

An interesting detour from Arecibo is to take the coast road (Route 681) past Mar Chiquita to another headland, Punta Caracoles, on which is the Cueva del Indio (Indian Cave). A short walk leads to the hole in the cliff, inside which are some (supposedly) pre-Columbian drawings.

There are prettier cities on this island, but few are prettier to approach than **Arecibo** ❼. Forty-eight miles (77 km) west of San Juan, Route 2 takes a tortuous turn and reveals the second capital city of Puerto Rico's north coast backed by the blue Atlantic. Directly to the south of Arecibo lies the karst country, with typical landscapes of pine and mahogany in the Río Abajo forest.

The coastal road, Route 681, affords an even more dramatic perspective. This is in itself one of the most spectacular drives in Puerto Rico, running from Palmas Altas through Islote, past Desvio Valdes, through a settlement at Punta Caracoles, and by the big radio antennae of the Arecibo station WCMN before hitting the bay at Puerto de Arecibo. Here you will meet the city in truly spectacular fashion. Middle-sized apartment blocks and business premises seem to loom large and blue across an even bluer bay, and Arecibo takes on something of the air of a western Puerto Rican Eldorado.

The reality of Arecibo is a bit more worldly than you would assume from its externally Arcadian aspect. It's one of the oldest of Puerto Rican towns, and since its foundation in the 16th century has enjoyed one of the highest levels of prosperity on the island.

Operation Bootstrap, the project which was designed by Muñoz Marín and the US Congress to boost Puerto Rico into the industrial world, and Section 936, the

BELOW: limestone rocks by the Indian caves near Arecibo.

American legislation which offered tax incentives to companies investing in Puerto Rico, accelerated Arecibo's advance in the business world. Puerto Rico makes more pharmaceutical products than any other place in the world, and Arecibo lies at the center of the pharmaceutical manufacturing industry.

Map, pages 176–7

Oil for the wheels of life

Arecibo has been a leader in the art of manufacturing products that ease one along the troubled road of life since long before the pharmaceutical boom. The town also produces agricultural machinery, clothing, plastics, paper and sporting goods – although Ronrico, one the great rums of the island (which is itself the rum capital of the world), is probably the major industry in town, and Arecibo is proud of its part in the island's rum trade.

Arecibo's name comes from a local Indian chief called Jamaica Aracibo.

Arecibo's Chamber of Commerce even goes so far as to acquaint the tourist with the whimsical saga of Don Juan Piza Bisbal, the Catalán who left Barcelona *"con lágrimas en los ojos"* ("with tears in his eyes") to come to Puerto Rico and introduce Westerners to *Ron Llave*, "the key to happiness".

Salubrious surroundings

For a town in its situation, Arecibo is center to a surprising variety of terrain. It forms a semi-peninsula pointing northeastward at the delta of two rivers: the **Río Grande de Arecibo** and the **Canal Perdomo**. The roads from San Juan hug the shoreline here, giving pleasant views of the city from afar. Those roads were put here for a reason: to the east recede swamps of unmeasured depth and gloom. Be warned that the surrounding area is chock-a-block with irritating mosquitoes in the wet season.

BELOW: Arecibo, one of the oldest – and most prosperous – towns in Puerto Rico.

The century-old Punta Morillos lighthouse in Arecibo is now restored as a museum focusing on the city's heritage.

BELOW: Arecibo's attractive Plaza Luis Muñoz Rivera.

Arecibo itself disappoints some tourists who use the city as a way-station on their indefatigable search for all that is mundane and tacky on the island. It takes an intelligent and observant traveler to realize that Arecibo is one of the finer and more livable-in cities, not only on the island but also anywhere in the Caribbean. Its streets are broad, its citizens relatively well-off, and its shopping district has far more variety than one might expect from a city of only 80,000 inhabitants.

Moreover, Arecibo has cafés and theaters – not as commonplace as one might think in Puerto Rico – and its oldest building, a distinctive wooden structure, dates from 1884. **Calle Alejandro Salicrup**, at the tip of the semi-peninsular wedge, is one of the best thoroughfares on which to see such timbered architecture, which is as unique to Arecibo as the southwestern townhouse style is to San Germán. In a somewhat different vein, the **Iglesia San Felipe**, between *calles* José de Diego and González Marín, boasts an unusual cupola and an anti-nuclear, anti-torture mural.

The **Alcaldía** (town hall), tucked in at the intersection of *calles* José de Diego, Romero-Barceló and Juarregui, is among the prettier offices in Puerto Rico, and its inhabitants are among the friendliest and most receptive. A trip there will garner for you information galore – its pamphlet, *Historia de Arecibo Como Capital de Ron*, is a big favorite among rummies and hangers-on – and perhaps a cup of coffee.

Formerly the Plaza Mayor, now the **Plaza Luis Muñoz Rivera**, this must be the prettiest plaza in Puerto Rico, with the cathedral facing over an idiosyncratically landscaped park surrounded by wrought-iron railings and multicolored Spanish colonial architecture. The plaza has undergone an astounding number of transformations in the past 100 years. In the mid-1890s, it was burnt to ashes

during a fire that consumed much of the city. In 1899, a hurricane and the ensuing surf, which was not far short of a tidal wave, pounded it into disrepair.

Arecibo was one of the first of the Puerto Rican cities to jump off the Spanish imperial bandwagon and to honor its own native heroes. The monument in memory of Queen Isabella II of Spain, which for so long stood in the middle of the plaza, was replaced in 1927 with an obelisk honoring local hero and politician Luis Muñoz Marín. It's the centerpiece of the town and one of its most scenic features.

Notwithstanding its history of natural disasters, about the only bad thing one can say about the layout of the town is that the river, the Río Grande de Arecibo, is a volatile creature, and the town does flood with alarming frequency. This, however, only enhances its prestige as an attractive shopping town; regular floods mean regular flood sales of damaged goods.

The radar/radio-telescope at the Arecibo Observatory is equal in size to 13 football fields.

Star attraction

Anyone who has ever taken sixth-grade or first-form science should have some familiarity with Arecibo. On one of those big, full-page spreads that fill up space in astronomy textbooks, the **Arecibo Observatory** ❽ is generally featured prominently.

A complicated trip 20 miles (32 km) south of the town of Arecibo into the karst country will bring you to the mammoth complex. From downtown Arecibo, follow de Diego to Route 129. Bear left on Route 651 and follow it for the 4 miles (6 km) before it becomes 635. Travel about the same distance until you come to a T-intersection, at which you'll turn right (onto Route 626) and travel a few hundred yards before making a left onto 625, at the end of which

BELOW: bustling business in an Arecibo market.

Arecibo Observatory

Hidden among the mountains of northwestern Puerto Rico, where the stars shine undimmed by city lights, sits the most sensitive radio telescope on Earth.

The Arecibo Ionospheric Observatory is so huge that you can spot it from a jumbo jet at 33,000 ft (10,000 meters). Yet on the ground, first-time visitors need a detailed road map to find its guarded entrance.

Located at the end of winding Route 625, in the heart of Puerto Rico's karst country, the observatory has been the focus of numerous astronomical breakthroughs over the years, ranging from Alexander Wolszcan's 1992 discovery of planets outside our own solar system to NASA's $100-million Search for Extra-Terrestrial Intelligence.

In 1993, the Arecibo "dish" gained world prominence when two American astronomers, Russell H. Hulse and Joseph H. Taylor, Jr, won the Nobel Prize for Physics for work done using the Arecibo facility.

The observatory owes its existence largely to Puerto Rico's political status as a United States Commonwealth and to the island's geographic position 17° north of the Equator. That makes it ideal for the observation of planets, quasars, pulsars and other cosmic phenomena. The telescope is so sensitive that it can listen to emissions from places 13 billion light-years away.

Built in 1960, the Arecibo Observatory is funded by an annual $7.5 million grant from the National Science Foundation, though its day-to-day affairs are managed by Cornell University of Ithaca, New York. The observatory counts 130 full-time employees among its staff, and has hosted more than 200 visiting scientists from countries as diverse as Argentina, Bulgaria, Brazil and Russia. No military experiments of any kind are conducted here, and, despite the presence of security guards, there's nothing secretive about this place.

The "dish" itself, suspended over a huge natural sinkhole, is by far the largest of its kind in the world. Spanning 1,000 ft (300 meters) in diameter, it covers 20 acres (8 hectares) and is composed of nearly 40,000 perforated aluminum mesh panels, each measuring 3 ft by 6 ft (1 by 2 meters). A 900-ton platform is suspended 425 ft (130 meters) over the dish by 12 cables strung from three reinforced concrete towers.

Underneath the dish lies a jungle of ferns, orchids and begonias. In fact, until recently tourists could get only as far as a viewing platform high above the site. The dish itself is off-limits, and visitors were limited to a five-minute audio tape describing the facility and a display area explaining the telescope's construction together with some current scientific results. However, this situation was remedied when Cornell University built a $2-million visitors' center (open Wed–Fri 12–4pm; weekends and most holidays 9am–4pm; open to students and groups Wed–Fri from 10am), including a 120-seat auditorium, a 4,000-sq. foot (370-sq. meter) scientific museum, a gift shop, and a trail leading to a viewing platform from which the telescope can be seen at close range.

The observatory can be seen in the movie *Contact*, in which Jodie Foster played an astronomer seeking extraterrestrial life. ❏

is the renowned observatory. (For further details of this, one of the most important research observatories in the Americas, see the panel on the facing page.)

Map, pages 176–7

The karst country

Puerto Rico is one of those places blessed to an almost unfair extent with an
enormous variety of beauty of landscape. But such places are legion, and
what do you give in Puerto Rico to the tourist who has everything? The answer
is not hard to find: the dark green sector of the island's northwest where the
land rises in regular green-and-white hillocks and appears to be boiling – the
intriguing area known as the karst country.

Limestone sink holes

Karst is one of the world's oddest rock formations and can occur only under
the most fortuitous circumstances. Some geologists claim there are only two
places on earth where rock formations resemble those of the northwest of the
island: one just across the Mona Passage in the Dominican Republic, and
one in the former Yugoslavia.

Karst is formed when water sinks into limestone and erodes larger and larger
basins, known as "sinkholes". Many erosions create many sinkholes, until one
is left with peaks of land only where the land has not sunk with the erosion of
limestone: these are *mogotes*, or karstic hillocks, which resemble each other in
size and shape to a striking extent, given the randomness of the process that created them. All this leads you to realize that the highest point on the highest
mogote in the karst country is certainly below the level which the limestone
ground held in earlier days when the first drop of rain opened the first sinkhole.

LEFT: the dish at the Arecibo Observatory is hidden in a natural sinkhole.
BELOW: a valley amid the karstic hills near Arecibo.

TIP

If you have the time, take advantage of the 2-hour-long free launch trips on Lago dos Bocas put on four times a day (7am, 10am, 2pm and 5pm) by the Public Works Department.

BELOW: Lake Caonillas, one of many nestled into the hills of the north.

It's hard to say where the karst country begins. Some say at Manatí, though there are two hills not 10 minutes' drive west of San Juan which look suspiciously karstic. From Manatí, they carry on as far west as Isabela, and are at their most spectacular a short drive (5 miles/8 km) south of the major cities of Puerto Rico's northwest.

It's just as hard to say wherein their appeal lies. Part of it must be in the odd symmetry of the things – despite the fact that it is the holes, not the hills, which have undergone the change over eons.

These hills are impressive mountains only a hundred feet high – they are probably the grandest landscape within which humans can feel a sense of scale. They encompass a startling variety within their regularity; certain *mogotes* can look like the Arizona desert tucked in for bed in the Black Forest.

Cars to karst

Arecibo is the capital of the karst country, and some fine drives can begin from there. The easiest is certainly Route 10 south to **Lago dos Bocas** ❾. Taking Route 129 southwest to Lares is a pleasant jaunt flanked by *colmados* (grocery stores), which never lets you stray into the Cordillera, as the Route 10 trip is prone to do.

If you like karst a lot, though, head west on Route 2, turn left on Route 119, and follow the road to **Lake Guajataca** for perhaps the finest views of the water and limestone that made the whole unfathomable but evocative landscape possible.

Make it a point, if at all possible, of getting out to the karst country. The unique beauty is staggering, and is worth a visit by itself. Even more, though,

THE KARSTIC FORESTS

Puerto Rico's Department of Natural Resources has recognized the beauty and fragility of its unique karstic landscape. It has created four national forests in which it is protected: **Cambalache** (east of Arecibo, with plantations of eucalyptus, teak and mahoe trees), **Guajataca** (west of Arecibo, offering some 25 miles/40 km of hiking trails), **Río Abajo** (south of Arecibo, it is home to 223 plant and 175 wildlife species; 70 trails criss-cross its 5,780 acres/2,300 hectares), and **Vega Alta** (west of Toa Baja).

Not all the karst country is limited to these forests; in fact, they are woefully small, comprising only about 4,000 acres (1,600 hectares) in total, with Río Abajo accounting for over half of these. All are ripe for hiking, yet the trails in the karst country never seem as crowded as those up El Yunque and other Puerto Rican mountains. Perhaps this is owing to the dangers involved with this sort of landscape. Sinkholes are not like potholes, but they can come as unexpectedly, especially in heavy brush.

Get a trail map from the visitors' center at whatever reserve you try. Otherwise, *The Other Puerto Rico* by Kathryn Robinson offers helpful advice, and one read of it will convince you that there's nowhere in Puerto Rico that's not worth risking your life to see.

the sight of karst will add another dimension to this tropical paradise too often labeled as a place for a "beach vacation".

Frontier town

If this tiny island has a frontier town, surely **Lares ❿** is it. It sits at the western edge of the Cordillera Central's main cluster of peaks, and rests at the southernmost spur of the karst country. Lares is about as far from the sea as one can get in Puerto Rico, and to its west stretches a placid corridor of plains land running just north of the hills of La Cadena and just south of Route 111 and the sleepy Río Culebrinas.

Like many of the towns in this area, where plains meet uplands to produce eerily spectacular vistas, Lares is as scenic to approach as it is to leave. Arriving from the south on either Route 124 or Route 128, the traveler is greeted by a tiny, toylike and close-packed community perched on a gentle rise across a valley and shadowed by rugged twin karstic *mogotes*. Emerging from the east on Route 111 from the karstic clusters of the Río Abajo Forest Reserve, you are hit by surprise at Lares' anomalous urbanity.

The town itself exudes much of the toylike ambience which you may well have perceived from afar. It's an attenuated cluster of little businesses, bars and shops snaking along two main one-way streets that run in opposite directions. In the center of the town is an imposing 19th-century Spanish colonial church, whose pale pastel façade and gracefully arched roof give it something of a Middle Eastern look.

If Lares has a stern side, pride rather than inhospitality is its source. For as the scene of the "Grito de Lares", Puerto Rico's glorious and ill-fated revolt

Map, pages 176–7

Puerto Ricans pride themselves on their friendliness and warmth.

BELOW: coffee and banana farm near Lares.

against Spanish colonial rule, the town is generally considered to be the birthplace of modern Puerto Rican political consciousness.

The Grito de Lares

The "Grito de Lares" ("Shout of Lares") was not merely a Puerto Rican historical event; its roots lay in political grievances that were to sweep Spain's Caribbean colonies in the mid-19th century and result, some decades later, in their ultimate loss.

When, in 1867, native Puerto Rican guards demonstrated in protest at discrepancies between their own salaries and those of Spanish guards, many liberals were expelled from the island, including Ramón Emeterio Betances, a distinguished physician and certainly the most prominent voice in Puerto Rican politics at the time. He went to New York, Santo Domingo and Saint Thomas, where he rallied support for abolition and self-determination.

On September 23, 1868, hundreds of Emeterio Betances' followers seized Lares and began to march on nearby San Sebastián. There they were met by Spanish forces, and easily routed. Though Emeterio Betances was merely exiled to France, and the revolution came to nought, the "Grito de Lares" led Puerto Ricans to think differently of their land and their aspirations for it, and the spirit of that September day lives on – not only in the streets of Lares but also in the hearts and on the tongues of Puerto Ricans throughout the island.

Speleology and scatology

Also significant, but in a rather different way, is the unspectacular town of **Camuy** ⓫, just far enough west of Arecibo, just far enough north of Route 2,

Plaque commemorating the 1868 revolution in Lares.

BELOW: flower shop brings a splash of bright color to Lares.

to appear almost untouched by the life of modern Puerto Rico. What appeal Camuy has is more primordial – a bewildering maze of one-way streets that will never accommodate automobiles; a lifestyle tranquil to the point of torpor; a few vestiges of an older era, like shops that sell salves and incense for the appeasement of various saints; and, most primordial of all, one of the largest cave systems in the Western world.

Most easily reached by driving due south on Route 129, the cave system is actually a series of karstic sinkholes connected by the 350-foot-deep (106-meter-deep) Río Camuy, which burrows underground through soft limestone for much of its course from the Cordillera to the Atlantic. The largest of these entrances has been developed for tourism, with attractions of the "fun for the whole family" variety.

The **Río Camuy Cave Park** ⓬ (open Tues–Sun, pub. hols 8am–4pm; last trip 3.45pm), which is managed by the Puerto Rico Land Administration, contains one of the most massive cave networks in the Western hemisphere. This 268-acre (106-hectare) complex includes three crater-like sinkholes and one cave. The Taínos considered these formations sacred; their artifacts have been found throughout the area. The park's main attraction is 170-foot high (52-meter-high) Clara Cave, which is specially lit, and accessible only by trolley and only in guided groups.

The cave entrance looks like a cathedral façade, with a broad row of toothy stalactites descending from the bushy hillside. Inside the cave's overhang, the light becomes bluish, and a weird silence descends, broken only by the chirp of bats on the ceiling and minute distant echoes. Could it be the far-off sound of water dripping through yet undiscovered passages?

Map, pages 176–7

The part of Río Camuy that runs underground forms the second largest subterranean river in the world.

BELOW: the impressive Río Camuy caves.

TIP

If you're thinking of taking some photographs in the caves, bring a tripod along for the best results.

It could be, but it's not. It's bat droppings, and you won't have to travel more than a dozen steps to realize that much of it is very likely to fall on you in the course of your perambulations. Natives claim that the droppings are potentially extremely toxic. But don't let this keep you away. Wash afterwards, or cover up well but visit. There's nothing quite like it.

Leaving the cave park, you have two excellent choices for lunch not far away. The **Restaurante Las Cavernas** and the **Restaurante El Taíno**, both located along Route 129, pride themselves on traditional Puerto Rican cuisine, bilingual waiters, family atmosphere and fairly reasonable prices. At Las Cavernas, the house specialty is *arroz con guinea* (rice with hen), served on a large plate with beans, and *amarillos* (fried bananas) for dessert.

If you're an avid spelunker, there's still more for you to see: close to Río Camuy is the privately owned **Cueva de Camuy** (open daily 9am–5pm, Sun to 8pm) on Route 486. Although smaller and less interesting, it too has guided tours as well as "family-oriented" activities that include a swimming pool and waterslide, amusements, a café, ponies and go-karts. And not far from *that* is **Cueva del Infierno**, but the 2- to 3-hour tours at this location have to be pre-arranged (tel: 898-2723).

Some 2,000 caves have been discovered in the karst region. They provide homes for 13 species of bat, the tiny *coquí*, the *guavá* (an arachnid), crickets and other species.

More caves are to be found near the town of **Hatillo**, on the north coast just east of Camuy, which produces most of the milk consumed on the island. But Hatillo's biggest attraction is in late December, when one of the most popular mask festivals in Puerto Rico is held here. Hundreds of people from around

BELOW: ready for cruising: Lares man and his customized 1960s Chevy.

the island gather at the town's main square to enjoy the colorful festivities, which sees locals dressing up with typical masks to enact King Herod's soldiers running after newborn boys with murder on their minds.

Map, pages 176–7

San Sebastián and back to the coast

Of all the prosperous provincial towns of Puerto Rico's northwest, **San Sebastián** ⓭ stands out both as the most representative of the region and in the most noticeable contrast to the gloomy villages of the Cordillera Central which lie to the south and east.

Perhaps this is because it is the first of the towns which is truly out of the highlands and secure in its footing as part of the low-lying northwest. Perhaps too it has something to do with the cornucopia of food products which come from the region, for this is the heart of many of the island's oldest and most traditional food industries.

San Sebastián is surrounded by green and moist rolling grassland, and stood as one of Puerto Rico's sugar boom towns in the cane industry's heyday. Now the area is given over to scattered dairy farming and various agricultural pursuits which used to be associated with other parts of the island. Tobacco grows in many a valley, and coffee plants, once the preserve of Yauco and other towns in the island's arid southwest, can be seen growing on local hillsides.

With close to 40,000 residents, most of them living in the shady main streets that cluster about a lovely plaza, San Sebastián has more of an urban ambience than most of the northwest. It lacks the historical reputation of Lares, and as a commercial center it is utterly overwhelmed by the tuna fishing port of Mayagüez which is just 10 miles (16 km) away on the east coast.

BELOW: the plaza in San Sebastián.

Map,
pages
176–7

But San Sebastián is within easy driving distance of these places and has a number of charming features that they lack: it is the most provincial of moderate-sized Puerto Rican cities, with a thriving local culture and most of the modern amenities; big salsa groups like El Gran Combo de Puerto Rico play here, as do first-run films.

This is not to say San Sebastián is devoid of scenic charms either. There's no better spot from which to explore the wondrous karst country. There's also the famous Pozo del Virgen, a well that is a religious shrine which attracts thousands of devout Catholics every year. To the north, Lake Guajataca boasts nature walks and a couple of *paradores* (country inns), as well as excellent fishing. And any drive into the countryside will invariably lead to scenic surprises.

Surprising town

The most amazing story Puerto Ricans tell about the town of **Quebradillas** ⓮ concerns basketball. During a close regular season game between the Quebradillas team and arch-rival Isabela, the score became close, and tensions and tempers began to run high. When Isabela took the lead on a surprise basket and its supporters began to cheer and taunt, Quebradillas's town dignitary, Mayor Hernández, rose from the stands with a revolver and fired into the opposing stands, injuring several spectators.

This is not to point to the people of Quebradillas as being especially violent – if anything, their friendly and welcoming attitude will convince you the opposite is the case – but rather to show that in this isolated northwestern municipality anything can happen, and quite often anything does. Quebradillas itself adds to the appealing oddities you expect from the towns west of Arecibo – spiritualist herb shops, narrow streets and houses sloping towards the waterline – with some geological oddities that make it a town well worth going out of your way for.

A short drive or walk northwest of town, **Playa Guajataca**, described paradoxically by locals as a "nice, dangerous beach", is to be taken with care. Deep waters, white sands and raging surf make it highly attractive for surfers and bathers, but highly dangerous for those incapable of swimming the English Channel. Even experts should exercise caution.

The **Río Guajataca** is another spot as beautiful as it is forbidding, pocked with a cave system which, though not completely charted, appears to be as extensive and awesome as that of the caves at Camuy.

Nearby **Lake Guajataca** ⓯, 7 miles (11 km) south on Route 113, is man-made, as are the rest of Puerto Rico's lakes, but offers a splendid natural retreat, with two *paradores*, Vistamar and El Guajataca, both situated on the coast, serving as convenient bases for hikes into the rolling **Aymamon Mountains** in the **Guajataca Forest Reserve** ⓰, located just to the west. Both *paradores* are very good: El Guajataca's rooms open onto the Atlantic, and the dinners – blending Creole and international dishes – are remarkable; Vistamar, one of Puerto Rico's largest *paradores*, features beautiful gardens and the opportunity to fish in a green-water river near the hotel. ❑

BELOW: geese await their fate at the Friday flea market in San Sebastián. **RIGHT:** view of the dammed Lago dos Bocas.

THE WEST

Aguada and Aguadilla are attractive seaside centers, Rincón has spectacular surf, Mayagüez mixes tuna packing and hedonism, and San Germán is the island's second oldest town

Map, page 196

The part of Puerto Rico furthest from San Juan is, not surprisingly, the part most tourists would choose to visit had they an inkling of what awaited them there. Mayagüez sits at the center of the region, a city with a vibrancy and beauty which has led Puerto Ricans to ruminate, despite Ponce's recent rehabilitation, "What's Puerto Rico's second city, Ponce or Mayagüez?"

None of the surrounding area, however, will make one sorry one left Mayagüez; there is San Germán, home to several rare examples of Gothic architecture and Puerto Rico's second oldest city; Boquerón, surf capital of the southwest; Parguera, with a phosphorescent bay; Guánica, where U.S. forces landed in 1898; and Punta Jagüey, which boasts not only spectacular beaches but also one of the most beautiful lighthouses in the Atlantic Ocean.

Isabela ❶, along the northern coast, is a florilegium of all the charms of this corner of Puerto Rico, with a cluster of brilliant, whitewashed houses tumbling out of the hills to some of the island's most justly renowned surfing and swimming beaches.

The city has that look of stability and purposefulness which is so characteristic of the region, due perhaps to flourishing shoe and textile industries. But Isabela has not bought serenity at the price of industrial over-expansion; it has retained a high proportion of its small farms.

If history has been somewhat kind to Isabela, nature has not. Located just south of the tectonically fickle Milwaukee Trench, Isabela has been victimized by earthquakes and tidal waves for as long as it has been permanently settled.

Breeding and beaches

Horse enthusiasts should make their way to **Arenales ❷**, to the south, where a number of the fine *pasofino* stables have made Isabela a renowned equine breeding center. Most visitors to Isabela, however, come to ride waves, not steeds, and **Jobos Beach ❸**, just west of town on Route 466, is the place they head for.

The beach is made even more beautiful by the high cliffs which back it. One of these, **El Pozo de Jacinto ❹**, is the source of a charming – though rather sad – local custom. A farmer named Jacinto used to pasture his cows near the edge of the cliffs. One day, part of the cliff collapsed and Jacinto's finest bovine tumbled to her death. Jacinto, enraged, ran to the cliff's edge and cursed fate. Fate disapproved; Jacinto too fell off the cliff and died. Today, Isabela schoolchildren stand at the edge of the cliffs and yell: *"Jacinto! Damne la vaca!"* (Damn the cow!) It's said to bring good luck.

Also near Isabela is a beach known as **The Shacks**, where scuba divers and snorkelers gravitate to swim among its coral caverns and reefs.

PRECEDING PAGES: colorful *yolas* at Aguadilla. **LEFT:** pensive Puerto Rican. **BELOW:** Jobos Beach near Isabela.

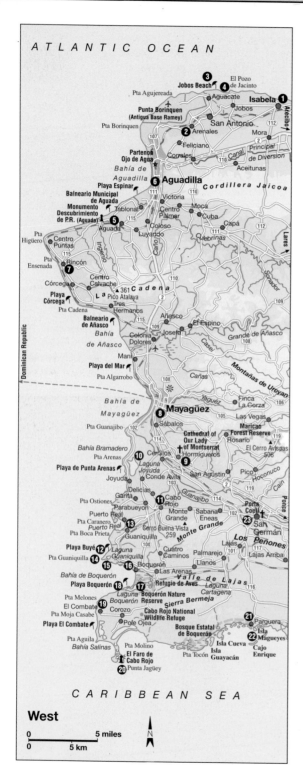

Rival resorts

The two lovely seaside towns of **Aguada ❺** and **Aguadilla ❻** on the west coast have a running rivalry over which was the spot where Christopher Columbus first landed in Puerto Rico. Its residents might therefore be taken aback to find that most of the handful of visitors who come each year have a hard enough time telling the two towns apart, let alone judging the primacy of their respective claims.

In defence of its claim, **Aguada** has erected a seaside **Parque de Colón** a mile northwest of the town on Route 441, dead center of **Playa Espinar**, a 2,500-foot (760-meter) white-sand beach so enticing that Columbus buffs will wish their man had landed there, regardless of historical fact. Aguadillans, meanwhile, certainly have logic, if not an airtight argument, on their side in claiming that Columbus's men stopped for water at the spring which now forms the focus of their own **Parque El Parterre**.

Aguadilla is the more prosperous and picturesque of the two towns, and has more places to stay, including the *parador* El Faro. It's laid out like a Mediterranean resort, bleeding along a mile of coast with very little penetration inland. **Avenida José de Jesús Esteves** (Route 440) is a prim and polychromatic seaside boulevard, a little Caribbean equivalent of the Promenade des Anglais in Nice; parallel streets are punctuated with attractive if unspectacular parks. *Mundillo* lace and wicker hats are the twin prides of Aguadilla's active artisan community, and both are ubiquitous in the shops located in the commercial district.

Flyers and *playas*

Many though its charms may be, Aguadilla can't claim, like Aguada, to have a pleasant *balneario* (swimming area) at its doorstep. Aguadilla's is just a bit too rocky for any sane people to have a go at.

Most of the townspeople, therefore, head north on Route 197 to do their bathing at **Playa Boqueron Sur**, known locally as Crash Boat Beach in honor of the vessels which used to take off from there to rescue errant fighter planes from the former **Ramey Air Force Base** just to the north, which has the longest runway in the Caribbean. No longer in service, the base area is now called Punta Borinquen.

Map, page 196

International waves

Rincón ❼, southwest of Aguadilla on a point on the way to Mayagüez, is certainly not a place for bathing enthusiasts, except for those whose idea of a good time is being thrown face-first onto rock flats or jagged reefs. Nor, although nightlife here is fast and loose enough for any taste, is it partying that draws so many young people to Rincón from San Juan, which is by now 100 miles (160 km) away. In fact, what Rincón has lures the young and the strong from much further than just San Juan. The town has a dazzling and varied offshore surf which has drawn board enthusiasts for decades, and has made Rincón, since the World Surfing Championships were held here in 1968, the surfing capital of the Caribbean area.

Though *rincón* means "corner", the town actually sits at the flat, regular end of the peninsula shaped like a pointer's snout. This is **La Cadena**, the westernmost spur of the rugged Cordillera Central, and nowhere in Puerto Rico do mountains meet coast more dramatically than they do here. The view most surfers see from offshore is of deep green hills and shimmering groves of mango backing bright, white sand and turquoise sea, and it's highly probable that this unique vista draws as many surfers to Rincón as the sport itself – those who tend to spend more time admiring the views than they do riding the waves.

Whale-watchers are becoming increasingly attracted to the Rincón shores; a bit further out is a wintering place for humpback whales.

BELOW: airborne in the Aguadillan surf.

Tunnel vision

Still, it's hard to imagine better surfing anywhere. Rincón is not just one beach but six, bordered by picturesque and prominent coral reefs and shoals, stretching from Puerto Rico's rough Atlantic coast on the north side of the peninsula to the placid and eminently swimmable turquoise waters of the Caribbean south. The quality and size of the surf vary all the way along the peninsula, leaving boardmen with a choice of rides at all levels of difficulty. The effect is rather like that of a year-round ski resort with a great number of delightful trails.

The town of Rincón is pleasant and quiet, with a number of trendy, surfer-infested restaurants ranged along Route 115. An old disused nuclear power plant standing next to the town's quaint little lighthouse lends the area an eerie look and gives Rincón an other-worldliness perceptible even to the non-surfers who end up here by mistake.

A big attraction in Rincón has nothing to do with the surf: the Horned Dorset Primavera Hotel here is considered one of the best hotels in the whole of the Caribbean.

Mayagüez

The third largest of Puerto Rico's three major cities is the only one which can claim the sort of cosmopolitan-cum-hedonistic lifestyle that makes a certain type of traveler fall in love with a city. San Juan and Ponce have other, perhaps deeper, charms, but both are a bit too hardworking and serious to compete with the relaxing atmosphere of their little sister out west. There's something about Mayagüez's modernism – this is not to say lack of history – which lends an irresponsible, vaguely Californian ethos to life there. Add to this beautiful ocean breezes and some of the best swimming and surfing on the island, and one is left with a holiday spot for those who wish to relax and be self-indulgent, rather than those who want to do a great deal of sightseeing or culture seeking.

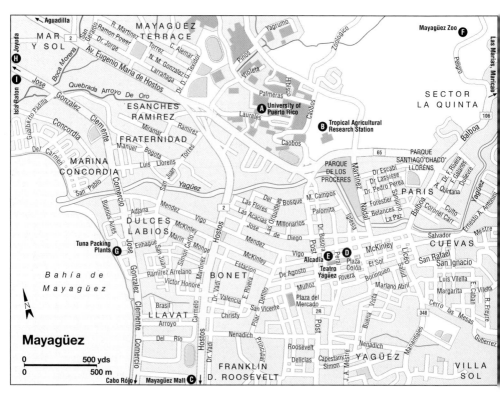

For all its charms, **Mayagüez ❽** remains off the beaten tourist path. Those who reach it tend to guzzle the local beer with the vengence only those who have worked hard for their holidays can understand.

Fishy business

Not all is beer and skittles in this western metropolis; in fact, the isolation of those who engage in high living from those who are stuck making a living is in large degree responsible for the particular pace of life in Mayagüez. Pared down to its most basic, Mayagüez is a fish-packing town with a university. The town lives on tuna, at least indirectly; over 60 percent of the tuna eaten in the United States is tinned here, and a substantial number of residents make their living from the stuff. It is also an important departure-point for deep-sea fishing and the port for exporting agricultural produce from the surrounding hills.

Mayagüez's college, located on Route 108, is an outpost of the **University of Puerto Rico (UPR) ❹**. It's primarily an engineering and agricultural college, so the ferment over issues political and literary which is so much a part of the University of Puerto Rico in Río Piedras doesn't really penetrate much here. But the college is right next to one of the finest places for learning that Puerto Rico has to offer, the **Tropical Agricultural Research Station ❸** (open Mon–Fri 7am–4pm). Run by the US Department of Agriculture, these gardens, built on the site of a former plantation, boast one of the largest collections of tropical and semi-tropical plants in the world. Across the street is the **Parque de los Próceres**, adorned with fountains and walkways and a perfect place for relaxing. Nearby is the new and somewhat hyper-modern **Mayagüez Mall ❹**, a scaled-down version of San Juan's Plaza Las Américas.

Maps:
City 198
Area 196

UPR's Mayagüez campus is a major engineering recruiting center for NASA and other US Government intelligence and military agencies.

BELOW: sprawling modern Mayagüez.

Tuna Territory

Driving along Mayagüez Bay, you can literally smell Puerto Rico's tuna industry a mile away. The stench is an unpleasant but necessary part of life in this small metropolis, where, despite the industry's gradual decline in recent years, thousands of jobs still depend on the export of canned tuna-fish to the US.

A chain-link fence separates the sprawling operations of rivals Bumble Bee International and StarKist Caribe, two of the world's largest tuna processors, who between them supply about half the US's canned tuna.

The fence ends at the water's edge, where both companies, in identical but separate operations, unload frozen tuna from different holds of the same vessel. The companies are here mainly because of Section 936 of the United States Internal Revenue Code, a tax holiday that has exempted them from federal income tax on local profits.

The canneries aren't open to the public;

even local journalists have a hard time getting in, so secret and competitive is the business. Traditionally, Bumble Bee controls the market in albacore tuna, while StarKist's strength lies in yellowfin and skipjack. In the early 1990s the industry suffered a major setback when controversy erupted over the strangulation of thousands of dolphins in tuna nets. Since the mammals swim mainly with yellowfin, adopting so-called "dolphin-safe" policies meant giving up nearly 300,000 tons of yellowfin tuna annually. While pleasing environmentalists, this policy has led to higher costs and smaller profit margins.

Even before the dolphin-safe issue arose, Puerto Rico's tuna industry was being hit by low-wage Far East competition. In 1986, the island had five canneries employing close to 8,000 people. Today, there are only three, with a combined workforce of 5,080.

StarKist's 600,000-sq. ft (55,700-sq. meter) Mayagüez facility remains the world's largest tuna cannery, though employment there has dropped from 4,300 to 3,500. Employment at its next-door neighbor, Bumble Bee, was slashed from 2,000 to 1,200 shortly after the company became a subsidiary of Thailand's Unicorp in 1991. And in Ponce, Caribe Tuna – owned by Mitsubishi Foods of Japan – has reduced its workers from 800 to 380. The Van Camp packing-plant in Ponce closed in 1991 after an Indonesian firm, P.T. Mantrust, bought the company and transferred its facilities to American Samoa. Another cannery, Neptune Packing, was closed the same year by its Japanese owners, Mitsui & Co. Inc.

In one recent year, StarKist, Bumble Bee and Caribe Tuna exported 181,000 tons of processed tuna to the US east coast, where it sold for $475 million. Tuna workers earn about 12 times the average hourly wage of their rivals in the Far East.

In addition to much higher labor costs, canneries here must contend with stricter environmental regulations, high transportation costs and greater distance from the world's leading fisheries. For this reason, most economists expect the remaining canneries to simply pack up and leave Puerto Rico once Section 936 tax incentives finally come to an end in the year 2006. ❏

Maps:
City 198
Area 196

Ladies of Barcelona

All this is only about a half-mile north of Mayagüez's main plaza, the **Plaza Colón D**. A statue dead-center commemorates Christopher Columbus, and round about are 16 different bronze statues of courtly ladies brought from Barcelona. The ground in the plaza is as smooth and shiny as an ice-skating rink, and the buildings around it are dignified and imposing, particularly the neo-Corinthian **Alcaldía E**, with its lovely crimson-and white-façade.

There is plenty more happening around Mayagüez. The **Mayagüez Zoo F**, (open Wed–Sun 9am–4pm) about 15 miles (24 km) outside the town, is one of those zoos that is something like a nature park, as animals roam about not in cages but in an environment as close to their native habitats as is possible in a climate where it almost never drops below 70°F (21°C) or rises above 80°F (27°C). It's an enjoyable family place, with such wild animals as ringtailed lemurs and Bengal tigers.

The tuna-packing plants **G** at the waterfront (*see panel opposite*) lend a unique flavor to this staid town, while along the shore, the **Joyuda H** section features one seafood establishment after another. Just offshore, within sight, is **Isla Raton** (Rat Island) **I**, where visitors go for a peaceful afternoon, perhaps fishing or just taking in the view – sans rats.

Mayagüez as it was

Mayagüez is not without history. The native Taíno Indians found the place every bit as alluring as today's beach-bums and pharmaceutical companies, and when Columbus landed here, on his second voyage to the Caribbean, he found a great number of welcoming natives. The name Mayagüez means

TIP

While in Mayagüez, try the local gastronomic specialty: traditional *mofongo* stuffed with shrimps.

BELOW: Plaza Colón and the Alcaldía, Mayagüez. **LEFT:** unloading frozen tuna.

The Spanish influence is evident throughout Puerto Rico – even in the little touches.

BELOW: a favorite (and serious) Puerto Rican pastime: dominoes.

"place of many streams" and the confluence of so many tributaries gives an open-to-the-sea feeling to the city. One of these, the Río Yagüez, gives the city its name. Should the Spanish and Taíno constituents of this odd name for a body of water be translated into similar English, we'd be left with the infinitely descriptive monicker of the "Water River".

Devastation

As a Spanish settlement, however, the city dates only from the end of the 18th century, when fishermen found the riches of the Mona Passage too alluring to pass up. Tragically, Mayagüez's history under Spanish dominion has been all but lost to us. The earthquake which rocked the entire western part of the island in 1918 fairly devastated Mayagüez, with the result that the town was almost depopulated.

Five miles (8 km) south of Mayagüez is the tiny *municipio* of **Hormigueros ⑨**, which is a suburb only in the sense that it is below its parent city on the map. This is a city with the pace of the northwest and the layout of a Cordillera town, with narrow, winding streets and one of the finest cathedrals on the island.

The **Cathedral of Our Lady of Montserrat** is at once awesome and unassuming. Bone-white towers of varying dimensions rise to domes of crimson topped with austere white crucifixes of wood. Elevated slightly above the town, the cathedral appears to soar into the sky with an effect that is, oddly enough, best appreciated on a cloudy day. Yet its proximity to the streets which surround it, its everyday color scheme and something in the ordinary way in which Hormiguerans go about life with such a treasure in their midst keeps the cathedral a friendly-looking place with no pretensions.

Hormigueros itself is worth a day-excursion from Mayagüez, if only to catch a glimpse of the cathedral and do a bit of shopping on the city's main avenues.

Back on the coast, west of Hormigueros, lies **Laguna Joyuda** ⑩, a mangrove swamp which is a sanctuary for birds native to the region. Mangroves are among the most hospitable of environments for semi-tropical bird life, and this sanctuary has them in higher concentration than any other area in the western half of Puerto Rico. This 300-acre (120-hectare) expanse is home to herons, martins and pelicans, including the lovely maroon pelican. The lagoon itself is full of fish, and is phosphorescent on moonless nights, due to a preponderance of the dinoflagellate *pyrodinium bahamense*.

The infamous Spanish buccaneer Roberto Cofresí made Cabo Rojo his home during 17th-century raids on European merchant ships.

To the point

Surrounded by coral-studded Caribbean waters, bathed in dry tropical heat year-round and sculpted into an odd network of cliffs, lagoons, promontories and swamps by fickle surfs and tides, the *municipio* of **Cabo Rojo** ⑪ shows Puerto Rico's seaside landscape at its eeriest and most alluring.

Stretching south along 18 miles (29 km) of coast from Mayagüez, this area is among the remotest on the island; whether approaching from Ponce or from Mayagüez, one notices the landscape growing drier and more hummocky, the population more sparse, and the scenery more beautiful.

For those to whom the name "Cabo Rojo" has become synonymous with isolated retreats and breathtaking vistas, Cabo Rojo town can come as something of a disappointment. It is unquestionably a quaint and pretty town, however, and full of history: its 10,000 residents are well up on local lore.

BELOW: Playa Boquerón, one of the island's finest beaches.

A battery of beaches

Everyone in Puerto Rico has his or her favorite beach, but **Playa Buyé** ⑫, just southwest of Cabo Rojo on Route 307, gets more votes than many others. With its wispy rows of pine hooking around a promontory to the bay known as **Puerto Real** ⑬, and pleasant views of the tiny village of Elizabeth across the water, Buyé makes up in charm what it lacks in size. The landscape changes with shocking suddenness just south of Buyé, as the cliffs of **Punta Guaniquilla** ⑭ give way to the swamps and mangroves of the tiny **Laguna Guaniquilla** ⑮.

The cliffs and lagoon are best reached either by making the shortish ¾-mile (1-km) walk south or by taking the dirt road that leads out of the tiny settlement of **Boca Prieta** at the southern end of Buyé.

Competing beaches

Seven miles (11 km) south of Cabo Rojo on Route 4 and 101, **Boquerón** ⑯ is a fishing port of staggering beauty. It is blessed with a mangrove forest which shelters some of Puerto Rico's loveliest birds – the Laguna Rincón and surrounding forests have been designated a bird sanctuary as one of the three parts of the **Boquerón Nature Reserve** ⑰.

But it is hardly bird-watching that brings most visitors to the town. For Boquerón sits at the mouth of a 3-mile-long (5-km-long) bay whose placid, coral-

TIP

The cabins around
Boquerón's beach are
popular among
weekenders; to rent
one, contact the
Department of
Recreation and Sports
in San Juan at least
four months in
advance.

flecked waters and sands backed by palm groves make **Playa Boquerón** ⓲ almost without question the finest beach on the island. In a place like Puerto Rico, where regional rivalries are intense, the fact that even some Luquillo residents will admit as much is significant.

Tucked into Puerto Rico's southwestern corner at the end of Route 301, a circuitous 6 miles (10 km) south of Boquerón, **El Combate** ⓳ is yet another beach of renown, with a charming row of fishing shacks and a crowded jetty.

Route 301 travels even farther south, past **Pole Oleja**, a not-terribly inspiring salt settlement. Two miles (3 km) on, however, at the southwesternmost extremity of Puerto Rico, is the crowning glory of Cabo Rojo and one of the most scenic spots in the entire Caribbean. This is **Punta Jagüey** ⓴, a kidney-shaped rock outcrop connected to land by a narrow isthmus and straddling two lovely bays, **Bahia Salinas** and **Bahia Succia**.

Herons and eelgrass

Here too is a nature reserve of grand proportions; both the peninsula and the surrounding waters are protected as part of the same Boquerón system that embraces Laguna Rincón. But there is more to Punta Jagüey than herons and eelgrass. **Cabo Rojo Lighthouse** is a breathtaking specimen of Spanish colonial architecture, with its low-lying, pale-sided main building and squat, hexagonal lighttower. It perches atop dun-colored cliffs at the very extremity of the peninsula and commands views of almost 300 degrees of the Caribbean.

The lighthouse is at its most awe-inspiring when given a faint blush by either sunrise or sunset. It's more likely you'll see the latter; many excursions to Cabo Rojo are conceived as day-trips and somehow carry on into the evening.

BELOW: jetty spans
white sand and
turquoise waters at
El Combate beach.

Southwest tip

Parguera ㉑ leads a dual life as a quiet coastal town and – on summer nights and weekends – a party town alive with young *sanjuaneros* and thrill-seeking tourists. This is not to say the place is spoiled; it serves the very useful function of diverting the inevitable crowds from the area's more delicate attractions.

Map, page 196

Boats ply the waters between the village and the bay itself with reassuring frequency. For a few dollars, you'll most likely get an hour in the flying Caribbean spindrift and one of the rare opportunities Puerto Rico affords to make use of a warm sweater. Leaving the docks, cruises run through the yachts and fishing boats of Parguera's poorly-sheltered harbor and past a tiny chain of islets whose focus is **Isla Magueyes ㉒**, home to a large colony of lizards.

As cruise boats enter the bay itself, their wakes turn an eerie pale-green. Captains invite the passengers to trail their hands over the gunwales and into the water to produce odd, remarkable patterns. A bucket is generally brought on board for the curious to play with, and in cupped palms the water breaks into shapes resembling splattering mercury. The phosphorescence is produced by billions of micro-organisms which belong to the family of dinoflagellates known as *pyrodinium bahamense*. Try to see this unique phenomenon on a cloudy night with a light breeze, when no other light sources muddle the brilliance of the waters, and wavelets make ever-changing patterns on the surface. Unfortunately, in recent years the effect has been reduced owing to pollution.

San Germán

Seeds of colonization in the New World have not always brought culture, but they have generally brought overpopulation, and the large cities of the Americas,

BELOW: a lively night in Parguera.

TIP

When planning a trip to San Germán, take note that, as it is a university town, it can be difficult to get cheap accommodation in term time.

with their millions of citizens, were generally in place, if only as minor outposts, a couple of centuries ago. **San Germán ㉓**, with its population of 30,000, is a different sort of locale – it is one of those major towns of the 16th century which has been blessed by never having been too thoroughly dragged into the squalid rat-race of the modern world. Although old, it has never grown into a sprawling urban center.

San Germán – Puerto Rico's second-oldest town – is a diamond in an emerald setting, a pearly-white town tucked into an uncharacteristically lush and verdant section of the island's south coast, about halfway between Ponce and Mayagüez on pretty Route 119.

Founded in 1573 by the second wave of Spanish colonists, San Germán was San Juan's only rival for prominence on the island until the 19th century. Forces invading or retreating from San Juan, notably the English, French and Dutch, not uncommonly stopped here to arm themselves or lick their wounds. In the 19th century it became one of Puerto Rico's great coffee towns, with magnates building some of the truly unique homes on the island.

Today, San Germán owes its prominence and cultural vibrancy to the Inter-American University, with its 8,000 students and well-tended grounds, and the diligence with which it has preserved some of the earliest European architectural works to survive in the Western hemisphere.

Heaven's gate

BELOW: picturesque main street in San Germán.

The **Porta Coeli Church** (open Wed–Sun 9am–4.15pm; free) is San Germán's – and arguably Puerto Rico's – greatest architectural inheritance. Founded in 1606, it is the oldest church under the United States flag. It is also one of only

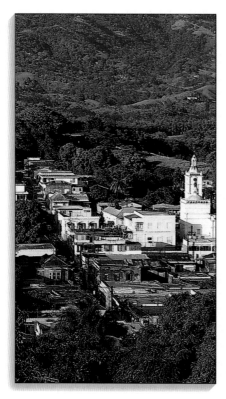

THE ART OF JOSÉ CAMPECHE

It is no surprise that the work of José Campeche adorns San Germán's Porta Coeli, one of Puerto Rico's most architecturally important churches. Many of the island's churches – as well as the cathedral in Old San Juan – feature paintings by Campeche, Puerto Rico's first native painter and its first artistic genius. He was born José de Rívafrecha y Jordán in 1751; his father, Tomás Rivafrecha y Campeche, was a black freeman and his mother, María Jordán y Márques, was a Spaniard from the Canary Islands. Campeche, like his brothers, learned about art and painting through Tomás, who was a master gilder and carver, a painter and an ornamentalist.

But José excelled at more than art: he was also a professional musician, sculptor, surveyor and decorator, and an architect. Well-educated and a devoted Catholic, he was considered a gentleman. He was fortunate to live after Puerto Rico's towns and cities were established: before that, not much emphasis had been given to the arts. Through his approximately 400 paintings of religious themes and historical events, and portraits of politicians and local landed gentry, he gained a reputation as "the most gifted of Latin American rococo artists". Campeche died in 1809 and is buried in San Juan Cathedral.

Map, page 196

a few buildings in the New World constructed in the Gothic architectural style. It is one of the great glories of Spanish colonization that the conquest came about early enough to ensure that this neo-medieval style, which peppered all the countries of Europe with some of the greatest monuments to man's artistry, could also flourish in the New World.

Porta Coeli means "heaven's gate" and, indeed, its portals are of great importance to its artistry. It's a squat little whitewashed building standing at the top of a broad, spreading stairway of scrabbly brick and mortar. Its large doors are of beautiful *ausubo*, a once-common Puerto Rican hardwood.

Inside, the pews and altar are all original, with embellishments. The altarpiece was painted by the first great Puerto Rican artist, José Campeche (*see panel opposite*), in the late 18th century, a fact that would indicate the church was fairly well-established as a historical landmark even by then. Today the church is a small religious museum containing some ancient *santos*, carved figures of saints. Porta Coeli overlooks one of the most beautifully landscaped plazas in Puerto Rico, with its terraced benches and beautifully groomed trees.

One of the many santos displayed in the Porta Coeli Church, now a museum.

Name that church

San Germán, like Ponce, is a two-plaza town, and its second, the **Plaza Francisco Mariano Quiñones**, is no less impressive than that overlooked by Porta Coeli, with the same lovely walks, period lamplights and marvelous topiary. But it also has a church to rival Porta Coeli in appeal, if not in age. **San Germán de Auxerre Church** commemorates the French saint who is the town's patron. Its steeple does not face the plaza directly but has its façade on a nearby side street. While less important than much of San Germán in historical terms, it dominates the town, and is particularly impressive when viewed from the surrounding hills on a bright and sunny day.

BELOW: the second of San Germán's pretty plazas: Mariano Quiñones.

Ancient homes

San Germán's oldest attractions – the two churches, in particular – have always captured the attention of visitors, but there is much more: 249 noteworthy sites, to be exact. (San Germán is one of only two Puerto Rican cities – the other is San Juan – to be included in the National Register of Historic Places.) But few have stopped to examine the general layout and ambience of this ancient town with the rigor and delight that tourists have always brought to San Juan and Ponce. Marvelous haciendas of the late 19th-century coffee barons are abundant, and demonstrate a style which, while it can be seen throughout the southwest – in Yauco, for example – is as much San Germán's own as Porta Coeli.

These houses must be entered to be appreciated, as much of their charm lies in the way in which the interior spaces are divided. Beautiful *mediopunto* carvings – delicate lacy half-screens of snaking wood – create conceptual divisions between rooms without actually putting up substantial physical barriers. Some of them are astounding harbingers of art nouveau, as are the simple and sinuous stencilings which grace the walls of many of the houses. ❑

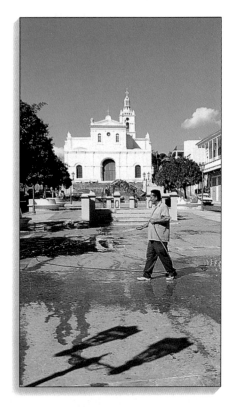

PUERTO RICO'S FANTASTIC FLORA

One would expect luxuriant flora on a tropical island, but Puerto Rico's exceeds all expectations, and much of it is protected in forest reserves

Everything grows in Puerto Rico – and in abundance. This lush, green island produces a vast array of flora which ranges from myriad varieties of orchid to a cornucopia of trees, many of them fruit-bearing.

Puerto Rico's flora is as colorful as the many other aspects of the country. Visitors will at once notice the exotic splashes of bougainvillea that adorn homes, businesses and even bridges. Gardenias and jasmine fill the air with their fragrance, while pink oleander and red hibiscus dot the countryside and towns. Bamboo, mahogany and *Lignum vitae*, the hardest wood in the world, are cultivated for local use as well as export.

The 200-acre (80-hectare) Botanical Gardens in Río Piedras (*see page 147*) is a particularly good place to see much of the island's tropical plantlife in one location. Along similar lines, the Tropical Agricultural Research Station in Mayagüez (*see page 199*) has one of the largest collections of tropical and semi-tropical plants in the world.

Although various hurricanes have taken their toll, Puerto Rico also provides ample locales to explore the island's flora in its natural state, including the Caribbean National Forest – better known as El Yunque (*see pages 157–60*). There are also well-kept hiking trails in the Guánica Forest Reserve, which is known for its birdlife as well as for its endangered plant species. Puerto Rico's wild karst country (*see pages 183–4*) can also be discovered via the trails running through that area's four national forests.

▷ **LUSH RAINFOREST**
More than 100 billion gallons of rain falls annually in El Yunque, creating an environment in which bromeliads, palms and ferns like these thrive.

△ **LOCAL EXOTICA**
The island's beautiful flora isn't limited to reserves – in nearly every garden and around every corner are brilliant tropical blossoms.

▷ **DELICATE BLOOMS**
The Caribbean National Forest (El Yunque) is home to 240 species of tropical trees, flowers and wildlife, including more than 20 kinds of orchid.

FRUITS OF A FERTILE LAND

It would probably come as no surprise to a Puerto Rican if a planted toothpick took root, so fertile is the soil. Fruit-bearing trees are a prime example: oranges, limes, mangos, papaya and guava grow wild on the island, although many fruits – and vegetables – are also cultivated. The country's most unusual fruit has to be the weird, head-sized breadfruit, which islanders prepare in a number of ways, but most commonly as *tostones* – fried green breadfruit slices – that accompany many main courses. More familiar to visitors is the banana, which grows in abundance here, alongside its close relative, the plantain, which cannot be eaten raw. You'll see plantains on menus everywhere, most commonly in the form of appetizer *tostones* or fried up in *mofongo*, a particular island favorite.

△ **TOP GARDENS**
The University of Puerto Rico's Botanical Gardens at Río Piedras are considered to be one of the best in the Caribbean.

◁ **FLAMING BEAUTY**
Bright red blossoms of the flamboyant tree, or poinciana, light up the Puerto Rican countryside in June and July.

▷ **DRY FOREST FLORA**
Guánica Forest, west of Ponce, is a dry and dusty region unexpectedly brimming with beauty. Some 750 plant and tree species grow here – 48 of them endangered and 16 indigenous.

Map,
page 215

THE SOUTH

*Salinas is known for its fish restaurants, Coamo and Ponce
are rich in history, Guayanilla is a good base for touring,
and birdwatchers head for the Guánica Forest Reserve*

San Juan

Until the completion in 1975 of the Expreso Las Américas, now a toll road known as the Autopista Luis Ferré toll road, San Juan natives considered the prospect of driving to Ponce only slightly less daunting than that of swimming to Miami. Indeed, Puerto Rico's south coast used to be so isolated by the Cordillera Central and its winding one-lane roads that most northern Puerto Ricans saw their southern compatriots in terms of a number of bizarre and often unflattering stereotypes. These were the proud, stubborn farmers, whose accent was slightly odd; they were a simple people with something of a gift for politics, but with a culture you wouldn't envy if you lived at the bottom of the ocean. Their only inheritance was a landscape as gorgeous as it was remote.

All that has changed, and it's no longer possible to entertain those stereotypes. The south has charms that are drawing northerners an hour down the highway to take up residence. Ponce, recently much refurbished, with a glittering double plaza and the greatest art museum in the Caribbean, is as pleasant and cultured as any city of its size anywhere.

Salinas's seafood restaurants rival San Juan's best, and Jobos Bay is as pleasant a spot for picnicking as it is for sailing. All along the coast is the alluring, typically southern landscape of golden plain stretching between lush mountain and blue Caribbean. And from Ponce, it's now only 90 minutes to get to San Juan. Most *ponceños* would tell you it's not worth the effort.

Eastern allure

Salinas ❶ is one of the most enjoyable and undersung towns on this island. It has more of a western ethos than most of the urbanizations surrounding it. There are several possible reasons for this: one could be that it maintains a shade of cosmopolitanism of the sort practiced in Ponce and Mayagüez, which have expatriate populations. Another is perhaps that its many excellent seafood restaurants serve up redfish, lobster and other *criollo* specialties of a quality that reminds one of the Mona Passage – the stretch of water between Puerto Rico and the Dominican Republic.

Despite its western orientation, most of Salinas's allure lies to the east. Its downtown is an attractive one, but after a brief stop you may want to get on the road to Aguirre to visit one of the most lively and patronized *galleras* on the island.

A *gallera* is a ring for cock-fighting, a sport many people find distasteful. And this country cock-fighting scene is a far cry from the organized, plush *gallera* in the San Juan suburb of Isla Verde. But if you want to stay for the experience you will see men knowledgeable about fighting cocks wager hundreds of dollars

PRECEDING PAGES:
Ponce's celebrated
Parque de Bombas.
LEFT: Salinas
Beach.
BELOW: Puerto
Ricans have
practiced
hammock-weaving
for many centuries.

TIP

While in Salinas, kids will probably enjoy spending some time at the Albergue Olímpico Germán Rieckehof, the Puerto Rican Olympic athletes' training facilities. Attractions here include a mini-mall, a botanical garden, the Puerto Rican Museum of Sports, a water park, and a playground.

BELOW: side-stepping on one of Puerto Rico's fine *pasofino* horses.

on the local birds in fits of frenzied passion. Be careful though. The sport is bloody and hardly for the fainthearted (it often ends with one of the birds being killed), and there will be plenty of people willing to take your wagers. (And be aware there aren't any odds posted.)

Not too far away, **Punta Salinas** offers a slew of unpretentious seafood restaurants, several of which look out on the peaceful **Bahia de Rincón**, and all of which serve seafood the likes of which would cause the most finicky chef in San Juan to turn green with envy, and perhaps even tempt some of the east coast's most scrupulous fishermen to order another plate.

Historic city

Moving westward across the mountains from Aibonito, Route 14 goes directly to **Coamo ❷**. One of the oldest cities in Puerto Rico, Coamo was founded in 1538. On the plaza, a **historical museum** located in a sunny courtyard displays 450 years of artifacts, documents and pictures. Several rooms are furnished with antiques to re-create a typical (and prosperous) 19th-century household. Enter the museum through a pediatrics clinic just off the plaza.

Even before the Spaniards came the Taínos considered the waters of Coamo holy and healing. In the early part of the 20th century, **Coamo Springs** was a major Caribbean resort with an international clientele. President Franklin D. Roosevelt took the waters here in the 1930s. After World War II, however, the resort went bankrupt and fell into decay.

Today a new resort stands on the ruins of the old one. The **Parador de Coamo**, part of the system of *paradores*, was built in 1975. The crumbling 1848 walls of the original hotel are cleverly used to help support some of the

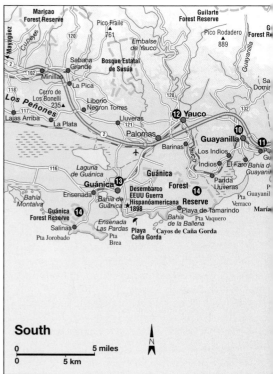

South

0   5 miles
0   5 km

new structures, and they lend a picturesque air to the site. Water at a temperature of 110°F (45°C) is pumped from the springs into a large pool. Its mineral content is remarkably high.

A Mediterranean health spa in the mountains of Puerto Rico? That's what it seems, with healthy young men and women jogging on the road outside the *parador,* and tanned bodies sunning by the swimming pool with iced juices in hand. Most guests are vacationing Puerto Rican families. There are also public baths at the springs for those who come only for the waters. Find the springs on Route 546; signs point the way to the *parador.*

Outside Coamo, farms and ranches raise beef cattle and fine horses with an island-wide reputation. The tradition of the gentleman-farmer still lives on.

Continuing west, the one-time sugar and coffee center of **Juana Díaz ❸** now produces marble and mangoes. Founded in 1798 by a woman of the same name, the town preserves the Three Kings tradition in January as the visit of the Magi to Bethlehem is celebrated with a horseback procession and re-enactment which draws hordes of visitors. A monument dedicated to The Three Wise Men stands in the town square.

Ponce and surroundings

No one ever claimed that Puerto Ricans were not a proud people, but it still shocks even *sanjuaneros* to hear a *ponceño* refer to his or her birthplace as *"La Perla del Sur"*, or "The Pearl of the South". It's to be expected that tourism companies and travel agencies will exploit such a sobriquet, but should the natives themselves be waxing lyrical – remembering that nowadays there are close to 200,000 of them?

Maps:
City 216
Area 215

Bloody big business: cock-fighting, while distasteful to many, is a popular sport in Puerto Rico, particularly in Salinas.

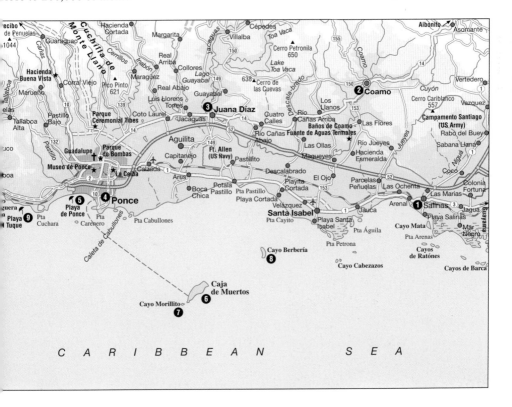

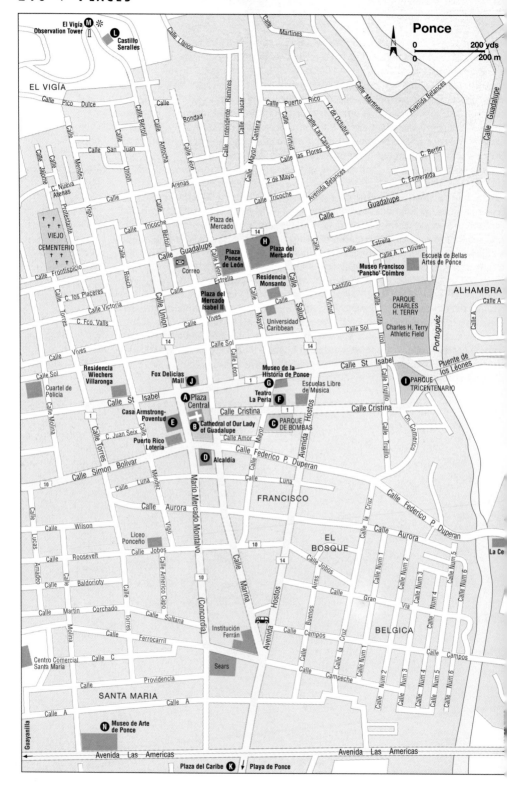

Ponce

El Vigía **M** ☀
Observation Tower **L**
Castillo Seralles

EL VIGÍA

Calle Pico Dulce
Calle
Calle Martines
Calle Llanos
Calle Bondad
Calle San Juan
Calle Arenas
C. Nueva Atenas
Mendez
Vigo
Protestante

VIEJO CEMENTERIO

Calle Frontispicio
C. los Placeres
Calle Victoria
C. Fco. Valls
Vives
Calle Sol
Residencia Wiechers Villaronga
Cuartel de Policia
Calle Molina

Calle Puerto Rico
12 de Octubre
Calle Las Casas
Calle Martines
Avenida Betances
C. Berlin
C. Esmeralda

Calle Guadalupe

Plaza del Mercado
14
Plaza del Mercado H
Museo Francisco 'Pancho' Coimbre
Plaza Ponce de León
Correo
Estrella
Residencia Monsanto
Escuela de Bellas Artes de Ponce

ALHAMBRA

Plaza del Mercado Isabel II
Vives
Universidad Caribbean

PARQUE CHARLES H. TERRY
Charles H. Terry Athletic Field

14
Calle Sol
Calle St. Isabel
Puente de los Leones

Fox Delicias Mall **J**
Museo de la Historia de Ponce G
Escuelas Libre de Música

Plaza Central A
Casa Armstrong-Poventud **E**
Teatro La Perla F
I PARQUE TRICENTENARIO

Cathedral of Our Lady of Guadalupe B
PARQUE DE BOMBAS C
Calle Cristina

Puerto Rico Loteria
Calle Amor
Alcaldía D
Calle Federico P. Duperan

Calle Simon Bolivar
Calle Luna
Calle Aurora
FRANCISCO
Calle Luna

Calle Wilson
Liceo Ponceño
Calle Jobos
EL BOSQUE
Calle Aurora

Calle Roosevelt
Calle Baldorioty
Institución Ferrán
10
14
Calle Jobos
Gran
Via

Calle Martin Corchado
Sears
Calle Campos
BELGICA

Centro Comercial Santa Maria
Providencia
Calle Campos
Calle Campeche

SANTA MARIA
Calle A

N Museo de Arte de Ponce

Avenida Las Americas

Plaza del Caribe **K** ↓ Playa de Ponce

0   200 yds
0   200 m

Perhaps the most surprising thing is that **Ponce ❹**, Puerto Rico's second-largest city, actually *is* a pearl of sorts. Though not so distant in the imagination of travelers as Mayagüez, it's still far enough away from the San Juan/Cerromar/Palmas del Mar circuit most travelers cling to. However, Ponce is an easy 90-minute drive from San Juan on the Autopista Luis Ferré, and there's very little excuse for not heading south to see what all these southerners are bragging about. On an island where self-congratulation is a way of life, the people of Ponce have the reputation of being almost haughty. And anyone outside deepest San Juan will admit that *ponceños* have a right to be aloof.

Hot stuff

To begin with, Ponce has the best weather on the island. It's located in what ecologists call a "rain shadow"; the afternoon storms which beleaguer the north coast are stopped dead by the peaks of the Cordillera Central. You can see the rain from Ponce – it's in those purple clouds pulsing above the hills 10 miles (16 km) north – but you're not going to feel any of it.

The landscape surrounding the city is a typical southwestern palette of purple and lavender skies against tumbling grasslands, parched to gold by the Caribbean sun. This is no Atlantic coast – although a place as far south as Ponce can take on that ocean's hostile cobalt aspect – as a look from the hills above the town will demonstrate. Especially from El Vigía, the view across Ponce shows the coral and white of the town's stately houses, the turquoise waters of its Caribbean harbor and the stripes of green mangrove and travertine coral formations of the archipelago surrounding the isle of Caja de Muertos.

This is not the impression you'll get as you enter the town on Route 2, the

---

Maps:
City 216
Area 215

"Ponce is one of the oldest towns on the island …. It is located on a big plain covered with trees … 115 houses form an irregular square. The parish church [Guadalupe], which is small and deteriorated, is on one side; 5,038 souls live here."

– HISTORIAN IÑIGO ABBAD Y LASIERRA, 1784

BELOW: view of Ponce from El Vigía.

antiquated proto-expressway. Here, your first sight of Ponce is of the Ponce bypass, which links highways 52 and 2, traveling through a neighborhood of unmitigated tedium.

The inland port

But Ponce proper – and if there's a proper city in Puerto Rico, it's Ponce – is not as far away as one might expect. This is perhaps the archetype of a strangely Puerto Rican sort of city: a bustling port with an enviable natural harbor which has nonetheless developed around a city center some distance inland. A left turn will take you, not to the center of a bustling waterfront town, but to the interesting outpost at **Playa de Ponce ❺** – a collection of old brick warehouses and more modern storage areas – and the wharf at **Muelle de Ponce**. Evenings and weekends, a popular gathering place for lovers and families is **La Guancha Board Walk**.

To get into the heart of Ponce, continue in a northwesterly direction on Route 133 as it passes over the sluggish Río Portugues and becomes **Calle F.P. Duperan**, which is the main commercial street of the town, also known as Calle Comercio.

Here, you'll see the results of the $450-million "Ponce en Marcha" program, begun in 1986 by former Governor Rafael Hernández Colón, himself a *ponceño*. The massive beautification effort resulted in the burying of unsightly phone and electric cables, the repaving of streets, and the renovation of nearly every structure in the downtown district. Hernández Colón is no longer governor, and the program has recently run out of money, but its astounding success was enough to turn Ponce into one of the Caribbean's most beautiful cities. Its image

There is a continual raging academic controversy about how Ponce (pronounced Pon-tsé) got its name – some say it's from the first governor of the island, Ponce de León; others argue that it was taken from his great-grandson.

BELOW: the ornate Casa Armstrong-Poventud.

FANTASY FIRE STATION

What must be the oddest – and certainly most whimsical – fire station ever built, Ponce's Parque de Bombas, was originally erected as an exhibit for the 1882 Trade Fair. It was one of two structures built in Arabic architectural style for the fair; the other, known as the Quiosco Arabe, was destroyed in 1914, although a glassed-in scale model of it can be viewed in the Industry Room at the Ponce History Museum. The Parque de Bombas was put into use as a fire station the year after the fair, and it remained the headquarters of the Ponce Fire Corps for over a century, until 1989. The following year the remarkable red-and-black wooden structure was restored and reopened as a museum featuring fire department memorabilia. The old fire-fighting equipment on display includes antique fire trucks and hand-pulled tanks, which needed the movement of rushing to the scene of a fire to build up the pressure. The exhibits in the upstairs museum also detail fire-fighting techniques of the late 19th century and provide interesting information on the Great Fire of 1906. With its playful collection of poles, sideboards, crenellations and cornices, the Parque de Bombas is a gaudy and riotous building with a playful, truly *ponceño* spirit – and has come to symbolize Ponce itself.

was further boosted in 1993 when Ponce hosted the 17th Central American and Caribbean Games.

A square deal

At the end of Calle Duperan is the cluster of architectural beauties which gives Ponce its reputation as one of the most Spanish of Puerto Rican cities. Here the magnificent **Plaza Central Ⓐ**, lush and beautifully landscaped, sits pounded by sunlight amidst a pinwheel of centuries-old streets. It's actually a double plaza, with **Plaza Degetau** and **Plaza Muñoz Rivera** sitting kitty-corner across Calle Cristina. Both are similarly landscaped, with huge fig-trees in lozenge-shaped topiary and large, shady islands of grass. Broad paths of rose-colored granite weave through the parks; they're lined with slender old lamp-posts which make the plaza both attractive and accessible in the evening.

Plaza Degetau is dominated by the **Cathedral of Our Lady of Guadalupe Ⓑ**, named for the patron saint of Ponce. It's a pretty, low, pinkish structure, reminiscent in its colors and rounded turrets of San Juan Cathedral. Though not as old as San Juan's, having been begun in the late 17th century, Ponce's cathedral makes ample use of the flood of reflected sunlight from the plaza. Its silvery towers – a characteristically Puerto Rican touch in religious architecture – are shaped like little hydrants, and glow oddly at midday. This gives the cathedral a bright, inviting look, against which the eerie stillness of its interior is a shocking contrast.

Photo opportunity

Our Lady of Guadalupe may hold the religious high ground, but the building right behind it cuts more ice with the tourist crowd. This is the **Parque de Bombas Ⓒ** (open Mon–Fri, 9.30am–6pm; closed Tues), Ponce's unmissable Victorian firehouse and perhaps the most photographed building in all of Puerto Rico (*see panel opposite*). The **Alcaldía Ⓓ**, diagonally across the plaza from the two buildings, has a pleasant hacienda feeling to it and contrasts in a lively way with its two more renowned neighbors.

Off the same plaza, **Casa Armstrong-Poventud Ⓔ** houses offices of the Institute of Puerto Rican Culture and the Tourism Company. The 19th-century edifice comes complete with ornate design and interior courtyard, and also has a very small museum with Spanish artifacts and some period pieces.

About a block away from the cathedral, at the corner of *calles* Cristina and Mayor, is the stately **Teatro La Perla Ⓕ**, where stage plays are performed by local theater companies. On occasion, plays shown in San Juan go on the road to Ponce. Built in 1864 but partially destroyed in the 1918 earthquake, it is also the home of Ponce's annual Luis Torres Nadal Theater Festival.

Around the corner on Calle Isabel, history comes to life at the **Museo de la Historia de Ponce Ⓖ** (open weekdays 10am–5pm, Sat 10am–8.30pm, Sun 11.30am–7pm; closed Tues). A fascinating feature outside is a 1,500-lb (680-kg) marble bathtub, built

Maps:
City 216
Area 215

An island license plate: públicos – the cars and minibuses providing low-cost public transport – have the letters "P" or "PD" following the numbers.

BELOW: Ponce Cathedral.

The El Vigía Observation Tower, or Cruz del Vigía (Virgin's Cross), is a 100 ft (30 m) structure with lateral arms measuring 70 ft (21 m) long.

BELOW: Plaza del Mercado, full of many surprises.

by Samuel B. Morse, inventor of the telegragh. The museum was inaugurated on December 12, 1992 – Ponce's 300th anniversary – and is considered Puerto Rico's best civic museum. Two hours in this place, and you'll emerge an expert on all aspects of Ponce's history: geographic, economic, political, racial, medical, educational and industrial. The museum is housed in the former residence and office of Dr Guillermo Salazar Palau.

Around town

There are plenty of peaceful perambulations to be made in this most historic part of Ponce. **Calle Cristina** and **Calle Mayor** are particularly renowned for the wrought-iron grilles and balcony work which evoke in Ponce, as in San Juan, the spirit of European cities. Even the highly commercialized Calle Duperan boasts a number of quaint shops and a shady marketplace. The finest market in town, however, is in the **Plaza del Mercado Ⓗ**, which is located two blocks north of the Plaza Central on Calle Atocha between *calles* Estrella and Castillo. Here, merchants haggle with customers over anything that can be worn, ogled or eaten, in an ambience as charged with excitement as any market in San Juan.

Also worth a visit is the **Parque Tricentenario ❶** and the Puente de los Leones (with its twin lions) and the **Fox Delicias Mall ❶**, which was a functioning movie theater from 1931 to 1980 and today contains an assortment of fast-food outlets and boutiques. Shopaholics can also enjoy spending plenty of time and their money at Ponce's **Plaza del Caribe ⓚ** south of the city center, a vast shopping center rivalling San Juan's Plaza Las Américas, where you can purchase anything from a Sony TV to a $1,000 frock. Children especially love its full-scale carousel.

The people and the city

Ponceños have always been a breed apart from other Puerto Ricans. Their insularity and haughtiness are legendary, and some Puerto Ricans claim that even the dialect here differs slightly from that spoken almost universally on the rest of the island. They're also racially different: you'll see more people of African descent in town than anywhere else on the island save Loíza Aldea, because Ponce's prominence as a port antedates slavery.

As a result, a great deal of African and other regional custom lives on in the city. Every February, at the Festival of Our Lady of Guadalupe, Ponce natives parade around the city in weird, spiked horror-masks made of local gourds. The tradition actually derives from medieval Spain, but it's unquestionable that such a transoceanic transplant required a soil as culturally fertile as Ponce's in which to take root.

A walk on the nice side

There's no better way to take in all the beauty and diversity of this city than to stroll north of Plaza Central to **El Vigía**. This hilly neighborhood is so beloved of the natives that you'll surely be directed to the place if you show the slightest interest in the city. From the winding road to the top you can see the mansions of Ponce's great families, the roofs of its 17th- and 18th-century townhouses and the greenish-blue Caribbean, which does more than any questions of demography, government or economics to shape the daily life of the proud *ponceño*. The most important of these mansions is the **Castillo Serrallés ⓛ** (open Mon–Sun, 9.30am–5.30pm), located right next to the huge cross-shaped **El Vigía Observation Tower ⓜ**.

Maps:
City 216
Area 215

In March every year, the largest artisans' fair on the south coast is held in Ponce. In addition to some wonderful handiwork, this Regional Craft Fair features folklore shows, plentiful Puerto Rican food and a children's folk-music contest.

LEFT:
Castillo Serrallés.
BELOW: a shopper's delight, the Fox Delicias Mall.

Ponce Art Museum

In addition to having one of the Caribbean's most beautifully renovated downtown districts, Ponce also prides itself on having the region's best art museum: the **Museo de Arte de Ponce**  (open daily, 10am–5pm).

Governor Luis A. Ferré, a *ponceño* and the founder of the pro-statehood New Progressive Party, dreamed up the museum in the late 1950s. The institution was born in 1959, and seven years later moved into its present home – a long, low-slung modern building designed by American architect Edward Durrell Stone (designer of New York's Museum of Modern Art). It is located along busy Avenida Las Américas, across the street from the Catholic University and down the road from another Ponce landmark, a gnarled, 550-year-old *ceiba* tree.

Ferré started the Ponce Art Museum off with 71 paintings; today it possesses more than 1,800 registered works, many of them European masterpieces. A marble plaque at the entrance states the museum's purpose: "To broaden the understanding of our own and other cultures through the contact with and appreciation of the visual arts, thus to enhance the quality of life in Puerto Rico."

Inside the museum is a honeycomb of skylit hexagonal rooms. Its interior highlight is its modernistic, scallop-shaped, wooden central staircase, which leads to a magnificent cluster of Renaissance paintings. To appreciate the museum fully, visit its galleries in chronological order. The best way is to start in the lobby surrounding the unusual staircase. Here are the oldest paintings in the collection, 14th-century works such as *Madonna and Child* by Luca di Tommé and *A Hebrew Prophet* by Giovanni del Biondo, and Leandro Rosanno's 16th-century masterpiece, *The Flood*.

Upstairs, in the Spanish School gallery, are masterpieces like Alonso Sánchez Coello's *Lady With a Pink*, and two works by José de Ribera, *St Paul* and *St Jerome*, as well as Pedro de Mena's lifelike sculpture, *Sorrowing Virgin*. In the adjacent Flemish School gallery can be found Peter Paul Rubens' *The Greek Magus* and David Teniers' *The Temptation of St Anthony*.

Three adjoining galleries are dedicated solely to Italian art. They are the Northern Italian School (Giovanni Battista Langetti's *The Torture of Ixion*), the Florence and Bologna schools (Ludovico Cigola's *St Francis of Assisi*) and the Rome and Naples schools (*Antiochus and Stratonice* by Pompeo Girolamo Batoni).

The Dutch School gallery contains both Peter Verelst's *The Philosopher* and the *Vanitas* still life of 1678 by Pieter Roestraeten. The last gallery on the second floor is the French School, containing, among other works, *The Origin of Painting* by Louis-Jean-François Cagrene and *Greek Lady at the Bath* by Joseph Marie Vien.

Downstairs, behind glass in the British School gallery, is Sir Frederick Leighton's *Flaming June*, completed in 1895, the year before his death. This painting has become a symbol of the museum itself. Above it hangs *Sleeping Beauty* by Sir Edward Burne-Jones, and on the entire far wall is Burne-Jones's masterpiece, *The Sleep of King Arthur in Avalon* – one of the largest works in the entire collection.

The two final galleries on the other side of the lobby are dedicated to the Puerto Rican School. There's enough here for a whole day; few places in Puerto Rico are more worth visiting than the Ponce Art Museum. ❏

Castillo Serrallés was formerly the home of Don Juan Serrallés, whose family became rich and powerful during the rum- and sugar-boom years of the early 20th century. The castle itself was designed, by architect Don Pedro Adolfo de Castroy Besosa, in the "Spanish revival" style popular throughout the 1930s. The Serrallés family moved in around 1934 and stayed until 1979. In 1986, the city of Ponce bought it from the estate for $500,000 – an unbelievable bargain – and spent the next three years restoring it in painstaking detail.

Among the castle's highlights are a formal dining room with the table set for 12; a vestibule decorated with furniture of the era; an 1865 rum-distilling unit in the central interior patio, and an octagonal fountain with tiles imported from Spain. Even the kitchen is preserved with its original stove and refrigerator made of metal and porcelain. An upstairs terrace offers a spectacular view of Ponce and the Caribbean.

Just outside Ponce are two other interesting sites. The **Tibes Indian Ceremonial Park** (open Tues–Sun, 9am–4pm) is the first; it is a 15- to 20-minute drive north of the city. An archeological treasure, it features rectangular ballcourts and ceremonial plazas dating from AD 300 to AD 700. The second is **Hacienda Buena Vista** (open Fri–Sun, by reservation; tel: 722-5882), about 7 miles (11 km) north of Ponce on Route 10. This is a restored coffee and corn plantation from the late 19th century, complete with working original machinery, that details every step in the coffee-harvesting process.

Southern isles

It's almost true that it never rains in Ponce, but at times the weather on Puerto Rico's sun-bombarded south coast can get so hot and steamy that you wish that some of those clouds would make it over the Cordillera Central. Fortunately, however, the environs of Ponce offer strategies for cooling off as diverse as they are effective. Nautical enthusiasts head their boats into the breezy waters for a trip to the fascinating rock archipelago that is located 8 miles (13 km) south. You'll probably need to know someone with a boat, or else find one to charter, in order to get there.

This string of Caribbean islets centers around **Caja de Muertos** ("Dead Men's Coffin") ⑥. Largest of the islets at 2 miles (3 km) long and 1 mile (1½ km) wide, Caja de Muertos is as popular with birdwatchers and botanists as it is with boatmen. This being one of Puerto Rico's driest regions, the majority of Caja de Muertos' flora resembles that of the Guánica Forest Reserve on the mainland. Some of the more prevalent plant species are certain herbs, dwarf forests of white mangrove, and loads of bindweed.

Four of the plant species on Caja de Muertos are extinct on the Puerto Rican mainland and classified as endangered. This is also a haven for endangered reptiles; iguanas and wall-lizards abound, and two species of Culebra lizard live here.

In different keys

Caja de Muertos is only one of the three islets that make up the **Caja de Muertos Nature Reserve**. The others, though far smaller, are no less enticing. **Cayo**

Map,
page 215

Ferries to Caja de Muertos run from Playa de Ponce on weekends, leaving the city in the morning and returning in the afternoon.

LEFT: one of many treasures at the Museo de Arte de Ponce.
BELOW: tying the knot – Puerto Rican style.

Some beautiful architectural touches grace the homes of Yauco.

Morillito ⑦, just a few hundred yards across flats, is the smallest, with only a few acres of territory, but contains more endangered birds than the other two combined. Among these is a variety of gulls, pelicans and sea eagles.

Cayo Berbería ⑧, which is the closest of the keys to the mainland at 3 miles (5 km), is blessed with a fauna no less extensive and no less idiosyncratic. Most of the fish – many of them endangered species – for which the southern isles are famous, populate the waters around its shores, and consequently some of them put in an appearance on the menus of the south coast's seafood restaurants.

Guayanilla and Guánica

Though the charms of the rippling, brown-green, semi-arid landscapes of Puerto Rico's southwest are well known to those who love the island, few travelers make the effort to visit some of its charming cities. Nonetheless, the scenic, historic and hedonistic pleasures Guayanilla and Guánica offer are enough to repay a visit of several days.

Route 2 moves westwards out of Ponce and hugs the shore for about 2 miles (3 km). It meets the coast at one of Greater Ponce's most popular beaches, **Playa El Tuque ⑨**, 3 miles (5 km) outside the city. One of the tinier swimmable beaches on Puerto Rico, it lies on the western shore of a tiny node of land, most of which is occupied by the marshy lands surrounding the **Laguna de las Salinas**, 5 miles (8 km) outside Ponce. From certain points there are good views of Ponce, its bay and the sea.

The beach you'll pass just to the left of the highway is known as **Balneario Las Cucharas** (Spoons Bathing Area), and the name is apt: it appears to have been scooped into a crescent by the calm waters.

BELOW: Yauco, once the "coffee capital".

Ports and pretty towns

From Balneario Las Cucharas, Route 2 runs the 6 miles (9 miles) into **Guayanilla ⑩**. This is a pretty town with a very southwestern flavor. It lies a little over a mile inland, though, and is somewhat quiet. The real attractions of Guayanilla are to the south.

A mile away, at the mouth of the Río Guayanilla, is the desolate and hushed fishing port at **Playa de Guayanilla ⑪**. The bay itself is an amazing natural formation: 3 miles (5 km) wide and embraced by two large peninsulas – **Punta Gotay** and **Punta Verraco** – it is surely one of the most auspiciously formed natural harbors in the Caribbean. A number of peninsulas within the harbor give it at least five sheltered sub-inlets.

The Isle of Java

The charming town of **Yauco ⑫** lies 3 miles (5 km) west of Guayanilla on Routes 2 and 127. The latter is probably the more pleasant drive, except when it rains, which on this arid coast is about once every millennium. Anyone with the most cursory experience of driving in the southwest knows that those little oily bushes huddled on the brown hillsides are coffee trees, but few know the pre-eminence that the Yauco area holds as a coffee capital. By the late 19th century, Puerto Rico had developed the most advanced coffee industry in the world. In the coffeehouses of late-colonial Europe – in Vienna, London, Paris, and Madrid – Puerto Rican coffee was considered the very best that one could drink. "Yauco" was that coffee's name.

Whatever can be said about its other effects, the 20th-century presence of Americans on the island removed Yauco from this position of pre-eminence,

Map, page 215

BELOW: Yauco is known for its outstanding architecture.

Map, page 215

Among the flora found in the Guánica Forest Reserve is the knotted guayacan tree, or lignum vitae *– a wood so hard it was once used to replace metal propeller shafts and ball-bearings.*

BELOW: beach in the Guánica Forest Reserve.
RIGHT: girls show off their national dress in Ponce.

as emphasis on manufacturing and cane production sapped the industry's resources. Fortunately, vestiges of that halcyon era remain – the stately homes of Yauco's coffee barons.

Owing to the variety of sub-climates in the southwest, coffee was a mobile industry, and its gentry and their residences were no less itinerant than their crops. As a result, Yauco shares with San Germán and Mayagüez an architecture that is distinctively Puerto Rican and among the best Spanish-influenced work of its day. Some of these old residences are open to the public; for information on the southwestern style and how to see it, the best source is the **Colegio de Arquitectos**, located in the Casa Rosa, not far from El Morro, in Old San Juan.

Even more fortunate is the fact that Yauco has regained some of its old prominence as a coffee-producer and exporter. One of Puerto Rico's most successful brands, Yauco Selecto, is now sold in Japanese gourmet coffee shops for over $20 a pound.

Warships by woodlands

On to **Guánica** , 5½ miles (9 km) past Yauco on Route 116. About the same size as Guayanilla, but with an understandably more oceanic ambience, Guánica might be worth visiting even without the historical significance which draws so many travelers and historians. In the mid-summer of 1898, at the height of the Spanish-American War, General Nelson Miles, having had no success in a month-long attempt to break the Spanish defenses around San Juan, landed in Guánica with a detachment of troops before going on to Ponce. He had come, he said, "to bring you protection, not only to yourselves but to your property, to promote your prosperity, and to bestow upon you the immunities and blessings of the liberal institutions of our government".

Out of this promise came American Puerto Rico, and the degree to which the promise has been kept or breached has defined almost all political arguments on the island for the past century. The commemorative stone placed at the edge of Guánica harbor by the local chapter of the Daughters of the American Revolution is encased in a wrought-iron cage guarded by lock and key – presumably to protect the marker against political vandalism.

In fact, Guánica was the focus of observances in 1998 – the 100th anniversary of the US occupation.

The birds

Guánica is the ornithological capital of Puerto Rico. Covering 1,570 acres (635 hectares) of subtropical dry forest, the **Guánica Forest Reserve**  is home to half of Puerto Rico's bird species. Most treasured among these is the highly endangered Puerto Rican whippoorwill (found here in the 1950s, some 80 years after it was thought to be extinct), but there are plenty of other birds to see as well. This low-lying area also has 48 endangered plant species, 16 of which are endemic to the forest. Well-kept hiking trails and a pleasant beach make the reserve a good respite in a hectic sightseeing schedule. UNESCO has designated it a World Biosphere Reserve, and it is also part of the US National Forest network. ❑

CORDILLERA CENTRAL

*The Ruta Panoramica cuts through this heart
of the island, which features characterful villages,
forest-covered mountains and some spectacular scenic views*

Map,
pages
232–3

The Cordillera Central or "central spine" towers over the middle of the island, its peaks and valleys stretching 60 miles (96 km) from east to west. It is a region of superlatives and extremes – the highest, the deepest, the roughest, the coldest. And also the remotest: most visitors to the island choose to ignore its allure, staying on the beaches or in San Juan.

This is perhaps due to lack of publicity. It is true that the charm of the Cordillera has little to do with the shops of Old San Juan or the sun-drenched beachfronts of Dorado and Humacao. Rather, it offers cool mountain lakes and streams, isolated green spots and remote country inns. The temperature in the mountains drops one degree for every 500-foot (150-meter) increase in elevation. This means that when San Juan is broiling, you just might need a sweater on Cerro de Punta. The contrast between Puerto Rico's urban industrial character and its countryside is both delightful and thought-provoking.

The best way to see the Cordillera is by automobile. Allow at least two full days, and find a good road map of the island. Getting around in the mountains is half the fun. Two-lane blacktop is the rule for mountain roads; some two-lane roads are major ones, others minor, and others again turn into dirt tracks half-way up deserted hillsides. Be prepared for some arduous driving on hairpin and switchback curves. The roads connecting most mountain towns run from plaza to plaza, making for easy navigation. Here, you are never more than a few minutes away from the next *colmado* – a roadside store selling cold drinks, groceries and perhaps a sandwich or two.

The Cordillera was the last retreat of the once-ubiquitous *jíbaro*, the hardy Puerto Rican mountain peasant, whose exploits had been the stuff of legend and literature from the chronicles of the early settlers to the stories of Emilio Belaval. The virtually extinct *jíbaros* were to Puerto Rican consciousness what cowboys are to the Americans, or bushrangers to the Australian. The *jíbaro*, frequently the butt of jokes by more sophisticated city slickers, was nevertheless shaped by an exacting landscape and possessed of pride, resourcefulness and a wry pessimism.

Along Highway 52, just after the Cayey turn-off on the way to Ponce, stands the Monumento al Jíbaro Puertorriqueño – a huge white statue dedicated to these diminutive, scythe-swinging philosophers who today live on only in songs, paintings and the memories of their descendants.

Eastern Cordillera

Two roads connect San Juan with **Caguas ❶**, 20 miles (32 km) to the south; Route 52, the fast modern tollway that runs all the way to Ponce, and the older

PRECEDING PAGES: view over Utuado. **LEFT:** the Cordillera is one of the most remote parts of the island. **BELOW:** entrance to caves, Aguas Buenas.

Puerto Ricans are fiercely proud of their multi-faceted island.

and slower Route 1, with no toll collectors. Caguas, whose 133,000 people make it the largest city in the island's interior, lies in the broad and fertile **Turabo Valley**. Three different mountain ranges form the valley's walls, accounting for its unusual expanse. To the north and east rises the **Sierra de Luquillo**, which runs almost to the coast. To the south, the **Sierra de Cayey** climbs rapidly, blotting out the horizon. And to the west, the Cordillera Central stretches up and across the island.

Caguas is named after the Taíno *cacique* Caguax, who ruled the people of the Turabo Valley area at the time of the Spanish Conquest. Caguax was one of the two *caciques* who made peace during the Indian uprisings of 1511. The Indians, fearing reprisal after drowning a Spanish boy, revolted. Several *caciques* led guerrilla bands on raids in the following weeks, but Ponce de León, with the help of peaceful *caciques*, soon restored order. A large allegorical painting, depicting Caguax's conversion to Christianity, exists.

In many ways Caguas typifies the Latin American city of moderate size. **Plaza Palmer**, one of the most charming plazas in Puerto Rico, is the center of civic and spiritual life. Almost as large as the one at Ponce, it is dominated by two ancient rubber trees with benches built into their huge trunks. Pigeons inhabit the plaza, some in an aviary and others flocking freely. In the middle, a solemn statue of the 19th-century poet José Gautier Benítez, Caguas's most famous son, stands on a pedestal. Goldfish sun themselves in a mossy pond, and, on weekends, musicians bring salsa rhythms to a small bandstand. There is also the Daliesque **Relój Florido**, a giant clockface planted with flowers.

The large **Cathedral of Caguas** faces one side of the plaza, directly across from the *alcaldía* with its 1856 façade. The church has been rebuilt and enlarged several times as hurricanes destroyed the original building. On any afternoon the plaza attracts a good number of people. Couples sit quietly holding hands, old men move from bench to bench, always keeping in the shade, and kids plan mayhem while their mothers shop in nearby stores. An evangelist, accompanied by a lone guitarist, exhorts a small crowd. Every city or town in Puerto Rico has its plaza, but few as lively or picturesque as this.

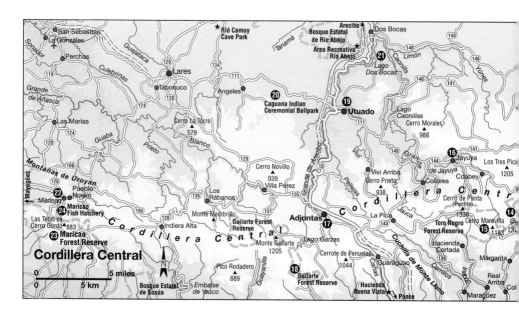

A walk down Calle Ruíz Belviz reveals a tiny 19th-century **Baptist church**. Farther along, on a side street, the historic **Piedra de Polanco** can be found. This large rock was once used to mount and dismount from horses. Today it is part of a jewelry store.

The southern tip of **Lake Loíza** ❷ may be reached by taking Route 796 northeast out of town. The road skirts the lake's banks with several likely picnic or fishing spots, before circling back to join Route 1 north of Caguas.

Rising mountains

The 6 miles (10 km) between Caguas and **Aguas Buenas** ❸ to the west mark a profound change in the landscape. Route 156 begins to climb as soon as it leaves the city behind. Aguas Buenas is perched on a hill that is part of the far northeastern extension of the Cordillera Central.

Mountain palms and bamboo start to line the roadside. The lush green miniature valleys glimpsed through the breaks in these trees are a rugged preview of the contours of the Cordillera, and the hills and curves of Route 156 serve as a beginner's course in Cordillera driving. Is it the change in temperature? The sweet, cool air? The first sight of a little boy leading a skinny black-and-white island cow? Whatever it is, the city seems much farther than a few miles away, and the intangible yet universal mountain mind-set of isolation and wonder begins to take hold.

Aguas Buenas is dashed across the hillside as if with one hurried stroke of a paintbrush; the town extends much farther along the face of the hill than up or down. A modern church and a school struggle for space on the small plaza, which often fills with children.

The town was once known for the nearby **Aguas Buenas Caves**. The Department of Natural Resources once ran tours on weekends, but the caves have been closed for some time. It is, however, possible to enter them off Route 794, but only experienced spelunkers should attempt serious exploration. Route 794, at any rate, has some interesting views as it leads down out of the town and then up to rougher country.

Map, pages 232–3

Economic activity in Caguas includes diamond-cutting, tobacco processing and the manufacture of leather goods, glass and plastic products, electronic equipment, clothing and bedding.

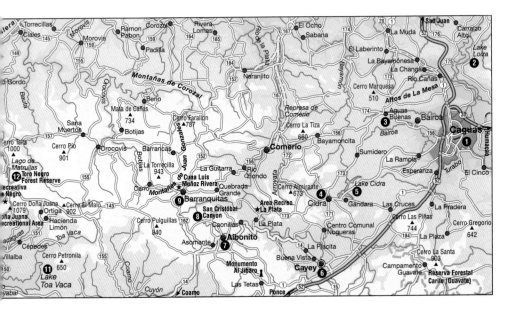

TIP

Look for the roadside fruit stands along Route 172 between Caguas and Cidra, where you can pick up some delicious local fruits and vegetables (some varieties of which are never seen in San Juan), or a bunch of fresh flowers for your hotel room.

BELOW:
market shopping
in the hills.

Dammed Cidra

Nine miles (14 km) southwest of Aguas Buenas is **Cidra** ❹, which can also be reached from Caguas on Route 172. This road offers excellent panoramic views of the entire **Turabo Valley**, including Caguas. With more than 30,000 residents, Cidra is a larger town than it seems. There is always a line of young people waiting to play video games at Café la Estrella, one block off the plaza.

In Cidra, in three closely guarded factories only a few miles from one another, Coca-Cola Inc. and Pepsico Inc. produce the top-secret flavoring concentrates that are eventually shipped to Coke, Pepsi and Seven-Up bottling plants around the world.

Lake Cidra ❺, 5 miles (8 km) long, supplies water to San Juan, Cataño and other cities. The lake, an artificial one, was dammed in the 1940s. While there is no boating, residents claim that the fishing is well worth a try. The houses around the lakeshore, with their serene views, give quiet testimony to the gracious lifestyle of their lucky inhabitants. A restaurant on the shore with outdoor tables shares the view.

An interesting local legend of buried treasure dates from the turn of the century. One night during an epidemic of smallpox, a wealthy peasant fearful of losing his fortune rode his horse into the forest and buried a quantity of gold. Upon returning home the man fell sick and soon died without disclosing the location of his treasure. To this day the old peasant appears as a skeleton atop a black horse, unable to rest because his sons inherited nothing.

Between Cidra and Las Cruces on Route 787, **Rancho Pepón** provides a pleasant family *pasadía* (picnic ground). Rancho Pepón looks like the country ranch that it is. Its facilities include a large covered patio, a swimming pool

Map,
pages
232–3

and a restaurant open on weekends. The Caraballo family runs the facility, which can accommodate groups of up to 300.

Cayey

Whether you follow either the tollway or the lesser Route 1 south of Caguas, the next major town is **Cayey** ❻, 12 miles (19 km) away. The first view of Cayey is of a modern strip-cum-shopping-center at the highway exit. Founded in 1773, Cayey is a city of nearly 50,000 people, with a university and bustling industry. The city sits on the northern slope of the Sierra de Cayey; from the *autopista* you can see the huge AT&T earth stations that carry most of Puerto Rico's long-distance telephone calls.

Southeastern Puerto Rico is a tobacco-growing region, and Consolidated Cigars has a large plant in Cayey. Here popular brands like Muriel and Dutch Masters are manufactured.

Cayey's **Plaza** features a large church, built in 1813, with an extremely long nave, a single square tower and a dome overlooking the transept. The museum at the university displays works by major Puerto Rican artists.

Road with a view

The Ruta Panoramica avoids Cayey, passing several miles to the south, but that doesn't mean the city's vistas are second-rate. It does mean, though, that Cayey is a good place to pick up the Ruta Panoramica from San Juan, little more than half-an-hour's drive from Condado. Route 1 becomes the Panoramica about 2 miles (3 km) past the town. Care should be taken, for the Panoramica shifts to Route 772 after another 3 miles (5 km).

The Sierra de Cayey is home to the 6,000-acre (2,400-hectare) Carite (Guavate) Forest Reserve, which harbors some 50 species of bird, plus waterfalls and a small pool with water of an incredible blue color.

BELOW: typical view from the Ruta Panoramica.

Even the smallest buildings in the Cordillera – like this barber shop – are splashed with color.

BELOW: going for a stroll in Cayey.

The Ruta Panoramica, as its name suggests, is rich with vistas. Remember, though: Cordillera driving is no picnic. Don't forget the essential map for winding road navigation, and pack some Dramamine (for motion sickness) – you never know.

Valley jewel

Set in a narrow valley, **Aibonito** ❼ is a pretty jewel of a place. The Ruta Panoramica narrowly misses the town, which can be reached from Cayey via Route 14, a road rivaling the Panoramica both for valley viewing and for its number of curves. Aibonito, at 2,500 feet (760 meters), has the highest altitude of any town in Puerto Rico, and the lowest average temperature. In 1911, the temperature reached 40°F (8°C).

One story of how Aibonito was named features a wandering half-starved 17th-century bandit who stumbles on the valley and then exclaims "*Ai, que bonito!*" (How pretty!). Another – possibly more plausible – explanation is that it is derived from the Indian name for the town, *Jatibonuco*, which means "river of the night". In 1887 Aibonito was the provisional capital of the island for seven months. In that year, known as *El Año Terrible*, an independence movement was bloodily suppressed by a military governor, the hated General Palacios González. The general moved his troops and government to the mountains in order to be better prepared to chase down the *independentistas*, and also perhaps to enjoy the cooler climate. The plaza here has a movie theater, a diner that would not be out of place in Des Moines, and a shining white 19th-century Catholic church with two small towers. Weathered wooden porches around the plaza give it an air of genteel neglect.

A slit in the hills

Near Aibonito is the **San Cristóbal Canyon** ❽, the deepest gorge on the island. Formed by the Río Usabon, this canyon, with walls up to 700 feet (210 meters) high, is so deep and narrow that from the air it looks like a slit in the hills. From the ground, the only way to see it is to stand on the very rim. The view is indeed impressive.

To approach the canyon, follow Route 725 to the north. In this area, businesses tend to call themselves El Cañon – Tienda el Cañon, Ferrenta el Cañon, and so on. One of the most *simpático* of these establishments is the **Bar el Cañon**, at Km 4 on Route 725. Among its attributes are a juke box and canned beer at country prices. The canyon can be reached from here, but it is a rough hike, so it's better to go on to Km 5.5, where a narrow unmarked side road comes a little closer to the edge. From there it is a short hike down to the canyon, and a 100-foot (30-meter) waterfall.

Hills and heroes

Four miles north as the crow flies, but double that by car, the town of **Barranquitas** ❾ overlooks the other side of San Cristóbal Canyon. The best place to view the canyon is on Route 156 east of the town. At Km 17.7 the Lions Club has a view which gives the traveler a much better perspective.

Barranquitas is known as the birthplace of Luis Muñoz Rivera, the famous autonomy-minded statesman (*see panel below*). Muñoz Rivera and his equally famous son Luis Muñoz Marín, governor of the island from 1948 to 1964, are buried near the plaza in a small complex that includes a museum full of Muñoz Rivera memorabilia.

Map, pages 232–3

The annual Aibonito Flower Festival is a popular summer event in this area. The competition features acres of lilies, anthuriums, carnations, roses, gardenias, begonias and much more.

BELOW: practicing the Puerto Rican art of relaxation.

A MAN WHO MADE A DIFFERENCE

Luis Muñoz Rivera, one of the most famous men in the political history of Puerto Rico, devoted his life to the struggle for his country's autonomy. Born in Barranquitas on July 17, 1859, he attended a local private school and later worked in his father's store. Muñoz Rivera was one of the founders of the Autonomist Party and its newspaper "voice", *La Democracia*. In 1897, he was appointed as Secretary of State and Chief of the Cabinet of the newly independent Government of Puerto Rico. After the Americans arrived on the scene in 1898, he again turned to journalism, founding the newspaer *El Territorio* and later, while living in New York, the *Puerto Rican Herald*.

After returning to Puerto Rico in 1904, he became one of the founders of the Unionist Party and served in the House of Delegates until 1910, when he was elected Resident Commissioner to the US House of Representatives. Here, Muñoz Rivera pushed to amend the Foraker Act. His work led to the passing of the Jones Act, which, among other things, gave Puerto Rico more autonomy and granted US citizenship to Puerto Ricans. He did not live to see the bill signed into law by President Wilson in 1917; Muñoz Rivera returned to Puerto Rico in September 1916, ill with cancer, and died on November 15 of that year.

TIP

If you're interested in Puerto Rican political history, you may want to visit the small museum in the Barranquitas house where Luis Muñoz Rivera was born.

Sad to say, Barranquitas lacks the charm of its cross-canyon neighbor. Its narrow streets and tightly packed houses have a sinister feel despite the mountain setting. Even the people seem more sullen. Perhaps the lack of an inspirational and mellifluous name like Aibonito has something to do with it. In Spanish, *una barranca* means a cliff or gorge, but it can also mean great difficulty or an impassable obstacle.

One attraction in Barranquitas, however, is the annual Artisans' Fair in July where some 130 Puerto Rican artisans sell their work at reasonable prices – the perfect time to buy a painting, a flute, or jewelry made from local stones. Traditional music and food are also a major part of the fair, which began in 1964, making it the island's oldest crafts fair.

There is another more direct route from San Juan to Aibonito and Barranquitas, a pleasant drive through hilly country. Take Route 2 from San Juan to Bayamón, and from there take Route 167 south until it intersects Route 156 which goes to Barranquitas. This route looks less taxing on the odometer; in reality, it involves nearly 30 miles (48 km) of demanding two-lane roads. If you plan any mountain driving beyond Aibonito or Barranquitas, it is probably better to take the *Autopista* to Cayey.

Route 167, though, is worth a trip in itself, especially on a Sunday afternoon. Immediately south of Bayamón, the road begins playing a game of peek-a-boo with the **Río de la Plata**, named after the mighty South American river, and its subsidiary streams. The streams jump back and forth across the road until at last, near **El Ocho**, a panorama of the broad river unfolds.

Another feature of the road, starting just outside Bayamón and continuing its entire length, is the green and white colors of the PIP (Puerto Rican Independ-

BELOW: Barranquitas, birthplace of Puerto Rican statesman Luis Muñoz Rivera.

nce Party) splashed on walls and houses, trees with great regularity. Whether his attests to a rural base of support for the *independentistas* is a matter of conecture; perhaps graffiti are more noticeable in the country.

Route 167 passes through or near settlements with rustic names: Pájaro Puertorriqueño, Sabana, Naranjito (Puerto Rican Bird, Savannah, Little Orange). On Sunday afternoons in nearly every one of these little towns, musicians will be tuning up in bandstands and *colmados*. They will start to play as the sun's rays stretch out, singing to audiences of 20, 30 or 50. If there are no musicians around, a group of men in a bar will begin to sing and keep singing until long after sunset. Thus the country people – and the city visitors – squeeze every moment out of the weekend.

Toro Negro

In the southwest of the Cordillera, the town of **Villalba** ❿ is surrounded by some of the most incredible scenery on the island, including Puerto Rico's highest peak. From Coamo, Route 150 reaches Villalba in 14 tortuous mountain-miles (22 km).

Villalba itself is not as interesting as the nearby peaks and forest reserves. A drive on its streets, choked and dusty at midday, awakens the desire to escape back to the cool green heights. North of town, Route 149 begins to climb in earnest. And you thought you were in the mountains! A stop at the *colmado* **La Collaloma**, within sight of the intersection with Route 514, feels like a reward for leaving civilization behind. Here you can catch your breath sipping a *bebida* (drink) and sitting on a handmade bamboo bench. From this vantage point, Villalba and **Lake Toa Vaca** ⓫ spread out far below, and in the distance the blue

BELOW: couple watch the world go by from their colorful home.

Caribbean shimmers. High above, terraced gardens line the slopes, and farther up still, the peaks disappear into the mist.

Route 149 continues to climb until it intersects Route 143 inside the **Toro Negro Forest Reserve ⑫**. Route 143 is an east/west road that follows the backbone of the Cordillera Central from Adjuntas to a point near Barranquitas. This 30-mile (48-km) section of road is the longest continuous stretch of the Ruta Panoramica; views along here stretch north and south to both coasts.

To the east of the intersection is the **Dona Juana Recreational Area ⑬**, a *pasadía* viewpoint that features a large freshwater swimming pool and several trails through dense forests of large mountain palms. There is a campground, and a ranger station. A trail leads from the pool to a deserted lookout tower about 2 miles (3 km) away; the first quarter of the trail is paved with uneven, mossy stones, and moss turns very slippery with the smallest amount of water, so watch out on wet days. The **Dona Juana Falls**, a 200-foot (60-meter) waterfall, is nearby.

Climbing the peaks

West of the intersection, the road climbs into the silent peaks. **Lago Guineo ⑭** (Banana Lake), the highest lake on the island, hides at the end of a gravel road marked only by a wooden sign reading *"Prohibido Tirar Basura"*. A dam across the Toro Negro River keeps the lake full. It's difficult to find, walled about by steep red clay banks choked with bamboo. Only the high-pitched chatter of the *coquí* disturbs the perfect isolation of this little round lake. The clay banks demand caution; clay is another surface that gets very slippery when wet.

Farther west (and higher up) the road passes **Cerro Maravilla ⑮**, a lofty peak that bristles with antennae and relay towers. This mountain, at 3,970 feet (1,210

BELOW: serene village portrait.
RIGHT: crosses at Cerro Maravilla.

meters) one of the island's highest, occupies a tragic place in recent history: on July 25, 1978, two young independence supporters planning to blow up the WRIK-TV transmitter atop the mountain were killed by policemen who had been tipped off. The deaths triggered an investigation and an ongoing political controversy.

Oddly, no sign directs visitors to the spot where it all happened, and the gravel road leading to Cerro Maravilla – Route 577 – doesn't appear on the official highway map. If you make a left at 577 and ascend the hill for half a mile, however, you'll see two stone crosses marking the graves of the two revolutionaries murdered there – Arnaldo Darío Rosado and Carlos Soto Arriví. The graves are surrounded by flowers and Puerto Rican flags. Don't be surprised to find several people at the site. Since the events of 1978, it has become a shrine for those who support the cause of Puerto Rican independence.

Across the road from the peak, a grassy picnic area overlooks the entire south coast. A gravel parking lot on the north side of the road at Km 16.5 marks the base of **Cerro de Punta**, at 4,390 feet (1,340 meters) the island's highest peak. The peak's summit can be reached on foot or by car up a treacherously steep paved road considerably less than one lane wide. On top, the solitude is shared by more antennae and a shed. On a clear day you can see for 50 or 60 miles (80 to 100 km). The view includes San Juan, unless of course a stray cloud gets in the way. To be on Cerro de Punta when the mists roll in is a powerful experience.

A few miles directly north of Cerro de Punta, **Jayuya** ⑯ nestles in its valley; unfortunately for the driver, no road connects the two. Take Route 144 to the town from either east or west. Among the monuments there are the Catholic church, a statue of Nemesio R. Canales and the bust of the Indian leader Jayuya by the Puerto Rican sculptor Tomás Batista.

Map, pages 232–3

A religious tile on the side of a building serves as a reminder of a strong faith.

BELOW: Jayuya coffee plantation.

TIP

A good time to visit
Jayuya is in November
during the Jayuya
Indian Festival, which
focuses on the Taínos'
culture and traditions,
including their music,
food and games.

In Jayuya, a visit to the stately **Hacienda Gripiñas**, a *parador* situated on an old coffee plantation, might prove tempting. A wide porch on the restored 200-year-old house overlooks a cool valley. As the sun goes down so many *coquí* begin singing that the *parador* lists this performance as a distinctive feature in its brochure. A trail connects the *parador* with Cerro de Punta just a short distance away.

The Western Cordillera

West of Toro Negro, the mountains change character once again. The stately peaks give way to rougher, lusher country. The valleys are smaller, shallower, more numerous. The tall mountain palms yield to bamboo, ferns, and hardwoods like teak. Flowering bushes sometimes line the road.

The town of **Adjuntas** ⑰ marks this area of transition. It is a rugged town filled with no-nonsense hardware stores and lumberyards; local produce includes coffee, bananas, oranges and other fruits. Adjuntas also has the **Monte Río Hotel**, a clean establishment near the plaza. In 1950, the first Health Center in the island was founded here. Adjuntas is nicknamed "the town of the sleeping giant", a reference to the outline of the mountains above.

Guilarte – land of the *jíbaros*

The **Guilarte Forest Reserve** ⑱ west of Adjuntas is another good place to get back to nature. A hillside *pasadía* is set near a eucalyptus grove whose fragrant, blade-shaped leaves litter the ground. A few hundred feet up the road, a well-marked trail leads to the top of 3,900-foot (1,190-meter) **Monte Guilarte**. Watch out for slippery clay on the trail.

BELOW: Coffee at
Hacienda Buena
Vista, a restored
plantation south of
Adjuntas.

Between Adjuntas and Monte Guilarte are many small farms, tended by the last of the *jíbaros* (mountain smallholders). This area is one of the few places on the island with such a concentrated population of these legendary people. The Ruta Panoramica passes right through their farmland, and they enjoy the opportunity to talk to travelers in a Spanish that is nasal, twangy and high-pitched.

North of Adjuntas toward **Utuado** ⓳, the Cordillera begins its descent to the coastal plain. But that does not mean the land gets flat. The haystack karstic hills north of Utuado march all the way to the Atlantic.

Land of the Indians

West of Utuado on Route 111, the **Caguana Indian Ceremonial Ballpark** ⓴ (open Wed–Sun, 9am–4.30pm) should not be missed. Built by the Taínos nearly a millennium ago, the ballpark includes 10 *bateyes* (ball courts) on which the early Indians played a lacrosse- or *pelota*-like game in a blend of sport and religious ceremony. Overlooking the courts, a small rocky peak has been guarding the park for centuries, and looks as though it will continue to do so for centuries to come. Strange sounds echo back and forth over the landscaped grounds. An owl hoots. A dry leaf rasps across one of the *bateyes*. The Taíno gods Yukiyu and Juracán continue to make their presence felt here.

North of Utuado on Route 10, **Lago Dos Bocas** (Two-Mouthed Lake) ㉑ curves into a U-shape around steep hills. Near its shores, a roadside stop called **Los Chorros** provides a restaurant, swimming pool and *pasadía*. At Km. 68, Route 10 skirts the lake shore. From there, a launch service carries passengers back and forth across the lake. Boats leave every two hours, starting at seven in the morning, on what is a worthwhile side-trip.

Land of the baby fish

On the far western edge of the Cordillera, not far from Mayagüez, is **Maricao** ㉒, one of the smallest *municipios* in Puerto Rico. Route 120 approaches the town from the south through the **Maricao Forest Reserve** ㉓. By the roadside in the middle of the forest is a castle-like stone tower, four stories tall, which overlooks the entire western half of the island from 2,600 feet (800 meters). There is also a campground.

Maricao's tiny plaza features a rustic cream-and-brick colored church. Just outside town is the **Maricao Fish Hatchery** ㉔, where many species of freshwater fish are hatched and raised, then dumped in 26 lakes around the island to replenish their indigenous stocks. On the road to the fish hatchery is a mountainside shrine, a haven of serenity and dignity.

The **Hacienda Juanita** in Maricao is yet another coffee plantation converted into a *parador*, surrounded by groves of oranges, bananas and avocados. Guests are invited to pick their own breakfasts. For the lazy ones, bowls of fragrant fruits are always within reach, and bunches of bananas hang from 150-year-old beams. Some of these beams are hewn from precious *ausubo*, a type of ironwood native to Puerto Rico. This wood, prized for its resistance to rot and termites, was once plentiful, but today it is among the rarest of the world's hardwoods. ❑

Map, pages 232–3

The Los Chorros restaurant at Lago dos Bocas takes its name from a nearby cave, which can be reached on foot.

BELOW: one of the Cordillera's many lovely *paradores*, the Hacienda Juanita in Maricao.

THE OUTER ISLANDS

Map, page 248

Off the east coast of Puerto Rico, Culebra and Vieques beckon with their pristine beaches and wild horses, while untouched Mona, far off the west coast, has unique charms of its own

Six miles (10 km) off the east coast of Puerto Rico lies **Vieques**, with twice the acreage of Manhattan and twice the charm of some islands many times its size. Like Culebra, Vieques belongs geologically to the Virgin Islands, but this is not all that separates it from mainland Puerto Rico. The island has grown in popularity among expatriates, although traditional ways live on. Islanders still refer to crossing the sound as "going to Puerto Rico", and the more formal *Usted* form of second person address, which is extinct on the mainland, is still heard in everyday conversation here.

Much of Vieques looks like Californian cattle-country: dry, rolling hills, scattered lazy herds and flocks of white egrets. But the island also enjoys scores of beaches, a small rainforest, exotic wild-flowers and a healthy population of tree frogs, mongooses and horses. A hundred or so beautiful *pasofino* (fine-gaited) horses, descended from 16th-century Spanish steeds, roam wild over the island. (If you can catch, feed and train one, it's probably yours.)

The Taíno Indians who first settled the island called it *Bieques*, or "small island"; Columbus named it *Graciosa* (gracious). English pirates called it "Crab Island" for the still-common land crabs they'd depend on for a tasty dinner. And the Spanish (who built the lighthouse and an unfinished fort) called Vieques and Culebra *las islas inutiles* – the "useless islands" – because neither had gold. The island took a direct hit in September 1989, when Hurricane Hugo passed directly overhead, its 200-mph (320-kph) winds destroying many houses and businesses before moving onto "mainland" Puerto Rico.

PRECEDING PAGES: the tiny *coquí*, Puerto Rico's "mascot". **LEFT:** Sun Bay Beach, Vieques. **BELOW:** slice of life in Isabel Segunda, Vieques's only town.

Isabel Segunda

Vieques is accessible by air from San Juan or by sea from Fajardo (a twice-a-day, 18-mile/29-km journey). The latter is the preferable route, offering an exhilarating excursion through brisk, choppy waters, a distant view of stormy El Yunque, and – with luck – a full double rainbow stretching for miles across blue waters.

Near the ferry landing, **Isabel Segunda ❶**, Vieques's only town, offers the staples of any modest Puerto Rican municipality. Many of the island's 8,000 residents live here or nearby. Some work in factories, but unemployment remains high. Sugar cane is the island's principal crop, but it also produces coconuts, grains, sweet potatoes, avocados, bananas and papayas. The town has the distinction of having the last fort built by the Spaniards in the New World, **El Fortin Conde de Mirasol**. Although it was never completed, what was there has been well restored and has an excellent historical museum (open Wed–Sun, 10am–4pm; other days by appointment; tel: 741-1717). There's also an interesting exhibit (and great views) at the **Punta Mulas Lighthouse** (open daily, 8am–4.30pm) to the north of town.

Both Vieques and Culebra are known for their pristine, uncrowded beaches.

The place to be

Only a 10-minute drive across the 25- by 4-mile (40- by 6-km) island, **Esperanza ❷**, a small fishing village, consists of little more than a strip of guesthouses and restaurants overlooking the water. Do not be fooled: this is *the* place to eat well, sleep well, sunbathe and explore.

The real gem of Esperanza is a tropical plantation house right out of a Somerset Maugham story, the **Casa del Francés** – "the world's most laid-back hotel". A near-jungle of orchids, coconuts, bananas, mangoes, aloe, bamboo and all sorts of other tropical flora surrounds the house and rises dozens of feet in the atrium. (Do not be surprised if you find an enormous toad in the foyer during a rainstorm.) From 17-foot (5-meter) ceilings, gentle fans turn. Drinks arrive on a checkered veranda which overlooks a pool, stables and grazing horses and colts.

A lovesick French army general turned sugar-plantation owner bought the house in 1910 for his pretty young bride. Word has it that the spoiled girl was impressed with neither the island nor the house, nor even the husband, and promptly fled back to Paris. Irreverent Bostonian Irving Greenblatt acquired the property in the 1950s, and today his longtime manager, Frank Celeste, personally oversees the general's fantasy.

Visit the **Esperanza Museum** (open Tues–Sun, 11am–3pm) for a historical look at pirate and Indian life around these parts. If it's nightlife you're after, try Banana's, Tradewinds and (Saturday nights) Cerromar. Saturday nights are especially lively, when pretty much the entire town turn out along the sea front to promenade in their finest, talk and flirt. During the *Patronales* (patron saint's) festival in the last two weeks of July, things really hop.

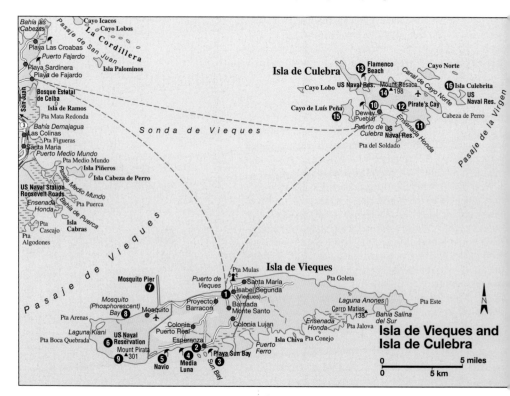

Isla de Vieques and Isla de Culebra

Just outside Esperanza, **Sun Bay** (Sombé to locals) ❸ glistens with a popular crescent-shaped beach. Camping is permitted here, as long as campers have the free permit. Beyond Sun Bay, and more secluded, lie **Media Luna** ❹ and **Navio** ❺ beaches. Final scenes from Peter Brook's classic 1963 movie *Lord of the Flies* were shot at Navio, a favorite spot for locals. The other good beaches to visit are not far away but are within **US Navy land** ❻.

In 1941 the Navy acquired over 70 percent of Vieques to use for land and sea exercises. About once a year it stages maneuvers, and the blasts of artillery batteries and fighter planes' target practice can be heard across the island.

As an impediment to development, the Navy has been partly responsible for the island's charm. Though inhabitants have protested at the military presence, the Navy does build roads, lets cattle owners use Navy land and leaves reserves open for public access to beaches.

Colorful beaches

With characteristic imagination, the Navy named three of the island's beaches Red, Blue and Green. Merely getting to these places is a small adventure; rocky approach roads wind through thick seagrape overbrush. **Red** and **Blue** beaches are ideal for swimming, snorkeling and scuba-diving. Seventy-five yards (68 meters) off Blue Beach lies a cay to swim to and explore for helmet shells and coral. The way to **Green Beach** is long, bumpy and tortuous. If you make the trek, stop to see **Mosquito Pier** ❼, a mile-long dock built earlier in the century when sugar production still flourished.

Vieques has a good number of minor expeditions on which to embark, should you muster the energy. Get a local fisherman to take you out at night in a boat

Map, page 248

Vieques has some 40 palm-lined white-sand beaches on its 60-mile (96-km) coastline. Although some are on US Navy property, anyone can visit them, provided that there are no military maneuvers going on. You might be asked to produce some photo identification, however.

BELOW: ponies abound on Vieques.

A gallon of water from Mosquito Bay may contain almost three-quarters of a million tiny (¹⁄₅₀₀ inch) bioluminescent swimming creatures, which are a type of dinoflagellate called pyrodinium bahamense.

to **Phosphorescent (or Mosquito) Bay** , considered the best in the world. Billions of luminescent microscopic creatures emit a green fluorescence when the water stirs. It is best on a moonless night, when swimming here becomes a scintillating experience.

Or climb to the cave atop **Mount Pirata** ❾, where the ancient *cacique* Bieque allegedly hid his tribe's treasure once he realized the conquistadors' intentions. Islanders say the cave's ceaseless roar attests that the great chief's ghost still rages. And while on the subject of superstitions, on Vieques' north coast near **Roca Cucaracha** (Cockroach Rock) is **Puerto Diablo** (Port Devil), said to be the third point of the notorious Bermuda Triangle.

Pirate's Cay

From Isla Grande Airport, the short flight to isolated **Culebra** to the north of Vieques overlooks dramatic coastline, dozens of varied cays and a patchwork of blue, turquoise and green Caribbean Sea. Columbus reportedly discovered this island on his second voyage in 1493. The first known inhabitants, the Taíno Indians, sought refuge on Culebra after the Spanish started colonizing the Puerto Rican mainland.

Before long, pirates and privateers began to use Culebra's Pirate's Quay as a protected hiding place and supply base before sailing off to raid ships in the Virgin Islands. Infamous corsairs, including the swashbuckling Welshman Sir Henry Morgan, may have buried treasure on and around Culebra; according to legend, a road near Punta del Soledado, a bend on Los Vacos Beach, a clump of large trees near Resaca Beach, and a rocky mound at the end of Flamenco Beach might be good spots to start looking for the 17th- and 18th-century fortunes.

BELOW: music plays an important role in the day-to-day lives of Puerto Ricans.

By 1880, settlers from Puerto Rico and Vieques were braving severe droughts and swarms of mosquitoes to build a colony which grew tamarind, mango, cashew and coconut trees. Then, a few years after the Spanish-American War of 1898, the US Navy opened facilities on Culebra, making Ensenada Honda its principal Caribbean anchorage. About this time, the island's town moved from what is now Campamento to Dewey (named after the victorious commander of the US Navy's Asiatic fleet, Admiral George Dewey). In 1909, one of President Theodore Roosevelt's last executive orders established Culebra as a National Wildlife Refuge, one of the oldest in the US.

By the end of World War II, the US Navy had begun to use Culebra for gunnery and bombing practice. Sea vessels and fighter planes from the United States and its allies pummeled target areas; islanders recall days and nights of constant bomb bursts.

The Culebrans protested bitterly for many years. In 1971, Navy personnel and Culebrans exchanged tear gas and Molotov cocktails, for which some islanders were imprisoned. Finally, President Nixon decided that all weapons training on Culebra should be terminated. President Ford's National Security Council reaffirmed the decision, and Culebra was left alone in 1975.

Probably the most important feature of Culebra is its arid climate; with only 35 inches (89 cm) of rain a year, there's always some sunshine here. Its 24 islands comprise 7,700 acres (3,100 hectares) of irregular topography and intricate coastline. Due to the dryness, most of the terrain is good only for pasture, forest or wildlife. Much of the land is administered by the US Fish and Wildlife Service, which aims to maintain the diverse fauna and flora of the islands. Culebra's cays provide flourishing nesting colonies for a dozen marine bird

Map, page 248

Grazing livestock and fishing are the principal activities of Culebra's inhabitants.

BELOW: Culebra's beautiful Flamenco Beach.

species, including the humorously named brown boobies, laughing gulls, sooty terns and Bahama ducks. The brown pelican, an endangered species, can often be spotted in mangrove areas. Rare leatherback turtles nest on many of Culebra's beaches from April through July. Turtle-watchers on Resaca Beach frequently stay up from 6pm to 6am in order to catch a sight of the large, lumbering amphibians delivering and protecting their eggs.

Because the island has no freshwater streams, sedimentation is low, and Culebra enjoys one of the healthiest coral ecosystems in the Caribbean. Remarkable reefs make for an abundance of fish species and clear water.

More than 2,000 people now live on Culebra, many in pastel-colored houses amid scrubby hills. Roads and front yards abound with jeeps and chickens. Time passes slowly; the atmosphere is one of tranquility and *bonhomie*.

Main town

The town of **Dewey** ❿ (which locals defiantly call **Puebla**), a 10-minute walk from the airport, covers only several blocks. (Be sure to remember Culebran law – no walking around town without a shirt!) At one end of town, the Fajardo ferry docks. Near the docks you will find a diving shop, some guesthouses and the highly recommended **Marta's Deli**. Down the road are two markets, the bank, the post office and **El Pescador**, which has inexpensive burgers, pricey seafood and a bar.

Just beyond town is one of the few drawbridges in the Caribbean. Nearby is **Ensenada Honda** ("Deep Bay") ⓫, surrounded by mangrove forests and one of the most secure hurricane harbors in the area, not to mention a nice spot for windsurfing. Smack in the middle of the bay is **Pirate's Cay** ⓬,

TIP

To see giant leatherback turtles laying their eggs between April and July is a truly worthwhile experience. The best beaches for seeing this happening are Resaca and Brava; you may wish to go with a guide.

BELOW: Culebra ferry comes into port at the harbor in Dewey.

where Culebrans enjoy lively holiday parties of beer and *arepas* (a local dish of sweet, fried bread).

While on Culebra, make a point of seeing **Flamenco Beach** ⓭. A *público* can take you there, or you can make the long walk from Dewey. This is the sort of beach you have always heard about – soft white sand, clear blue water and no one to kick sand in your face. A few hundred yards down the beach rest two archaic US Marine Corps tanks. Hikers occasionally find unexploded shells in the vicinity. Another fine beach is **Zoni Beach**, on the island's northeastern edge, some 7 miles (11 km) from Dewey.

Half-a-mile uphill and east of Flamenco Beach stands **Mount Resaca** ⓮, the highest summit on Culebra, with a formidable 360-degree view of cays and some of the Virgin Islands. Resaca hosts a dry subtropical "rock forest" where exotic Caribbean flora thrives amid thousands of large boulders. Last officially sighted in 1932, the Culebra giant anole, a huge lizard, is still believed to survive in the forested areas of the mountain.

The best way to see Culebra is by packing a picnic and hiring a boat for the day. Do some snorkeling or scuba-diving from the boat as you travel to otherwise inaccessible beaches, lagoons, forests and rocky bluffs on **Cayo Luis Peña** ⓯ and the mile-long **Culebrita** ⓰. Here you will find the most exuberant wildlife on the island. On Culebrita, you can also see an operating stone lighthouse built in 1874 by the Spanish colonial government.

Untouched island

Throughout the Caribbean it's hard not to feel that, however beautiful the landscape may be, it must *really* have been heart-stopping before the European settlers

Maps, pages 248, 253

Welcoming smiles come from all ages.

LEFT: Mona Island's non-operational lighthouse.

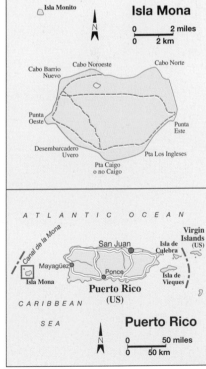

Isla Monito

Isla Mona

N

0   2 miles
0   2 km

Cabo Barrio Nuevo   Cabo Noroeste   Cabo Norte

Punta Oeste   Punta Este

Desembarcadero Uvero   Pta Los Ingleses

Pta Caigo o no Caigo

ATLANTIC OCEAN

Canal de la Mona

San Juan   Isla de Culebra

Virgin Islands (US)

Mayagüez

Isla Mona   Ponce   Isla de Vieques

Puerto Rico (US)

CARIBBEAN

SEA

N

Puerto Rico

0   50 miles
0   50 km

Map, page 253

TIP

If you decide to make the long journey to Mona, make sure to take everything you need (including water); there are no facilities.

BELOW: the unspoiled beauty of Mona Island. **RIGHT:** enjoying a peaceful island vacation. **FOLLOWING PAGE:** doorway in Old San Juan.

arrived. There are still a few places that the hand of civilization has not reached, though, and one of them, the tiny **Isla Mona**, belongs to Puerto Rico. Stuck 45 miles (72 km) out to sea, in the Mona Passage halfway to the Dominican Republic, this rugged island of 25 sq. miles (65 sq. km) is a haven for some of the oddest and most interesting wildlife in the Antilles, and remains as bizarre and uninhabited as it is difficult to reach.

Mona is now protected by the Department of Natural Resources, which also supervises the use of Cabo Rojo and other spots of great scenic beauty on the mainland's west coast. Nobody lives there now, but Mona has actually had a long history of inhabitation. Christopher Columbus found Taíno Indians there when he landed on the island, and Spanish settlers visited for many years in hopes of finding livable and pleasant spots to settle. For centuries it was the stronghold for some of the most notorious of European and Puerto Rican pirates.

It is rumored that treasure lies buried on the island to this day, and perhaps it does. For a brief period a century ago, certain prospectors carried out a brilliant scheme to mine not gold, not silver, not copper from the caves of this remote island, but … well, bat-droppings. For fertilizer. The scheme never got off the ground. Nor did an ambitious 1973 plan by Fomento, Puerto Rico's economic development agency, to turn Mona into a major petrochemicals and refining center. Outraged environmentalists stopped the proposal in its tracks. Since then, only a few naturalists and hermits have visited the place, as the scheme never succeeded.

As they left it

The landscape these solitary types have found is reported to be astounding.

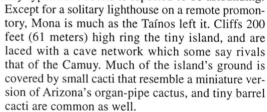

Except for a solitary lighthouse on a remote promontory, Mona is much as the Taínos left it. Cliffs 200 feet (61 meters) high ring the tiny island, and are laced with a cave network which some say rivals that of the Camuy. Much of the island's ground is covered by small cacti that resemble a miniature version of Arizona's organ-pipe cactus, and tiny barrel cacti are common as well.

Some of the vegetation on the island is known nowhere else in the world. The fauna is even more astounding, and is often compared with that of the Galápagos. Here are found the biggest lizards in Puerto Rico, ugly iguanas growing to 3 feet (1 meter) long, as well as three species of endangered sea turtle. Besides an extensive variety of gull, there lives on Mona a red-footed bird beloved by visitors and known disrespectfully as the "booby".

The perils of travel

There are those who would claim that anyone who wished to visit Mona could be called a booby as well. Those hardy souls who are not dissuaded would be best advised to charter a boat or private plane in Mayagüez. Apparently, planes can be chartered from San Juan's Isla Grande Airport as well. Official information on hiking trails and on the island's topography is hard to come by, but try writing to the **Departmento de Recursos Naturales** in San Juan. ❏

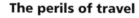

INSIGHT GUIDES

Travel Tips

Insight Guides portray destinations in depth, providing the complete picture and the top photography

Insight Pocket Guides focus on the best choices for places to see and things to do and include large fold-out maps

Insight Compact Guides' portability makes them the perfect books to carry with you for on-the-spot reference

Three types of guide for all types of travel

INSIGHT GUIDES Different people need different kinds of information. Some want *background information* to help them prepare for the trip. Others seek *personal recommendations* from someone who knows the destination well. And others look for *compactly presented data* for on-the-spot reference. With three carefully designed series, Insight Guides offer readers the perfect choice. Insight Guides will turn your visit into an experience.

The world's largest collection of visual travel guides

CONTENTS

Getting Acquainted

The Place 258
Geography 258
Climate 258
Government 258
Economy...............................258
Public Holidays 258

Planning the Trip

Visas and Passports 259
Customs 259
Money Matters.......................259
What to Wear/Bring 259
Tourist Offices Abroad 259
Getting There 259
Specialist Tours....................260

Practical Tips

Business Hours 260
Tipping 260
Media 260
Postal Services 260
Telecommunications 260
Embassies & Consulates 261
Emergency Numbers.............261
Medical Treatment 261

Getting Around

By Air....................................262
By Bus 262
By Water 262
By Car....................................262

Where to Stay

Choosing a Hotel...................263
Hotels 264
Paradors 266

Eating Out

What to Eat 268
Where to Eat 268

Culture

Museums...............................272
Galleries................................272
Concerts 273
Ballet 273
Movies 273

Nightlife

Nightclubs & Discos 273
Casinos.................................274

Festivals

Events...................................274

Outdoor Activities

Fishing 274
Hiking 275
Golf.......................................275
Watersports 275
Cockfighting..........................276

Shopping

Where to Shop 276
Bookstores............................276
What to Buy 277

Language

General 277
Words & Phrases...................277
Emergencies 278
On the Road 278
Numbers, Days & Dates 278
Shopping 279
Sightseeing...........................279
Dining Out.............................280

Further Reading

General 282
Arts & Customs 282
Other Insight Guides.............282

Getting Acquainted

The Place

Area: 3,421 sq. miles/8,860 sq. km
Situation: Latitude 18.5 degrees; longitude 66.9 degrees
Capital: San Juan
Population: 3.5 million (San Juan: 1.5 million)
Language: Spanish and English
Religion: Roman Catholic
Time Zone: Atlantic Time Zone, four hours behind GMT and one hour ahead of Eastern Standard Time
Currency: US Dollar
Weights & Measures: Metric and Imperial
Electricity: 110 volts
International dialing code: 787
Puerto Rican song: *La Borinqueña*
Puerto Rican motto: *Joannes est nomen ejus* (John is His Name)
Puerto Rican flower: *La Maga*

Geography

Puerto Rico is an island facing the Atlantic on the north and the Caribbean on the south. It is the smallest of the Greater Antilles, running 100 miles (160 km) east-west and 35 miles (56 km) north-south.

Three offshore islands of significant size complete its territory: Vieques and Culebra, geologically and geographically part of the Virgin Islands; and Mona, an uninhabited islet halfway between Puerto Rico and the Dominican Republic in the Mona Passage. The Puerto Rico trench, which runs 30,000 ft (10,000 meters) down just north of the island, is the deepest part of the Atlantic.

The Cordillera Central ("central spine"), a mountain range whose peaks reach well over 3,000 ft (900 meters), takes up most of the island's area and is surrounded by foothills. To the northeast, odd haystack-shaped limestone formations make up the karst country, a unique and fascinating landscape of rock cones and caves. Puerto Rico is ringed by palm-lined, white-sand beaches and by coral reefs, and is veined with rivers and streams. The island has no natural lakes. San Juan is one of the finest natural harbors in the Caribbean.

Climate

Puerto Rico has one of the most pleasant and unvarying climates in the world, with daily highs almost invariably at 70–85°F (21–29°C). The island is at its wettest and hottest in August, with 7 inches (18 cm) the average monthly rainfall and 81°F (27°C) the average daily high. During the rainy season, sudden late-afternoon squalls are common.

Regional variations are noticeable: Ponce and the southern coast are warmer and drier than San Juan and the north. It is coldest in the higher altitudes of the Cordillera, where the lowest temperature in the island's history was recorded near Barranquitas: 39°F (4°C).

Average daily high temperatures for San Juan range from 75°F (24°C) in January and February to 81°F (27°C) from June through to September.

Government

Puerto Rico's official status is *Estado Libre Asociado*, or "Free Associated State." It is commonly referred to as the "Commonwealth of Puerto Rico." Under an agreement dating from 1950, Puerto Ricans are American citizens, with almost all the economic and personal rights and responsibilities pertaining thereto.

Heading the island's government is an elected governor; Puerto Rico has an elected Senate and House of Representatives, which work much like the US system.

While Puerto Rico has presidential primaries, Puerto Ricans are not permitted to vote in national elections. However, they are represented in the US Congress by a resident commissioner who can sit on committees but cannot vote. Puerto Rican residents do not pay federal income tax.

Economy

Manufacturing is the largest sector of the local economy. Puerto Rico is the world's largest producer of pharmaceuticals. Petrochemicals are another strong industry, as is tourism. Puerto Rico is the banking center for most of the Caribbean.

The island's per capita income is $7,000 – lower than the United States. Twenty-three percent of the work force is employed by the government. The island's gross domestic product is over $25 billion, by far the largest in the Caribbean and one of the largest in Latin America.

Public Holidays

The annual Public Holidays are:
● **1 January** New Year's Day
● **6 January** Three King's Day
● **10 January** Eugenio Maria de Hostos Birthday
● **17 January** Martin Luther King Day
● **21 February** George Washington's Birthday
● **22 March** Celebration of the abolition of Slavery
● **March/April** Good Friday
● **18 April** José de Diego Day
● **30 May** Memorial Day
● **4 July** US Independence Day
● **18 July** Luís Muñoz Rivera Day
● **25 July** Constitution Day
● **5 September** Labor Day
● **12 October** Columbus Day
● **11 November** Veterans' Day
● **19 November** Celebration of the discovery of Puerto Rico
● **3rd Thursday in November** Thanksgiving Day
● **25 December** Christmas Day

Planning the Trip

Visas and Passports

No visa or passport is required for US citizens entering Puerto Rico from the United States. Those with permanent residence, however, are advised to bring their green cards.

Foreign nationals are required to present the same documentation and papers required for entry into the continental US.

Customs

Customs regulations resemble those of the United States, and are carried out with similar thoroughness. It is illegal to transport perishable foods, plants, drugs or animals into or out of Puerto Rico except with prior permission. This stipulation applies to those traveling to and from the United States as well.

Duty-free shops are open for all international flights, and for flights to the United States and US possessions in the Caribbean.

Money Matters

All business in Puerto Rico is transacted in US dollars, and foreigners are advised to buy their travelers' checks in that currency. Travelers' checks are accepted all over the island.

Most restaurants and hotels in well-traveled areas honor American Express, MasterCard, Visa, Carte Blanche and Diner's Club. Ideal and Discover cards are accepted at a smaller number of establishments. There are a number of American Express Travel Services on the island: offices are located in Aguadilla, Anasco, Caguas,

Condado, Hato Rey, Isabela, Manati, Mayagüez (2), Ponce, Río Piedras, Sabana Grande, San Germán, San Sebastián, Utuado and Yauco. For more information contact **Travel Network**, 1035 Ashford Ave, Condado, tel: 725-0960.

Banking

Puerto Rico is the banking center of the Caribbean Basin and as such has almost all of the leading North American banks, as well as many European and native Puerto Rican ones. ATM machines are installed in most towns around the island.

Banking hours are Monday–Friday, 9am–2.30pm. Certain branches of each bank may open on Saturday and, in some cases, evenings.

Tax

Puerto Rico has no sales tax. There are taxes on alcohol and cigarettes, though these are included in marked prices and do not appear as surcharges. An excise tax applies to incoming automobiles, electronics equipment and luxury items.

What to Wear/Bring

Puerto Rican dressing is extremely casual: jeans, shorts and long trousers are common. Only in a very small number of clubs are jackets and ties really necessary, and businessmen often remove their jackets in the course of the workday. Colorful, medium-length dresses are versatile evening wear for women.

Anything more than a light sweater is seldom necessary, even on winter nights in the Cordillera. An umbrella will come in handy, especially in late summer on the island's northern coast.

However, sunscreen will be necessary for those who plan to spend even a minimal amount of time outdoors.

Airlines

The following airline offices are in Puerto Rico. The area code is **787**. Numbers preceded by 800 are only toll-free on the island and in the US.
- **American Airlines**, tel: 749-1747.
- **British Airways**, tel: 791-7222.
- **Caribair**, tel: 791-1240
- **Continental Airlines**, tel: 725-7711.
- **Copa Airlines**, tel: 722-6969.
- **Delta**, tel: 791-0045.
- **Flamenco Airways**, tel: 253-0810.
- **Iberia**, tel: 791-1741/721-5630.
- **Lacsa**, tel: 791-6400/1332.
- **Liat/Dominair**, tel: 791-3838.
- **Northwest**, tel: 253-0206.
- **Tower Air**, tel: (800) 34-TOWER (348-6937)
- **Trans World Airways**, tel: 791-2121
- **United**, tel: (800) 241-6522.
- **US Air**, tel: (800) 872-7440.
- **Vieques AirLink**, tel: 722-3736.

Tourist Offices

On the US mainland, call the Puerto Rico Tourism Company toll-free at (800) 223-6530. Outside the United States:
Canada: 41–3 Colbourne Street, Toronto, Ontario, M5E 1E3, tel: (416) 368-2680.
France: 5 Bis, Rue de Louvre, 75001, Paris, tel: (1) 44 77 88 00.
Germany: Abraham Lincoln Strasse 2, 65189, Weisbaden, tel: (611) 977-2312.
Italy: Via Dante 2/53, 15121, Genoa, tel: (010) 553-1169.
Spain: Calle Serrano 1, 28001 Madrid, tel: (91) 431-2128.

Getting There

Air

San Juan's **Luís Muñoz Marín International Airport**, just west of the city center in Isla Verde, is one of the largest airports in the Caribbean, serving not only as Puerto Rico's main port of tourist entry but also as a stopping point for most US and European flights to the Virgin Islands and many other Caribbean islands. The most important international carriers serving San Juan include American Airlines, Pan American, Delta Airlines, Iberia, TWA and United.

Free buses run to most car rental agencies not in the airport, and those operated by the Metropolitan Bus Authority run to various parts of the city for only a small charge. Taxis from the airport operate on a fixed-rate zonal system for tourist areas; meter charges apply for areas not considered tourist locations.

Sea

While regular passenger service to Puerto Rico is rare, cruise ships are commonplace. San Juan is the most popular cruise port in the Caribbean, receiving over 1 million visitors annually. Several modern "tourism piers" have been constructed at the harborside in Old San Juan, with the result that most cruise companies plying the South Atlantic make at least an afternoon stop in San Juan.

Specialist Tours

The following tour companies can be contacted:
Borinquen Tours, tel: 725-4990, 725-2460.
Fuentes Bus Line, tel: 780-7070.
Gray Line Sightseeing Tours, tel: 727-8080.
Rico Suntours, tel: 722-2080.
United Tour Guides, tel: 721-3000 ext 2597.

Practical Tips

Business Hours

Business hours follow the US rather than the Latin tradition, and the afternoon *siesta* is generally not practiced. Most stores are open Monday–Friday 9am–6pm, banks 9am–2.30pm. Some selected stores of major supermarket chains are open 24 hours a day, 7 days a week.

Tipping

Puerto Rico has a service economy resembling that of the United States, and this means tipping for most services received. Follow the American rules of thumb: 15 percent in restaurants, including *fondas* and *colmados* but not including fast-food joints; 10 percent in bars; 10–15 percent for cab drivers, hairdressers and other services. Fifty cents per bag is a good rule for hotel porters, and a few bucks should keep the person who cleans your room happy.

Media

Print

Puerto Ricans are avid readers of periodical literature, and the national dailies, published in San Juan, cover the spectrum of political opinion.

Of the Spanish papers, *El Nuevo Día* is probably the most popular, a meaty tabloid with special features and book excerpts. *El Vocero* is a slim paper with more local, sensational news; while the new *La Era* is beginning to make waves. The *San Juan Star* publishes editions in English and Spanish.

Puerto Rio produces few magazines, but gets most of the

weeklies from the United States and Spain. American newspapers are available here on the day of publication: in Spanish, *Diario de las Americas*, published in Miami; in English, *The New York Times, The New York Post, The Miami Herald* and *The Wall Street Journal*.

Television and radio

Puerto Rico has more than 100 radio stations, including the English-language WOSO (1040 on the AM dial), which is quite versatile, combining fine local coverage with network news. English-language WBMJ is a religious station, and the St. Thomas station may be picked up by some radios, particularly in the eastern part of Puerto Rico. Recommended Spanish music stations are Radio Uno and, on FM, Radio Fidelity.

The island has at least half a dozen Spanish-language TV stations of its own, but there are no English-language stations, save for the offerings on cable and satellite TV, which come from the United States and include all the American television networks. The government station, WIPR, broadcasts local programs in Spanish and some PBS programs in English.

Postal Services

Puerto Rican postal services are administered by the US Postal Service. Regulations and tariffs are the same as those on the mainland. Stamps may be purchased at any post office; most are open from 8am–5pm, Monday–Friday and from 8am–noon on Saturday. Stamps may also be purchased from vending machines located in hotels, stores and airports.

The US Postal Service Authorized Abbreviation for Puerto Rico is PR.

Telecommunications

The international area code for Puerto Rico is **787**.

Coin-operated telephones are common and cost either 10¢ or

25¢ for local calls, depending on the particular pay phone. When you hear the dial tone, you may dial the seven-digit number. If the call is long-distance within Puerto Rico, extra charges will apply. For calls to the US Virgin Islands, dial 1-340 and the number; to the Dominican Republic, dial 1-809 and the number. Every Caribbean island now has its own area code; check your directory for the complete list. For calls to the US and Canada, dial 011, then the area code, then the number. An operator will tell you how much money to deposit.

If you wish to place a call through an operator, dial "0." Directions are usually printed on the phone, and are always printed in the first pages of the phone directory.

The phone directories in Puerto Rico are in Spanish, with a special section in English providing commercial and government telephone numbers and giving translations of the Spanish headings under which information can be found.

Telegraph facilities are available through Western Union or Telex. Western Union telegraphs and cash transfers arrive at food stores of the Pueblo chain.

Local Tourist Offices

The Puerto Rico Tourism Company has its main office at La Princesa, Old San Juan (tel: 721-2400); the company also has an office on the US mainland, tel: (800) 223-6530 (toll-free).

Embassies and Consulates

Because Puerto Rico isn't an independent nation, it cannot have diplomatic relations with anyone. Hence, there are no embassies in San Juan – but plenty of consulates and honorary consulates.

Consulates
Canada, Scotiabank Plaza, Piso 13, Hato Rey, tel: 250-0367.
France, Edif Mercantil Plaza 720, Hato Rey, tel: 753-1700.

Germany, Santa Bibliana 1618, Río Piedras, tel: 755-8228.
Italy, Amatista 93, Río Piedras, tel: 793-5284.
Spain, Edif Mercantil Plaza, Hato Rey, tel: 758-6090.
UK, Taft 1, 5-E, Condado, tel: 728-6715.

Security and Crime

In recent years, the crime rate in Puerto Rico has skyrocketed, but following a crackdown by police the annual murder rate has dropped. It is a place with high unemployment and a tourist population which is often gullible and vulnerable. Travelers would be wise to take certain precautions.

Nevertheless, petty theft and confidence scams are more prevalent in Puerto Rico than violent crimes. Always lock your rooms, especially in smaller lodgings. Never leave luggage unattended or out of your sight. Most hotels will store bags at the front desk, as will many restaurants and shops. Never leave any valuables in your room. It is advisable to leave your room key at the front desk when you leave your hotel or guest house for any length of time.

Always lock automobiles, regardless of whether you have left any valuables inside, as the car radios which come with most rentals are extremely valuable, easily saleable and much coveted by thieves. As travelers' checks are accepted all over Puerto Rico, there is no reason to carry more than the cash you need.

Puerto Rico has an island-wide emergency number. To contact the police, fire service and for medical emergencies call 911. Most dispatchers understand some English.

Medical Treatment

Puerto Rico's health care resembles that of the United States in that it has no de jure national health service, and the sick are cared for on a pay-as-you-go basis.

Useful Numbers

San Juan:
● **Emergency** call 911
● **Police,** tel: 343-2020.
● **Fire,** tel: 343-2330.
● **Medical Center of Puerto Rico,** tel: 754-3535.
● **Assist** (for medical emergencies), tel: 343-2222.
● **Coast Guard,** tel: 729-6770.
● **Rape Hotline,** tel: 765-2285.
● **Poison Treatment Center,** tel: 754-8536.
● **American Red Cross,** tel: 759-7979.

In practice, however, Puerto Rico's health care is administered on a far more lenient basis than in the United States. In general, fees are much lower and, since many Puerto Ricans have medical insurance, being hospitalized is far less of a financial nightmare than it is in the continental United States. Most hospitals have 24-hour emergency rooms but, if possible, check the yellow pages of the telephone book under *Servicio Emergencia de Hospitales*.

Puerto Rico is full of competent medical professionals. If you could choose where to fall ill, you'd doubtless elect San Juan, as the number of universities and clinics there make it full of doctors and medical personnel. Still, facilities in other areas, though often old and disheartening, are generally run by capable physicians and nurses.

Below are listed some of the larger hospitals with emergency rooms and some of the more popular (not necessarily 24-hour) pharmacies in San Juan. For listings in provincial cities, check the yellow pages in the phone book.

Hospitals
Ashford Presbyterian Community Hospital, tel: 721-2160.
De Diego Hospital, 310 De Diego Ave, Stop 22, Santurce, tel: 721-8181.
Metropolitan Hospital, 1785 Carr. 21, Las Lomas, P.V., Río Piedras, tel: 783-6200.

Hospital Auxilio Mutuo, Hato Rey, tel: 758-2000.
Hospital San Pablo, Bayamón, tel: 747-4747.
Hospital Pavia, Santurce, tel: 727-6060.

Pharmacies

Old San Juan
Puerto Rico Drug, tel: 725-2202.
Walgreens, tel: 722-6290; also 1130 Ashford Ave, Condado, tel: 725-1510.
Farmacías El Amal, 617 Europa, Santurce, tel: 728-1760.

Mayagüez
Walgreens, Mayagüez Mall, tel: 832-2072.

Ponce
Walgreens, Ave Fogot, tel: 841-2077.

Special Considerations

Puerto Rico has few of the dangerous bacteria and diseases that plague other semi-tropical areas, but one deserves special mention. Almost all of the island's rivers are infected with the bacteria *chisto*, which can cause severe damage to internal organs. Some say that river water is safe to drink and swim in on the upper altitudes of mountains, provided it is running swiftly, but this guide does not recommend it. Tap water is safe.

Getting Around

By Air

Puerto Rico is dotted with airports. While most international and many domestic flights to San Juan use **Luis Muñoz Marín International Airport** in Isla Verde, many others use San Juan's second airport, **Isla Grande**, just across an estuary south of Puerta de Tierra. Ponce and Mayagüez have modern, if small, airports which give residents 20-minute access to the capital. Also, part of Ramey Air Force Base near Aguadilla has been converted to a civilian airport which serves domestic flights as well as charters and some international flights from Canada. Dorado, only a 45-minute drive west of San Juan, has an airport which services its resorts. Vieques has a fine airport, and the Vieques Air Link, which leaves Isla Grande and costs only $40 each way, is a pleasurable means of getting to and from that charming island.

Small planes can be chartered at Isla Grande Airport.

By Bus

Puerto Rico's major cities are linked by *públicos*, small vans which assemble at stands all over San Juan and in pre-established locations in the smaller cities. *Públicos* are good value and comfortable to ride in, and probably the best alternative to having one's own car.

San Juan, Ponce and Mayagüez all have very efficient local bus services. Buses can be hailed where you see signs reading *Parada de Guaguas*.

Water Transportation

As Puerto Rico is fairly rectangular in shape, with few awkward peninsulas and bays, it lacks the extensive water transportation networks of other islands in the Caribbean. There are some exceptions: the ferry from the tourist piers of San Juan to Cataño, a mile across San Juan Bay, is a time-saver and a real bargain. Ferries leave the docks at Fajardo twice daily (9.15am and 4.30pm) for Vieques. Ferries from Fajardo to Culebra leave at 4pm Monday–Saturday with a 9am boat on Saturday, Sunday and holidays. Boats can be chartered in Mayagüez for the arduous but fascinating 45-mile trip to the Isle of Mona.

Driving

Car hire
Puerto Rico has one of the highest per capita rates of car ownership in the Americas, and an automobile is a necessity for anyone who wants to see the island extensively. Puerto Rico therefore has an inordinately high concentration of car rental dealerships. A complete listing can be found by looking in the local yellow pages under *Automóviles Alquiler*. Avis, Budget, Hertz and National rental offices are located in the arrival terminal at Muñoz Marín Airport; others are just a short shuttle-bus trip away. Most have unlimited mileage. Smaller companies often have excellent automobiles and are less expensive. Insurance usually costs extra; be sure to get it, and always check the terms of the coverage before signing anything.

Most rental agencies stipulate that you be at least 25 years old and carry a major credit card. However, some will take a large cash deposit in lieu of the card. Foreign drivers may be required to produce either an international driver's license or license from their home country. US licenses are valid in Puerto Rico.

Rental Agencies

Avis, tel: (800) 331-1212; Isla
Verde (airport), tel: 791-0426;
Mayagüez, tel: 833-7070; Ponce,
tel: 848-4188.
Budget, tel: (800) 527-0700;
Condado, tel: 725-1182; Hato
Rey, tel: 751-4330.
Charlie, tel: 728-2418.
Discount, tel: 726-1460.
Hertz, tel: (800) 654-3131;
Condado, tel: 725-2027; Isla
Verde (airport), tel: 791-0840;
Puerta de Tierra, tel: 721-0303;
Ponce (airport), tel: 842-7377;
Mayagüez (airport), tel: 832-
3314.
L&M, tel: 725-8307.
National, tel: (800) 328-4567;
San Juan, tel: 791-1805.
Target, tel: 783-6592.
Thrifty, tel: (800) 367-2277; Isla
Verde (airport), tel: 791-4241.

Rules of the Road

Speed limits are not often posted in
Puerto Rico. They are listed in
miles, paradoxically – distance
signs are in kilometers. The speed
limit on the San Juan–Ponce
autopista is 55 mph (90 kph).
Limits elsewhere are far lower,
especially in residential areas,
where speed-bumps (*lomos*) provide
a natural barrier to excess.

Puerto Rico's older coastal
highways take efficient routes but
can be slow going, due to never-
ending traffic lights. Roads in the
interior are narrow, tortuous, ill-
paved, and always dangerous.
Often, they run along dizzying
cliffsides. Frequent landslides
mean that roads often wash out.

Hurricanes, too, take their toll on
the roads and drivers: traffic
signals are often out of commission
and drivers begin to go at their own
pace, which usually means too fast
and weaving in and out of traffic.

By law, you must wear seat belts
in Puerto Rico, and occasionally a
driver may be stopped by the police
for not wearing one. As in the US,
turning right on a red light when
traffic allows is permitted – except
at a few intersections, where a sign
advising you not to do so is
indicated.

Slow down if you see a sign
reading *Desprendimiento*
(Landslide). *Desvio* means detour
and *Carretera Cerrada* means Road
Closed. You'll see plenty of these
signs on a trip through the beautiful
country roads of the Cordillera.

Neither hitchhiking nor picking up
hitchhikers is advised.

In general, most Puerto Rican
drivers tend to follow the rules of
the road, but a formidable group do
not, which can make driving
hazardous. The best advice is to be
aware of where you are at all times
and don't take anything for granted.
Traffic signs and lights may not be
heeded by all.

Where to Stay

Choosing a Hotel

Puerto Rico has a wide range of
accommodations unusual for a
Caribbean island which draws
droves of tourists. As one would
expect, big resorts set the tone.
Still, guest houses, beach houses,
grand hotels, and camping grounds,
as well as a host of less
conventional settings round out an
encouraging, if expensive, lodging
situation.

Puerto Rico's big resorts are of
two types. The first comprises richly
equipped, beautifully landscaped
beachfront resorts, best typified by
the **Caribe Hilton**, of the tropical
Hiltons, in Puerta de Tierra; the
Hyatt Dorado Beach Hotel and
Hyatt Regency Cerromar, resorts
just west of San Juan in Dorado;
Fajardo's **El Conquistador** and
Humacao's famous **Palmas del
Mar**. These tend to have casinos
and several bars. Except for the
Caribe Hilton, all have beautifully
groomed golf courses. Each is
characterized by big swimming
pools, excellent facilities for tennis
and exercise and long stretches of
lovely beachfront. Another thing
these places have in common is
that they are extremely expensive.

The second tier of resort hotels
are somewhat less lavish, may lack
casinos and tend to be about half
as expensive as the others. These
are typified by the big, white high-
rises of San Juan's Condado and
Isla Verde areas. They tend to cater
less exclusively to holiday-makers
and draw a more diverse crowd of
guests. Many of these are
businessmen, and the Condado
hotels in particular have made great
efforts over the past several years
to draw conventions.

Guest houses are perhaps the most pleasant lodging option. These tend to be smaller and more intimate than the resorts, averaging around a dozen rooms. Many of them are on beaches and offer the guest the opportunity to walk across the patio, not a check-out lobby, for a morning swim. About half have bars; almost all have swimming pools.

A self-catering vacation may be to your taste. Contact **San Juan Vacations**, Marbella del Caribe Oeste Local S-5, Isla Verde, PR 00979, tel: 727-1591; fax: 268-3604 for comprehensive details of a selection of condominiums available on the island.

There are a certain number of run-down, sleazy hotels, most of them in major cities, which have gone to seed and tend to be full of bugs and dirt. They don't have bars. They're not air-conditioned. They tend to stay in business by boarding illegal immigrants and state-supported residents. They are extremely cheap, however, and the real budget tourist may be persuaded to brave the bugs.

Hotel Listings

Condado
Best Western Pierre
105 De Diego
Tel: 800-468-4549; 721-1200
Located a few blocks from the beach, this traditional hostelry caters to families and business men and women. Its 184 units are well-proportioned and are equipped with air conditioning and cable-TV. The Metropol restaurant next door offers Cuban fare at very reasonable prices and fine service. **$$**
Casa del Caribe
57 Caribe Street
Tel: 722-7139
Nine intimate units remodeled and graced with Puerto Rican original art. Complimentary breakfast can be taken on wrap-around veranda. **$**
Condado Plaza Hotel and Casino
999 Ashford Avenue
Tel: 800-624-0420; 721-1000
Centrally located, ideal for business

travelers, this is considered Condado's best full-service hotel. Top-notch restaurants such as La Posada, Mandalay, Tony Roma's. Large casino, pool, discotheque, executive floor and business center. **$$$**

Hotel Prices

- **$ = Budget** under $150
- **$$ = Moderate** $150–250
- **$$$ = Expensive** $250+

Prices are per double room in winter high season

Diamond Palace
55 Condado Avenue
Tel: 800-468-2014; 721-0810
Moderately priced hotel one block from the beach. Small but crowded casino frequented by mostly locals. A good choice for those who want to economize, yet stay close to where it's happening. Popular restaurants, Martino's on penthouse floor and the Green House on ground level. **$$**
Days Inn Condado Lagoon Hotel
6 Clemenceau Street
Tel: 800-858-7407; 721-0170
Near beach, the Condado Lagoon is a watersports center. Reasonable priced hostelry contains 48 units. **$**
El Canario Inn
1317 Ashford Avenue
Tel: 800-533-2649; 722-3861
Charming small hotel near the water; lots of character. Deemed a bed and breakfast inn, this hostelry goes back to the days when Condado underwent rapid development 30 years ago, and it remains a popular choice. **$**
El Canario by the Lagoon
4 Clemenceau Street
Tel: 800-533-2649; 722-5058
Comfortable bed and breakfast hotel on the Condado Lagoon, where windsurfing and waterskiing are available. Close to the beach. **$**
El Canario by the Sea
4 Condado Avenue
Tel: 800-742-4276; 722-8640
Small 25 unit guest house near San Juan Marriott Hotel. All rooms are air conditioned with private bath. Complimentary breakfast. **$**

El Consulado
110 Ashford Avenue
Tel: 723-8665
Elegant European style bed and breakfast, formerly a restaurant, retains fine qualities of a Spanish mansion. 29 rooms. **$**
El Prado Inn
1350 Lucchetti Street
Tel: 800-468-4521; 728-5925
Quiet, charming location at Cervantes Park a few minutes walk to the beach and hotels. A quiet getaway, with all rooms furnished with air conditioning, private bath and ceiling fans. Spanish-style patio provides European atmosphere. **$**
El Portal
76 Condado Avenue
Tel: 721-9010
Centrally located, traditional small hotel of the Condado dating back to its halcyon days. Inexpensive with 48 well-equipped units. **$**
Iberia Hotel
1464 Wilson Avenue
Tel: 723-0200
In residential neighborhood, this inexpensive 30-unit hotel includes air conditioning, phone, bath in cozy Spanish style. **$**
San Juan Marriott
1309 Ashford Avenue
Tel: 791-1000
One of Condado's newest, this hotel was formerly the Dupont Plaza Hotel and Casino, which was closed after the New Year's Eve 1986 fire that killed 97 people. Now, the 525-unit grand hotel enjoys great popularity, usually crowded with locals and guests, with immense busy casino and fine restaurants including Tuscany (Italian) and Cherry Blossom (Japanese). **$$$**
Radisson Ambassador Plaza
1369 Ashford Avenue
Tel: 800-468-8512; 721-7300
Formerly Howard Johnson's, still has a famous ice-cream parlor; pleasant piano bar adjacent to casino. Recent expansion cost $45 million now featuring lavish concierge floor with 2-room suites. Three restaurants and 2 lounges with live music. **$$$**

Ramada Condado
1045 Ashford Avenue
Tel: 723-8000
Located on the beach, with
swimming pool, this 96-unit
unobtrusive hotel caters to tourists
and business people. **$$**

Regency Hotel
1005 Ashford Avenue
tel: 800-468-2823; 722-2909
Newly renovated air-conditioned
rooms, primarily for residence type
accommodations. Deluxe suites
with refrigerator, private balcony,
cable TV. First class dining room for
banquets and other activities. **$$**

Tanama Princess Comfort Inn
1 Joffre Street
Tel: 888-826-2621; 724-4160
Centrally located within walking
distance of Condado Lagoon and
beaches. 112 units with chic
restaurants and shops. **$**

Ocean Park

Hostería del Mar
1 Tapia
Tel: 800-742-4276; 727-3302
Charming 17-unit hostelry on the
beach. Thrilling view of the Atlantic.
Restaurant offers natural foods
menu. **$**

Isla Verde

Casa Mathieson Inn Hotel
14 Calle Uno
Villamar
Tel: 800-667-8860; 726-8662
Lovely 46-unit hotel located just off
the beach. Award-winning restaurant
features Spanish cuisine. **$**

Colony San Juan Beach Hotel
2 Tartak Street
Tel: 253-0100
Beautiful view of the ocean, this 71-
unit hideaway offers privacy right on
the beach. **$$**

Crowne Plaza Hotel and Casino
Route 187, Km. 1.5
Tel: 253-2929
Near Boca de Cangrejos and
Piñones public beaches. Large
casino and banquet halls. **$$**

El San Juan Hotel and Casino
Isla Verde
Tel: 800-468-2818; 719-1000
Many consider this Puerto Rico's
finest hotel. Lavish resort with 389
rooms, certainly has the most

interesting lobby in the Caribbean.
The casino is fashioned after a
Monte Carlo gambling establishment.
Also has some of San Juan's best
restaurants, including Yamato
(Japanese), La Piccolo Fontana
(Italian) and Back Street Hong Kong
(Chinese), where the facade was
brought from the New York 1964
World's Fair. **$$$**

Embassy Suites Hotel and Casino
8000 Tartak Street
Tel: 888-791-0505; 791-1423
Short walk to beach, this spacious
300-unit luxury facility offers one-
bedroom suites with living/working
area. Large casino and huge
banquet hall. **$$$**

Hotel Prices

- **$ = Budget** under $150
- **$$ = Moderate** $150–250
- **$$$ = Expensive** $250+

Prices are per double room in
winter high season

Green Isle Inn-Hotel
30 Calle Uno
Villamar
Tel: 800-677-8860; 726-4330
Management boasts cleanliness
and comfort in 36 units.
Considered one of the best deals in
town. **$**

Hampton Inn
6530 Isla Verde Road
Tel: 800-HAMPTON; 791-8777
This 200-unit facility features two-
room suites with lounge, bar,
meeting rooms and fitness center. **$**

ESJ Towers
6165 Isla Verde Avenue
Tel: 800-468-2026; 791-5151
On the beach, this 450-unit building
features air-conditioned studios and
apartments with fully-equipped
kitchens and private balconies. Fine
art in modern lobby. **$$$**

Mario's Hotel and Restaurant
2 Rosa Street
Tel: 791-3748
This low-priced 59-unit hotel is
known for its restaurant featuring
Greek, Italian and tropical cuisine.
Satellite TV, cocktail lounge and live
entertainment. **$**

**Ritz-Carlton, San Juan Hotel
and Casino**
6961 Road 187
Tel: 800-241-3333; 253-1777
Luxurious 401-unit resort offers
casino styled after Monte Carlo, set
in Spanish design. A fine fitness
center, private dining room and chic
boutiques and shops. **$$$**

San Juan Grand Hotel
Isla Verde
Tel: 800-443-2009; 791-6100
Beautiful, modern, full-service
hotel. Las Vegas-style
entertainment at night. Has five
restaurants including Ruth's Chris
Steak House. **$$$**

Travelodge of Puerto Rico
Isla Verde Avenue
Tel: 800-468-2028; 268-0637
Deluxe rooms on executive floor
complete with jacuzzi, cable TV. **$**

Puerta de Tierra

Caribe Hilton
Calle San Jeronimo
Tel: 800-468-8585; 721-0303
The granddaddy of big resorts, the
650-room Caribe Hilton was
inaugurated in 1949 and is still the
only hotel in Puerto Rico with its
own private beach. VIPs and foreign
dignitaries usually stay here.
Restaurants include Peacock
Paradise, one of the finest Chinese
restaurants in Puerto Rico, El Batey
(fine seafood) and Rotisserie II
Giardino (Italian). **$$$**

Radisson Normandie
Avenida Muñoz Rivera
Tel: 729-2929
Art deco designed hotel shaped like
the Normandie; one of the early
cruise ships. Most rooms include a
parlor with working and sitting area
and sun room. **$$**

Old San Juan

El Escenario Guest House
152 San Sebastián
Tel: 721-5264
Pleasant 7-room guest house above
lively bar, this may be Old San
Juan's best lodging bargain. Rates
include breakfast on rooftop
terrace. **$**

Galeria San Juan
204 Norzagaray
Tel: 722-1808
Art gallery and eight-room guest
house in 16th-century mansion
restored by sculptor and local
personality Jan D'Esopo. Purchases
of her art available. From the
house, the artist's sculpture of
Christopher Columbus looks toward
the sea. **$**

Gran Hotel El Convento
100 Cristo
Tel: 800-468-2779; 723-9020
Historic convent, dating back to the
16th century, the building was
converted in the 1960s into a 100-
room hotel. An ideal base for
exploring Old San Juan. **$$**

Hotel Central
202 San José
Tel: 722-2751
Right off Plaza de Armas; caters
mainly to black Caribbean islanders
on shopping or business trips. **$**

**Wyndham Old San Juan Hotel
and Casino**
100 Brumbaugh Street
Tel: 800-WYNDHAM; 721-1111
This 242-room hotel, the Old City's
largest, built as part of waterfront
expansion, contains 240 rooms,
restaurant and two lounges
overlooking huge meeting place.
Roof-top pool and large casino. **$$$**

Miramar
Hotel Excelsior
801 Ponce de León
Tel: 800-289-4274; 721-7400
Businessman's hotel in commercial
area, but within easy access to Old
San Juan, the Condado. **$$**

Hotel Toro
605 Miramar Avenue
Tel: 725-5150
Basic accommodation for the
budget traveler. **$**

Olimpo Court Hotel
603 Miramar Avenue
Tel: 724-0600
In residential area, with guest
rooms and studio apartments
containing fully equipped
kitchenettes. **$**

Dorado
Hyatt Dorado Beach Hotel
Route 693
Tel: 800-233-1234; 796-1234
The finest resort in Puerto Rico
features 2 championship Trent
Jones golf courses, tennis courts, a
casino and Su Casa restaurant, a
former plantation house, from when
the property was a grapefruit farm.
Its long stretch of pristine beach
accommodates all major
watersports activities. **$$$**

Hyatt Regency Cerromar
Dorado Beach
Route 693
Tel: 800-233-1234; 796-1234
Upscale resort with world-renowned
golf course and $3 million river
pool. Fine choice of restaurants
including Sushi Wong's. It is also
the site of the annual Puerto Rico
Manufacturers' Association
Convention. **$$$**

Río Grande
**Westin Río Mar Beach Resort
and Casino**
6000 Rio Mar Blvd.
Tel: 888-6200
Set on the beach and amongst the
hills, the resort is ideal for a
secluded private getaway. The
beauty of Puerto Rico becomes
more vivid with El Yunque in view
and as a backdrop for the two
championship golf courses. Tennis,
fitness center and casino along with
10 restaurants make for a pleasant
stay. **$$$**

Paradors

The one unique lodging option
Puerto Rico offers is the *parador*.
These state-run country farm-
houses, often old coffee or sugar
haciendas, offer the authentic
ambiance of Puerto Rican rural
life. Beautiful old furniture, elegant
dining facilities and the opportunity
– at some – to pick one's own food
for dessert make these well worth
trying for those who prefer to see a
side of Puerto Rico that won't
remind one of Nice or Miami
Beach. They are about the same
price as guest houses.

Many of the *paradores* out on
the island are restored 19th-
century coffee plantations, and are
located in particularly scenic
areas. Rates are very reasonable,
usually not more than $60–80 a
night for a double, and the food is
often much better than what you
would find at nearby restaurants.

From the US mainland, *parador*
reservations can be made through
a central toll-free number, (800)
443-0266. In San Juan, dial 721-
2884; from outside the metro
area, call (800) 981-7575 toll-free.
At the moment, 18 *paradores* are
certified by the Puerto Rico
Tourism Company, as follows:

Baños de Coamo, Coamo
Tel: (787) 825-2239. **$**
Boquemar, Boquerón
Tel: (787) 851-2158. **$**
Casa Grande, Utuado
Tel: (787) 894-3939. **$**
El Faro, Aguadilla
Tel: (787) 822-8000. **$**
Guajataca, Quebradillas
Tel: (787) 895-3070. **$**
Hacienda Gripiñas, Jayuya
Tel: (787) 828-1717. **$**
Hacienda Juanita, Maricao

Tel: (787) 838-2550. **$**
J B Hidden Village, Aguada
Tel: (787) 886-8686. **$**
Joyuda Beach, Boquerón
Tel: (787) 851-5650. **$**
La Familia, Fajardo
Tel: (787) 863-1193. **$**
Martorell, Luquillo
Tel: (787) 889-2710. **$**
Oasis, San Germán
Tel: (787) 892-1175. **$**
Perichi's, Rincón
Tel: (787) 851-3131. **$**
Posada Porlamar, La Parguera
Tel: (787) 899-4015. **$**
Sol, Mayagüez
Tel: (787) 834-0303. **$**
Villa Antonia, Rincón
Tel: (787) 823-2645. **$**
Villa Parguera, La Parguera
Tel: (787) 899-3975. **$**
Vistamar, Quebradillas
Tel: (787) 895-2065. **$**

Fajardo
Anchor's Inn
Route 987, Km. 2.7
Tel: 863-7200
Located on a bluff overlooking the sea, the 14-unit inn features an excellent seafood restaurant. **$**

Hotel Prices

- **$ = Budget** under $150
- **$$ = Moderate** $150–250
- **$$$ = Expensive** $250+
Prices are per double room in winter high season

El Conquistador Resort and Country Club
Route 987, Km. 4.1
Tel: 800-468-8365; 863-1000
This 918-room resort has everything a well-heeled tourist could want, including a 10-acre private island accessible by ferry boat. A funicular takes guests down to the beach. The 18-hole championship golf course hosts international tournaments. **$$$**
Fajardo Inn
52 P. Beltran
Tel: 860-6000
With a panoramic view of the Atlantic, this 42-unit hotel is located on five lush acres. Voted "Green Hotel of 1996." **$**

Humacao
Wyndham Palmas del Mar Resort
170 Candelero
Tel: 800-PALMAS-3; 852-6320
Only 45 minutes from San Juan. This 255-unit suite resort includes an 18-hole golf course designed by Gary Player, 20 tennis courts, horseback riding, scuba diving and a variety of restaurants. **$$**

Patillas
Caribe Playa
Route 3, Km. 112
Tel: 800-221-4483; 839-1817
Beachfront studios have equipped kitchens in 29 units. Seaview terrace restaurant, barbecue, hammocks, kiddie pool. **$**

Guanica
Copamarina Beach Resort
P.O. Box 805
Tel: 821-0505
Luxury resort set in 18 acres of mangrove cays, coconut palms and Guanica's famous dry forest. In recent years, the hotel has been well renovated. Ideal for families. **$$$**

Aguadilla
Cielo Mar Hotel
84 Montemar Ave.
Tel: 882-5960
With breathtaking panoramic view of the ocean, 40 rooms come complete with all amenities. **$**

Mayagüez
Best Western Mayagüez Resort and Casino
Tel: 832-3030
Situated on 20 acres of landscaped gardens with a hilltop view of Mayagüez. Family hotel. On weekends, there are scores of kids in the pool and elsewhere. Its Rotisserie Restaurant serves themed buffets daily. **$$**
Holiday Inn Mayagüez
2701 Highway 2
Tel: 833-1100
Centrally located with 152 units, air-conditioning, cable TV, lounge and non-smoking rooms. A good stopover when driving through the west. **$$**
La Palma Hotel
Mendez Vigo and Peral
Tel: 834-3800
46 comfortable guest rooms with direct-dial telephone, air-conditioning, cable TV. For the budget-minded. **$**

Ponce
Belgica
122 Villa
Tel: 844-3255
In the heart of town, 60 units next to the old trolley route, Las Delicias Plaza and the old fire house. **$**
Days Inn of Ponce
Route 1, Km. 123.5
Tel: 800-329-7466; 841-1000
Family accommodations with kiddie pool, laundry, courtyard and international restaurant. If it's value you want, this is the place. **$**

Holiday Inn Ponce
Highway 2, Km. 221.2
Tel: 844-1200
Part of the international chain; overlooks the Caribbean. **$**
Hotel Melia
2 Cristina
Tel: 842-0260
Charming hotel in heart of restored district; the ideal place to stay for discovering downtown Ponce. Friendly staff; room price includes breakfast on rooftop terrace. Mark's at the Melia restaurant is worth the trip. **$**
Ponce Hilton
Highway 14
Tel: 259-7676 or 259-7777
This government-owned hotel, the city's most luxurious, has a casino and 18-hole golf course. **$$**

Rincón
Horned Dorset Primavera
Route 429, Km. 3
Tel: 823-4030.
Privacy, elegance and fine service in this beachside Mediterranean-style property with 30 secluded suites. Restaurant serves gourmet, price-fixed dinners. **$$$**

Where to Eat

What to Eat

Aside from having a delectable and historic native cuisine, Puerto Rico benefits from its American and Caribbean connections in having just about all the "ethnic" cuisines you'd find in the largest cities of the United States. Spanish, US, Mexican, Chinese, French, Swiss, Brazilian, Japanese and other food is plentiful, especially in San Juan.

Puerto Rican cuisine differs from that of its Spanish neighbors in the Caribbean almost as much as it differs from that of the mainland US. Relying heavily on beans, rice and whatever Puerto Ricans haul out of the sea, it is a mild, filling, well-balanced style of cookery. See the feature on Puerto Rican Cuisine, page 75, for details.

Where to Eat

You can get Puerto Rican food in all manner of spots: in the modest urban *fondas*, where a rich *asopao de camarones* will run you under five bucks; in the rural *colmados* where roast chicken is the order of the day; and in the posh restaurants of Old San Juan and the Condado, such as **La Mallorquina**, the Caribbean's oldest continuously operating restaurant. The restaurants of San Juan tend to be concentrated in certain areas.

While *fondas* are all over town, European cuisine tends to be concentrated in the trendier parts of Old San Juan and in the more expensive areas of the Condado and Santurce, such as Ashford Avenue. There must be a higher concentration of American fast-food joints than anywhere else on earth. These are in the Condado and the modern shopping malls in Carolina and Hato Rey. Bars are everywhere.

Old San Juan

Amadeus
106 San Sebastián
Tel: 722-8635
Puerto Rican. Traditional dinners, fresh seafood and delicious *ceviche* on Plaza San José, where the bar is usually well-stocked and very crowded. **$$**

Amanda's
424 Norzagaray
Tel: 722-1682
Mexican. Nice drinks and ocean view, but French-Mexican dishes and vegetable plates are overpriced. Slow service. **$$**

Ambrosia
250 Cristo
Tel: 722-5206
Italian. Fresh pasta served in a sidewalk-café atmosphere. **$**

La Bombonera
259 San Francisco
Tel: 722-0658
Puerto Rican. Traditional cafeteria-style bakery and the best place in Old San Juan for a cheap, satisfying *arroz con pollo* and coffee with local pastry. **$**

Café Berlin
407 San Francisco
Tel: 722-5205
Vegetarian. Owned by a German baker, this "gourmet vegetarian" eatery fronting Plaza Colón offers fresh pastas, organic foods and a delicious salad bar. Portions on the small side. **$$**

Chef Marisol
202 Cristo Street
Tel: 725-7454
Contemporary. Romantic patio restaurant features contemporary cuisine by Marisol Hernandez, winner of many gold medals in international culinary competition. Local foods prepared nouvelle style. **$$$**

Hard Rock Café
253 Recinto Sur
Tel: 724-7625
American. Crammed like all other Hard Rocks with musical memorabilia, this restaurant also features delicious food (try the "veggie burger"), large video screens and surprisingly quick service. Great Old San Juan dining experience – if you can stand the noise. **$**

Il Perugino
105 Cristo Street
Tel: 722-5481
Italian. Located in a restored home, chef-owner Franco Seccarelli prepares specialties such as *pasta a la vongole*, carpaccio of lamb and marinated salmon. Appetizers include tomato with bufalini mozzarella. Fine wine collection. **$$$**

La Chaumière
367 Tetuán
Tel: 722-3330
French. The Old City's only French restaurant offers treats such as baby rack of lamb with herbs, scallopine of veal with medallion of lobster topped with asparagus and Béarnaise sauce. Very expensive; reservations recommended. **$$$**

Price Guide

- **$** = Inexpensive
- **$$** = Moderate
- **$$$** = Expensive

La Mallorquina
207 San Justo
Tel: 722-3261
Puerto Rican. Oldest restaurant in Puerto Rico, dating from 1848. House specialties are *asopao de marisco* and *arroz con pollo*. Worth a visit if only for interior courtyard. Reservations recommended. **$$**

Mango's Café
2421 Laurel
Punta Las Marias
Tel: 727-9328
Caribbean. Delicious Jamaican, West Indian and Creole food, drinks and music. **$**

Parrot Club
363 Fortaleza
Tel: 725-7370.
Contemporary. A new Latin bistro and bar featuring live music. Home of the original Parrot Passion Cocktail. Sunday brunch. **$**

Yukiyu
311 Recinto Sur
Tel: 721-0653.
Japanese. Teppanyaki restaurant
and sushi lover's paradise.
Celebrities flock here for the best
Japanese food in town. Try the
California Roll, Spicy Tuna or
Salmon sashimi. Expensive;
reservations required. **$$$**

Puerta de Tierra
El Hamburger
402 Muñoz Rivera
Puerta de Tierra
Tel: 725-5891
American. Rustic eatery overlooking
the Atlantic; nearly blown away by
Hurricane Hugo in 1989. Before
fast food restaurants landed on the
island, El hamburger was the place
to go, and it still draws the crowds.
Enjoy the best flame-broiled burgers
in town while listening to guitar-
playing "Calypso Man." **$**
Marisqueria Atlantica
7 Lugo Vinas
Puerta de Tierra
Tel: 722-0890
Seafood. Prides itself on "friendliest
fresh food and fish restaurant in
town." Spanish-style preparation.
Try the daily specials. **$$**

Miramar
Augusto's Cuisine
Hotel Excelsior Miramar
Tel: 725-7700
Continental. Voted the best
restaurant in San Juan as winner of
the prestigious Golden Fork Award
for 4 years. Owner Augusto Shriner
was the chef at the Caribe Hilton in
its heyday. It usually gets the nod as
the best restaurant on the island. If
not, it's up with the best. **$$$**

Condado and Ocean Park
Ajili Mojili
Joffre and Clemenceau streets
Tel: 725-9195
Puerto Rican. Authentic local
cuisine with a gourmet twist:
*mofongo relleño, arroz con pollo,
fricasé de cabrito ó guinea,
piononos, piñon* and *serenata de
bacalao.* Top dollar for local fare
which may cost far less in other
establishments. **$$$**

Antonio
1406 Magdalena Avenue
Tel: 721-2139
Spanish gourmet cuisine in elegant
atmosphere. Table settings are
majestic. Service impeccable.
Steaks, chicken and seafood deluxe
complemented with fine stock of
Spanish wines. **$$$**

Price Guide

- **$** = Inexpensive
- **$$** = Moderate
- **$$$** = Expensive

Big Apple Deli
1407 Ashford Avenue
Tel: 725-6345
American. New York style deli
featuring favorites such as pastrami
and corned beef sandwiches,
knishes, smoked fish, apple strudel
and bagels. Legendary Dr. Brown's
sodas available. **$$**
C'est La Vie
Ashford and Magdalena avenues
Tel: 721-6075
French. Indoor-outdoor café on
Condado's Plaza de la Libertad.
Features crêpes, *fajitas*, sirloin
burgers; pricey. **$$**
Caruso Restaurant
1104 Ashford Avenue
Tel: 723-6876
Italian. Classic cuisine which
features usual pasta dishes,
homemade lasagna , spaghetti,
ravioli and flaming desserts. **$$**
Cherry Blossom
At San Juan Marriott Hotel
Ashford Avenue
Tel: 723-7300.
Japanese. Steak house and sushi
bar featuring teppanyaki
preparation. Well appointed bar on
second level, where you may order
dinner. Service is fast and caring.
Chart House
1214 Ashford
Tel: 728-0110.
Steak and seafood. Converted
plantation-style house. Fresh
seafood, prime-rib, salad bar with
verandahs looking out over tropical
garden. Popular yuppie-type
hangout. **$$$**

Chayote
603 Miramar Avenue
Olimpo Court Hotel
Tel: 722-9385
Contemporary Caribbean cuisine in
both elegant and casual
surroundings. Chayote, a Caribbean
vegetable, is prepared in
imaginative ways in the kitchen,
then served elegantly. **$$$**
Chili's
1004 Ashford Avenue
Tel: 725-5657
American. Stateside franchise
restaurant loaded with atmosphere
and usually lots of diners.
Hamburgers, grilled chicken, *fajitas*,
rich desserts and lots of beer.
Various Chili's restaurants are now
spread around the island. **$**
Compostela
106 Condado Avenue
Tel: 724-6088
Spanish. Rated "excellent" by *San
Juan City Magazine*, which
recommends Royal Pheasant with
raspberry sauce and chocolate-and-
coffee mousse for dessert.
Reservations required. **$$$**
Daniel's
1104 Magdalena Avenue
Tel: 721-7754
A French touch of seafood and
steak creations. Originally at
Palmas del Mar resort where it
became well known for fresh fish
and meats, homemade desserts
and extensive wine cellar. **$$$**
Dunbar's
1954 McLeary
Ocean Park
Tel: 728-2920
American. Favorite *gringo* hangout
and pick-up joint with buffalo
chicken wings and dart games.
Good value for money. Try the
ratatouille and their pasta
specialties. **$**
Green House
Ashford Avenue
Diamond Palace Hotel
Tel: 268-0546
Short orders and full dinners well
prepared at popular meeting place
eatery. Hamburgers, fresh fish,
local favorites. **$$**

Hermes Creative Cuisine
1108 Ashford Avenue
Tel: 723-5151
Contemporary. Restaurant with an incredible list of close to 200 wines from around the world including 25 varieties of Port. Specialties include lamb with tequila and goat cheese sauce, wild boar and ravioli. Quite creative. **$$$**

Houlihan's
1309 Ashford Avenue
Tel: 723-8600
American. Traditional favorites including herb-garlic stuffed mushrooms, barbecued baby back ribs, *fajitas* and Santa Fe linguine. Big screen TV for sports events. Sunday brunch. **$**

Il Grottino
1372 Ashford Avenue
Tel: 723-0499
Italian. Informal yet elegant atmosphere with typical appetizers and pasta dishes complemented with a vast array of wines. **$$**

José José
1110 Magdalena Avenue
Tel: 725-8496
Named after its two owners, this restaurant serves Creole-style and international cuisine, including Ostrich with Chutney. **$$$**

La Fonda de Cervantes
1464 Wilson Avenue
Tel: 722-6933
Continental. Serves entrées from southern Europe in a traditional atmosphere. Specialties include seafood and meat casseroles, old fashioned potage and Paella Valenciana. **$$$**

La Scala
Ambassador Plaza Hotel
Tel: 725-7470
Italian. Northern Italian cuisine featuring gnocchi, tortellini and black pasta. For dessert you can't miss the Zuppa Inglese. **$$$**

Mandalay
Condado Plaza Hotel
Tel: 722-0940
Oriental. The *New York Times* hails this as one of the very best restaurants in Puerto Rico. The menu features Szechuan, Hunan, Mandarin and Cantonese cuisine, and the only *dim sum* on the island. Reservations recommended. **$$$**

Martino's
55 Condado Avenue
Diamond Palace Hotel
Tel: 722-5264
Italian. Chef Martin Acosta presides over some of the finest fare from northern Italy this side of Milan. Special ravioli, gnocchi, seafood specialties and definitely the best pasta sauce on the island. **$$$**

Price Guide

- **$** = Inexpensive
- **$$** = Moderate
- **$$$** = Expensive

Metropol
De Diego Avenue
Tel: 268-3045
Cuban. Traditional fare in an informal atmosphere at very reasonable prices. Specialties include smoked chicken, steaks Cuban style and grilled dorado (*mahi-mahi*). It may be more economical eating here than at home. **$**

Miro
76 Condado Avenue
Tel: 723-9593
Catalan/Spanish. Fresh fish and shellfish cooked Mediterranean style with emphasis on Catalan preparation. Plates of squid, octopus, oysters, clams and *langostinos* abound. **$$$**

Pikayo
Hotel Tanama
Tel: 721-6194
Creative cuisine combining gourmet recipes with local produce and seafood. At one time considered the best restaurant in San Juan. **$$$**

Ramiro's
1106 Magdalena Avenue
Tel: 721-9049
Puerto Rico's finest restaurant featuring imaginative international specialties with a Spanish flair. Chefs/owners Luis and Jesús Ramiro prepare a table that you will remember with delight for years to come. Par excellence desserts and fine wine list. White sangria a must. Reservations definitely recommended. **$$$**

St. Moritz
Regency Hotel
Tel: 724-0999
Continental cuisine in Old World atmosphere. Impeccable service. Specialties include veal piccata, sauerbraten and grilled red snapper. **$$**

Sweeney's Scotch and Sirloin
Ambassador Plaza Hotel
Tel: 723-5551
American. Baked stuffed Maine lobster, seafood stew are house specialties,. Sirloin, filet mignon and New York cut steaks are done to perfection. Owner Larry Sweeney, known for his expertise, puts together a scrumptious salad bar complete with loaves of homemade corn bread and black pumpernickel. Drinks are generous and the piano bar draws repeat clients. Reservations recommended. **$$$**

Tony Roma's
Condado Plaza Hotel
Tel: 722-0322
Ribs. Baby back ribs accompanied by barbecued beans and coleslaw are a pleasing lunch or dinner. The Cajun spiced ribs are special. **$$**

Via Appia
1350 Ashford Avenue
Condado
Tel: 725-8711
Italian. Always busy sidewalk café featuring pizza and pasta dishes. Indoor tables are available where Italian foods are displayed and sold grocery-style. **$**

Zabo
14 Candina Street
Tel: 725-9494
Set in the heart of Condado, this old beach house features "grazing" cuisine, where you may choose from a variety of appetizers or a large selection of entrées. **$$$**

Hato Rey and Río Piedras

El Zipperle
352 F.D. Roosevelt Avenue
Hato Rey
Tel: 763-1636
German/Spanish. Old-time eating and meeting place of business men and women and politicians. Specializes in favorite dishes from the old country set in European decor. **$$**

Jerusalem
O'Neill I-6
Hato Rey
Tel: 764-3265
Arabic. Palestinian owners offer delights such as grilled leg of lamb, stuffed grape leaves and cardamom coffee; Arab grocery and video store available in the back. **$$**

La Terraza
Plaza Las Americas
Hato Rey
Food court houses vast array of fast food restaurants including Sizzler, Cajun Grill, Kyoto, Orange Julius, and Gyros. Usually jam-packed. **$**

Price Guide

- **$** = Inexpensive
- **$$** = Moderate
- **$$$** = Expensive

Margarita's
1013 F.D. Roosevelt Avenue
Puerto Nuevo
Tel: 722-9583
Mexican. Well known, of course, for its margaritas. Dishes include enchiladas with mole and pork, chicken, beef and turkey fajitas. Entertainment by Mariachi musicians. **$$**

Metropol 3
124 F.D. Roosevelt Avenue
Hato Rey
Tel: 751-4022
Cuban. Long-time favorite among locals. Daily specials usually include meat, chicken and fish dishes with rice and beans and fried plantain. Try Natilla and Cuban coffee for dessert. One of three Metropol establishments in San Juan area. **$**

Middle East Restaurant
207 Padre Colón
Río Piedras
Tel: 751-7304
Arabic. Nicely decorated eatery in heart of San Juan's tiny "Arab Quarter," specializes in felafel, hummus and full course traditional Arabic dinners; belly-dancing on weekend nights. **$$**

Tierra Santa
284 F.D. Roosevelt Avenue
Hato Rey
Tel: 763-5775
Arabic. Hummus, baba ganouch, tabuleh and shish kebab are favorites here. Entrées include kustaleta (lamb chops) and gambary (shrimps Arab style). **$$**

Santurce

Casita Blanca
351 Tapia
Tel: 726-5501
Puerto Rican. Outstanding local cuisine in café-restaurant with outdoor patio, located, unfortunately, in one of Santurce's worst neighborhoods. Its specialties, from *gandinga* to *pastelón de amarillo*, have been mentioned in both *Gourmet* magazine and *The New York Times*. **$**

La Casona
609 San Jorge
corner Fernández Juncos
Tel: 727-2717
Spanish. Very expensive restaurant in an old Spanish-style home replete with tropical gardens and immaculate service. Lobster salad, stuffed rabbit loin and the best *paella* in Puerto Rico make this a popular lunch or dinner spot – especially for executives on expense accounts. **$$$**

Isla Verde

Back Street Hong Kong
El San Juan Hotel
Tel: 791-1224
Chinese. Set in a pagoda used as the Hong Kong Pavilion in the 1964 New York World's Fair. Besides delicious Mandarin, Szechuan and Hunan dishes, this restaurant features a huge salt-water aquarium and 19th-century Chinese antiques. Excellent service, reasonable prices; reservations required. **$$$**

Che's
35 Caoba
Punta Las Marias
Tel: 726-7202
Argentinian. Specialties include *parrilladas*, *churrasco* and *chimichurri* as well as international grilled steaks and pasta. **$$**

La Piccola Fontana
El San Juan Hotel
Tel: 791-0966.
Italian. Elegant, Northern Italy fare served in classic surroundings. Fettuccini Alfredo, veal scalloppine and tip-top Caesar's Salad are recommended. **$$$**

Lupi's
Route 187, Km. 1.3
Tel: 253-2198
Mexican. Bar and sports *cantina* with a decidedly American flavor. Delicious *fajitas* and flying fish, and best margaritas in San Juan; impeccable service. **$**

Yamato
El San Juan Hotel
Tel: 791-8152
Japanese. Outstanding service in classic teppanyaki and sushi restaurant. Saki and Sapporo beer are served. **$$$**

Cataño

La Casita
27 Manuel Enrique
Tel: 788-5080
Seafood. Fancy restaurant in a very poor neighborhood serves delicious fresh fish; specialties include a delicious octopus cocktail and *mofongo relleño* with lobster. **$$$**

Fajardo

El Conquistador Resort and Country Club
1000 Conquistador Avenue
Tel: 863-100
This upscale resort contains a bevy of world class restaurants such as Isabela's Grill, Otello's, Blossoms, Casave Seafood Grill, Stingray Café, Ballyhoo, Ciao Mediterranean Café, Las Brisas Terrace and Café. **$$$**

Joyuda

Pino's Restaurant
Road 102, Km. 14.6
Tel: 255-3440
Seafood. Typical Puerto Rican seafood restaurant near Mayagüez, specializing in salmorejo and *mofongo relleño* with *mariscos* (mashed, spiced crab meat and fried plantain stuffed with seafood). **$$**

Ponce
Mark's at the Melia
2 Christina Street
Hotel Melia
Tel: 284-6275
Continental. Award-winning chef
Mark French creates classic dishes
using local ingredients. Elegant
atmosphere. **$$$**

Healthy Options

There is a great movement
toward health foods in Puerto
Rico. Dozens of stores have
cropped up around the island
dispensing vitamins, herbs
and organically-grown foods.
These establishments also
provide small restaurants
where you may have lunch,
which might consist of a
soyburger and sprouts
sandwich and natural orange
juice. Recommended: **Salud**,
1350 Ashford Avenue,
Condado (Tel: 722-0911) and
Good Earth, Plaza Las
Americas, third level. **Fresh
Mart** is an organic-food
supermarket. The main store
is located on Road 887,
Carolina (Tel: 782-7890).

Pito's Café and Restaurant
Road 2
Las Cucharas
Tel: 841-4977
Seafood. *Mofongo relleño* is this
charming eatery's specialty. This
favorite island dish is made up of
stuffed fried plantain which may
contain seafood, meat or chicken.
$$
Restaurant El Ancla
Avenue Hostos on Ponce Playa
Tel: 840-2450
Seafood. Specialties from waters of
Puerto Rico include Caribbean
lobster, red snapper and shrimps,
Creole style. **$$**

Culture

Sources of Info

Visitors may pick up free
publications which give information
on places to go, sights to see,
history, and general information on
the island. Most readily available
are *Que Pasa* and *Bienvenidos*.
These are usually found at the
hotels and tourist offices. La
Princesa in Old San Juan is the
main tourist office, while a kiosk
near the Condado Plaza Hotel also
provides tourist literature.

Museums

Puerto Rico's museums place great
emphasis on the colorful history of
the island and its people. The
island's most famous museum, the
Ponce Art Museum, is primarily
devoted to classic paintings which
represent schools from around the
world. San Juan's Museum of Art
and History depicts the story of the
city dating back to the 16th century,
while The Museum of the Americas
houses a collection of items from
New England to Mexico, with a
strong emphasis on Puerto Rican
life. Most museums do not charge
for admission and are open daily.
Try to plan a museum trip during a
weekday, as there are fewer visitors
at that time.

Art Galleries

Almost all of Puerto Rico's cities
sell their native crafts, from
Aguadillan lace to Loízan *veigante*
masks, but an art "scene," as
understood in New York, exists only
in San Juan. Here, the combination
of a radiant light and an active
network of patronage have worked
to draw most of the finest painters

of Puerto Rico and many from North
America and Europe. Sculpture
thrives, as do the crafts of Puerto
Rico and other Latin American
nations. Most galleries are huddled
together on a few of Old San Juan's
streets, but you'll find plenty of
pleasant surprises in San Juan's
other neighborhoods and even out
on the island. Here are some of the
better spots in the metropolitan
area:
Art Students League
San José St
Old San Juan
Tel: 722-4468
A small, changing display of some
of San Juan's up-and-coming
artists, with a tendency toward the
vanguard and the experimental.
Open: 8am–4pm Monday to
Saturday.
Galería Diego
51 Maria Moczo St
Ocean Park
Tel: 728-1287
Changing exhibits of local painting
and sculpture. Open: 10am–6pm
Monday to Friday, until 9pm on
Thursday, and 10am–1pm Saturday.
Galería Labiosa
312 San Francisco St
Old San Juan
Tel: 721-2848
Paintings and sculpture. Open:
9.30am–5pm Monday to Saturday.
Galería Palomas
207 Cristo St
Old San Juan
Tel: 724-8904
A fine collection of Puerto Rican
paintings and graphic design. Open:
10am–6pm Monday to Saturday.
Galería San Juan
204–206 Norzagaray St
Old San Juan
Tel: 722-1808
A sizable changing collection of
fine paintings in an elegant, old
building. Open: 10am–5pm Tuesday
to Saturday.
Galerías Botello
208 Cristo St
Old San Juan
Tel: 723-9987
Fine Haitian paintings, among other
things, in an artist-operated gallery.
Open: 10am–6pm Monday to
Saturday.

Concerts

The San Juan Symphony Orchestra has progressed in a few short years to a position of great respectability. Frequent concerts are held in the Fine Arts Center Festival Hall, known locally as the "Bellas Artes," in Santurce. Chamber music ensembles are numerous at the university and among private concert-givers. The highlight of the classical music year comes in early June, when the San Juan Symphony's performances at Bellas Artes are complemented by guest appearances from musicians from around the world, some of them as renowned as Yitzhak Perlman and Maxim Shostakovich.

Ballet

There are plenty of opportunities to see ballet in San Juan. The Friends of San Juan Ballet periodically host performances with the Symphony Orchestra at Bellas Artes. The San Juan City Ballet are frequent performers at the restored Tapia y Rivera Theater in Old San Juan, and give matinee performances. Rounding out dance offerings are the modern dance shows given at the Julia de Burgos Amphitheater in Río Piedras as part of the UPR Cultural Activities.

Libraries

Puerto Rico is not long on public libraries; most are in universities and private foundations, and much exchange of books rests on person-to-person lending. Here are two exceptions:
Ateneo Puertorriqueño, Ponce de León, Stop 2, Puerta de Tierra, tel: 722-4839.
Volunteer Library League, 250 Ponce de León, Santurce, tel: 725-7672.

Movies

Puerto Rico is woefully understocked with movie theaters, even in San Juan. A handful in Santurce show first-runs and oldies, but it's best to look them up in the phone directory under "*Cinemas*" and ring to find out what's playing on the day.

Good films can be seen at unexpected places, however. The Amphitheaters at the University of Puerto Rico frequently show art films, especially in the UPR Cultural Activities series, whose showings are at 5pm and 8pm every Tuesday. For more information, tel: 764-0000, ext 2563.

Video

Games: One of the most popular and most used video arcades is Time Out on the third level of Plaza Las Americas in San Juan, which has all the latest video games and more. Video game rooms are also located at most hotels.
Sales and Rental: Video rental establishments fill the San Juan area and do very well around the island. There are many locations of Blockbuster Video, popular for rental. Other rental stores include Video Ave in Río Piedras (Tel: 274-0868) and Televideo in Hato Rey (Tel: 250-1131). Suncoast Movies, located on the first level of Plaza Las Americas, just sells videos.

Nightlife

The nightlife of Puerto Rico ranges from the tranquility of coffee and conversation to the steamy, fast-lane excesses of San Juan's clubs. On cool nights in the Cordillera, nightlife resembles what Puerto Ricans have probably enjoyed for decades, if not centuries. Townspeople gather round local plazas and sing to the accompaniment of guitars, finding time between tunes for a couple of sips of Don Q or Medalla.

San Juan duplicates much of this rural nightlife – on weekends in the old city, youths of high school and college age mill about the Plaza San José by the hundreds, stopping in bars, restaurants and coffee houses, and trying to get groups together to go dancing.

But in San Juan and other cities, partying is in general taken with more reckless abandon. The whole city is crowded with bars and dancing establishments of all description. In Old San Juan, **El Batey, Los Hijos de Borínquen** and **El Patio de Sam** provide good spots for drinking and talk.

Sources of Info

Free publications such as *Que Pasa* and *Bienvenidos*, usually found at the hotels and tourist offices, provide up-to-date information on local nightlife.

Nightclubs/Discos

Amadeus
106 San Sebastián
Old San Juan.
Popular hangout for Old City crowd.
Egipto
1 Roberto H. Todd
Tel. 725-4664

Imaginative decor.
El Batey
Cristo St, Old San Juan.
Small, loud, great juke-box. Open
until 6am.
Hard Rock Café
253 Recinto Sur
Old San Juan
Tel: 724-7625.
Delicious food and loud music, with
lots of rock-n-roll memorabilia.
Krash
1257 Ponce de León
Santurce
Tel: 722-1390.
Gay bar.
Laser's
251 Calle Cruz
Tel: 721-4479.
Loud teen disco.
Lupi's
Route 187, Km. 1.3
Isla Verde
Tel: 253-2198.
Mexican bar and sports *cantina*.
Delicious margaritas, fabulous
fajitas and live music.
Maria's
204 Cristo St
Old San Juan.
Singles' bar.
Small World
San José St
Old San Juan.
Expats' drinking hangout.
1919 Lounge
Condado Beach Hotel, Condado
Tel: 725-2302.
Ritzy piano bar. Open until 3am.

Casinos

Gambling is legal in Puerto Rico.
Casinos offer blackjack, roulette,
poker, slot machines and all
manner of games of chance, though
they have somewhat lost their
novelty for US visitors since the
laws were liberalized in the States.

Casinos are permitted only in
hotels, and tend to be open from
noon until early morning.

Festivals

Almost every holiday is the
occasion for a festival in Puerto
Rico, many of them legislated,
others informal. Every town has its
patron saint, and every saint his or
her festival. These, known as
patronales, are the biggest events
of the year in their respective
towns. A complete list of these
would be impossible to compile, but
the most famous is probably Loíza's
Fiesta de Santiago Apostól in July.
The largest is certainly San Juan's
Bautista Night in late June.

A year-long festival has been
established by the Puerto Rican
Tourism Company. The **Le Lo Lai
Festival** is for those who happen to
stay in hotels which participate in
the Le Lo Lai program. Le Lo Lai
generally involves nightly shows of
Puerto Rican music and dance
programs staged in hotels. Consult
the Puerto Rico Tourism Company
(tel: 800-223 6530) for details.

Outdoor Activities

Fishing

Freshwater fishing has existed in
Puerto Rico's 12 man-made lakes
for years, but the sport itself has
become popular only in the past
decade.

Some 14 clubs fish the dozen
lakes, which were constructed in
the 1930s as a source of drinking
water and irrigation. Bass, both
large-mouth and peacock, are local
favorites, though at least seven
other native species are fished as
well. Plastic worms are the most
popular choice of bait among bass
fishermen. The lakes are stocked
with more than 2,000 baby fish
from the Maricao Fish Hatchery
(*Los Viveros* in Spanish), an
interesting site in itself.

Here's a list of the island's 12
freshwater lakes and the clubs that
fish them:
Carraizo (Loíza) Lake: At 32 sq.
miles (84 sq. km) the island's
largest lake, Carraizo is bordered by
Caguas, Gurabo and Trujillo Alto
and is accessible by Routes 175
and 739. (Gurabo Fishing Club).
La Plata Lake: Measuring 26 sq.
miles (67 sq. km) this is Puerto
Rico's second largest lake. It is
located between Toa Alta, Bayamón
and Naranjito, and accessible by
Route 167. (San Juan Bass and
Bayamón Fishing Club).
Cidra Lake: only (1 sq. mile) 3 sq.
km, this is one of the island's
smallest lakes. It's between
Bayamón and Cidra along Route
172. (Cidra Fishing Club).
Carite Lake: Off Route 179, Carite
Lake is located near Guayama and
the Carite National Forest. (Guyama
Fishing Club).
Toa Vaca Lake: Just south of

Villalba off Route 150, but to fish in here, you need a permit from the Water and Sewer Authority. (Freshwater Fishing Federation).
Guayabal Lake: Measuring 6 sq. miles (16 sq. km) and located in the Barrio Pastillo section of Juana Díaz. (Southern Bass Fishermen).
Caoníllas Lake: South of Utuado, this lake covers 7 sq. miles (19 sq. km) and can be reached by Route 607. (Utuado Fishing Club).
Dos Bocas Lake: At 16 sq. miles (41 sq. km), this unusually shaped lake is the third largest in Puerto Rico. It is located between Arecibo and Utuado just off Route 10. (Fishing Association).
Garzas Lake: Located off Route 518 in Adjuntas and among the island's smallest lakes. (Adjuntas Fishing Club).
Guayo Lake: Located in Lares, right off Route 129. (No local club).
Guajataca Lake: Off Route 119 in San Sebastián. (Backlash Fishing Club and Lares Bass Fishing Club).
Yauco Lake: Fed by the Yauco River and located 4 miles (6 km) outside the town of Yauco. (No local club).

Hiking

There are quite a few hiking trails in Puerto Rico, and many offer spectacular vistas. Particularly good hikes can be had in the Caribbean National Forest at El Yunque, as well as in the Guánica State Forest and on Mona Island. Río Camuy Cave Park and Las Cabezas de San Juan Nature Reserve offer more "walks" than hikes, but are still enjoyable. The Puerto Rico Department of Natural Resources in San Juan (tel: 724-3724) can provide more information on many of the country's trails.

Golf

Golf courses and tennis courts are scattered throughout the island, though most of the better ones are in the larger, more expensive resorts. It is possible, however, to arrange with these resorts to use their courts and courses on a user-fee basis.

Among the resorts with 18-hole championship golf courses are:
Hyatt Regency Cerromar Beach, Dorado, tel: 796-1234, ext. 3013.
Hyatt Dorado Beach, Dorado, tel: 796-1234, ext. 3239.
Palmas del Mar, Humacao, tel: 852-6000, ext. 2525.

Physical Fitness

Gymnasiums devoted to physical fitness are springing up all over Puerto Rico. These gyms are fully equipped with the latest exercise machines, saunas, showers, instructors and a variety of activities. Membership is available at reasonable rates or for use on a daily basis. Recommended in San Juan: **Powerhouse**, Avenida Pinero (tel: 783-6380) and **Caparra Fitness Club**, Avenida Kennedy (tel: 782-8585).

Sailing

Most of Puerto Rico's sailors head to Fajardo for weekends on the water. Boats of all sizes and descriptions are available for rental. For more information, consult:
Villa Marina, tel: 863-5131.
Puerto Chico, tel: 863-0834.

Scuba Diving

Ringed by a submarine forest of coral and subject to some of the greatest variations in underwater depth in the world, Puerto Rico is prime scuba territory for those with the expertise. Those who would like to learn to dive can get lessons at:

San Juan
Caribbean School of Aquatics, 1 Taft St, Suite 10-F Condado, tel: 723-4740.
Caribe Aquatic Adventure, Caribe Hilton, Puerta de Tierra, tel: 724-1307.

Out On The Island
Fajardo: Carlos A. Flores, Puerto Chico Marina, tel: 863-0834.
Isabela: La Cueva Submarina, Plaza Cooperative, tel: 872-3903.

Fajardo is probably the island's capital for water sports. For a relaxing sailing and diving adventure and an exploration of some of the smaller cays off Puerto Rico's east coast, contact: **Jack Becker**, Villa Marina Yacht Harbor, Fajardo, tel: 863-1905.

Snorkeling

Snorkeling is also popular among diving enthusiasts. Equipment can be rented or purchased at most dive shops and in certain department stores.

Surfing

Puerto Rico has almost ideal conditions for surfing – warm water, brilliant sunshine and heavy but even tubular surf. Many of the most popular spots are convenient to San Juan: **Piñones**, off Route 187 in Isla Verde, is probably the most renowned, and **Aviones**, so named because of the airplanes that fly over from nearby Muñoz Marín Airport, is just a bit farther down the road in Piñones. In the northwest, **Punta Higüero**, off Route 413 in Rincón, is world famous, and hosted surfing's world championships a few years ago. In the southwest, Jobos Beach proves popular among Mayagüez residents.

Swimming

Puerto Rico is ringed with sandy beaches, some of them outrageously popular, others secluded and quiet. Many are balnearios, public bathing facilities complete with life-guards, refreshment stands, dressing rooms and parking lots. Of those around San Juan, the most popular are probably those at **Luquillo** and **Vega Baja**. But all of Puerto Rico's beaches are exceptional, and all beachfront – with the exception of the Caribe Hilton – is public. Swimmers are advised to be careful of strong surf and undertow at certain beaches, especially in the northwest.

Windsurfing

Windsurfing is popular all over the island. Boards can be rented at most dive shops, including some of those listed above.

Cock Fighting

For a truly Puerto Rican sporting experience, cockfighting is hard to match. Although the sport seems inhumane to many, its popularity on the island cannot be denied. In this sport, dozens of the proudest local cocks are matched one-on-one in a tiny ring, or *gallera*. The predominantly male crowds at most events are almost as interesting as the fights themselves. These highly knowledgeable enthusiasts are often familiar with a cock's pedigree through several generations. The shouts are deafening, the drinking is reckless, and the betting is heavy. Betting is done on a gentlemanly system of verbal agreement, and hundreds of dollars can change hands on a single fight.

Gallerias are scattered all over, and the fights in even the most rural areas can draw hundreds. Admission can be expensive but the beer is cheap. For information on cockfighting in the San Juan area, consult:
Club Gallistico de Puerto Rico, Carr. Isla Verde, Isla Verde, tel: 791-1557.
Club Gallistico Río Piedras, Km 4.2. Carr. 844, Trujillo Alto, tel: 760-8815.

Spectator Sports

Puerto Rico has a national pastime – it is baseball. The island has produced some of the greatest stars ever to play the game, and you can find someone to talk baseball with in almost any bar.

The **Caribbean League** season runs from October to March, and there are teams in the largest cities. Many aspiring big-leaguers (and not a few has-beens) play in Puerto Rico. Games are almost daily, and tickets generally inexpensive. Those who want to keep abreast of American and National League action will find complete box scores in all the local papers. Also, Atlanta Braves games are televised on certain national stations.

Basketball is another team sport that is now really popular on the island: the *Federación Nacional de Baloncesta de Puerto Rico* has teams in almost all the island's larger cities.

Horse racing in San Juan is at **El Comandante Racetrack** in Canóvanas, 10 miles (16 km) east of the city. Races are held on Wednesdays, Fridays and Sundays at 2.30pm; small admission charge. For more information on races, tel: 724-6060.

Shopping

Where to Shop

In San Juan, the more upmarket shopping areas tend to be concentrated in the Old City and the Condado. Old San Juan boasts the more boutiquey atmosphere of the two. It is probably also what one could call more "authentic," with plenty of shops selling tourist baubles, curios, T-shirts and various other items. Among the better stores in the Old City are its jewelry shops, especially numerous along Fortaleza Street, which have signs reading "Joyería." Other specialties include leather and arts and crafts, ancient and modern.

The Condado lures customers with slightly more money to spend, and thus sells more goods of

Bookstores

The following have a good selection of books in both English and Spanish:
Bell, **Book and Candle**, 102 De Diego Ave, Santurce, tel: 728-5000.
Parentesis, Plaza Las Américas, Hato Rey, tel: 753-7140.
Casa Papyrus, 357 Tetuán, Old San Juan, tel: 724-6555.
Cultural Puertorriqueña, 1406 Fernández Juncos, Stop 20, Santurce, tel: 721-5683.
Librería Hispanoamericana, 1013 Ponce de León, Río Piedras, tel: 763-3415.
Librería La Tertulia, Amalia Marín and González, Río Piedras, tel: 765-1148.
The Book Store, 255 San José, Old San Juan, tel: 724-1815.
Thekes, Plaza de las Américas, Hato Rey, tel: 765-1539.

lasting value. Clothing, porcelain, crystal, jewelry – each is represented in at least a handful of shops which are called "Boutique" or "Shoppe." There's less of a marketplace ambiance in Condado, and a decidedly touristic tone to the merchandise there.

Hato Rey, Santurce and Isla Verde are more workaday marketplaces for permanent residents, places you'd go to buy a refrigerator, television set or car.

An exception is **Plaza de Las Américas**, the Caribbean's largest shopping mall, in Hato Rey. This is the best place on the island to go for merchandise of all kinds. It is rivaled by the **Plaza Carolina** shopping center in Carolina. Other malls exist on the island, like the **Plaza del Caribe** in Ponce and the **Mayagüez Mall** in Mayagüez. Cities as small as Caguas and Cayey have malls of good size.

For traditional (barter) shopping in San Juan, the best marketplace is the **Plaza del Mercado**, a bustling outdoor affair in Río Piedras. Primarily a fruit market, the Plaza del Mercado nonetheless trucks in merchandise of all kinds. Prices are often unlisted and haggling can be intense. Miramar also has a smaller market.

What to Buy

Cigars have caught on in Puerto Rico, even though smoking in public is frowned upon. There are even laws prohibiting smoking in most public buildings, yet in a short time dozens of tobacco and cigar shops have opened up. There are many in Old San Juan, and the Tobacco Shop on the first level of Plaza Las Américas is well stocked, although prices are a bit high. Recommended: **Habanacuba**, located on San Patricio Avenue in San Patricio, and **International House of Cigars** on Avenida Miranda in Río Piedras. Most well-known brands are available at reasonable prices. El San Juan Hotel has a "cigar boutique", which sells fine cigars from the Dominican Republic, Honduras and Jamaica.

Language

General

The language of Puerto Rico is Spanish. While it is by no means true that "everyone there speaks English," a majority of Puerto Ricans certainly do, especially in San Juan. Almost everyone in a public service occupation will be able to help in either language.

The Puerto Rican dialect of Spanish resembles that of other Antillean islands, and differs from the Iberian dialect in its rapidity, phoneme quality and elisions. For a more detailed look at this rich tongue, *see The Language of Puerto Rico on page 69.*

There are many excellent Spanish-English dictionaries, but **Barron's**, edited at the University of Chicago, is particularly recommended for its sensitivity to the vocabulary and syntax of the Latin-American idiom. Cristine Gallo's *The Language of the Puerto Rican Street* is an exhaustive lexicon of the kind of Puerto Rican slang most dictionaries would blanch at printing.

Basic Rules

English is widely spoken in most tourist areas, but even if you speak no Spanish at all, it is worth trying to master a few simple words and phrases.

Generally, the accent falls on the second-to-last syllable, unless it is otherwise marked with an accent (´) or the word ends in D, L, R or Z.

VOWELS

a as in father
e as in bed
i as in police
o as in hole
u as in rude

CONSONANTS are approximately like those in English, the main exceptions being:

c is hard before **a**, **o**, or **u** (as in English), and is soft before **e** or **i**, when it sounds like **s** (as opposed to the Castilian pronunciation of **th** as in think). Thus, *cen*so (census) sounds like senso.

g is hard before **a**, **o**, or **u** (as in English), but where English **g** sounds like **j** – before **e** or **i** – Spanish **g** sounds like a guttural **h**. **G** before **ua** is often soft or silent, so that agua sounds more like awa, and Guadalajara like Wadalajara.

h is silent.

j sounds like the English h.

ll sounds like y.

ñ sounds like ny, as in the familiar Spanish word *señor*.

q is followed by **u** as in English, but the combination sounds like **k** instead of like **kw**. *¿Qué quiere Usted?* is pronounced: Keh kee-ehr-eh oostehd?

r is often rolled.

x between vowels sounds like a guttural **h**, e.g. in México or Oaxaca.

y alone, as the word meaning "and", is pronounced **ee**.

Note that **ch** and **ll** are a separate letter of the Spanish alphabet; if looking in a phone book or dictionary for a word beginning with **ch**, you will find it after the final **c** entry. A name or word beginning with **ll** will be listed after the **l** entry.

When addressing someone you are not familiar with, use the more formal "usted". The informal "tu" is reserved for relatives and friends.

Words & Phrases

Hello *Hola*
How are you? *¿Cómo está usted?*
How much is it? *¿Cuánto es?*
What is your name? *¿Cómo se llama usted?*
My name is... *Yo me llamo...*
Do you speak English? *¿Habla inglés?*
I am British/American *Yo soy británico/norteamericano*
I don't understand *No comprendo*
Please speak more slowly *Hable más despacio, por favor*

Can you help me? *¿Me puede ayudar?*
I am looking for... *Estoy buscando*
Where is...? *¿Dónde está...?*
I'm sorry *Lo siento*
I don't know *No lo se*
No problem *No hay problema*
Have a good day *Que tenga un buen día,* or *Vaya con Diós*
That's it *Ese es*
Here it is *Aquí está*
There it is *Allí está*
Let's go *Vámonos*
See you tomorrow *Hasta mañana*
See you soon *Hasta pronto*
Show me the word in the book *Muéstreme la palabra en el libro*
At what time? *¿A qué hora?*
When? *¿Cuándo?*
What time is it? *¿Qué hora es?*
yes *sí*
no *no*
please *por favor*
thank you (very much) *(muchas) gracias*
you're welcome *de nada*
excuse me *perdóneme*
hello *hola*
OK *bién*
goodbye *adiós*
good evening/night *buenas tardes/noches*
here *aquí*
there *allí*
today *hoy*
yesterday *ayer*
tomorrow *mañana (note: mañana also means "morning")*

now *ahora*
later *después*
right away *ahora mismo*
this morning *esta mañana*
this afternoon *esta tarde*
this evening *esta tarde*
tonight *esta noche*

On Arrival

I want to get off at... *Quiero bajarme en...*
Is there a bus to the museum? *¿Hay un autobús al museo?*
What street is this? *¿Qué calle es ésta?*
How far is...? *¿A qué distancia está...?*
airport *aeropuerto*
customs *aduana*
train station *estación de tren*
bus station *estación de autobuses*
metro station *estación de metro*
bus *autobús/público*
bus stop *parada de guaguas*
ticket *billete*
return ticket *billete de ida y vuelta*
hitch-hiking *auto-stop*
toilets *servicios*
This is the hotel address *Ésta es la dirección del hotel*
I'd like a (single/double) room *Quiero una habitación (sencilla/doble)*
... with shower *con ducha*
... with bath *con baño*
... with a view *con vista*

Does that include breakfast? *¿Incluye desayuno?*
May I see the room? *¿Puedo ver la habitación?*
washbasin *lavabo*
bed *cama*
key *llave*
elevator *ascensor*
air conditioning *aire acondicionado*

Emergencies

Help! *¡Socorro!*
Stop! *¡Alto!*
Call a doctor *Llame a un médico*
Call an ambulance *Llame a una ambulancia*
Call the police *Llame a la policia*
Call the fire brigade *Llame a los bomberos*
Where is the nearest telephone? *¿Dónde está el teléfono mas próximo?*
Where is the nearest hospital? *¿Dónde está el hospital más próximo?*
I am sick *Estoy enfermo*
I have lost my passport/purse *He perdido mi pasaporte/bolso*

On the Road

Where is the spare wheel? *¿Dónde está la rueda de repuesto?*
Where is the nearest garage? *¿Dónde está el taller más próximo?*
Our car has broken down *Nuestro coche se ha averiado*

Numbers, Days and Dates

NUMBERS				DAYS OF THE WEEK	MONTHS
0 *cero*	16 *dieciseis*	10,000 *diez mil*		**Monday** *lunes*	**January** *enero*
1 *uno*	17 *diecisiete*	1,000,000 *un millón*		**Tuesday** *martes*	**February** *febrero*
2 *dos*	18 *dieciocho*			**Wednesday**	**March** *marzo*
3 *tres*	19 *diecinueve*			*miércoles*	**April** *abril*
4 *cuatro*	20 *viente*	SAYING THE DATE		**Thursday** *jueves*	**May** *mayo*
5 *cinco*	21 *veintiuno*	**20 October 1999,**		**Friday** *viernes*	**June** *junio*
6 *seis*	30 *treinta*	*el veinte de*		**Saturday** *sábado*	**July** *julio*
7 *siete*	40 *cuarenta*	*octubre de mil*		**Sunday** *domingo*	**August** *agosto*
8 *ocho*	50 *cincuenta*	*novecientos*			**September**
9 *nueve*	60 *sesenta*	*noventa y nueve*			*septiembre*
10 *diez*	70 *setenta*	(no capital letters		SEASONS	**October** *octubre*
11 *once*	80 *ochenta*	are used for days		**Spring** *primavera*	**November**
12 *doce*	90 *noventa*	or months)		**Summer** *verano*	*noviembre*
13 *trece*	100 *cien*			**Fall** *otoño*	**December**
14 *catorce*	200 *doscientos*			**Winter** *invierno*	*diciembre*
15 *quince*	*quinientos*				
	1,000 *mil*				

I want to have my car repaired
Quiero que reparen mi coche
It's not your right of way *Usted no tiene prioridad*
I think I must have put diesel in my car by mistake *Me parece haber echado gasoil por error*
the road to... *la carretera a...*
left *izquierda*
right *derecha*
straight on *derecho*
far *lejos*
near *cerca*
opposite *frente a*
beside *al lado de*
car park *aparcamiento*
over there *allí*
at the end *al final*
on foot *a pie*
by car *en coche*
town map *mapa de la ciudad*
road map *mapa de carreteras*
street *calle*
square *plaza*
give way *ceda el paso*
exit *salida*
dead end *calle sin salida*
wrong way *dirección prohibida*
no parking *prohibido aparcar*
motorway *autovía*
toll highway *autopista*
toll *peaje*
speed limit *límite de velocidad*
petrol station *gasolinera*
petrol *gasolina*
unleaded *sin plomo*
diesel *gasoil*
water/oil *agua/aceite*
air *aire*
puncture *pinchazo*
bulb *bombilla*

On the Telephone

How do I make an outside call? *¿Cómo hago una llamada exterior?*
What is the area code? *¿Cuál es el prefijo?*
I want to make an international (local) call *Quiero hacer una llamada internacional (local)*
I'd like an alarm call for 8 tomorrow morning *Quiero que me despierten a las ocho de la mañana*
Hello? *¿Dígame?*
Who's calling? *¿Quién llama?*
Hold on, please *Un momento, por favor*
I can't hear you *No le oigo*

Can you hear me? *¿Me oye?*
He/she is not here *No está aquí*
The line is busy *La línea está ocupada*
I must have dialed the wrong number *Debo haber marcado un número equivocado*

Shopping

Where is the nearest bank?
¿Dónde está el banco más próximo?
I'd like to buy *Quiero comprar*
How much is it *¿Cuánto es?*
Do you accept credit cards? *¿Aceptan tarjeta?*
I'm just looking *Sólo estoy mirando*
Have you got...? *¿Tiene...?*
I'll take it *Me lo llevo*
I'll take this one/that one *Me llevo éste/ese*
What size is it? *¿Que talla es?*
size (clothes) *talla*
small *pequeño*
large *grande*
cheap *barato*
expensive *caro*
enough *suficiente*
too much *demasiado*
a piece *una pieza*
each *cada uno/la pieza/la unidad*
bill *la factura (shop), la cuenta (restaurant)*
bank *banco*
bookshop *librería*
chemist *farmacia*
hairdressers *peluquería*
post office *correos*
department store *grandes almacenes*

MARKET SHOPPING

Supermarkets (*supermercados*) are self service, but often the best and freshest produce is to be had at the town market (*mercado*) or at street markets (*mercadillo*), where you place you order with the person in charge of each stand. Prices are usually by the kilo, sometimes by gramos (by the gram) or by unidad (by the piece).

fresh *fresco*
frozen *congelado*
organic *biológico*
flavor *sabor*
basket *cesta*

bag *bolsa*
bakery *panadería*
butcher's *carnicería*
cake shop *pastelería*
fishmonger's *pescadería*
grocery *verdurería*
tobacconist *estanco*
market *mercado*
supermarket *supermercado*
junk shop *tienda de segunda mano*

Sightseeing

mountain *montaña*
hill *colina*
valley *valle*
river *río*
lake *lago*
lookout *mirador*
city *ciudad*
small town, village *pueblo*
old town *casco antiguo*
monastery *monasterio*
convent *convento*
cathedral *catedral*
church *iglesia*
palace *palacio*
hospital *hospital*
town hall *ayuntamiento*
nave *nave*
statue *estátua*
fountain *fuente*
staircase *escalera*
tower *torre*
castle *castillo*
Iberian *ibérico*
Phoenician *fenicio*
Roman *romano*
Moorish *árabe*
Romanesque *románico*
Gothic *gótico*
museum *museo*
art gallery *galería de arte*
exhibition *exposición*
tourist information office *oficina de turismo*
free *gratis*
open *abierto*
closed *cerrado*
every day *diario/todos los días*
all year *todo el año*
all day *todo el día*
swimming pool *piscina*
to book *reservar*

Dining Out

breakfast *desayuno*
lunch *comida*
dinner *cena*
meal *comida*
first course *primer plato*
main course *plato principal*
made to order *por encargo*
drink included *incluida consumición/bebida*
wine list *carta de vinos*
the bill *la cuenta*
fork *tenedor*
knife *cuchillo*
spoon *cuchara*
plate *plato*
glass *vaso*
wine glass *copa*
napkin *servilleta*
ashtray *cenicero*
waiter, please! *camarero, por favor*

Table Talk

I am a vegetarian *Soy vegetariano*
I am on a diet *Estoy de régimen*
What do you recommend? *¿Qué recomienda?*
Do you have local specialties? *¿Hay especialidades locales?*
I'd like to order *Quiero pedir*
That is not what I ordered *Ésto no es lo que he pedido*
May I have more wine? *¿Me da más vino?*
Enjoy your meal *Buen provecho*

Liquid Refreshment

coffee *café*
  black *sólo*
  with milk *con leche*
  decaffeinated *descafeinado*
sugar *azúcar*
tea *té*
herbal tea *infusión*
milk *leche*
mineral water *agua mineral*
  fizzy *con gas*
  non-fizzy *sin gas*
juice (fresh) *zumo (natural)*
cold *fresco/frío*
hot *caliente*
beer *cerveza*
  bottled *en botella*
  on tap *de barril*

soft drink *refresco*
diet drink *bebida "light"*
with ice *con hielo*
wine *vino*
red wine *vino tinto*
white *blanco*
rosé *rosado*
dry *seco*
sweet *dulce*
house wine *vino de la casa*
sparkling wine *vino espumoso*
Where is this wine from? *¿De dónde es este vino?*
pitcher *jarra*
half liter *medio litro*
quarter liter *cuarto de litro*
cheers! *salud*
hangover *resaca*

Menu Decoder

BREAKFAST AND SNACKS
pan **bread**
bollo **bun/roll**
mantequilla **butter**
mermelada **jam**
confitura **jam**
pimienta **pepper**
sal **salt**
azúcar **sugar**
huevos **eggs**
  cocidos **boiled, cooked**
  con beicon **with bacon**
  con jamón **with ham**
  fritos **fried**
  revueltos **scrambled**
yogúr **yoghurt**
tostada **toast**
sandwich **sandwich in square slices of bread**
bocadillo **sandwich in a bread roll**

MAIN COURSES
Carne/Meat
buey **beef**
carne picada **ground meat**
cerdo **pork**
chivo **kid**
chorizo **sausage seasoned with paprika**
chuleta **chop**
cochinillo/lechón asao **suckling pig**
conejo **rabbit**
cordero **lamb**
costilla **rib**
entrecot **beef rib steak**
filete **steak**
abalí **wild boar**
jamón **ham**

jamón cocido **cooked ham**
jamón serrano **cured ham**
lomo **loin**
morcilla **black pudding**
pierna **leg**
riñones **kidneys**
salchichón **sausage**
sesos **brains**
solomillo **fillet steak**
ternera **veal or young beef**
lengua **tongue**
a la brasa **charcoal grilled**
al horno **roast**
a la plancha **grilled**
asado **roast**
bién hecho **well done**
en salsa **in sauce**
en su punto **medium**
estofado **stew**
frito **fried**
parrillada **mixed grill**
pinchito **skewer**
poco hecho **rare**
relleño **stuffed**

Pollo/Poultry
codorniz **quail**
faisán **pheasant**
pavo **turkey**
pato **duck**
perdiz **partridge**
pintada **guinea fowl**
pollo **chicken**

Pescado/Fish
almeja **clam**
anchoas **anchovies**
anguila **eel**
atún **tuna**
bacalao **cod**
besugo **red bream**
bogavante **lobster**
boquerones **fresh anchovies**
caballa **mackerel**
calamar **squid**
cangrejo **crab**
caracola **sea snail**
cazón **dogfish**
centollo **spider crab**
chopito **baby cuttlefish**
cigala **Dublin Bay prawn/scampi**
dorada **gilt head bream**
fritura **mixed fry**
gamba **shrimp/prawn**
jibia **cuttlefish**
langosta **spiny lobster**
langostino **large prawn**
lenguado **sole**
lubina **sea bass**

mariscada **mixed shellfish**
mariscos **shellfish**
mejillón **mussel**
merluza **hake**
mero **grouper**
ostión **Portuguese oyster**
ostra **oyster**
peregrina **scallop**
pescadilla **small hake**
pez espada **swordfish**
pijota **hake**
pulpo **octopus**
rape **monkfish**
rodaballo **turbot**
salmón **salmon**
salmonete **red mullet**
sardina **sardine**
trucha **trout**

VEGETABLES/CEREALS/SALADS
vegetables **verduras**
ajo **garlic**
alcachofa **artichoke**
apio **celery**
arroz **rice**
berenjena **eggplant/aubergine**
cebolla **onion**
champiñon **mushroom**
col **cabbage**
coliflor **cauliflower**
crudo **raw**
ensalada **salad**
espárrago **asparagus**
espinaca **spinach**
garbanzo **chick pea**
guisante **pea**
haba **broad bean**
habichuela **bean**
judía **green bean**
lechuga **lettuce**
lenteja **lentil**
maíz **corn/maize**
menestra **cooked mixed vegetables**
patata **potato**
pepino **cucumber**
pimiento **pepper**
puerro **leek**
rábano **radish**
seta **wild mushroom**
tomate **tomato**
zanahoria **carrot**

FRUIT AND DESSERTS
fruta **fruta**
aguacate **avocado**
albaricoque **apricot**
cereza **cherry**

ciruela **plum**
frambuesa **raspberry**
fresa **strawberry**
granada **pomegranate**
higo **fig**
limón **lemon**
mandarina **tangerine**
manzana **apple**
melocotón **peach**
melón **melon**
naranja **orange**
pasa **raisin**
pera **pear**
piña **pineapple**
plátano **banana**
pomelo **grapefruit**
sandía **watermelon**
uva **grape**

flan **caramel custard**
helado **ice cream**
natilla **custard**
pastel **pie**
postre **dessert**
queso **cheese**
tarta **cake**

Further Reading

General

Adventure Guide to Puerto Rico, by Harry S. Pariser, Adventure Guide Series (1997). Traveling around the island with the author takes the reader to out-of-the-way spots as well as to the best known. As the title implies, this guide focuses on the unusual. Pariser explores parks, reserves and the offshore islands, while including fine dining and exclusive accommodations. Easy to read. Well-written impressions of Puerto Rico should motivate the reader to explore the island.
The Disenchanted Island: Puerto Rico and the United States in the Twentieth Century, by Ronald Fernandez, Praeger Publishing (1996). A study of the Puerto Rico/United States relationship which goes back to the beginning of the 20th century. The author asserts that despite the island's economic progress it is heavily dependent on the US. Fernandez, who is a professor of sociology at Central Connecticut State University – as well as the author of *Los Macheteros, the Violent Struggle for Puerto Rican Independence*, places emphasis on the independence movement, claiming that the US has hampered the Puerto Rican economy and has contributed to its social problems. Fernandez illustrates his claims with supportive figures.
Island Paradox: Puerto Rico in the 1990s (1990 Census Research Series), by Francisco Rivera-Batiz/Carlos E. Santiago, Russell Sage Foundation (1997). Rapid improvement in social and economic conditions also gives rise to problems of unemployment and wide divergences in income levels. The authors claim that growth brought about by United States assistance also has led to

difficulties in establishing international connections, and improving living conditions has its drawbacks as political ideals may take a back seat. A must-read to better understand Puerto Rico's economic and social dilemma.
Puerto Rico: A Political and Cultural History, by Arturo Morales Carrion, W.W. Norton and Co. (1984). Island history as interpreted by Puerto Rico's leading historian. Carrion traces Puerto Rico from the early days of Spanish rule in the 1600s to the 1980s when modern trends considerably changed the way of life. Carrion is assisted by four other contributing writers. The text tends to favor the Commonwealth political status while ignoring many achievements of the Statehood Movement.
Puerto Rico: A Profile by Kal Wagenheim, Hudson Publishing (1974). Highly regarded history of the island. Told in simple language by a journalist who spent more than a decade on the island. Wagenheim is assisted by his wife, Olga Jimenez, who is well-prepared in relating lifestyles in Puerto Rico. The simple text has been used by high schools in their history classes. One of the few books that tells the story of the *jibaro* (Puerto Rico's country peasant) in an accurate fashion.
Puerto Rico Mio, Four Decades of Change, photographs by Jack Delano (1990). A collector's item for lovers of Puerto Rico. Black and white photographs tell the story of Puerto Rico from the 1940s to the 1980s by one who loved the island and its people dearly.
Teodoro Moscoso and Puerto Rico's Operation Bootstrap, by A.W. Maldonado, University Press of Florida (1997). Puerto Rico made giant strides to pick itself up economically and socially in the 1950s to reach its secure position today. Operation Bootstrap was the brainchild of Teodoro Moscoso, who steered the island out of the backwaters of poverty into the sea of prosperity. The program was successful in that it attracted large groups of capital investors which

brought industrialization to the island. Moscoso, who rose to head of the Alliance for Progress, has his professional life recounted here.
Kicking Off the Bootstraps: Environment, Development and Community Power in Puerto Rico, by Deborah Berman Santana (1996). In the modern era, Puerto Rico faces new challenges, such as control of the environment, which has undergone major changes during the island's industrial period. Community relations has taken on a completely different look as populations shift from country to city and a measure of prosperity bring drastic changes at various social levels.

Fiction

Family Installments, by Edward Rivera. New York: Morrow (1982)
Macho Camacho's Beat, by Luis Rafael Sánchez. New York: Pantheon (1981)

Cuisine

Puerto Rican Dishes, by Berta Cabanillas and Carmen Ginorio. Río Piedras: Editorial de la Universidad de Puerto Rico (1993)
The Spirit of Puerto Rican Rum: Recipes and Recollections, by Blanche Gelabert. San Juan: Discovery Press (1992)
Puerto Rican Cuisine in America, by Oswald Rivera. New York: Four Walls Eight Windows (1993)
Rice and Beans and Tasty Things: A Puerto Rican Cookbook, by Dora Pomano. San Juan (1986)
Puerto Rican Cookery, by Carmen Aboy Valldejuli. Gretna: Pelican Publishing (1993)

Arts, Customs & Social

Puerto Rican Woman, by Edna Acosta-Belén and Eli H. Christensen. New York: Praeger (1979)
Divided Borders: Essays on Puerto Rican Identity, by Juan Flores. Houston: Arte Publico (1993)
Puerto Rican Culture: An Introduction, by Raoul Gordon. New

York: Gordon Books (1982)
Antonin Nechodoma, Architect 1877–1928, by Thomas S. Marvel. Gainesville: University of Florida Press (1994)
Puerto Rico 1900: Turn-of-the-Century Architecture in the Hispanic Caribbean, by Jorge Rigau. New York: Rizzoli (1992)
Trapped: Puerto Rico Families and Schizophrenia, by Lloyd H. Rogler and August B. Hollingshead. Maplewood: Waterfront Press (1985)
When I Was Puerto Rican, by Esmeralda Santiago. Reading: Addison-Wesley Publishing (1993)

Other Insight Guides

Apa Publications offer the discerning traveler more than 400 titles in its three series of travel guide books. *Insight Guides* provide a full cultural background and top quality photography; *Insight Compact Guides* combine portability with encyclopedic attention to detail and are ideal for on-the-spot reference; and *Insight Pocket Guides* highlight recommendations by a local host and include a full-size pull-out map.

The vivid text and spectacular photography in Insight Guide: Caribbean is just one of the well-informed, up-to-date titles covering the region. It brings to life the serenity, the allure, the diversity of this part of the world – from the beauty of a Caribbean sunset to the charm of the Caribees.

Insight Guide: Belize
Discover the beauty of Belize with
the aid of breathtaking photography
and articles written by local
experts.

Insight Guide: Costa Rica
This is a fascinating book full of
creative pictures and interesting
information about this small island
of Costa Rica, its people and
customs.

Insight Pocket Guide: Bahamas
comes complete with a pullout map.
The book, written by a local host, is
based on a series of itineraries
designed to help visitors get the
most out of the Bahamas during a
short stay. The tours divide
between four main bases: New
Providence & Paradise Island,
Eleuthera and the Family Islands
and Grand Bahama.
Other Caribbean titles in the Pocket
series are Insight Pocket Guide:
Barbados and Insight Pocket Guide:
Jamaica, again written by local
hosts and with pullout maps.

A perfect companion, *Insight Pocket
Guide: Puerto Rico* offers a series
of tailor-made itineraries designed
to help readers get the most out of
Puerto Rico during a short stay. It
also includes a large-scale pull-out
map which can be used
independently from the guide.

Insight Compact Guide titles which
highlight destinations in this region
include Bahamas, Barbados, Costa
Rica, Cuba, the Dominican Republic
and Jamaica.

ART & PHOTO CREDITS

All photography by Bill Wassman
except for:
APA Photo Agency 87
Archive Photos 46
Tony Arruza 1, 2B, 4B, 18/19, 28,
45, 49, 50, 59, 68, 70, 71, 74,
92, 93, 97, 100, 103, 104/105,
114/115, 121T, 130, 131,
152/153, 156T, 157, 159, 161,
162, 172/173, 174, 178, 180,
181, 183, 185, 186, 188, 189T,
190, 191, 192/193, 197, 202,
202T, 214, 215T, 224, 224T, 225,
231, 239, 240L, 241, 241T, 253,
253T, 254, 255, 256
Mary Evans Picture Library 20, 27
Robert Fried 51, 85, 90/91, 119,
132T, 168T, 180T, 199T, 217, 218,
221, 248T, 251, 252
Stephen Frink 98/99
Glyn Genin 108/109
Robert Harding Picture Library 14
Hulton Getty 34
Image Bank 21, 43, 95
**Courtesy of Jamaica National
Library** 36
Kobal Collection 47
Bob Krist 2/3, 5BL, 57, 58, 69,
75, 77, 80/81, 82, 84, 94, 102,
122, 123, 125, 127, 143, 144,
145, 154, 158, 160T, 164/165,
171, 187, 223, 226, 227,
244/245
Larry Luxner 200, 240R, 250
Edmond Van Hoorick 6/7
**Reproduced from *Historia de
Puerto Rico,* by Salvador Bran**
34/35, 37, 38/39, 41

Picture Spreads

Pages 64/65: *Top Row, left to
right*: Tony Perrottet, Tony Arruza,
Bob Krist, Jose R. Channón
Bottom Row, left to right: Bob Krist,
Tony Perrottet, Tony Arruza
Pages 88/89: *Top Row, left to
right*: Bill Wassman, Tony Arruza,
Tony Arruza, Bill Wassman
Bottom Row, left to right: Bob Krist,
Bill Wassman, Tony Arruza, Tony
Arruza
Pages 150/151: *Top Row, left to
right*: Bill Wassman, Bill Wassman,
Private Archive
Centre Row, left to right: Bill
Wassman, Courtesy of Rum of
Puerto Rico
Bottom Row, left to right: Courtesy
of Rum of Puerto Rico, Bill
Wassman, Bill Wassman
Pages 208/209: *Top Row, left to
right*: Tony Perrottet, Bill Wassman,
Tony Arruza, Martin Rosefeldt/APA
Bottom Row, left to right: Tony
Arruza, Bill Wassman, Bill
Wassman, Tony Arruza

Map Production Berndtson &
Berndtson Productions.
© 1999 Apa Publications GmbH & Co.
Verlag KG (Singapore branch)

INSIGHT GUIDE
PUERTO RICO

Cartographic Editor **Zoë Goodwin**
Production **Stuart A Everitt**
Design Consultants
Carlotta Junger, Graham Mitchener
Picture Research
Hilary Genin, Monica Allende

Index

Numbers in italics refer to photographs

a

Abercromby, Ralph 33, 129
Adjuntas 242
Africans 60–1, 155–6, 221
  food 75, 76
  language 69
  music 69, 93
  religion 16, 65, 156, 221
  slavery *see main entry*
agriculture 39, 46, 169, *176*, 189, 195
  avocados 243, 247
  bananas *185*, *209*, 243, 247
  cattle 29, 30, 33, *59*, 155, 215, 251
  coconuts 247
  coffee *see main entry*
  conducos 24
  European 76
  fruit *54–5*, 76, *176*, 177–8, *185*, *209*, 243, 247
  ginger 29, 30
  grains 247
  horses 30, 33, *52–3*, *214*, 215, 251
  oranges 243
  papayas 247
  pineapples *176*, 177–8
  plantains *54–5*, 76, 209
  plantations 29, 223, *241*, 243
  slavery *see main entry*
  sugar *see main entry*
  sweet potatoes 247
  Taíno 24
  tobacco 29, 33
  Tropical Agricultural Research Station 199
Aguada 33, 196
Aguadilla *192–3*, 196, *197*
Aguas Buenas *231*, 233
Aguirre 170
Aibonito 236, 237
air travel 144, 247, 250
Albizu Campos, Pedro 42
alcohol *see* **food and drink; rum**
Alomar, Roberto 47, 101
Alomar, Sandy 101
Alonso, Manuel A. 69–70
Añasco *70*
Añasco, Luis de 27
Anthony, Marc 94
Arawaks *see* **Indians: Arawaks**
Archeology *see* **Indians**

architecture
  Arabian 124, 218
  Arecibo 180
  Art Deco 121–2, 141
  baroque 124
  Colegio de Arquitectos 226
  Gothic 124, 195, 206–7
  haciendas 206, 207, 223
  medieval 124
  National Register of Historic Places 207
  neo-classical 124
  Ponce 217, 218, 219, *221*, 223
  San Germán 195, 206–7
  San Juan *118*, 119, 120, 121–2, 124, 129, 130–1, 139, 141, 145–6, *256*
  Spanish colonial *52–3*, *118*, 119, *121*, 124, 129, 180, 185
  timber 180
  Yauco *224*, *225*, 226
Arecibo 60, *68*, 69, 111, 178–81
  Alcaldía 180
  architecture 180
  industry 48
  karst 183–5
  lighthouse *180*
  markets *181*
  nationalism 46
  Observatory 181–3
  Plaza Luis Muñoz Rivera 180–1
  restaurants 180
  shopping 180, 181
  smuggling 33
Arenales 195
Arroyo 170
arts and crafts 47, 63, 83–6
  see also names of individual artists
  Centro Nacional de Artes Populares y Artesanías 126
  ceramics 83
  fairs, festivals 88, 149, 221, 238
  folk 84, 88–9, 90–1, 94, *213*
  galleries 83, *84*, *85*, 86
  hammocks *88*, *213*
  Indian *24–5*, 178
  Institute of Puerto Rican Culture 83, 85, 88, 124, 126, 130, 131, 139, 219
  jewelry 88
  markets 88
  masks *see* **festivals**
  modelling *88–9*
  mundillo 88

  museums 83–4, 85, 86, 130, 131, 149, 213, 222, 235
  Operation Serenity 46–7
  painting 63, *82*, 83, 85–6, 88, *89*, 206, 222
  poster-making 46–7, 86
  printmaking 86
  santos 83, 84, 88, *127*, *207*
  sculpture 63, *80–1*, 86, 88, *128*, 129, 131, 241
  weaving *213*
automobiles 49, 57, 59, 60
autonomy
  see **politics**: independence
Avellanet, Chucho 94

b

Bacardí family 148–9
Baerga, Carlos 101
Baez, Myrna 86, *87*
ballet 94
Balosi, John 86
Barceloneta 48
Barranquitas 237–8, *238*
Bayamón 77–8, 149
beaches *255*
  Arroyo 170
  Balneario Las Cucharas 224
  Balneario Lucia 169
  Cataño 149
  Culebra 61, *248*, *251*, 253
  Dorado 175–6
  El Combate *66–7*, 204
  El Ojo Del Buey 175
  Fajardo 161
  Flamenco 61, *251*, 253
  Guánica Forest Reserve 226
  Icacos 163
  Isabela 195
  Jobos 195
  Luquillo 160
  Media Luna 249
  Navio 249
  Palmas del Mar 167
  Patillas 170
  Playa Boquerón 197, *203*, 203–4
  Playa Buyé 203
  Playa de Guayanilla 225
  Playa de Vega Baja 176–7
  Playa Dorado Sardinera 175
  Playa El Convento 162
  Playa El Tuque 224
  Playa Espinar 195
  Playa Guajataca 190
  Playa Humacao 167
  Playa Mar Chiquita *6–7*, 178
  Playa Sardinera 161

Playa Soroco 162
Playa Tortuguero 177
Ponce 224
Puerto Maunabo 170
Punta Jagüey 195
Punta Tuna *169*, 170
Rincón 197–8
Salinas *212*
San Juan *110*, *141*, 142, *143*, 144–5
Sun Bay *246*, 249
Vieques *246*, 247, *248*, 249
Benitez, Lucesita 94
Benitez, Wilfredo 102
Benítez, José Gautier 232
Bermuda Triangle 250
birds *see* **wildlife**
Bithorn, Hiram 47, 103, 146
Blades, Rubén 96, 97
Blanco, Sylvia 86
Boca de Cangrejos 33, 145, 155
Boquerón 195, 203–4
Borinquen 23, 69
Botello, Angel 86
Britain
    American War of Independence 34
    English invasions 31–2, 33, 123–4, 129, 130, 132–3, 134, 141, 206
    piracy 30, 31, 247, 250

c

Cabo Rojo *8–9*, 33, 203, 204
Caguana Indian Ceremonial Ballpark *22*, 23, 84, 101, 243
Caguas 48, 69, 231–3
Caja de Muertos 217, 223–4
Cajiga, Luis 86
Camacho, Hector "Macho" 47
Cambalache National Forest 184
Campeche, José 85, *124*, 131, 206, 207
camping *see* **sport**
Camuy 186–8
Caribbean National Forest *see* **El Yunque**
Caribs *see* **Indians:** Caribs
Carite (Guavate) Forest Reserve 235
Carmoega, Rafael 139
carnivals *see* **festivals**
Caro, Nydia 94
Carolina *see* **San Juan**
Carrión, Arturo Morales 147
Casals, Pablo 93, 94, 130, 147
Cataño 60, 121, 148–9
caves 23, 178, 187–8, 190,

231, 233, 243, 254
Cayey 235, *236*
Cayo Berbería 224
Cayo Morillito 223–4
Cayo Santiago 167–8
Cepeda, Orlando 47, 70–1, 101
Cerro de Punta 241, 242
Cerro Maravilla *240*, 240–1
Chacón, Isabel 96
Chayanne 94
Cidra 234
Clemente, Roberto 47, 70–1, 101, 146
climate 15, 157, 160, 167, 217, 223, 236, 251
Clinton, Bill *and* **Hillary** 50
Coamo 214
Coamo Springs *41*, 214–15
coffee 57, *185*, 206
    haciendas 207, *242*
    hurricanes 40
    imported 76
    plantations 223, *241*, 242
    Yauco *224*, 225–6
Colón, Diego 27–8
Colón, Willie 96–7
Columbus, Christopher
    expeditions 15, 23, 27, *28*, 125–6, 131, 195, 201, 247, 250, 254
    statues *119*, 201
Condado *see* **San Juan**
Cofresí, Roberto 149, 203
coral reefs 162, 163, 195, 217, 249, 251–2
Cordero, Angel, Jr 47
Cordillera Central 111, *228–30*, 231–43
    see also individual placenames
Creoles 29
crime 49, 57, 59–60, 61, 63, 134, 141
cruises 120, 121, *147*, 205
Cruz, Celia 97
Cuchilla de Pandura 169, 170
Culebra 111, 247, 250–3
    agriculture 251
    beaches 61, *248, 251*, 253
    Cayo Luis Peña 253
    climate 251
    coral 251–2
    Culebrita 253
    Dewey 251, 252
    Ensenada Honda 252–3
    ferries 61, 161, 252
    fishing 251
    Flamenco Beach 61, 250, *251*, 253
    hotels 252

hurricanes 158, 252
lizards 223, 253
Mount Resaca 253
National Wildlife Refuge 251
Pirate's Cay 252–3
Pirate's Quay 250
population 60, 252
restaurants 252
Taínos 250
US Navy bases 251
wildlife 251–2
Cumberland, Earl of 31–2, 123–4, 133

d

dance 57, 64, *65*, 69, 94, 95, *96*
Delano, Jack 94
D'Esopo, Jan *80–1*
Dewey 251, 252
Díaz, Justino 94
Dona Juana Recreational Area 240
Dorado 175–6, *177*
Drake, Francis 31, 123, 132–3
drugs 47, 59, 75, 179

e

earthquakes 195, 202, 219
economy 57
    see also **industry**
    agriculture *see main entry*
    Operation Bootstrap 46, 47, 178–9
    Section 936 47–9, 178–9, 200
    Spain and 32–3, 34
    USA and 16, 40, 41–2, 46–9, 200
education 39, 49
    see also **University of Puerto Rico**
El Conquistador Resort & Country Club 162
El Gran Combo 96, 97, 190
El Yunque *152–3*, *156*, 157–60
    camping 159
    El Portal Center *158*, 159
    flora *156*, 158, *160*, 208, *208–9*
    hiking trails 158, 159–60, *161*
    La Coca Falls 159
    La Mina Falls *154*, 159
    rainfall 157, 208
    trees 158, 159
    wildlife 157–8
Emeterío Betances, Ramón 37, 38, 39, 40, 186

emigration 46, 49
England *see* Britain
Esperanza 248
Espinosa, Susan 86
Estrada, Erik 47
exports *see* economy

f

fairs 149, 221, 238
Fajardo 33, 61, 161, *163*
family life 63
Feliciano, José 47
Fernandez, Gigi 102
Ferré, Luis A. 222
Ferrer, José 47
Ferrer, Rafael 86
festivals 58, 64–5
  Aibonito 237
  asaltos 95–6
  Casals 93, 94
  craft 88
  flower 237
  Hatillo 64, 188–9
  Indian 242
  Jayuya 242
  Juana Díaz 64, 215
  Loíza 64, 89, *155*, 156–7
  Maricao 64
  masks *17, 64–5, 89, 155,*
    156–7, 189, 221
  mourning 69
  music 93, 94, 130
  Ponce 64, 89, 221
  religious *17,* 64, *64–5,* 65, 75,
    77, 89, 94, *155,* 156–7,
    188–9, 215, 221, 248
  San Germán 64
  San Juan *57, 64, 65,* 93, 94,
    130
  San Sebastián *62–3, 97*
  sugar 169
  theater 219
  vejigantes 17, 64–5, *89, 155,*
    156–7
  Vieques 248
  Yabucoa 169
  Yauco 64
films 47, 143, 190, 236, 249
  West Side Story 46, *47*
flag *40,* 61, *130*
flora 158, *160,* 208–9, 226,
  242, 247, 253
  bindweed 223
  Botanical Gardens 147, 199,
    208, *209*
  bougainvillea *123,* 208
  cacti 254
  ferns *156,* 158, 242

gardenias 208
herbs 223
hibiscus 208
jasmine 208
oleander 208
orchids 156, *208*
poinciana *208–9*
see also national forests/
  parks/nature reserves; trees
food and drink 57, 75–9
  see also agriculture;
    restaurants
  adobo 58–9, 79
  African 75, 76
  alcapurrias 59
  arepas 253
  arroz con guinea/pollo 77,
    95–6
  asaltos 95–6
  asopao 78
  barbecued 144
  beans 58, 77
  beef 76, 79
  beer 78
  bread 75, 149, 253
  breadfruit 209
  carnecita 79
  cassava 29, 75
  chicharrón 77–8, 149
  chicken 59, 77, 78, 95–6, 149
  Chinese 78
  Christmas 77
  coco frío 155
  coffee 40, 57, 76, 79, *185,*
    206, 226
  comida Criolla 58
  coquíto 58
  corn 29, 75, 77
  desserts 77, 188
  fast-order 78
  festivals 64
  fish *44, 45,* 47, 59, 75, 77,
    78, 149, 160, 161, 189,
    199, 200, 201, 213, 224
  flan 77
  fritters 77
  fruit 29, *54–5,* 58, 76, 77, 78,
    176, 177–8, 188, *209,*
    234, 243
  German 78
  guava con queso 77
  herbs 76
  Italian 78, 122
  Japanese 78, 122
  lechón asado 58, 69, 70,
    72–3, 77, 95
  majarete 77
  maví 70
  meat 59, 76, 77, 79

Mexican 78
milk 188
mofongo 79, 201, 209
pasteles 58, 77
pernil 58
piña colada 126, 151
piñon 76
pork 59, 78
rice 29, 58, 76, 77, 188
rum *see main entry*
sandwiches 78
seasoning 76–7
serenata 77
shellfish 47, *60,* 75, 77, 149,
  160, 213, 247
sofrito 77
sorrullos 77
Spanish 75–6, 78, 148
spices 29, 30, 76–7, *142*
Taíno 24, 75
Thai 78
tostones 209
toytiyas 70
tuna *45,* 189, 199, 200
vegetables 29, 58, *74,* 75, 76,
  77, 95
yautías 77
yuccas 95
Foraker Act 40–1
Ford, Gerald R. 251
forests *see* national
  forests/parks/nature reserves;
  rainforests; trees
Frade, Ramon 86
France 15, 30, 33, 34, 206
fruit *see* agriculture; food and
  drink

g

gambling *58,* 102, *106–7,* 120,
  121, 127, 141, 175, 214
gardens *see* flora
gold 24, 27, 28
Gomez, Rubén 101
Gomez, Wilfredo 102
Gonzalez, Juan "Igor" 101
González, Palacios 236
Guajataca Forest Reserve 184,
  190
Guánica 195, 224, 226
Guánica Forest Reserve 208,
  209, 226
Guayama *43, 52–3,* 170
Guayanilla 224, 225
Guaynabo 69
Guilarte Forest Reserve 242
Guzman, Pedro 94

h

haciendas 206, 207, 223, *242*
Hatillo 64, 188–9
health 49, 59, 147–8, 159, 214–15, 242
Hendrikszoon, Boudewijn 32, 124
Hernández Colón, Rafael 47, 60, 218
hidalgos 28
hiking see sport
Homar, Lorenzo 86
Hormigueros 202–3
hotels
　Adjuntas 242
　Aguadilla 195
　Coamo Springs 214–15
　Culebra 252
　Dorado 175–6, *177*
　El Conquistador 162
　El Guajataca 190
　Fajardo 161
　Hacienda Gripiñas 242
　Hacienda Juanita 243
　Maricao 243
　paradores 190, 195, 214, 242, 243
　Rincón 198
　San Juan 121, 127, 141, 142
　Vieques 248
　Vistamar 190
Humacao 48, *51*, 167
hurricanes 16, 39–40, 42, 50, 69, 158, 232

i

Iglesias, Pablo 42
immigration 15–16, 29
　see also slavery
independence
　see politics: independence
Indians
　Arawaks 15, 69
　art *24–5*, 178
　Caribs 60, 69, 75
　caves 178, 187–8
　Museo del Indio, San Juan 24, 130
　Spain and 15, 24, 27, 28–9, 69, 75
　Taínos 15, 23–4, 60, 75
　agriculture 24
　archeology 84
　art *24–5*
　batey 23, 84, 101, 243
　crafts 24
　Caguana Ceremonial Ballpark *22*, 23, 84, 101, 243

Caguas/Caguax 232
Columbus and 201
Culebra 250
drugs 75
festivals 242
food 24, 75, 242
gold 24
Isla Mona 254
Jayuya 241, 242
Mayagüez 201–2
museum 248
music 94, 242
religion 16, 23, 65, 75, 214, 232, 243
slavery 28–9
Spain and 15, 24, 27, 28–9, 232
sport 23, 84, 101, 242, 243
Tibes Ceremonial Park 23, *85*, 101, 223
Vieques 247, 248, 250
villages 23
industry 169
　see also economy
　agricultural machinery 179
　chemicals 169
　Coca-Cola 234
　coffee *see main entry*
　diamond-cutting 233
　electronics 233
　glass 233
　leather 233
　oil 169
　Operation Bootstrap 46, 178–9
　paper 179
　Pepsi-Cola 234
　pharmaceuticals 48, 169, 179
　plastics 179, 233
　rum *see main entry*
　Section 936 47–9, 178–9, 200
　Seven-Up 234
　shoes 195
　sporting goods 179
　sugar *see main entry*
　textiles 169, 179, 195, 233
　tobacco 233, 235
　tuna *44*, 199, 200
Isabela 195
Isabel Segunda 247
Isla Magueyes 205
Isla Mona 111, 254

j–k

Jayuya 48, 241–2
jíbaros 15, 42, 231, 243
　El Gíbaro 69–70
　"Jíbaro Jazz" 94
　music 94, 95, 96
　pava 45
　The Jíbaro 86
Jimenez, Juan Ramón 147
Jobos Bay 170, 213
Jobos Beach 195
Juana Díaz 64, 215
Juliá, Raul 47
karst 183–5, 187–8, 208, 243

l

La Borinqueña 42, 61, 63, 69, 95
Lago dos Bocas 184, *191*, 243
Lago Guineo 240
Laguna Guaniquilla 203
Laguna Joyuda 203
Laguna Tortuguero 177
Lake Caonillas *184*
Lake Cidra 234
Lake Guajataca 184, 190
Lake Loíza 233
Lake Toa Vaca 239
languages 16, 60, 69–71, 221
Lares 111, 185–6, *186, 188*
Las Cabezas de San Juan Nature Preserve 162–3
Lavoe, Hector 96
lighthouses
　Arecibo *180*
　Cabo Rojo *8–9*, 195, 204
　Culebrita 253
　"El Faro" 162
　Isla Mona 253, 254
　Port of San Juan *132*, 133
　Punta Mulas 247
　Punta Tuna 170
　Rincón 198
literacy 39, 49
literature 57, 63, 69–70, 125–6, 147, 232
Loíza Aldea 23, 60–1, 64, 89, 93, 155–7
Luquillo 70, 77, 160

m

Mameyes 158
Manatí 48, 177–8, 184
Maricao 48, 64, 243
　Fish Hatchery 243
　Forest Reserve 243

Marín, Augusto 86
markets *59, 234*
  Arecibo *181*
  San Juan 88, *129*, 143, 147
  San Sebastián *71, 190*
Martin, Ricky 47, 94
Martorell, Antonio 86
Mayagüez 69, 111, 195, 198–202, *199*
  Alcaldía 201
  Columbus 201
  earthquakes 202
  food 201
  independence movement 38
  Isla Raton 201
  Joyuda 201
  Mayagüez Mall 199
  Mayagüez Zoo 201
  Plaza Colón 201
  Tropical Agricultural Research Station 199, 208
  Taínos 201–2
  tuna *45*, 189, 199, 200, 201
  University of Puerto Rico 199
McKinley, President 40, 41
Mendez Miller, Carmina 103
Menéndez de Valdes, Diego 31
Menudo 96
mestizos 29
Mona *see* **Isla Mona**
Moreno, Rita 46, *47*
Morgan, Henry 250
Morse, Samuel B. 170, 220
Muñoz Marín, Luis *21*, 45, 46, 63, 94, 178, 237
  memorials 144, 181
Muñoz Rivera, Luis 39, 41, 45, 237
  memorials *139*, 141, 145, 180–1, 219
museums 83
  Casa Blanca, San Juan 134
  Casa del Libro, San Juan 125–6
  Casa del Rey, Dorado 175
  Casa Roig, Humacao 167
  Cayey University 235
  Coamo 214
  El Fortin Conde de Mirasol, Vieques 247
  Esperanza, Vieques 248
  Graphic Arts, San Juan 86
  La Princesa, San Juan 129
  Muñoz Rivera, Barranquitas 237, 238
  Museo de Arte de Ponce 83–4, 85, *86*, 213, 222
  Museo de Arte e Historia de San Juan 83, 134

Museo de la Historia de Ponce 219–20
Museo de las Américas, San Juan 131
Museo del Indio, San Juan 24, 130
Museo Felisa Rincón, San Juan 129
Museo Francisco Oller, Bayamón 149
Museo Pablo Casals, San Juan 130
Museum of Pharmacy, San Juan 130
Parque de las Ciencias, Bayamón 149
Porta Coeli, San Germán 206–7
San Juan Museum of History and Art 130
University of Puerto Rico, San Juan 83, 84, 85
music 57, 63, 64, 93–7, *250*
  African 69, *92*, 93, 95, 97
  aquinaldo 95, 96
  bands *171*, 239
  bomba 93
  Casals 93, 94, 130, 147
  Conservatory 94
  danza 95
  décima 96
  festivals 93, 94, 130
  instruments *89, 92*, 93, 94, 96
  jazz 47, 94, 95
  La Borinqueña 42, 61, 63, 69, 95
  merengue 96
  Mi Terra Borincana 57
  opera 94
  plena 93, 94
  salsa 47, 93, 94, 95, 96–7, 190, 232
  Spanish 93, 95
  symphony concerts *90–1*, 94
  Taíno 94
  traditional *92*, 94

n

national anthem 42, 61, 63, 69, 95
national forests/parks/nature reserves
  Boquerón 203, 204
  Caja de Muertos 217, 223–4
  Cambalache 184, 208
  Carite (Guavate) 235
  Cayo Santiago 167–8

Culebra 251
El Morro 132–3
El Yunque *152–4, 156*, 157–60
Guajataca 184, 190, 208
Guilarte 242
Guánica 208, *209*, 226
karstic 184, 208
Laguna Joyuda 203
Laguna Tortuguero 177
Las Cabezas de San Juan 162–3
Maricao 243
Río Abajo 184, 208
Toro Negro 240
Vega Alta 184, 208
nationalism
  see **politics**: independence
nature reserves *see* **national forests/parks/nature reserves**
Nazario, Ednita 94
Netherlands 30, 32, 124, 130, 206
Nixon, Richard M. 251
North 175–90
  see also individual placenames
Northeast 155–63
  see also individual placenames

o

O'Daly, Tomas 134
Oller, Francisco 85–6, 149
O'Neill, Mari Mater 86
Operation Bootstrap 46, 47, 178–9
Operation Serenity 46–7
O'Reilly, Alejandro 33, 134
Ovando, Nicolas de 27

p–q

Palmas del Mar 167
Palmer 158
Parguera 195, 205
Pasarell, Charlie 102
Patillas 170
phosphorescence 195, 205, 250
Piñero, Jesús 45
Piñones 145, 155
piracy 30, 31, 149, 161, 203, 247, 248, 250, 254
plantations 29, 223, *241*, 243
plants *see* **flora**
Playa ... *see* **beaches**
politics 21, 49
  colonialism 40–1, 45
  commonwealth status 16, 45–6, 49–50, 182, 226

El Año Terrible 236
"Grito de Lares" 38, 185–6, *186*
independence 37–9, 40, 41, 42, 46, *49*, 50, 185–6, *186*, 236, 238–9, 240–1
Muñoz Rivera Museum, Barranquitas 237, 238
Partido Independentista Puertorriqueño (PIP) 50, 238–9
Partido Nuevo Progressivo (PNP) 50
Partido Democratico Popular (PDP) 45, 50
statehood 46, 50, 101
Ponce 60, 111, 195, 213, 215–23, *227*
Alcaldía 219
architecture 217, 218, 219, *221*, 223
beaches 224
Caja de Muertos 217, 223–4
Calle F.P. Duperan (Comercio) 218–19, 220
Carnival 64, 89
Casa Armstrong-Poventud *218*, 219
Castillo Serrallés *221*, 223
Cathedral of Our Lady of Guadalupe 219
El Vigia *217, 220*, 221
festivals 89, 219, 221
Fox Delicias Mall 220, *221*
Hacienda Buena Vista 223
markets 220
La Massacre 42
Museo de Arte de Ponce 83–4, 85, *86*, 213, 222
Museo de la Historia de Ponce 219–20
music 94
name 218
nationalism 46
Parque de Bombas *210–11*, 218, 219
Parque Tricentenario 220
Playa de Ponce 218, 223
Playa El Tuque 224
Plaza Central 219
Plaza del Caribe 220
Plaza del Mercado 220
"Ponce en Marcha" 218
shops 220, *221*
sport 219
Teatro La Perla 219
Tibes Indian Ceremonial Park 23, *85*, 101, 223
tuna 200

weather 217, 223
Ponce de León, Juan 15, *20, 26*, 27–8, 30, 232
San Juan 30, 127, 130, 131, 134, 149
population 15–16, 29, 33, 37, 39, 42, 49, 60–1
Power, Ramón 86
Power Giralt, Ramón 33–4
public transport
ferries 61, 121, 161, 223, 247
free 120
guaguas 170
públicos 119, *219*, 253
Puente, Tito 47, 95
Puerto Maunabo 170
Puerto Real 203
Punta Guaniquilla 203
Punta Jagüey 204
Punta Tuna *169*, 170
pyrodinium bahamense 205, 250
Quebradillas 190
Quijano, Nicky 86
Quiñones, José María 37

r

rainforests 157, 247
Ramey *103*
Rancho Pepón 234–5
religion
African 16, 65, 156, 221
Arawak 69
Christianity 16, 58, 77, 156, 232, *241*
see also **arts and crafts:** *santos*; **festivals:** religious
spiritualism 16
Taíno 16, 23, 65, 75, 214, 232
restaurants 59, 78
see also **food and drink**
Aibonito 236
Arecibo 180
colmados 184, 231, 239
Culebra 252
Dorado 175, 176
El Guajataca *parador* 190
El Taíno 188
fondas 59, 78, *79*, 143
friquitines 160
Lago dos Bocas 243
Lake Cidra 234
Las Cavernas 188
Los Chorros 243
Maunabo 170
Mayagüez 201
Palmas del Mar 167

Patillas 170
Playa Sardinera 161
quioscos 144
Rancho Pepón 234–5
Salinas 213, 214
San Juan *77*, 119, 121, 122, 126, 141, 142, 143, 146, 148, 149
Vieques 248
Rincón 197–8
Rincón de Gautier, Felisa "Dona Fela" 129
Río Abajo National Forest 184
Río Camuy Cave Park 187–8
Río de la Plata 238
Río Grande de Loíza 156
Río Guajataca 190
Río Piedras *see* San Juan
Rivera, Danny 94
Rivera, Geraldo 47
Rivera, José Manuel 57
Rodriguez, Ivan "Pudge" 101
Rodriguez, Juan "Chichi" 47, 102, 176
Roosevelt, Franklin D. 45, 214
Roosevelt, Theodore 39, 251
Roosevelt Roads 163
Rosa, José 86
Rosario, José "Chapo" 102
Ruiz, Noemi 86
rum 29, 34, 46, 69, 96, 150–1, 179
Bacardi 121, 148–9, 151
Ruta Panoramica 111, 169, 170, *235*, 235–6, 240, 243

s

Sabana Seca 61
Salinas *212*, 213–14, *215*
San Cristóbal Canyon *12–13*, 237
San Germán 64, 111, 195, 206–7
San Juan *14, 104–5, 114–15*, 119–49
adoquines 119, 121, 124
Alcaldía 122
Antiguo Asilo de Beneficienca 131–2
architecture *118*, 119, 120, 121–2, 124, 126–7, 129, 130–1, 139, 141, 145–6, *256*
Archives and General Library of Puerto Rico 139
art 85, 86, 88, 119, 121, 126, *128*, 129
Ateneo Puertorriqueno 141

Banco de Santander Building 145–6
Banco Popular de Puerto Rico 121–2, 146
beaches *110*, *141*, 142, *143*, 144–5
Biennial Graphic Art Exhibition 86
Botanical Gardens 147, 208, *209*
calesas 130
Calle del Cristo 124–8
Caparra Heights 60
Carnival *57*, *64*
Carolina 48, 144
Casa Blanca 24, 30, *32*, 134
Casa Candina 83
Casa de España 139
Casa de la Contrafuertes 86
Casa del Callejón 120
Casa del Libro 125–6
Casals Festival 93, 94
Casa Rosa (Rosada) 134, 226
casinos *58*, *106–7*, 120, 121, 127, 141
Centro de Bellas Artes Luis A. Ferré *84*, 94, 143
Centro Médico 147–8
Centro Nacional de Artes Populares y Artesanías 126
Coliseo Roberto Clemente 146
Condado *96*, *136–7*, 141–2, *144*
crime 60, 134, 141
Cristo Chapel *84*, *124*, 125
Cuartel de Ballajá 131
Dominican Convent 124, 130
El Boquerón 31
El Capitolio *138*, 139
El Gran Convento 127
El Morro 31, *32*, 123, 124, *131*, 132–3, *134, 135*
Estadio Hiram Bithorn 103, 146
festivals *57*, *64*, *65*, 93, 94, 130
Fort Buchanan 148
Fort Cañuelo 149
Fort San Gerónimo 141
founded 27, 30
Frente Portuario 121
Fuerte San Cristóbal *10–11*, *40*, 134
Galerías Botélo/Palomas 86
garitas 133
Graphic Arts Museum 86
Hato Rey 111, 103, 145–6
hotels 121, 127, 141, 142
Institute of Puerto Rican

Culture 83, 85, 88, 124, 126, 130, 131, 139, 219
Isla de Cabras 149
Isla Verde *143*, 144–5
La Fortaleza (Santa Catalina) 30–1, 123–4
La Perla 134
La Princesa 129
La Puente de San Antonio 31
La Rogativa *128*, 129
markets 88, *129*, 143, 147
Metropolitan 139–49
Museo de Arte e Historia de San Juan 83, 134
Museo de las Américas 131
Museo del Indio 24, 130
Museo Felisa Rincón 129
Museo Pablo Casals 130
Museum of Pharmacy 130
Ocean Park 142
Old Casino of Puerto Rico *106–7*, 120
Old City Wall 128
Old Town 119–34
Palo Seco 149
Parkville 60
Parque de las Palomas 124–5
Parque Luis Muñoz Rivera *139*, 141
Paseo de Diego 147
Paseo de la Princesa 88, 128–9
Plaza Colón 119–20
Plaza de Armas 94, 122
Plaza de la Dársena 88, 94
Plaza del Quinto Centenario 131
Plaza Las Américas 146
Plaza San José *129*, 130
population 60
Port 120–1, *147*
Port of San Juan Lighthouse *132*, 133
public transport 119, 120
Puerto de Tierra *138*, 139
Puerto Nuevo 148
Punta la Galiena *110*
Punta las Marias 144–5
Punta Salinas 149
quioscos 144
restaurants *77*, 119, 121, 122, 126, 141, 142, 143, 146, 148, 149
Río Piedras 85, 111, 145, 147–8, 208
San José Church 124, 130–1
San Juan Batista festival *65*
San Juan Cathedral 30, 124, 126–7, 131

San Juan Cemetery *133*, 133–4
San Juan Gate 128
San Juan Judicial Center 146
San Juan Museum of History and Art 130
Santa Elena 31
Santurce 33, 83, *84*, 94, 143
shops 83, 120, 121, 122, *144*, 146
sieges 33, 124, 129, 133
Tapia Theater 119
Torrimar 60
Totem Telurico 131
University of Puerto Rico *34*, 83, *84*, 85, 145, 147, 168
US Customs House 120–1
Yacht Club *108–9*
San Sebastián 111, 189–90
arts 190
battle 38
festivals *62–3*, *97*
markets *71*, 190
moto-cross racing *172–3*
plaza *189*
Santa Rosa, Gilberto "Gilbertito" 96
Santurce *see* **San Juan**
separatism *see* **independence**
Serrallés, Don Juan 223
shopping
Arecibo 180, 181
Bayamón 149
Cayey 235
Mayagüez 199
Ponce 220, *221*
San Juan 83, 120, 121, 122, *144*, 146
Sierra de Cayey 232, 235
Sierra de Luquillo 157, 159, 160, 232
siesta 57–8, 59
slavery
Africans15, 29, 32, 37, 69, 156, 221
descendants 60–1, 156, 221
Indians 28–9
numbers 33
trade 34, *35*
smuggling 33, 161
society *56*, 57–63, 69–70, 75, 155–6, 221
South 213–26
see also individual placenames
Southeast 167–70
see also individual placenames
Spain 15, 24, 27–34, 37–9
see **Columbus, Christopher; Ponce de León, Juan** and *individual placenames*

El Año Terrible 236
encomienda system 28
gold 24, 27, 28
governors 33, 34, 37
"Grito de Lares" 38, 185–6,
  186
repartimientos 28
rule ends 39
settlement 15, 24, 27–34
situado 32, 33
Spanish-American War *36*, 39,
  133, 134, 226
sport 101–3
  Albergue Olimpico Germán
    Rieckehof 214
  American football 103
  baseball 47, 70–1, 101, 146,
    149
  basketball 101, 190
  batey 23, 84, 101
  boating 102, *108–9*, 111,
    161, 163, 170, 223, 253
  boxing 47, 101, 102
  camping 159, 161, 163, 170,
    240, 249
  caving *see* **caves**
  cock-fighting 213–14, *215*
  fishing 102–3, 167, 170, 190,
    233, 234
  football 103
  golf 47, *51*, 101, 102, *162*,
    167, 175, 176
  handball 103
  hiking 158, 159–60, *161*, 184,
    190, 208, 226, 240, 242
  horse racing, riding 47, 102,
    166, 167, *214*
  international 50, 101–2, 103,
    197, 214, 219
  kayaking 102
  moto-cross racing *172–3*
  motor racing 103
  Pee Wee football 103, 148
  pool *142*
  racquetball 102
  running 103
  sailing 102, *108–9*, 111, 161,
    163, 213, 223
  scuba-diving *98–9*, 195, 249,
    253
  shooting 103
  snorkeling 141, 163, 195,
    249, 253
  soccer 103
  stickball 103
  surfing 102, *103*, 111, 155,
    195, 197–8
  swimming 129, *167*, 176,
    195, 198, 240, 249

tennis 101, 102, 167, 175
touch football 102
volleyball 102, 103, 167
water *98–9, 100*, 102–3, 129,
  141
windsurfing *100*, 102, 252
Suárez, Jaime 86, 131
sugar 15, 16, 34, 37, *43*, 168–9
  see also **rum; slavery**
  collapse 32, 169, 170
  festivals 64
  hurricanes 40
  imported 76
  ingenios 29–30
  San Sebastián 189
  Vieques 247

t

Taínos *see* **Indians:** Taínos
Tañon, Olga 96
Tapia y Rivera, Alejandro 119–20
theater 63, 119–20, 143, 180,
  219
Tibes Indian Ceremonial Park
  23, *85*, 101, 223
Toa Baja 175
topography 15, 183–5, 231, 251
Toro Negro Forest Reserve 240
Torrecilla Baja 156
Torres, José "Chegui" 102
Torres, Luis Llorens 63, 219
Torres, Miguel de la 37
tourism 46, 58
trade *see* **economy; industry**
trees 158, 159, *168*, 209
  see also **flora; national
    forests/parks/nature
    reserves**
  ausubo 243
  bamboo 208, 233, 240, 242
  coconut palms 169
  eucalyptus 242
  guayacan (*lignum vitae*) 208,
    226
  mahogany 208
  mangrove swamps 156, 162,
    203, 217, 252
  mountain palms 233, 240
  rainforests 157, 247
  teak 242
Truman, Harry S. 45, 46
Tufiño, Rafael 86
Tugwell, Rexford Guy 45
Turabo Valley 232, 234

u

University of Puerto Rico
  Botanical Gardens 147, 208,
    209
  Mayagüez 199
  San Juan *34*, 83, 84, 85, 145,
    147, 168, 208, *209*
USA 16, 21, 34, 39–42, 45–50,
  195, 225–6
  citizenship 40, 41, 70
  colonialism 40–1
  commonwealth status 16,
    45–6, 49–50, 182, 226
  emigration from 16
  flag *34, 40*, 61
  Foraker Act 40–1
  immigration to 46, 49, 70
  Operation Bootstrap 46, 47,
    178–9
  Operation Serenity 46–7
  Spanish-American War *36*, 39,
    133, 134, 226
  statehood 46, 50, 101
  trade 34
  US Air Force bases 197
  US Army 148
  US Navy bases 61, 163, 249,
    251
Utuado 84, *228–9*, 243

v

Vacia Talega Beach 155
Vega, Tony 47
Vega Alta National Forest 184
Vega Baja 177
Velasquez, Juan Ramón 86
Vieques 111, 247–50
  agriculture 247
  beaches *246*, 247, *248*, 249
  Casa del Francés 248
  El Fortin Conde de Mirasol 247
  Esperanza 248
  ferries 61, 161, 247
  festivals 248
  hotels 248
  hurricanes 158, 247
  Isabel Segunda 247
  Media Luna 249
  Mosquito Pier 249
  Mount Pirata 250
  museums 247, 248
  name 247
  Navio 249
  Phosphorescent (Mosquito)
    Bay 250
  population 247
  Punta Mulas Lighthouse 247

restaurants 248
Sun Bay *246*, 249
Taínos 247
US Navy 249
wildlife 247, 249
Villalba 239

w

weather *see* **climate**
West 195–207
see also individual placenames
wildlife
see also **flora; national forests/
parks/nature reserves**
Bahama ducks 252
bats 188
birds 157, *164–5*, 170, 177,
203, 223–4, 226, 235,
247, 251–2
brown boobies 252
brown pelicans 252
coquí 57, 93, 157, 188, 240,
242, *244–5*, 247
crabs 247
ducks 252
egrets 247
fish 224, 252
folk art 88
guavás 188
gulls 224, 252, 254
herons 203
horses 247, *249*
iguanas *162*, 223, 254
insects 188
laughing gulls 252
leatherback turtles 252
lizards *162*, 205, 223, 254
martins 203
mongooses 247
parrots 157, *164–5*
pelicans 203, 224, 252
rats 169
red-footed boobies 254
sea eagles 224
snakes 157–8
sooty terns 252
turtles 252, 254
whales 197
whippoorwills 226
women 50, 65, 75, 101

y–z

Yabucoa 168–9
Yauco 64, 69, 76, 207, *224*,
225–6
Zeno, Jorge 86
zoos 149, 201

The World of Insight Guides

400 books in three complementary series cover every major destination in every continent.

Insight Guides

Alaska
Alsace
Amazon Wildlife
American Southwest
Amsterdam
Argentina
Atlanta
Athens
Australia
Austria
Bahamas
Bali
Baltic States
Bangkok
Barbados
Barcelona
Bay of Naples
Beijing
Belgium
Belize
Berlin
Bermuda
Boston
Brazil
Brittany
Brussels
Budapest
Buenos Aires
Burgundy
Burma (Myanmar)
Cairo
Calcutta
California
Canada
Caribbean
Catalonia
Channel Islands
Chicago
Chile
China
Cologne
Continental Europe
Corsica
Costa Rica
Crete
Crossing America
Cuba
Cyprus
Czech & Slovak Republics
Delhi, Jaipur, Agra
Denmark
Dresden
Dublin
Düsseldorf
East African Wildlife
East Asia
Eastern Europe
Ecuador
Edinburgh
Egypt
Finland
Florence
Florida
France
Frankfurt
French Riviera
Gambia & Senegal
Germany
Glasgow

Gran Canaría
Great Barrier Reef
Great Britain
Greece
Greek Islands
Hamburg
Hawaii
Hong Kong
Hungary
Iceland
India
India's Western Himalaya
Indian Wildlife
Indonesia
Ireland
Israel
Istanbul
Italy
Jamaica
Japan
Java
Jerusalem
Jordan
Kathmandu
Kenya
Korea
Lisbon
Loire Valley
London
Los Angeles
Madeira
Madrid
Malaysia
Mallorca & Ibiza
Malta
Marine Life in the South
China Sea
Melbourne
Mexico
Mexico City
Miami
Montreal
Morocco
Moscow
Munich
Namibia
Native America
Nepal
Netherlands
New England
New Orleans
New York City
New York State
New Zealand
Nile
Normandy
Northern California
Northern Spain
Norway
Oman & the UAE
Oxford
Old South
Pacific Northwest
Pakistan
Paris
Peru
Philadelphia
Philippines
Poland
Portugal
Prague

Provence
Puerto Rico
Rajasthan
Rhine
Rio de Janeiro
Rockies
Rome
Russia
St Petersburg
San Francisco
Sardinia
Scotland
Seattle
Sicily
Singapore
South Africa
South America
South Asia
South India
South Tyrol
Southeast Asia
Southeast Asia Wildlife
Southern California
Southern Spain
Spain
Sri Lanka
Sweden
Switzerland
Sydney
Taiwan
Tenerife
Texas
Thailand
Tokyo
Trinidad & Tobago
Tunisia
Turkey
Turkish Coast
Tuscany
Umbria
US National Parks East
US National Parks West
Vancouver
Venezuela
Venice
Vienna
Vietnam
Wales
Washington DC
Waterways of Europe
Wild West
Yemen

Insight Pocket Guides

Aegean Islands★
Algarve★
Alsace
Amsterdam★
Athens★
Atlanta★
Bahamas★
Baja Peninsula★
Bali★
Bali Bird Walks
Bangkok★
Barbados★
Barcelona★
Bavaria★
Beijing★
Berlin★

Bermuda★
Bhutan★
Boston★
British Columbia★
Brittany★
Brussels★
Budapest &
Surroundings★
Canton★
Chiang Mai★
Chicago★
Corsica★
Costa Blanca★
Costa Brava★
Costa del Sol/Marbella★
Costa Rica★
Crete★
Denmark★
Fiji★
Florence★
Florida★
Florida Keys★
French Riviera★
Gran Canaria★
Hawaii★
Hong Kong★
Hungary
Ibiza★
Ireland★
Ireland's Southwest★
Israel★
Istanbul★
Jakarta★
Jamaica★
Kathmandu Bikes &
Hikes★
Kenya★
Kuala Lumpur★
Lisbon★
Loire Valley★
London★
Macau
Madrid★
Malacca
Maldives
Mallorca★
Malta★
Mexico City★
Miami★
Milan★
Montreal★
Morocco★
Moscow
Munich★
Nepal★
New Delhi
New Orleans★
New York City★
New Zealand★
Northern California★
Oslo/Bergen★
Paris★
Penang★
Phuket★
Prague★
Provence★
Puerto Rico★
Quebec★
Rhodes★
Rome★
Sabah★

St Petersburg★
San Francisco★
Sardinia
Scotland★
Seville★
Seychelles★
Sicily★
Sikkim
Singapore★
Southeast England
Southern California★
Southern Spain★
Sri Lanka★
Sydney★
Tenerife★
Thailand★
Tibet★
Toronto★
Tunisia★
Turkish Coast★
Tuscany★
Venice★
Vienna★
Vietnam★
Yogyakarta
Yucatan Peninsula★

★ = Insight Pocket Guides
with Pull out Maps

Insight Compact Guides

Algarve
Amsterdam
Bahamas
Bali
Bangkok
Barbados
Barcelona
Beijing
Belgium
Berlin
Brittany
Brussels
Budapest
Burgundy
Copenhagen
Costa Brava
Costa Rica
Crete
Cyprus
Czech Republic
Denmark
Dominican Republic
Dublin
Egypt
Finland
Florence
Gran Canaria
Greece
Holland
Hong Kong
Ireland
Israel
Italian Lakes
Italian Riviera
Jamaica
Jerusalem
Lisbon
Madeira
Mallorca
Malta

Milan
Moscow
Munich
Normandy
Norway
Paris
Poland
Portugal
Prague
Provence
Rhodes
Rome
St Petersburg
Salzburg
Singapore
Switzerland
Sydney
Tenerife
Thailand
Turkey
Turkish Coast
Tuscany

UK regional titles:
Bath & Surroundings
Cambridge & East
Anglia
Cornwall
Cotswolds
Devon & Exmoor
Edinburgh
Lake District
London
New Forest
North York Moors
Northumbria
Oxford
Peak District
Scotland
Scottish Highlands
Shakespeare Country
Snowdonia
South Downs
York
Yorkshire Dales

USA regional titles:
Boston
Cape Cod
Chicago
Florida
Florida Keys
Hawaii: Maui
Hawaii: Oahu
Las Vegas
Los Angeles
Martha's Vineyard &
Nantucket
New York
San Francisco
Washington D.C.
Venice
Vienna
West of Ireland